Evangelical Christians *in the* Muslim Sahel

African Systems of Thought
Ivan Karp, editor

Contributing editors
James W. Fernandez
Luc de Heusch
John Middleton
Roy Willis

Evangelical Christians *in the* Muslim Sahel

Barbara M. Cooper

Indiana University Press
Bloomington and Indianapolis

This book is a publication of

Indiana University Press
601 North Morton Street
Bloomington, IN 47404-3797 USA

http://iupress.indiana.edu

Telephone orders	800-842-6796
Fax orders	812-855-7931
Orders by e-mail	iuporder@indiana.edu

The paper used in this publication meets
the minimum requirements of American
National Standard for Information
Sciences—Permanence of Paper for
Printed Library Materials, ANSI
Z39.48-1984.

Manufactured in
the United States of America

Library of Congress Cataloging-in-Publication Data

Cooper, Barbara MacGowan.
    Evangelical Christians in the Muslim sahel / Barbara M. Cooper.
        p. cm.—(African systems of thought)
    Includes bibliographical references and index.
    ISBN 0-253-34739-4 (cloth : alk. paper)   1. Missions—Niger.   2. Sudan Interior
Mission.   3. SIM (Organization)   4. Christianity and other religions—Islam.   5. Islam—
Relations—Christianity.   6. Christianity—Niger.   7. Islam—Niger.   I. Title.   II. Series.
    BV3625.N48C66 2006
    266'.0096626—dc22

                                                                                        2005032590

1 2 3 4 5 11 10 09 08 07 06

To Hawa and Ayyuba
May peace be with you.

Contents

Acknowledgments

The work required to produce this book occurred on three continents with the assistance of a host of institutions and individuals. Critical funding for this work was provided by the National Endowment for the Humanities. Without continued support from federal funding, U.S. scholars have little hope of a deep understanding of international issues, and I am deeply grateful to the NEH for support at a formative juncture in this project. The American Historical Association provided similarly crucial support in the form of a Bernadotte E. Schmitt Research Grant. Bryn Mawr College provided faculty research support through a Madge Miller Fund Faculty Research Grant, and New York University provided a particularly generous Research Challenge Grant. My current institution, Rutgers University, has unfailingly provided funding, logistical support, and a warm and intellectually stimulating environment.

My husband, Richard Miller, and my daughters Cara and Rachel have been wonderful companions throughout this project, offering wry humor, insightful observations, and an indispensable sense of perspective. I am grateful for the emotional and intellectual support of my colleagues at the Rutgers Center for African Studies, including (among others) Ousseina Alidou, Abena Busia, Dorothy Hodgson, Allen Howard, Julie Livingston, and Rick Schroeder. Kari Bergstrom, Rob Glew, Ibrahim Hamza, Ken Harrow, Jean Hay, Adeline Masquelier, Joel Matthews, Jim McCann, Steven Pierce, David Robinson, and Sue Rosenfeld offered thoughtful comments and questions on earlier iterations of this work. Alia Hanna assisted in editing an unruly manuscript. The inimitable Kate Babbitt copy edited the manuscript with extraordinary care and improved it immeasurably.

All historians are particularly beholden to the archivists who make it possible to find traces of the past. I would like to thank Bob Arnold of the SIM International Archive in Fort Mill, South Carolina, for working so hard to make the treasure trove of SIM station records, photographs, pamphlets, memoirs, and periodicals accessible to me. His imaginative and enthusiastic assistance has been invaluable. Before SIM transferred its holdings to the archive I received gracious assistance from Jo-Ann Brant at the SIM International Resource Center in Charlotte, North Carolina. In France, the staffs of the Centre des Archives d'Outre-Mer and of the Bibliothèque nationale de France have been unfailingly helpful and efficient. Work on French colonial perceptions of medical work of SIM was particularly difficult to retrieve—I would like to extend special thanks to Mame N'Gor Faaye and Saliou Mbaye for assistance in the Archives du Sénégal at a messy moment when the documents I needed were destined to be microfilmed. Sometimes research is full of necessary dead ends—Monsieur Yataga of the Mairie in Maradi patiently assisted me as I waded through dusty and crumbly civil records to retrieve the irretrievable. In Niamey, Gazali Abdou Mahamane helped me with the more satisfying task of tracking down the colonial-era *rapports de tournée* for Tsibiri and Maradi in the Archives nationales du Niger. In Maradi, EERN president Abdou Lawali made records of the Evangelical Church available to me, and MIDP director Joel Matthews gave me access to materials on SIM's recent development initiatives.

Sometimes private letters, informal filing cabinets of papers, and generously shared personal writings shed more light on the past than formal archival materials. I have been very fortunate that so many individuals have been willing to share these more or less private materials with me in the interest of furthering an understanding of the past and the present. Missionaries Rita Salls and Immie Larsen shared their private letters with me; Pastor Abdou Lawali, Peter Cunningham, and Joel Mathews shared their own published and unpublished writings; and journalist Illia Djadi forwarded his precious but difficult-to-find articles about religion and politics in Maradi. Neal Childs shared tapes of radio sermons that would otherwise have been utterly lost to history. All of these acts of generosity opened important windows of understanding to me, and I am very grateful to each of these individuals for their courageous openness to sharing with a secular scholar.

Over the years I have accrued a tremendous debt to retired SIM missionary Liz Chisholm, who has on several occasions assisted me in contacting missionaries who have worked in the Maradi region and has graciously hosted me in her home. I would like to thank her and her sister Ruth for their kindness and generosity (and, I suspect, a few prayers) over the years. Rita Salls and Ray de la Haye have recounted their experiences faithfully on numerous occasions. I am very grateful to them and to all the other retired missionaries who consented to be interviewed and whose perspectives on the past have provided invaluable material for this book.

This book would never have been written if Tony and Liz Rinaudo had not invited me into their home in Maradi many years ago, introduced me to Christian converts, and offered me the use of their telephone. The SIM International and Vie Abondante missionaries working in Niger today have been equally helpful and kind. They are too numerous to name here, but I would like to thank in particular Philippe Hutter for encouraging me as a secular scholar to work on the history of the SIM mission. Joel and Alice Matthews have become good friends and models from whom I have learned much about what a Christian family life might be. Susan and Andrew Strong made me feel welcome and safe in the SIM guest house in Maradi. Vie Abondante missionary Neal Childs and his mother Jerry Childs were generous in offering their perspectives on Christianity and mission work with me. Barbara Kapenga was a wonderful neighbor at the EERN guest house, and I value her balanced reflections on language and spirituality more than I can say.

Most of all I must offer my deep thanks to all the Nigérien Christians in Maradi and Niamey who have assisted me in this project, befriended me, and tolerated my eccentricities. Professor Addo Mahamane of the History Department at the Université de Niamey has been a wonderful colleague. Pastor Abdou Lawali passed many hours with me chatting about what evangelical Christianity means, about the spiritual landscape of Maradi, and about his own writings. I enjoyed staying in the EERN guest house immensely as a result of his friendliness and his intelligent observations of Maradi life. My stays there were also made all the more pleasant by Habsatu and her husband Soji, who also took me in as something of an adoptive daughter during my visits. Warm appreciation to all the members of the congregation of Église Sonitan, which has been so generous in opening its community to me, and especially to the women of the *zummutar mata*. Pastors Cherif and 'dan Nana were extraordinarily generous with their time, experiences, and wisdom. My old friends Delphine Toussaint, Amina Diyar Sarki, and Malam Habou Magaji provided much-needed distance from this project, spaces in which I could genuinely celebrate Muslim life in Niger, and the critical perspectives that helped me see how others experience the growing Christian presence in Maradi.

This book is dedicated to two Christians without whom it could not have been written and who embody both the difficulties Christians face and the promise they represent for the future of Niger. The first is Hawa Mahamane, who is the first Christian in Maradi I became friends with many years ago. She wrapped me in the warmth of her friendship then and has never ceased to keep me in that embrace. I will always think of her as Malama—the woman who marched fearlessly around Maradi with a Hausa Bible in hand, ready to argue with any man, woman, or child who dared to take her on. Without the energy and courage of women like her, Christianity in Niger would have no dynamism and no soul. The other is my assistant, Ayyuba Abudu, who in myriad subtle and not-so-subtle ways worked to shape this book in order to proffer a frank and unflinching appraisal of Christianity in Niger. But he also, less consciously, revealed to me the courage some of his generation have exhibited in their efforts to face the past without bitterness and the imagination of some to envision a more hopeful future. *To, Hawa da Ayyuba, sai in ba ku aya mai dace gare ku Matta 5:16: "haskenku ya ri'ka haskakawa haka a gaban mutane, domin su ga kyawawan ayyukanku, su kuma 'daukaka Ubanku da ke cikin Sama."*

Acronyms

AOF   Afrique-Occidentale Française; French West Africa
CAOM   Centre des Archives d'Outre-Mer
CMS   Church Missionary Society
ECWA   Evangelical Church of West Africa
EERN   Église Évangélique de la République du Niger; Evangelical Church of Niger
FIMA   Festival International de la Mode Africaine; International Festival of African Fashion
FMNR   farmer managed natural regeneration
MIDP   Maradi International Development Project
SIM   Sudan Interior Mission, later known as SIM International
UEEPN Union des Églises Évangéliques Protestantes du Niger
EESN   Église Évangélique Salama du Niger
PPN   Parti Progressiste Nigérien, the local branch of the RDA
RDA   Rassemblement Démocratique Africaine
SIMIA   SIM International Archive

Evangelical Christians *in the* Muslim Sahel

Introduction:
Fundamental Differences

> *Our gap in knowledge about fundamentalists'*
> *foreign missions . . . is more than an esoteric*
> *corner of American (and global) religious*
> *history. It is a critical missing piece.*
>
> —J. Carpenter, "Propagating the Faith Once
> Delivered," 1990, 93

Avant propos

On market day in Maradi, one can experience one of the finest pleasures in life: sitting in the tiny buvette on the street corner southeast of the marketplace and watching the passing crowds. Sipping a cold soda from the kind of thick, heavy bottle that Americans of my generation associate nostalgically with the innocence of childhood, enjoying the sensation of a slight breeze lifting in the late afternoon as happy villagers prepare to pray before making their way back home, one can take the pulse of what passes for a major commercial center in Niger. It's a thoroughly Muslim environment—on the way into town from both north and south one passes an imposing mosque and smaller neighborhood mosques dot most every major street corner. The town is oriented with respect to these mosques and the Friday mosque opposite the traditional ruler's palace, just down the road heading west from the Grand Marché. Most men wear the characteristic Muslim garb of this region, a long-sleeved *riga* tunic that comes below the knee over matching slacks, complemented by a small hat known as a *hula*. Of course it is a city, so there is some variety to what one sees: some younger men wear western-style jeans and shirts, and male civil servants often wear vaguely military safari suits. Relatively few women are on the streets—market day is largely a masculine affair, although village women may come to sell a tasty cooked dish to hungry buyers. A handful of older women, carefully wrapped in their colorful *zane* cloths so that their heads are covered and their ankles are modestly out of sight, make purchases for their daughters' weddings. Market women, who are often from other regions of Niger or Nigeria, sell their plastic goods and enamelware. Farm women from the Maradi valley sell their carefully stacked tomatoes and chat with other vendors. But the big *commerçants* are men—they sell cloth and bulk quantities of grain and expensive vegetables shipped in from Nigeria.

Despite my modest-to-the-point-of-dowdiness research attire, I am quite clearly an outsider. As a white woman on foot I am also an anomaly. With my overflowing backpack of vegetables and the time, money, and temerity to stop with the young men on the corner for a soda on my way home, I have little in common with either the white woman passing in an expensive air-conditioned World Vision SUV or with the local women scurrying home on foot in happy chattering groups in an effort to fit their prayers in before cooking dinner. In the past there were more Peace Corps volunteers whose informal and low-budget style of inter-action with local people more closely matched my own. U.S. government interest in Niger as measured through Peace Corps personnel has quite visibly declined of late; they have been replaced by the "thousand points of light" of a scattering of religiously affiliated NGOs such as World Vision. Later I will hop indecorously on the back of a motor-scooter taxi, unhampered by the narrow lines of a *zane* cloth and undeterred by the visibility of my ankles. But most women will walk miles to their homes elsewhere in the city or they will squeeze into the back of a bush taxi laden with goats and peanut sacks.

When *azahar* (afternoon) prayer time arrives, prayer calls rise over the town from all directions, and gradually the streets lining the market clog with men and boys all facing Mecca in collective prayer. My *buvette* owner and his buddies disappear briefly—their Levi's jeans and American T-shirts don't mean that they are not practicing Muslims—leaving me to my enjoy my drink alone seated on a plastic milk carton. A radio repair man with a little portable tabletop shop keeps me company, and we chat quietly as he works. A tiny number of elderly women may join the men in prayer, but most of the straggling women will wait to perform their prayers in the privacy of their homes. A sense of peace settles over the city, a sense of a shared set of values, a shared culture, a shared movement through the day. Even as an outsider to Islam I pace myself according to that tempo and take intense pleasure in the sounds and movements of my Muslim environment.

But I have also learned to see and hear things that someone else might miss, even a Muslim who knows the city quite well. As the bustle of city life resumes after prayer, I glimpse a Hausa friend passing on a bicycle. Hey, he says, you want to buy some peanut butter? I say, Yes, but I don't have a container, and he agrees to drop it off where I am staying later on. As we are conversing, a mutual Fulani acquaintance comes out of the tiny bookshop across the street; he is on his way to make a recording at the radio station for his show later in the week. He looks very impressive in his market-day attire, a majestic purple *riga* and matching *hula*. As we chat, a third man, who is disabled, hails us enthusiastically as he makes his way past us on an ingenious locally made bicycle design he pedals by hand. From the back of a passing bush taxi a young man in a white lab coat shouts a greeting. He has taken advantage of the greater taxi traffic on market day to come to town to replenish his little mobile pharmacy. As I say goodbye to my friends, I decide that on the way home I will stop by one of the shops and pick up some locally canned fruit juice and preserves to liven up my breakfast of bread and instant coffee. In the store, I pause to chat with a woman friend making purchases on her way home from work. She is the secretary in one of the government offices I frequent for my research. She wears the elegant attire of functionary women—high heels, a hand-crocheted shawl, and a patent leather handbag.

To the uninitiated, all of this would appear to be very much in keeping with the Muslim tenor of this contemporary city—nothing about these men and this woman marks them as outsiders to Maradi life. And yet all of these interactions bear the marks of the long presence of the evangelical Christianity purveyed by a largely American evangelical mission, the Sudan Interior Mission (now SIM International) in the region: the evangelical bookstore where Maradi's Muslim schoolchildren buy their pens and paper, the peanut butter entrepreneur who knows that Peace Corps volunteers and American researchers like peanut butter sandwiches because he has spent much of his Christian life in the company of missionaries, the disabled Muslim man appreciative of the specially designed bicycle made in a mission workshop, the Christian radio shows (both sermons and development programs) recorded and transmitted in the private Anfani radio station, the locally produced fruit preserves from the Christian-owned and-operated factory, the itinerant pharmacy made possible by some rudimentary training in a mission health care facility, the rare educated Hausa woman schooled by missionaries in Nigeria. Even the ambivalent radio repair man, who is a Christian in town and a Muslim in the village where his first wife resides, occupies a particular social space. All are evidence of a lively but largely invisible Christian subculture that has contributed substantially to the quality and texture of life in this region of Niger. This book explores the history of the emergence of that world, its complex relationship to American fundamentalism, and its place in a culturally Muslim but politically secular nation.

SIM and the Maradi Context

By the time the Sudan Interior Mission came into being in 1893, Christian missionaries had been working in Africa for centuries. Ethiopia, of course, had encountered evangelism in the medieval period, leading to a distinctive brand of Christianity as the highlands became isolated from the rest of the Christian world by the expansion of Islam. The kingdom of Kongo was recognized as Christian by Europeans by the late sixteenth century, a consequence of the long interaction of the region with slave traders and Portuguese missions (Thornton 1992). Christianity in this instance became deeply bound with the trans-Atlantic slave trade, resulting in complex cross-fertilization between Portuguese, Afro-Brazilians, and Africans both in the practice of Christianity and in the forms of resistance to the slave trade (Thornton 1998; Gray 1990). In the eighteenth century, freed English-speaking slaves such as Olaudah Equiano collaborated with British abolitionists to create safe havens in coastal West Africa for converts who hoped in turn to convert their former countrymen to their new faith (Hastings 1979). With this development, mission work became more closely associated with abolitionist movements than with the slave trade proper.

By the late eighteenth century, missions of a bewildering array of denominations had entered the continent, sometimes competing with one another for converts, with particular violence in the case of the kingdom of Buganda. Missions tended to be funded through particular denominational mission boards that drew upon gifts raised in networks of denominational churches. Often businessmen were lured into backing missions on the promise that linking missions with commercial ventures would simultaneously eliminate the slave trade and promote Christian piety. Each mission strove to instill one brand of Christianity or another in converts, re-creating in Africa some of the tensions and schisms of the European church even as commercial rivalries echoed national competition for spheres of influence. These missionary efforts tended to be focused geographically on coastal regions and areas accessible through river networks. As a result, Christianity developed earliest along the coastal belt of West Africa, into the Congo River basin, in the Great Lakes region, and so on. The Sudanic belt was by and large neglected in these earliest efforts, in part because it was less easily reached and in part because Islamic civilization rendered it less obviously in need of moral intervention. Missions often strove to transform African Christians to match a certain nostalgic vision of an idealized European civilization: converts were encouraged to wear western clothing, to speak western languages, to build and maintain western-style homes, to adhere to mores often honored more in the breach than the observance in the sending countries. The watchword of the era, Christianity, Commerce, and Civilization, characterized the general impulse of the nineteenth-century mission movement. It was assumed that Christianity would go hand in hand with the "legitimate trade" that would replace the slave trade and that western-style Christian practice would civilize Africans. After an initial period of emphasizing preaching, missions consistently began to build schools to teach Africans western languages and to domesticate African family life. They worked to create a class of Africans who would become teachers, nurses, and, eventually, the political elite of much of Africa (Comaroff and Comaroff 1991, 1997).

Over time, missionaries with long experience interacting with Africa's organic intellectuals began to shift away from a daunting insistence upon sin, salvation, and the end times and toward an emphasis on Christianity's common ground with existing beliefs concerning creation and divinity (Hastings 1994, 273–273). Late-nineteenth-century missionaries might learn from local spiritual specialists or they might be influenced by their peers among the elite converts with whom they increasingly shared the labor of evangelism. Yet this class of articulate Africans—whose polish, aspirations, and intellectual achievements equaled or rivaled those of some of the missionaries—generated unease among some colonial administrators and missionaries. Urban life in trade centers and the growing hubs of colonial administration was unruly, complex, and hybrid. Some late-nineteenth-century missionaries chose to embrace that complexity.

Others, however, sought a return to a more pure era of evangelism. Just as the coastal areas had become saturated with missionaries and just as African converts were beginning to make their own marks upon Christianity as evangelists, scholars, and church leaders, some more-conservative missionaries became disillusioned with the model of Christianity that had propelled much of the evangelical revival and impatient with its gradual liberal accommodation with local beliefs and leadership. The tension over and rejection of the leadership of Bishop Samuel Crowther as head of the Church Missionary Society's Niger Mission was of a piece with this general shift in orientation among a particular brand of late-coming and highly critical conservative missionaries (Hastings 1994, 388–393; Isichei 1995, 171–173, 273). The faith mission movement, epitomized by the China Inland Mission (CIM), which was founded by James Hudson Taylor in 1865, emerged as the conservative solution to the dilemmas that had crystallized with the maturing of the denominational mission movement.

SIM, very much in sympathy with the CIM, emerged in this period of reflection and reconsideration of what evangelical Christianity and Christian conversion might mean. Turning its energies to the as-yet-unreached Sudanic region, the mission made its entry into the mission fields with a "new" and more authentic vision of the mission enterprise and the ideal African convert. As an interdenominational mission, SIM would abandon the denominational rivalries of the existing mission boards. Unhampered by the expectations of such boards or local Christian intellectuals, the mission would no longer devote its energies to "social" mission work such as building schools and hospitals—it would return to the "pure" activity of preaching. The link with commerce would be replaced with an emphasis on "industry" and hard work. Each missionary would simply go into the field to preach, and prayer alone would raise the necessary funds. There would be no preset budget raised by the boards to dictate who could be a missionary and where they could work and no preset program of action dictated by the boards. This would be a movement driven by faith alone—a conceit that led to the movement becoming known as the "faith mission" movement. At the heart of the faith mission enterprise would be the generation of converts and churches, not "civilized" school-leavers and schools. Converts would instead remain vernacular Christians who would not be permitted to become westernized—they would be discouraged from taking on the finery of westerners or aspiring to the material life of westerners. They should be driven by the same evangelical impulse as the missionaries themselves, but they should not be drawn to the trappings and moral pitfalls of western civilization. Over time, of course, "faith" missions developed much the same infrastructure as any mission, relying upon networks of churches and donors (often businessmen) in sympathy with a general set of understandings of Christianity and creating a formidable foundation of educational institutions for training like-minded Christians for mission work. The difference in emphasis in the faith missions lay primarily in their sense of being distinctive in placing evangelism before social transformation, in their willingness to take on missionaries who were eager to serve but might have little in the way of training or resources, and in a fundamentalist understanding of Christianity and salvation (to which I will return in a moment) that was not rigidly adhered to by all missionaries of the evangelical revival era. SIM strove to protect its distinctiveness and tended to isolate itself as much as possible from the work of more liberal or ecumenical institutions as the twentieth century progressed.

SIM's three Anglo-American founders—Scotch Canadian Walter Gowans (a Presbyterian), English Canadian Rowland Bingham (who was affiliated with the Salvation Army and in sympathy with the Plymouth Brethren), and American Thomas Kent (a Congregationalist)—felt a particular burden to advance Christianity in the vast "unreached" Sudanic interior of Africa. All three were trained by the renowned faith healer and founder of the Christian and Missionary Alliance, Dr. A. B. Simpson, at what was later known as Nyack Bible College in South Nyack, New York (Turaki 1993; Bingham 1943). The different affiliations of the three men marked the nondenominational character of the new mission from the outset, while their countries of origin seemed to signal an international, if rather Anglo-Saxon, orientation.

Of the three, only Rowland Bingham survived the initial attempt to reach the Sudanic regions in 1893; as the most significant leader of the early mission, it is his nondenominational, noncharismatic vision that has shaped the philosophy of the mission, and it is his emphasis on adult baptism by immersion that has marked it most visibly in terms of ritual practice. Bingham espoused an approach to interpreting the scriptures known as premillenial dispensationalism, which held that the divine creation of the world occurred in 4004 BCE and that the Bible is an inerrant account of and guide to human history until the Second Coming of Christ. According to this approach, history could be divided into seven different "dispensations," in each of which God revealed himself to humanity in ways appropriate to the times. The current (sixth) age would be succeeded by a millennium of rule by Christ over earth before the final conflict between good and evil and the last judgment (Kraphol and

Lippy 1999, 35). In Bingham's mind, there was a great urgency to the task of sharing the gospel with as much of the world as possible, for evangelism to the whole world would trigger the beginning of the new age and the Second Coming of Christ.

The principal characteristic of SIM's practical interventions is its reluctance to engage in social services for the sake of charity or social uplift. The purpose of the mission is not to perform good works but to plant churches that will sustain Christian communities. In other words, the mission's unabashed goal is the conversion of non-Christians to Christianity, not the provision of social services such as education, medicine, or emergency services. SIM historically has had little patience with the social ministries of the earlier denominational missions; its reluctance to engage in such work has marked every stage of its history in the region. After a brief flirtation with the name "Sudan Industrial Mission," the mission reverted to its earlier name, Sudan Interior Mission, for fear that the word "industrial" would imply an engagement with worldly monetary pursuits it eschewed. The goal of the mission was an industrious and self-supporting local church, not industry in some more commercial sense.

SIM's field of operation over the years advanced gradually from Nigeria to much of West Africa, Sudan, and Ethiopia. Today, through mergers with other missions, it has truly global operations and has over time adjusted its acronym, SIM, to stand for Society for International Missions and, more recently, Serving in Mission. SIM's personnel have over the years represented more and more of the Anglo-American world, including staff from the United States, Canada, Great Britain, New Zealand, and Australia. Through the many changes, however, and despite the growing internationality of its personnel, SIM International has retained a resolutely American character (its founders and leaders have largely hailed from Canada and the United States) and a frank emphasis on church-building over servicing physical needs. Its central offices have gradually shifted southward from Toronto to New York and are now to be found in Charlotte, North Carolina, in the heart of the American Bible Belt.

Telling the story of SIM's interactions with Africans in the southern region of Niger is complicated by the fact that SIM is multilayered and has changed over time—there are many SIMs. There is the SIM of founder Rowland Bingham, who oversaw the mission from its central offices in Canada and later in the United States for fifty years. His writings and personal charisma inspired many missionaries to join the mission. He was also an important figure in a broad network of evangelical

Christians in America. The central administration handled major policy decisions and vetted the applications of missionaries to ensure that motivations and doctrinal beliefs were in keeping with the spirit of SIM. As the mission became established in the 1930s, two field offices were created, one to oversee the Western Sudan (including Nigeria and French West Africa) and the other to oversee the Eastern Sudan (to handle the Anglo-Egyptian Sudan). Once missionaries were in the field, it was to this office that they would send reports. The culture of the mission in Niger was set in the field offices in Nigeria. SIM missionaries in Niger went to Nigeria regularly for medical checkups and for vacations and generally transited through Nigeria in coming to and from the field from home. SIM's main publication, *The Sudan Witness*, was edited and printed from the field offices in Nigeria. SIM missionaries participating in translation work on the Hausa Bible worked on this project in Nigeria, and the earliest medical work—in particular the mission's leprosaria, which dated from the late 1930s—was located in Nigeria.

The history of SIM in Nigeria is a key part of the story of the emergence of a Christian community in Niger. Nevertheless, in their day-to-day work reaching Africans in Niger, missionaries reported to a district superintendent who headed one of the larger stations in Niger. For most of the history of the mission in Niger, that district office was in either Tsibiri or Maradi. The tone of work in French West Africa was affected by the personalities and attitudes of the district superintendents in Tsibiri and Maradi. Finally, each individual missionary interpreted and acted upon his or her understanding of the call to perform mission work in particular ways—some missionaries were generous and charismatic, others were condescending and judgmental.

SIM's history in Nigeria has been much more richly detailed by historians than its history in Niger (see Shankar 2003; Turaki 1993). However, Niger had a special place in the advance of the mission; facing obstacles to access to direct evangelism to native Hausa speakers in Nigeria, the mission began in 1924 to attempt to make more direct contact with the Hausa-speaking peoples for whom the founders had such a deep sense of spiritual responsibility. By entering into the territories held by the French, the mission could circumvent some of the restrictions placed on missionaries in northern Nigeria (limited to work in Zaria and Nupe). While the French administration was certainly not, as we shall see, supportive of evangelism, the distance of the region from central sites of decision making meant that the mission could work directly with Hausa-speakers without drawing much attention to itself until the outbreak of

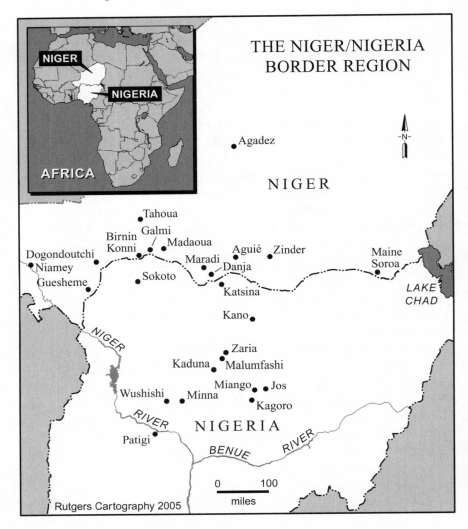

THE NIGER/NIGERIA
BORDER REGION

NIGER

NIGERIA

AFRICA

-N-

Agadez

NIGER

Tahoua

Birnin Galmi
Konni / Madaoua

Dogondoutchi
Niamey
Guesheme

Sokoto

Aguié Zinder

Maradi
Danja

Katsina

Maine
Soroa

LAKE
CHAD

Kano

NIGER

Zaria
Kaduna Malumfashi

Miango Jos

Wushishi Minna

Kagoro

RIVER

NIGERIA

Patigi

BENUE RIVER

0   100

miles

Rutgers Cartography 2005

World War II. In principle, the mission was forbidden to evangelize, but in practice missionaries engaged in preaching to and evangelizing among Hausa-speakers (and other Muslim and non-Muslim peoples in the region) more directly than was possible in the British territory to the south in the same period.

The region into which it moved, the Maradi region that borders on the northern emirates of Nigeria, had a complex history. Although the mission seemed never to remark upon the distinctive history of this re-

gion, this was not just another emirate of the Sokoto and Gwandu Caliphates, for the Maradi region was home to the many aristocratic Hausa
lines that rejected the jihad of Usman 'dan Fodio. The leaders of the
kingdoms of Maradi (where the recusant forces of Katsina made their
home) and Tsibiri (where the fiercely resistant forces of Gobir resettled)
retained a rich and complex relationship with the pre-Islamic practices
of the region, while they themselves continued to espouse a highly tolerant and adaptive form of Islam. The kingdoms of Maradi and Tsibiri
were a thorn in the side of the leaders of the jihad of Usman 'dan Fodio,
for they never conceded that the jihadists' vision of Islam was the correct
one and made periodic raids upon the caliphates throughout the nineteenth century. Unlike the scholarly outpost of the Bornu empire, Zinder, the Maradi region had a long history of pragmatic tolerance and
respect for the different nodes of authority and power that multiple forms
of spiritual practice made possible. This perhaps explains why with the
advent of colonialism, the traditional rulers of Tsibiri and Maradi, unlike
the emirs of northern Nigeria and scholarly elite of Zinder, were willing
to experiment with Christian missionary interlopers whose beliefs and
presence might at some point prove useful.

Maradi, always at the crossroads of major trans-Saharan traffic flowing toward Katsina, became a major commercial center with the growth
of the peanut economy under colonial rule and the explosion in cross-
border trade that the Pax Britannia and the Kano railhead made possible.
Maradi was to become simultaneously a major transit center for goods
from north, south, east, and west and a key agricultural center for the
production of cash crops for consumption and export. Millet production
in the region fed the commercial center, and peanut sales filled the colonial coffers. Agricultural production in the region is bound up with
commercial life, and today there is hardly a major civil servant or merchant who does not also engage in farming in one form or another. As
the town of Maradi has grown in importance as an administrative center,
the population of civil servants, nongovernmental organizations (NGOs),
and missionaries has increased over time.

However, to Nigériens from other parts of the country, Maradi is
known most for its extremely conservative atmosphere and its links—
commercial, familial, cultural—with northern Nigeria. One of the ironies
of colonial rule is that the enmities between the jihadists and the kingdoms of Maradi and Tsibiri were increasingly effaced by the ever-increasing integration of the region. Cross-border trade has been the life-
blood not only of Maradi but of Niger as a territorial entity. Because at

various moments both the colonial and postcolonial governments wanted a greater cut of the profits generated by this relatively productive agricultural and commercial region, much of this trade has of necessity been driven underground. But continue it has, and the constant flow of people, goods, and ideas between southern Niger and northern Nigeria has meant that religious dynamics in Nigeria have tended to overflow into the Maradi region. As anti-Sufi sentiments have grown in Nigeria, so too a parallel Islamic reformist movement has emerged in Niger. As tensions have flared up between Christians and Muslims in Nigeria, so too have tensions grown between faiths in Niger. The conservative identity politics of Muslims in northern Nigeria have left a strong imprint on the character of beliefs in Niger, in spite of a history of an adaptive and tolerant Islam in the recent past.

The strategies the mission used with Hausa-speakers in both Nigeria and Niger and toward Muslims in general shifted over the decades. Muslim resentment at Christian missionary intrusion was and is quite intense and had a very significant role in shaping the practice of Christianity in the region: in setting the parameters for Christian community, in dictating the language of belief, and in determining where and how evangelism could be practiced with any hope of success. This book opens with two chapters that reflect on contemporary tensions between Christians and Muslims over the radio ministry of a relative newcomer to the scene, the Vie Abondante American Pentecostal mission. They also shed light on the kinds of tensions that characterized SIM's experiences in the 1920s and 1930s as it struggled to gain a foothold in Niger through direct preaching, "giving the Word." Over the years, the mission's attentions and strategies of necessity shifted in the face of the sustained resistance of Muslims, in response to the demands and expectations of converts, and in reluctant recognition of the requirements of the French colonial order. This book is structured as a series of engagements with the various evangelical strategies the mission adopted over time: open preaching, Bible translation, medical work, educational work, and, finally, relief and development work.

As a small community of converts began to emerge, the mission had to address the expectations of converts whose aspirations far exceeded the modest vision of the vernacular Christian the mission purveyed. The mission endeavored to discipline the church, to determine who would become the leaders of the emerging community, and to define proper behavior for women as wives. For its part, the community of Christian converts struggled mightily to compel the mission to provide the kind of education that would make it possible for them to succeed materially in the French colonial world. Converts argued among themselves over whether older social hierarchies that emphasized aristocracy and geron-tocracy would prevail over the newer values of the church and mission: piety, literacy, fundamentalist values, and youthful enthusiasm. While the Christian community that emerged was explicitly patriarchal in orienta-tion, women carved out significant roles for themselves and in some ways kept the church alive over the longer term as internal competition be-tween male leaders of the church threatened to fracture the community beyond repair. Struggles over the language and content of education are a leitmotif of the history of the mission in the region; the failure of SIM to produce technically trained Christians skilled in the languages of the metropole was to cast a shadow over almost every subsequent enterprise taken up by the mission.

Until World War II, the mission remained largely unnoticed by the French administration, and although many of its activities could not be formally recognized because they did not meet the requirements of French regulations, the mission could function quite well by remaining more or less out of view. After the fall of France, the "Anglo-Saxon" mission fell under tremendous scrutiny and many of its activities were severely curtailed. The mission survived in large part as a result of the covert activities of committed converts. With the rise of de Gaulle the fortunes of the mission were utterly reversed in many ways: avenues that had been closed to the mission suddenly became available and the "doors were opened" in ways that they had not been before the discrediting of the pro-Catholic policies of the Vichy regime. The mission began to expand on the medical work it had found so productive in northern Ni-geria; it established a model farm school, and it began to enter into formal education in a manner that it had not in the interwar years.

The book explores the many tensions and contradictions that emerged as a mission that was reluctant to take on physical ministries found itself ever-more-deeply engaged in providing social services. The manly self-image of the original founders as crusaders offering "the Word" to men who would in turn go on to preach to other men was deeply troubled by the reality in the postwar period that far more women than men entered into mission work. Their attentions were focused on providing services to women and children in schools and hospitals. Such women were charged with teaching African women how to become good wives to Christian men, but they themselves often remained unmarried to remain faithful to their vocations as missionaries, an irony that was not lost on African populations. Other, more masculine domains were not without contradiction, for by promoting plow agriculture the mission inadvertently promoted conceptions of land ownership that were consistent with the expansion of Islamic conceptions of family life, property, and law.

When the effects of the Great Sahel Drought began to be felt in the early 1970s, the mission found itself even more deeply committed to simply saving bodies, not souls. The gender inequalities at the heart of the poverty dynamics in the region became difficult to ignore, and year after year the mission serviced the needs of the women and children who were the most vulnerable in times of stress. Yet it had neither the personnel nor the analytical capacity to make sense of these dynamics. Today the mission continues to adapt and change (in part in an attempt to respond to just these sorts of issues), so much so that newer mission personnel are often at a loss to understand the history that has generated the deep wounds and resentments that seem regularly to undermine the success of the most well-intended efforts. In recent years the mission has shifted to a philosophy of "contextualization" that is intended to render its interventions more culturally sensitive, but this sensitivity is not reducible to some sort of liberal cultural relativism. Its ideal family form remains firmly patriarchal, and Islam will always be, in the optic of this faith mission, an impediment to true belief.

Of Fundamentalisms in Time

While this is not a book about fundamentalism as a broad social phenomenon, one reason I wanted to explore the history of Protestant Christianity in Niger was that I came to feel that an extremely important dimension of U.S. intervention in global affairs has been neglected in secular scholarship, especially the scholarship on Africa (see Brouwer, Gifford, and Rose 1996). The influence of institutions that emanated from the Protestant fundamentalist movement in the United States seemed to me to be largely invisible in historical accounts of religion in Africa and neglected in discussions of American foreign policy, capital flows, and cultural transfer. I suspect that a large reason for this has been an antipathy on the part of evangelical fundamentalist Christians to engage with secular scholars and disdain on the part of scholarly elites outside religious studies toward treating religious phenomena with any real seriousness.[1] In French-language scholarship on Africa, for example, there are few studies of missions, Christian groups, or religious phenomena in Africa that are not authored by a scholar who has a personal involvement in the movements in question.[2] Many of these studies represent excellent secular scholarship, but the fact that secular scholars outside these religious traditions do not take up the important study of missions in Africa perhaps reveals a residue of an anticlericalism in French academic culture that has outlived its usefulness.

Scholarship in English on religion in Africa has greater breadth and depth but nevertheless has significant blind spots—well-meaning colleagues hinted that they didn't see why I was doing a study of Protestantism in a former French colony, since obviously the more significant group would be the Catholics. Yet by its own reckoning the Catholic church had very little success in converting local populations in Niger to Christianity; of some 20,000 Catholics in Niger at the close of the 1990s, only 500 or so could be said to be from among the indigenous populations (Berthelot 1997, 249). Today, in the town of Maradi alone, there are more than 500 members of evangelical congregations from among local ethnic groups and evangelical churches dot the landscape of the entire region beyond the city of Maradi proper. This does not include the churches in what is known as Arewa, or the burgeoning Fulani Christian community, or the Christian churches that have burst on the scene in the capital of Niamey as mobile Christians establish new communities there. The *indigenous* Christian church in Niger is Protestant, not Catholic. The assumption that Protestantism, particularly American evangelical Protestantism, is a marginal and largely irrelevant phenomenon in Francophone Africa has meant that there are few serious historical studies of Protestantism outside the former British colonies. This is a striking silence, given that the tense relations between France and the United States in the global arena today have largely unrecognized religious dimensions. While scholars of Africa may be blind to this phenomenon, administrators in postwar French colonial Africa certainly were not, and they went to considerable lengths to maintain surveillance of the worrisome American missionaries.

Yet even within the Anglophone ambit little work has been done on the specifically twentieth-century fundamentalist evangelical impulse and its consequences for Africa (the important exception being Carpenter and Shenk 1990). Much of the most prominent historical literature on missions focuses on the European-dominated eighteenth- and nineteenth-century "Christianity, commerce and civilization" wave of missions, missing altogether the twentieth-century surge of American-led missionization that is far less amenable to analysis as handmaiden to the Euro-

pean colonial enterprise.[3] The American-led modern missionary movement—that "autumnal child of the Evangelical Revival" (Walls 1996,
79)—differed substantially from its more-European forebears.
American-led missions depended initially on the financial mobilization
of American businessmen centered in Chicago and Toronto to fund mission work rather than wealthy sponsors, modest tithing parishioners, or
the state. They held to a rather naive conviction that a doctrine of separation of church and state guaranteed that their interventions were by
definition apolitical, and their "methodological common sense" led them
to see statements of belief (often codified as doctrinal statements) as tests
of membership and fellowship—of "real" commitment to the fundamen-
tals of Christianity (230–234; the quoted phrase originated with Mark
Noll). Despite its heavy dependence on the U.S. capitalist economy, this
movement did not by any means espouse externally oriented legitimate
commerce for Africans, nor did it envision an educated African acculturated to Euro-American life as the ideal Christian. The anti-intellectualism and insularity of the American faith mission movement in particular has left few literary traces to attract the attention and interest of
the secular scholar—one searches in vain for intellects on a par with
Placide Tempels, Spencer Trimingham, David Livingstone, Bengt Sund-
kler, Geoffrey Parrinder, Trevor Huddleston, or John Taylor among the
American evangelical missionaries (cf. Hastings 1994, 567–568). "The
scandal of the evangelical mind," remarks evangelical insider Mark Noll
with some sadness, "is that there is not much of an evangelical mind"
(1994, 3). Noll's own contemporary writings on the evangelical movement in American history are an extremely welcome and self-critical exception to that rule, but he does not focus specifically on the missionary
dimension of that movement (1994, 2001).

It is striking that there seems to be little awareness among Americans
who are not themselves part of the evangelical subculture in the United
States that our country has had and continues to make a mark in Africa
and elsewhere through the informal voluntary associations of missions.
U.S. diplomatic and military engagement with Africa has always been
sporadic (which is not to say that it has not had occasionally catastrophic
effects), while the engagement of U.S. capital with the continent is, by
comparison with European nations, relatively modest.[4] American secular
scholars have perhaps become complacent about the degree to which we
ourselves are implicated in the religious dynamics of the continent. But
as any evangelical Sunday school student can tell you, Americans have
engaged deeply and consistently with the spiritual life of Africa through

missionization for more than a century. Virtually every evangelical church in the country sponsors missionaries in the field, invites missionaries as regular speakers to report on their work and to seek prayers and financial support, and takes the "great commission" of Matthew 28:19 to be a literal commandment from Jesus to share Christianity in every nation in the world: "Go then, and make disciples of all nations, baptizing them in the name of the Father, the Son and the Holy spirit, and teaching them to observe all that I have commanded you."[5] That's what it means to be evangelical. Paul Gifford offers a perceptive assessment of the significance of this phenomenon for both Africans and Americans:

> We have stressed throughout that Christian missions are now very important for Africa; perhaps the biggest single industry in Africa. But missions are an enormous industry in the United States as well. . . . For [small American churches], especially, part of the involvement is not specifically about Africa at all; it is the commitment to Africa that drives and focuses church activity back home. Here too the churches display the dynamic observable in the international aid community; the aid industry "needs" Africa, as does the mission industry. (Gifford 1998, 315)

Indeed, today major philanthropies such as the Gates Foundation, faced with weakened states in Africa, "need" religious NGOs to absorb and distribute their largesse on the continent.[6] The tradition of American capital supporting the efforts of evangelical voluntary organizations is very much alive and well.

What are the key elements of this odd "industry," this American-led evangelicalism? Evangelicalism emerged in the early eighteenth century as a protest against the empty formalism of establishment piety (in particular that of the Anglican and Lutheran churches), emphasizing instead religion "of the heart" that celebrated the "good news" of God's redemption of sinners through the work of Christ. Gathering force throughout the century, the movement was characterized by large revival meetings in which powerful public preaching of repentance and grace gave rise to intense emotional experiences of personal transformation, transformations captured in such powerful hymns as John Newton's "Amazing Grace" (Noll 2001, 11). Within the existing denominations, evangelical subcultures emerged, often promoting a more populist approach to religion that was less beholden to establishment clergy and emphasized the power of prayer and preaching over scholarship and ritual. Over time these groups developed their own modes of organization and activity that were characterized by a high degree of volunteerism and an antipathy toward hierarchy and centralization. New "free" denominations formed that were strictly evangelical, such as the Baptists and Methodists, that emphasized autonomy, individual action, and volunteerism.

These Protestant evangelical groups, which were in general sympathy with one another despite their differing churches of origin, found common cause with one another, sharing publications, favoring particular popular preachers (Dwight Moody and Billy Graham represent two such major leaders), cooperating in translation activities, and developing a network of Bible schools and missionary organizations that crossed traditional denominational lines. Within the United States and Canada, white evangelical Christians, the dominant social and cultural force until the early nineteenth century, often saw themselves as inheritors of a tradition of reform that began with the Puritans, conceiving of the continent as the New Jerusalem, a space of spiritual renewal, and the site of the enactment of God's greater plan for mankind. That sense of election and destiny was profoundly troubled by major waves of immigration that brought Catholics, Jews, and Eastern Europeans to the major cities of the United States, transforming what had by and large been a taken-for-granted cultural milieu into a self-conscious movement to protect "tradition" and the perceived foundational values of the nation.

American evangelicalism has a number of specific features that I would hesitate to attribute to evangelicals across the globe, however, which is one reason the word "fundamentalist" was coined. While Africa has seen many evangelical missions, it is the American latecomers that have been the bearers of Protestant fundamentalism to the continent, and it is with just such a mission that this book is concerned.[7] American evangelicalism is most closely associated with insistence on a number of core beliefs that are often tagged as "fundamentalist" even when the institution or individual in question might not self-identify as fundamentalist.[8] The doctrinal statement of the SIM International mission (the most important mission for the history that follows), with which any SIM missionary must agree, is entirely consistent with those key benchmarks: the Bible is the "inerrant" word of God (a rejection of historically grounded Biblical criticism); God consists of three persons (Father, Son, Holy Spirit); all humans suffer from original sin and must be reborn; humans will go to heaven or hell in the afterlife as a consequence of their spiritual condition (their rebirth or failure to be "born again"); Jesus was born of the Virgin Mary, he atoned for human sin with his bodily resurrection, and his Second Coming is imminent; Satan exists literally (not simply figuratively) and acts in the world; the Christian church is the whole body of those who have been reborn (implicitly excluding Christians who are not "born again"); and Christ's great commission was to order his followers to share these "truths" to every people (therefore to be a Christian is to evangelize).[9]

But there is more to Christian fundamentalism than a set of "fundamental principles"—Christian fundamentalism as a self-conscious *movement* implies political activism within the United States and abroad concerning key social issues (supporting school prayer, opposing abortion, promoting the teaching of creationism). Christians who chose to channel their religious activism into the "great commission" of mission work, rather than focus on U.S. politics, often imagine themselves to be apolitical, despite the links between their missionary enterprise and the broader Christian right in the United States. In particular, evangelicals who associate the word "fundamentalism" with a naive creationism that they themselves find distasteful may choose to distance themselves from the term, arguing that they are not themselves literalists; rather they insist upon biblical inerrancy. There are divisions among fundamentalists concerning the degree to which separatism from corrupt secular culture is necessary, which kinds of political alliances are appropriate (such as the alliance of conservatives with Catholics and Mormons over abortion and homosexuality), and where the line is between activism and rebellion. There have also been rather long-standing tensions over the degree to which charismatic/ecstatic dimensions of religion can be admitted into a movement founded upon the assumption that the rational reading of the Bible by ordinary laypeople can provide solutions to all spiritual, social, and political questions. Pentecostal movements, with their historically rural, populist flavor and their emphasis on the gifts of healing and speaking in tongues, have often been slighted within the broader urban-focused evangelical and fundamentalist movements, despite their adherence to the same core principles. The "born again" Pentecostal movement in Africa, with its appealing emphasis upon this-worldly blessings and healing, is particularly vibrant and relevant today, so much so that, as Paul Gifford points out, even mainline churches appear to be increasingly "Pentecostalized" (1998, 306).

To the scholar observing the movement as a whole over a long century, however, some of these distinctions seem rather slender when compared with the far greater divide between the committed secularist and those who would transform the United States and the globe according to a narrow moral order modeled on a patriarchal family and founded upon an assumption that the world and its affairs can be interpreted as a cosmic struggle between God and Satan, good and evil, black and white. For me as a secular scholar who struggles daily with ambiguity and complexity, this stark and simplistic dualism is the central distinguishing characteristic of fundamentalisms of all kinds. While I count myself as a Christian, it is my rejection of such dualism that sets me utterly apart from most of the missionaries and converts whose history I have attempted to capture in this book. It also sets me apart from many Islamist activists who, with a similarly Manichean vision and a similarly patriarchal template for family life and social order, would remake the world according to their own version of the True Way.

Many Christian missionaries of an evangelical bent (partly as a result of the use of the term "fundamentalist" to describe the Muslims in opposition to whom they often conceive themselves) have come to reject the term originally invented to describe their core convictions. This does not mean that they no longer hold to those "fundamental" beliefs but rather that they seek to distance themselves from the irrationalism, the antiprogressivism, and the antimodernism that purportedly characterize Islamists and from the open political engagement (and occasional embarrassments) of the strident fundamentalist movement in the United States. For their part, radical Muslims (and those who study them) often resent the imposition of a term historically associated with American Christianity to describe Islamic reform movements. Islamic reform movements have an extremely long history that is not readily reducible to reactions to western modernism. Muslim regions of the globe have long oscillated between periods of adjustment to local needs, practices, and customs and periods of reform. To mark off the current moment of reform as somehow radically different from other moments of reform and renewal, and in the process reduce that activism to mindless reactionary rejection of modernity, strikes many as simply more evidence of the solipsism and arrogance of the west. In other words, both parties (Christian and Muslim) resist the use of the term "fundamentalist" and consequently complicate any analytical strategy that attempts to discern whether such movements have some kinship with one another. And yet the dualistic thinking and nostalgia for an ideal order modeled on the patriarchal family seem so unmistakably similar that it is difficult to defer to the insiders on this issue of their fundamental difference from one another.

As a historian, I am struck by both the parallels and the important differences. First, the "family resemblance" between the movements is

worth pointing out, even if in the end their specific qualities and historical trajectories begin to seem more important than the general commonalities when it comes to understanding particular moments of encounter in time. Precisely because both evangelical Christians and
Islamic reformists would be startled at the suggestion that their movements bear strong resemblances to one another, sketching out those resemblances might be one of the most powerful ways to induce all parties
to engage in deeper reflection and introspection and in particular to encourage a more nuanced and historically informed engagement among
and between them.

Martin Riesebrodt's study of two fundamentalist movements in parallel phases of historical development has been particularly useful to me
in my reflections on the prospects of such a comparison.[10] Riesebrodt
compares the rise of Protestant fundamentalism in the United States
from 1910 to 1928 with the rise of Shi'ite fundamentalism in Iran from
1961 to 1979, tracing with care the social origins of the leaders, the
demographic background of supporters, and the specific ideological emphases of each movement. His study sheds light on the "reactionary modernism" of early SIM missionaries. Because the Iranian revolution has
come to serve as a model of committed Islamism even for Sunni Muslims
in Africa in the contemporary moment, his reflections on Iranian fundamentalism are also revealing, if less immediately relevant. He chooses
two salvific millenarian movements that are explicitly political for comparison, making it possible to think about the relationship between salvation history and social critique. Such movements read the social practices of the present both in terms of their falling away from an ideal
order established in the past (the time of the early church, the time of
Mohammed's early community) and in terms of their significance in the
linear march of history from creation to the end times. Both the Christian and Shi'ite fundamentalist movements, he argues, are "instances of
a traditionalism that has become reflexive and radicalized"; in other
words, they are "mobilized traditionalism" as opposed to either quiescent
traditionalism or unchallenged orthodoxy (Riesebrodt 1993, 177). Believers faced the disintegration of a supernatural view of life at the hands
of modern science, cultural pluralism that undermined the universality
of their convictions, and a growing separation of private and public
spheres that increasingly made religion a personal matter rather than a
principle of social control and cohesion. The battle to restore the ideal
moral order was for both a supernatural battle of good against evil, leading toward the culmination of God's will on earth.

Both movements, contrary to the assumptions of many outsiders, were primarily urban in origin and cut across class and other social boundaries—they were neither specifically lower class nor evidence of a reactionary rural premodernism.[11] Movement leaders, however, did not come from among leading theologians but were mostly religious practitioners from traditional rather than elite educational institutions (Bible schools and *madrasas*) whose middle-class expectations of prestige and social advancement through education were under threat. Fundamentalism, Riesebrodt argues, "is the means by which the traditional middle class conveys to a part of the population of urban migrants the principles of its statutory, ethical, rationalized conduct. Fundamentalism is thus a radical-traditionalist protest movement within the rapidly growing cities by means of which rural migrants are socialized into their new social environment. At the same time, it sponsors the integration of the city-dwelling traditional middle class and the new urban migrants" (1993, 178). In both cases, fundamentalism had close links to bourgeois trade and industry (the bazaar and the industrial base of the United States) and a marked hostility toward the secular educated elite.

Fundamentalism aims to preserve and re-create particular ideal structural forms through patriarchal structural principles; its innovations are therefore always neopatriarchal. Proper relations between men and women, elders and juniors, are templates for social order as a whole. Revitalizing the respect for a particular patriarchal family order simultaneously restores middle-class prestige and protects values seen as central to the realization of an ideal theocratic republic: "A common central characteristic is the restoration of the universal validity of traditional patriarchal social relationships and morals in the family, in consumer and leisure-time behavior, in politics, the economy, law, and culture" (Riesebrodt 1993, 201). Thus, fundamentalism regulates female sexuality and labor through dictating dress, attacking prostitution, and idealizing women's ordained position as mothers in the domestic sphere; it directs leisure time by attacking alcohol consumption, secular entertainment, and gambling; and it promotes personalized relations and individual work over government bureaucracy as remedies for social inequity or economic decline.

In part because of the lack of gender or class uniformity in such movements and in part because of movement participants' rejection of depersonalized bureaucratic relations in favor of personalistic and patriarchal structural principles, Riesebrodt finds Weber rather more useful for his thinking than either Marxist class analysis or feminist theories of institutional male dominance: "Only when the personalistic principle of piety has been replaced by the depersonalized principle of performance are the foundations of legitimacy of social relationships transformed and does dramatic change become possible precisely in the relationship between the sexes as well" (1993, 207).

The presumed universal validity of the social and moral precepts under threat is, of course, why fundamentalisms are so regularly missionary in outlook. Yet when the fundamentalism Riesebrodt describes is exported, interesting complications develop. Today in Niger a U.S. fundamentalism in the late stages of its absorption into the mainstream (the consequence of consistent engagement with political reform) comes head to head with a mosaic of Islamic fundamentalisms of varying age and militancy that are, in some senses, equally imported and therefore have a very complex relationship to "tradition" in the region in question. The recent entry on the scene of a freshly militant Christian fundamentalism—this time of a strongly Pentecostal bent, represented in this study in the Vie Abondante mission—heightens the sense of embattlement of the Islamists and places the more-established evangelical Christians on the defensive. The personalistic piety of Islamists is under threat from the assumption that the Christian view of patriarchal order is universally valid, and vice versa. Both Christian and Muslim fundamentalisms are under assault from the expansion of notions of secularism, feminism, and human rights purveyed by international development organizations and global financial institutions of precisely the centralized, bureaucratized, and depersonalized kind that, Riesebrodt argues, fundamentalists reject. This is why Muslim and Christian fundamentalists alike revile the United Nations as demonic. At the same time, Christians, Islamists, and secularists all agree that some "traditional" practices are backward and dangerous—in short, incompatible with modern life.

Riesebrodt insists that these movements are not antimodern but that they offer alternative modes and milieus for adjusting to the stresses and demands of modern urban life. While they may reject the assumptions of modernism, they do not reject modernity. Thus, contrary to the common thinking of those outside the two movements, both fundamentalist Christians and Islamists in Maradi today see themselves as active participants in shaping modern life by drawing upon divinely ordained values and practices in the service of promoting God's greater design.

At least three central differences between the Christian and Muslim movements, however, must be addressed lest the comparative impulse render real historical understanding impossible. Theologically, of course, the understanding of the particular form through which human salvation will occur differs substantially. For evangelical Christians it is acceptance of Jesus as Savior that ensures individual salvation, and individual Christians have access to spiritual renewal through God's word by reading the Bible in translation. For Islamists, adherence to the "way" set forth by God through the vehicle of the Prophet Mohammed ensures salvation— for Sunni Muslims in Africa, this is generally reduced following to the Shari'a as interpreted by the Maliki school of Islamic law. This means that while fundamentalist Christians globally have no coherent political agenda beyond promoting a climate favorable to evangelism (they can, for example, claim to promote democracy and at the same time support Charles Taylor), Muslim fundamentalists generally quite explicitly engage in political activism in an attempt to integrate Islamic law fully into all aspects of life: judicial, social, political, and moral (see Gifford 1998, 341–342). For both groups, a rationalist reliance upon the interpretation of revealed texts is key, but since Muslims tend to equate the "way" with a set of laws, in practice it is those who can claim to know and uphold the law who have greatest authority in dictating what is and is not salvific or ethically acceptable behavior. It is not enough to be able to read the Koran. Furthermore, many (but not all) Islamists explicitly reject the notion of a vernacular sacred text, making a deep grasp of the Koran or any other sacred text in Arabic a rather distant prospect for that majority of Muslims outside the Arab-speaking world who have little access to literacy in Arabic. Thus, a religion that has no clergy is, ironically, heavily dependent upon a particular scholarly class for its understandings of morality and politics.

The second central difference is geopolitical and concerns the interpretation of the relationship between western imperialism and Christianity. American Christians of the evangelical movement see the universality of their faith as transcending cultural, historical, and political particularities. Christianity is therefore (they believe) separable from the excesses, indecency, and violence of colonialism. They do not see themselves as participating in imperialism. This sort of naiveté is less available to, say, an Anglican mission that has a long history of work in a former British colony or to the Catholic Church in Latin America; most mainline denominational churches and more-liberal missions today are quite self-conscious and forthright about the ways in which missionization in the past has been implicated in violence and imperialism.

Islamists, on the other hand, regularly see core Islamic values as being under threat by the west and tend to conflate the intrusions of the colonial bureaucratic state with neocolonial international organizations and with western missionaries—groups that can in fact have histories of quite-intense mutual antagonism. All are alien, and all promote the decadence and immorality that threatens the social and spiritual well-being of the Islamic community. Seen as participants in broader global processes, then, Christian fundamentalists and Islamic fundamentalists have radically different readings of global politics. The differences between them are even more pronounced when one takes into account their very different stances vis-à-vis Israel. Christian fundamentalists have often seen the establishment of Israel as part of the working out of prophecy and as part of a greater movement toward the end of time in which the forces of good and evil will do epic battle in the Middle East (Ammerman 1991, 35). Fundamentalist Muslims in sympathy with displaced Palestinians often see Israel in satanic alliance with the west. Thus, the Arab-Israeli conflict takes on heightened and often eschatological meaning for both parties. The tendency, given the Manichean proclivities of both sides, is to read global politics in terms of conspiracies in which the Islamic world is pitted against a Judeo-Christian alliance.

The third important difference lies in divergent conceptions of democracy. American evangelicals have tended to take for granted that Christian values and American values are synonymous, not because Christianity is culturally American but because to them America is ideally ethically and constitutionally Christian. This is, of course, a matter of intense political debate in the United States. However, Christian missionaries and converts tend to believe that an ideal democratic state would uphold and protect Christianity. For Islamists, the words "secular" and "democracy" are often associated with the west, with the dominance of Christian-educated elites, and with a political conception hostile to the integration of Islamic precepts into all domains of life: social, familial, legal, political, and economic (Kane 1997). Thus, regardless of the actual disposition of any given democratic state to either Christianity or Islam, as a rhetorical and strategic matter, the notion of democracy has very different valences within the two movements. This is not to say that Islam is undemocratic; to the contrary, historically Islam has often been associated with anti-authoritarian, representative, and generally egalitarian populist movements. But in the contemporary historical moment, ideologues on both sides often see promoting secular democracy as being inconsistent with Islam. Most Christian fundamentalists share with Muslim fundamentalists a mistrust of secularism, but that mistrust is inconsistent and ambiguous, for mission work relies on the guarantee of religious freedom that is frequently couched in terms of the separation of church and state.

In other words, while both Islamic reformists and American evangelical missionaries might be characterized as fundamentalist, there is much to be gained from seeing these two movements, as they encounter one another in this particular time and place, through a particular set of historical conjunctions. Although it has made sense within the United States to see Protestant fundamentalism as a reaction against a number of key elements of modernism, once that impulse has been carried abroad to the mission field its oppositional dimension is quite differently configured. No longer a movement against modernism, it instead comes to stand for a particularly American brand of progress, a particular kind of modernism, and a particular mode of western intervention.

This means that we will need to attend to a number of key diacritical differences in thinking about the history of this encounter of Christian fundamentalists with Muslims that begins in a colonial context. What specific elements of modernity have been critiqued and to what degree are they separable from the west—how possible is it for Christian fundamentalists to step out of the very modernism they critique? SIM missionaries today, who take it for granted that they themselves are purveyors of modernity, seem rather oblivious to their mission's historical rejection of modernism. In this complex dance of alternate rejection and embrace of the modern, focusing on the shifting conceptions of the various parties with respect to tradition, secularism, progress, gender, and rationality will be perhaps more helpful than attempting to apply the loose and diffuse terms "modernity" and "fundamentalism."

What is the nature of this "tradition" that serves as both a nostalgic reference point and as the marker of the ignorance of the past that must be rejected? Colonial administrations regularly turned to "custom" and tradition as the source of stability and authority on which to ground their control of local populations, despite a sense that the colonial enterprise would free Africans from the thrall of the practices of the past. Tradition seems to be a remarkably slippery reference point for administrator, historian, missionary, and Islamic reformist alike. Because "tradition" has been at the heart of so many conflicts among and between these parties, rather than see the fundamentalist movements that come into confluence in this region as "radical traditionalists," I hope to illustrate how complex the notion of "tradition" was to become and how unstable a riverbed it could be for the flows of ideas and cultures in the Niger of the twentieth century. In the chapters that follow, I will take up how "tradition" and custom play out in struggles over what leadership roles converts should have, the nature of education, gender norms, and conceptions of law and property. While this is not a book that focuses exclusively on women, the significance of struggles over the "traditional" roles and practices of women is very much at the heart of the book, making an analysis of gender conceptions and relations an important thread.

Similarly, by exploring the specific consequences of various understandings of secularism, we gain a clearer understanding of the implications of French colonialism, Protestant fundamentalism, and Islamic reform as concrete historical configurations rather than as ideal abstractions. French anticlerical secularism made the work of missions in French West Africa extremely difficult. A more Anglo-American conception of secularism as the guarantor of freedom *of* religion (rather than freedom *from* religion) would have had rather different implications for evangelism. Furthermore, U.S. evangelical fundamentalism has historically defined itself in opposition to secular academic elites, which has had great consequences for the interventions of faith missions in the realm of education. While the mission might espouse secular government for its own pragmatic reasons, it did not see itself as an ally of secularism. SIM's rejection of secular scholarship and education, as we shall see, flew in the face of the most ardent aspirations of the Africans the mission hoped to shepherd into the fundamentalist Christian fold, with lasting implications for church-mission relations in the present. I take up the complex question of just what secularism might entail in chapters that explore contemporary violence, the tensions of World War II, education, and law.

The study of an evangelical Christian community in the heart of the Muslim Sahel, a Christian community founded by missionaries whose conceptions of modernity and secularism were deeply at odds with those of the colonizing power, can hardly be reduced to a binary "encounter" between mission as colonial agent and African as colonized. Furthermore, in this setting an instrumentalist interpretation of conversion seems particularly unsatisfactory: there was little to be gained and considerable hardship to be had from conversion to a North American brand of evangelical Christianity in a French colony in the Muslim Sahel. I have attempted throughout this study to maintain a sense of the multiplicity of players and discourses at issue, the unresolved quality of many of the struggles, and the different kinds of analyses insiders and outsiders of various kinds bring to the same sets of phenomena. One way to underscore the complexity of this setting is to set out a few of the kaleidoscopic affinities that momentarily emerge and just as quickly disappear: Christians and Muslims against "pagans" in the context of property relations, African converts and "pagans" against Muslim reformists in the context of constructions of gender, French administrators and African converts against "American" missionaries in the context of education, male native evangelists and women missionaries against racist patriarchal mission discourse in the context of medical evangelism, Muslim reformists and evangelical Christians in the context of traditional authority. These are affinities, not fixed or self-conscious alliances, but they are suggestive of just how fragmented the terrain of religion can be, how provisional the moments of bricolage, and how tenacious personal religious commitment must be to endure.

In a region in which to be Hausa is implicitly understood to be Muslim, the identity of an individual as simultaneously Hausa and Christian is complex. The book traces the ever-shifting space of Christian practice in Niger as individuals negotiate between the hegemonic assumption that to be Hausa is to be Muslim and the missionary insistence that to be Christian is to be an evangelical fundamentalist. The reality that many Hausa-speaking Christians are not ethnically Hausa is very much obscured by the proclivity of the church to adopt the cultural and ethnic mantle of the region's most prominent and politically relevant ethnic group. Drawing upon archival materials, participant observation, interviews, popular pamphlets, sermons, popular plays, church records, and songs, this book sketches the contours of a religious practice that is both Christian and distinctively Hausa—the kind of complex Christianity, at once predictably conservative and unpredictably independent of "the west," that one finds throughout the "two-thirds world."

Although much of the discourse of both the mission and the formal church bodies emphasizes the work of particular named male figures, a close examination of the Hausa-speaking church suggests that it is the ongoing labor of unnamed women that sustains the Christian community. Far more than either missionary or male convert would be inclined to recognize, the vitality of this church depends on the energy and imagination of women. As Adrian Hastings observes, the Christianity of African women "is undoubtedly Christianity's principal asset in Africa today" (Hastings 1993, 124; see Hodgson 2005). The role of women and gender issues have consistently provided the grounds of debate in the history of the mission and the church: the mission debated the essentially (white) masculine nature of the task of evangelism, the proper understanding of monogamy in the growth of the church and church leadership, the proper behavior of the Christian wife, the type of schooling suited to women, the nature of family and female labor, and the conception of womanhood among the Muslims it hoped to convert. For its part, the church has consistently denied women recognized roles, but as in churches throughout Africa, some of the most important social and political spaces such as choirs (Gifford 1998, 342) and fellowship groups have been dominated by women. Yet any open recognition of the importance of women to Christian life would undermine some of the central patriarchal tendencies of evangelical Christianity. Christians are ever mindful of how Muslims would interpret any open recognition of women as religious leaders in public settings. As has occurred in other regions, women's centrality in forging and sustaining a distinctive form of Christian associational life is not matched by recognized authority within formal institutional structures.

One final theme that emerges from a consideration of the complex history of evangelical Christians in Niger is how powerfully the Christian missionary enterprise in Africa was shaped by the preexisting and competing missionary thrust of Islam. Most missions chose to work where competition with the literate traditions and social capital of Islam was less intense, preferring "pagan" areas over Muslim regions. During the earlier wave of missionization, some missionaries even felt that Islam was a positive and admirable force and were happy to concentrate their efforts in non-Muslim regions. SIM's entry into the Sudanic belt coincided with a shift in perceptions about Islam and a growing feeling among evangelical missionaries that Africans must be saved by Christianity before they became contaminated by Islam.

The inevitable Muslim resistance to this variety of Christian encroachment shaped the mission's activities in numerous ways: it contributed to the uneasy relationship between the colonial governments and the mission, to mission decisions about where stations were to be placed, to the rhetorical and linguistic apparatus developed to work in the region, and to SIM's eventual focus on medical and development work. This book reveals that at virtually every stage, SIM's activities in the region were affected by the reality that African populations in Niger expressed their preferences politically, socially, and spiritually in ways that dictated much of what the mission could accomplish. One might state this in a positive way to say that Christian converts had a significant role in shaping the mission's interventions by contributing to translation and evangelism and emphasizing schooling and technical services. But Muslim resistance also came into play, for it often dictated the form and the location of mission activities. In very significant ways, Muslim intermediaries had a hand in shaping the translation of the Hausa Bible. Christian practice in an overwhelmingly Muslim milieu bears the imprint of Hausa Christians' awareness of Muslim expectations and unconscious acquiescence to a range of local cultural assumptions about spirituality. SIM and later evangelical groups succeeded in fostering a lively Christian minority community. However, they have not done so under conditions of their own choosing.

This work provides a sustained exploration of the complex relations between Christians and Muslims in a milieu in which a substrate of local spiritual practices exerts profound influence on understandings of space, nature, and the body, but the more striking and sustained division the book sets out is that between the community of Hausa-speaking Christians and the SIM mission. I did not intend, when I began this study, to write a book about the tensions between mission and church, but those tensions have profoundly shaped the history of Christianity in this region and the perceptions and experiences of the missionaries and Christian converts I interviewed. This study is in many ways a cautionary tale about the long-term costs of the failure to invest in education, about the insidious consequences of unrecognized racism, and about the near-impossibility that individuals so differently situated culturally and economically can fully understand and respect one another's motives. Most of the parties to this history, I should observe, would agree that we are all the children of Adam ('yan Adamu). Not surprisingly, then, this story is full of all-too-human slights and injuries, failure to forgive, and the sin of pride. I hope my various readers (including those whose story it is I tell) will not experience this book as accusatory or reproachful. My intention is not to cast proverbial stones but to suggest just how complex intercultural encounters can be—how deep and fundamental the conceptual and ideological divides among allies often are—and to trace the inescapable legacy of choices made in the past for those who find themselves struggling to do the right thing in the present. Only by facing up to these kinds of legacies can we, in the United States, come to some understanding of why it is that those we think we have come to save so regularly seem to feel little but mistrust, anger, and resentment in return.

1

Anatomy of a Riot

> *In the Name of God, the Merciful, the Compassionate . . .*
>
> —Koran 1:1 (Arberry trans.)
>
> *And the scribes and Pharisees brought unto him a woman taken in adultery; . . . They say unto him, Master. . . . Moses in the law commanded us, that such should be stoned: but what sayest thou? . . . He lifted up himself, and said unto them, He that is without sin among you, let him first cast a stone at her.*
>
> —John 8:3–11

On the morning of November 8, 2000, hundreds of young Muslim men, angered, among other things, by the opening of the International Festival of African Fashion (FIMA) in the capital of Niamey, took to the streets of Maradi and damaged or destroyed numerous drinking establishments, the Vie Abondante church and food stores, property of the SIM mission, lottery booths of the Pari Mutuel Urbain, cars, and the homes of purportedly immoral single women. Little noted in the press was the attempted murder of the *iya*, the titled aristocratic leader of the local spirit-possession cult of the region and sister of the traditional ruler of the region of Maradi. Her home was set ablaze and she was thrown back into the flames by protesters as she attempted to flee the conflagration. She survived the attack but suffered severe burns. Other women were publicly abused and beaten and their homes and modest property were destroyed. There have been no official reports of deaths resulting from the violence, although rumors on the street insisted that at least one infant died in the burning of a straw-hut refugee village outside of town. The failure of any news media to report the attempt on the *iya*'s life suggests to me that the government of Niger went to some pains to keep the real depth of the violence under wraps. It took local authorities well into the evening to bring the city to uneasy order; they arrested close to a hundred protesters. The government dissolved eight Islamic associations in the wake of the disturbances, and some of the accused leaders were held for a month before being given a trial date. The burned skeletons of lottery kiosks and gutted cars continued to mark the landscape of Maradi long afterward. The riot was a watershed in Niger's recent history, the moment in which it became unmistakably clear that the secularist discourse of the national government could no longer hide the rise of Islamism in Niger. It also marked a significant turning point in my own thinking about religion in Niger, for as an eyewitness to the riot I could no longer be complacent about Niger's immunity from the kind of intercommunal violence seen in neighboring Nigeria. I continue to mourn the loss of a country I had always experienced as a haven of kindness and tolerance.

This riot was in part the result of the complex local experience of several intersecting processes: the fitful effort of Niger since 1990 to democratize; the resurgence of monotheistic religious discourses, both Islamist and charismatic Christian, at the expense of spiritually plural practices; the perception that western donors control the decision making of the state; and the playing out of these tensions on the bodies of women. I will provide evidence for a reading of the riot as carefully orchestrated and targeted, an interpretation of the events that runs counter to the way some, including Niger's government and many Christians, have chosen to understand it. To see the violence as principally directed at Christians—as has been the case in the western media and in Nigérien political discourse—is to underemphasize a more sustained assault on the rights of single women (most of whom are Muslim). Furthermore, the highly embodied spirit-possession activities of both women and men in the region have been violently suppressed, a dimension of the assault on religious freedom that has gone entirely unremarked.

Nilüfer Göle has recently pointed out in a penetrating study of the social imaginary in Turkey that the public sphere "is not simply a pre-established arena: it is constituted and negotiated through performance" (2002, 183). Göle's study illustrates the importance of women as visible markers in struggles to define the public sphere and reform or adapt modernity in response to critiques of the west. "Social imaginaries," she points out, "are carried by images" (177), and the image of women is among the most potent in shaping a nation's sense of self. Urban settings are precisely the arenas where such struggles to define the social imaginary are enacted, for it is in these concentrated spaces that the juxtaposition of different globalizing discourses and modes of self-representation force a reconsideration of the taken-for-granted social and cultural forms that often characterize more-rural settings. The urban centers of Niger, in this instance Niamey and Maradi, are sites of confluence and contradiction where national (Nigérien), transnational (Muslim, Hausa, *bori*), and subnational identities (Gobirawa, Aderawa, Arna) coexist. They are also sites where the habitus of "tradition" is challenged and the grand progressive assumptions of unreconstructed modernism are regularly discredited. As the settings in which the educational and communications infrastructures are most advanced, they are also the prime arenas for the generation and propagation of alternative visions to both tradition and enlightenment modernity. Even when their occupants reject western modernism, they remain spaces that have little tolerance for the attributes of "bush" life, which is regarded as "backward" or "ignorant."

Urban settings throughout Hausaland are highly textured and often contain disparate elements that historically have been held together only by political dexterity, religious pragmatism, and, occasionally, force. Maradi's fragmented urban landscape, revealed through the names of her neighborhoods, contains previously animist Arna populations that have only recently Islamicized (Maradawa), traditionalist families with long histories of Islamic scholarship (Limantchi, "the neighborhood of the imam"), aristocratic families whose claim to power resides in their ability to mediate between these two disparate populations (Yan Daka, "children of the court"), newer areas where the commercial wealth of men known as *alhazai* (pilgrims to Mecca) has created alternative trajectories to power (Sabon Gari, Sabon Carré, and Zaria) and from whence have emerged less-accommodating interpretations of Islam, and, finally, the residential zone originating in the colonial and early independence era where the elite functionaries of the state (often from other regions of Niger) live alongside western expatriates who work in the fields of development and missionization.[1] The small population of evangelical Christians is concentrated in three newer neighborhoods, Sabon Carré (near the SIM mission compound), Soura Bouldé (where there are two churches), and Zaria (where newer immigrants to the city build homes in a neighbor-

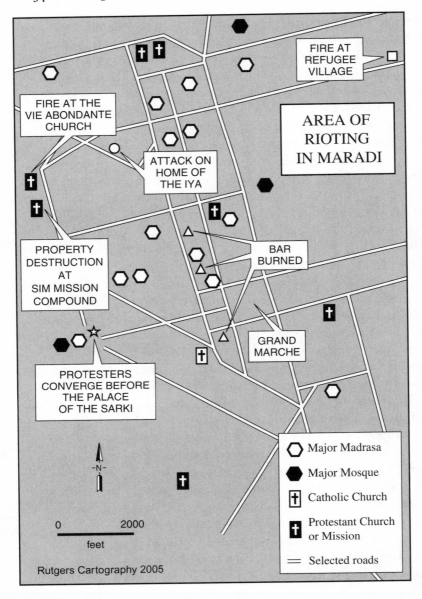

FIRE AT REFUGEE VILLAGE

FIRE AT THE VIE ABONDANTE CHURCH

ATTACK ON HOME OF THE IYA

AREA OF RIOTING IN MARADI

PROPERTY DESTRUCTION AT SIM MISSION COMPOUND

BAR BURNED

GRAND MARCHE

PROTESTERS CONVERGE BEFORE THE PALACE OF THE SARKI

-N-

0   2000

feet

Rutgers Cartography 2005

Major Madrasa

Major Mosque

Catholic Church

Protestant Church or Mission

Selected roads

hood that is expanding rapidly eastward). While some Christians have homes in scattered pockets elsewhere in the city, the security and sociability of living near other Christians is highly valued.

Christians and Islamists are often relative outsiders to establishment

Maradi society (the aristocracy and the traditionalist scholars), and they tend to live in the same relatively new neighborhoods at the northern end of town.[2] Indeed, some of the most vocal reformist Islamic scholars have schools in the same neighborhoods populated by the Christians. One of the most unfriendly mosques from the vantage point of Christians is a stone's throw from the largest Christian neighborhood, and Christians in Soura Bouldé must pass it to visit friends in the other concentrated Christian enclaves in Zaria. Christian women in particular are very conscious of which routes they must travel to avoid hostile students sitting outside in front of an informal Koranic school, a mosque full of men at prayer time, or the flood of *madrasa* students as they leave formal Islamic school at the end of the day. The spatiotemporal landscape for Christians, then, is conditioned by the location, activities, and movements of Islamists.

Of course, it is not just Christian women who must be careful about their movements. Muslim traditionalist and secularist women are equally cautious; many of my Muslim female friends have significantly altered their veiling habits and visiting patterns in recent years as a result, eschewing western clothes and veiling their heads more carefully than in the past. Women's difficulty in moving about the city has been greatly increased by the dearth of taxis, one of the consequences of Niger's long economic decline. In the past women could travel in safety and a kind of limited seclusion in private cars and taxis, but those days are gone. Where men may ride on the back of a *kabukabu* (a motorbike taxi), women's dress and sense of propriety inhibit them from making use of this new form of transportation. Women of all social backgrounds now find that they must navigate Maradi's complex social terrain on foot, which renders them both vulnerable and subject to intense criticism. By adopting relatively conservative dress, women can insulate themselves somewhat from opprobrium. Mature Christian women tend to dress in the same conservative Hausa-style garb as Muslim women of their generation; however, the cloth they choose to make up their outfits often bears Christian symbols and quotations from the Bible. Thus, while they do not hide the fact that they are Christian, their dress does not differ remarkably from that of their Muslim female peers. Younger Christian women, on the other hand, are often quite cosmopolitan in their tastes, sporting elegant pantsuits and following broader West African fashion trends. All, however, cover their heads regularly and tend to avoid miniskirts. In this respect they, too, resemble many Muslim schoolgirls of their own age group. Christian women and traditionalist or secular Muslim women seem on the whole to share the same sensibilities with regard to dress. Islamist women, on the other hand, distinguish themselves by wearing multicolored body coverings similar to those worn in Saudi Arabia, known locally as *hijabi*. This form of veiling is a very recent introduction into the region. An even smaller number of women wear such veils in white or black and cover their faces entirely. Such women perform their religious and social affiliations regularly in their public appearance.

Similarly, while the *madrasas* often have signs up in Hausa and Arabic advertising the school, Christian establishments are generally quite circumspect. Many churches are unmarked and can be found only if one is aware of the name they are known by locally by congregation members. On the map of Maradi, I deliberately give only a rough indication of the location of some of the sites that were under attack during the riot. Similarly, I indicate only the approximate location of some of the best known of the Christian establishments, only enough to assist the reader in following the argument.

These differing neighborhoods make up an extraordinarily complex social mosaic; the one common denominator shared by all but westerners, missionaries, and converts to Christianity is faith in Islam. Far from the taken-for-granted "tradition" that might serve as a shared social lubricant, Islam is itself subject to ongoing debate. In the different neighborhoods, one finds enacted radically different interpretations of the relationship between public space and appropriate gender relations. In some neighborhoods (Limantchi and Zaria), Muslim women are strictly secluded, in others they openly sell cooked food on the street, and in still others they own homes and make a livelihood by servicing men's sexual and domestic needs. One of the defining differences in the lived experience of urban modernity across the neighborhoods of Maradi is the degree of tolerance for female mobility and visibility. Women's social, political, and economic options are thus profoundly linked to their spatial mobility, which conditions their ability to tap into discourses, resources, and self-representations associated with a range of geographic scales (Cooper 1997a, 1997b). The state functionary accesses national-level discourses of patriotism and citizenship to legitimize her employment outside the home, but she also does so by residing in and working in particular settings. Islamist women, on the other hand, enjoy a certain mobility in their neighborhoods as long as they are veiled in their distinctive fashion and their destination is legitimated through an interpretation of Islam that emphasizes their right to access Islamic learning. In the capital of Niamey, some discourses have greater salience in legitimating female spatial access than in Maradi: the educated Muslim or Christian schoolgirl (who often wears a miniskirt in Niamey and whose visibility and mobility there is underwritten by her sense that a cosmopolitan modernity is her privilege and a mark of Niger's secularism) may find that in Zinder and Maradi her dress is seen as justifying physical violence against her.

In Maradi, the gradual encroachment of Christian and secularist visions of Niger's future has meant that increasingly heated struggles over whether and how to define an appropriately Islamic modernity have characterized the past twenty years. Muslims have struggled to determine where to position themselves along a continuum from the kind of excessive secularism Göle describes in Turkey (which actually prohibits women from veiling in official state settings such as the Parliament) to the excessive Islamism all too familiar across the border in Nigeria (which treats adultery as a capital offense but threatens women disproportionately over men). Nigérien citizens who are proud of Niger's secular identity shudder as they watch state after state in Nigeria endorse Shari'a law. Nigeria's choices are not simply a matter of distant interest, for the Maradi region in particular experiences the social and economic fallout from that process as scores of Nigerian single women flee to the relative safety of an emerging red-light district to the north of the Niger border or to thatch (*karakara*) refugee villages within the city of Maradi. Maradi's entrepreneurial women find it less and less attractive to attempt to conduct trade across the border, given the constant reproach their mobility occasions. Such trade has historically been one of their most significant sources of income and social mobility and has been a key pillar of Maradi's economic structure (see Cooper 1997a).

The presence of Christians in Niger weighs heavily in debates about secularism and modernity. Their significance rhetorically is out of proportion with their numbers, which are very small in this overwhelmingly Muslim setting. Unfortunately there is very little real data upon which to substantiate claims about the size of the Christian population. For many years the Muslim population was argued to be on the order of 98 percent, a figure derived from demographic data dating from 1988 that placed the total Christian population at 0.39 percent. These figures, however, did suggest that in urban areas the concentration of Christians could be far more significant, at 1.54 percent, particularly in Maradi (République du Niger, Ministere de l'Économie et des Finances 1992). Since then little credible data collection has been done that would shed light on religious affiliation in Niger. No doubt it is the ever-increasing visibility and audibility of Christians that has emboldened some to reduce estimates of the Muslim population to the suspiciously round figure of 80 percent, leaving the remaining 20 percent of the population as "Christian and other," but the data upon which these estimates rest are not evident in these sources.[3]

Christians have become a kind of symbolic reference point in debates about how Niger should define its relationship to secularism and modernity. In practice, Christian families tend to be monogamous and the women tend to have some sort of salaried employment. Christians sustain linkages with Christians in Nigeria and the United States. They are the embodiment of a certain vision of male-female relations that locally reads as "modern" and "western" despite the hegemony of Hausa culture within the multiethnic Christian community and despite the conservative patriarchy characteristic of the evangelical tradition. The outward visibility of this Christian presence prompts debates about secularism, modernity, westernization, and Islam that are rendered all the more volatile by the American links of the Christian missionaries and an economic crisis that forces Niger to rely heavily on western aid.

Competition to define Niger's modernity transpires through predominantly oral/aural media (radio, television, amplified sermons, and the circulation of cassettes) that are now privately produced, edited, and distributed. Niger's commercial center of Maradi is abuzz with the electrified and amplified efforts of various parties to define and control the new Nigérien modernity through the circulation of what I think of as a kind of audible capital (Cooper 1999). These struggles are effected on the whole by men who themselves remain safely invisible—or, at any rate, out of reach. The Muslim call to prayer is emblematic of this ever-escalating competition—the reformists broadcast an additional morning prayer call at high volume an hour earlier than the traditionalists in a show of greater piety and asceticism.

If the mode of dissemination of these debates is oral/aural, the anxieties that are both expressed and generated by them regularly crystallize in concerns about female visibility, sexuality, and morality. As Valerie Hoffman notes, in the Islamic world, contemporary social and political problems are often perceived to be "ultimately moral in nature" (Hoffman 1995, 211). Islam emphasizes adherence to external rather than internal constraints; thus, it is the role of government to protect Muslims from temptations by rigorously applying the law. The "perceived epidemic of immorality" is caused not by a lack of male self-restraint but by a failure of government to regulate female visibility, the source of temptation and moral decline (212–213). Muslim reformists attack traditionalist Muslims for their relaxed interpretation of veiling and seclusion, for their tolerance of Sufism and spirit possession, and for their cooptation by what reformists regard as a western-controlled puppet state. Yet despite the potentially radical implications of their critique of the central nodes of political authority in Niger, much of the specific content of Muslim sermons on the radio concerns the control of women's dress and movements. Young women in western dress or skirts deemed to be too revealing are regularly hospitalized after attacks by reformists in the cities of Zinder and Maradi.

Much of the violence that emerges as a result of contemporary malaise is directed against or enacted upon the bodies of vulnerable and visible women. Young men, boxed out of marriage and licit sexual relations by the inflation of wedding expenses in an economy starved for sources of income, instead direct their resentment of gerontocracy and a state that relies on a foundation of paternal authority toward the single women who seem to simultaneously arouse and humiliate them. For most ordinary Muslim reformists enraged by their sense of powerlessness, the United States is a target that is well out of reach. Local women, on the other hand, are not. Diffuse rage in the face of impotence and uncertainty is regularly channeled into attacks on those least capable of defending themselves, those most subject to the ill effects of Niger's fragile economy. Women who are thrust into the most marginal of Maradi's economic niches, rather than being seen as the victims of global processes that disadvantage Africans quite broadly, have come to be seen as the bearers of western contagion.

Audible media, then, are not simply the invisible arena of the public sphere. They are central in generating social tensions, informing the social imaginary, and organizing violence (Hintjens 1999). Their geographic reach means that struggles over the definition of the social that first crystallizes in urban settings can go much farther afield into more-homogeneous rural settings and can implicate populations across national boundaries. Cities serve, then, as seedbeds for alternative articulations of modernity and as platforms for their propagation. As we shall see in a moment, social dynamics in Maradi have a strong rural-urban component and can involve highly mobile populations that regularly traverse the border between Niger and Nigeria. The social imaginary of Niger bears the marks of multiple conjunctions and migrations of peoples and ideas despite the conservatism of rural areas. In the ensuing struggle to shape the social imaginary of Niger it is not simply Christianity or Islam that is subject to debate, but also, and this is important, the figure of the Nigérien woman who so regularly seems to embody an idealized or demonized social whole. In the competition between globalizing monotheisms, the highly localized and spiritually plural practices of many women have come under particularly vicious attack. Whatever else she may be, the ideal woman of Niger is not to be permitted to embody or promote the "ignorance" of demonic rural spirit worshipers or superstitious urban *bori* adepts.

Moral Discourses of Development

Niger has, since 1990, embarked intrepidly on a rocky road toward democratization after decades of military and one-party rule. There is a poignancy to efforts to institute genuine democratic reform in an era of globalization—at a moment when the relevance of territorially based democracy is difficult to discern and at a time when the moral and financial resources at the disposal of Nigérien state have eroded significantly. The Nigérien state is a peculiar entity that has had little revenue of its own to draw upon since the collapse of the uranium market and the decline in peanut prices. France's unilateral devaluation of the CFA in 1994 contributed to a sense of the state's irrelevance and to popular feelings of disempowerment. A significant portion of the state's revenues comes from international loans that are subject to externally imposed conditionalities, and Niger qualifies for special consideration with the International Monetary Fund and the African Development Bank because of its status as a heavily indebted poor country.

The power and ubiquity of largely western donors in Niger's economic and political life breed deep resentment, an index of which can be found in Niger's mixed response to the attack on the World Trade Center. Niger's government immediately expressed sympathy for the United States. Yet two of Niger's prominent Muslim leaders, Souleymane Inoussa and Boukari Hadj Issa, addressed the following comment to President Bush: "Know that if you and your allies threaten Osama Bin Laden, Afghanistan, or any other innocent people, you will face the jihad of the Islamic Umma which aligns itself with all people devoted to peace and justice" (Anza 2001, my translation). The Nigérien government took this message to be a threat and dissolved the Islamic associations to which the two imams belonged. The comment reveals the perception of many that the west, and the United States in particular, hypocritically makes demands on others to uphold "democracy" and "human rights" when it is unwilling to hold itself to the same standards.[4]

Public debate in Niger is increasingly bound up with social movements that have extralocal linkages, in particular the resurgence of Islam and the explosion of charismatic Christian missionizing. Capital and ideas from other Islamic regions have taken on increased importance as a counter to the presumptions of western donors. Similarly, Pentecostal Christianity provides an appealing moral and financial alternative in a region in which the population has grown disillusioned by figures of authority who have consistently sought political legitimacy through Islamic social and cultural capital but who have failed to improve the lives of ordinary Nigériens, who are among the poorest on the globe.[5] Where the Islamists see the moral failings of the state as deriving from western intrusions and moral decay, the charismatics see those failings as resulting from the hypocrisy of politicians who veil their self-interest in a spiritless Islamic piety.

Neither Islam nor Christianity, obviously, is entirely new to West Africa. Islam has influenced politics and culture in the region since the fourteenth century; Catholicism in the region is linked to the French colonial presence from the turn of the twentieth century, while Protestant Christianity was introduced into the region more recently in the 1920s by the American-led Sudan Interior Mission. Pentecostal Christianity has exploded only in the past five years or so, and it is extremely difficult to get reliable figures on the percentage of the population affected by the phenomenon. Pentecostal Christianity has had particularly great success in enclaves where Islam historically has had little purchase. Rural areas in which highly localized spirit veneration is practiced by Hausa-speakers known as Arna are in some ways the most marginalized within the competing religious discourses of Niger; it is these areas that are responding vigorously to Pentecostalism. Using the city of Maradi as a base, Pentecostal preachers develop materials, raise funds, set up training centers, and transmit radio sermons to rural populations that feel to some degree estranged from the hegemony of Islamic discourses in Niger. Itinerant preachers based in the city venture into rural areas to show Christian films and preach. Rural populations are drawn to Bible study at centers in Maradi, where they receive training, materials, and spiritual support.

The accelerated, superheated character of contemporary capital, media, and population flows in the context of state crisis and economic collapse in Niger has powerful implications for the tenor of urban life.

Since the early twentieth century, Niger has been increasingly exposed to competing and conflicting currents, a *brassage* of ideas and people that generates an uneasy feeling of loss of control, a countervailing sense of possibility, and intense competition over how to control the outcome of unpredictable global processes. The waves of Islamism in Niger share an ideological affinity with Wahhabi currents from Saudi Arabia. Islamists can be quite sophisticated in their use of modern media in the service of a reformist agenda; namely, the creation or adaptation of the state such that all dimensions of life for Muslims can be governed by a scripturalist/ legalist understanding of Islam. As Niger struggles to define what democracy might mean, drafting and redrafting its constitution with each regime change, Islamist groups have regularly argued against a freedom of religion clause while Christian groups have rallied to safeguard an element they regard as absolutely critical to their survival (Djadi 1999b). Niger's self-definition as a secular state is thus very much at the heart of the religious struggles of the past several years.

One major change in Niger in the past ten years, then, has been the growth of a lively public sphere as part of the effort to democratize. Citizens are free to debate policies, politics, and the doings of public figures in ways that were simply unimaginable in the past. Most of the infrastructure and media outlets relevant to this public sphere are located in urban centers, and Maradi is now among the most active sites of debate with its two radio stations. The effect is intoxicating. But in Niger, which has historically been a relatively peaceful and stable country, the growing expansion of a global public sphere has also in some ways had a disruptive impact, particularly in urban centers, where exposure to cosmopolitan ideas is greatest and where social frictions are most intense. The state has neither the strength nor the legitimacy to act as mediator among and between the various parties sparring in the public sphere. Rather than act as arbitrator and guarantor of peace, the state periodically represses one element or another of the media, feeding a dynamic of mistrust and resentment. As is so often the case, democratization has had the ironic effect of leading to the periodic suppression of voices of dissent that are perceived to threaten democracy. This is a pernicious process—nothing is so radicalizing as exclusion from political life (Juergensmeyer 1995).

The social tensions that emerge with the suppression of religiously inflected political discourses of reform can lead to unrest significant enough to trigger a return to military rule and systematic media repression. But Nigériens have now come to expect freedom of the press, perhaps because labor migration, fax machines, and the Internet make it impossible for the government to contain the flow of the information that has in the past been more forcefully censored. International media and rights groups, as well, have been consistent in supporting both international correspondents and local reporters and editors in protesting repression of the press. The election of Tandja Mamadou in 1999 brought the reinstatement of democratic rule, and the public sphere is once again the uneasy site of noisy and contentious debate.

The failure of the Nigérien state to halt the cataclysmic economic decline of the region prompts Nigériens (reasonably enough) to seek alternative solutions from within available local discourses; some see a moralistic approach to political and social reform as appropriate and authentic. Increasingly, political discourse is colored by moralist theories of underdevelopment shared by almost all parties, whether they be Muslim, evangelical Christian, or Pentecostal Christian. These groups agree that moral failing leads to God's wrath being visited upon humans in the form of poverty, AIDS, and political corruption. It is only through moral purification that regeneration and development can occur. A commitment to such regeneration often fuels a reformist spirit within religious communities and a sense of religious renewal.

The most religiously activist of the Christian communities at the moment is the Pentecostal. Pentecostalism can be read in light of a kind of theory of wealth formation and economic development: those with true belief, whose prayers draw the power of the Holy Spirit, are blessed with wealth. If Islamic communalist discourse is often treated as a response to the individualistic tendencies of western modernism, the highly embodied practices of Pentecostalism (speaking in tongues, faith healing) might just as reasonably be seen as a reaction against the excessive rationalism of both the western heritage of Enlightenment and Islamist rejections of immanence (in attacks on Sufism and spirit possession) (Brown 1994).

Within its own terms of reference, this eclectic array of moral discourses—the strangely discordant common currency of so many in the region—is not so much antimodern as antimodernist. The group that is most consistently reviled by all of the moralist reformers is the *bori* spirit practitioners, whose activities are seen by all as backward and satanic— the epitome of the ignorance (*jahilci*) of the past that must be expunged. Traditionalist Muslims are readily marked by Islamists as *kafirai* ("pagans") for their absorption of and tolerance for pre-Islamic beliefs and practices related to this spiritual world. In such an environment it is easy to understand the sentiment of the relatively adaptive and tolerant Mawri spirit-cult practitioner whose beliefs are increasingly marginalized and demonized, to whom it can seem that "prayer has spoiled everything" (Masquelier 2001).

Audible Capital and the Struggle for the Public Sphere

The first major assault on the Christian community of Maradi occurred in April 1998 on the occasion of a protest march to demand the resignation of Ibrahim Mainassara, whose reintroduction of military rule in Niger after five years of civilian rule was extremely unpopular.[6] Mainassara had close ties with a number of well-educated Protestant Christians in Niger and gave an evangelical Christian economist a ministerial post. During the 1998 protest march, opposition activists targeted the church in Maradi most closely associated with that official during a crowded Sunday service, causing a great deal of material damage and permanently blinding a male elder of the church in one eye.

Protestant Christians have, until recently, been largely invisible in the political domain, keeping very much to themselves. However, as the evangelical church has grown over the twentieth century, the importance of a few well-educated second-generation Protestant Christians in a country woefully lacking in highly trained personnel has made it harder for Christians to remain in the background. The more visible Protestant Christians become in the political domain, the more their personal failings (or the unpopularity of the administration to which they contribute) tend to open Christians more broadly to attack. Some Christians in Maradi felt that no Christian should have accepted a position in the unpopular Mainassara government, while others felt that it represented a significant step forward for Christians to take part in the government. All seemed to agree that the visibility of evangelical Christians under Mainassara had made the churches more vulnerable to attack. Since that time, the evangelical church in question has not replaced the sign that was destroyed, and the outer wall has taken on a more defensive posture than it had in the past. The blinded elder now attends a different church.

Subsequently, however, threats to Christians have focused not on the older and more self-effacing evangelical church but on a newer Pentecostal church that first came to Niger in 1993, known as the Vie Abondante. This charismatic church has roots in Nigeria and draws its pastors from among the many Pentecostal ministers fluent in Hausa in Nigeria. However, the mission that oversees the church and the funding upon which it relies come largely from the United States. The Vie Abondante church took up the crusade of converting the unsaved in Niger with a vigor and success that took the older evangelical churches and the SIM mission entirely by surprise. One important dimension of the Vie Abondante outreach has been radio ministry. While the evangelical church traditionally had a weekly radio show through free airtime on the government station, Vie Abondante seized upon the potential represented in the newer private Radio Anfani station in Maradi. Vie Abondante offered more shows and developed a more lively and daring format that was hosted by a pastor from Nigeria. Broadcasts featured interviews and guest sermons from local Hausa-speaking converts, often from rural areas, about their conversion experience and the power of the Holy Spirit in their lives. The effect was to generate a sense of embattlement among Islamists and the feeling that potential and actual Muslims were being lost to Christianity.

Disputes over the content of the Pentecostal radio show soon became endemic in Maradi, causing Radio Anfani to be closed down periodically and occasioning regular intervention by the police to prevent vandalism to the radio station. Evangelical Christian leaders (and some Catholics, who have largely remained out of the fray because they have never been given to particularly active evangelism) came to feel that the charismatic preachers had an unnecessarily confrontational approach, and they faulted them for endangering both the Christian community and broader social tranquility in Maradi. Crafting a radio show that would not offend Muslims requires a great deal of experience, diplomacy, and subtlety in Hausa, or so the thinking seemed to go, and therefore charismatic ministers (who are generally new to the region and often not native Hausa-speakers) should not take to the airways in incendiary ways. Critical evangelicals implied that Nigerian and American charismatics should not be allowed on the airways at all. Of course, this slightly xenophobic criticism ignored the reality that some of the most inflammatory sermons were in fact made by native Hausa-speakers with deep roots in the region who were invited to serve as guest preachers on the radio show, which I will discuss in the next chapter.

By 1999, tensions had reached such a peak that one of the Muslim leaders of Maradi had openly proposed that Muslims should burn the churches of Maradi as a result of a radio show that he regarded as particularly offensive to Islam and the Prophet Mohammed. This disagreement, combined with friction over the questions of whether Jesus should be referred to as the "son of Allah" (which is seen by Islamists as a blasphemous suggestion that God is human) and whether it is appropriate to assert that there is no salvation except through Jesus, came to a head in the Muslim cleric's attempt to incite a riot during a sermon at Friday prayer in response to the radio broadcast. The police intervened in advance to prevent any further escalation of the tensions (Djadi 1999a).

Later tensions were of a similar nature but even more acute, for the shared conviction that God conveys messages through human intermediaries opens the way to interpret the differences between Islam and Christianity as evidence of false prophesy and, by extension, of Satan's work in the world. Malam X, the Muslim cleric who has been the most prominent in these radio debates and cassette ministries, is infamous among secularist Muslim intellectuals in Maradi for inflammatory radio sermons in which he claims, among other things, that whites are using the polio eradication program to commit genocide in Africa by deliberately killing children with bad vaccine and that the AIDS epidemic is a myth designed to prevent Africans from procreating. Both of his claims, unfortunately, have a kind of surface plausibility among a population justifiably wary of health care interventions by the government and NGOs.[7] Malam X's antiwestern diatribes resonated readily with local resentments about western intrusion, anger about the corruption of government officials, and outrage at the continuing disparities between the life prospects of Niger's elite and ordinary Nigériens.

In the next major incident involving the radio show, which took place not long before the riot, the American missionary for the Vie Abondante church gave a sermon on one of the epistles of Paul that Malam X took to be an attack on Mohammed, since it seemed to suggest indirectly that Islam was a false religion whose emergence the early Christian church anticipated. When I discussed the incident with the missionary in question, he remarked innocently that he never mentioned the words "Islam" or "Mohammed" in any of his sermons. But the effect of offering up a sermon about the importance of evading the temptations of false religions in a majority-Muslim region was, as evangelical missionaries critical of the sermon pointed out, quite predictable. By implication, Mohammed was to be seen as a false prophet, an emanation of Satan. Because a violent Muslim reaction was so predictable, local thinking on many sides (Christian and Muslim) seemed to be that the offensive sermon was deliberately incendiary. If Christianity is the religion of love, Muslims wondered aloud, why are its evangelists provoking hate? The friction that resulted from this incident prompted the government to close down Radio Anfani and prohibit both Vie Abondante and Malam X from preaching until things cooled down. It was in this general climate, in which unfettered speech conflicted with public order, that the riot occurred.

"Culture, Peace, and Development"

The proximate cause of the November 2000 riot was an international fashion festival held on the banks of the Niger River that was publicized under the theme "Culture, Peace and Development." The second annual International Festival of African Fashion, known by its French acronym FIMA, was supported in part by the United Nations Development Programme (UNDP) as an effort to support the development of a fashion industry and artisanal workshops in Niger. While haute couture might seem an unlikely economic specialization in a nation largely populated by impoverished farmers, there was a certain logic to the notion. Niger has long produced "Moroccan" leather goods made from goatskin that are much in demand in particular markets, and with a pool of inexpensive labor already skilled in handcrafts and in particular in sewing, fashion designer Sydnaly Sydhamed Alphady's dream of a distinctively African fashion industry built on relatively accessible intermediate technologies was not altogether implausible.[8] From the point of view of international development institutions such as the UNDP, the scheme had the added appeal of targeting women: in the words of one UNPD representative, "because cottage industries are essentially feminine, they present us with tools for eradicating poverty" (Panafrican News Agency 2000, my translation). Thus, the successful Nigérien designer's expressed hope was to counter the negative media image of Africa as conflict- and famine-ridden with a view toward attracting foreign investment to Niger, and his preferred tools had significant gender implications.

The festival offered a highly feminized and sexualized image of the new modern Africa. In the wake of years of war between the state and Tuareg rebels, a more pacific and feminine image was, perhaps, attractive to global donors.[9] The festival's stated intention was to create jobs, attract tourism by televising Niger's exotic landscape globally, and raise money for Niger's development. In an atmosphere of trust and in a period of relative prosperity perhaps those intentions would have been taken at face value, but it is hard to see how the overwhelmingly Muslim population of Niger could ever have found this vision of development appealing. The entire scheme seemed symptomatic of a development community and a national government far out of touch with local sentiment.

Thus, the media-savvy designer (who had all the major news organizations interested and a Web site to promote the event—one could watch video clips of some of the fashions on the BBC's Web site) went head to head with media-savvy Muslim reformers (who well knew how to use television and radio to raise a protest) in Niger's increasingly open and unruly media environment.[10]

The event, held on November 9th through 12th of 2000, attracted thirty-four fashion designers, including Yves Saint Laurent, Paul Gauthier, and the Senegalese designer Oumou Sy. The photogenic event was very much in the public eye on the televised news: images of internationally known fashion figures and glamorous nonwhite models in provocative dress dominated the local imagination. The extraordinary disconnect between these images and the generally modest Islamic dress and decorum of Niger's capital city of Niamey was jarring. The profound global imbalances in wealth and privilege, without which the high fashion industry would not exist, were everywhere in evidence. In this surreal environment, economic and cultural elements came increasingly to be fused—the unequal distribution of wealth and power was embodied, quite literally, in the dress and bodies of female fashion models.

Questions were raised about who would profit from this event and whether the costs, moral and otherwise, would be borne entirely by the people of Niger. Cheik Abdoulahi of the Association for the Influence of Islamic Culture (ARCI) suggested that Alphady would personally retain all of the profits. "You can't allow someone's pet project to be more important than the survival of an entire community, a project which also undermines the moral fibre of Muslim society," Cheik Abdoulahi reportedly said (Arji and Tedegnon 2000). However, the economic dimension receded rather rapidly into the background as the moralist discourse on development increased the tension. Religious figures expressed their opposition to the festival as contrary to the tenets of Islam because of the scanty dress of models and other women at the festival. This lack of modesty, it was claimed, would undermine the foundations of Islamic society. Thus, the discontentment over the festival was almost immediately framed in terms of women's bodies rather than in terms of the sources of funding or the lack of local control over how development in Niger would be defined. Resentments over a sense of impotence at outside intrusions into Niger's economy, however mediated by Niger's cosmopolitan elite, were actualized in an impulse to control women, their movements, and their bodies.

The tensions over the festival also were related, albeit diffusely, with a growing discourse of contamination and contagion that went in tandem with Niger's creeping awareness of and response to the AIDS epidemic. The event's highly visible impresario brought to the surface a homophobia that is rarely voiced in Niger. Homosexuality is so thoroughly rejected within local moral systems, both Muslim and Christian, that few in Niger would openly admit to being gay. Malam Yahaya Mohamed of the group ADINI ISLAM voiced this strand of the discourse of protest: "We know that at FIMA, all kinds of people who engage in practices contrary to our religion get together. The most notable of these is homosexuality, which is condemned by God and the Prophet Mohammed." FIMA would contaminate the youth of Niger, as Sheik Abdoulahi put it: "I am convinced that people who participate in FIMA want to give our youths Satanic habits" (Arji and Tedegnon 2000). The event was the work of Satan and would, it was claimed, promote prostitution and AIDS.

In the weeks prior to FIMA, it was becoming more and more clear that the fall 2000 harvest had been a disaster and that the country would have to gear itself up for an extremely difficult hungry season. Other disquieting news was in the air—a teachers' strike did not seem to have yielded any significant gains in pressuring the state to pay some part of the twelve months' arrears the teachers were owed. The functionaries desperately needed that money to make good the debts they had accrued and to weather what was certain to become a year full of visits from importunate rural kin who would be hungry and in poor health. Recent studies of health in Niger sponsored by such groups as UNICEF and CARE had made it clear that AIDS was an increasingly urgent problem with the acceleration of labor migration of men to the coast and North Africa during the dry season, so that AIDS and AIDS prevention through the use of condoms was a subject of greater media and government attention than in the past. To the east, in Maradi, the contaminated water supply in the neighboring town of Tsibiri was very much on everyone's minds.

In this apocalyptic climate, Muslim resurgents, incensed by the festival, staged their own media event on Wednesday, November 8th, holding anti-FIMA meetings in mosques and denouncing the festival in sermons. Muslim activists then marched on the National Assembly in protest, and when the crowd was dispersed by security forces with teargas, the crowd attacked betting-office kiosks, bars, prostitutes, and women in western dress. The sermons and protest were televised and reached an audience across Niger's urban centers. On the following day, Maradi had its share of the violence.

Madame, est-ce que vous nous aimez?

The riot broke out on the morning of November 9th as I was visiting a prominent evangelical Christian pastor who has given temperate, if by all accounts uninspiring, sermons over the airways of Niger's national radio. His home is in the center of the neighborhood known as Sabon Carré. As we were talking, he suddenly lifted his head and said with quiet urgency, "They're marching." There are often marches in Maradi, to celebrate the arrival of government dignitaries, to promote cultural events, or to protest the precipitous decline of the schooling system of Niger. But the pastor knew immediately that this march must have something to do with the television news broadcast he had seen the previous evening about the FIMA protests in Niamey. At the pastor's house, we felt a growing wave of anxiety, and somehow as we listened to the growing hubbub of the marchers, our conversation turned to somber subjects, such as the emerging news of the season's failed harvest. As we said our goodbyes, the pastor prayed for us and for the country in a time that looked very much to him like the beginning of the end of the world.

But things were heating up on the street, and one of the pastor's teenage grandsons came home from school and said he didn't think I should go out yet. Things were looking ugly, and he thought that he had heard rumor that the marchers had set fire to the *karakara* village—a refugee camp for women from Nigeria on the outskirts of town full of huts made of highly flammable sorghum and millet stalks. We watched from the doorway as a stream of young men and boys, dressed in unremarkable white Islamic dress, flowed along the larger thoroughfare to the east of us. These were not on the whole people of means and they were exclusively young and male. Some were dressed in the clothes characteristic of the newer Islamic schools; the majority seemed to be the kind of aimless and occasionally surly young men one sees all over the city, school-leavers with few employment prospects and illiterate men with even less to look forward to. They were accompanied by a swarm of small ragged boys carrying bowls, hungry mendicant students from the villages preparing to wait out the dry season in town.

When, sometime later, it seemed that the crowd had passed, the pastor suggested that his grandson accompany me home. So his grandson and his close male friend, both of whom were about sixteen, reluctantly agreed. We got a few blocks from the pastor's house, only to discover that the crowd to the east had somehow circled around to the west, north, and south of us, quickly closing behind us like a wave as we made our way west toward the SIM mission compound where I was staying. The streets were suddenly clogged with crowds of young men in worn white *riga* gowns beating violently on metal things with what appeared to be the pestles women use to grind millet peacefully in the early morning. Targets of particular attack were the ubiquitous metal gambling kiosks and the rare car still on the road in Niger despite the extremely high cost of petrol. The clanging din of pestles against metal and the clamor of the crowd were on all sides. The air was electric with noise and a frenzy of violence.

In the midst of it all, a calm and well-dressed middle-aged man with a carefully groomed beard was speaking on a cell phone in the middle of the street. He appeared to be orchestrating the different streams of protest. He did take the time to interrupt his conversation to look at me, evidently assuming I was a missionary, and ask contemptuously in a re-fined Parisian accent, *"Madame, est-ce que vous nous aimez?"* (Madame, do you love us?) Just how willing would the Christians be to turn the other cheek when they are the ones who feel violated, he seemed to be asking. The intimacy of the challenge took my breath away.

We didn't linger to respond or find out more about the targets of the crowd. We wove our way quickly through the streets, trying to keep off the bigger thoroughfares. One portion of the crowd seemed poised to move toward us, when, like a school of fish, it suddenly darted in the other direction. We ducked into a doorway briefly, then ventured out again. Everyone we encountered in the doorways was jittery and the town was abuzz with rumors—of the numerous bars owned by Christians that had been burned, of women and children trapped in the *karakara* fire. People speculated about whether the *sarki*, the local ruler and leader of the traditionalist Muslims, did or did not support the demonstrators, about whether he himself had or had not been attacked, about whether the gendarmes had or had not responded. The sound of teargas canisters exploding to the south of us closer to where the gendarmerie was located suggested that there was some sort of response under way, but there was no sign of the authorities anywhere near us. We came out in what ap-peared to be a lull and ventured westward again, and as we walked I could see billows of black smoke from the direction of the mission com-pound.

Ahead of us a steady stream of young men swarmed down the main western road, moving towards the *sarki*'s palace. Behind us saucy young girls sporting fashionable purple *hijabi* veils—they were the only women other than me who were on the street rather than peeking from doorways—called out to us "Allahu Akbar," the preferred cry of the rioters. Just as we were within sight of the road to the mission, a woman popped out of a doorway. Calling out my name conspiratorially, she pulled us in from the street, saying, "They've set fire to Vie Abondante church." And so we ducked into a Christian compound. But the waiting was excruciating. Unable to restrain ourselves for long, we poked our heads out as the sound receded somewhat. Another Christian friend ran up, tears streaming from her eyes, telling us not to go to the mission.

We ducked quickly back into the house and the sounds of teargas explosions came more frequently, but the explosions seemed to recede, like an ocean wave, to some other corner of the town farther to the south. We sat quietly drinking cold water in an unreal calm while the smoke billowed from the western roadway and the noise of the crowd continued to buzz angrily around us. The noise was overwhelming, a swell of thuds and bangs, cries and explosions. It was clear that the rioting was going on all around us, that the crowd had split and encircled much of the city.

At length the noise of the crowd subsided. The woman of the house ventured out veiled as modestly as her Muslim neighbors, slipping with my male companions into the anonymity of the crowd. I stayed put, knowing that nothing marked my protectors as Christians so clearly as my presence alongside them. It seemed that they were gone forever. When the woman finally came back, she said, "It's nothing but Christians in the compound now; they did a lot of damage but no one is badly hurt." Once inside the compound, my sense of relief was unutterable. No one had been seriously hurt. The older and more organized element of the crowd had systematically destroyed all of the mission vehicles, and two buildings had been set afire. The youngsters in the crowd had left their own childish mark: my bananas had been eaten and the missionaries' children's toys had been tossed all over the compound.

Controlled Chaos

While my own experience of the riot was conditioned by the fact that I was doing research on Protestant Christians, it soon became clear to me as I gathered information from people from around the city that Christians were not necessarily the primary objects of rage. The crowd started congregating in Zaria to the northeast of town, not far from where the prominent Islamist Al Hajj Y has built his mosque and where many of the younger and more prosperous Islamists reside. The assembled crowd set fire to the *karakara* refugee village in Zaria as their first act of violence, assaulting the women and their children who had left northern Nigeria to escape the violence against single women and prostitutes that had been unleashed by Islamist discourse there and the growing ferment surrounding the institution of Shari'a law.

The Hausa-speaking region has a long history of exiling and harassing single women in times of stress, and in this instance the women had fled north into Maradi for refuge. Consistent with a dying tradition of tolerance of the local practice of Islam, the local governing authorities—traditionalist Muslims and state functionaries—not only tolerated their presence but gave them permission to build huts in a number of designated areas on the outskirts of Maradi. There are specific spiritual contours to this long-standing Hausa harassment of single women in times of stress. On the one hand, zealous religious authorities threaten such women with violence or expulsion if they fail to marry immediately. On the other hand, during droughts, the *bori* spirit-possession cult, which has numerous single women as participants, is often called upon to perform a kind of propitiatory ritual to bring rain in the bush outside the cities—in a sense acknowledging the possibility that the spirit activities of women have an efficacy in this world. In other words, there is a complex and ambivalent cultural association between years of poor rainfall and famine, female power, and the perceived moral and spiritual imperfections and practices of women. In attacking the *karakara* village, the protesters were carrying forward a long tradition of scapegoating single women, particularly those who are seen either as prostitutes or as members of the *bori* cult.[11]

Having thus successfully violated Maradi's most vulnerable population, the protestors then flooded into the quarters farther to the west, ignoring the Protestant Christian neighborhood with its two churches near the northern gate of town. While their first target was the refugee village, and presumably the prostitutes in particular, their second target was the home of the *iya*, the leader of the traditional *bori* spirit-possession cult, a bit to the south of the largest Christian neighborhood. For me, this is the most disturbing element of the violence; I have many friends among the *bori* network of Maradi. Once again, there is a linkage with prostitution, since some of the women who take part in *bori* activities are single, and single women are often assumed to be prostitutes. Once the marchers had attained the *iya*'s compound, they set fire to it with her in it. When she attempted to run out of the burning house they picked her up bodily and threw her back into the fire. Her legs and arms were severely burned. The violence against her was the most extreme and the most personal of all the attacks that happened that day. She and her home were clearly objects of particular rage.

The protest happened immediately prior to Ramadan, the Muslim month of obligatory fasting, a period of tremendous importance to the Islamic community as a time of cleansing and spiritual renewal. In Maradi, the period prior to Ramadan triggers a major moment in the annual cycle of *bori* cult activities, for while *bori* practitioners acknowledge the existence of Allah, the Muslim God, they focus on a variety of activities in this world to control or regulate the spirits. In the past, *bori* dancing has been openly and noisily held in the heart of Maradi in Yan Daka, in a compound next to the *sarki*'s palace that was occupied by the previous head of the *bori* cult. As Islamist hostility has grown toward *bori* practices, the dances of the cult have gone farther and farther underground. My *bori* friends mourn what they experience as the gradual extermination of their religious practices. As spirit practitioners in the urban center of Maradi have been increasingly repressed, their followers have instead clustered around traditional *bori* leaders in more-rural areas that are farther afield and harder to control. The neighboring village of Tsibiri has become the epicenter of *bori* activities, and those activities are now far more closely in sympathy with rural Arna pre-Islamic practices than with reformist or traditionalist Islam. Nevertheless, in defiance of the general trend of capitulation to reformist preferences, in the year in question, *bori* dances were held for *yayal zana*, a ceremony to propitiate and say good-bye to spirits before they are "tied up" temporarily during Ramadan. During the week before the riots, the sound of *bori* drumming could be heard daily coming from the current *iya*'s compound in Sabon Carré.

One way of understanding the unaccustomed boldness of the *bori* practitioners in Maradi that season is to read it as a kind of demonstration of good faith in a ritual exchange between the *bori* community, which adheres to the Islamic lunar calendar, and Arna communities, which are regulated by the seasons. If the Arna would hold off their *bu'dar daji* (a solar year ceremony that would open the bush to hunters and free up bush spirits at the end of the harvest—the antithesis of the "tying of the spirits" prior to Ramadan), the *bori*-cult practitioners would make good their claim to honor the spirits by holding a significant *yayal zana* ceremony this year. The bush deities and their rural devotees could thus be confident that the spirits would indeed be released and celebrated in a particularly spectacular *bu'dar daji* ritual after Ramadan. *Bori* practitioners see themselves as Muslims, and it is important to them that the sanctity of Ramadan be respected. There was perhaps an urgency to the *yayal zana* ritual this year in honor of (rather then despite) a traditionalist understanding of Islam. After the violence to the *iya*, dispirited *bori* members speculated ominously about what the implications of this disruption of the spiritual cycle might be for the future of Niger.

Having thus thrown the spiritual world into utter disarray, the crowd split and surged in two streams, which is why my companions and I suddenly found ourselves surrounded. Part of the crowd threaded its way along an easterly route toward the market and the administrative center, targeting every bar along the way before converging with the other protesters in the open plaza before the *sarki*'s court. The destruction of property was extensive, and because many of the bars are owned and run by Christians, the impact on the Christian community was considerable. Once again, however, it is not entirely clear that Christians as Christians were under attack; rather, the target was a night-life culture that promoted alcohol and prostitution.

If the original impetus of the protest was not directed in any immediate way against Christians, how did the Pentecostal Vie Abondante church and evangelical SIM mission come under attack? As far as I can tell, the other stream of the crowd made its way to the westernmost road in town and was headed along that route toward the *sarki*'s court. I suspect that the gentleman with the cell phone was orchestrating much of this at the moment we encountered him. Clearly, if I am right about the flow of the crowd, this was not simply random violence but was rather a well-planned and carefully executed operation that took advantage of the presence of large crowds of disaffected young men (some evidently trucked in from elsewhere; rumor had it that they were Nigerian) and at least three leaders on the ground—the man I encountered and two others with phones leading the two main streams. Although the actions of individual protesters were unpredictable and opportunistic, the overall action was not chaotic. This westerly branch of the marchers, I believe, had been specifically directed to attack the Vie Abondante compound on that road. The sizable compound holds a church, a residential Bible school, and a childcare center for the children of the adult Bible students who come to Maradi from rural areas to increase their knowledge of Christianity.

The story on the street is that as the crowd was washing past the church, the church's disgruntled neighbors urged the protesters to attack the compound; otherwise, they would have passed it by. I am not sure what the appeal of that story is, beyond the well-known fact that the noisy amplified celebrations and sermons of the church have indeed managed to anger some of the Muslims of the neighborhood. While other older evangelical churches tend to be very wary of drawing attention to themselves through signs and noise, Vie Abondante had a conspicuous sign on the road and a boisterous presence in the neighborhood at the time of the riot. The trajectory of the crowd directly west to the point on the road where the Vie Abondante compound is located seems too calculated to fit with the story that it was the church's neighbors that urged the crowd to enter the compound as it happened to pass by—there are other, more direct ways to get to the *sarki*'s palace from the home of the *iya*. Indeed, given the layout of Maradi's streets, it is easier to flow toward the *sarki*'s palace than it is to head directly west toward Vie Abondante's compound.

In fact, the individual who is known to have led the westerly branch of the marchers, easily recognized by everyone in Maradi, was none other than Malam X, the nemesis of the Vie Abondante church and its radio sermons. Why would the protestors attack Vie Abondante in particular when it had spared all the other churches in town? (There are six other churches, none of which was touched.) I think there are two reasons. One has little to do with Vie Abondante's immediate neighbors and everything to do with the community's ubiquity as a result of their radio broadcasts over Radio Anfani. The protests in Niamey could be directly traced to the International Festival of African Fashion and the opportunistic use of television broadcast by Muslim reformists there, but in Maradi (where very few people have televisions and where the fashion show seemed a rather distant and irrelevant event) the proximate causes of the riot—which was far more destructive than in the capital—had more to do with the growing competition between Muslim preachers such as Malam X and charismatic preachers such as the Vie Abondante missionaries over Radio Anfani. The riot had become part of the escalating struggle to control the public sphere.

While some other missionaries, preachers, and evangelical Christians in Maradi might maintain the same views as the Vie Abondante preachers in private, only Vie Abondante has had the temerity in recent years to confront the Muslims over the prickly question of whether or not Islam supersedes Christianity. Muslims believe that Islam, as the most recently revealed of the Abrahamic traditions, improves upon the revelations of Christianity. Evangelical and Pentecostal Christians reject the notion that Islam can replace or improve upon the teachings and salvation offered by Jesus. With its noisy amplified services and its radio show, Vie Abondante aims to be heard, if not seen. As a result, it has become something of a lightening rod for resentment among Maradi's Muslims about externally funded intrusions and the importation of ideas and practices that threaten the vision of modernity resurgent Islam purveys.

Another characteristic of Vie Abondante distinguishes it from Catholic and older evangelical churches. Consistent with the Pentecostal tradition, Christians of Vie Abondante believe in the power of the Holy Spirit to heal and bring wealth. Their services gather the power of the Holy Spirit by using music and movement. Services are kinetic, embodied experiences that include loud amplified music, western-style drums, dance, and song. They feature faith healing, speaking in tongues, and the ingathering of the Holy Spirit. To Maradi's Muslims (and, it must be said, to more than a few disapproving evangelical Christians), this looks a great deal like *bori* spirit possession. Many recent converts come from traditionally animist enclaves. The coincidence of the rise of Pentecostalism with the extraordinary decline of Niger's economy and standard of living seems, in the minds of some, to be linked. It is this satanic activity that has drawn the wrath of Allah on Maradi, so the thinking goes, and it must come to an end. There was a certain associative logic to the flow of the rioters from attacking prostitutes (single women) to attacking the head of the *bori* cult (head of the many single women who engage in spirit-possession activities) to attacking the Vie Abondante church (purveyors of an apparent variation on such activities).

The damage done at Vie Abondante was systematic. The crowd used a log to crash through the locked gate (which took a good ten to fifteen minutes) while one of the church women stood with her hand up, praying that God would stop the crowd. As the protestors finally broke through, an Ibo pastor from Nigeria, who was entirely too familiar with the perils of sectarian martyrdom, yelled at her, "Just run!" Frantic Bible school students and teachers passed the children over the compound wall before climbing over themselves. The protesters burned the schoolrooms, the dormitories, the storerooms, and, most spectacularly, the church itself. The children in the mob trashed everything—the instruments, the sound system, the benches, the church doors. They took particular joy in destroying the amplification system of the church. "This is the last day," the little boys reportedly crowed in triumph over the loudspeaker, before it, too, was destroyed. Throughout the neighborhood, people could hear them taunting, "Testing, testing, this is the last time!" Most disturbingly, they destroyed with particular deliberateness quantities of grain in the storerooms.

As for the SIM mission compound, just a little farther down the same major westerly road, the attack there seems to have been equally calculated, if less successfully focused and perhaps less emotionally fraught. But again, the attack was not random: to get to the mission one has to know it is there; it is not visible from the street, and it has no sign outside. The crowd, led again, according to witnesses, by Malam X, streamed from Vie Abondante to the next major target, the SIM mission compound. Why, after sparing numerous other churches, the Christian neighborhood, two Christian bookstores, and the homes of the many prominent Christians who are well known in town, would the crowd attack a mission that has devoted decades to promoting the health care infrastructure and agricultural development in the region?

The answer lies, it seems to me, in which particular structures were most effectively targeted by the rioters. While there was a great deal of destruction of vehicles on the compound (expensive cars being the sign par excellence of western privilege) and trivial vandalism and theft done presumably by the children in the crowd, the most evident target was the building that in the past the mission had used to store relief grain during the many periods of famine Maradi has experienced since the mid-1960s. Once again rioters painstakingly used a battering ram to open the door, and they set fire to the building. The seeming irrationality of destroying food in what promised to be a famine year is stunning, but that seems to have been the goal of the more-structured part of the attack.

In Maradi, most Muslims who are aware of the SIM mission compound think of it as the place where "Tony," a particularly popular missionary who has since moved on to work for World Vision, provided relief grain in exchange for work. Not surprisingly, some unsympathetic Muslims read this relief work as an attempt to "buy" converts. But there is also a significant gender dimension here worth underscoring. The overwhelming majority of the recipients of the grain in Maradi proper were women—widowed, divorced, and abandoned women who had made their way from surrounding villages to the mission in times of stress to seek food for themselves and emergency assistance for their undernourished children. In my experience, most secular and traditionalist Muslims in Maradi speak of Tony with the kind of awe ordinarily reserved for saints. So it seems to me that in targeting the storeroom for grain, the protest organizers were once again attempting to regulate the activities and movements of single women. The aim was to discourage them from staying in the region and force them to conform to an image of dependent marriage that the Islamists believed would bring Maradi back into a proper relationship with Allah and result in *lafiya:* peace, fecundity, prosperity, and good fortune. Once again the logic seems to be that the money and values of westerners have supported the rise and presence of "immoral" women and their activities that imperil the health of the *umma* (Islamic community). Hence, at both Vie Abondante and the SIM compound the grain store became a particular target, even in a famine year.

What, in the end, was the damage? For the mission and church, frankly, very little. Because of insurance coverage, a flood of donations from sympathetic supporters in the United States, and a certain stock of moral capital because none of the Christians returned violence for violence, if anything they may have come out ahead. Local bar owners probably would have had less success getting insurance for their property, so the impact on the local Christians as individuals was probably much more significant. But in the end the most effective destruction was not done to property. My friend Mary, a divorced Protestant Christian woman, was very upset by the events of the day, having seen clearly what mission leaders and the media evidently did not; namely, that single women had become a particular target of aggression. In tears, she described watching helplessly as an unmarried Muslim female friend accused of sexual impropriety was dragged out of her house and all of her things were burned. While the most visible destruction was done to property, the more long-lasting psychic violence was done to single women, whether Muslim or Christian, *bori* members or Arna, who all over Maradi now feel themselves to be extremely vulnerable. My Protestant Christian friend is at the moment contemplating a marriage as the second wife of a Muslim man she does not love because she is so frightened. She has lost many nights of sleep and can't eat because she doesn't know what to do and is afraid that if she marries him she will be ostracized by the church that is the center of her emotional and spiritual life. There is no insurance to cover that kind of damage.

I have emphasized the gender dimensions of this riot in order to avoid casting the struggles in Niger as political combat between established religiopolitical communities (Christians versus Muslims). Instead, the violence emerges out of much larger struggles to define Niger's social imaginary and thereby to reshape its relationship to modernity, secularism, and the gendering of space. The "problem" with conservative religious reformists is not, as seems often to be assumed, that they are insufficiently schooled in secular Enlightenment thinking (see for example Danfulani and Fwatshak 2002). A self-conscious rejection of secularism is what motivates their activism in the first place—indeed, the leaders of such movements often have quite-developed thoughts about secularism, modernity, and religious freedom. Religious violence in Niger is also a form of protest against the highly undemocratic intrusion of economic actors (largely western) into Niger's social, cultural, and political life. In rejecting FIMA's sexualized image of the new Niger, Islamic reformists also staked a claim to the right to define the terms of Niger's participation in global modernity. In Maradi, the response to FIMA was compounded with and ultimately transformed into a struggle to forcibly capture the public sphere (through the missions' radio transmissions, the amplified services at Vie Abondante church, and the noisy drumming at the home of the *iya*) and to set limits on women's movement and visibility. It was also a determined attempt to set limits on the forms of spirituality women would be permitted to engage in—the spirit-possession activities that have enlivened the spiritual world for countless women in the region were violently assaulted. If in Niamey the critique of global capital, international aid agencies, and the excesses of western conceptions of modernity was cathected on the bodies of female fashion models, in Maradi, the violence moved beyond the reformulation of an ideal image of Niger to actual violence on single women and active attempts to intimidate them in an effort to control their access to space and redefine the boundaries of gender relations and spiritual life. For women in Niger, the struggle to shape the national imaginary has also become a struggle to control the social, spiritual, and spatial mobility of ordinary women. It is an irony that the struggle to reclaim a certain right to self-determination in the realm of the nation has become articulated with a systematic effort to deny that same right to women in Maradi in the realm of urban life. What is often lost in discussions of the global religious conflict is any awareness that those whose spiritual beliefs are not confined to Christian or Muslim monotheism are in some settings under the most violent assault. This is not in any simple way a struggle between Islam and the west, or Christians and Muslims, for it reveals deeper struggles over the very nature of modernity and the rights of actors to choose how they will engage with global modernity and how they will navigate spaces and discourses, from the neighborhood to the globe.

2

Love and Violence

> *And, behold, a certain lawyer stood up, and*
> *tempted him, saying, Master, what shall I do*
> *to inherit eternal life? [Jesus] said unto him,*
> *What is written in the law? how readest thou?*
> *And he answering said, Thou shalt love the*
> *Lord thy God with all thy heart, and with all*
> *thy soul, and with all thy strength, and with*
> *all thy mind; and thy neighbour as thyself. And*
> *he said unto him, Thou hast answered right:*
> *this do, and thou shalt live. But he, willing to*
> *justify himself, said unto Jesus, And who is*
> *my neighbour? And Jesus answering said, A*
> *certain man went down from Jerusalem to*
> *Jericho, and fell among thieves. . . .*
>
> —Luke 10:25–30
>
> *The* bori *spirits aren't Satan; Satan is the*
> *evil that humans do to one another.*
>
> —*Bori* practitioner commenting on the
>   violence done to *bori* members by Islamists
>   during the November 8, 2000, riot

*A*fter my experience in the riot, I found myself haunted by the question posed to me in the street that day by the insouciant gentleman with the cell phone: *"Madame, est-ce que vous nous aimez?"*—Madame, do you love us? I needed to understand why, of all the things he might have chosen to say to me at such a moment, he chose to ask whether people like me (Christians? missionaries? westerners? whites?) were truly capable of love. Nothing in my experience of the riot led me to feel that love was at the heart of it, and yet clearly, in some perverse way, it was. Prior to the riot I had gathered sermons from the Vie Abondante radio show, *Muryar Ceto* (*The Voice of Salvation*) in an effort to begin to understand the recent explosion of the Pentecostal movement in Maradi. After the riot, I tried to listen to them not simply to understand the history of recent conversion but also (with an awareness that these were some of the very sermons that had fed the violence that day) to understand the sense of injury among some Muslims. What were the arguments resurgent Christians (in this case, charismatic Pentecostal Christians) were using to convince their Muslim neighbors to convert? And why might these arguments be experienced by some as hurtful and violent?

Even before the riot, some traditionally evangelical Christians had a sense that there was a kind of violence to the preaching parvenu Pentecostal Christians were delivering. After the first round of planned violence against the Vie Abondante church in 1999 was successfully prevented by the state, an unnamed Christian pastor denounced the virulence of the radio program to reporter Illia Djadi, commenting, "You can't hope to share the Good News to someone by making comments that are hurtful [*blessants*] in the local context" (Djadi 1999a).

This chapter will set out some of the characteristic tensions and impasses Christians and Muslims of a literalist stripe in this region are likely to encounter in debating the nature of monotheism with one another. While the Pentecostal ministers have been extremely aggressive in evangelizing in recent years, the older evangelical church and SIM mission often took the same kind of injurious approach in the early days of missionization in the region. Indeed, one virtue in reflecting on this rather rich contemporary material from the recorded radio shows is that it helps shed light on the less easily documented preaching done by SIM missionaries in marketplaces I will be discussing in the chapters that follow; the repertoire of scriptural passages preferred by broadly evangelical missionaries has remained relatively constant over many years. While there are differences of style and emphasis between Pentecostal preachers and the conservative evangelical SIM preachers of the early years, those differences have largely to do with SIM's abandonment of faith healing early in its experience in Africa as the heavy toll tropical diseases took on its personnel brought home the limitations of that theology. SIM missionaries at the inception of the mission could readily have declared, as Pentecostal preachers do today, that Christians needed to return to the simple prayer and faith of the early Christian church: "In the early church, they didn't have time for orphanages, gathering offerings for the poor. In the early church there were no hospitals for the sick. They went everywhere preaching and praying and in every city they healed the sick, they raised the dead" (Gifford 1987, 76).

In an eerie way, current Pentecostal proselytizing recapitulates the history of earlier SIM approaches. In the 1940s the SIM mission attempted to convert Muslims in Zinder by broadcasting inflammatory sermons in Hausa and Arabic over a loudspeaker. Of these efforts a SIM quarterly report said, "This is a new venture and we cannot predict the extent of its usefulness, but the Word is going forth to a large number of people in a way that avoids the endless and utterly useless arguments in which the strongly Moslem people of this town love to indulge."[1] Unlike radio transmission, these kinds of broadcasts could not be turned off, so they were far more intrusive than the current radio shows: "As was to be expected, the Malams have become wrought up over the broadcasting of the Gospel message; they cannot hinder the people from hearing, nor can they answer back with their time-worn arguments."[2] When the mission moved the amplifier into the Old Town, the broadcasts prompted such anger that the African evangelist at the time, Abba Musa, felt that with so much noise and stone-throwing he could not concentrate well enough to deliver a good sermon.[3] By 1949, the French administration's patience had worn thin and the *commissaire de police* would no longer permit the mission to broadcast.[4]

While SIM continues to make considerable use of radio, it abandoned this kind of intrusive approach as it matured or restricted its use to more-distant and untouched mission fields, for example among the Tuareg. But in Maradi proper, the SIM mission and the Église Évangélique de la République du Niger (EERN) churches now struggle with the complex and often bitter legacy of many of those earlier encounters with the local populations. This history is the reason for the undisguised criticism of some of the older members of the evangelical community in the face of what appears to them to be callow, insensitive, and inflammatory preaching. Voicing this position, one elder remarked, "You don't feed children food that is meant for adults." After its reluctant abandonment of faith healing, SIM gradually found itself taking on the kinds of institutional infrastructures that it had criticized mainline denominational missions for building (schools, orphanages, hospitals). I anticipate that in time Vie

Abondante will go through the same gradual shift to building schools and eventually to some kind of medical intervention. One young Pentecostal missionary with children remarked to me that she wondered whether, the power of the Holy Spirit notwithstanding, some of her flock wouldn't benefit from understanding more about hygiene and nutrition. The mission already includes Bible schools and nursery schools as part of its approach, and those schools are becoming very popular as the educational system of Niger continues to decline.

Pentecostal services and revival meetings include the laying on of hands and an insistence that the Holy Spirit will bring health and prosperity. They stress the contemporary experience of miracles such as the curing of blindness and the restoration of fertility.[5] But those dimensions of Pentecostal belief do not seem to enter prominently into the style of oral evangelism to Muslims that one encounters in Vie Abondante's radio program in Maradi which, evangelical Christians conceded, was entirely consistent with SIM and conservative evangelical doctrinal beliefs. When conservative evangelicals (whether missionaries or members of evangelical congregations) criticize the Vie Abondante, they criticize the aggressive mode of evangelism, not the theology.

Varieties of Radio Evangelism

The longest tradition of radio programming by Christians in Niger originates with the Catholic church, which has for many years aired its Sunday service live from the cathedral in Niamey over the national radio. This program is not specifically intended for a Muslim audience; rather, it provides Catholic fellowship in French for those who are not able to attend Mass. In a modest effort to provide balanced programming, the government has, since the wave of democratization in the 1990s, offered a free time slot to the established churches of Protestant Christians of the Maradi region once a week, which is transmitted from the Maradi station. Because most of the Protestant community originated in the Hausa-speaking regions of Zinder, Maradi, and Dogondoutchi, that programming has always been in Hausa. In contrast with the emphasis in the transmissions of the Catholic church, this program, which is produced by the EERN, has always been conceived by the evangelical community as a means of reaching the unconverted, particularly Hausa-speaking Muslims.

When the Vie Abondante Pentecostal mission arrived on the scene in the mid-1990s it saw the opportunity to make a much more significant impact through a recently established independent private radio station in Maradi, Anfani Radio. Rather than using the free slots on the state radio, the Pentecostal mission began paying the new private station for the use of a regular time slot at 3:30 every Sunday afternoon for a full-length sermon of approximately half an hour. The time slot was particularly well chosen in terms of reaching Muslims: the mission's program comes at a moment when many people are resting at home but are beginning to rouse themselves to prepare for late-afternoon prayers, which are held at about 4:00. The radio is often on in the background as people enjoy the gradual cooling of the afternoon and begin organizing the last tasks of the day. Christians and crypto-Christians both in Maradi and in more distant villages who cannot make it to church on Sunday morning can find some sense of community through listening to this sermon.

While both the EERN and Vie Abondante target Muslims in their radio programs, the EERN program is far less combative and builds on the strong shared cultural base of Muslims and Christians in this region. The position of the EERN pastors is that evangelizing to Muslims is a very complex task, best left to native Hausa-speakers who are urbane, mature, well trained theologically, and highly experienced. One EERN minister writes his sermons out in advance, so that each sermon is a carefully scripted performance. His sermons tend to emphasize a belief that many Muslims and Christians share, namely that the contemporary sins of immorality (prostitution) and disrespect (of the young for the old) are marks of the beginning of the end of the world. Another EERN minister, who is younger, does not rely exclusively on a text written in advance but does carefully rehearse the sermon, for which he prepares an outline. The theme of the sermon is calculated to interest a Muslim audience without offense. However, consistent with the interests of many of the younger generation, he reflects less on the end of the world than on immediate social relations between men and women, husbands and wives. Respect of husbands and wives for one another, for example, is a fertile topic. During a period when the Muslim radio sermons were attacking the prostitutes who were fleeing to Maradi from Nigeria, he gave a sermon reflecting on male adultery with prostitutes, gently raising the issue of male responsibility for and participation in the sexual sinfulness that both Christians and Muslims decry.

Because this younger (middle-aged) pastor has the primary responsibility for preparing and offering the EERN program on Niger's national radio, it is worth sketching a concrete example of one of his sermons, which he recorded in advance at the national radio station. He often prefers to give sermons using texts with metaphors that will carry the argument for him symbolically rather than literally. In January 2001, he offered a sermon on a passage from Mark (10:46–52) in which the story of a blind man who was cured by his faith served as an allegory for how, through belief, we come to see the truth. Lightly skirting the issue of what "belief" and "truth" would consist of, he allowed the story of miraculous healing and the trope of lightness and darkness to speak for themselves. He at no time argued that only through Christian faith could one please God or enter heaven, and the passage he chose did not refer to Christ as the son of God. Opening music in the broadcast consisted of women praying in a general way for the well-being of Maradi. As this transmission illustrates, while the EERN programs are targeted at non-Christians, they are neither aggressive nor fiery. The tone is moderate and measured, with little or no reference to any other potential religious tradition. EERN sermons are the product of many years of interactions of Hausa-speaking Christians with their Muslim relatives and neighbors. They seem to be largely inoffensive, but it is not clear that they are effective modes for "saving souls," for inspiring listeners to convert to evangelical Christianity.

Where the evangelical community now tends toward carefully scripted and text-based radio sermons, the born-again Pentecostal approach bears far stronger marks of a heavily oral culture. Pentecostalism emphasizes baptism through the Holy Spirit and takes as its key text the Acts of the Apostles in which, after the death and resurrection of Christ, Christ's followers were given the power of speaking in tongues through the intervention of the Holy Spirit. Speaking in tongues at services and during moments of shared prayer is a mark of membership in the community of believers, one which sets the Pentecostal Christians apart during larger interchurch gatherings of evangelical Christians. In other words, having the power to speak, to share orally the enthusiasm brought forth through the baptism of the Holy Spirit, is part of the perceived power of Pentecostalism. It holds the power to heal, to bring material well-being, and to guarantee eternal salvation. That lively force, that spontaneous oral inspiration, could be edited from the radio show only at great cost. The radio shows I will be discussing are far less scripted and far less self-consciously edited than the programs produced by the EERN.

Neither the state radio nor Anfani Radio are owned or controlled by the local churches or the missions. Their staff is mostly Muslim, as are their audiences. Interestingly, one effect of the various Protestant Christian–derived radio programs is that the non-Christian personnel at both stations, hungry for more programming and for journalistic balance, regularly seek out extra material from the various participants. Christian music to provide some color and variety on Christian holidays is now part of the staple programming of the stations. Simply having pastors whose shows include music in the station has opened the way for tapes of Christian music, both professional recordings from Nigeria and more amateur recordings of church choirs in Niger, to become a larger part of the local cultural landscape. The delicate task of choosing which songs to air is left entirely to the radio stations, which are seen to be responsible for any public reaction. If demographic figures for Niger regularly disguise the importance of Protestant Christians in the country, radio programming provides a very different impression of the size and significance of the Christian population in Niger.

The Notion of Sin: Zunnubi

In the months preceding the June 1999 attack, Vie Abondante's Pentecostal radio program, *The Voice of Salvation*, sponsored emotional appeals by recent Hausa converts to other non-Christian Hausa-speakers to convert and a series of guest preachers whose sermons were highly charged. One reason for inviting guest speakers was precisely to counter the impression that Vie Abondante is a foreign mission staffed by non-Hausa Nigerian personnel full of alien American ideas. Each of the guest pastors was invited to establish where they preached, where they were born, and how they became followers of Jesus. In this way the host, a middle-belt Christian from Nigeria named Pastor Sahiru, made it clear that the real evangelization in rural areas outside Maradi is in the hands of local Hausa populations; it is not "foreign" or western. Pastor Sahiru's standard opening question to his guests—"How did you come to accept Jesus as your Savior?"—is an awkward one, guaranteed to produce uncomfortable responses, as I have reason to know myself from posing similar questions in an effort to understand the sociology of conversion. To converts, spiritual transformation is the work of the Holy Spirit and therefore the role of humans in effecting such a change is in a sense irrelevant. Each of the preachers was reluctant to reply, and there was regularly a moment of confusion in which the guest preacher avowed that this was indeed an important question, suggesting that the answer could only be a mystery.

Nevertheless, Pastor Sahiru did seem to want to establish the social process of conversion for the radio audience, and with a bit of encouragement, managed to elicit such responses as "from observing the lives of relatives who are followers of Jesus," "through a friend of mine, Chef Musa, who took me to church with him," "I was in Tamroro and I met up with some evangelists and I said yes [na'am] to the truth of what they said." Through this brief preliminary interview, Pastor Sahiru humanized the guest preachers and established that in fact there is a sizable, if often invisible, Christian population scattered throughout the region and that it is through observing the quality of Christian life that many convert. The process of conversion was thereby revealed to be a slow one, requiring sometimes years of listening and watching, calling for the patience of loving relatives, neighbors, and friends whose personal contact with the convert prompts change. And finally, conversion was shown to require that the convert make a conscious act of acquiescence. It would not result from the impositions of a foreign outsider.

Having thus framed the sermons, the guest preachers (who were all male) could then assume the role of the interested and loving insider—the neighbor, friend, or relative who hopes to share his own faith with the listener. In all of these sermons the ministers regularly appealed to the audience, which was conceived explicitly as including both women and men, as "my brothers and sisters," using the more affectionate of the available terms in Hausa. The effect was of an intimate encounter with a familiar figure speaking in folk images and cadences in the kind of rural Hausa dialect that would not put off the many relatively poorly educated listeners in the Maradi region. This was a direct emotional appeal, not a theological exercise.

Some of these preachers came from pockets of the Maradi region that had only recently converted to Islam ('Kiriya and Tamroro, for example); these geographic origins would have signaled to the listener that these converts were deeply conversant with the local spirit veneration (arnanci) of such milieus. Their recently Islamicized kinfolk tend to practice a form of Islam laced with folk beliefs that many of Maradi's Muslim reformists reject as pagan. These pastors' origins rendered them particularly adept at speaking in ways that would be powerful to a rural audience that was only tenuously woven into the Islamic umma, but the "pagan" tincture of their upbringing would immediately raise suspicions of idolatry (kafirci) to a Muslim reformist in the city. Hence it is not surprising that many Muslims in Maradi associate Pentecostalism with spirit veneration, given the origins of many of its recent converts and its emphasis on the Holy Spirit. Such a listener would be particularly alert to any hint that

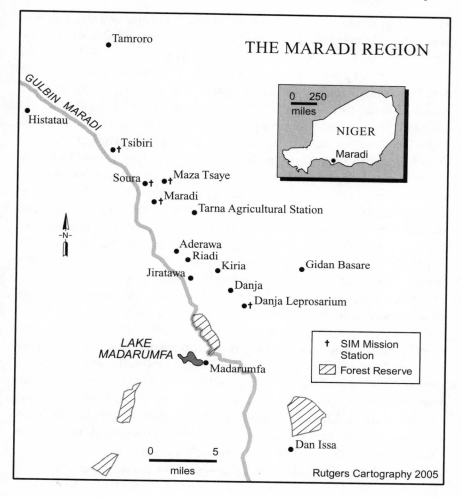

THE MARADI REGION

the preacher was attempting to draw vulnerable and immature Muslims away from veneration of the one true God, Allah, toward the pagan worship of multiple unworthy (and possibly satanic) gods or spirits. Let us see how this already inauspicious beginning played itself out over the next year.

The first of the guest sermons I will be discussing was offered in March 1999 by Pastor Iro. It began with the statement, "Hallelujah! Today's talk will be an admonition regarding the conquest of sin—*nasara da zunnubi.*"[6] The sermon, then, began with the assumption that the listener *needed* to conquer sin, which is not necessarily a perception that is common among the listening audience. Muslims, as John Esposito points out, do not have the same conception of irremediable original sin as Christians; sin is a failure to submit to God's will by following the straight path of Islam (Esposito 1998, 28). I cannot recall hearing the word "*zunnubi*" used with any frequency until I began my research among Christians in Maradi. Clearly it is a loanword from Arabic, but one with little currency in people's personal reflections on one another's behavior. The one context in which, it seems to me, Muslims now use it with increasing regularity (perhaps because they hear it used by Christians) is in reflections on the collective failings of the Muslim community in moments of crisis. The "sins" of the community (*zunnubanmu*, "our sins," as a collective possessive) must be behind Allah's failure to send the rains. In such moments, rather than attending to their own personal behavior, Maradi's more self-righteous Muslims tend instead to act in punitive ways toward those groups of people, single women in particular, who are seen to threaten the moral well-being of the Islamic *umma*.

Much discussion among Maradi's Muslims is devoted to debating what sorts of actions and daily practices are lawful and unlawful (*halak* and *haram*) within Islam, but here the sense often has less to do with moral blemish than with obeying proscriptions and obligations. Failure to meet those requirements leads to a measurable offense before God, the sum of which (*alhaki*) at the end of time (the day of accounting, *ranar hisabi*) will determine whether an individual will go to Paradise or not. Because many of Maradi's Muslims have little formal schooling in Islam, they live in considerable fear that they will unintentionally fail to meet those proscriptions; to shore up against that possibility they attempt to build up a kind of moral balance through extra prayer, pilgrimage, and almsgiving. While individuals do worry about the balance of their *alhaki*, they don't by and large conceive of those offenses as "sin" in a Christian sense, and they don't use the word "*zunnubi*" to refer to them. Working to redress a moral imbalance is a community effort, and participating actively in the life of the Muslim community is on the whole sufficient to guarantee the position of an individual in the afterlife.

Reformist Muslims put considerable effort into increasing the understanding of Islam among the local population through schooling so individuals will be less vulnerable to what anti-Sufi reformists see as the superfluous claims and practices of the Sufi orders. Most people can point to sinners around them—prostitutes, for example—and may argue that their misbehavior makes it difficult for the community of Muslims to remain pure. But Maradi's Muslims do not, on the whole, dwell on sinfulness as an indelible and immutable human characteristic. Improper behavior can be redressed through extra performances, better training, and the imposition of social constraints from without (such as driving away prostitutes).

Evangelical Christianity, on the other hand, begins with the presumption of original sin. At its foundation is the assumption of the need to conquer the sin that we all, as humans, necessarily bear. Thus, Pastor Iro's sermon begins with an assumption of fault that some Muslims could experience as an assault on the integrity of their personal observance of the obligations of Islam and on the relevance of their meritorious actions (such as sponsoring the trip to Mecca or giving alms). If one meets the requirements of Islam (prayer, fasting, and so on) and takes part in the *umma*, that should be enough; there need be no *presumption* of sin.

Yet Pastor Iro insists that God's words in the New Testament warn us to "flee the foolishness of youth, and persist instead in righteous works, and faith, and love ['*kauna*], and peace, together with those who pray God with a pure heart" (II Timothy 2:22).[7] The listener should presumably avoid those who pray without a pure heart; indeed, the oblique message of the sermon is that there is a danger of engaging in the wrong sort of prayer. One of the recurrent tensions in the preaching of Christians, and indeed in the very act of translating scriptural passages, is over how to translate the word "God." As we shall see in a subsequent chapter, the availability and ubiquity of the Muslim term "Allah" in the region before the arrival of Christianity virtually required that Christians take up the same term to refer to God. Of course, the Arabic word "Allah" is in some ways closer to the original Aramaic and Hebrew words for God than is the English word "God," which is a borrowing from Teutonic mythology (Massey 2004). There is nothing problematic for Christianity about the Arabic word "Allah" in itself; the question is rather how the word resonates in a context in which Islam determines the word's meaning.

However, the pre-Islamic term for the creator God, "Ubangiji," was also available and had been used by Muslims as a kind of epithet for Allah. In the translation Pastor Iro used, the word "Ubangiji" was used for God rather than the word "Allah." He went on to remark with increasing feeling that one must flee the foolishness of youth because this earthly world is full of sin. The only remedy for this sin is to affirm the word of God. It is the Holy Spirit that is the remedy for sin, and the Holy Spirit is the Word of God. Subsequent passages, which the pastor read at breakneck speed, reinforced this sense that there is a danger of becoming an "instrument of unrighteousness," or in Hausa "a thing to do evil works" (Romans 6:13), and that it is only through tremendous effort that one can "resist the devil" (James 4:7). The interpretation of the passages seemed to be of little import; it was the accretion of numerous passages full of exhortations to avoid the dangers of falling into the easy sins of Satan that mattered. It was not clear entirely what those sins might be; the important point was that it was urgent that the listener flee Satan. It was only toward the close of the increasingly excited sermon that we learned that Jesus Christ the Savior, who is the Word of God, can save us from sin, that only be accepting the Savior can we defeat sin.

The textual authority for the claims of the pastor would be ambiguous at best in the local context. While Muslims do generally acknowledge that Jesus, as a prophet, is to be associated with a sacred text, known as the Linjila, few would actually possess such a text and most would dispute the notion that any contemporary Christians are in possession of an accurate version. To succeed in its goal of reaching Muslim listeners, the radio ministry would need to use more emotional or experiential arguments. Perhaps aware that this particular sermon (which, in addition to being obliquely tendentious, was quite incoherent) was not likely to be compelling to the audience, program host Pastor Sahiru closed the show by emphasizing the power of the Holy Spirit in us to lead us on the right path: "Let us not become distracted, let us seek out knowledge because ignorance is poison, and it can kill. . . . Let us not allow ignorance to destroy us." The word for ignorance, *"jahilci,"* is an Arabic loanword that would normally refer to ignorance of proper Islamic practice when used by a Muslim; in other words, paganism. In broader secular usage, the word has come to mean something more like "superstition and illiteracy," but the strong Islamic resonance remains. Here Pastor Sahiru cast ignorance as a dangerous lack of understanding of Christianity. He then went on to invite the listeners to visit the Vie Abondante churches, where life-saving knowledge could be acquired. He offered precise information on where and when they could meet with other Christians of the Pentecostal tradition. Pastors Iro and Sahiru both chose to hint that there is an urgent danger, a seductive poison, which can deter humans from finding the right path to God.

If Maradi's traditionalist Muslims don't, on the whole, see themselves as being in need of salvation, then how does the persistent evangelist go about instilling a fear of sin in them? The shared traditions of the Old Testament provide a promising foundation, from the vantage point of the fundamentalist Christians, for convincing Muslims of a need for change. Because Muslims, Christians, and Jews share a familiarity with the figures of the Hebrew Bible, Old Testament stories in many ways offer more-compelling evidence to work from than the New Testament. Among those stories, one of the most promising for instilling a fear of sin is the story of Noah and the flood. One of the next radio shows that aired in 1999, which was devoted to "God's justice and mercy," drew on the text of Genesis 6. This time the guest preacher was Pastor Daniel, the pastor in Garin Sarkin Yamma Sabowa.[8] Rather than treating the familiar story as a charming children's tale with a magical boat and animals marching two by two (the admittedly banal approach familiar in liberal Christian settings), Pastor Daniel dwelled on the terrifying prospect that God's just anger about human sinfulness would lead him to destroy his entire creation. Pastor Daniel's harrowing sermon, offered at a fevered pitch, made an explicit parallel between the failure of sinners today to believe in Jesus as Savior and the failure of sinners at the time of Noah to believe that God would destroy the world through a flood. Jesus, he explained, was the saving vessel today just as Noah's boat was God's merciful concession to repentant humans at the time of the flood. God's justice is inescapable, though it is tempered by his mercy. But there is a limited amount of time for sinners to repent, after which they will, like the desperate humans who repented too late at the time of the flood, suffer utter annihilation. Pastor Daniel's sermon emphasized the cries of the drowning masses pleading with Noah to let them on the boat, having learned too late that they could ill afford to dismiss Noah's prophecy of a coming flood with contempt for his "crazy talk." Pastor Daniel's rendition of their earlier rejection of Noah's preaching and their subsequent cries for help was highly effective; it mimicked the language a contemporary Hausa-speaker would use to dismiss the claims of evangelical Christianity and it conjured a desperate moment in the future when the world would again be destroyed, this time by fire.

In one of the most effective passages in the sermon, Pastor Daniel likened those who wanted to escape God's wrath by choosing some other path than Christianity to Maradi's many ordinary smugglers who attempt to escape the notice of the authorities by traveling on little-used country roads and cattle paths along the border between Niger and Nigeria. "There is a perfectly good road," he said, "yet they choose not to use it. Why? So that they won't meet up with customs authorities, with those in power. But," he bellowed, "there is only one road to heaven! You can't hide from God!" Just as virtually everyone in Maradi is implicated in one way or another in illegal transborder activity, so all humans, he implied, are engaged in sin, and all would like to evade responsibility. As the sermon drew to a close, he asserted boldly, "My brothers and sisters, *addini* cannot save you. *Addini* has become like clothing that you take on and off as you please whenever you want to enjoy earthly pleasures. Only faith in the Savior can save you." The word "*addini*" within Islamic usage designates the opposite of paganism, and so by extension it has come to be used in Hausa to refer to the major religious traditions of monotheism, from Christianity to Judaism to Islam. But in the context of the sermon, it is fairly clear that Pastor Daniel was asserting to the audience that Islam would not save them from the wrath of God. By using the word "*addini*" rather than the term for Islam more directly (Musulunci), he could claim to be speaking of empty religious practice more broadly. But the ordinary Muslim listener would likely experience this language as an assault on Islam's capacity to bring humans into favor with God. For someone from a rural background who was only partially socialized into Islam, the sermon would seem to indicate that there is no purpose in developing a more mature understanding of Islam when the "true" path to God is through Christianity. Little wonder, then, that Maradi's warring traditionalist Muslim scholars and Islamist reformists began to tune in to the radio program regularly with increasing anxiety and anger.

God's Love

One reason many Christians prefer the animals in the tale of Noah and the flood to the image of drowning humans is that few today care to dwell upon a wrathful God so unlike the paternal figure of the New Testament. Within Christianity, God figures regularly as the Father, and in keeping with our sense of human love, this God should have an infinite capacity to forgive our sins, just as parents are ideally expected to provide unconditional love to their imperfect offspring. Despite Pastor Daniel's claim that the God of the Old Testament is merciful, the tale of Noah and the flood does not readily project a loving or merciful God. Having worked to instill a fear of the consequences of sin in the radio audience, it was now necessary to emphasize the Christian God as a loving God.

Pastor Huseini provided a sermon on God's love toward humans two weeks after the sermon by Pastor Daniel.[9] Having guest preachers on the radio show made for some unevenness and unpredictability in the program, however. The rural and relatively unschooled pastors were often poorly equipped to deliver a compelling sermon. The authority of Muslim scholars rests heavily on their mastery of reading and recitation of texts. This speaker's imperfect mastery of literacy and his stumbling over the relevant texts potentially undermined his credibility with Muslims, quite apart from the texts themselves. Yet his energy and conviction were compelling.

To establish human sinfulness and God's judgment upon that sin, he turned to a series of passages from the prophet Isaiah (64:6; 59:1–3). When we pray to God and he doesn't answer our prayers, it is because we are full of sin, the pastor asserted. Humans would rather engage in evil acts and walk in darkness than hear God's call. But in his great love for us, God has given us Jesus Christ, the Savior, who will take upon himself all the sins of those who have faith in him. Throughout his sermon Pastor Huseini was far more likely to refer to God as "Ubangiji" than as "Allah." Ubangiji, he asserted, loves us. God has prepared a path of salvation for us through Jesus Christ. But God does not force us to do anything; there is no requirement (*Allah ba ya tilasa mutane*) to have faith in Jesus. That is a choice each human must make. Where Islam generates a series of obligations, he implied, Christianity emphasizes free will. Other religious practices are, in a sense, voluntary forms of enslavement. Some may choose to worship (*bauta*—to serve, to be enslaved by, to revere) the sun or their ancestors' graves or trees or cows—each of these examples clearly refers to the folk practices of rural populations only recently converted to Islam. It is interesting that he tactfully omits to mention the most common religious usage of the word *bauta*, which in the phrase "*bautar Allah*" means to practice Islam, to be a "slave of God," in the Islamic idiom.

In his next move, the preacher took the reader to a passage in the Gospel according to Matthew, "Come unto me, all ye that labor and are heavy laden, and I will give you rest" (11:28). When we are weary, the burden we suffer under is our sins, the preacher explained, and that is what Jesus offers to lift from us. He emphasized that all of us have such a burden—no matter who the listener might be, he or she has sin. "If you think you don't have sins you are deceiving yourself and the truth of God is not with you," he asserted forcefully. In a far more direct assault on Islam, he went on to insist that "*ibada ba za ta raba ka da zunnubi ba*"—service to God through habitual religious practice (*ibada*)—will not separate you from your sins. The word "*ibada*" is in this region virtually synonymous with Islamic religious practice because it conveys the daily and yearly obligatory performances of Islam and the original Arabic term relates to Islamic observances. The preacher avoided referring directly to Islam, but his meaning would have been clear to any local audience.

It was at this point that Pastor Huseini introduced the text of John 3:16, "For God so loved [*agape* in the original Greek; to love in a social or moral sense] the world, that he gave his only begotten Son, that whosoever believeth in him should not perish, but have everlasting life." Evangelical and Pentecostal Christians refer to this text regularly as one of the most important proofs that it is *only* through belief in Jesus as Savior and son of God that humans can enter heaven, since the corollary (which is not directly stated in the scriptures) would seem to be that whoever does *not* believe in Jesus will perish in damnation. Like many liberal Christians, I find the purported corollary inconsistent with the rest of Jesus' message, and therefore I confidently reject it. Of the many passages in the Bible in which one of the three central Greek words for "love" appears, it is one of the least revealing about what God's love might consist of beyond requiring (if one insists upon the supposed corollary) that we believe in Jesus as Savior if we hope to have salvation.

Most evangelical Christians seem to find this introduction of the word "love" to be adequate and do not go to great lengths to reflect on the peculiarity of this way of speaking about "love." But it has always felt somehow wrong to me and very different from the kind of demanding but readily understandable love Jesus emphasizes in the parable of the good Samaritan. My encounter with the gentleman on the street in Maradi has only heightened for me the strangeness of this fundamentalist manner of approaching love. Why is it loving to destroy any human who does not find the messages delivered through flawed human carriers sufficiently convincing to give up the practices of Islam? In the absence of a compelling explanation, the Muslim hearer would be inclined to reject this as an implausible accounting of a God who is known from the Koran to be infinitely merciful.

If the sermon had ended here, perhaps the listener would simply have gone his or her way, puzzled by Christians but happy enough to leave them to their odd understanding of God. But Pastor Huseini went on to assault the integrity of traditionalist Muslim scholars and to inveigh against the common Muslim funeral practice of offering prayers requesting forgiveness for the dead. "If you die, there is nothing more to be done. You see some people, if someone dies, they [Muslim scholars, or *malamai*] gather together and give prayers for the forgiveness of some woman—that's a worthless activity. They are just confusing you, and why? So that you will give them money to put in their pockets. They know the truth, but they won't tell you, this thing you are doing, it's just something for this world." It is hard to see how the traditional Muslim scholars of Maradi could be anything but offended by this attack on their integrity. But the more ordinary listener would also likely be deeply offended, having found solace in prayers for those they have loved and lost. In the strange logic of the evangelical, Christianity is a form of freedom while Islam is a form of compulsion, and yet it is Christianity that seems to imperiously require a particular set of beliefs that fly in the face of the most ordinary understandings of love, mercy, and freedom: the beliefs that human love for other humans at the moment of death is irrelevant and God cannot be moved by it, that humans are not truly "free" to practice anything other than Christianity and failure to meet that requirement is cause for the most severe and irreversible of imaginable punishments, that God's "infinite" mercy is so finite and contingent that it cannot be invoked after death.

In closing the program, Pastor Sahiru added insult to injury by making two startling claims. First, he argued that if you ignore God's path then you are following Satan. Those who go to hell (all those, as we have seen, who do not believe in Jesus as Savior) are followers of Satan, he said, and that is why they go to hell. It is but a small step to conclude that Islam is a satanic practice. And then he went on to argue that in order to prepare ourselves for God's mercy we cannot rely on laws. The scriptures tell us, he averred, that the law of Moses (*doka ta Musa*) cannot save us. But in glossing the word "*doka*" as "*shari'a*," he was stating that adherence to Islamic law cannot bring us into favor with God. The familiar Christian move of arguing that faith in Jesus Christ supersedes Old Testament law is thereby transplanted in this context to mean that Christianity must supersede Islamic law. If the traditionalist scholars would have been immediately outraged by the assault on their integrity in Huseini's sermon, reformist Muslims attempting to enhance the scope of Shari'a in Niger could only be deeply threatened by this barely disguised assault on the notion that moral order can be found through following the Shari'a. In one sermon, Pastor Sahiru and Pastor Huseini of Vie Abondante had virtually guaranteed an alliance between former foes, the traditionalist scholars and the resurgent Islamic reformists. And this in the name of love.

Son of Adam, Son of God

Thus, three months before the first incitement to riot, Vie Abondante had paved the way for a concerted protest against the assaults on Islam in their radio sermons. But the pastors had been remarkably clever in not attacking Islam directly or ever mentioning either the word "Islam" or the name of the Prophet Mohammed. Despite the transparency of these attacks on Islam, the show had succeeded in preserving its ability to claim that, according to the letter of the law, so to speak, it had never attacked Islam. There was nothing in the sermons that would have violated the understanding of acceptable free speech in the United States. Everyone in Maradi knew that the sermons were causing friction, but there was little anyone could do about it. Then, in the next major broadcast, a sermon by Pastor Isa on April 25, 1999, the radio show took up the single most contentious issue separating Islam and Christianity—the status of Jesus as "son of God."[10]

This is not simply a question of whether Jesus is understood to be one of the prophets (Annabi Issa, as he is known to Hausa-speaking Muslims) or is actually divine himself. If the claim of Christianity was that God became manifest in human form and was known as Jesus, then the shape of debates between Christians and Muslims would be rather different. The point of contention rests on Christianity's insistence that Jesus was actually born and that God is his father. In its iconoclastic rejection of any form of worship that might lead to human worship of idols or other humans, Islam refuses any representation that Allah is akin to a human. In Islam, Allah is distinguishable from humans because Allah neither begets nor is Allah begotten—to suggest that the creation of Allah is in any way related to human procreation is blasphemy. Allah is not, strictly speaking, gendered as male or female to begin with—the very conception of gendering is so fully bound up with human procreation that it can reveal little about God. Thus, Christianity's simultaneously literal and metaphoric use of kinship relations to describe both God and God's relations to humans is anathema to Muslims. God is not a Father figure, for to imagine God in such a way is to slip toward idolatry. Neither does Allah procreate, so to use any form of language that implies that Jesus is God's "son" is deeply offensive.

In Hausa, men are regularly referred to as the son of their fathers—a man might be known as 'dan Mamman or 'dan Magaji or, more famously, as 'dan Fodio. This use of teknonyms binds humans to one another in broad webs of social relations that suggest that humans are important or worthy to the degree that they are connected to other humans. The naming practice resonates strongly with the importance of wealth in people, of having extensive networks of clients, kin, and affines. Thus, to use the expression "Issa 'dan Allah" is to bind God into a web of human relations and to measure God's worth in human terms. While Christians might find this way of thinking about God comforting and humanizing, Islam goes to great lengths to emphasize the difference between God and humans. God is great, and one attribute of that greatness is that it can't be reduced to human social relations. Jesus is a prophet, and he is referred to by Muslims as the son of Mary, not the son of God.

Pastor Isa began his sermon by stating that it is a mistake to think that Christians have given Jesus the name "son of God." Referring to Matthew 3:17, Pastor Isa argued that this manner of speech comes not from Christians but from the word of Allah, for it was the voice of Ubangiji himself that referred to Jesus as "my son" upon his baptism by John the Baptist. In Luke 1:34, the angel Gabriel had told Mary that the Holy Spirit would cause her to give birth to a child who would be called "son of God." In the transfiguration passage in Matthew 17, God referred to Jesus as "my beloved son." So, insisted the pastor, despite the anger and dispute of Muslims whenever Christians refer to Jesus as 'dan Allah, the son of God, Christians have not only a right but a duty to refer to him fearlessly as Jesus, son of God.

The preference of Pastor Isa for the word "Ubangiji" over "Allah" in this context is both striking and utterly natural. The word "Ubangiji" contains within it the word "uba," or "father." Pre-Islamic Hausa understandings of the creator God clearly encompassed a sense of God as a kind of father of many households and heavens, the presiding master of creation and of hosts of creatures of different kinds that were in some sense his offspring. God in this rendering is indeed gendered as male and is the progenitor of a locally bound pantheon of spirits of the land, trees, and waters. Humans enter into this creation as a kind of second generation of offspring, often similarly bound to particular spaces and places. Indigenous peoples, then, are known as 'yan 'kasa, ("children of the earth"), and are understood to have a particularly close relationship with the spirits of that territory. While the Hausa creator god was rather distant—one did not make sacrifice to Ubangiji but to lesser intermediate spirits and forces—he was imaginable and readily comparable to humans. Christianity in the region has tended to combine this humanized understanding of God with the stature and greatness implied in Islamic conceptions of monotheism by referring to God through the two terms combined, Ubangijin Allah. An English translation of that pairing as "Lord God" would not be inaccurate, yet it would somewhat obscure the awkwardness of the formula from the vantage point of an Islamic purist. It is one thing to borrow a local term as one epithet of hundreds that can be suggestive of Allah's infinite greatness. It is another to use the term literally as a fixed attribute of God.

For evangelical and Pentecostal preachers, however, it is this literal and figurative language of divine fatherhood and birth that is absolutely key. The entire notion of rebirth in the Holy Spirit relies upon a prior imagery of Christ as son of God and the salvation that is the inheritance of a child of God. To evacuate Christianity of this literal and figurative equation with birth and regeneration would, from their vantage point, empty it of its central significance. Within this equation, "love" serves as the central middle term, but this is not love in an emotional sense. Pastor Isa went on to argue, on the basis of I John 5:1, that if one did not believe in Jesus as the son of God, one did not truly love Allah because whoever loves the one who gives birth also loves the child. Pastor Isa insisted that what it meant to "love" Jesus was to accept him as the son of God. The argument, if it is an argument, is circular. It claims that love is not so much human emotion or compassion as an oddly dispassionate acquiescence to the *requirement* that one believe in Jesus as God. Only by accepting that Jesus is the son of God can humans overcome this world and defeat sin. To accept that Jesus is the son of God is to be reborn in the Holy Spirit and to be saved. But in the course of making the argument, Pastor Isa stated outright that if one is not an evangelical Christian in precisely this sense, one does not love Allah.

Defiantly anticipating the objections of his audience, Pastor Isa noted that if they timidly followed the word of their Muslim teachers in rejecting the language of birth rather than the word of God, they were putting humans before God. Christians would always refer to Jesus as the son of God, he asserted, regardless of what their neighbors thought, because this is the word of God and only those who believe in his name will be part of God's family. Pastor Isa didn't hesitate to throw gas on the flames he had kindled. He turned to Galatians 1:6–10, a passage in which Paul lays some of the critical groundwork for the separation of Christian faith from the requirement that gentiles adhere to the Old Testament Hebrew law when they become followers of Jesus. In other contexts this idea is empowering—Christians need not conform to some prior legalistic conception of proper practice, they need only believe in Jesus. In this setting, however, the legalism of the Old Testament blurs into the legalism of Islam, the rejection of heterodox texts becomes the rejection of the Koran, other interpretations of proper relations with Allah become "perversions" of the gospel of Christ. By this reckoning, no other gospel can bring us to God except that of Jesus Christ. Evangelical Christianity had made its jealous and exclusive claim to access to God and salvation in unambiguous terms.

In the sermon that was widely seen to have been the straw that broke the camel's back for Maradi's increasingly disturbed Islamic leaders, Pastor Sahiru preached on the notion of covenant in the Bible, discussing Noah, Abraham, and David.[11] Whatever God has promised will come to pass, he argued. He then turned to the "new covenant," discussing God's promise to Mary that she would have a child, the prophecy that Jesus would come from the house of David, and gravitating eventually to that key evangelical text, I John 5:10 "He that believeth on the Son of God hath the witness in himself: he that believeth not God hath made him a liar; because he believeth not the record that God gave of his Son." God had promised his son, Pastor Sahiru argued, so anyone who does not accept that Jesus is the son of God has made God out to be a liar and is, by implication, a liar himself.

The first epistle of John is where two of the more significant passages referring to the antichrist occur—in Hausa literally the "enemy of the Savior." Sahiru and his colleagues in subsequent sermons obliquely suggested that Islam might impede salvation because of its "false" understanding of prophecy. But in using the language of "lying," they invoked the deceiver, or the antichrist, a figure that is quite familiar within Muslim popular discourse. The most prominent attribute of al-Dajjal, the antichrist in Muslim tradition, is that he is a liar. Muslim scholars in the region, ever alert to the anti-Islamic undercurrent of these sermons, picked up the implication that Mohammed, in rejecting Christ's status as "son of God," was in effect himself the antichrist. In Muslim lore, the figure of the antichrist is accepted and is understood by some Muslims to be the personification of evil. There is debate over when the antichrist is to appear and whether this force is Satan, a human individual, a regime, or a zeitgeist (materialism or western secularism, for example). True Christians (those who reject the divinity of Jesus) and Muslims will, according to some interpretations, join together at a critical juncture in time to defeat irreligiosity (Saritoprak 2003, 298). Given that Muslims accept that there is a force of evil associated with that liar who rejects the Messiah Jesus, any implication that Islam or Mohammed itself is a "liar" is deeply offensive. It is not entirely clear that the Christian pastors, who are relatively unschooled in Islam (and in the case of Sahiru, a second-language speaker of Hausa), understood the force of some of the passages they quoted. It was not long after this that the first incitement to riot on purely religious grounds in Maradi occurred. The planned uprising was quelled in advance, but it caused the radio station to be closed temporarily until tempers had cooled.

The 1999 transmissions reveal the underlying logic of conceptions of love by those who have been "born again" in part because they were so unguarded. The Vie Abondante mission became somewhat more gentle and circumspect in subsequent radio emissions, but it did not significantly alter the thrust of its message. In 2000, immediately before the riots described in the preceding chapter, Pastor Sahiru preached two radio sermons designed to illuminate the concept of love. In a rare deviation from the strong emphasis in these sermons on the epistles and the Gospel of John, Pastor Sahiru turned to Matthew 20:1–16,[12] the parable of the householder who hired workers for his vineyard yet paid those who toiled all day the same wage he paid those who came to be hired only in the eleventh hour. Pastor Sahiru recast the story in a more colloquial style so that in unspoken ways it resonated deeply with the contemporary local landscape peopled with unemployed young men eager to find work, women refugees encamped in the outskirts of town, and successful pious Muslims performing their prayers and giving alms with regularity. Christians, he suggested, are endlessly willing to accept the lost and forgotten on terms that are equal to their acceptance of those who are hardworking and virtuous. This is the paradox of God's love—it is not fair. It shows no preference for those who work long and hard and who adhere to a strict moral code. All these sinners need to do to have salvation is accept God's gift of Jesus as Savior.

If, in the secular or liberal west, missionaries are seen as the carriers of puritanical prudishness about dress, smoking, drinking, and sex, in this Muslim context where dress and bodily practice are already quite closely monitored, the notion of salvation solely through the acceptance of Jesus as Savior sounds like a license to give in to sin and immorality. For Muslims across a very broad and in some ways mutually antagonistic spectrum, such preaching could be seen as threatening. The extreme corrective, given that the government was not inclined to close down this consistently offensive preaching permanently, would be to purge the city of spaces in which license occurs, to rein in the sphere of dangerous heretical Christians by instilling fear in them, and to eliminate the grain that strange householders might use to draw the immoral eleventh-hour sexual laborers to the city and toward this brand of Christianity.

Islam does recognize Jesus as a central and unique prophet, and many Muslims would like to learn more about Christian teachings. But orthodox Islam rejects the notion of immanence quite strongly; the only way to understand the deification of Jesus is to see it as a perversion of true Christianity. The attacks on the Vie Abondante church and the SIM mission were not attacks on Christianity as Muslims understand it. They were rejections of the implied demonization of Islam in the radio sermons and an attempt to contain the licentiousness an ethically empty approach to salvation seemed to invite. And thus was violence born of "love." The propensity within evangelical preaching to work through this negative conception of love and to interpret any alternative understanding of Christianity as an unloving rejection of God—indeed, as placing one in the camp of "the enemy"—has created a long-standing habit of demonizing Islam that has profoundly troubling consequences. The following chapter takes us back to the turn of the twentieth century to see how a similar logic was played out at the inception of the work of the Sudan Interior Mission.

3

From "Satan's Masterpiece" to "The Social Problem of Islam"

> *Finally, those who have not yet received the Gospel are related in various ways to the people of God. . . . [The] plan of salvation also includes those who acknowledge the Creator. In the first place amongst these there are the Mohamedans, who, professing to hold the faith of Abraham, along with us adore the one and merciful God, who on the last day will judge mankind.*
>
> —Vatican Council II, *Lumen Gentium*, 1964, 16

$\mathcal{T}$he rhetoric of demonization has, as we have seen, been common in the religious discourse of almost all parties in the region at one point or another (with the notable exception of the Catholicism of the post–Vatican II era, as the above epigraph suggests) and has a logic that is extraordinarily destructive. However, the image of Islam SIM missionaries in the region have held has not been static and bears the marks of ongoing adjustment in the face of shifting global politics, deepening understanding of local practice, shifting opportunities for interaction with Africans, and the demographics of missionary recruitment. SIM evangelical missionaries working a century ago began with attitudes similar to those of the Vie Abondante mission today but found themselves adapting and adjusting to the realities and necessities of the mission field in which they worked. By tracing those shifting attitudes among missionaries devoted to converting Hausa-speakers of Nigeria and Niger to

Protestantism, I hope to offer a broad overview of the circumstances that have shaped the mission's interventions, provide a the history of changing strategies that will structure the succeeding chapters, and offer an introduction to the race and gender dynamics of this complex intercultural encounter. This chapter is based primarily upon publications of the Sudan Interior Mission, particularly *The Sudan Witness,* a periodical sent out to mission supporters and potential donors. Most of the articles were written by missionaries in the field; articles by administrators in the United States were generally authored by former field missionaries who had moved into administration later in their careers. Articles, letters to the editor, photographs, and cartoons in this and other SIM publications give a good sense of the shifting perceptions SIM missionaries had of Muslims. They also provide narrative descriptions of the strategies the mission pursued at different historical moments. The publications reveal how the mission presented itself to its supporters, its recruitment strategies, and (indirectly) how the populations the mission encountered reacted to the mission. Most important, the mission's presentation of its work to like-minded Christians offers a window on evangelical perceptions of Islam over time. Obviously such representations are discursive in the sense that they tell us little about actual Muslims and a great deal more about what evangelical Christians sympathetic to faith missionary activity took for granted or found perplexing about Islam.

The earliest figurations of the Muslim in Africa in SIM discourses at the turn of the century would include the despot king slaver, the Hausa merchant as potential evangelizer, and the Muslim as fanatical scholar. By the 1920s, the rhetoric of Islam as "Satan's masterpiece" had emerged forcefully in evangelical writings. Gradually, with greater exposure to Muslims on the ground, missionaries modified that image to emphasize Muslims as slaves to empty ritual; later still, they began to see Islam as a social problem. As the African mission fields moved closer to decolonization, Islam came to be seen as one of a number of threats, part of the rising tide of isms that included nationalism and Marxism. At the close of the colonial period, with the mission's growing success in medical ministry, missionaries began to feminize Islam in their characterizations and to see Muslims as victims of underdevelopment. Most recently, missionaries have begun to see Hausa Muslims as "nominal Muslims" at the "soft underbelly of Islam," amenable to conversion and perhaps different in kind from the dangerous "green menace" that has become a familiar part of contemporary discourse emanating from the United States. But throughout these imaginings and reimaginings, the specter of Islam as the archenemy of Christianity has had an enduring appeal as a result of the binary thinking characteristic of American evangelicalism.

Most of these representations have been available throughout the history of SIM in Niger; however, I am interested in how and why particular images seem to surface more forcefully at a given moment. The kaleidoscopic figurations of the Muslim over the course of a century are the outcome of the interplay of a number of central elements. First, larger geopolitical forces have contributed to the mission's understanding of its task and have affected the resources available to it. Second, and more important, Muslim resistance in the face of mission intrusion and colonial domination has conditioned almost every aspect of what the mission has done, from where it has worked to how it has translated. The mission's experiences with real Muslims contributed to broader strategic shifts in evangelization throughout the mission's fields: however overblown the rhetoric of the mission board at any moment might be, devoted missionaries struggled to find approaches that would actually influence the living and breathing individuals with whom they spent much of their lives in the field. The mission went from a highly masculine strategy of market preaching to itinerant strategies carried out by married couples to door-to-door work done largely by women, until in the late 1950s it stumbled upon the strategy that has made the mission the success it is today, namely medical work performed predominantly by female missionaries.

Most recently the mission has become deeply engaged in development and relief work with the ultimate goal of converting Hausa and Tuareg to Christianity and with the less-explicit goal of rendering mission work more appealing to men. The repertoire of missionary activities has expanded over time, but in a sense the older strategies (translation, itinerant preaching, home visits) have also been carried forward into relatively untouched "pioneering" territories, often adapted to new technologies: the "Jesus film" has replaced the phonograph that was to attract a crowd and open the door to outdoor sermons. As the mission's emphases, strategies, and resources have shifted, so also has its own demographic profile: at its inception, the mission pioneers were exclusively white males, but the mission very rapidly built its early foundations on the labors of married couples, and gradually white female volunteers, many of whom were single, came to outnumber male applicants by two to one (compare Tucker 1990, 252). The imagined figure of the African

Muslim has been shaped by the dispositions and experiences of gendered and raced missionaries.

A number of SIM's characteristics have also shaped this dialectical interplay. First, the mission was and is marked by a rejection of materialism that, paradoxically, is only possible because of the mission's links with North American surplus capital. The history of the mission is bound up with the social and economic history of the United States in particular; the fortunes of the mission have followed the flows of capital and political ideology within the U.S., beginning in the Great Lakes region, shifting to New York City, and finally settling in the southern Bible Belt at Charlotte, North Carolina. Second, this mission has a strong anti-intellectual bent. This has had, I think, profound consequences for the ability of the mission to attract African American missionaries. One of the defining characteristics of the faith mission movement has been a hostility toward education and social improvement as ends in themselves. Sandy Martin's work on black Baptist missionaries in West Africa suggests that African Americans may have been interested in mission work for reasons that were ultimately incompatible with the central tenets of the faith missions such as the Sudan Interior Mission, despite the strong interest of both white and black Baptists in mission work in the late nineteenth and early twentieth centuries. Martin argues that black Baptists felt a special obligation to improve both the material and spiritual well-being of their African brothers and sisters and that this interest carried an implicit critique of racism—theirs was a "practical Christianity" with a deep commitment to education and a quiet, if inconsistent, concern for injustice (Martin 1989). African American networks and institutions relating to mission work strengthened the African American community at home even as they served Africans abroad.

White Baptists felt no special burden for Africa; in fact, they were more likely to be attracted to China as a field. White missionaries were less able to see their own engagement in mission work as political, and many white Baptists have been drawn to the China Inland Mission, the faith mission to which SIM is most closely related in philosophy. SIM, like other faith missions, has consistently insisted on a naive decoupling of religion and politics, refusing to address the ways in which its own activities have political consequences. For SIM, mission work is fundamentally apolitical. Yet the rise and operation of the evangelical movement has been intimately tied to political and economic currents at play in the United States and Canada.

The Post-Keswick Context: Mission Work at the
Turn of the Century

"The modern missionary movement," observes Andrew Walls, "is the autumnal child of the Evangelical Revival" (1996, 79). To make sense of how SIM has constructed Islam it is important to take a moment to understand the forces that shaped the mission's initial entry into the Sahelian regions. The evangelical movement emerged in protest over the perceived inadequacies of Christian society itself. Walls argues that the evangelical revival succeeded by drawing on deep wellsprings of western culture:

> It combined the traditional framework of the Christian nation and the established church . . . with serious recognition of individual selfhood and personal decision. That reconciliation bridged a cultural chasm in Christian self-identity. It helped to make evangelical religion a critical force in Western culture, a version of Christianity thoroughly authentic and indigenous there. To use the appalling current missiological jargon, the evangelical Revival contextualized the gospel for the northern Protestant world. (84)

Of course the mission movement in its earlier eighteenth- and early-nineteenth-century guise saw itself as drawing on the cardinal virtues of Christianity, commerce, and civilization to counter the evils of the slave trade, binding the expanding trade economy to evangelism. However, unlike the standard missionary of the earlier period, who was by and large "a fairly homespun character with few formal attainments" (106), the late-nineteenth-century missionary agents, particularly in the case of English missions, were relatively highly educated. The younger generation of missionaries had little patience with the compromises and priorities of the earlier missions, from promoting the slave trade to building schools. By this later period, as the Atlantic slave trade was waning, and as "the pyramids of gin bottles built up in [African] villages and townships . . . it was no longer obvious that the interests of Christianity and commerce marched together" (107). The notion that taking on Western clothing and practices was to be seen as evidence of inward change was under attack; similarly, prosperity through successful engagement in "legitimate" trade was no longer an unambiguous mark of incipient membership in the Christian community.

The success of missions in coastal regions had generated a class of educated African Christians acculturated in a variety of ways to western habits whose "presumptions" were troubling to colonial administrators.

The Black Englishman or "modern Coast negro" presented a challenge to missionaries not simply because his claims to equality could threaten the implicit racial hierarchy within missions but also because colonial administrators were reluctant to support "disruptive" mission efforts in newer, more interior, territories (Barnes 1995). Particularly in regions with sizable Muslim populations, debates raged among educated Africans over whether Christianity truly suited the African and whether Islam might not better serve the advancement of Africa (Sanneh 1996, 67–83). Some colonial administrators saw Africans' capacity to understand Christianity as limited and therefore believed that Islam had a role in guaranteeing public order due to its "civilizing effect" (Barnes 1995, 428).

It was during this later period of missionization that the SIM made its entry into West Africa. At precisely the moment when Islam was being considered by some, Africans and administrators alike, as a reasonable alternative to the expansion of Christianity, the Sudan Interior Mission took up the quixotic task of converting the "unreached" Sudanic interior of Africa. The mission, of course, continued to attempt to draw on the familiar tropes of abolitionism to justify its endeavor: "The Moslem kings of the north," asserted Rowland Bingham (one of the three founders of the mission), "gathered their armies together every year to raid the pagan areas for slaves. . . . Any one [sic] resisting the waiting troops was shot down; the rest of the people were gathered together and chained man to man, woman to woman, child to child, and marched off to the distant slave-market. There they were sold without the slightest regard to the ties of nature" (Bingham 1943, 12).

However, by the 1890s, such rhetoric had inevitably lost some of its force, both among the public and among colonial administrators buffeted by the demands of missionaries, their superiors in the metropole, and the populations they governed. Once the British took control of northern Nigeria, the "slow death" of slavery was already set in train under conditions carefully engineered by Lugard and his successors with or without the support of missionaries (Lovejoy and Hogendorn 1993). Frederick Lugard, high commissioner of the Protectorate of Northern Nigeria, did not regard conversion to Christianity to be a prerequisite to the eventual elimination of slavery. In French territories, attitudes toward Islam were highly contradictory. For administrators such as François Clozel, lieutenant-governor of Upper Senegal and Niger, "an intimate and almost exclusive link between Islam and slavery was one of the cornerstones of French Islamic policy" (Harrison 1988, 99); the long-standing French fear of Islam led to Clozel's policy "opposing Islam with a strong centralized and self-conscious fetishism" (100). Maurice Delafosse, on the other hand, would argue that the "mixed" Islam of West Africa was neither good nor evil but that local religions were probably preferable (105). Despite the profound differences among all these stances toward Islam, it is clear that none was particularly promising for launching a new mission enterprise in the Muslim belt of West Africa. Joseph-Roger de Benoist's excellent study of the often-difficult and always-ambivalent relations between the French colonial administration and Catholic missionaries during the same period in colonial Soudan shows that even French missionaries faced almost insurmountable obstacles to mission work in the Muslim belt (1987). Prospects for a Protestant mission staffed largely by Americans were, *a fortiori*, likely to be daunting.

Features of both the overall mission enterprise of the later period and the missionary personnel in the field were therefore distinct from those of an earlier period. With the launching of the Student Volunteer Movement in 1893, with its motivating watchword, "the evangelisation of the world in this generation," missions enjoyed a swell of enthusiastic recruits who aimed to blanket the globe with evangelists in order to hasten the second coming (Yates 1994, 17–21). These young American and British missionaries were generally highly educated (at such institutions as Princeton and Cambridge Universities) and were eager to push back the mission frontiers in a reformist spirit and through the renunciation of the material world and an emphasis on preaching over lengthy engagement with populations (Walls 1996, 106). Denominational mission boards had their pick of highly educated and energetic male recruits, who displaced the female missionaries and their boards. With the swell of recruits resulting from the revival movement, less-educated men and women were no longer in demand in the denominational missions, and the faith missions took in this surplus and turned the relative lack of education into a virtue. From the outset, the China Inland Mission and SIM accepted women as significant partners in the project of evangelism and placed relatively low educational demands on their recruits.

Within this broader movement, then, there were a number of distinguishing features of the new faith missions, of which SIM was one. I shall raise three, namely a deemphasis on education and scholarship, a profound linkage with American capital and organizational acumen, and a certain naiveté concerning the degree to which religion and politics could be divorced from one another. As Walls notes, in the wake of many of the inspirational conferences and conventions of the revival movement, mission recruitment of relatively educated men swelled; however, "a corresponding increase . . . of candidates without education came in the same period; the new 'faith' missions to which most of them went were slow to institute formal training, but came eventually to do so" (1996, 188).

One reason for the relative lack of attention to this large and influential mission among historians and anthropologists, I suspect, is that it produced no scholar-missionaries in the tradition of Spencer Trimingham, David Livingston, Sister Marie-André du Sacré-Coeur, and Father Placide Tempels. SIM missionaries were active in Bible translation and produced tracts—the Gaskiya Corporation of northern Nigeria, for example, owes its existence in part to SIM interest in producing vernacular texts. However, missionaries within SIM never authored richly detailed, introspective, or intellectually provocative writings. SIM mission publications were and still are, by and large, pitched at an unsophisticated reader of a literalist bent, with a view toward motivating others for mission work or raising funds for the mission. They bear the marks of the kind of black-and-white dualist thinking that Mark Noll likens to a kind of evangelical Manicheanism (1994, 52).

All of these qualities have discouraged extended historical or ethnographic study of the mission either from within or from without. This antipathy toward secular scholarship has become increasingly problematic for the mission over time as it has become more and more international in its recruitment. Many of the younger missionaries within the mission today (from Australia, France, Switzerland, Korea, and Great Britain as well as the United States and Canada) have a willingness to engage with secular scholarship and ecumenical dialogue that makes it hard for them communicate well with more-senior (often American) missionaries. They are often poorly prepared to understand or respond to the problematic legacies that SIM's characteristically American evangelical anti-intellectualism has left to them in the mission field.[1]

Second, practically speaking, the disengagement of Christianity from commerce meant that missionization had to be de-linked from trade, making the mission far more dependent on voluntary contributions emanating from the industrialized centers of the west. It is an irony that in separating Christianity from commerce, missions were binding themselves ever more profoundly to the surplus production of the capitalist centers. As Walls acutely observes in an attempt to make sense of the increasing importance of American missions as the twentieth century progressed:

For the voluntary society to operate overseas implies the existence of cash surpluses and freedom to move them about. It cannot operate if the surplus of production is marginal or if the movement of surpluses is controlled by the wider community. America provided *par excellence* the economic capability for voluntary societies to operate overseas, just as it had provided a favorable social and political climate for their development. (1996, 225)

Thus while the faith missions emphasized their willingness to commit to mission work even before funds for any given missionary had been secured, in reality this seeming divorce from monetary concerns was made possible only because of the circulation of surplus capital in Canada, the United States, and, decreasingly, Great Britain. The success of SIM derived from informal but powerful links with a network of American evangelical institutions (including the Moody Bible Institute, the Bible Society, and Park Street Church in Boston). Dwight L. Moody, whose career as an evangelists took off during a revivalist preaching tour of the British Isles in 1873, was central to the institutionalization of this network, for "he produced and mobilized Christian businessmen, who munificently supported missions at home and abroad" (230; see also Krapohl and Lippy 1999, 280–281). Moody's urgent and restless earnestness embodied a central dimension of late-nineteenth-century North American life: in this modestly educated man were combined an unapologetic drive for success in business and an unassailable confidence in the need to crusade "to wrest this State from the power of Satan and take and hold it for Christ" (quoted in Findlay 1969, 79). Moody represented the strongest link between the work of the evangelical movement and the secular work of North American Protestant businessmen. An ethos of practical diligence and a sense of responsibility as stewards of wealth in a context of a rejection of materialism among evangelical Christians combined to generate an extraordinarily potent form of philanthropy: "The philanthropic activities generated by the evangelical rationale . . . not only financed many of the missionary efforts of the evangelical denominations, but ultimately made these groups dependent on the business community for much of their economic support. In Moody's day, businessmen and evangelicals saw eye to eye not only because they thought alike but also because their economic interests coincided" (85). The organizational skills of American business were thus brought successfully to bear in the expansion of faith missions. As Joel Carpenter observes, faith missions were to become the "foreign policy" wing of the evangelical movement (1990, 99).

Finally, SIM writings show a lack of interest in the ways in which politics and religion overlap or intersect. Walls remarks on this characteristically American pattern: "Modern American missions have some-

"Mr. D. M. Osborne, Graduate of Moody Bible Institute of Chicago, Preaching in a Moslem Village: The First Witness for Christ." Courtesy of SIMIA (N-1034), photographed by R. Bingham (?), 1929

times displayed a curious political naivete, as though by constantly asserting that church and state were separate they have somehow stripped mission activity of political significance. Even the elementary political implication of their presence, let alone of patriotism, has not always been recognized" (1996, 233). While the fundamentalist movement in the United States eventually shed its political quietism to become a potent force, the mission enterprises that emerged from the same roots retained a sense that politics and mission activity must be carefully separated, at least in the mission field. A certain willful blindness to the political nature of religious intervention in itself was combined with a reluctance to entertain engagement with politics on behalf of recently converted Christian communities in mission territories. This did not (and does not) prevent those who support SIM from acting politically on behalf of "Christian values" at home and "religious freedom" abroad through political processes in the United States.

While civilization was no longer directly equated with Christianity, it is not clear that the missionaries, however critical of the worldly bent of earlier mission endeavors, fully severed their sense of moral superiority from the technological advantages of the west. In a novelistic rendition of his experiences in interwar Nigeria, Raymond Davis contrasts the worlds of his own wife, a missionary nurse, and the abused African woman she treated:

> The two presented a striking contrast. One born in God-favored America in a Christian home, loved and cared for as an intelligent being, with the knowledge of salvation and assurance of sins forgiven. The other, poor and weak, born in a hovel made of cornstalks and mud, without the meanest experience of human love, much less the love of God, now lying there, brought low by the hand of her husband, whose chattel she was, without even so much as once before having heard the name of Jesus. (1944/1966, 18)

The spiritual wealth and well-being of the "God-favored" American woman in a clean and safe home is opposed to the material and spiritual poverty of the Hausa woman as if spiritual and material/political wealth were somehow parallel to one another. The implication is that somehow God has chosen to favor America (meaning both Canada and the United States, two of the major points of origin of SIM missionaries) by endowing it with technological superiority as a handmaiden for its participation in Christendom.

Furthermore, in terms of SIM attitudes specifically directed toward Islam, it would be unwise to overemphasize the breaks with early-nineteenth-century attitudes. SIM founders such as Rowland Bingham and Walter Gowans were motivated by the moral discourse of their Victorian predecessors, and these images in turn shaped their early understanding of Islam. As Adrian Hastings observes, for missionaries, "darkness" was associated with a lack of Christian belief, superstition, and abhorrent practices such as human sacrifice:

> Wesley was only too insistent upon the darkness of the villages and slums of England. There was nothing so different about missionary references to darkness in Africa. It was no more than the common discourse of Evangelicalism. For Pilkington, speaking in 1896, there were 'three forms of darkness' to be found in Africa, 'Heathenism, Mohammedanism and Popery.' . . . [Darkness] had come to represent the unacceptable superstition of any religion other than one's own. (Hastings 1994, 300–301)

Late-nineteenth- and early-twentieth-century missionaries moving into Muslim areas carried on the image of "Mohammedanism" as a kind of spiritual shadow casting a sinister pall over portions of Africa. To this early casting of Islam, let us now turn.

Hausa Traders and Cannibal Evangelists

The evangelical impulse of the North American SIM missionaries was countered by an equally forceful outward thrust by Muslim Hausa traders into non-Muslim regions to the south. The missionaries found themselves engaged not only in an enterprise to convert the Muslim but also in a competition to see which spiritual imperialism would win the as-yet-unclaimed souls of *kafirai*, or "heathens." Islam in West Africa has long been intimately linked to expanding trade networks, making even a relatively unschooled Muslim trader an agent in the spread of Islam. Missionaries into the Hausa regions were, as Elizabeth Isichei notes, dismayed to find that "the expectation that the Hausa would rise against the Fulani, and that 'the whole Hausa world is waiting for Christ' proved groundless" (1995, 273). British officials, wary of the unrest Christian intrusion might foment and protective of what they perceived to be the superiority of "Northern" Islamic peoples and states, restricted the entry of missionaries into the Hausa emirates of northern Nigeria not long after conquest. Early SIM preaching in Nigeria was limited to market areas outside the Hausa heartlands.

One of the most prominent of the early members of the mission, Dr. A. P. Stirrett, a druggist turned missionary, provides telling glimpses of the experiences of the mission as it attempted to reach the Hausa masses. Stirrett was drawn to service after reading the SIM pamphlet *Burden of the Sudan*, about the earliest efforts of Gowans, Bingham, and Kent in West Africa in the 1890s. He sold his drugstore to join the mission and took a crash course on tropical medicine in Liverpool before shipping out with SIM to Nigeria in 1902. When he first arrived, he was disappointed to find that SIM was not permitted to work among the Hausa, for whom he felt a particular spiritual responsibility after reading the pamphlet. It was only later, when a station opened in Wushishi in 1904, that he began to be able to reach the Hausa, still indirectly, by preaching to Hausa traders as they passed through the town:

> In those days Wushishi lay on the great caravan route from Hausaland south, and many traders were constantly passing through the town. The main part of the work was preaching to these traders at their halting place just outside the town walls. And in this way hundreds, yes probably thousands, who had never

before heard the gospel story hearkened to the message and carried it with them to all parts of Hausaland. (1935c, 23)

This notion that the Hausa trader would become the evangelist for Christianity proved to be far-fetched. Far from working with the Christians, Muslim traders came quickly to represent the spiritual nemesis of the mission. Blocked from serious work within Hausaland, the missionaries found themselves in competition with Muslim Hausa cultural expansion within those southerly territories of the Sudanic belt into which missions were permitted to enter. Hausa traders, rather than seeing Christianity as liberating, seem to have gone out of their way to heighten fears about the activities of the Christians. In a piece entitled "Atmosphere, Attitudes, Antagonisms," John Hall reported back to his sponsors and supporters in 1923 about the kinds of beliefs prevalent among Tangale non-Muslims. Relating "stories circulated and believed," he was not amused to find that the Christians whose mission was to convert cannibals had been cast by Hausa traders as cannibals themselves. Here is his account of the sorts of stories Tangale reported to him:

> Hausa traders tell us: "The White Man eats the flesh of men. He says he and his people do not eat human flesh, but that they are ruling the world. It is a lie. He deceives you. He is a cannibal like yourselves. Some of that meat which you see him taking out of cans, when you see it, you ask whatever kind of meat it is. And he tells you it is meat of bush. It is not; it is flesh of men. We Hausas know the world and all things that happen in it. We know. The White Man is your own kind; uncircumcised and a cannibal." (Hall 1923, 13)

In his article Hall does not attempt to account for this story, which would seem to underscore the universal appeal of the image of the Other as cannibal. Christian emphasis on the consumption of the body and blood of Christ might account in part for this unflattering picture of "the White Man." Of course, one residue of the Atlantic slave trade was also a common perception in West Africa that whites "consumed" the humans who disappeared into the bowels of slave ships. Hall's account of "stories circulated and believed" continues in just such a vein, well after the slave trade had ended. Criminals taken by the whites are fattened up for consumption, according to the tales. Some are canned, while others are sold:

> Some of these men whom you see the White Man bind are taken home by him and sold. The White Man's many clothes, boxes and possessions in general are the proceeds of the sales. When he takes a man captive, he carries him off to the edge of the sea. He turns the head of the victim round so that the back of his neck is where the front used to be, and he stands the man up in that position on

the shore. Then writes on the sand the price he wants for the captive back, and retires. One of the people who live in the sea rises out of the sea, and, coming ashore, finds the captive as the White Man had left him, and sees the price written on the sand. He erases that and writes his own, following upon which he brings a great quantity of goods, expensive things, piles them on the shore for the White Man to get when he returns, and descends with his slave back into the sea. (Hall 1923, 13)

Hall seems disinclined to examine the resonances of such tales or to make the connection between the metaphoric content of African stories about white cannibals and the likely metaphoric content of his own stories of Black cannibals. The pointed linkage in the Hausa trader's tale between white people's trade goods and the evils of the cannibalistic slave trade would have made his own goods appear less morally compromised. One can't help but enjoy the irony here of whites claiming the superiority of their own goods and religion on the grounds that African traders are evil slave merchants while Hausa traders extol the merits of their own religion and merchandise in precisely the same terms. As the ensuing remarks show, however, one need not assume that the Tangale received either set of claims uncritically. In response to Hall's criticisms of what he sees as Tangale Africans' inordinate affection for feasting, he is told that in the past feasting was a form of worship. Hall attempts to impress his interlocutors with the virtues of abandoning such older practices and prompts only laughter: "Indeed they laughed at all I had to say, and I am not sure but that it was all scoffing" (Hall 1923, 14). Like most semi-hidden transcripts, this laughter is hard to read, but it does suggest that whether or not the Tangale fully believed the stories they passed along, the tales authorized a kind of contempt for the moral claims of the whites. It is no surprise that the Hausa trader comes to figure in much of the SIM literature as the competing and confounding spiritual emissary, one whose word is trusted before the missionary's and whose contempt for the whites' assumptions of moral superiority is infectious.

The "Gapman" and the Malam

SIM's growing hostility to the figure of the Muslim Hausa trader was shaped in part by the mission's hostility to worldly advancement. Missionary writings often depict Muslims in a strongly disapproving tone, as if prosperity were a sign of moral failure: "The 'MALLAM' sitting before me had the usual Mohammedan air of self-righteousness and superiority, an air which is undoubtedly developed by too little introspection and too much outward show. His turban and flowing robes were perhaps contributory factors to his self-satisfaction, contrasting as they did with the dress or undress of the pagans with whom he was constantly surrounded." (Jackson 1935). Although much Protestant mission activity in Africa was linked to an ethic of prosperity through hard work and commercial enterprise, the faith missions emphasized a rather different set of values. SIM referred to itself as the "by prayer" mission, meaning that its success was to be underwritten not by subscriptions guaranteed in advance but by prayer. Any qualified missionary who presented him or herself would be sent to the field on the assumption that funding would follow. As Bingham remarked of his initial departure to Africa, "Not one of us had sufficient money to carry us through to the field, but we made the necessary deposit in faith and by the time the date set to sail was reached, we had paid the money in full for our passages to Lagos, West Africa" (Bingham 1943, 15). The mission trusted that prayer would inevitably bring forth the necessary funds to support the worker.[2]

One reason SIM did not emphasize lengthy theological training may have been that the mission had a strong interdenominational character even from the very outset, so that doctrinal differences had to be set aside in favor of the common purpose of evangelical work. One characteristic of the faith missions of the era was an insistence on moving beyond the sterile theological divides of the formal denominations. The three initial adventurers were Presbyterian, Congregationalist, and Brethren. Bingham was later to become a Baptist minister, but he nevertheless believed strongly in interdenominational mission work. SIM work came to emphasize neither any single brand of Protestant theology nor the kind of scholarly tradition of the Catholic missionaries to much of French West Africa under Cardinal Lavigerie, the Pères Blancs (White Fathers). Instead SIM missionaries believed that simple and direct exposure to the Scriptures in local languages combined with an emphasis on redemption would be sufficient to bring Africans to the light of Christianity:

> What our mission has sought to do has been to get the Scriptures translated into the tongue of the people and then to let the Word of God do its own work in their hearts. In doing this there has been begotten a oneness that we believe is nearer unity than anything which could be obtained in any single denomination. (Bingham 1943, 115–116)

Many SIM missionaries, if they had training at all, had been schooled in the spirit Dwight Moody promoted at the Moody Bible Institute: "Never mind the Greek and Hebrew. . . . Give them plain English and good Scripture. It is the sword of the Lord and cuts deep" (quoted in Findlay 1969, 329). Moody, himself a lay evangelist, saw an urgent need for laymen to fill the gap between the limited number of seminary graduates available to preach and the massive number of "unreached," whether they be in urban North America or in the Sudanic belt of Africa. In many ways, the SIM recruited what Moody called "gapmen"—volunteers whose enthusiasm for preaching would make it possible to evangelize the world, as the Student Volunteer Movement hoped, "in this generation."

Where other denominations and missions might choose to find common ground with Islam over theology, ritual, or shared moral claims, SIM's emphasis on the primacy of the translated scriptures meant that there was little sense of a shared human spiritual endeavor with Muslims. It would be impossible, for example, to imagine a SIM tract stating the sentiments of the first Catholic bishop to Niger: "Our aim is not to make Muslims change their religion, but together to be converted to a greater faithfulness to God."[3] Although Catholics could understand and respect Islam's emphasis on daily ritual, SIM missionaries had only contempt for the "vain repetitions" of the five daily prayers. It is no surprise that the very evident contempt of the missionaries for this ritual spawned local resistance to missionary intrusion that took the form of even more ostentatious attention to the ritual of *salla*:

> Every evening at dusk all good Mohammedans say their evening prayers. Nothing is allowed to interfere with the performance of this rite. Even in the middle of a conversation a Moslem will walk away a few steps and say his "salla" (prayers), without even asking to be excused. Two men in a village one day asked me to read to them from the Bible. While I was turning up the place, they did "salla" and I had to await their convenience. (Whale 1937)

Having distanced itself from the notion that commercial prosperity is evidence of spiritual election, and having adopted a stance that did not call for deep scholarship in the scriptures, the missionaries inevitably found themselves at a disadvantage in their attempts to outshine the prosperous Muslim trader and the itinerant Muslim scholar. Once they had retreated from the earlier evangelical insistence on linking commerce and Christianity, the later missionaries to Muslim regions were poorly equipped to compete with the commercial vitality of the Hausa trader. Because the early missionaries in Hausa-speaking regions, at least initially, were not deeply grounded either in theology or in Islam, they were also sometimes ill prepared to cope with Muslim scholars' attempts to catch them up in logical or theological contradictions. One way Muslim scholars seem to have worked to keep the missionaries from spending much time talking to less-trained Muslims was to engage the evangelists in scholarly debate. Edward Morrow, one of the pioneers in Hausa Niger, relates an experience in Zinder when he stopped to chat with "an especially bigoted and fanatical group of Moslems":

> Since they are Moslem teachers, the conversation is easily turned to religious matters and soon I find myself referring to Christ with the Koranic title "Spirit of God" and explaining to them that while His human body was born of the virgin Mary (a fact that the Koran also affirms), yet the breath (spirit) of that body was the very breath of God—the life of God—eternal life. One of them, no doubt with some intention to catch me up, asks, "Where is the life?" Thinking it a good opportunity to introduce the need for the shedding of blood, I turn to Lev. 17:11 and say, "Well, in the Torah of Moses (they are familiar with these names though not with the books) we read, 'The life of the flesh is in the blood . . . it is the blood that maketh an atonement for the soul.'" I start to explain when one of them, getting a bright idea, bursts out laughing and says, "Now we know that your book is a counterfeit. It says the life of the flesh is in the blood, but a locust has no blood yet it has life." I must confess that this about bowled me over,—it was the first time that I had ever had that one flung at me. How would YOU have answered him? By the time their gloating laughter had subsided I remembered that, in Lev. 17:11, God was speaking of the redemption of a human life, not that of a locust; but they were so pleased with their little victory that it was not possible to get any further with them. (Morrow 1941, 8–9)

The passage is revealing, for it conveys something of the dismay of the SIM missionary in the face of the formidable argumentative powers of those trained in the Koranic tradition.

The Pagan as Potential Convert

The gradual realization that mere dogmatic assertion of the superiority of Christianity was not compelling to Muslims, combined with the political reality that in Nigeria the British were highly resistant to the mission's overtures within Hausaland meant that for many years SIM focused its efforts on evangelizing among the "pagan" neighbors of the Hausa. Stirrett's reminiscences are revealing about the growing attitude toward Islamic "contamination" among SIM missionaries as the recalcitrance of Muslims became clear and as Islam began to spread with the colonial-era peace:

> Both Patigi and Wushishi were strongly Moslem centres, but now a new programme was entered upon, viz. Missions to the remaining pagan tribes. The first

of these was opened in the Yagba tribe by Mr. Titcombe in 1908, and from that time until the year 1926 the great urge in our Mission was to get missionaries out among these pagan tribes and win them for Jesus *ere they became contaminated by Moslemism.* (Stirrett 1935c, 24; emphasis added)

For several decades, then, the mission focused on translation and evangelization for language groups other than the Hausa. However, as such regions became saturated in the 1920s, the mission rethought its strategy and determined that it should make a more systematic effort to use the lingua franca of Hausa to continue its expansion:

In the year 1926 there came somewhat of a change in our general missionary programme, because God had so blessed us and the other Societies working in this land that it now became hard to find a *large* pagan tribe having a distinct language of its own where missionaries of the Cross were not already at work. All the pagan tribes which remained were small ones, and were mostly reachable through the Hausa language. Hausa then became *the* language for our new workers to study, instead of the pagan languages. (Stirrett 1936; 20, emphasis in original)

The choice of Hausa was an ironic recognition of the expansive cultural and economic power of the Hausa trader and was in a sense an effort to co-opt that expansive potential in the service of Christian evangelism:

This is because Hausa, like English, is the great language of commerce. As tribe after tribe open their borders to trade and civilization, in goes the Hausa language and that to stay, so that Hausa has been and is today rapidly on the increase.... This, as I see it, is the great task which lies before us—to get this Hausa Bible and especially the Hausa New Testament into the hands of the youth of these millions just as quickly as we can, *to combat the Devil's masterpiece, the Koran.* (21; emphasis added)

In a sense, then, it was precisely the success of the Hausa trader, the vigor of the Hausa commercial enterprise, and the strength of the cultural core underpinning Hausa commercial expansion that demanded that the mission simultaneously co-opt Hausa strengths and demonize the Islamic core at their heart.

Thus, despite its initial goal to convert Hausaland, the mission ended up focusing much of its energies on Africans who were quite different from Hausa Muslim population of the Sudanic belt. The paradigmatic figure of the native in spiritual peril had become "pagan" rather than Muslim, while the Muslim Hausa became the negative contagion to be fought.

A Fundamental Problem: Satan's Masterpiece

One senses in the 1920s and 1930s a shift and hardening in the rhetoric of the mission toward Islam. The reasons for this were complex and multiple. This was the dawning of what Mark Noll refers to as the age of fundamentalism within American evangelicalism, a period when influential evangelical figures such as James Gray, president of Moody Bible Institute, interpreted major international events (including the creation of the League of Nations and the Interchurch World Movement) in apocalyptic terms, seeing in each major political development the immanence of the "end of the age" and evidence of the battle of light and dark, God and Satan. In such a Manichean dispensationalist context, the analysis of Islam and the Middle East tended to be carried out through obscure prophetic interpretation rather than careful historical or political analysis (Noll 1994, 164–169). On the ground in Africa, missionaries were finding that in the face of the British and French colonial administrations' concern for the gradual and relatively peaceful restructuring of societies, their well-worn critiques of slavery were no longer effective in shaping policy or raising funds. Islam, from the administrators' perspective, did not appear to be terribly threatening. In what may have been an effort to heighten the urgency of its work, SIM began to portray Islam not merely as a flawed rival but also as positively demonic. In an article entitled "The Easy Way," SIM missionary F. Merryweather breezily asserts: "Mohammedanism has been described as Satan's masterpiece, and it is also known as the easy way; and such it is. The Evil one devised a plan by which he secured a great victory, and entrapped millions of precious immortal souls. They are in his snare; and are taken captive by him at his will" (Merryweather 1925, 13–14).

However, this representation is also related to broader movements afoot to rethink the relationship between Christianity and other world religions. Merryweather's claims rested on what was regarded at the time as a profound theological problem for Christians who were attempting to understand God's purpose in producing the other religions of the world. The growing knowledge of the different religions of the world had, by this period, produced some deeper reflection among missionaries more broadly; a position was emerging that saw other major religions as "preparing the way" toward Christianity in an evolutionary progression that began with primal religions, developed into "primitive" monotheism (which often had scriptural traditions), and ended with the crown of Christianity (see Walls 1996, 63–65). More-liberal theologians and missionaries began to reflect more deeply on the relationship between Christianity and other religions, sometimes coming to the conclusion that Christianity's universalist claims needed modification. One eventual outcome of the ongoing introspection was the tremendous shift within the Catholic church brought about by Vatican II, which was signaled in the epigraph with which this chapter opens.

In the context of such debates, SIM came to identify itself as "fundamentalist." Where in the first decade of the century it had distinguished itself largely with its mode of fund-raising and its interdenominational profile, by the 1920s it had begun to define itself increasingly in opposition to more-liberal brands of Christianity that were growing more tolerant of difference. Mission writings from the 1920s and 1930s reflect a sense of deep mistrust of the developing ecumenical movement and a growing sense of embattled isolation vis-à-vis other Christian groups. In this broader context, SIM's hostility toward Islam bears the marks of an anxiety about Christianity's sense of purpose in the face of other religions as the divide between fundamentalism and modernism deepened (Turaki 1993, 249–254).

The problem for SIM, of course, was that within any emerging paradigm in which the world's religions could be seen as preparing the way toward Christianity, Islam could only be seen as a *retrogression* from the natural trajectory of spirituality toward recognition of Christ's special role as redeemer, since Islam was historically a successor to Christianity rather than a forerunner. Any such deviation from the divine plan had to have been prompted by Satan: "The antagonism is between the Old Serpent the Devil and Jesus Christ. Mohamet in coming after, is placed before, and his book, described as 'The Final Revelation,' is given preeminence to the Word of God" (Merryweather 1925, 13). Stirrett, who had made translation of the Bible into Hausa his life's project, was particularly insistent upon the evils of Islam: "Now, brethren, we have a strong enemy—the Devil with *his* book the Koran—the *lie* of the devil—and there is no remedy but the Lord Jesus Christ with His Book the Bible, the truth of God" (1932, 6).

The demonization of Islam, of course, had contradictory implications for work in a Muslim region, for the missionaries had to sustain an interest in Muslims as individual souls while at the same time casting their religion, practices, and expansion as the work of Satan. The thrust of Merryweather's article was, in fact, to argue that the missionary must not give up on the Muslim:

A God-given-up people! Is this not true? How many have gotten out of the tangle? How many Missionary Societies or missionaries care to work among them? If the attitude of His servants is any criterion at all, may we well not think; they are given up!!; and Governments cry; "Stand back!" Are they not given up? and the Devil says, "They are mine." . . . Most difficult is it for God to meet this class, as the only way to Himself is despised; but there is hope in that He may honour the faithful ministry of His servant. (Merryweather 1925, 14)

The argument for proselytizing among Muslims is, in a sense, the challenge of its difficulty. In the face of Muslim pride, government intransigence, and Christian repugnance, so the argument goes, the dedicated missionary does not turn back. SIM missionaries projected the familiar image of slavery on the Muslim, who was "chained in sin, enslaved to Satan" (Kapp 1935, 16).

The longer the mission worked in Muslim regions, however, the more difficult it became to sustain the contradictory impulses of demonizing Islam while engaging with individual Muslims. The Muslim populations themselves were far from demonic and indeed bore many traits the missionaries could only with difficulty cast as uncivilized. Where "pagan" populations closer to the coast were "indecent," the most that could be said of the Muslim was that he was "overdressed." Strict Muslims and Christians alike decried the spirit-possession activities that could more readily be identified as demonic, and the family life of the Muslim was no more objectionable than that of other polygynous peoples of the region. By the mid-1930s a textured image had emerged of Muslims of the region as belonging to rival ethnic groups with different histories and differing degrees of adherence to Islamic practice.

The representations of Islam in SIM publications were therefore of necessity ambivalent. Rather than focusing on the religion itself and representing it as a product of Satan, missionaries such as Newton Kapp presented sympathetic portraits of the suffering Muslim, depicted as slave to ritual performed out of fear of a despotic God: " 'God is great,' proclaims the Muezzin, but it is futile if this greatness is only that of a despot looking from behind the azure skies ready to exercise his tyrannical power simply because He is God. Naturally those that are under this fear will rush through their ablutions in order to do their genuflections and repeat the stereotyped Koranic prayers in Arabic" (Kapp 1934, 20). Similarly, missionary Ed Morrow, in a voyeuristic piece on a neighbor's sorrow on losing a son, reports: "As the sustained notes [of the call to prayer] pealed out Malam Kassam stood motionless, gaunt despair written on his face. When he had said his prayer at two o-clock, his son was still alive, and while there is life there is hope; but since then he had died, the funeral service had been held and the child was buried. Mechanically, following the habit of years' standing, Malam Kassam turned facing the east and lifted his hands in the first of the several body positions assumed during the Moslem prayer. Lifted his prayer to what? . . . Only Allah. Allah who is more of a judge than a father, more ready to punish than to love, more quick to destroy than to resurrect" (Morrow 1934, 4).

This is not to say that missionaries ceased to regard Islam as a falsehood propagated by Satan. But by the mid-1930s this understanding of Islam had to yield, in day-to-day transactions with Muslims, to a more humane vision. Parallel to this ambivalent vision of the Muslim proper, missionaries began to insist that Muslims in the region were only partially Islamicized. They claimed that practices were by and large syncretic among the broader populace, leaving the *malams* and traders as the primary propagators of the rival faith. If the Muslim religion was to be seen as satanic and "fanatical," actual Muslim individuals were understood to be performing empty, and therefore presumably harmless, rituals. It was the spirit-possession practices such as *bori* that received greater condemnation as emanations of The Evil One by missionaries on the ground (Ray de la Haye interview).

SIM missionaries in the field between the mid-1930s and 1950s looked to the publications of former CMS missionary and Princeton College Seminary professor Samuel Zwemer for some form of theological and intellectual imprimatur for their intolerance of Islam. Zwemer's stand on the question of Islam's position within the evolution toward Christianity in the early 1940s was ambiguous. Having sketched out, for example, earlier western understandings of Mohammad as the romantic prophet (in the vision of the writer Thomas Carlyle) and as the Antichrist (according to nineteenth-century missionary S. W. Koelle), Zwemer declined to fully repudiate the latter reading of Islam, reiterating the "historical problem" Islam poses for Christians:

> But whatever may be the conclusion to which one comes, the question of the rise of Islam remains a historical problem, because *this religion was in no sense a preparation for Christianity*, but was a retrogression. Of other non-Christian religions we may hold that they were in God's sovereign providence some sort of preparation for the coming of the world's Redeemer. . . . This religion and its Prophet claimed not to prepare the way for Christ but to supersede or supplement His divine mission. (Zwemer 1941, 30; emphasis in original)

After effectively skirting the issue of whether Islam is Christianity's spiritual nemesis, Zwemer, like many missionaries before and after, turned to the condition of women and children under Islam to lend urgency to his call to convert the Muslim. In the context of global war and the rise of fascist and totalitarian states, it was inevitable that he would cast Islam in the language of the times:

> Islam was originally conceived as a totalitarian state, and therefore its legislation includes every detail of personal and family life. Words such as polygamy, concubinage, slavery, the rights of womanhood, illiteracy and superstition, enfold whole chapters, as it were, regarding social evils and social problems which had the same character in every part of the Moslem world, but which have reached different degrees of solution. The Moslem theory of education, of the place of the child, is in itself a problem for all who are trying to uplift society. There is a vast literature on this single aspect of Islam; namely, Moslem womanhood and childhood. And some of the best books on the subject have been written by educated Moslem leaders of the new era, who advocate the abolition of the veil and the emancipation of womanhood. . . . The greatest changes in the world of Islam have been in social and economic life due to the impact of western culture and not least to the education of Moslem womanhood which was in nearly every case initiated by the early missionaries. (35)

"Needed MEN Urgent": The Social Problem of Islam and the Problem of Mission Demographics

While this preoccupation with "the social problem" that Zwemer suggested Islam presents was not altogether new, the foregrounding of the condition of women and children took on far greater urgency in the postwar period. Slavery had disappeared as a motivation for mission intrusions, and the popular image of the fanatical Muslim was unlikely to arouse much compassion among politicians, potential missionaries, or funders. To stir sensibilities at home, SIM (and Zwemer) needed to turn to familiar paternalistic tropes. Additionally, the context on the ground in Nigeria and Niger was shifting with the advent of decolonization. For many years the mission had been prevented from engaging in serious work within the Hausa heartlands of Kano, Katsina, and Sokoto, but in the late 1950s, the British administration rethought its exclusionary policies. The mission was invited to take over a number of leprosaria. With the growth of more effective treatments, it became more desirable from the standpoint of the colonial administration to draw on mission capital and labor to carry the medical work forward. SIM enthusiastically embraced the opportunity to enter into these areas and grew by leaps and bounds from that period forward.

However, I suspect that of equal importance in the growing emphasis

Table 1. SIM Mission Staff in Maradi and Zinder, Niger, by Gender and Marital Status, 1929–1995.

Period	Married Couples	Single Women	Single Men	Ratio of Women to Men
1929–1944				
Zinder	6	1	1	7:7
Tsibiri	5	6	6	11:11
Maradi	5	0	0	5:5
Total	16	7	7	**23:23**
1945–1960				
Zinder	12	4	2	16:14
Tsibiri	11	12	4	23:15
Maradi	9	11	0	20:9
Total	32	27	6	**59:38**
1960–1974				
Maradi Department	11	10	1	**21:12**
1980–1989				
Maradi Department	11	13	3	**24:14**
1990–1995				
Maradi Department	8	5	1	**13:9**

Source: These figures are compiled from SIM "Prayer Guides." The guides indicate who is posted at which stations and who is on leave. I have counted the total number of individuals associated with a given post during the time span in question—not all would necessarily have been present at the same time because of furloughs. As mission activities have shifted into areas that do not yet have an established church, the number of missionaries posted to Maradi has declined in favor of other regions.

on the needs of women and children was the shifting demography of the SIM missionary population itself. Table 1 provides a glimpse at the gender composition and marital status of the missionaries stationed in the Maradi region over time. Clearly in the postwar period the number of women presenting themselves for service with the mission skyrocketed, and this group included many single women. Relatively few single men seemed to take an interest in mission work, although the mission continued to have a strong foundation in married couples.

Despite the success of the mission's strategic shift toward service, the mission administration located in North America saw the corollary demographic shift within the personnel of the mission as a failing. From the late 1940s to the mid-1970s, repeated calls went out in the mission's publications for young men to come to the mission fields of West Africa, despite the fact that women were clearly succeeding where earlier missionaries had failed. In some ways, the mission's ongoing sense of crisis over the failure of young men to present themselves as workers should come as a surprise. As a faith mission that was heavily indebted to the model provided by Hudson Taylor and the China Inland Mission, one might have expected that SIM would see female missionaries as particularly suited to the enterprise of reaching inland peoples who had proven particularly difficult to reach: they might be seen as the "missing link" critical to reaching the unreachable (Williams 1993, 48). As Peter Williams observes, the democratic revivalist impulses of the faith missions contrasted sharply with the rational gradualist approach of the more clerically oriented missionary societies. The evangelical vision of the China Inland Mission, for example, "was self-consciously different and in it the use of women missionaries was but one part of a generally subversive, anti-establishment, anti-clerical radicalism" (47). Far from being restrictive, the notion of surrender to God's will and the injunction of female submissiveness tended, paradoxically, to open for women unprecedented and highly responsible roles in mission work from the early decades of this century (61–64; Noll 2001, 80–101).[4] The China Inland Mission celebrated female missionaries from its inception in 1865.

By the time SIM was flourishing in Nigeria and Niger in mid 1930s, the role of women in mission fields, while not always seen as central, was accepted by both the denominational and the interdenominational evangelical missions (Beaver 1968/1998).[5] Why, then, at a moment when its own success seemed guaranteed largely through the work of female missionaries, was SIM anxious about the diminished profile of male missionaries, captured in the regular appearance of such headlines in the *Sudan Witness*, the mission's fund-raising magazine, as "Needed MEN Urgent" (Playfair 1949, 1)?

The key imagery that motivated the senior men who controlled the mission's administration hearkened back to an earlier literature steeped in a more masculine and martial authority, as is revealed in Walter Gowans's final epistle, written in 1893, the year he died:

> Wherever the faithful missionary seeks to rear the blood-stained banner of the Cross, there is the Spirit of Christ, consoling, encouraging, inspiring. He is the companion, and His is the Spirit that enables the missionary and martyr to labor, to love, to endure, to suffer, and to die. Hallelujah for the Cross! The Sudan for Jesus, and, blessed by God, Jesus for the Sudan! (SIM 1953, 30–31)

Gowans anticipated the martyrdom of Africa's missionary servants, his own death after the writing of this letter lending it something of a prophetic air. Gowans instilled in his companions and the mission itself the fervor of the medieval crusader against Islam, embodied in his letter in the figure of Bruce of Scotland:

> When Bruce of Scotland lay dying, he charged his valiant Douglas to have his heart interred in the Holy Land. Douglas accordingly had the heart encased in a casket, and immediately set about to fulfill the trust. One day, however, in an engagement with the Moors in Spain, his little band was like to have been overwhelmed by the very number of the enemy. His men were beaten back from his support. The Moors swarmed in on every side. It was a critical moment. Suddenly raising himself for a supreme effort, Douglas hurled the casket into the thick of the enemy, exclaiming, "Onward, gallant heart, as thou wert wont. We follow thee or die." Thus rallying his men, who saw the heart of their champion in the midst of the enemy, he led them on victorious. (30)

Wantonly blending Scottish patriotism, Christian missionizing, and the abolitionist spirit, Gowans goes on to remark:

> Wherever men are trodden down by feet hurrying and heedless, in greed of gain; wherever they are held captive in the chains of sin; wherever they are feeling if haply they may find God, there is the great heart of Christ moved with compassion on beholding the multitude as sheep having no shepherd, groaning in utterance, but there is no voice. Oh! shall we not all say, "Onward, heart of Christ, as Thou are ever wont. By Thy grace, we will follow Thee or die!" (30)

The mission's male administrators and potential male recruits preferred this "crusading" and "pioneering" work of masculine men. They regarded the "social" ministries in which female missionaries were engaged as less challenging (and, one suspects, less romantic). Engaging in tasks that were maternal, domestic, and in some sense servile, women missionaries altered the tenor and culture of SIM as a whole. As both the personnel and clientele of the mission shifted more and more toward women, the missionary project was, in effect, feminized, producing a sustained crisis for a mission founded with a rhetoric of spiritual conquest and a rejection of the physical ministries of earlier denominational mission efforts.

In the postwar period, mission publications made repeated calls for more men to enter the mission field, for women volunteers were outnumbering men by roughly two to one (SIM 1949, 1951a, 1951b, 1955, 1961; Wall 1953a; Bishop 1957; Troop 1956; Ockers 1958). Many of these women were nurses and teachers who staffed the growing medical and educational infrastructure of the mission. Others worked among home-bound women and fostered women's groups. Even as the mission cried out for more male missionaries, the kinds of articles published in mission magazines increasingly featured the problems of African women. Evangelical missionary theorist and theologian Samuel Zwemer had argued that "one could make a strong case for missions to the Moslem solely on the social conditions in Moslem lands, and the crying needs of its childhood and womanhood" (1941, 38). The paternalistic trope embedded in Zwemer's depiction of the "social problem," which reiterated the much older vision of the denominational women's mission boards, tended to draw more women to missionary work. Practically speaking, addressing the problems of women and children called for the labor of female missionaries—Muslim heads of household were unlikely to permit male evangelists to have contact with the women and children who SIM saw as the direct targets of missionary work by the 1950s. North American women and men perceived the kind of work engaged by addressing the "social problem" to be appropriately women's work.

Dana Robert has argued persuasively that women in the faith missions faced a missiological impasse: having rejected the ethic that celebrated "woman's work for woman" in favor of an emphasis on evangelization, these women found themselves in fact performing precisely those feminized social tasks in a context in which they were explicitly devalued (Robert 1997, 189–254). White male preachers (known respectfully as "Reverend") did the public preaching, while women performed the slow and in the end far more effective task of drawing converts using a more holistic understanding of the needs of both the body and the soul. The slow labors of white female medical workers in leprosaria cultivated a generation of male African evangelists who in turn began, at last, to have success in presenting Christianity to local populations in ways that were compelling, leading to large-scale conversions for the first time in the 1950s. As we shall see in subsequent chapters, white women missionaries together with (by and large) male African evangelists eventually made possible the emergence of the core Protestant community of Maradi. However, this complex social process is largely invisible in the mission's own perception of its history and is undervalued in the privileged image of the (white) male preacher.

The interest of North American women in missionary work, particularly after the end of World War II, was also bound up in the social and economic dynamics of American life. White women who had educated themselves for careers suddenly found themselves on a trajectory toward domestic lives. Single women drawn to the mission were often nurses and teachers who had pursued an education in the name of helping others. Evangelical women missionaries were complex and contradictory creatures who fled, largely unconsciously, the limitations of a life as 1950s-era American housewives by using the discourse of paternalism to justify entry into challenging careers as missionaries. Many never married, yet all espoused a discourse of Christian heterosexual patriarchal marriage. As the evangelical movement within the United States became more institutionalized in the 1940s and 1950s, the tolerance for highly visible women in positions of authority declined and gender roles hardened (Noll 2001, 93). Evangelical women may have found in the mission field opportunities for self-actualization that were closing down for them within their communities at home, and this may account somewhat for the striking increase in single women as applicants to SIM after 1945.

The demography of the mission staff was an enduring mystery to the mission itself, which persisted in imagining the ideal missionary as a crusading male evangelist in the face of the reality that by the 1950s the majority of its applicants were women. A 1961 report that explores why so few men were drawn to missionary work provides a sense of some of the consequences of the combination of an emphasis on Islam as a "social problem" and the mission's shift to providing social services in order to gain entrée for evangelism. The article discussed a survey of evangelical men that was undertaken to gain some understanding of their reluctance to enter into mission work. The authors noted:

> "Too much missionary appeal is on the children's level," was an opinion which many [of the men surveyed] shared. A man was not likely to be challenged by something which sounded like a woman's job—social service, teaching, nursing, children's work. Men responded less quickly to emotional appeals: they needed a definite challenge. (SIM 1961, 4)

The Rising Tide of "Isms"

World War II and the Cold War period produced shifting preoccupations at the mission. The rise of fascism in Europe and the complexity of global politics made it less likely that Islam alone would be cast as the nemesis of Christianity. During this period, the mission literature began to express concern over "the rising tide of 'isms'" (SIM 1939, 15), casting Islam, alongside communism and modernism, as just one of a disturbing range of forms of godlessness. In roughly the same period, the mission found itself in competition with other "cults" of Christianity and devoted much of its Hausa-language literature to responding to these propagandists as well as to Islam.

The mission's successful shift toward social services in the postwar period and its growing competition with secular ideologies meant that its preoccupation with the dangers of Islam receded to the background. Mission literature emphasized the recruitment of skilled men. The power of western biomedicine began to tell in the region, and the anxieties of the mission were for a moment far less cathected on the question of Islam and the figure of the Muslim. Nurse Martha Wall wrote, "Here in this forgotten, untouched desert land, the physical and spiritual needs of multitudes cry for still others to help. Medical work in the name of our Lord is the wedge that allows the wonderful Light of Life to stream into cold, death-bound hearts, warming and softening them to accept a life that will never end" (Wall 1952, 10). Missionary writings of the 1950s reveal an emerging sense of the mission field as part of the "underdeveloped world" and reiterate the nineteenth-century sense that technological progress will make spiritual salvation possible.

The shifting depiction of Islam, oddly, came full circle in the postwar period, for in the absence of a rationale for demonization of the religion, SIM returned to the familiar nineteenth-century trope of the sensual Oriental, sans the slave trade:

> Learn of their foul system of polygamy and concubinage. Live with them and know of their deceit towards all whom they class as 'infidels'. With their spiritual "malams" selling charms to ward off disease, disaster and death; or guaranteeing them invisibility for thieving, you have the background of Mohammedanism which to many at home is merely a picturesque religion of men in flowing robes repeating the name "Allah." Here is the degrading, debasing religion of the east, whose sole appeal is sensuality and carnality. . . . What Moslems need is not a dead prophet but a LIVING SAVIOUR! (SIM 1948)

Perhaps of a piece with this resurgence of nineteenth-century tropes is the suggestion that Muslims pray not to God but to Mohammad. This implausible casting of Muslim practice was encapsulated in the persistent characterization of Muslims as "Mohammedans," suggesting that they viewed Mohammad as God in the same manner that Christians regard Jesus as God. This, of course, is willfully inaccurate. A 1953 photograph in *The Sudan Witness* depicts the Muslim bowing in prayer, accompanied by the misleading caption, "On the sands of the Sahara. Bowing to the false prophet" (Berdan 1953, 14).

The Muslim, then, for much of the post–World War II period, was seen within SIM circles as more misguided than threatening, an idolater like the heathens around him. It was Christianity (in the form of American missionaries) that had technological power, not Islam. SIM missionary publications present possession of that power as evidence of God's hand in support of the mission, while the ravages West Africans faced were the means by which God drew them toward the mission and salvation. This is not to say that the notion of Islam as a force to be countered had altogether disappeared. To the contrary, all of God's force, to this way of thinking, successfully combated Islam through the agency of the American missionary. In the words of Albert Helser, who was the third SIM general director:

> As Christians we have every good thing the world has and, in addition, the mighty power of Christ. That is why the Sudan Interior Mission is ministering to the thousands upon thousands of lepers in the Sudan. Mohammedans are doing nothing for the lepers—they do not have the power—only the Jesus people have that power. (Helser 1940, 42)

In the post–Cold War era and with the rise of Islamist terrorism, there has been another sea change in the ways that Christian evangelicals think about Islam. In the wake of the attack on the World Trade Center on September 11, 2001, the rhetoric of Christian evangelists of all persuasions has tended toward a resurgence and legitimation of the older discourse of demonization of Islam with the implicit if not explicit support of a large subset of an emotional and angry American public. The Manichean and martial thinking that makes possible the unreflective demonization of Islam is never far from the surface in a certain brand of evangelical American thinking (as President Bush's unfortunate use of the word "crusade" in his original responses to the attack reveals). The crisis has had the effect of temporarily flushing out into the open and authorizing such revealing comments as Jerry Falwell's characterization of the Prophet Mohammed as a "terrorist," Pat Robertson's remark that the Prophet was "an absolute wild-eyed fanatic," and Franklin Graham's (Billy Graham's son) disparagement of Islam as "a very evil and wicked religion" (O'Keefe 2002). Some prominent evangelical Christians see the contemporary war on terror not simply as a battle against particular Muslim enemies but as a battle against the Enemy. In the era of political correctness, however, liberals immediately criticize the underlying intolerance that gives rise to these kinds of statements, which are generally grudgingly retracted. But this kind of rhetoric originates in a current of evangelical thinking that has ebbed and flowed but has never entirely disappeared. A policy paper offering guidance on whether and how to draw upon local culture to "contextualize" Christianity in order to make it more appealing to Muslims reveals that as recently as 1988 SIM explicitly understood its work in Muslim areas as "spiritual warfare" (SIM 1988, 2). SIM missionaries today would be extremely unlikely to use this kind of language. However, the Pentecostal missionaries of Vie Abondante do speak quite openly of their work in Niger as a "power encounter" in which the superior force of the Holy Spirit will conquer the occult power of spirits and of Islam. Vie Abondante missionaries frankly admit in informal conversation that in their understanding, Islam and local spirits have real spiritual power or potency and that Christians are called upon to counter that power through the Holy Spirit in Jesus' name. The directness with which they address this issue may account in part for the appeal of Pentecostalism today among recent converts to Christianity. But it is not hard to see why this attitude leads to practices that generate great friction with Maradi's Muslims.

4

A Hausa Spiritual Vernacular

Allah mai cetona ne. ("Allah is my Savior,"
a retort to the common Christian
pronouncement, "Jesus is my Savior.")

—Bumper sticker on a Muslim taxi driver's
cab in Niamey

*B*ecause of the emphasis on direct access to the Bible in evangelical Protestant Christianity, the first and most essential task of missionaries in West Africa was to translate the Bible into local languages. The Christianity propagated by evangelical Protestantism was, by contrast with older Christianities, remarkably textually oriented, anticlerical, inflexible in its disposition toward other sacred texts, and dismissive of other modes of religious instruction and practice (philosophical argument, pilgrimage, meditation, liturgy, song) (see, for example, Sugirtharaja 2001). Because they placed so much emphasis on the text of the Bible, evangelicals made the act of translating and transmitting "the Word" the paradigmatic act of evangelism. But it was an emphasis with complex consequences—it entailed engaging with interpreters, creating networks of printers and colporteurs, and investing tremendous energy into teaching illiterate populations how to read. In this chapter, I explore the history of the translation of the Hausa Bible to take up the challenge raised by Derek Peterson and Jean Allman that scholars "talk meaningfully and at the same time about both coerciveness of missionary discourse on the one hand and the invention and creativity of African Christians and their missionary interlocutors on the other" (Peterson and Allman 1999, 7). The translation of the Bible into Hausa involved the engagement and mediation of western missionaries, Muslims who were native Hausa-speakers, and Hausa-speaking Christians, each of whom brought specific sensibilities, skills, and agendas to the table.

In recent scholarly work, the missionary encounter is thought of very much in terms of a discussion, debate, or conversation in which the missionary and the African may engage with one another in a variety of ways (Comaroff and Comaroff 1991, 1997; Hunt 1999; Sanneh 1994). But what if the missionary enters the scene to join into a conversation that was already ongoing among Africans themselves? In that scenario, "the Word" becomes yet another element in debates among and between Africans, a vehicle for different claims and a rhetorical mode through which to reframe ongoing political and social contests (Peterson 1999). The notion of a missionary or colonial "encounter" may offer too constricted a time frame and privilege relations between missionaries and their converts over other equally relevant contests and conversations. Furthermore, the notion that there are two parties to the conversation (missionary and African) or even three (missionary, middle figures, and unschooled Africans or perhaps missionary, colonizer, and colonized) may be too simple. Many interlocutors were struggling to have their voices heard, producing what Bruce Berman and John Lonsdale have called a multivocal clamor (1992).

Of course, the metaphor of conversation, however apt it may be for moments of translation, may overemphasize the self-consciousness of the kind of hybridization and interaction at play in the encounter of a universal religion with the complexities of African social, political, and spiritual life. Jean-Loup Amselle would insist on the ongoing hybridization that affected the missionary encounter with Africa. Taking the example of Islam rather than Christianity, he finds no "zero degree paganism" and no "White Islam" to serve as originary interlocutors in the imagined conversation. Rather, he argues, the successive waves of Islam in Africa (characterized by oscillation between periods of reform and periods of synthesis with local practice) make for very supple paganisms, very mixed Islams. In this plural and fluid encounter there are no recoverable fixed systemic wholes; the multidirectional flow of cultural interaction is, indeed, poorly captured in the kinds of binaries the dialogic models (however richly nuanced they may be) tend to imply (Amselle 1998). The epigraph at the beginning of this chapter captures some of the unexpected and disorienting quality of these flows: in distinguishing himself from the Christian, this Muslim taxi driver absorbs and co-opts a Christian vocabulary of salvation that one would not ordinarily associate with Islam.

In the spirit of Amselle, I hope in this chapter to foreground the problem of disentangling Islam, Christianity, and "primal" beliefs from one another, a project guaranteed to be troubling to all who see their own spiritual practice as distinct and authentic. It is also likely to be troubling to those who hope to find a pure point of departure from whence to launch an argument about the colonial encounter, for by emphasizing a genealogy of hybridity and intermingling rather than a "long conversation" I must inevitably imply a process with no beginning. My point is not that there are no differences among and between these spiritual practices, for clearly there are—chapter 2 is my attempt to make an honest appraisal of just how significant those differences can be. My point is that despite those differences, there are significant ways in which spiritual practices on the ground mutually define and inform each other; they are shot through with family resemblances both welcome and unwelcome. The combative reformist spirit that drives claims to authenticity aims to seize the moral and political ground from others by articulating nodes of fundamental distinction. Yet the reality of practice is far more complex; indeed, the contests themselves have the effect of simultaneously creating marks of difference and reiterating the shared logics that give those differences meaning. Historically, Islam has had tremendous respect for the prior traditions of Christianity and Judaism and has borrowed quite unapologetically from them even as it has (somewhat less openly) retained reworked elements, such as the *hajj*, of the pre-Islamic spiritual practices of the Hijaz (Peters 1994). The result of such real histories of intermingling, refusal, and embrace in religious encounters is what one might think of as a swelling and turbulent reservoir of collective moral problems, symbols, and lexical elements. In this chapter, I shall explore these issues in the context of the generation of the Hausa Bible.

The twentieth-century mission initiative with which we are concerned engaged North American Christian missionaries in a colonial setting in which their national and spiritual agenda could not in any simple way coincide with that of the colonizing powers. The missions faced a shifting kaleidoscope of identities, statuses, and ethnicities that already had long histories of interaction with universal monotheism because of Islam's sustained history in the region. Mission translation teams blindly entered this unknown terrain and profoundly shaped the logics through which those identities might be formed and contested. However, they did so without full intention or understanding. Most important, they relied on an extraordinary range of middle figures to assist them in their attempts to transparently "give the Word" to Hausa-speaking Africans.[1] Throughout their quixotic quest to produce an unambiguous and "correct" translation of the Bible, they referred to an idealized and singular understanding of universal Christianity. They wanted to produce a pure and authentic version of the Hausa Bible, although the conception of what such a Bible would be changed over time. At first they favored a literal word-for-word translation, but this approach yielded over time to a philosophy that favored a translation that would be culturally meaningful for a Hausa-speaker while remaining faithful to the "real meaning" of the original.

Hausa-speaking middle figures, for their part, alternately enhanced, reinforced, created, and rejected other modes of identity and spirituality around which claims to "authenticity" might be made: Islamic, ethnic Hausa, Hausa Christian, Kanawa, Nigerian. This chapter explores the hybridity of this Hausa-language landscape, highlighting the ambivalent and multidirectional interactions between "native assistants" and their missionary interlocutors. Various potential audiences haunted the translation teams, shaping the text through imagined and real conversations with Muslim adversaries, "pagan" innocents, and Christian critics alike. My purpose is to trace a few of the lineaments of the complex and layered *métissage* that emerged from that encounter, the Hausa spiritual vernaculars that are rather taken for granted today.

Scriptural Translation and Muslim Hausa Hegemony

Missionaries entered the Hausa-speaking regions rather late in the colonial enterprise, gathering force only after medical work became a central activity after the 1930s. It was only as the coastal regions were saturated by the denominational missions and as knowledge about the more-Islamicized interior regions spread within Europe and the Americas in the second half of the nineteenth century that missionaries, spurred by the evangelical revival, began to turn their gaze to the Sudanic belt. At precisely the moment when Islam was being considered by some Africans and colonial administrators alike as a reasonable alternative to the expansion of Christianity, the Sudan Interior Mission took up the quixotic task of converting the Hausa (Barnes 1995).

The initial attempts of SIM founders Walter Gowans, Rowland Bing-

"Tamajeq man with vernacular illustrated publication in Arabic script." The work of translation and vernacularization is ongoing. Courtesy of SIMIA (NR 27), photographed by Raymond Davis, 1972.

ham, and Tom Kent to enter the Hausa emirates in 1894 were thwarted by ill health, the uncertain conditions created by the slave trade, and the open hostility of Muslim rulers:

> A slave raiding ruler, the Emir of Kontagora, had surrounded the little town in which Mr. Gowans awaited the return of Mr. Kent [with supplies from the coast]. For two weeks the people fought against the enslaving army until they finally were starved into submission. . . . Having captured and enslaved the natives, the old king let the white man and his black servants go free, but took the whole of his trade goods, promising to send him money for them. A few days later he dispatched to him a string of slaves, whom Walter Gowans indignantly refused. (Bingham 1943, 27)

When a later expedition of CMS missionaries attempted entry into the region they met with similar frustrations:

> The Moslem Emir of Kano was a slave-raiding ruler. When he learned of the purpose of the missionaries, he gave them three days to leave his city and they were compelled to flee. They withdrew to the adjoining city of Zaria, which on their way up had seemed friendly; but hearing what the King of Kano had done, the King of Zaria issued a similar order—three days' grace to get out of the city. (28)

The missionaries were therefore quite enthusiastic about the British conquest of the region in 1903. According to Bingham, Sir Frederick Lugard and his forces were God-sent, "an expedition to break the power of the slave-raiding Moslem kings of the Central Sudan." SIM histories ritually invoke an early meeting between missionaries and Lugard as proof that the British "pro-Moslem policy" that excluded them from any meaningful activity in the Moslem north was a deviation from the initial pure and Christian intentions of the conquest (29–30). SIM almost immediately found that the British did little to encourage missionary work in the central emirates such as Kano. Not surprisingly, colonial administrators and Muslim rulers of the early twentieth century were not terribly supportive of what they saw as a potentially disruptive intrusion, and they colluded to delay the entry of missionaries into Hausaland proper through a variety of stratagems.

Finding its work in Kano too constrained and seeing the more southerly work at Patigi and Wushishi as limited, the mission sought permission to do work in Hausa Niger under the French. The French acquired the Hausa-speaking territory to the north of the British northern Nigerian Protectorate in 1899 by conquering the forces of the kingdom of Zinder, but only after the infamous Voulet-Chanoine expedition had ravaged the countryside between the Niger River and Lake Chad in a particularly sordid episode in the history of colonial conquest. In part the havoc the column wrought was in retribution for the murder of military explorer Captain Cazamajou and twelve of his men the preceding year in Zinder (Charlick 1991, 34; Baier 1989, 96–97). Because of the difficulty of controlling extremely disaffected holdings so distant from the French center of power in Senegal, Niger was treated as a "military territory" and was governed by the French forces stationed in Zinder for two decades. In 1922, after intermittent Tuareg rebellions were finally brought under control, Niger was officially declared a colony. Once the French had consolidated control over the western portion of Niger in 1927, they transferred the capital of the colony to Niamey on the banks of the Niger River, permanently shifting the center of power away from Hausa-speakers in favor of the Zerma-speakers of the west.

Edward Rice made his initial venture into the Hausa-speaking region of Niger in 1923, at a moment when the French at last felt confident of their control of the territory, and just as civilian administrators were taking over command of Zinder. In this atmosphere of relaxation and openness, Rice found the French colonial officials "very friendly" and was permitted to established SIM's first work in a majority-Hausa-speaking region in Zinder. By contrast, in northern Nigeria, SIM missionaries had little direct access to or exposure to native Hausa-speakers in the core Hausa regions of Kano, Katsina, and Sokoto until 1937, when the colonial government turned over its leprosaria in those provinces to the mission. SIM missionary exposure to Hausa language and culture prior to 1934 was derived from encounters with Hausa traders, ex-slaves, and non-native speakers outside the Hausa-speaking heartland of the Kano, Katsina, and Sokoto emirates. However, the missionaries' passion to reach Hausa-speakers was combined with their pragmatic recognition that Hausa was a useful lingua franca for reaching the many smaller ethnic groups of colonial Nigeria; these two factors meant that the translation of Christian texts into the Hausa language was a matter of some importance. Missionaries who were prevented from entering directly into the Hausa-speaking regions to evangelize counted on the power of the translated word in print to reach Muslims there.

The mediated way in which these early evangelical missionaries gained access to the Hausa language is worth underscoring, for it had important implications for the kinds of translations they produced. Because missionaries often found themselves working outside of Hausaland, they drew on a variety of dialects and informants opportunistically, depending on who among the Hausa-speaking population (whether native Hausa-speaking migrants or traders who had learned Hausa in the marketplace) was willing to help them. This contributed to a certain incoherence in terms of dialect, grammatical imperfections, and unintended infelicities in word choice. The earliest Hausa grammar, which was written by a CMS missionary of German origin, Rev. J. S. Schön, was probably assembled in part from notes assembled by Samuel Ajayi Crowther, who accompanied the ill-fated Niger Expedition of 1841. Crowther was an acute observer and brilliant linguist himself, but he was not a native Hausa-speaker. Schön had learned Hausa from escaped slaves in Sierra Leone, whose dialect seems to have been the Sokoto dialect rather than one of the more widely spoken dialects. Because he did not speak Arabic, he seems not to have been aware of the many Arabic loanwords in his list or to have known that there was a strong literary tradition in Hausaland (Robinson 1899/1925, xii).

Schön consulted with various colonial figures stationed in Nigeria to revise that text and produced a translation of much of the New Testament and a number of books from the Old Testament. This work, which he did in England, called once again for the help of expatriate Hausa-speakers. Schön provoked the ire of the famous explorer Henry Barth by taking in two young men (Abega and Durugu) Barth had brought back to England, native informants who, for undisclosed reasons, opted not to continue with him in his travels. Durugu was a Hausa-speaker who had been enslaved in Bornu. Rather than release the young man to his parents in Hausaland as promised, Barth took him to Europe, where Durugu succeeded in establishing a limited and ambiguous freedom under Schön's patronage (Aliyu 2000, 107–109). The two undoubtedly assisted Schön in his 1876 revision of the dictionary and grammar. Later in 1877, Crowther arranged for a Sierra Leonean clergyman of Hausa-speaking parentage, T. C. John, to go to England to help Schön prepare portions of the Bible. With this motley array of experiences, tools, and mediating figures, Schön prepared a draft Bible, which he shared and compared with the translations undertaken by William Baikie, who had been British consul at Lokoja, outside Hausaland proper (Schön 1876/1968, iii–vi). All of these elements went into the publication of the first Hausa New Testament, which appeared in 1880.

The next significant translation work was done by Dr. Walter Miller of the Church Missionary Society (CMS). Miller's own draft translation "was largely the Katsina dialect, because he had for his helper a boy called Audu, a native of Katsina, who had gone with his father on 'pilgrimage' and had landed up in North Africa, where Dr. Miller had gone to study Hausa" (Stirrett 1945, 10). Once again one sees hints of the influence of a variety of native informants, in this case precisely the kind of highly literate Muslim most likely to engage in reflection, critique, and reform. Miller's initial effort was a translation of the Gospel of John into Hausa that was printed in Arabic script and is still used to evangelize among literate Muslim Hausa-speakers. By printing the Hausa text in Arabic script (a form of writing known as *ajami*, which in Arabic implies non-sacred texts in any vernacular), Miller could introduce Christian writings to Muslims who were already literate. This text had a profound effect on proselytization until the 1930s and influenced later translation work. Given the reliance of Miller and others on literate Hausa Muslims and pilgrims for the earliest drafts, it is not surprising that many of the most important proper nouns in his translation come from Arabic: Allah (God), Ibrahim (Abraham), and Dauda (David).

That "God" should appear as "Allah" in this initial translation is extremely important. SIM missionaries and others in the field later debated whether it would have been better to use another term such as the Hausa term for the creator God that antedated the influence of Islam in the region. Had the use of the pre-Islamic word "Ubangiji" come into exclusive usage early, the resonances for Hausa-speakers of the Christian God might have been quite different. The word is an intriguing one, for it plays on the very ordinary word "*ubangida*," which simply means the head of an extended household—the father of the house. The more common term today would be "*mai gida*"—the owner of the house. A variant of that term that seems to have been much more commonly in use at the turn of the century is "*ubangiji*," yet the resonances it carried were, it seems to me, somewhat more deeply linked with slaveholding. That is, an *ubangiji* was likely to be head of a large household that included not only the homes of sons but also the dwellings of slaves. The *ubangiji* was master, not simply father. One is left with the impression that the variant "*giji*" is in fact a kind of contraction of the plural for *gida, gidaje*. Thus, when "Ubangiji" rather than "Ubangida" or "Mai Gida" is used to refer to the creator God, a number of potential resonances are available; God is the father of all households and, significantly, the master of all masters, possessor of all slaves. It is a term that is at once humane (since it contains a highly paternal image of God as father), imbued with potency and wealth (since slaveholding was both a form of wealth and a means of accruing wealth), and extraordinary (since it transforms and amplifies the quotidian). I am struck by the many potential resonances such a term would have had in a slaveholding society with Christian notions of mercy, salvation, and redemption. Indeed, Christians today regularly refer to the Christian God as "Ubangijin Allah," a marker that at once suggests commonality with and distinction from Muslim belief in Allah.

The figure of Ubangiji circulated in non-Muslim stories of creation that had clearly endured a long admixture with Islamic stories of creation and Paradise. Despite the surface evidence of Islamic influence, an Arna creation story that was collected by Guy Nicolas in the Maradi valley in the 1950s has distinctive features that at once highlight a paternal understanding of God and sanction the veneration of the spirit world:

In the beginning there was on earth only one supernatural being called *Ubangiji* (Father of the house or Dominus). He created the first man, named *Adamu*, who then got up and set off in search of companions. He went in each of the cardinal directions one by one, each time returning to his point of origin. On his fourth return *Ubangiji* struck him and drew out of him a woman named *Adama* (note that she is not named *Hawa*, or Eve, although that name is known to the *Arna* and attributed to the wife of the bush god). (Nicolas 1975, 111–112)

Thus Adam's wife is his twin (Hausa twins are regularly given matching names such as Hassan and Husseina), and the cosmos is centrally structured around pairs of beings. The primal couple then gave birth to seventy pairs of twins, and out of shame at this seeming redundancy the couple hid half of the offspring in trees, rocks, and termite mounds. This deception angered Ubangiji, who retaliated by declaring that the beautiful hidden ones would remain unseen forever and their human counterparts would henceforth offer their cousins, the *iskoki* (wind/spirit), animal sacrifices to appease them. For the Arna, then, parallel human and spirit worlds have a deep kinship with one another, implying significant ritual obligations.

Nicolas notes that local Muslims tell a similar myth involving Adamu and Hawa, but in this version the hidden twins become the Arna (who historically did indeed hide out in the bush in the face of various outside intrusions), while those visibly present before Allah are the ancestors of the Muslims. Where the first myth sets up a kinship between the realm of the spirit and the realm of humans, the second establishes a ranking between human groups, placing one set closer to God than the other. Clearly a myth that made spirits kin to humans and explained their ritual worship as sanctioned by God would have been problematic for Christian missionaries. Nevertheless, the sense that God as the father of creation is an active overseer of human behavior could conceivably have helped in the mission's attempts to distinguish Christianity from Islam in the region and might have helped strike a chord with Arna who were marginalized and othered within Islam. To recapitulate the Arna version of the myth in slightly more abstract terms, one central source of being gave rise to multiple manifestations, one human and embodied, the other invisible and spirited. This sort of story, with some careful recasting, might have paved the way well for the Christian understanding of sin, the Holy Spirit, and the Trinity.

Indeed, Muslim Hausa seem to have used the word "Ubangiji" to refer to Allah as early as the time of the earliest missionary entry into West Africa. John Peel notes that Yoruba who had long exposure to Muslim influence had come to think of God in ways that were strongly influenced by Islam even though they might not be Muslim. One of the Yoruba expressions that Peel notes as having a Muslim origin is in fact probably a deformation ("Obangiji") of the pre-Islamic Hausa term for the Supreme Being, Ubangiji (2000, 196). In other words, the epithets for Allah that Hausa traders carried into Yoruba-speaking regions included a vernacular term they had borrowed from the Arna. For Muslims, of course, the slaveholding resonance that I argue seems to have been a dimension of the term at the turn of the century might have fit well with their own understanding of the believer as a slave of God, one who submits to God's will. The migrations and borrowings of meanings, which are powerful precisely because they were multivocal and highly resonant, took many unexpected turnings and detours.

It is therefore striking that Miller, who was dependent on devout Muslim Hausa migrants in North Africa, used the term "Allah" when clearly even Muslims were comfortable using the term "Ubangiji" as an epithet for God. "Allah" is of course the more broadly useful term for Muslims, and one which, reasonably enough, would have underscored the commonalities between Christianity and Islam and reiterated their shared Abrahamic heritage. Yet by preferring the word "Allah" over "Ubangiji," Miller's Muslim interlocutors were foregrounding the rather abstract Islamic understanding of God, and one can't help but wonder whether this choice was calculated. The central difference between evangelical Christianity and Islam is the very different understandings of the means of access to salvation. Evangelical Christians believe that humans are by nature sinful and that humans can have salvation only through God's mercy in ransoming souls through the sacrifice of his own son. The term "Ubangiji" would seem to encapsulate much of that understanding of God and provide it with a grounding in indigenous beliefs. "Allah," on the other hand, in this context suggests instead that it is Islam that is the original monotheism, grounded in the sanctity of Arabic as sacred language and exemplified through particular ritual acts. Christianity, then, is merely a derivative parvenu carried by outsiders deficient in ritual performance who do not themselves speak Arabic. None of the imagery of paternalism, slavery, and redemption is necessarily embedded in the term "Allah."

Some of the responsibility for preferring Arabic terms over other available terms for God undoubtedly rested with the missionaries. Recent work by William Worger on missionization in nineteenth-century southern Africa reveals a complex interpretive dynamic that may have given rise to a perception among some missionaries that "barbarous" peoples lacked fundamental concepts and the attendant vocabulary to convey theological ideas: "The most 'immense difficulty' [Moffat] found was in 'translating theological ideas. Kingdoms, crowns, thrones, and scepters are unknown here'" (Moffat, quoted in Worger 2001, 419).

As Worger nicely demonstrates, the impasse Moffat experienced is less one of a conceptual vacuum than a struggle over the central metaphors through which theological beliefs are to be conveyed and the political implications of those figures of speech. The movement of missions into the Sudanic region in the second half of the nineteenth century may very well have been accompanied by a growing perception that indigenous African metaphors were contaminating Christianity. This is why Schön was enthusiastic in 1841 about Hausa and its seemingly unambiguous theological vocabulary:

> Hausa . . . is rich, and admits of [an] additional number of words being formed legitimately; and the influence which Mohammedanism has gained over the people in the interior has supplied it with many religious terms and words which we sought for in vain among the vocabularies of Pagan nations. (Schön, quoted in Aliyu 2000, 99)

Frustration over an inability to fully control the central terms of Christianity because of the richness of local languages is likely to have colored missionary perceptions about the uses of African languages as the nineteenth century progressed. Worger's observations suggest that it was not exclusively "religious terms" that translators struggled to find parallels for, that terms for government and economy were in some ways the central metaphorical currency of the Bible itself. Stateless societies did not have "kings, crowns, thrones and scepters"—and, indeed, did not want them. But highly centralized states in the Islamic belt often did have corollary institutions. For example, in Hausa, "kingdom" could be translated with the Arabic loanword "*mulki,*" which means something closer to "government." Islam carried an understanding of heaven, which the Hausa associated with the sky. Thus, "Kingdom of Heaven" could be rendered "Mulkin Sama." By 1896, some mission circles were upholding Arabic, Hausa, and Swahili as the great African languages through which missions "shall enter readily into the minds and views of the people of Africa" (103). However in sidestepping the complexities of a possibly richer and older language about God that antedated Islam and centralized states, early translators of the Hausa Bible may well have robbed it of the metaphors that would have rendered Christianity most resonant within the region for the many non-Muslims who populated the countryside before the explosion of Islam under colonial rule. At the same time, they privileged and exported understandings of social structure, authority, and government that were associated with centralized kingdoms.

The problems inherent in using the theological vocabulary of Islam became clear very rapidly as missions moved beyond evangelization in the middle belt and attempted to convert Muslims directly. The earlier entry of Islam and Arabic inevitably made Christianity appear to be a heretical sect rather than the authentic precursor to a degenerated monotheism. Translators of the Bible had attempted to forestall the Islamic interpretation of Christ as simply one of many human prophets by translating "Jesus" as "Yesu" or "Jesu" rather than using the Koranic name for Jesus, "Annabi Issa." Nevertheless, because of the heavily Arabized vocabulary of Christianity, some of the most important passages the missionaries quoted regularly were inevitably refracted through Muslim lenses.

By 1908 or so, the British and Foreign Bible Society had called for a complete translation of the Bible into Hausa and initiated the formation of a translation committee with representatives from various missions. Miller, having established his credentials as a translator, was called upon to head the new translation committee. One of the earliest issues the committee had to address was "which was to be considered the classical language, Arabic or English?" (Stirrett 1945, 12). That neither Arabic nor English is ordinarily considered to be a classical language of Christianity seems to have been lost on the translators, for reasons which will be more clear in a moment. Another key issue was whether to continue with the *ajami* version of the Bible or to print the new version in Roman characters. Largely for the convenience of western missionaries but also in an effort to be consistent with the growing western schooling of the colonial period, they decided to adopt Roman type (12).[2] In both of these debates, at issue was a perceived need to seize the Christian scriptures out of the clutches of a creeping Islamicization.

Although the translation committee in principle drew on the expertise of numerous government officers and clergy, according to Andrew Stirrett, by the end of the twenty-year effort only two medical workers, he and Dr. Miller, along with "a young Hausa office helper from Zaria" remained to finalize the work (Stirret 1945, 11). Invisible in the written materials produced by SIM but evident in the reminiscences of missionaries and the memoir of John Mamman Garba was the hand of Ethel Miller (Rita Salls and Ray de la Haye interview; Garba 1989, 391), Dr. Miller's sister. Despite Stirrett's self-aggrandizing claim that he and Miller worked alone, the central importance of a number of African intermediaries emerges when one looks closely at how this edition was prepared. Throughout his work, which was carried out in numerous locations from Zaria to Kano, Miller relied heavily on his "typist," presumably the unnamed "office helper" Stirrett referred to. John Garba offers an extremely rich portrait of these otherwise unnamed assistants:

> Among the "boys" who came along with him from Zaria were M. Tafida (John Tafida Omaru); Barau (Dr. Russell Aliyu Barau Dikko); Musa (Arthur Musa Benson); Ango (Mark Ango Ibrahim); Ibrahim (Frank Ibrahim Musa), Bagudu (Peter Bagudu Omaru), Garba Labar (G. N. Hassan), and perhaps one or two others. Mallam Tafida (later in life, Dan-Galadiman Zazzau) . . . used to come to the bookshop in order to assist Dr. Miller with the work of typing out the translated passages of the Bible. When the job of translating and typing was completed, Mallam Tafida got an appointment in 1930 at the Murtala Muhammed Hospital as an assistant warden. (Garba 1989, 389–390)

The invisibility of these "office helpers" in the narrative of the mission is strikingly out of keeping with the obvious political and social prominence of these "boys"—Malam Tafida would become a major figure within the local native administration, and Garba himself went on to become an important national political figure and diplomat. Although Stirrett tended to erase these "middle figures," Miller had a close, even intimate, relationship with them throughout their lives—Garba thought of Miller as a father figure in some ways and quotes at length from their correspondence with one another in his memoirs.

Other colonial officers and missionaries who contributed sporadically to the work of the committee also relied on middle figures, local informants whose identities are fugitive but who seem to include one Malam Fate, a Hausa Christian, and one Malam Bello, a Muslim, evidently of one of the most eminent Fulani families. As Musa Gaiya points out, western translators, few of whom were highly trained in theology and none of whom was a linguist, "used the [English] Revised Version to translate from, while the informants used the Arabic Bible to give the appropriate words in Hausa. There is no indication that the Hebrew or Greek texts were used" (Gaiya 1993, 56). Under the circumstances, the missionaries relied very heavily on the largely unidentified informants who were literate in Arabic script.

Miller's initial translation choices, which used Arabic proper nouns, were to have a long-term impact on the language of Christian missionizing, for even when a complete revised Bible appeared, residues of the earlier translation had to be retained, causing inconsistencies in the translation:

> It was decided that *English* should be the classical language, so that now we find nearly all the proper nouns in the Old Testament [translated later] are spelled

as in English, whereas those in the New Testament [translated earlier] are spelled as in Arabic. It was agreed, however, that the names of persons in the Old Testament with which the infant church was already familiar, such as Allah, Ibrahim and Dawuda (God, Abraham, David), should retain the Arabic spelling, but that all new, unfamiliar names such as Reuben, Simeon, etc. should be spelled as in English. Hence there has come about the lamentable condition of having the name spelled in the Old Testament as in English (e.g. Reuben, Simeon, etc.) and in the New Testament as in Arabic (Ra'obainu, Shimi'una, etc.). (Stirrett 1945, 12)

Furthermore, the habits created by the early introduction of "Allah" into the initial Miller translation were difficult to shake off. The improved translation, which appeared in 1932, recast the critical lines of John 14: 6 to read "*Yesu ya che masa, Ni ne hanya, Ni ne gaskiya, Ni ne rai: ba mai-zuwa wurin Uban sai ta wurina*" ("Jesus saith unto him, I am the way, the truth, and the life: no man cometh unto the *Father*, but by me"; emphasis added) and that rendition was retained virtually word for word in the 1979 edition of the Bible. But veteran missionaries I interviewed who worked in Niger in the 1930s and 1940s were more likely to quote the earliest translation that used "Allah" rather than "Uba" from habit when they spoke informally. Although the 1932 translation made it possible to emphasize God the Father (a notion that was quite distant from Muslim notions of Allah and was closer to "Ubangiji"), the early use of the word "Allah" presented a way to link Christian practice with the known God of the Muslims. In his initial encounter with Muslim Hausa in Jiratawa in 1941, for example, Ray de la Haye deliberately sought out what he called "bridges." On this occasion he seized on the chance event of a blind man who became confused when he came upon de la Haye's newly built home, which blocked his familiar path:

I said [to the villagers], "Today you've prayed four times, you have one more time left . . . and in your prayers you begin with the *fatiha* (which is the first chapter of the Koran), and you pray to God the Almighty ascribing to him praise and greatness and so forth, but you also say lead us in the way of those to whom thou hast been gracious." . . . I guess they kind of were listening, cause I had learned that just as a point of contact with them, a little of Islam, so I might build a bridge—and I says "Yes, but this person [the blind man] who had been over that road for so many years said, 'Well if this is not the right way then lead me to it.' So I'm here to teach you that there is another way." It was then I gave them John 14:6 in Hausa, *Ni ne hanya ni ne gaske, ni ne rai, ba mai zowan Allah sai ta wurina*, and there was one person only that made a response, which we followed up, but it was a good contact, that people were not negative, they welcomed us, and it was not done with too much force, and we became one with them in a wonderful way. (Ray de la Haye interview)

It was difficult in the same moment to create bridges of familiarity with Muslim audiences and at the same time hold to the peculiarly Christian understanding of God as Father.

In a sense by keeping missionaries out of the Hausa heartland, Muslims inadvertently succeeded in guaranteeing that the Christians' introduction to Hausa language was powerfully shaped by Muslim pilgrims, traders, and acculturated Hausa slaves. Missionaries were caught between two quite different strategies. One would have used language that targeted non-Muslims by distinguishing Christianity from Islam and building on the spiritual and figurative ground prepared by pre-Islamic practices. The other would have preferred language that emphasized the shared Abrahamic heritage of the "religions of the book." As it happened, it was the *less* Islamicized Hausa population that consistently proved the most fertile ground for missionizing, and therefore the first approach would undoubtedly have been the more profitable. However, the language the mission actually used was formed by the initial language training missionaries received and by translation work among Hausa Muslims. The mission's language choices betrayed a prejudice within this later mission movement against "pagan" figurations of God or power and in favor of the higher civilization of Islam—an adversary worth contending with. In any case, missionaries preached in a context in which ignoring or bypassing Islam would have been quite difficult.

The missionary impulse in Hausaland, then, was directed in important ways by the expansive currents of Islamic Hausa society and by often-unnamed middle figures who were Muslims. Nancy Hunt, in her insightful semiotic approach to the "colonial lexicon" of birth ritual, medicalization, and mobility in the Congo, has signaled the ubiquity of these little-noted intermediaries in the shaping of colonial representations. Her own focus is on the medical discourses that emerge in the colonial era, and she argues "that such middle figures were . . . central to processes of translation in a colonial therapeutic economy" (Hunt 1999, 2). My interest here is obviously a bit more literal than her own work on transactions and exchanges, and I am less concerned with medicalization (for the moment) than with the most immediate ways in which Hausa-speaking Africans came to encounter textualized and verbalized representations of Christianity. Middle figures mediated not simply between a broader African population and colonial-era missionaries and agents, they in effect intervened in a spiritual economy that they themselves for the most part eschewed.

In this instance, one might reformulate Hunt's attention to the often-unheralded role of African interpreters to note that Muslim middle figures were often unrecognized players in the process of vernacularization through which cultural and spiritual capital for Christians (who were marginalized within the colonial enterprise) was to be negotiated. In intervening in the most primary acts of colonial-era missionary translation, Muslim intermediaries profoundly shaped some of the most persistent and taken-for-granted elements of the Hausa Christian lexicon. It is interesting that the borrowings of indigenous practices within Islam in combination with Christianity's subsequent borrowings from Islam have generated a terrain in which all parties strive to demonstrate their "authenticity" in order to make distinctions, while at the same time all share a great deal of unacknowledged common ground.

One final irony is worth entertaining, although it would be difficult to document without becoming a biblical scholar myself. Because the missionaries who worked on the translation of the Bible did not themselves have access to the original-language texts, they treated the Revised Standard Version of the Bible, in English, as their "classic" text. Their Muslim assistants, on the other hand, were drawing on the Arabic translation of the Bible as their "classic" text. Arabic is, of course, a language that is far closer to the classical languages of the Bible than is English, and the Arabic Bible was one of the earliest translations of the Bible. It benefited from the fact that its translators knew all of the central languages of the Bible intimately and were Christian. It is entirely possible that the Arabic text these Muslim scholars worked from was a good deal more faithful to those classic texts than was the English version. The goal of the translators was to produce what is referred to as a "formal correspondence" variety of translation, in which the words and forms of the original text should have precedence over the functionally equivalent meaning. By refracting the Hausa Bible through the Arabic Bible, it is conceivable that the mediation of these Muslim middle figures was healthy and positive, given that the goal was to match the language of the original texts. Where there was disagreement it may well have been the missionaries, who were limited to the English text, who were producing the problems. One can hardly fault the native Hausa-speakers for the many grammatical errors in the 1932 translation—in their confidence in the superiority of their own understanding the non-native speakers seem to have frequently had the upper hand, to the detriment of the translation. In other words, it is entirely possible that the Muslim translators contributed dimensions to the text that should have been highly valued by literalists, insights into the original text of the Bible that are unavailable in the English version. There are those whose preference for the 1932 translation rests on the argument that it is a more faithful rendition of the original text than the later 1979 translation, which, as we shall see, is a meaning-based translation.

Hausa Christians as Middle Figures

Missionaries in other regions faced the problem of the role of Arabic loanwords in translations of the Bible—the intermission disputes and philosophical disagreements SIM and its collaborators faced troubled the translators of the Swahili Bible also (Mojola 2001). It was all very well to use Hausa or Swahili—literary languages and vehicles of trade with a rich spiritual, political, and legal vocabulary borrowed from Arabic—in the areas where they were spoken as a first language. But using highly Arabized versions of the local lingua francas with populations farther afield that had not already been exposed to Islam presented the risk of either rendering the text opaque to non-native speakers or inadvertently propagating Islamic beliefs.

There was, not surprisingly, a call for another translation of the Bible to be prepared not long after the death of Stirrett in 1948. Work by individual SIM missionaries evidently began on a New Testament as early as 1949, but it was many years (and many collaborators) before the full Bible produced through the United Bible Societies appeared in print in 1979 (Kirk 1950). A number of serious concerns had emerged by the 1960s that led missionaries of different stripes as well as Hausa-speaking Christians to take an interest in preparing a revised version of the Hausa Bible. An interview with two retired SIM missionaries illustrates the kinds of things that missionaries, who by that point were far more fluent in Hausa after over fifty years of work in the region, found troubling about the 1932 edition (Salls and de la Haye interview). The interview also sheds light on some of the tensions between different missionary societies as their differing philosophies about translation became an increasingly significant distinguishing difference in the context of the deepening division between fundamentalism and modernism. Among the issues they struggled over were how to relate to Islam, how to choose middle figures, and what a "good" translation of the Bible might look like. I began the interview by posing some questions to Ray de la Haye, who had assisted with the translation of the 1979 edition of the New Testament, but some of the interjections of Rita Salls, a seasoned missionary who was fluent in Hausa, offer some confirmation of his comments.

De la Haye and Salls agreed that the central problem with the earlier edition was a kind of literalness that missed what they took to be the real meaning and spirit of the Christian text—precisely the kind of spiritless and pro forma translation one might expect from a nonbeliever, they seemed to imply. But the literalness was also a predictable outcome of an emerging mission strategy at the close of the nineteenth century of evading richly figurative speech. The goal of the 1932 translations was to create a text that offered a formal correspondence, word for word, with the original. However, the literal translation seems to have regularly missed the mark in terms of meaning. Salls offered an example: "In talking about wrapping the Lord Jesus in swaddling clothes . . . they had used the word for 'rags' or something" (Salls and de la Haye interview). And indeed the 1932 translation of Luke 2:7 can't help but strike any observer of Hausa life as unnecessarily arcane. In ordinary speech one would simply say that the child was wrapped in a *zane*, an ordinary cloth, since women swaddle children in *zane* to this day. But the 1932 translation says that Mary wrapped the baby in *tsummoki*, or "rags," as if there were something remarkable about the cloth itself. The Hausa word for "rags" is also an epithet for a prostitute. The original Greek word "*sparganoo*" does refer to the kind of strips of cloth a Hebrew woman would have used to wrap her baby, but the significant issue presumably wasn't that the cloth was in strips but rather that Mary wrapped the infant Jesus just as any baby would be wrapped. Salls, who spent much of her time in the field wrapping babies at a mission orphanage, clearly found this particular passage wildly out of keeping with her own experience, as it must also have struck the Hausa women she spent much of her time evangelizing. No loving and honorable woman would wrap her baby, much less the Savior, in rags.

De la Haye, in the kind of telling critique that was available to better-educated male missionaries coming to the field in the 1930s and 1940s, objected to direct translation from English instead of any real attempt to find a Hausa equivalent to the Greek or Hebrew. As he delicately noted, one of the central translators of the new translation didn't know Greek or Hebrew and relied heavily on a well-known Muslim who had assisted in the preparation of the 1934 Bargery dictionary.[3] Because most of the participants were not scholarly authorities in the biblical languages, Malam Musa's linguistic authority as a native Hausa-speaker and experienced translator would have weighed heavily in the discussions. The more-conservative participants to the translation effort did not like working with a Muslim who was so self-confident and who worked with a missionary from the more-liberal CMS mission. According to de la Haye, "And when this Malam Musa, the helper for the Bargery, uh, they formed a very formidable team. . . . True. And when Hausas read it, they said, 'Oh, that's wonderful.' But then, I'm talking about those who were unsaved Hausas. And to those who were members of the body of Christ—Hausas who were saved and redeemed—they would have another viewpoint when they started to read it" (Salls and de la Haye interview). De la Haye places the blame for the poor translation from the original languages at the feet of the Muslim assistant to Bargery, when in reality the fault may have lain with the missionaries' insisting on the priority of the English translation and on literalness over Hausa equivalents.

As an example of the sort of translation issue that troubled missionaries and Hausa Christians, de la Haye and Salls offered their thoughts on a favorite Bible verse, John 3:16: "For God so loved the world, that he gave his only begotten Son, that whosoever believeth in him should not perish, but have everlasting life." De la Haye noted that the 1932 Hausa translation was grammatically incorrect, which would grate on anyone whose Hausa had not been learned in the marketplace and would give Muslim Hausa listeners the impression that Christians lack a central attribute of Hausa urbanity, namely articulateness and poetic skill with language. Salls noted that the word that in the King James Version appears as "perish" is rather poorly captured by the Hausa word "*lallace*," which is much weaker and less linked to volition, since it means "spoil." A better Hausa word with stronger figurative resonances would have been "*halaka*," which implies destruction, damnation, and agency. These kinds of differences, she noted, mattered to one's understanding of Christianity (Salls and de la Haye interview). And indeed, the improved 1979 translation of the Hausa Bible did correct the two mistakes Salls and de la Hay noted in the older translation. Of Dr. Miller's efforts in the earlier translation, de la Haye simply tactfully remarked, "He was a medical doctor with many other responsibilities besides translation" (Salls and de la Haye interview).[4]

John Garba's reflections on Miller in his memoirs suggest that there was considerable tension between the liberal impulses of Miller and some of the CMS missionaries and the conservative evangelical Christianity of SIM and the Sudan United Mission (SUM).[5] Miller felt strongly that mass education was one of the most important contributions of missions and colonial intervention: "To educate partially is to make a nation of miserable pundits and discontented, literate nondescripts; we cannot have men too well trained for this work of education now" (quoted in Garba 1989, 403). It is probably no coincidence that his "boys" and a few girls went on to higher education and distinguished careers in medicine, government, and diplomacy. Miller, who was forward looking for his time, also espoused coeducation. Unlike SIM missionaries of the same era, Miller advocated English-language instruction, despite his fame as the translator of the first Hausa Bible. One reason Miller promoted the Roman script for the Bible was that it would facilitate children's entry into schooling in European languages. He also envisioned advanced schooling in "the three great religions of the world—Christianity, Buddhism, and Islam" and fearlessly promoted the interests of commoners over those of indigenous rulers (403–407). It is not at all clear that he was doctrinally committed to the notion that Christianity was the only path to human salvation—a difference in disposition from SIM missionaries that would very likely have led to quite heated differences over how to translate and who to trust as an assistant (417–418).

Whatever one might conclude about Miller and his assistants, clearly the earlier edition was flawed from the perspective of a Christian fluent in Hausa. And by the late 1960s there was a large number of Christian converts in Nigeria, many of whom could read and write in Hausa, although very few were themselves native Hausa-speakers. Most were from the ethnically and linguistically diverse middle belt and very few had converted from Islam. Indeed, as evangelical missions began to have some success in attracting converts, it became more and more clear that the most promising mission prospects were not Muslims and were not necessarily ethnic Hausa. These Nupe, Igala, Gbari, and Tiv Christians had become church leaders and some had succeeded in acquiring higher theological training. But the success of the mission among "pagans," many of whom did not speak Hausa as their mother tongue, meant that the missions and emerging churches faced difficulties in attempts to improve on the original translation. One extremely interesting issue that emerged was, in fact, the problem of whether the Hausa language fully belonged to native Hausa-speakers anymore. The Hausa-language church was by this time largely made up of converts for whom Hausa was a second language, the lingua franca of the marketplace and the idiom in which much Christian practice was conducted. Like Igbo converts to Islam, these converts in a sense called into question the hegemony of the Hausa-Fulani Islamic nexus (Anthony 2000). An "authentic" Hausa-language Christianity had emerged outside of Hausaland, rupturing the ethnic, religious, and geographic locus of Hausaness.

United Bible Societies began systematic work on a full revision of the Bible with the Nigerian Bible Society in 1969, drawing on the large pool of Christian converts in Nigeria. One team was to work on the Old Testament except for the Psalms, while another was to handle the New Testament and Psalms. The first team was headed by Nigerians—Reverend D. N. Wambutda, Reverend Chisawa Kaburuk, and Malam Paul Yusufu. Wambutda later left the committee to take up another appointment but continued to contribute revisions. Ray de la Haye's memories of work on the New Testament team in the 1970s reveal the complexities of such a collective enterprise:

> There were three groups: the Sudan United Mission, the SIM—the mission of which we're members today—and also the CMS—Church Missionary Society, which was Anglican. And we three would meet. And from time to time, after having done our work separately, we'd come together and discuss the revision of the work being done. We started in the New Testament. And about, uh . . . there was good progress made for a time. And I must say—it's safe to tell you frankly—that one of the members was using the chief translator of the Bargery dictionaries . . . Malam Musa [presumably Malam Musa Nahann Danjuma]. He's French [sic] and he's a Muslim. He never changed [meaning he never converted]. But he was Bargery's greatest helper. And, uh, must have been . . . and we got to know him. He was on our committee working with this other SUM worker [possibly Cyril Sanderson]. And he gave it a Muslim flavor which, uh, our checkers detected and didn't like. Uh, some words were, uh, Arabic, uh, used in Hausa. But their connotation was more toward the religious aspect [of Islam]. (Salls and de la Haye interview)

Obviously Arabic permeated the Hausa language and had entered into some the most ordinary expressions—it was neither desirable nor feasible to eliminate all Arabic from the new translation. At issue presumably was whether central religious concepts should be expressed in ways that reflected Muslim beliefs (emphasizing ritual, merit, and adherence to law) or evangelical Christianity's understanding of redemption through Christ's sacrifice. The possibility that Christianity as refracted through the eyes of a Muslim who was literate in Arabic might in fact be truer to the original text seems never to have entered the minds of evangelical missionaries such as Ray de la Haye, but it may very well have colored the approach of the more-liberal participants. The presence of a Muslim with strong views and the authority of a native speaker on the committee clearly ruffled the feathers of the SIM participants in the translation. The SIM missionaries' reservations about the evolving translation prompted numerous interventions and objections that ultimately had a significant impact on the final product.

Musa Gaiya's description of the translation process suggests that there were a great many cooks in the kitchen, making inconsistency a serious likelihood in the drafts that emerged: a Hausa team at Wusasa would do a draft, which would then be reviewed by a review committee in Kano, and those comments would be reviewed and amplified by a Christian named Paul Yusufu and passed on to Reverend Wambutda in Ibadan. Once the draft of the Old Testament had been completed by the translation committee, it would be reviewed by two experienced SIM missionaries, Helen Watkins and Ruth Warfield, who worked ostensibly to "insure that an up-to-date, quality (Kano) Hausa was maintained and that the whole of the translation work was in line with the recommendation of the Hausa Language Board" (Gaiya 1993, 57). Given the kinds of grammatical mistakes in the 1932 edition, this review was important to efforts to regain some of the intellectual and linguistic capital lost in the earlier translation. Gaiya's description of their work suggests that their role was simply to provide consistent Kano-dialect grammar.

However, Helen Watkins and her secretary, Ruth Warfield, actually became involved in the review of the draft when Watkins discovered that, as she put it:

> There was not a man whose mother tongue was Hausa [on the translation committee]. Well, that upset me! So I wrote the Bible Society . . . and said to them I felt they should have men whose mother tongue was Hausa doing the work. And I got back a rather snippy letter, "If you know any men whose mother tongue is Hausa, let us have their names—and who are Christians." (Helen Watkins interview)

She submitted a list of names that included Reverend Sule Garko, Reverend Mai Ku'di Kure, and Reverend Tambaya Hassan, who all in various ways ended up contributing to the translation work. Reverend Mai Ku'di Kure more or less replaced Reverend Wambutda on the translation committee for the New Testament in the final stages, while Reverend Sule Garko performed less-visible and less-recognized labor on the Old Testament review committee that went over the final drafts and the various comments submitted by the other committees. It is not clear that these men had converted from Islam—Sule Garko, for example, came from one of the enclaves of non-Muslim Hausa known in Nigeria as

Maguzawa. While they were "authentically" Hausa, they interrupted the long-standing pattern in translation work that associated Hausaness with Muslimness. Reverend Garko was also a well-known preacher who had impressed congregations in Nigeria and Niger with powerful sermons. These men were not merely converts; they were experienced evangelists themselves. The fact that they were unknown to the Bible Society seems indicative of a growing separation between the milieu of the evangelical fundamentalists and the more liberal milieu of some of the other participants in the translation work. Watkins had selected men whose Hausa was impeccable but whose familiarity with their Muslim neighbors prompted them to preempt certain kinds of infelicity, misunderstanding, and ridicule.

While in principle the translation work was to be done from Greek and Hebrew, in practice it is clear that, once again, few individuals working on the translation were capable of consulting the original texts. Watson and Sule Garko's review, which significantly affected the final product, was done with the assistance of an array of English translations rather than the original languages. Because Sule Garko was blind, Watkins read the entire draft to him out loud and entered any corrections he suggested. This painstaking labor of love reveals the kinds of interventions Hausa Christians introduced into the new translation and the rather intimate work transcultural mediation involved. Watkins attempted to be faithful not so much to the classical texts of the scriptures as to the texture and richness Hausa believers expected the translation to convey.

As Derek Peterson's wonderful work "Translating the Word: Dialogism and Debate in Two Gikuyu Dictionaries" illustrates, the act of translation engaged European and American missionaries in a "sustained dialogue with native others" that was "inevitably shot through with meanings" beyond the control of the missionary (1999, 6, 32). Peterson's work suggests that even as rudimentary a text as a dictionary could be a site through which local debates about power, already under way as the missionary entered the scene, could be framed. As a result, the new hybrid language that emerged "gave voice to meanings and ideas which neither language [English or Gikuyu] could express, and marked out a potentially radical interpretive terrain for Gikuyu converts and politicians" (32). Peterson's work raises the possibility that the Hausa Bible was a fruitful site for marginal groups (Maguzawa converts, middle-belt converts, and descendants of slaves) to stake out the terms by which local politics and ethics could be judged and to map out the contours of a utopian future.

One striking dimension that emerges in Watkins's description of her work with the blind Reverend Garko is that for Hausa Christians, a deep love and reverence for the landscape of the Holy Land was part of the pleasure of reading and envisioning the events in the Bible. For Muslims, the territory of the Saudi Arabian Hijaz is an important part of the spiritual imagination and real pilgrimage, but for Christians the Holy Land invited equally vivid imaginings grounded in an actually existing geography:

> He would pick up different geographical things, now he said, "Where is that in relation to, uh, Jerusalem?" And so I'd tell him, "It's north," or "it's east." And when we came to the words, word Goram [sic], which is in part of the land— well, I mean, it was divided up between the tribes. Just a series of names. And he said, "Is that the same as Golan Heights?" He had heard it on the radio. And I said, "Yes," and he was thrilled! He had such a keen mind to pick up little details. (Watkins interview)

What for the missionary was "just a series of names" in Deuteronomy 4:43 and Joshua 20:1 was for the blind Christian evangelist who was imagining the relationship between the familiar world of the Scriptures and the known world of modern media and politics a point of intersection between the sacred and the profane. It mattered that the word used for the territories of ancient tribes corresponded to the name used to describe contemporary geopolitical struggles. The list named the cities of refuge into which anyone who committed unintentional homicide might flee for sanctuary. Associating the name in the text with a site on the map was one way of establishing the credibility and relevance of the scriptures. The contemporary world was sacralized, while the world of the scriptures was in a sense ratified by its continued existence in the present. The meaning of the city in the Old Testament had a bearing on Israel's claims over the same land in the present. Finally, contemporary struggles between Jews and Arabs could provide parallels through which Christians in Garko's audience might reflect on their own predicaments in a majority Muslim region.

Sule Garko's concern for a vivid and physically rich image of events depicted in the scriptures that could serve as a figurative parallel to felt experiences in the present emerges in another example, the translation of 1 Samuel 17:49, the culmination of the story of David and Goliath. Watkins recalls, "When Goliath fell, he fell—in our English Bible—'he fell forward.' And he said, 'Well, how did he fall? Did he fall to his knees and then go forward? Or did he fall stiff?' . . . Well, it was a different

Hausa word!" (Watkins interview). For a Hausa Christian surrounded by indifferent or hostile Muslims who was imagining a battle that was emblematic of the struggles of the weak and small against powerful and dominant enemies, it mattered not simply *that* Goliath fell but also *how*. In the King James and American Standard versions, the Hebrew was rendered word for word with English parallels: "he fell [*naphal:* to fall, to be laid low, to be judged, to be overwhelmed] upon his face [*paniym:* face] to the earth ['*erets:* firm ground, earth]." The original 1932 Hausa translation, whether following the English or the Hebrew, pursued the rather stilted strategy of matching the language word for word: *ya fa'di a fuskatasa har 'kasa* (he fell upon his face to the ground). The sequence of descriptive words parallels the Hebrew precisely but is rather awkward in Hausa. Biblical figures might fall in such a manner, but ordinary people do not.

Abandoning the word-for-word literal translation in favor of a more evocative and idiomatic approach, the translators of the 1979 Bible rendered the passage *ya fa'di rubda ciki*. The expression "*fa'di rubda ciki*" conveys the same sense that Goliath fell on his face, but by choosing a more idiomatic expression, the translators succeeded in bringing the passage to life, describing an event that could be envisioned and expressed in the same terms as one would use in everyday life. The Hausa words for "face" or for "earth" do not appear; instead, the phrase conjures an image of the whole body prostrate on the dirt, the belly and face hidden. There is an onomatopoeic and emphatic quality to the expression "*rubda ciki*" that is missing in the wordiness of the original translation. When Goliath falls in this version, he falls with a satisfying and definitive thunk. The Hausa listener would know from this that Goliath didn't fall backward or to his seat, as a *bori* medium might during a dance. He fell, as we might say today in idiomatic English, flat on his face. Although the original 1932 translation is truer to the specific syntax of the original, the 1979 translation seems to be more faithful to the spirit.

The experience of reencountering the familiar Scriptures through the mind's eye of a Hausa Christian evangelist who was experienced in helping others "see" the truth was, as Watkins put it, "a great blessing" to her (Watkins interview). Watkins's experience served to deepen and enliven her own reading of the Bible. Her recollections of this work illustrate once again the potential for multidirectional hybridization in the translation encounter. The most famous example of such an encounter is, of course, Bishop John Colenso's rejection of a literal understanding of the Bible at least in part as a result of the probing questions posed by

Africans during his evangelical work (Sugirtharajah 2001; Draper 2000). In Watkins's case we have less a rejection of the literal than a deeper appreciation for the power of vivid imaginings and the implications of locating the Bible in the culture and politics of the present. Working with her assistant did not cause her to ask "Do I really believe this?"— unlike the liberal Colenso, she had no inclination toward the biblical criticism that would have made such a question imaginable. Colenso found that he had to rethink how he would frame Christianity for the nonbeliever in view of his own mathematical and scientific skepticism. Watkins, by contrast, was taught to envision the Bible differently by a fellow believer, to see the world of the Bible as contiguous with her own.

Although they were in principle charged with the review of the Old Testament, Watkins and Reverend Garko also insisted on a number of changes to the revised version of the New Testament. After she and her assistants had reviewed the draft version, Watkins submitted a report on its shortcomings that was scathing. Understanding the text would depend on proper intonation, which would be an invitation to misunderstanding and a hurdle for non-native Hausa-speakers; the spelling, dialect choice, and plurals were inconsistent; there were too many unnecessary English loanwords. But most damning was their discovery of a consistent mistake no native Hausa-speaker would make that touches on the very understanding of God's distinctness from humans. The draft evidently contained many passages in which the English "God can" or "God may" was rendered *"Allah yana iya."* But in Hausa to use the verb *"iya"* ("to be able to do something") implies that one can imagine its converse, the inability or incapacity to do something. Hausa-speakers, she pointed out, only use the expression *"Allah yana da iko"*—"God has the power" when speaking of God's potency (Gaiya 1993, 60). The understanding of Allah as the possessor of the unqualified power of rulers (rather than as having a reversible capacity or entitlement akin to commoners, spirits, and humans more generally) that has been imprinted on the Hausa language may well be the most significant way in which Islam has shaped quotidian understandings of the Supreme Being. The defect was remedied throughout the translation, but the mistake was far from minor and suggests the degree of influence Watkins and Garko had in their review and how big a difference it made that she insisted on the participation of native Hausa-speakers.

Watkins and Garko were also troubled that the word for "Savior," which in the older version had been "Mai Ceto" (the one who brings liberation) had been changed to "Maceci" (rescuer), which, they conceded, was perfectly good Hausa grammar. "But the Muslims who want to misread it anyway would not say 'Maceci,' they'd say 'Macuci' [deceiver or rogue, and, by extension, Satan]. . . . Yes, and sometimes they say '*maceci*,' which is very similar. But it's 'servant'" (Watkins interview). Obviously Garko was acutely sensitive to the abusive readings Muslims might bring to the new text and hoped to control some of the resonances of a term as central to Christianity as "Savior."

Because Christianity amplified on an existing Hausa lexicon of enslavement and redemption, Muslims could use that vocabulary to denigrate the status and sophistication of Christians. The word that Watkins says had come to mean "servant" undoubtedly derived from the Hausa word "*bacuceni*," defined in the Charles Robinson *Dictionary of the Hausa Language* as "a sort of household servant who could not be sold" (Robinson 1899/1925, 26). Robinson's translation obliquely signals the slave ancestry of the *bacuceni*. Abraham's translation suggests a more complex social negotiation born of the intimacies of domestic slavery: "Person born in slavery of slave-parents (so called as knowing the secrets of the family, he thinks to himself '*cuce ni n cuceka*' 'you blab about me and I'll blab about you!')" (Abraham 1958, 54). The play between "*cuce*" (to cheat) and "*cece*" (to redeem) oscillates in the figure of the member of a household who could no longer be sold. Christianity's inevitable resonance with an earlier vocabulary of slavery and redemption yielded an ambiguous legacy, for evidently hostile Muslims were happy to play on it in casting Christians and their Savior as low-status slaves who were intimate in the ways of their Muslim masters and lacking in the kind of honor and restraint common among the truly civilized. Muslims might be slaves of God, but the expression of that submission through an Arabized vocabulary elevated and sacralized it. The enslaved Hausa Christian, by contrast, was simply a low-status member of society, a heretic and an outcast. Given the marginal social origins of many Christian converts, Maguzawa and middle-belt groups that had long been the prey of slave raiders, refusing such associations was in a sense a political act.

Despite Watkins and Garko's vigilance about Muslim misappropriations of Christian vocabulary, there were some instances of the formalization of what one might characterize as an orthodox Islamic vocabulary in the 1979 translation. An example suggests that translators were alert not only to how orthodox Hausa Muslims would read the text but also to how "pagans," Maguzawa Hausa and Hausa-speaking Muslims who had accommodated *bori* spirit possession, might read it. It also reveals some of what is at stake in choosing a "meaning based" translation over a literal one, for if many of the translators' choices did, in my view, improve the Bible dramatically, all assumed that there was a single "meaning" to the passage in question and that the translators had some sort of privileged access to that meaning.

The critical New Testament passage on demon possession is Mark 5:2, in which Jesus drives the spirits possessing an outcast man into a herd of swine. The 1932 translation rendered the first encounter with the *kazamin ruhu* ("unclean/impure spirit"), using the Arabic loanword *"ruhu"* (often rendered as *"roho"* in Hausa) for "spirit" or "soul." The translation was an attempt at a word-for-word translation of either the Greek, *"pneuma akathartos,"* or the English, "unclean spirit." The word *"ruhu"* was also used to refer to the Holy Spirit, Ruhu Mai Tsarki ("the clean/pure spirit"; *"pneuma hagios"* in the original Greek). Keeping the same word for the two appearances of the word "spirit" was consistent with both the original Greek and with the English rendition, although a closer parallel that captured the sense of an invisible presence such as breath or wind would have been the Hausa word *"iska."* This suggests either that the translators were working from the English rather than the Greek or that they deliberately chose to prefer an Arabic loanword over the local image with all its uncontrollable resonances.

Later in the passage, the term *"aljanu"* is used without a modifier to refer to the legions of spirits that Jesus drove into the swine. The term in the original Greek is *"daimon,"* a far more complex and philosophically fraught term than "spirit" or *"pneuma,"* since it evokes both evil spirits and the kind of inspiration that comes with the blessings of the gods. However, the word is regularly translated as "demon" in the English, retaining only the negative valence of the word. *"Aljanu,"* the word used to translate "demons," are the *jinn* ("concealed ones") that Islam and Arabic folklore recognize as active agents in the world. The word may have positive connotations in some cultural contexts, but in Nigeria and Niger, *aljanu* have come gradually to be rejected as demonic within reformist Islam.

In the context of Maradi, however, *"aljanu"* is a simply a synonym for the *bori* spirits. Muslims who have reconciled spirit possession with their practice of Islam do not regard such spirits as demons, nor do they aim to exorcize such spirits. True madness or illness comes from a failure to come to terms with such spirits, especially from outright rejection of them. The appropriate response to discovering that one has "inherited" spirits is to develop a positive and mutually rewarding relationship with them through ritual, gifts, and animal sacrifice. Some *bori* spirits are "good" or "white" and cause no harm. Others are dangerous or "black" and can be the source of illness if they are not handled well. But to reduce a shifting and morally ambiguous spirit world to such "black and white" binary terms is to do violence to their complexity—indeed, some *bori* are red! All spirits are the potential source of some sort of power and benefit, for it is only by appeasing spirits that one can cure certain illnesses (especially certain forms of paralysis) or remedy certain conditions (such as infertility).

The 1932 translation was, therefore, quite confusing within the local understanding of the spirit realm. Although the Holy Spirit is distinctive within Christianity, the use of the word "*ruhu*" with two different adjectives ("dirty" and "clean") and then the equation of the "dirty" spirit with "*aljanu*" would have placed the third person of the Trinity within the realm of the *bori* spirits, perhaps as a relatively benign spirit. This is not necessarily inconsistent with the multiple uses of the word "*pneuma*" in the Greek. On the other hand, the failure to describe the *aljanu* as "white," "black," or otherwise would leave the committed *bori* practitioner puzzled about what kind of spirit was driven away and why. Perhaps the mad rush of the swine over a cliff and into the sea answers the question through the narrative itself by showing that the spirits, in this instance, were willfully self-destructive. Jesus, in speaking to and commanding the spirits, could be likened to a spirit medium.

In the later edition of the Bible, translators chose to segregate the language for the Holy Spirit from the language of spirit possession, deliberately violating the literal wording of the passage. "*Ruhu*" was used exclusively to describe Ruhu Mai Tsarki, the Holy "Clean" Spirit, while "*aljanu*" was used to describe possession. Rather than describe the spirit as "unclean," which seemed to invite comparison with the Holy Spirit, the *aljanu* were described as "black," which is roughly consistent with the categorization of dangerous spirits within *bori*. However, in this context, "black" designated evilness rather than a particular kind of potency. The newer translation simultaneously adopted wholeheartedly reformist Islam's rejection of *aljanu* as necessarily satanic and placed the legions of *bori* spirits within a single category, "black."[6] In a sense, Christianity was explicitly aligning itself with reformist Islam in its rejection of all *bori* spirits as demonic. It is interesting that in segregating *ruhu* as positive from *aljanu* as negative, the translators opened the way for the later Pentecostal movement to employ a language of spiritual healing through the power of the Holy Spirit that could be conceptually separated from the healing of *bori*. Of course, in practice, while Pentecostal Christians insist on their rejection of the demonic, the reality that healing and unseen forces are the province of *bori* has meant that to outsiders, faith healing simply appears to be *bori* in disguise. Whether one regards such healing as demonic depends, of course, on whether one regards all spirits as evil; however, in aligning itself with Islam against *bori*, Christianity made it far less likely that faith healing could be viewed positively by outsiders to the practice. To the revisionists, it was obvious that the "real" meaning of the passage in question is that "unclean spirits" and the Holy Spirit are utterly different in kind, but the slippage toward seeing them as akin within the Hausa worldview defies the controlling impulses of the translators.

Conclusion

Watkins, Garko, and other contributors hoped to forestall willful misreadings, denigrating ridicule, or categorical confusion, but they were not solely consumed with imagining the native Hausa reader. In fact, much of the appeal of the new translation was that it would make scripture far more transparent and vivid to the average non-Hausa reader—the sizable pool of non-Muslims who had acquired Hausa as a second language and whose access to the scriptures would be through the lingua franca of Hausa. The only African woman who seems to have been involved in the translation served, in a sense, as the final arbiter of the clarity of the translation. When I asked if any women were involved, Helen Watkins at length recalled that there was one non-Hausa woman named Mariamu. She was asked to read the entire translation "to see that it made some kind of sense to a Hausa-speaking non-Hausa. And she said, 'Oh, this is so plain!' And she read it with her 1932 Bible on her lap. And she said, 'Now I can understand it.' She said, 'I couldn't understand it before'" (Watkins interview).

But that hard-won clarity is the fruit of a complex and lengthy struggle and collaboration, a contra dance in which Muslims who were literate in Arabic provided some elements, evangelical missionaries others, and Christian converts (both native and non-native speakers) yet others. At times, Islam provided the negative space against which Christianity hoped to define itself, at others *bori* practices and other "pagan" practices served that function. But in order to make sense, to be "clear," the translation has to participate in the very symbolic economy it hopes to transform. The Hausa spiritual vernacular is an uncontrollable confluence of converging and diverging ideas, practices, and beliefs rather than a codified lexicon. Perhaps this should not be surprising given the history of *brassage* that characterizes this sociocultural region (see Alidou 2005). As Peel observes of Yoruba religious dynamics, "Where the internal critics of Yoruba Islam were most anxious to upgrade its Islamic credentials, the most persistent demand on Yoruba Christianity has been to prove its African ones. . . . To translate the Bible into Yoruba was not only just the start but was itself the template of Christianity's whole project of realizing itself as an African religion" (2000, 190). This was a complex enterprise, given that Africans in this region had long been exposed to Islam: Islam could in a sense stand for "authentically African." So the question of the degree to which Islamic elements color the translation of the Hausa Bible is an interesting and important one, and one which immediately complicates the very notion of authenticity. A vernacular is rich and multivocal; it borrows shamelessly from other vocabularies and revels in the improvisations of real users in messy settings. In the end, it refuses formalization and fixity. The "authentic" African element or Christian element or Islamic element or, for that matter, western element is a chimera, a fiction that is passionately sought after but upon closer inspection betrays its hybrid origins.[7] For one seeks explicit evidence of an authentic conception only when its taken-for-grantedness has been flushed out into the realm of an articulated ideology—in other words, when it has already come into contact with other forces and modes of thought.

The fixity of a printed text gives the illusion of a final "clear" version, but in attending closely to the complex process of translation, one mustn't fall into the trap of imagining that texts alone define religion—however much fundamentalists of various stripes might wish that were so. The complexity, mobility, and multidirectionality of the Hausa spiritual vernacular suggest the need to attend to practice as well as text. A fuller grasp of the story of Protestant Christianity in Maradi will require us to look at how texts are used or not used, at the practices surrounding them, and at the struggles that the emphasis on text-based Christianity set in train. Both historically and conceptually we must turn to the critical question of literacy, for the evangelical emphasis on the vernacular Bible meant that, as Sugirtharajah observes, "reading had now become a new state of grace" (2001, 169). But what kind of reading, for what purpose, and under whose terms?

5

African Agency and the Growth of the Church in the Maradi Region, 1927–1960

> *The ones who have a red number, Almasihu [Savior], that's not just anyone . . .*
>
> —Song sung in Tsibiri ridiculing the earliest converts, who wore a red number issued by the mission (Barmo Abdou interview)

Introduction

When I spoke with Christians in Maradi about the history of their community, I was often puzzled by the deep resentment of Christians toward the mission that had introduced Christianity into the region. Why did they convert if the mission was so terrible? If Christianity is the central pillar in their lives, then why weren't they grateful to the mission? For the secular scholar it is rather difficult to come to terms with the reality that for missionary and convert alike, agency in the moment of conversion rests not with humans but with the Holy Spirit. Missionaries did not "give" Africans Christianity. And African converts did not convert without, in effect, being actively "turned" toward God and away from sin through the power of the Holy Spirit. As Brian Stanley has recently argued in a thoughtful overview of the ways scholars and converts have talked about conversion, "Whatever validity social scientific analyses of conversion may possess in relation to the general phenomenon of conversion from one religion to another, Christian theology cannot rest content with any understanding of conversion to Christ as purely a matter of human agency, whether on the part of the evangelist or the convert" (Stanley 2003, 320). Within their understanding of conversion, Christians don't feel beholden to missionaries—they don't concede that they have suffered some "colonization of the mind."

Converts are far more conscious than missionaries of the broad range of highly individual circumstances that contribute to the disposition of any particular individual who encounters evangelical Christianity: family training to reflect deeply about God, unhappy experiences in *makarantar allo* (Koranic school), prior exposure to Catholicism, private dreams and visions, resentment at being called a kafir by Muslim neighbors, a need to enter a loving community. . . . Christian converts in Niger do not tend to express gratitude to missionaries for their exposure to Christianity—the mission did not "give" them salvation. Jesus did.

SIM missionaries, on the other hand, have a harder time sustaining the humility their interpretation of history would seem to imply. They feel an urge to count their converts, to measure just what the mission has accomplished, and to tell glorious stories of the feats of the earliest "pioneers" in Niger. They somehow feel that Christian converts ought to feel grateful to the mission because they feel keenly the extraordinary sacrifices choosing the life of a missionary entails. Missionaries I spoke with did refer to "giving" the gospel to Africans; the urgency of taking part in that saving act governed their choices in life, sometimes at tremendous personal cost. Working in the service of God, however, makes it hard for missionaries to acknowledge mistakes—whether individual failings or misjudgments by the mission as a whole. When converts find it hard to forgive those unacknowledged mistakes, missionaries tend to see that failure of Christian forgiveness as a sign of spiritual immaturity.

The self-designation of Christians, *masu bin Yesu* (followers of Jesus), suggests a collective that is actively following Jesus. This is in contrast to the term sometimes used by Hausa-speaking Muslims to describe Christians, *'yan mission* (people of the mission), which calls to mind individuals drawn, like moths, to the resources of a mission. How did these earliest "people of the mission" become instead "people of the church," an independent and self-defining community of believers—*'yan eglise?* The song quoted as an epigram above suggests that one of the key problems for Christians was becoming more than simply a number, a statistic counted by the mission, branded with a humiliating red mark that separated them from their Muslim and Arna neighbors. The number assigned to them had the additional problem of giving the impression that in order to become a Christian one had to be from a certain set of families—aristocratic families, as it happened—not just anyone. Generating a genuine Christian community out of such beginnings would not be easy. The active choices and efforts of Africans—youthful seekers of spiritual knowledge, healed lepers turned native evangelists, foster parents modeling a Christian life—made the growth of an indigenous and autonomous evangelical church possible, Spirit-driven hermeneutics notwithstanding.

A variety of forces contributed to the timing, location, social configuration, and extent of the Protestant community in Niger. The colonial context shaped in countless ways the forms of access the mission had in its pursuit of sharing the gospel with the "unreached," prompting the mission to explore the possibility of work in Niger in the first place and then setting limits on the ways in which the mission could evangelize there. The reach of Islam and the resistance of Muslim scholars to Christian intrusion ensured that the mission would focus its energies in the Maradi region rather than in Zinder. The mission operated within the emerging Hausa spiritual vernacular, which both reiterated and reshaped earlier spiritual beliefs and practices. Finally, the preexisting social mosaic of the Maradi region profoundly affected the receptivity of different individuals and groups to Christianity so that the community that emerged of necessity reformulated prior social tensions in complex ways.

The growth of the church occurred in a series of stages related to the kinds of interventions the mission engaged in, and each stage entailed the introduction of new social groups into the church. The gradual accretion of a very broad range of social classes, ethnic groups, and age groups into the community made for a lively, varied, and occasionally contentious community in which individuals of different backgrounds contributed in differing ways to the growth of the church. It also led to tensions within the churches over authority, comportment, and the disposition to engage actively in evangelism. These differences in turn generated tensions between an increasingly socially differentiated church and the mission.

"The distractions are legion": Muslim Resistance to SIM in Zinder

On the eve of European colonial expansion, the territory that was to become northern Nigeria had been governed for a century by the leaders of the nineteenth-century jihad of Usman 'dan Fodio. The kings of the Hausa-speaking kingdoms of the region lost power to a new class of rulers who were supporters of the jihad or were Fulani members of Usman 'dan Fodio's extended family. Convinced that the original populations of the region chafed under the Islamic governance of the Fulani jihadists, missionaries imagined that a popular uprising would support the British conquest of the region. Hausa commoners did not rise up against their Fulani overlords, and many Hausa fled the advance of the infidel Christian army, retreating toward Mecca in imitation of the *hijra* of Mohammed prior to his own conquest of Mecca in the early days of Islam. After the fall of Kano and the defeat of Sokoto in 1903, the British did not overthrow the Fulani rulers so much as absorb them into a new colonial administrative structure. Existing institutions and ruling families became the means through which Great Britain administered the region, a practice known as indirect rule. Mission activities appeared to some colonial administrators to be too dangerously disruptive to this system to be permitted. The preferences of the Muslim emirs governing northern Nigeria were respected and missions were by and large prevented from working directly in the Hausa-speaking heartlands of northern Nigeria.

When SIM missionaries discovered that the British colonial administration of northern Nigeria was not, after all, going to permit direct evangelization to the Muslim Hausa for whom the original founders of the mission had conceived such a deep sense of "burden," they put their energies into evangelizing non-Muslim groups outside the Hausa-speaking heartland and producing Hausa-language materials that could be carried into the central emirates by traders and colporteurs. This work, while in some ways very successful, did not satisfy the enduring craving of the missionaries to reach their originally imagined audience. In 1923, Edward Rice made an expedition into the French territory of Niger to sound out the possibility of beginning evangelization there, for while the British had limited missionary presence to regions in which the emirs themselves were favorable to their presence, the French administration at the time was evidently in a less deferential mode with respect to local authorities. "The French officials have placed no restrictions on the evangelization of the Moslems," crowed Roland Bingham, "and the opportunities are unlimited" (Bingham 1938/1951). Finding the circumstances satisfactory, Rice established a station in Zinder in 1924.

As a Hausa-speaking outpost of the Bornu empire, Zinder had a long and venerable tradition of Islamic scholarship. Zinder was the seat of administration of the newly formed colony of Niger when SIM first entered into the French colony. The largest urban center of the Damagaram kingdom, Zinder linked the east-west axes of trade along the Sudanic belt (reaching from Senegal in the West to the Red Sea in the east) with the north-south trans-Saharan axis and was therefore at that time the largest and most important trade center in Niger. France marched into the Lake Chad region in 1899 to seize Damagaram in order to prevent Great Britain from controlling this complex network from its dominant trade position along the lower Niger River. Trade linkages and kinship ties guaranteed that Hausa was the language of trade and administration in Damagaram, although culturally and historically Kanuri was also an important language. Zinder maintained some social and political distance from the Hausa-speaking kingdoms of Maradi and Tsibiri farther to the west in the new colony but shared a resentment of the presumptions of the nineteenth-century jihadists whose descendants served within the colonial administrative apparatus of northern Nigeria.

Although the French and British competed at the turn of the century to seize control of key trade centers that might link their holdings across the continent, the late 1920s was a period of cordial relations between French and British colonial administrators in the interest of sharing information and concern about the activities of various Muslim movements on either side of the border The French administration saw the earliest SIM missionaries as benign spies for the British. When SIM first sent Rice and another missionary to Zinder, the French administrator ventured the following speculation: "Their religious zeal and their desire to make converts seem extremely modest. They are likely to meet with complete failure. I myself am inclined to believe that these two missionaries, whose attitude has hitherto been utterly proper, are simply agents sent here by the Intelligence Service of the neighboring colony."[1] Despite this sense that the odd Protestants were possibly spies, the French administration was initially quite tolerant of the mission's activities.[2] Unlike the British, the French did not formally absorb local traditional rulers into the administrative apparatus, preferring to handle administrative matters directly. The scholarly and ruling classes of precolonial Damagaram continued to have importance, and that importance tended to grow as the French found their own staff to be inadequate to meet the many demands of administering a colony. However, at the time of Rice's initial venture into Zinder, the French felt no need to consult with local authority figures about whether the missionaries should be given admittance into the colony.

Local Muslim scholars were less inclined to see the missionaries' religious activities as mere cover for intelligence activities. Relations with

Muslim authorities were cold from the very outset. For the most part, the missionaries posted to Zinder visited Muslims in their homes or in villages near the city and preached to them in hope that simply telling them "the good news" would lead to individual transformations. Because of hostility toward the westernized Christians produced by the older mission schools of mainline denominational missions, the mission did not envision setting up schools as a way of attracting the interest of the local population. But without some incentive to convert, the setting was not a promising one for engaging with Muslims. For example, a female missionary, Miss E. St. Germain, reported that the daughter of a leading Muslim scholar who had learned enough about Christianity to want to convert experienced repeated harassment from her kin (St. Germain 1935). Edward Morrow found that even when he was "itinerating" among villages outside Zinder, Muslim scholars who were "too busy copying a portion of the Koran to give us any time" found ways of snubbing him (Morrow 1935, 23)

By 1936, after more than a decade of evangelism, the Zinder station had yielded little fruit and was gaining a reputation as a particularly difficult posting: "Here our missionaries have laboured for over ten years with very little apparent success. The Lord of the Harvest has given to our workers who are at present stationed there the faith to labour on and to expect to see definite results, tokens of which present themselves even now" (Osborne 1936, 13). The following year the field director in Zinder, D. M. Osborne, remarked, "The Mission and missionaries are continually watched by the Malams, and anyone showing any interest in the Gospel is dealt with by them, and in most cases they are never seen again. Children are unmercifully beaten for coming to the compound" (Osborne 1937, 22). The persistent resistance of local malams to the mission's evangelism had succeeded in inhibiting the growth of any significant Christian community.

Female missionaries who entered into the women's spaces within compounds had the sense that they were being watched at all times, but they also found that Muslim women had an extraordinary repertoire of forms of passive resistance to the evangelical message. The failure of the mission in Zinder was brought about by their successful strategies of diversion and deflection: "The next compound we visit is a hum of business and excitement. . . . Waiting in vain for a lull, we eventually get the eye and ear of one woman. We seek to inveigle her into a coherent conversation; but *the distractions are legion.* Taking a sad leave, we wonder how much truth has been conveyed even to this one" (Whale 1938, 10, emphasis in original).

Finding that open engagement with the local population was unsuccessful, the mission began broadcasting sermons by loudspeaker from their rented house. If door-to-door work was not going well and if individuals were harassed for being seen with Christians, then perhaps the best way to reach interested souls was through public broadcasts rather than direct contact. However, "soon after this was started . . . an unprecedented storm of persecution broke upon [the preacher Abba Musa]. On one occasion an angry mob stoned his house. At another time a group of Malams gathered outside the Mission Compound gate to pronounce upon him and the missionaries curses and imprecations which he well knew possessed a subtle, Satanic power" (Morrow 1946, 22, 24). Beginning in 1943, the mission imitated the loudspeakers of the Zinder mosques, and missionaries believed that under a regime that respected freedom of religion, its broadcasts should be protected. Nevertheless, the mission's public broadcasting efforts were eventually forbidden by the colonial government as "an offence in a Moslem country" (Rev. and Mrs. Kapp 1950a, 15). Encounters with local Muslims were unnerving; Edward Morrow was given to understand by one *malam* that it was only French protection that prevented him from being put to death "at the point of a sword as they used to do" (Morrow n.d.). Excluded from meaningful work in the central Hausa heartlands of northern Nigeria until the 1930s and consistently thwarted in their efforts in Zinder by the hostility of the local community, missionaries of necessity began to focus its energies in other fields where the relationship between Islam, the colonial state, and the mission was less problematic.

The Tsibiri Station

One such locale was in the Maradi region, where the forces resistant to the Sokoto Caliphate had settled in the nineteenth century. Segments of the Katsina, Gobir, and Kano aristocracy and courtly class had migrated into the region and settled the towns of Maradi and Tsibiri to the west of Zinder. The region therefore had a rather different relationship to Islam than either the kingdom of Damagaram (which was centered at Zinder) or the Nigerian emirates (which were conquered by the jihadists). Maradi and Tsibiri had a greater tolerance for pre-Islamic practices, and because of their resistance to the hegemony of Sokoto, they did not define themselves exclusively in terms of adherence to Islam. In order to sustain the support of the indigenous population of the Maradi valley, the rulers of the newly established kingdoms refrained from aggressively promoting conversion to Islam. Thus, unlike Zinder, this was not a region known for deep Muslim scholarship or orthodoxy. The complex texture of the local spiritual and political environment opened up fissures in which the seeds of Christianity could profitably find purchase. And so it was that the field director, Reverend G. W. Playfair, ventured to visit Tsibiri in the late 1920s and found that Sarki Salao of Tsibiri was well disposed to his proposal to staff a mission station there. The village of Tsibiri had been the refuge of Gobirawa Hausa from the time of the jihad of Usman 'dan Fodio. Neighboring Maradi, the home of refugee Katsinawa, was the site of a sometime ally and recent military adversary. The chief of the Gobirawa was undoubtedly maneuvering to place himself in a more advantageous position with regard to the colonial administration (which was perennially confused about who should be designated as the *primus inter pares* among the chiefs and war leaders in the region) and relative to his adversaries to the north and east. Knowing little about the differences between French administrators and American missionaries, Sarki Salao may have calculated that having his own contingent of white missionaries would be useful, particularly as Maradi seemed to become more and more the center of French administrative attentions and as Katsinawa seized the ascendancy.

SIM's motives in targeting Tsibiri were probably as murky as Sarki Salao's. I have found no indication that the mission was specifically invited, and there are numerous significant villages it could have chosen other than Tsibiri. But reflecting on why those other villages might have been eliminated as prospects helps make sense of how Tsibiri emerged as the preferred site once Sarki Salao seemed to be open to his new visitors. Tessawa and Magaria were perhaps too close to Zinder, too reminiscent of the "Moslem stronghold" the mission hoped to escape, and too tainted with the presence of European trade houses. Tessawa suffered an attack on the administrative post in June 1927 in which a French administrator and two guards were killed. The attack was vaguely associated with Muslim "fanaticism," making it unlikely that Tessawa would be an improvement over Zinder, and it could hardly have seemed like a secure site.[3] Once he learned that the French administration supported the Muslim scholars in their rejection of various evangelical strategies, Playfair may have hoped to find a site in which the colonial administration had little presence, making Maradi, the more logical site at first glance (given its location on the road to Katsina and Nigeria), less desirable. Tsibiri offered the dual virtues of being unmistakably "mixed" in its relationship to Islam and at some small remove from the larger centers of French commerce and administration. It was still close enough to the major road from Niger to the mission's far more developed infrastructure in Nigeria to be practically workable. However, the mission could hardly enter into such a complex environment without automatically and unconsciously activating preexisting tensions: between Gobirawa (of Tsibiri) and Katsinawa (of Maradi), between sedentary Hausa and nomadic Fulani and Tuareg, and, perhaps most important, between non-farming aristocrats (the Habe rulers) struggling to find autonomous bases for authority and their powerful autochthonous hosts (the Arna).

Local Hausa in Tsibiri first saw Playfair as Mai Munduwa, "The One with a Watch," and he lived up to that name by moving quickly to establish the new mission. On Christmas Day of 1927, David Osborne and his wife Drusille were installed in the home of the *sarki* until a mission compound could be built, cementing for better or for worse the strong linkage between the Tsibiri aristocracy (*sarauta*) and the Protestant community that emerged: "On our arrival here we were made most welcome by the Chief and many of his people. He kindly offered us the use of one of his mud houses in his own compound, in the centre of the town. We gladly accepted and have been living here ever since. Conveniences are not plentiful and the task of training boys to do house work has been no light one."[4]

There were deep ironies in this relationship, for SIM had explicitly rejected an earlier mission philosophy that in order to build a Christian church in Africa one must begin by converting African kings, whose subjects would then of necessity follow within a Christian kingdom. SIM's ascetic philosophy and rejection of worldly power were unlikely to make for a comfortable pairing with an aristocratic elite whose authority was based upon wealth, patronage, and ostentatious gift exchange. Osborne and his first wife (who would die during World War II) obtained a reputation for maintaining a strict attitude of reserve and superiority toward the "natives" with whom they came into contact—no one was to enter the house without permission, no one was to interrupt early morning devotions or Mrs. Osborne's organ practice, and inferiors (whether African house servants or junior missionaries) were expected to jump in response to commands. With this kind of imperious bearing, Osborne may have seemed very much at home in the court of the *sarki*, which may account for why he was well received at the outset. But the mission philosophy of SIM sought to undermine pride, worldliness, and the search for power.

Despite these ironies, the mission immediately experienced much greater success in this region, into which it was propelled by the animosity it encountered in Zinder. As it happened, in its early years in Tsibiri, the mission found the local *commandant* to be very supportive; he helped the mission arrange lodging at government rest stations and organize transport. Thus, early in their stay Drusille Osborne was to write to the central office of SIM, "The Commandant and his wife have been very good to us. About every week they have sent us a bag of fresh vegetables.... They have gladly accepted a French Bible from us."[5] It seemed to be a quite promising setting. Mission statistics on baptisms show the stark contrast between the success of the Tsibiri station and the stagnation of the efforts in Zinder; by 1934 the Tsibiri station had an average attendance of forty-four students at Sunday school, while in Zinder, which was established a good eight years earlier, there were generally fifteen. Tsibiri could boast nine baptisms to Zinder's three (SIM 1934). However awkward the relationship into which the mission had gotten itself, it was clear that it would do well to concentrate its efforts in the Maradi/Tsibiri region rather than in Zinder.

A colonial report from 1928, the year SIM began work to establish a station in Tsibiri, characterized Tsibiri as the Islamic heartland of the region, noting that many marabouts had come there for their studies and that all spoke and read Arabic (Nobili 1928). However, accounts of the importance and size of the scholarly class differ substantially, depending upon which administrator made the assessment: by 1934 the Commandant de Cercle de Maradi M. Gosselin was to comment that Islam in the region consisted mostly of ritual and that there were few real scholars to be found. Neither the villages of Maradi nor Tsibiri appear in his list of significant centers of scholarship (Gosselin 1934). What seems clear is that Maradi and Tsibiri did have a modest scholarly class but that because of the complex spiritual and political texture of the region, that class did not seem to hold sway over the local population or the aristocracy with the same force that Muslim scholars did in Zinder. The missionaries found that they encountered resistance in Tsibiri and its environs as well that was sometimes quite reminiscent of the state of affairs in Zinder:

> In one place a devout young Moslem sought to hinder our work in every way he could. One of his tricks was to hide somewhere in a field close to the place where the children were being taught reading and Scripture verses, and right in the middle of the teaching he would appear and shout at the children and they

would scatter like rabbits. Now God has answered prayer for this young man, and instead of hindering the work, he has begun to seek the way of salvation himself. (Petersen 1938, 7)

As this man's conversion suggests, even the Muslim scholarly community in Tsibiri seems to have been slightly more receptive to the ideas of the mission than had been the case in Zinder. A sketch of the life at the mission by Newton Kapp hints that the scholarly community kept a vigilant eye on the children while turning a curious ear to the preaching of the missionaries:

The Tsibiri Mission Station is a play-ground for children and the rendezvous for grown-ups. They visit us from early sunrise till after dark. Many prejudices are broken by these contacts till even the Malams, the Moslem Theologians, come and are told that Christ has the claim upon their lives by His atoning death on Calvary. They listen attentively and the Missionary clings to the promise that His Word shall not return unto Him void, but it shall accomplish that which He pleases. (Kapp 1934, 20)

Although in this relatively large village at a crossroads that led to the emirates of northern Nigeria the mission faced a fairly Muslim milieu, the population of the village was not uniform in other respects, and it was probably the complexity of the social landscape that enabled the mission to gain entrée. The following recollections of Jadi Marafa, a member of the oldest Christian family in Tsibiri, give a glimpse of how David Osborne made his initial contacts in the region:

When he came it was in the time of Sarki Salao, when the village was in its old site in the river valley. They didn't have a house, he and his wife, when they came. So they slept over in the Sarki's palace until they had their own house built. Then one day, he came on horseback, he had a big white horse, and he saw our father on the dune above the village. At that time we hadn't seen a white man before, they were the first to come. You could say that because the first whites had come to do war on us, we [children] hadn't seen any whites before. So there he was on his horse, so we hid! No one would approach him but my father, and no one would let us children come out. But we did like this [peeking out] because we wondered what brought him. Then he got down and he asked my father's name and he answered, "Ibrahima Marafa." And he wrote that down. And he said, "Do you want a friend?" So [Marafa] said, "Yes." So he said, "Do you know what my work is?" [Marafa] said, "No." He said, "What brings me here is that I'm a *malam*, I want to stay with you." So Marafa said, "Yes, I'd like that." (Jadi Marafa interview)

Osborne's self-representation as a *malam*, the word used to refer to the Muslim scholars so familiar in the expansion of Islam, necessarily implied that he was interested in teaching his new acquaintances the arts of a literate religion. In acquiescing to Osborne's presence, local people in Tsibiri were simply showing their respect for learning and revealing their desire for even greater access to it. Christians who recalled Osborne's time invariably refer to him as "Malam Osborne," a title that was not necessarily given to other missionaries who were less closely associated with education and learning or who had a less-dignified bearing. Indeed, by referring to some missionary men as "Mista" (Mr.) rather than "*Malam*," or "*Monsieur*," converts subtly engaged in an indigenous ranking of the missionaries they encountered relative to both religious scholars and the French.

Osborne left Ibrahima Marafa and the children with a puzzling metal object that turned out to be a canteen, a cause for hilarity that Jadi Marafa used to good effect in recounting the story. Eventually after a number of visits, Ibrahima Marafa entrusted the new *malam* with a young man, Musa, to assist him in his work, and it was Musa Marafa, a member of the local aristocracy, who became the mission's first convert, a major mediator between the mission and the local population, between Christians and Muslims, and between colonial administration and mission. The mission's reliance upon the Marafa family had profound implications for the nature and character of the Christian community that emerged. The Marafa family, of the powerful Yacouba aristocratic line, was one of four lineage segments that issued from the pre-jihad Gobir Habe kingdom: the Yacoubawa, the Nafatawa, the Zangarzawa and the Gomkawa. Under colonial rule, the French found it unwieldy to continue the complex precolonial pattern of multidynastic competition for the central position of *sarki*. Over time the colonial administration restricted the throne to the Yacoubawa line.

As Pearl Robinson explains, this limitation of the potential contenders to the throne tended to mean that competition among lineage segments within the Yacoubawa line became the central mode of political competition in Tsibiri. In order to emerge as the most significant of contenders in an increasingly modern political environment, it was necessary to find ways to use traditional authority to create an expansive network of clients and transform that network into a political base that could be recognized within a party system. The holders of traditional office can then tap into the resources of the larger state, which enhances their ability to distribute the resources necessary for sustaining a client base and these claims to legitimate authority (Robinson 1983, 109–110). The

Marafa line's interest in the Christian missionaries was undoubtedly something of an experiment in acting as hosts to a set of "European" guests who might simultaneously provide resources and reinforce the Marafa claim to authority vis-à-vis other segments of the Yacoubawa.

Other members of the broader household of the Yacoubawa line of the aristocracy that were significant to the growth of the church included Abdou, Katumbe, Issaka, and 'dan Naya. These men encouraged a second wave of household members to study with Osborne, a wave that included Barmo and Jadi Marafa. Until the 1940s or so, the community was made up exclusively of members of the aristocratic lines. One of the most important developments for the early church was the inclusion of a commoner named 'dan Nana in that second-wave circle of believers. He was from a commoner family that was known as the "shavers of the sarki,"—clients of the sarauta families. Thus, two possible trajectories of expansion were opened, one through the major aristocratic families and another through the clients of those families.

Osborne's presence generated a need for substantial building projects—a home, a place "to teach us the letters of the alphabet," and a medical storeroom. Through the intervention of Musa Marafa, a number of local men and women were drawn into the labor of building. The novelty of being paid wages on a weekly basis for this work in itself attracted attention and interest, no doubt because a request for labor that emanated from the sarki's palace would not ordinarily have implied wages: "If you compared it with, say, 100 CFA today, you could say that when Malam Osborne came, it would be very hard to come by that much cash; there was no money in the village in those days. Now he, each week, whoever had done a reasonable amount of work he would call them and write their names down and pay them. When he had finished that work, he moved his things from the sarki's palace and they set to work making other buildings, like the one for the medicine" (Marafa interview).

Gradually the station came into being. It had generated a labor market and had established early links between mission work and writing, missionary and malam, cash and Christianity. Eventually Osborne and his wife were joined by other mission workers; there were generally between four and ten missionaries at the station for the first two decades or so, with others scattered in nearby outposts such as Jiratawa and Maradi as the reach of the mission grew. Jadi Marafa's account suggests that in those early days there were only two or three households in Tsibiri where "they would light a lantern at night and set to learning" about Islam, so the opportunity to learn was welcome and the competition with Islam relatively restrained.

Because the Marafa were linked to the royal household and the *sarki*'s court, they provided one kind of node in the emerging Christian community as members of that family drew on the potential intellectual and spiritual resources the mission presented. However, within the *sarki*'s palace, the complexity of the recruitment of "wealth in people" generated its own social texture; one of Musa Marafa's "mothers" was a Buzu woman named Tashibka, who had been enslaved by Marafa's father on a raid and was later married to him. Tashibka was a key pillar of the early church although she was blind and never learned to read. The very first generation of converts, which included such figures as Tashibka and another woman named Sa'a, is rather hard to reconstruct, since it was often such invisible members of households that acquiesced to the attendance of younger boys at the mission compound.

Those young men, the early students in the Bible school, were the ones who made names for themselves as leaders of the local church. The older women appear in mission records as "mothers of" various male converts, but one has to wonder how the mission came to have contact with the male children in the first place. Here agency is difficult to reconstruct. Did the women encourage the children or were they simply tolerant of novel contacts? Were the children overtaken by the *kwarciya* of youth—that mad propensity toward self-destructive experiments? Interviews with Christians do not place the agency with the missionaries. Numerous tales of the earliest male converts involve curiosity about schooling and literacy. It would be, I think, an erasure of the agency of young boys to see this as simply the "luring" of children by the mission; indeed, these converts recount with some pride tales of playing hooky from Koranic school or tedious household tasks to listen in at the mission. Some children were actively curious, others were not.[6] A small subset of early professing Christians came to the mission because they were already *almajirai* or Koranic students, and it may have been in part their theological curiosity that drew them (e.g., Nanaya, 'dan Nana, Almajir). Some evidence suggests that these children in turn succeeded in converting their parents, an unexpected reversal of influences. At the very least, the children carried traces of their exposure out of Sarki Salao's compound and into the town, as David Osborne remarked in a letter: "The children have unconsciously published the glad tidings in their homes and on the streets as they have sung the hymns and repeated the verses of Scripture taught them in school."[7]

The following recollections of 'dan Nana shed light on the way that the simple novelty of the mission in a remote setting combined with the potential for a new kind of learning led seven of the central early converts (all of whom were men) to the mission. There is a hint of rebelliousness in this account of his adventure of venturing into the white man's school with seven friends that suggests that some of these younger men would have found ways of disrupting the existing gerontocratic order and the rise of Koranic schooling whether the mission had appeared on the scene or not. When he was twelve, 'dan Nana reports, his father put him in a Koranic school under one Malam Zandaban. At the time, other people pointed out to him that another *malam* was teaching the white people's learning. "So," he said, "the seven of us, we thought that was an astonishing thing [*abin mai mamaki*], because you know, people could remember that the whites had defeated us, they had killed us. So we went just to see, at the *sarki*'s house."[8] 'Dan Nana was charged with the task of collecting grass for the horses of his father's house every day at about 2:30, and from there he was supposed to go to study with his Koranic teacher. But instead of going to his teacher, he hid and went to study secretly with Madame Osborne and the other boys and then returned home at the same time as the Koranic students. After Malam Zandaban protested, his ruse was discovered, and his father wearily decided to let him follow his own inclinations against his mother's judgment. Eventually the French government objected to this informal school because the instruction was not in French, but the mission persisted quietly, because, as 'dan Nana observed, they had come to this difficult setting in order to teach "chapter and verse in our own tongue." He and his friends learned to read Hausa together, and 'dan Nana gradually found himself reflecting more deeply on the verse, "For the wages of sin is death; but the gift of God is eternal life through Jesus Christ our Lord" (Romans 6:23). After thinking about sin and the prospect of heaven, he and his friends eventually declared themselves to be Christians (Pastor 'dan Nana interview, October 24, 2000). Once these young men had converted, the missionaries gathered them and some of the older converts such as Musa Marafa to form the original students of the mission's Bible school, which opened formally in 1947 (SIM 1968, 10).

Even from the outset, then, the mission's modest efforts in the realm of education were quite central to the interest local populations showed toward Christianity. Another anecdote that relates how early converts were attracted to the mission suggests that literacy had a mystery and power associated with the wealth of the whites that converts sometimes hoped to acquire for themselves. Ray de la Haye recounted a stock missionary tale of sending a young boy named Garba to Maradi to the canteen to pick up soap to be charged to his bill:

> So I wrote a little note because we had an account up there which we paid monthly, and I gave it to Garba, and said, "Would you kindly take this to Maradi and give it to the Frenchman there in the store, and he'll give you something, and you bring it back." He went . . . and toward the end of the day he arrived with a box of soap. . . . He said, "Teacher . . . oh, give me that power of asking for something without paying for it! . . . What did you do on that paper?" And that was a power he wanted because he know something had to be attributed to that paper, what I put on it. And I said, "Well Garba, I'll give you that power, but I won't assure you that you'll get everything you write on a piece of paper." (Ray de la Hay interview)

The colonial administration was increasingly ambivalent about SIM's activities and never entirely abandoned the suspicion that the evangelists were spies of some sort. The *commandant de cercle* of Maradi was clearly keeping a close eye on the mission's evolving operations in Tsibiri, as he noted in an annual report in 1930:

> [The Sudan Interior Mission consists of] Pastor Osborne, his wife, and a young woman claiming to convert the young blacks of the village to Protestantism. Some twenty children, all boys, regularly visit the mission. Religious instruction is given to them in Hausa, and in the meantime these catechumens are employed working the gardens. Small sums of money are given to the most diligent children. But I don't believe that the missionaries have had to this time many conversions. Some Muslims were even chased away for having pretended to be interested in conversion.[9]

"In the face of such unpromising results," the lieutenant-governor of Niger observed, "one can't help but wonder whether the apparent goal [of conversion] is truly the one pursued by the mission."[10] This suspicion that the mission had ulterior motives, probably intelligence-gathering, resulted in part from the administration's lack of understanding of how difficult it would be to convert even nominal Muslims to Christianity, an experience that casts somewhat into doubt the credibility of administrators' regular dismissive pronouncements about the character and depth of Muslim belief and the decline of Islam in Niger. Resolutely secular administrators were perhaps not particularly perceptive observers of religious life and clearly had no real understanding of the difference between Protestants professing Christianity and Catholic "catechumens." Because the missionaries produced so few converts, the government reasoned, they must be devoting their energies to something else altogether. Gradually, the higher administration's lack of confidence in its grasp of the motivations of anglophone missionaries prompted it to encourage the Catholic church to send French missionaries to Niger to counter the "foreign" influence of Protestant missions. At the encouragement of the French administration, Père Faroud of the Missions de Lyon began work to construct the first Catholic mission station in Niamey in 1931.

The sketch provided by the administration does nevertheless give some sense of the shape of the emerging community, which was made up mostly of young boys. It is also clear that from the outset the mission offered pay for farm labor. As a result of the agricultural activities of SIM and the novel introduction of cash, the early church gradually began to include elements of the local population that were not from among the aristocratic families. The many income-generating ventures the new mission engaged in (gardening, supplying milk and eggs, making chairs) were also significant means by which the missionaries made contacts and built trust. Many of the mission's earliest professing Christians were artisans and laborers who could provide services for the mission: 'dan Nana (a "boy"), Alita (the cook), Birache (a builder), Bagwari (a leather worker), Balla (a mud mixer), Gazau (a weaver), and Jatau (a gardener).[11] Each of these forms of labor and skill linked the mission to networks of individuals and communities of the laboring segment of Tsibiri society.

The nearby farming village of Guma (which is now a neighborhood within Tsibiri), in particular, became a focal point of converts as a result of the vegetable-gardening activities of a man named Guji.[12] Relatives of 'dan Nana provided another rural node that led to semi-Muslim villages and to the Arna, many of whom were peasant farmers. A later figure in the development of the church was Pastor Garba, whose family was traditionally from the low-status butcher caste. Originally from Maradi, Garba had come into contact with the mission in Nigeria when he sought treatment from Hansen's Disease, or leprosy. His family was Katsinawa rather than Gobirawa and was engaged in raising and trading cattle and in farming the rich *fadama* lands of the river valley near Madarumfa. As a result, he had stronger ties to Maradi than to Tsibiri; Garba's connection to the church made it possible for the mission to distance itself from the perception that Christianity was the religion of the Gobir aristocracy. As the Christian community grew, competition between Gobirawa and

Katsinawa, Tsibiri and Maradi, commoners and aristocracy, and competing strands of the Yacoubawa lineage created tensions that were a complex tangle of class, village, and subethnic rivalries.

Many of the early converts to Christianity were, like 'dan Nana and Jadi, workers within the households of the missionaries—close daily contact with the practices of the missionaries through employment was probably more significant in the recruitment of early converts than the itinerant preaching and home visits that the missionaries felt was their central task. Christianity rapidly became associated with employment in the homes of missionaries, creating a danger that the social hierarchy of missionary and convert would become embodied in the parallel hierarchy of employer and employee.

In its early phase, the mission tended to set up a station and a storeroom for medicine. The medical component was simply a way to promote hygiene and generate goodwill toward the mission, and few of the missionaries before the late 1930s had more than rudimentary training in medicine. This is why the lieutenant governor of Niger declared in 1933 that the mission could no longer engage even in the rudimentary medical work it had been doing (Cunningham 1996, 4). A close examination of the Tsibiri Church Records suggests that this restriction probably did not have a very significant effect, since relatively few of the early Christians who stayed with the church in this period were drawn to it through such rudimentary medical outreach. Shut out of formal education and medicine, the missionaries devoted their energies to preaching in the open in the Tsibiri market, hosting visitors at the mission (particularly on Sundays), and doing home visits in town. A small number of young children was invited to learn to read in Hausa at the mission compound at informal sessions in the afternoons.

The number of apparent converts from among the Tsibiri aristocracy was at first encouraging—by 1933, Osborne and his wife counted fifteen professing Christians from within the home of Marafa.[13] However it soon became clear to the mission that "there is not the zeal in the church that there should be" (Osborne 1937, 23), perhaps because the political ambitions of the aristocracy somewhat overshadowed their interest in evangelism. The fate of a young man named Isaka from the household of Sarki Salao is instructive on this account. When Mr. and Mrs. Osborne first came to the chief's compound in 1928, he "gave" the couple his son, Isaka, "and said," reports Osborne, "he was ours to do with him as we wished."[14] The young man was at that point about fourteen, and the Osbornes taught him to serve them as a cook. In 1930, Isaka converted and was baptized. However, Osborne notes with dismay that less than a year after his baptism:

> Isaka left our employ and went back to work for the chief, his father. He had married Mantai, who had previously made a profession of faith. Indications were not lacking that the chief, although he had said he had given [him] to us for all time, was anxious for Isaka to leave and work in the "sarauta" [the titled offices of the aristocratic class]. Isaka showed signs of a desire to be a big man. From this time on his backsliding was marked and rapid.[15]

Osborne's disappointment here has several facets. In a manner that was to be characteristic of the mission's inconsistent and self-serving attitudes toward local fostering practices, he and his wife imagined that when Isaka was "given" to them, they would have a permanent claim to his labor and attention. The difference between "giving" as fostering and "giving" as something akin to either permanent adoption or enslavement is rather murky here. The couple's disappointment that Isaka's father chose to bring him back to his own household for socialization into the skills of aristocratic courtly life in an Islamic idiom reflects an odd understanding of the claim they had over the young man in the first place. Isaka, it appears, made the choice to pursue the life of a prince in the court, taking his rare and valuable Christian bride with him. Such a choice seemed to the missionary to indicate a surrender to worldliness, a desire to be a "big man." However, this was the calling of a child of the *sarauta* class, just as the child of a butcher would become a butcher.

To SIM, to be a Christian was in effect to become a missionary. Christians who were not interested in energetically promoting the conversion of others seemed to be imperfect Christians within SIM's understanding of real faith. Whether converts were reluctant to evangelize because they did not have the same understanding of salvation as the missionaries or because they were afraid of the possible consequences of antagonizing kin and neighbors is difficult to know. It does seem likely that the pursuit of an enhanced client base called for a diplomacy that may have been incompatible with overt evangelism. Many of the ceremonial activities of members of the Tsibiri court needed to bridge the disparate communities of the autochthonous pagan Arna conversant with the spirits of the local terrain, the Muslim scholarly class insistent upon the demands of Islamic practice, and the highly syncretic urban culture of the Gobir immigrant court devoted to its *bori* spirit cult. Any member of the *sarauta* class who hoped to be effective politically would have to find ways of communicating with and mobilizing all of these groups, and ritual would be a key part of that communication. The exclusivity of evangelical Christianity in contrast with the tolerant Islamic practice of that era meant that it would be virtually impossible to be effective as a member of the courtly class while remaining a practicing Christian.

Osborne's further comments suggest that by 1937 the French administration did not embrace the presence of these American missionaries as much as Sarki Salao might have hoped, a fact that reduced the utility of this already problematic alliance of evangelicals and aristocrats: "Humanly speaking the work would have advanced more rapidly had it not been for the unfriendly attitude, and in some cases actions, of some of the French officials" (Osborne 1937, 23). Pursuing the active promotion of Christianity when there were few political advantages vis-à-vis the French may not have had much appeal to the core *sarauta*-class Christians. If the Muslim resistance of scholars in Zinder was to dictate where the mission was to place its energies, French colonial fears about a resurgence of Islamic unrest increasingly came to limit the mission's ability to determine unilaterally the kinds of activities it would engage in. Gaining the position of *sarki* or one of the many other key titled positions in the court called for the support of the French administration.

One residue of the protracted resistance of Islamic leaders to French conquest was a general wariness on the part of the French colonial administration with regard to any activity that might inflame Muslim passions. Appointing a Christian as *sarki* could be perceived to be a provocation by Muslims. As Christopher Harrison remarks of the contradictions of the Catholic missionary enterprise in the French territories, "However well [Catholic mission] charitable activities fitted with the rhetoric of the civilising and liberating mission of colonialism . . . the colonial authorities were nonetheless, with good reason, fearful of the political consequences of allowing the missionaries a free hand in strongly Muslim areas" (Harrison 1988, 18). While the Marafa line had cast its lot with the Christians, it was not at all clear what the political consequences of such a move would be, and other *sarauta* class lines were undoubtedly biding their time to see the outcome of this bold move.

SIM suffered under the further burden of neither being French nor promoting Catholicism. In the early years the French colonial administration was relatively tolerant of the SIM, but the colonial documents suggest that as time went on, the French grew increasingly suspicious of the predominantly North American personnel of the mission and more and more fearful that mission proselytizing might stir resentment among the Muslim population. This was particularly true during the World War

II years. However, long before that nadir in relations, the colonial government's policy requirement that all missionaries deposit a sum sufficient to cover their return costs home with the French colonial administration before they would be permitted to enter the country meant that SIM had a hard time getting a large number of missionaries to the field in Niger. A mission founded on funding "by prayer" was ill equipped to deal with the French predilection for security deposits in advance (Cunningham 1996, 4). Furthermore, the colonial government tried to insist that the mission focus solely on medical work and desist from any form of evangelization. Any specialized social services were increasingly regularized and professionalized by the French administration. Because the mission had no medical or educational professionals, it experienced these requirements as a ban on those activities. In 1934, Osborne delivered this report:

> The work in Niger Colony is carried on under more stringent governmental regulations. No dispensaries may be operated unless under the direction of a qualified doctor. Schools may only be conducted by teachers who have French certificates and the curriculum must be that of the Government syllabus, all in the French language. Missionaries, therefore, are not permitted to teach reading and writing in the vernacular of the people. This however, throws greater responsibility upon the native Christians to teach their fellows to read God's Word in their own language, against which there is no restriction. (Osborne 1934)

Obviously it would have been rather difficult for an overtaxed colonial administration to monitor particularly closely the day-to-day activities of the missionaries. SIM never entirely abandoned its efforts to teach Hausa-speakers to read the vernacular Bible, even though their efforts could not be formally recognized as "schooling." Osborne's observation of the importance of local Christians to the work of training their neighbors to read the vernacular Bible signals the kind of work he had hoped the emerging church members would show more "zeal" in pursuing. Finding urban and aristocratic Christians deficient, the mission seems to have focused its energies elsewhere.

Itineration and the Native Evangelist

"Latterly," Osborne remarked in his 1937 report, "more effort has been expended on work in the villages, and indications are such as to give encouragement to press on with this work" (Osborne 1937, 23). From relatively early in its endeavors in Niger, the mission devoted considerable time and energy to "itinerating" to visit the villages within a few days' ride of Tsibiri on horseback. This description of such "itineration" from the skeptical perspective of a French colonial administrator doing an administrative tour of the region during World War II offers a rare outsider's perspective on the evangelism of the early missionaries:

> Under a tree they gather women and children, and sing with the phonograph. They preach to these pagans a puritanical morality: they forbid drinking *dolo* beer, having two wives, eating cola nut, and they tell them to follow Issa [Jesus] in everything. To be more persuasive they give out generous gifts. One young man told me that he was given 105 francs . . . which didn't seem to prevent him from remaining a Muslim. I've made careful enquiries with people to find out whether any pro-English declarations make their way into these prayers; they tell me they've never heard anything of the sort. (Moncoucut 1941)

Colonial officers' observations of religion in the region make it clear that while Islam had a long-standing and substantial presence in the region, its effects were rather localized. Inspection tours regularly suggest that while the overall ratio of Muslims to animists was on the order of 75 percent to 25 percent by the late 1940s, many villages in the east of the region were exclusively animist, just as areas in the west were exclusively Muslim. In the many villages in which Muslims and animists lived alongside one another, there could be majority animist villages as well as villages in which substantial minorities of non-Muslims resided (Paumelle 1945a, 1945b; Leroux 1946). In other words, the mission was likely to have greater success in this region than near Zinder, for by itinerating they would inevitably come across pockets of non-Muslims. It was the non-Muslim Arna—those who Muslims and Christians alike regarded as having "no religion whatsoever"—who were to prove most responsive to Christian evangelism.

The mission, ever critical of the failings of the core Tsibiri Christians, seemed to have little understanding of the invisible spiderweb of networks leading out of the *sarki*'s palace that made its success in itineration possible. Rural sectors were represented at the court of the *sarki* by titled notables, some of whom were Muslim but most of whom maintained strong links to the practices and rituals that justified their power to levy labor, tribute, and taxes. One such powerful titled figure was the Sarkin Arna, without whom the legitimate offspring of the *sarki* could not be recognized, for his household was responsible for a ritual washing of each legitimate child. This was, in other words, one of the means by which the autochthonous population balanced the power of the Habe aristocracy. The Sarkin Arna oversaw a key set of Arna villages north of Tsibiri that would become a very rich zone for evangelization. Signaling unconsciously the ways in which the mission's access was mediated, missionary Karen Petersen reported:

> The people out in these villages are partly Moslem and partly beer-drinking pagans. The headman is called Sarkin Arna which means, the chief of the pagans. Of all of the headmen of the villages in Gobirland, he is the one who is most eager to hear the Gospel. He wants his people to hear too, and during a recent visit there he called the people together to hear the Message in two different sections of the village. Many times he has asked us to come and teach the younger people, so that they may be able to read "God's Book." In this village, there is just one Moslem teacher and he does not seem to have much influence over the people. (Petersen 1938, 7)

The importance of learning to read cannot be overstated here. The early schools the French administration created were explicitly designed for the "sons and nephews" of the aristocracy; the colonial regime did not consider the children of the Arna to be relevant to local governance. The children of slaves and minor lines of the aristocracy did, of course, end up benefiting disproportionately from that education as wary aristocratic families attempted to protect their biological children from the unwelcome intrusions of the colonial administration by foisting off less-valued household members as "sons and nephews." Some prescient notables, sometimes from within minor aristocratic lines or among their clients, evidently hoped to make the mission an alternative avenue to schooling and favor within the court.

However, despite the interest in social, political and economic advancement among those who first approached the mission and were attracted to the education it seemed to offer, it would be a mistake to read all of the interactions between local figures and the mission as merely cynical attempts to seize the advantage in a shifting political environment. Christians wanted *Christian* schools, not the schools provided by the state. Many early converts, despite the insufficiency of their "zeal" from Osborne's perspective, do seem to have developed a deep sense of responsibility for the spiritual welfare of their kin and neighbors. Just as Ruth Cox found in Nigeria that converts touched by the evangelicalism of SIM adopted wholeheartedly the "lifestyle evangelism approach" of the mission and devoted much of their lives to the patient work of bringing those they loved to Christianity (Cox 2000, 139), early converts in the Maradi/Tsibiri region often committed themselves to a life of informal or formal evangelism. Such deep and private commitments are, of course, extremely difficult to reconstruct at this remove in time, particularly as the earliest converts by and large were not literate and left little trace of their thoughts—although they left many traces of their actions. Some hint at the kind of deeply felt burden that early converts took on may perhaps be discerned in a dream Musa Marafa related to the missionaries at the end of a day of visiting villages with Mrs. Osborne outside Tsibiri:

> Before we separated one of these young men said, "I want to tell you something else. Last night I dreamed that a young man from the village to which we were to go was standing upon a pile of ashes left by the burning of his house. . . . I saw him begin to sink slowly into this fire. As he sank, he called out to me, 'Musa, save me'! I stretched out my hand, caught him, and pulled him out of the pit." (Wright 1935, 10)

SIM missionaries consistently underrecognized the labor of committed converts who hoped to themselves become evangelists while aspiring to a better material life in this world. Running throughout the reports, letters home, and memories of SIM missionaries is a striking failure to appreciate the significant labor of African evangelists, who often worked without pay or recognition. The many descriptions missionaries wrote of their brave and bold attempts to bring "the Word" to the "unreached" invariably underemphasized the role of domestic staff, converts, and local contacts in the work of itineration. Martha Wall, for example, offers a heroic vision of herself visiting a "forgotten" village outside of Tsibiri at great risk to her health, but slightly below the surface of the narrative it is clear that 'dan Nana had been visiting the village fairly regularly and that it had by no means been "forgotten" (Wall 1960, 277–278). Given the rudimentary language skills of many of the missionaries at the time of those pioneering visits, it is hard to know what a villager would be able to make of the visitors without the preaching of such local Christians. In some ways, the missionaries served more to attract a crowd with their unusual appearance (*babban abin kallo;* "something to look at") and their phonograph than to actually preach themselves, for it was often a local Christian who stepped in at that critical juncture.[16]

A report on a Bible conference in Tsibiri in 1946 gives an uncharacteristically rich glimpse into the importance of such convert-missionaries:

> As a rule Acts 1:8 pictures the Gospel being preached in the country of our birth with the circle ever-widening to include the lands of darkness. But what a thrill it was to hear Dan Nana, who is the first *missionary* from Tsibiri, interpret this

verse to mean the place of his birth, his tribe, and finally the regions beyond. It was evident to all who saw the speaker arrive the day before, accompanied by his family and at least fifteen keen young men, that he was putting into action the very words he spoke. Who may estimate the future results of such preaching and practice by one of this tribe which often opposes the Gospel messages [as] being the white man's religion. (de la Haye 1946, 20–21, emphasis added)

This passage offers rather rare confirmation that such men were essentially equivalent to the white missionaries—the convention was to refer to them as "native evangelists." Bible conferences such as this one in which the burgeoning Christian community took an increasingly greater part perhaps contributed to the mission's rather belated discovery of the significant activities of what one might characterize as the second wave of converts (including at that time Musa Marafa, Abba Musa of Zinder, Malam Naino, Malam Ba'ka, Malam Umaru, and, although he was somewhat younger, 'dan Nana). The next wave of converts were substantially influenced by the activities of such men, for although later converts sometimes knew and even lived alongside and worked for missionaries, it was the preaching of native Hausa speakers that was more significant to their interest in Christianity. Malam Kashalu lived near Ray de la Haye in Jiratawa and became aware of the Christians through him, but it was the preaching of 'dan Nana, Naino, and Umaru that exposed him to Christian beliefs regularly enough for him to be interested in conversion (Malam Kashalu interview).

Despite the persistent sense of disappointment in the writings of the missionaries about the evangelical vigor of their new church, it is clear that many early converts practiced evangelism from the moment they felt confident in their ability to read the Scriptures. As Cox observes of similar SIM converts in Nigeria, "a general pattern of basic literacy education followed by evangelism and teaching through itineration was established very early. After first learning to read, their new knowledge was put into practice among friends, relatives, and in nearby villages. The Scripture verses memorized in literacy classes served as texts for the message they would preach after they taught reading classes. Along with this, new believers gave testimony of what had happened to them" (Cox 2000, 140). Similarly, the Christians in the Maradi region that I interviewed had been encouraged to begin evangelism themselves almost immediately upon conversion, well before they themselves felt entirely ready for it. Many had extremely fond memories of giving their testimony, and some continue to manifest real pleasure in what they (like the Christian leaders of the ECWA churches in Nigeria that Cox interviewed) refer to as

"God's work." A few, however, felt unprepared and underqualified. One man remarked that he didn't see how he, as a mere boy, could have any positive impact upon adults, since in Hausa culture, age distinctions are felt acutely and social stature increases with age. He became comfortable preaching only much later as a mature man, after seeking out advanced theological training in France and Switzerland (Ali 'dan Buzu interview).

Those Christians who seemed to the mission to show zeal and promise were hand picked for more advanced training; access to further schooling therefore was closely linked to adhering to the mission's perceptions about the urgency of evangelism. I will discuss SIM's approach to education more fully in another chapter; however, at this juncture it is worth noting a few things that follow from the "lifestyle evangelism approach" of the mission. Education was conceived of first and foremost as necessary for literacy in the scriptures. Secondarily, education was necessary to train skilled evangelists. SIM never conceived of education as a means of enriching or edifying an *existing* Christian community either spiritually or materially, and missionaries never proposed it as a means of political advancement. Thus, the preaching in SIM gatherings was always targeted at those where were not yet committed to Christianity rather than to the spiritual needs of committed Christians facing a complex and sometimes-hostile setting. Because the goal of schooling was to train evangelists, the mission did not train Christians in technical skills on the whole or in the pastoral skills that sustain Christian communities. Christians who showed promise as preachers might be given ancillary medical training, but they were never given such training to become specialists themselves. Their task was to assist the missionary specialist and to use medical work as a means to evangelize. This extremely limited understanding of education became a central point of contention between the emerging Church and the mission.

Lifestyle Evangelism: Women and the Christian Home

The lifestyle evangelism approach entailed not simply the preaching of male converts, despite the tendency of both mission and church to tell the history of the rise of the Christian community by listing the names of prominent male pastors. Indeed, when men tell the story of the growth of the church it is almost impossible to detect the role of women at all, despite the fact that some of the central male figures in the church I interviewed remarked that "apart from [their] mother," they were the first Christian in their families. An ideological reason for this myopia is captured in the following remarks by Pastor Cherif:

> Women, most of the time, they follow the religion of their husband, right? You could say that since it was Adam who was born first, he was called forth first, and then it was from the rib of man that woman was made, that's why God said, "You will return alongside of your husband." And so that's why it wasn't women who entered [the Protestant church] first. It was men who were the first. Whatever a person [meaning a man] was to become, so also his wife would become. (Pastor Cherif Yacouba interview)

Within a fundamentalist reading of the Bible, then, God created Adam first and it is entirely natural that men, as heads of households, should determine the practices and beliefs of women, who are their subordinates. This is a reading that sits rather well with the local understanding of women as subordinate within Islam, and it is therefore not likely to be particularly startling to most West African Muslims. This universalized, mythologized, and naturalized understanding of the process of conversion, of course, flies in the face of much of the history of Christianity elsewhere in Africa, for in many regions slave women and women in flight from unwelcome marriages were attracted to missions and the Christian message before men were (Wright 1993) or were simply more receptive to spiritual concerns then men were (see, e.g., Hodgson 2005). While it is clear that in Tsibiri it was difficult for the mission to come into contact with younger women and girls, there were nevertheless a number of older women such as Tashibka whose age gave them a certain amount of license and whose moral authority made it possible for male children to come into contact with the missionaries. Women were extremely important contributors to the growth of the church in Niger, despite their relative invisibility. As the gender composition of staff of SIM came more and more heavily to reflect the enthusiasm of evangelical American women for missions, the interventions in which it engaged made it more possible to make contact with women. Women converts (who were cultivated through medical work and schools that were established to teach girls to become Christian wives) in turn anchored model Christian households, fostered children, raised their own Christian children, and used visits with other women to share their beliefs.

One of the most important ways that women contributed to the growth of the Christian community was through the fostering of Muslim children in Christian households, an enterprise that relied substantially upon the work of Christian women. Fostering could be part of a broader pattern of clientage, and is a very common practice among Hausa families. Often such children (known as *'yan ri'ko;* "children who are being supported") are treated in principle identically to birth children, and it is generally the responsibility of the woman of the house to ensure that they are well trained morally, that they have the necessary skills to become responsible adults, and that they ultimately marry and move to a home of their own. Christian households took in Muslim kin and disinherited neighbors from their farming villages and raised them, thereby exposing such children daily to Christian practices, beliefs, and mores. Because Maradi and Tsibiri towns eventually had relatively high concentrations of Christians (who gravitated to neighborhoods where they felt comfortable among other Christians), rural families took advantage of their connections with Christian kin in town in order to help their children gain access to schooling. Some Christian families quite self-consciously recruited Muslim kin to Christianity by hosting them while they went to school in town. Pastor Garba and his wife Hajjiya Umma Garba, for example, substantially altered the demography of the Christian community in this way, bringing in numerous children from the Madarumfa and Dogondoutchi regions to be raised in their home. Through their efforts the number of Katsinawa and Gobirawa Christians eventually became more balanced. While such children might regularly be referred to as "Pastor Garba's children" (he had no biological children of his own), it was inevitably his wife who attended to much of their early moral training, their understanding of hygiene, their food and clothing, and their health. Numerous other Christian households contributed to the rearing of Christian children in the same manner but on a smaller scale.

By the close of World War II, the mission in Niger had begun to work far more closely with the government health services of Niger. Up until that point its medical work had been superficial, for the staff had no real medical training. However, when the colonial administration agreed to turn over its large dispensary in Tsibiri to the mission to make up for the unpleasantness of the Vichy era, SIM suddenly had opportunities for contact with local populations of an entirely different order than it had experienced previously. The first trained nurse to "man" the dispensary was Martha Wall, who wrote a detailed memoir of her experiences as an SIM missionary. I will discuss the mission's medical work much more fully in a subsequent chapter. Here I would like to simply trace some of the consequences of that burgeoning medical work for the growth of the church. SIM's medical work in Niger ran parallel to its work in Nigeria, and because populations on both sides of the border were Hausa-speakers who crossed the border with considerable ease, it is difficult to discuss work in Niger without seeing it as linked to the work in Nigeria. The dispensary treated individuals who came to Tsibiri from villages many days' distant by foot. Through this work the mission could meet patients from a broad range of ethnic groups, including Buzu, Tuareg, and Fulani. Niger's pastoralist economy meant that many social groups were highly mobile, which made it difficult to evangelize to them systematically simply through itineration. With the Tsibiri dispensary, the "unreached" came to the mission. The effect of the medical work was twofold: it gave rise to a set of healed male converts who became committed evangelists, and it brought the mission into contact with women so that the demographic expansion of the church could proceed through fostering, marriage, and childbirth and not simply through conversion.

By the 1940s, the growing church was facing a demographic dilemma. While it had a number of influential male converts who were married or who were approaching the age of marriage, it had very few female converts. It had been far more difficult for the missionaries to reach women than to reach men. Local households were very protective of women and girls and tended to prevent them from being exposed to the preaching of the Christians. Young men had much more spatial mobility than women and girls. Married women were subject to the supervision of their husbands, who could physically punish them for misbehavior. Women could even find themselves divorced if their husbands became angered by their disobedience. Divorced women had no guarantee that they would continue to have custody of their children. The disincentives to flirtation with Christianity were numerous and substantial for women. Men had less to lose from exploring Christianity, but an unmarried man found that it was hard to find a spouse once he had converted.

The mission's medical work made it far easier to gain the ear of women, who sometimes had to remain at the dispensary for weeks or months at a time with their children for treatment. Later, when the mission also had a leprosarium at Danja, even more patients were exposed to Christianity. As the success of the mission's medical treatments became known, people brought infants and small children that would otherwise have been given up for lost. The difficulty of caring for some of these patients meant that the mission found itself in effect raising some of these marginal children itself. These "orphans" were eventually raised by the mission in its girls' homes at Soura and Dogondoutchi and its boys' home at Maza Tsaye. The girls in particular were trained to be-

"Audi Mammane—a bright Christian." Audi encountered missionaries when her mother was treated at the
Danja leprosarium. She was later schooled at the girls'
school in Soura. Courtesy of SIMIA (NR 24), photographed by Niger Challenge Press, n.d.

come Christian wives, and many made up the core of the Christian community of the Maradi region. Christian men began to find wives among
these women, and these wives raised Christian children. Dogondoutchi,
somewhat to the west of Maradi in a largely animist region of Hausa-
speaking Mawri, became a second focal point of development for building Christian communities, in part (and rather unconsciously) building
on the previous work of the Catholics in the region. Zeb Zabriskie and
his wife Irene began work in Dogondoutchi in 1945 precisely because it

was not Muslim and might prove, like the Maguzawa areas of Nigeria, more receptive to the Christian message. Zeb Zabriskie believed that the French administration tolerated this new station with some wariness mixed with curiosity, calculating that these Americans would pose less of a political threat in a pagan area than elsewhere among more Islamicized populations (Zeb Zabriskie interview).

In all of its stations, SIM found that it was left with "orphan" children well before it had formally envisioned orphanages or residential homes for children. Zabriskie and his wife raised the *métis* son of a local woman who they had taken in because she was pregnant and abandoned and was sleeping in the marketplace. A second child came to them because the co-wives of a polygynous man would not raise the son of another wife who had died in childbirth (Zabriskie interview). Ruth Jacobson recalled that as early as 1945 she was tending nine children that had been given to the mission in Tsibiri to raise. Some of them had been offered for schooling by older Christian women such as a rather unstable woman named Sa'a and the devout Tashibka. Others were given by men who did not feel capable of raising them, particularly if the girls were sickly (Ruth Jacobson interview). Such children presented both an opportunity and a quandary for individual missionaries, for the mission frowned upon the missionaries raising such children as full adoptive members of missionary families, fearing that this would be "culturally inappropriate" for the children, who would become deracinated from their "real" origins. But the children could not be abandoned. Somewhat in recognition of the fait accompli of mission fostering of children, the girls' and boys' homes were developed as a kind of intermediate solution. The children would be raised with the assumption that they would eventually remain within the Christian community in Niger rather than move with the missionaries if they went home on leave or left the field to retire. Emotionally, culturally, and financially, the individual missionaries retained some distance from the children, despite very evident affection for them.

"Thou canst make me clean": Leprosy and Native Evangelism

SIM's work in both Nigeria and in Hausa Niger was profoundly enhanced by its entry into medical work. The mission took over several leprosaria in Nigeria in 1936 and expanded this work in Niger, thus finding a niche for itself which both colonial governments and local populations were willing to not only tolerate but applaud. The establishment of the leprosaria created momentum for SIM's work in Hausaland. A headline for a photo spread in the SIM publication *The Sudan Witness* heralding the new leprosy work in Nigeria pronounced this to be "The Peaceful Invasion of the Northern Emirates of Nigeria" (SIM 1938). Medical work dovetailed nicely with the theme of healing in the New Testament, giving the missionaries an important reference for what might otherwise have appeared to be a distraction from the more-important work of testifying. Indeed, some of the mission literature suggests that over time tension emerged between those, particularly old-timers, who perceived pure traditional evangelization activities to be of paramount importance and the younger generation of "specialists" whose skills in medical work, teaching, and development work sometimes outpaced their abilities as evangelists and linguists (see, e.g., Bishop 1957, 7).

Because of the lengthy treatment required for leprosy before the development of sulfone drugs in the 1950s, patients at the leprosaria in Nigeria at Kano and Katsina were among the most thoroughly versed and dedicated of the converts to Christianity. Having been transformed from social outcasts to living examples of the saving and healing power of Christ, they had particularly powerful testimony to give on behalf of Christianity. It would be very difficult to do a systematic study of the geography and social networks of conversion in all the rural villages of Niger; however, in my own visits to numerous villages outside Maradi with substantial Christian populations it became very clear to me that the evangelism of former Hansen's Disease patients had been an extremely important factor in the spread of evangelical Christianity in Niger from 1950 on. Pastor Garba, for example, has become legendary in the Maradi region for his influence on the church. But the list of influential pastors and itinerant preachers who had become exposed to Christianity through the leprosaria and the Kano Eye Hospital is long and impressive. Not all were treated in Niger (the leprosarium at Danja in Niger dates only to the 1950s)—many had come to Niger from Nigeria after treatment, and others had been treated in Nigeria and returned home to be bearers of "the Word." These pastors were by and large modestly schooled commoners, men whose ability to work their fields was diminished by the gradual loss of limbs or by blindness but whose enthusiasm for life and willingness to preach was sparked by the transforming experience of entering a sustained Christian community for long periods of time. I will discuss their experiences and sense of identity more fully later, but it is important to underscore the significance of such individuals (both men and women) in the expansion of Christianity in Niger.

Christianity offered such individuals the possibility of having an important social role in an economy in which their physical disabilities would ordinarily render them simply burdensome. Leprosy, or *kuturta*, in particular was an emblem not only of burdensome dependency (as in the expression *kuturun dangi*, "poor relations") but of the very process of impoverishment itself (as in the expression *ya kuturta ni*, "he impoverished me," literally "he transformed me into a leper"). Individuals suffering from Hansen's Disease (better known colloquially as leprosy) had difficulty gaining access to and retaining land, and they had very little prospect of finding or keeping a spouse. Beyond curing Hansen's sufferers of their biological disease, the mission's Christianity went some way toward relieving their social stigma as "lepers." The vast majority of expressions in Hausa relating to leprosy have to do not with contagion or revulsion but with uselessness and vulnerability. The problem with leprosy is not simply that it is a progressive disease. Even after the bacillus responsible for the disease has been eliminated, the long-term damage to nerve endings means that patients often lose limbs to infections: "The classic effects of leprosy result as indirect consequences of permanent damage in infected nerves or skin cells" (Silla 1998, 21). In effect, to be "cured" of the contagion does not mean that one is be cured of its effects, both physical and social. For this reason I agree with Eric Silla that it is important to retain the term "leper" with all its social complexity to do full historical justice to the sense of identity of Hansen's Disease sufferers. While medical workers might wishfully insist that Hansen's Disease can be cured and that the stigma of the word "leper" should be abandoned, the reality for such patients is that the long-term side effects of the disease mark them permanently as social lepers. Hausa proverbs often pair leprosy with blindness, capturing the permanency of the stigma: leprosy can contribute to blindness, and both blindness and leprosy can have permanent disabling effects even when their original causes have been treated.

Disabled people in a labor-intensive agro-pastoral economy cannot always pull their own weight; the perception that they are no longer useful is an important part of their sense of isolation and rejection. Evangelical Christianity gave such individuals a raison d'être and supremely important work to do: God's work. To preach they did not need fingers, they need not be able to see, they did not need four limbs. The only skill they needed was skill with words, and this was something many of them had in abundance. As the preceding chapter on Bible translation shows, the blind preacher Sule Garko had a significant role in the 1979 translation of the Bible. He was one of the many Hausa-speaking Christians who preached in Niger and was well known and admired for his oratory (see e.g. SIM 1973, 12). Good preachers could make a modest living through the support of the broader Christian community, and this support would not simply be the alms given out by Muslims out of pity for charity but a real recognition of the value of their labor.

Men with a purpose in life thereby became desirable as spouses. Patients at leprosaria and other medical institutions sometimes found partners among others who, like them, had physical disabilities but nevertheless desired full and meaningful lives. This, as Eric Silla shows for Mali, is one of the important ways a sense of community emerged out of the colonial-era "treatment" of leprosy (Silla 1998). A man from Sokoto such as Audu might find a wife among Maradi's Christian women while spending time at the mission's leprosarium south of Maradi. The mission also actively facilitated the courtship and marriage of promising evangelists with the women in known Christian communities or the students of the girls' homes, a practice that linked distant communities and ethnic groups and crossed the otherwise intractable social boundary between the "healed" (*warkaku*) and the "healthy" (*masu lafiya*). Because the clientele of the medical mission included Fulani, Buzu, Tuareg, and Hausa in Nigeria as well as Gourma, Zerma, and Beriberi in Niger, the potential ethnic composition of the church expanded considerably. Pastor Garba, who had been treated in a mission facility, found a wife among women raised in distant Dogondoutchi, where the mission had a girls' home and had therefore developed social ties with local families. A Fulani man such as Adamu Na Mamayo might find a bride in Nigeria among the women being treated alongside him. In effect, the extended Christian community made it possible for people who might otherwise have endured a lifetime of rejection to become useful workers, fully adult men and women who had earned respect through marriage and childrearing (sometimes through fostering rather than biological parentage).

While such individuals may, as Silla suggests, have developed a strong sense of identity as "lepers," it is also important to recognize that for many converts it was their identity as *Christians* that was socially defining. Rather than live the rest of their lives with and among other "lepers," they often chose to make careers as evangelists, living among the healthy and raising children in the church. The colonial educational infrastructure did not regard such individuals as worth expending the time and money to educate (Silla 1998, 119), but the mission was more than happy to offer them literacy in Hausa and the respect that comes with being known as a *malam*—a scholar. With further training they could even earn the title of "Pastor." Within the Christian community, they could become respected elders within their churches and leaders of the women's fellowship groups. It is not hard to see why the emphasis upon Christ as healer in the Bible would have resonated for such former patients, or why the healed would be seen by healthy Christians as particularly appropriate carriers of "the Word" given such miraculous biblical passages as this one from the Gospel of Mark:

> And there came a leper to him, beseeching him, and kneeling down to him, and saying unto him, If thou wilt, thou canst make me clean. And Jesus, moved with compassion, put forth his hand, and touched him, and saith unto him, I will; be thou clean. . . . He went out, and began to publish it much, and to blaze abroad the matter, insomuch that Jesus could no more openly enter into the city, but was without in desert places: and they came to him from every quarter. (Mark 1:40–41, 45)

In both major translations of the Hausa Bible, the leper is not simply made clean, he is purified (*tsarkaka*), using the same root that is used to refer to the Holy Bible (Litafi Mai Tsarki). The lame, blind, and healed "lepers" I have encountered within the Christian community in Niger are often treated with a respect and deference that suggests that far from being ostracized, their embodiment of the ministry of Christ to those with physical ailments lends them a certain sanctity. The importance of giving alms (*sadaka*) within Islam means that encountering people with physical ailments and deformities presents an occasion for acquiring merit. In a sense, within Islam as well they may be endowed with a kind of sanctity—the most obvious place to look for such individuals is outside the mosque. While the social stigma of being useless and vulnerable that attaches to being blind, lame, or having leprosy might have reduced the stature of such individuals among ordinary villagers, their disfigurements and disabilities nevertheless conferred on them a certain license in a Muslim milieu. Where outraged abuse might well have been the response to an able-bodied individual preaching in a firmly Muslim enclave, the importance of charity within Islam offered them some protection. The social origins of some of the mission's most important evangelists were nevertheless, as one missionary remarked frankly, both "a blessing and a problem. The blessing was they were Christians. The problem was they could not minister in some areas because of stigma" (Chuck Forster interview).

The expansion of the church through the conversion of people whose infirmities marked them as social outcasts obviously meant that the social makeup of the church in Niger was becoming extremely complex. On the one hand, the earliest core converts were individuals with very high social standing as members of the Tsibiri *sarauta* class. Rather exceptionally for SIM's work among Hausa speakers, these earliest converts to Christianity came from among nominally Muslim sectors of the population. The gradual expansion of the church as workers and ordinary villagers were exposed to the mission and to earlier converts broadened the base to include Hausa farmers from villages within a day or two of Maradi and Tsibiri, but at the outset it was rather heavily focused in the larger urban centers. The medical work brought people of all kinds and backgrounds to the mission. But the significance of the leprosaria and Kano Eye Hospital to the overall work meant that a significant portion (and arguably the most conspicuous segment) of the growing church was made up of individuals who might otherwise be seen by Muslims as social outcasts. These committed believers then sought systematically to preach in villages around the leprosarium in Danja and in the broader Maradi region, targeting especially Arna populations that had not converted to Islam with considerable success. With the growth of this work more and more converts to Christianity were from among the *jahilai*—those rural peasants the urban Muslims regarded as ignorant heathens.

As the church expanded its social composition included more of the marginal and disreputable peoples when viewed from the perspective of an urban Muslim. Nevertheless, this growing and dynamic community grew and expanded through the agency of committed native Christians. It became ever more difficult for the mission to control the leadership of the church or the meanings of the practices of an increasingly autonomous and fractious church. As we shall see in the following chapter, the mission struggled to contain and control this increasingly independent community, while African men alternately competed for leadership of the church and cooperated with one another to contain Christian women's access to traditional female support systems and networks.

6

Disciplining the Christian:
Defining Elderhood, Christian Marriage, and "God's Work," 1933–1955

> *We wrestle not with flesh and blood but*
> *against spiritual hosts of wickedness in*
> *heavenly places.*
>
> —D. V. and C. M. Osbourne, 1937

*A*fter three years of struggling with little success in Zinder and another five breaking new ground in the Maradi region, SIM finally had, in 1933, the beginnings of a church in its more promising location in Tsibiri. The mission had attracted a core group of converts through contacts with the family of Musa Marafa, through the novelty of providing an alternative literate monotheism, and through the daily exposure to local populations as a major employer, and it took stock of its following in 1933, the first year for which records of the new church in Tsibiri were kept. There were sixty-one professing Christians. However, sustaining this hard-won success would not be easy. SIM missionaries of the 1930s were fond of likening their experience of evangelizing in Africa to the experience of Paul among the Gentiles. Paul's early Christian church faced obstacles orchestrated (or so the imprisoned apostle believed) by Satan. The best way to defend against the onslaughts of the "spiritual hosts of wickedness" was to shore up family life and proper hierarchical relations between masters and servants in the fragile communities of Christians in such key locations as Ephesus. In a parallel fashion, the slowly growing community of Christians in Tsibiri was hindered by satanic forces, as the early missionaries saw it. Church members were being

lost to the lure of polygyny and the "love of money and worldly companionships." In the letter quoted above, David and Drusille Osborne
ask their prayer partners to pray for three Christian men at the heart of
the small community who had been drawn by "Moslem intrigue" to violate monogamy and drop out of the church.[1] The landscape of religious practice was quite complex; in another letter, the Osbornes noted
that "besides Islam we are confronted with fetish worship, demon worship and sorcery."[2] Vulnerable and impressionable new converts needed
to be carefully trained so they would not be drawn toward the unchris-
tian practices that threatened to undermine the infant church. Their
struggles against satanic forces would be fortified through prayer and
discipline.

Tsibiri church records that debated and recorded *horo*, or the discipline meted out to members who violated the mission's understandings
of Christian behavior, are particularly rich sources for unpacking the
particular social, moral, and economic conflicts that emerged as the local
Christian community gradually grew and the mission struggled to retain
control over the definition of appropriate Christian behavior in the key
period of church growth from 1945 to 1955. For reasons that will become
clearer in chapter 7, in the early postwar period the French colonial
administration became far more sympathetic to the activities of Protestant missionaries, opening up the possibility for them to take over some
of the medical work the French did not have the staff to handle. In the
late 1940s and 1950s, the entry of more women into medical and educational work made it possible for the mission to reach more women and
children, balancing the heavily male make-up of the converts of the 1930s
and early 1940s. The farm school and the girls' and boys' homes established in the 1950s became poles of attraction for families in the region
that hoped to provide their children with more educational opportunity.
This gradually expanding and shifting work begun to result in a Christian
population that was large enough to begin to grow through marriage and
reproduction from the late 1950s on. But as it grew, friction could develop between the mission and the emerging community over who would
lead the new church, how families should be structured, how Christian
practice should be defined, and the work of evangelism. Converts who
saw themselves as having been transformed through the power of the
Holy Spirit were quite capable of distinguishing between the attempts of
the mission to regulate behavior and the requirements of Christianity.
The spiritual warfare the mission saw itself engaging in was also a struggle between missionaries and converts to define authority within the
growing church. As Brian Stanley has recently noted, "The process of

conversion to Christianity was less tightly regulated by the missionary than many critics suppose and, indeed, many missionaries desired" (2003, 326).

Catholicism on the whole treated individual sin as a matter to be handled through the sacrament of confession during which the individual parishioner revealed in secret to his or her priest spiritual failings and then rectified those failings through private individual acts of contrition. By contrast, evangelical Protestantism within SIM made individual spiritual failings a matter of concern to the entire church, in part to prevent the corruption that might ensue if spiritual cleansing was seen as a monetary affair between parish members and venal priests. Each individual served as a model of Christian behavior to the rest of the community— the church as a whole regulated behavior through *horo*, mechanisms of temporary exclusion. Individuals who were placed in discipline could not attend church, take communion, lead prayers, or preach. In effect, they were exiled from the Christian community and publicly humiliated for periods ranging from a month to several years. Reinstatement in the community entailed a public confession of guilt and repentance during Sunday service. To be placed under *horo* was no small matter to Christians whose social worlds revolved around participation in church life. Among Muslim Hausa-speakers, the word "*horo*" has two meanings that have a bearing on these struggles between the church and the mission. *Horo* is the kind of shaping discipline that parents impose upon a child or a Koranic teacher imposes upon a Koranic student—a well-raised child has been trained into appropriate behavior through the sometimes-severe punishments of parents and elders. Thus, the word suggests infantalization—someone who is under *horo* is like a child, and those who are empowered to administer discipline are implicitly senior and more highly schooled in matters of religion. It is also the kind of physical discipline one applies to animals—it suggests taming. This understanding of religious discipline applied forcibly from without is quite distinct from the prevailing sense of self-discipline captured by the Sufi term "*tarbiyya*." A well-disciplined initiate into Sufism learns a kind of introspection, reflectiveness, and *self*-control that is much admired among Hausa-speakers. The term "*tarbiyya*" has migrated from its initial Sufi context to refer in Hausa to good breeding and moral education more broadly.

One key question was who should be authorized to administer such discipline. Missionaries in Tsibiri were in a sense the resident authorities on Christian practice, but as the church grew it was necessary to establish some internal mechanism for regulating the behavior of local Christians. Until about 1939, the church was small enough to debate issues of general interest to the community as a congregation—or, one suspects, the men of the church engaged in these discussions; their voices are the only ones we find in the records of the meetings. This system became unwieldy as the church grew, and it is occasionally difficult to tell from the records what the consensus in any given meeting was. One senses that the outcomes of these open-forum debates were not always quite what the missionaries had intended. For example, in August 1938, David Osborne proposed that the church send money as a gift to the British and Foreign Bible Society; he then left the meeting to let the church make its deliberations. The men of the church chose instead to fund local evangelists and a new church building next to the mission station. They also expressed interest in charity toward the elderly and lepers and to strangers who needed burial.[3] These highly local concerns are rather telling, for the church led by Musa Marafa in effect decided that it was not interested in funding the missionary efforts of wealthy foreign Bible translators toward some abstract "unreached Africa" when there were known evangelists and destitute people in the Tsibiri region that the church could support.

In 1945, David Osborne, a missionary from New Zealand who was heading the Tsibiri station, established a council of elders, or *dattibai* in Hausa, to govern the growing Christian community. The converts had been meeting in a chapel on the mission compound, which had been built slightly outside the old walled town of Tsibiri. But in order for the community, which had grown to 250 converts, to become a self-sustaining church, it would need to begin to develop some autonomy from the mission. In keeping with its anticlerical leanings, SIM replicated in the field the evangelical model of semi-autonomous churches led by a group of church leaders whose decisions would be governed by prayer and close study of the Bible rather than by appeal to an established clerical hierarchy. As the long-discussed project of building a church in Tsibiri town outside the mission compound began to look like it might become a reality, Osborne compiled a list of the men he regarded as suitable elders to lead the new church. These men approved baptisms, marriages, and discipline for church members. They also, in principle, oversaw the collection of tithes and decisions about how to spend church money.

The decision to create such a council originated with the missionaries, who chose the individuals to serve and clearly saw themselves as having a higher order of understanding of Christianity than the Church Elders Council. The records also suggest that missionaries actually held the church treasury for the church and did all the bookkeeping, making the notion that the church could unilaterally decide how to spend money something of a fiction. The director of the station at Tsibiri evidently also set the agenda for the council meetings. When the outcome of council deliberations did not meet with the station director's expectations, he sent the agenda items back to the elders' council for reconsideration at the next meeting. As a source for the history of the church in the region, the minutes of the elders' council meetings are extremely interesting—there is a considerable disconnect between the agenda and the tone of the minutes. The council sometimes chose to ignore agenda items it was unwilling to consider or couldn't understand, it curtly dismissed issues that the mission regarded as "problems" but that the elders viewed with less anxiety, and it sometimes permitted criticisms of the mission to creep into the minutes of the meetings—an indirect way of conveying discontentment. Clearly, while the elders' council was in some sense a creature of the mission, it was not a mere puppet.

The choice to set up a council of elders implied that the principal of gerontocracy and seniority so familiar in the Tsibiri region would apply within the church. The Hausa word used to refer to these leaders, *dattibai*, is quite clearly related to age. It implies an individual of at least late middle age with stature and respectability in a community. The entirely male composition of the committee from the outset established that women as a group would be treated as minors, regardless of their age. The church would be patriarchal in conception. Yet as we have seen in the preceding chapter, those who were most drawn to Christianity were not "elders" at all; in local parlance, they were *yara*, or children. Osborne preferred young men with literacy skills over those who might be senior in age as members of the Church Elders Council. The mission also ignored Gobirawa Hausa understandings of the importance of older women within governance and local spiritual hierarchies, symbolized in titled positions for women (*inna, sarauniya, magajiya*) in the Tsibiri Gobir court (just as they were ignored by the French colonial administration; see Cooper 1997a).

The church records are therefore suggestive of tensions and struggles at multiple levels: the mission hoped to shape the church while maintaining a kind of paternalist illusion of church autonomy, church members struggled to make the church genuinely autonomous while at the same time trying to retain access to the critical resources of the mission, junior and senior men struggled to determine who would lead the church, and men struggled to maintain control of the women and children, who were to be socialized into proper Christian behavior through an uneasy alliance between the patriarchy of the mission and the patriarchy of the newly forming church. The unruly behavior of women both old and young is visible in these records in the many attempts of the men to regulate the dress, parenting, and wifely behavior of women through the authority of husbands and fathers.

First the mission and then the elders tried to control the behavior and family lives of the church members regarding a cluster of key issues: the conception of monogamous nuclear family life, the fear of contagion by Islam and paganism, the uneasy and unequal relations between missionary masters and Christian servants in collective labor on behalf of the expansion of Christianity, and the decisions about which visible practices could be used to mark Christians as a distinctive "reborn" community set apart from the unconverted Muslims and Arna surrounding them. But the effort to create a council of elders created its own tensions that were acted out in the building of the first Tsibiri church and the eventual defection of the legendary figure of Musa Marafa from Christianity altogether.

Defining Elders

The earliest list of elders for the church is dated 1945, when the first formal meeting of the Elders Council was held. The elders' list, in the order in which Osborne constructed it, included: Alita, a man from an unremarkable Tsibiri family who was twenty-nine years old but whose long service to the mission meant he was deemed to have "unusual honesty";[4] Barmo, the leader of the farming community in Guma who was a minor figure in the Tsibiri aristocracy at thirty, first referred by Osborne as "small and boyish for his age";[5] the commoner 'dan Nana, who was at this point twenty-six and was acting as an evangelist and teacher of twenty-two Bible students in a village named Sarkin Bora near Tsibiri;[6] Isaka, a 23-year-old Tsibiri commoner; Jadi, the only *sarauta*-class elder, at thirty still a young man and relatively unimportant within the gerontocratic aristocratic milieu as the son of a slave woman; Kulungu, 'dan Nana's 37-year-old brother, who worked in the mission dispensary; and Nayashe, a 27-year-old member of Musa Marafa's household. The youth of these men overall is striking.

Even more striking, however, is the absence of Musa Marafa from the list, the earliest convert, who, at thirty-seven, was older than all but one of these men. Musa Marafa's voice was everywhere in evidence in the records of full church meetings prior to 1945—he clearly had a strong say in anything decided by the church, including the disciplining of several of the young men who appeared on the list for theft, *tsarance* (a locally tolerated form of heavy petting among the unmarried), smoking, and other youthful offenses. Musa himself had not been subject to *horo* at that point and was authorized by the community to preach. He had been instrumental in the expansion of the church and had assisted in the baptism of several of his close kin. Itinerant preaching by the missionaries would not have been possible without the support of such eloquent early converts as Musa Marafa and his wife Habsu.[7] Yet the missionary gloss on Musa Marafa in 1933 was curiously ambivalent: "He has never learned to read well. Generally he has been staunch and loyal, and is very helpful in laboring and general repair work around the compound."[8]

Musa Marafa's limited ability to read and his "general" rather than unconditional loyalty meant that the mission never saw him as the heir apparent to Osborne. Indeed, his aristocratic origins may have meant that he *could not* become the leader of the church in the mission's eyes, regardless of his degree of literacy or his loyalty. One senses in the records of church meetings prior to 1945 a subdued rivalry between Musa Marafa and the young commoner, 'dan Nana, whose frequent peccadilloes were counterbalanced by a certain charisma and a fervent commitment to evangelism.[9] Musa Marafa's independence of judgment was a greater offense to the mission than 'dan Nana's repeated confessions of sin. Rather than draw upon existing leaders of the church, particularly Musa Marafa, Osborne devised the Church Elders Council to create an alternative pole of leadership more readily controllable by the mission than Musa Marafa. Musa Marafa's unassailable integrity, his considerable influence in the church, his independence from the mission, and his implicit political aspirations as a prince made him a threat to the mission. When the political fallout caused by the exclusion of Musa Marafa from the council eventually became clear some years later, missionaries professed dismay at their "cultural misunderstanding" of the importance of age in Hausa society. This strikes me as entirely disingenuous. The church council members were never referred to as "deacons" because that would have been misleading—the Hausa word the mission regularly used to refer to these leaders very clearly refers to age and implies a council of elders.

Also striking to a contemporary feminist is the absence of a number of memorable women such as Tashibka, Jadi's ex-slave mother, and Habsu, Musa Marafa's wife, from the Church Elders Council. The patriarchal fundamentalism of SIM guaranteed that the inclusion of such genuine church leaders in the Church Elders Council was never even entertained. Such women were "a great help" in itinerant preaching because they were skilled at opening the way for rural women to listen to and understand the mission's preaching.[10] The elderly Tashibka was among the *real* elders of the church—she was one of two women among the first six believers to be baptized and take communion for the first time with the missionaries.[11] Despite the thundering silence of women in the records of the church meetings prior to the formation of the Church Elders Council in 1945, we do hear a certain echo of Tashibka, who in 1935 had the temerity to speak up in support of the right of one young man in *horo* to preach.[12] Tashibka was something of a mythic figure in the recollections of female missionaries, a woman who was impressive not simply for her individual qualities but for the way she typified the unexpected authority of illiterate elderly women within the early community. Such women were deeply spiritual, gifted at prayer and oral arts more generally, and in the stories told about them, so attuned to the spiritual that they were in constant conversation with God. Elderly women were no doubt an embarrassment to the literate and rational young men of the early church. Speaking regularly to the Holy Spirit in public spaces was perhaps seen as eccentric, even mad. And the danger that these elderly women might lead the church back toward the spirit-possession activities for which women in this region are celebrated may have also colored men's perceptions of older women. One of the prominent aristocratic women in the early church, Magajiya, continued her *bori* spirit-cult activities, which the missionaries saw as engagement with the satanic realm. She eventually dropped out of the Christian community and was conveniently erased from the memory of the early church.

But Tashibka consistently appears in the oral narratives of women missionaries, and traces of her presence can be found in *The Sudan Witness* as well. She even dictated a letter exhorting more *turawa* (white Christians) to come to work as missionaries. The letter was translated and published to encourage potential mission sponsors: "I urge you young people, get ready and come quickly to help my people who are daily dying in their darkness and their sins. . . . What stops you from coming?" (Tashibka 1949). The editor's introduction to her letter declared, "Since her conversion a few years ago, [Tashibka] has grown in grace until today she is numbered among the strongest believers in Hausaland." Yet male converts seemed deeply embarrassed when I asked them to recall something about her—she did not fit with their sense of what the new church should be. A woman, a former slave, a medium of sorts, a "traditional" illiterate person, a poverty-stricken dependent of the mission—nothing about her was suitable as a model for the new Christian. And evidently she did not fit with what male mission leaders thought the new church leadership should be, either—literate, young, "modern," and masculine. She might have been useful for recruiting new missionaries, but she would not have a leadership role within the new church.

Building the First Church in "the Muslim North"

According to political scientist Pearl Robinson, Musa Marafa, "stifled by his status as a second-generation prince" and quite unlikely to attain the throne, channeled his considerable leadership qualities and intelligence into the church in pursuit of another route to prominence. His aspirations within the church were deliberately thwarted by an "American missionary pastor" because the missionary feared that "the Gobir prince-turned-evangelist would ultimately emerge as the dominant power on the church's governing board" (Robinson 1983, 117). Beginning in 1945 the Church Elders Council had discussed how to raise enough funds to build a proper church building in Tsibiri town, away from the mission compound. To succeed in this aspiration would require raising funds to cover the cost of the building. It would also call for securing a plot of land in the town of Tsibiri, which had only recently been relocated outside the flood zone of the Goulbin Maradi (a seasonal watercourse) as part of a colonial-era flood management and malaria reduction scheme. But the high cost of such a construction combined with the lack of support of the local colonial administration for any initiative that might anger the Muslim majority had caused the project to founder. The mission did not have the right to claim any new plot of land in the relocated town. Musa Marafa's decision to invite Tsibiri's Christians to build their new church on his land in 1947 may very well have been an effort to regain control of the church after his exclusion from the newly created Church Elders Council in 1945. Moving the church off the mission compound and into the town altered the dynamics of the church considerably, making it far more independent of the mission.

Marafa, as a member of the local aristocracy, had been allotted a sizable plot in the new town to build his family compound. It seemed to the Christians that there was no need to ask for permission to build on this plot. When word got out that the Christians intended to build a *makaranta*—a place to pray, read and teach—angry Muslim scholars objected to the local colonial authorities. In order to go forward with the project, the community of converts would have to make its case before the colonial administration. In the telling of the story of the construction of the church building, the young men who were at that time recognized members of the Church Elders Council such as 'dan Nana, Barmo, and Jadi recall themselves as central players in the negotiations with the French. In their recollections, Musa Marafa was simply one of many church members and indeed they were protecting him from reprisal by speaking to the French *commandant* for him (Barmo Abdou interview). The unstated implication was that Marafa was "old" and less comfortable about speaking French than the young leaders of the church. Their version of the story is, of course, somewhat self-serving. On the other hand, the erasure of the Church Elders Council from the version of the story the missionaries told is also self-serving. It suggests that what struck them most was the forceful figure of Musa Marafa, who had by no means been eliminated from the picture simply because Osborne did not include him on the Elders Council. In order to contain and control Musa Marafa's influence, missionaries needed to transform this from a tale of mature African initiative into a miraculous story of the struggle of the mission against the French administration and of the faith of an older steadfast convert. Recasting the story in this triumphal manner in an odd way evacuated it of any special political meaning.

The building of the first church in Tsibiri just before the rainy season of 1948 is a stock tale in the repertoire of both missionaries and Christians, one that reveals in both its statements and its silences the different perceptions of converts and missionaries about who the central actors were and what the critical conflicts were. At the heart of the difference between the versions the various players tell is the question of human agency. As Jadi Marafa tells the story, the number of people who gathered on Sundays had become too large for the room they had been using in the compound of Malam Osborne:

> People had started to "see Ubangiji" and it was time to move out into the open and create a church building. The missionaries said to the local converts, "You have the right to build your own church, a place where were can pray to God, since the number of people has grown so large." You could say the missionaries were involved but when it came to building we had more influence, we were born here and had our roots here, we had the land. So it wasn't that the mission went and did something and then said, "There it is." We went and we chose a

place, and we said, "Let's build." We made this decision amongst ourselves. (Jadi Marafa interview)

The local Christians chose a place, raised money from their farming, and made the bricks from clay by hand. Some helped with money, some with land, others with labor. So, he went on:

> When the Muslims began to see that we were building a church, they began to get angry. They said, "Ha! We don't agree to that! They're going to build a *makaranta* [a school] here, for the mission, for the Savior, in this town, we don't agree to that!" So they went off to make a complaint before the *commandant*, who was in Maradi. They said to him, "They're going to build a *makaranta*, we don't want that. They have to stop, we only [want] schools for Islam." So the *commandant* sent for us. There were a lot of us and we all went when he called us. So at that time he said, "Well, here's what the *malamai* have said, they say you are building a *makaranta* and that they don't believe in that, they say you should stop." So then we gave him our reply, we said, "Well, we are the ones who want to build a *makaranta*. Not the whites [*turawa*]. The Muslims have the right to make a *makaranta*, and we too have the right to do the same because we are all from this land. What they can do, we can do too. We don't keep them from doing what they do, so they can't stop us from doing what we hope to do. We are going to build a *makaranta*, and if they want to build one of their own they are free to do so." So the *commandant* said, "Yes, that's true. Whatever they have the right to do, you have the right to do, you are all *'yan 'kasa* [indigenous people of the land]. They had claimed that it was the whites who made you do it." "It has nothing to do with them, it doesn't belong to the mission. We were born here, and we have the right to do as we like." So the *commandant* said, "Yes, well, you go ahead with your work. But keep out of trouble." (Jadi Marafa interview)

This is a story of collective local Christian initiative, and almost all the leaders of the early church claim that they were present at that first meeting with the *commandant*. Note that the Muslims and Christians were struggling over who would control the spiritual education of the people of Tsibiri, for the building was explicitly referred to by all as a *makaranta* and was likened to a Koranic school even though the Christians clearly wanted to use it as a gathering place for worship. For Jadi Marafa, the story is largely one of conflict with a handful of Muslim scholars, and in it the rational colonial administrator is readily persuaded of the logic of treating Muslims and Christians equally in a secular state. Other Christians related the story in a similar fashion, commenting, for example, that the *commandant* confided to them that he, too, was a Christian and had no reason to stand in their way (Cherif Yacouba interview).

Building the church in Tsibiri. Courtesy of SIMIA, *The Sudan Witness* 3 (1966): 3.

For these Christians, the local French administration acted as intermediary to protect the rights of Christians against the claims of intrusive Muslims.

By contrast, the story as told from the vantage point of missionary Ray de la Haye becomes one about circumventing a hostile and recalcitrant French administration which would not permit the missionaries to build a church for the growing congregation away from the small mission compound:

> But this senior member, a man by the name of Musa Marafa, that's from a well known family there, had land, and he contributed that land to build a church building, which would be his, theirs. And he having owned the land he could do anything he wanted on it. And of course, when it got, became known by the Muslim chief and the others in the town . . . they were unhappy to think that when they thought that a transgression of the French law. [They] made a complaint to Maradi, the administrator there, who was a Frenchman, the *commandant*. And he asked that we account for what [had happened], when I said, we had nothing to do with it. "Then who did?" they asked. And we named Musa Marafa. So Musa Marafa was called in, he was one of the students of the school and he was a man about maybe 30 at that time, and mature, with a wife and two children, and respected. . . . Well, Musa told the administrator, "The land is mine, we are

now Christians, and we're building our own church, and . . . the missionaries have nothing to do with it. We invite them to come, we seek their advice, but this is ours." [The] *commandant* had nothing more to say, he says, "Very well, no problem there." The church was built. (Ray de la Haye interview)

Note that for Ray de la Haye the conflict was partly between the mission and the colonial administration. It is the cleverness of circumventing the colonial administration's limits on where the mission could build that is at the heart of the story. Unlike Jadi Marafa, he does not note the parallel between a Christian "church" and a Muslim "school." Here the integrity of a single loyal Bible school student forces the French administrator to back down. Gone are the crowds of Christians in Jadi's narrative and the sympathetic comment of the administrator in the narrations of others. By contrast, the story converts in Tsibiri told underscores Musa Marafa's success in forging a positive relationship with the French administrator and the demonstration of the size and strength of his following despite the obstacles thrown in his way by the *sarki* and by Muslim scholars.

Missionary Martha Wall, in a published memoir calculated to spur recruitment and financial support for mission work, read the story in the context of SIM's encounters with Islam in the broader region, including Nigeria. She emphasized what a coup it would have been to succeed in building a church within the walls of a Muslim town: "All of us were well aware of the fact that in the Moslem North no permit for a Christian church within city limits had ever yet been granted. Still, Tsibiri was not nearly so fanatically Moslem as Kano or Katsina, south of us, Zinder, to the east nor . . . Madaoua to the west" (Wall 1960, 228). According to Wall, when the town was moved from the river valley to its current site on the dune (a colonial effort at malaria eradication and flood management that was forced upon the local population), Osborne saw the opportunity to attempt to integrate the construction of a church into the development of the new town.

According to Wall, when the French administrator in Tsibiri found that the *sarki* and the *malamai* were opposed to a church, he summarily denied the mission permission to begin construction: "Satan had scored a definite victory but he had also played into the hands of a God who could turn such a defeat into a challenge for far greater exploit" (1960, 228). It is at this point in the account that Musa, "an older Christian of a royal lineage, and shrewd in native diplomatic matters as his patriarchal namesake, Moses," approached Osborne to say that he had staked out a large compound in the new town and would be willing to build a large *zaure* (an entry hall to a traditionally constructed compound that is often used by Muslim scholars as classroom space) for meetings in the town. Wall's narrative obscures the reality that the *sarki* and the *malamai* were opposed to the church precisely because it was the means through which the Marafa line was building a conspicuous following. Wall's narrative sees the hand of God in motivating "the believers to cease to lean on the missionaries for money, plans, and initiative" (228). Beyond contributing the land and reporting on the activities of Muslims, Musa Marafa then fades as a central figure in Wall's narrative.

For her, this is an epic struggle between Satan and God, and therefore a protracted description of every stage of construction is called for, culminating with a crisis over the roof. Within her narrative, the Muslims offer gifts of animals to the *malamai* in exchange for the making of "medicine that the rains [should] destroy our church" (Wall 1960, 232) before the roof could be built to protect the fragile mud construction. Christian prayers to withhold the rain were successful. According to Wall, it was only after the roof was finished and Ray de la Haye stood on it to give a prayer of thanks to God that the rains finally came to Tsibiri (233–234). When Rita Salls recounted the story, she added that the Christians came to Ray de la Haye the next day, infuriated because the rains had been too strong and had partly damaged the new roof. Why, they asked, did he tell the Lord to make it rain so hard? (Rita Salls interview).

It is interesting that this tale of prayer and rain-making does not make its way into any of the stories I collected from Christian converts. Many of the early converts, as I have suggested, were members of aristocratic families who would not normally have engaged directly in farm work themselves. For them, this is a story about being recognized as full and equal citizens with legitimate authority and autonomy within a rational regime of law, not a miraculous story of God's triumph over Satan in a primitive spiritual economy preoccupied with control of the rains. And in their versions of the story, both the French colonial administrators and their Muslim neighbors come to see the rationality of their request. Vigilance, hard work, and skill in disputation are what succeed in making the first church possible. Miraculous interventions, particularly those overseen by missionary prayer, were not called for and were not necessary to move the Christian community to take initiative on its own. The differences between the various versions of this stock tale offer an interesting glimpse into the different key players and the unrecognized centrality of Musa Marafa in the life of the church, despite the efforts of both elders and missionaries to shift the agency elsewhere.

The unwillingness of SIM missionaries to recognize Marafa as a leader in the indigenous church eventually led to an irreparable rupture between him and the mission. That the mission could make a decision that was so unpopular—that it could assume that it alone had the right to decide who would be a leader and could override the preferences of the oldest converts in the community—suggests that it was already quite disturbed by the power Marafa had within the church well before he entered formal political politics. When party politics began to emerge in Niger after 1946, Musa Marafa gradually transformed his client base into a political following within Tsibiri's Parti Progressiste Nigérien (PPN), which he led from 1959 to 1962. In an interview with Pearl Robinson in 1973 he recalled, "When I started in the PPN all my *barwaye* [clients] became (PPN). . . . At that time, they followed what I said. Each *barwaye* had the right to vote. And if there is a bond between two people, they are always going to walk together" (Robinson 1983, 113). Marafa combined his client base, the Christian community, and local PPN supporters in an attempt to build a political base "as an advocate for the commoners against Sarkin Labo and his retinue of traditional officeholders. During the years that Moussa headed Tsibiri's PPN party, the population became polarized into two mutually exclusive competitive groups. As one resident of Tsibiri explained, 'If you went to Moussa Marafa's compound, you did not go to the Sarki's palace'" (117).[13] Marafa's following under a populist banner became one major camp within Tsibiri, while *sarauta* class members loyal to Sarkin Labo made up another camp.

The anti-aristocratic and antimaterialist teachings of the mission may have shaped the particular political positions Marafa took, despite his negative experience within the church. I don't think that it is necessary to assume that Musa Marafa was cynically using Christianity or that he abandoned his major moral orientations in pursuit of party politics. Where he differed from the missionaries was in his sense that it was important to engage politically and that it was appropriate for Christians to do so. Rather than wait for God to remedy social inequalities, he was prepared to use the political arena. Unfortunately for his political aspirations, the populist approach he took, which defended the rights of commoners and eschewed political office, was difficult to reconcile with the broader orientation of the PPN, and Sarkin Labo succeeded in having him removed as the head of the party in Tsibiri in 1962 (Robinson 1983, 118).

The ever-widening rupture between the mission and Musa Marafa was never healed. Missionaries I interviewed were disapproving of the political activities of "one of our early Christians" and his name falls out of the official narrative of the development of the church altogether, despite the fact that some members of his broader household, Jadi Marafa in particular, continued as important members of the community. The fragmentation within the *sarauta* class over the populist strategy Marafa chose also meant that he would not be remembered fondly by all of the Christians, some of whom were members of the *sarauta* class he attacked as what Paul Robinson terms "an antitraditionalist crusader" (Robinson 1983, 117). I was told by members of his family that he eventually took a second wife and left the church altogether. In the wake of the rupture with the mission, many of his clients and followers, particularly those of the *sarauta* class, gradually left the church as well.

Disciplinary Inscription and the Work of God

There was, it seems to me, an intimate connection between the need to keep church records and the development of church discipline. The first record of a meeting of the Tsibiri church, dated June 4, 1933, begins:

> The church met on Sunday, June 4th in the morning after the preaching was finished. Malam [Osborne] said that he was not happy about what he was about to say, but it was necessary. He said that two Christians would speak for themselves. Then he called Audu to speak. Audu said that he had stolen from Madame [Osborne] on several occasions, but he was unhappy and was no longer able to pray as in the past. Yesterday Allah opened a way for him to declare his mistake. He knew he had sinned, but how he begged the entire church forgiveness, both black people and white, because he knew that as a result of his action he had brought shame upon the entire church.[14]

What emerges in the surrounding documents is that Audu and Nanaya, both of whom worked for the mission as servants, had begun evangelizing in villages in the afternoons instead of working at the mission. In order to engage in this evangelism they had to reduce the number of hours they could work for the mission. In effect, they lost money by devoting their energies to "God's work," the kind of work in which the missionaries engaged. As the missionaries' notes for the year's events elaborate: "From January to May Nanaya and Audu had been willing to accept less work and consequently less wages in order that they might have the opportunity to go out to the villages and preach each afternoon. This they did faithfully five days each week. Despite this they are now both hindered from it because of sin."[15]

A reading between the lines suggests that the mission was unwilling to pay such young men to engage in evangelism; it was willing to pay them only for the menial tasks the missionaries themselves did not wish to do. But evangelical theology saw evangelism as the highest form of labor and stressed the urgent need for such work. Young mission employees found it difficult to reconcile these rather dissonant messages and chose to recompense themselves for their evangelical "work" through pilfering from the missionaries. This expectation on the part of the mission that the most devoted converts should perform the work of evangelism without pay generated a pattern of pilfering that would be repeated over and over in various forms, feeding resentment on the part of the most zealous of Christians and mistrust on the part of the missionaries. If there was a single refrain that carried through all the interviews I conducted among early male leaders of the church, it was the complaint that it made no sense for the missionaries to be "paid" to evangelize when the Christian converts were not. If there was a single stereotype of "Africans" that characterized most pre-independence missionary documents and narratives, it was the notion that Africans had no real understanding of private property and were particularly prone to theft. The conceptual gap between these two ways of reading events in the community is rather striking.

The records of the church emerge in just such a moment of mutual misunderstanding: in order to clear the church of the shame brought upon it by its most devoted members, a period of exile and a public act of contrition was required. Audu ended up losing his job with the mission and was "sent out of the country," presumably because his presence was an unwelcome reminder that the most zealous preachers from among the Christians were unable to live up to the expectations of the missionaries. The "shame upon the church" was precisely this—that those who were most devoted to evangelism were also the very men whose private behavior seemed to call the higher moral claims of Christians into question. The other young man was permitted to endure his *horo* and return to the church. The community as a whole was exhorted to keep quiet about the affair; this was not something for the Muslims to know about. The church records came into being at this moment because they were needed to keep track of how long the *horo* had been and when it would be completed.

Nanaya's trajectory after this moment of discipline is suggestive of what happened to Christian men who could not establish themselves successfully within the mission's rigid logic of work and marriage. Notes in a letter from the Osbornes in 1937 report that "he took a second wife, says the Moslem prayers, and gives no outward evidence of being a christian [sic]. The Moslems glory in this situation frequently stating his case as proof of the superiority of Islam over Christianity. The love of money and worldly companionships have largely been the cause of his downfall."[16] A man with real drive to succeed and ambition to lead could not easily achieve his goals within the Christian community unless he was willing either to settle for servile status relative to the missionaries or perform significant labor for free. Once a man decided that neither of these conditions was tolerable, there was little to prevent him from making his mark within the Muslim community instead. "Backsliders" from among the Christians as a rule went on to become prominent men in an Islamic idiom, taking multiple wives (Isaka, the chief's son, took four) and engaging in public Muslim prayer.

Thus, the labor of preaching was very much at the heart of struggles between the mission and its protégés. Church records bring to light one rather important dimension of the postwar expansion into medical work that is completely neglected in the writings of the missionaries. The utility of such work for the mission was entirely a function of the potential to preach to patients in the waiting rooms of such facilities on a daily basis. Given the very slow growth of the church in Tsibiri, this rate of exposure to and preliminary interest in Christian ideas represented an acceleration of the mission's reach. At the Tsibiri dispensary, this critical labor—the work of preaching to patients—was left almost entirely in the hands of the local church. In other words, the labor of evangelizing to medical patients fell entirely to local Christians instead of to the missionaries, who were compensated for their work in the field. Records of meetings of the church as a whole and of church elders make it clear that preaching was considered a privilege and that the uncompensated labor of preaching at the dispensary was distributed in a rather ad hoc way among the men who were prominent in the church as elders or were students in the mission's Bible schools. When individuals were to be punished for transgressions, one key privilege that was taken away was the right to preach, to do wa'azi. Little wonder that preaching occurred on average only three times a week in 1945—the missionaries had little control over this highly effective but entirely voluntary labor force (Osborne 1945). The missionaries could determine who would have the privilege of preaching, but they could not guarantee that such unpaid preachers would actually take advantage of the privilege on any given day.

Why would local African Christians compete to volunteer their time to preach in the local dispensary? Missionaries continued to dominate the church community in Tsibiri even after the church in town was built. Elders were permitted to preach one Sunday per month—a coveted moment of public prominence and recognition for which individuals (all men) competed. Preaching to the church membership did not represent the highest calling of the evangelical Christian, however—reaching the "unsaved" occupied that lofty space. The dispensary opened another stage for public wa'azi, one that was slightly less controlled by missionaries and offered opportunities for up to six men a week to preach. The dispensary and other medical sites that emerged later offered access to an audience that was the equivalent of the audience of the white male missionary who was crusading to reach the unsaved. In such a moment the African evangelists were equal to their missionary counterparts without having to leave home. Indeed, they were superior to those white women missionaries whose medical work and limited language skills often prevented them from preaching themselves—in the rosters I have found of dispensary preachers the nurse was listed as a preacher only once. But they did not receive pay and therefore could only take advantage of these opportunities if other work obligations did not interfere.

Early converts were therefore eager to contribute to Christian expansion through preaching but suffered from a certain lack of parity in the understanding of their "work" relative to the work of the missionaries. Missionaries made preaching a life's mission; mission work became their livelihood, their vocation. Their furloughs were largely devoted to raising the funds necessary to continue such work in the field. To converts, however, a reasonable interpretation was that missionaries were "paid" to preach while they themselves were not. Furthermore, converts might be excluded from preaching for sinful behavior and then be paid to do construction work by the same missionaries who were pressing the Church Elders Council to place them in horo. This struck them as odd. Were not preaching and construction both work? Odder still was the fact that they might find themselves competing with Muslims for wage work.[17] If the work of preaching was sacred and reserved for Christians, perhaps all work that contributed to the life of the mission should fall into that category as well.

Fostering a Church: Dedicating Children to Christian Life

The very first moment of horo in the church records raised this interesting problem of the "work of God" and its compensation, but another early instance of horo in the church records sheds light on the importance the mission placed on children in the future growth of the church. Disqualifying women from leadership roles did not mean that they became irrelevant to either the mission or the church. Indeed, determining what to do about wives and their children was a central concern of the early church. Converting adults from Islam to Christianity proved to be extraordinarily difficult—missionaries found that those adults to whom they had access were very resistant to Christianity. Very few adults appear in the lists of early professing Christians—Musa Marafa of Tsibiri and Abba Musa of Zinder are exceptions to the general pattern rather than exemplars of Christian conversion, despite their prominence in mission lore. The earliest converts were generally quite young men—even Musa Marafa was twenty-two when he first converted, meaning that in local parlance he was still a "boy," or a *yaro*. Most, however, were unmarried teenagers who had no prospects for marriage yet.[18]

In order to continue to grow, the church had to seize upon every available opportunity to train youth and children in Christian belief and practice. Small children and infants became coveted targets of missionary attention, and very early on a key test of a male convert's maturity as a Christian became his willingness to commit his own children to a Christian life. The local practice of naming a newborn child after seven days according to a nominally Muslim rite in which a Muslim scholar was to choose a name from the Koran at random—a ceremony known as *zanen suna*—became a battleground over whether and how to dedicate children to a Christian life. The *zanen suna* is a very important part of social life in the Maradi region—through it a man publicly recognizes a child as legitimate, enjoins kin and neighbors to celebrate its birth, and marks himself and his wife as successful producers of children. While the *biki*, or celebration, is understood by most in the region to be Muslim—through it a child receives his or her "official" (but generally little-used) Muslim name—local practices bear many marks of pre-Islamic practice. The *biki* entails the sacrifice of a ram (which is slaughtered by a Muslim butcher) and a variety of arcane practices that reformist Muslims today find highly objectionable, such as having the birth mother step over the sacrificed ram four times for a girl child and three times for a boy child. Such ritual surrounding the sacrifice of an animal calls into question traditionalist Muslim claims that the animal is a form of alms (*sadaka*) rather than pagan sacrifice to appease powerful local spirits (*sabi*).[19] Various superstitions Muslim women attach to the ceremony suggest to me that women understand the *biki* to "tie up" dangerous spirits that might endanger the child and the mother—it is this ritual closure that is central to the *biki*, not simply the act of naming. Local Maradi women almost never utter the Muslim name of a child—the name's potency opens up a vulnerability in the child that can be exploited by anyone who is jealous and hopes to harm the mother or child. Mothers almost always refer to their children through affectionate descriptive nicknames that capture the spirit of the moment when the child was born. Thus, to choose a particularly relevant example, many girl children in Maradi are named "Maday" because a woman missionary or a government nurse (a "Madame") helped deliver the child. The *bikin suna* also situates newly born individuals relative to competing social groups in the region. Until the mid-1950s or so, a baby also received scarification markings that identified his or her clan and ethnic affiliations at this ceremony.

One can understand why such a socially and spiritually complex ritual might become critical to struggles among Christians to control behavior within the Christian community. Wouldn't the best practice simply be to forbid it? Interestingly, however, missionaries did not forbid the celebration of *bikin suna*—what they gradually encouraged was the Christianization of the rite so that at first missionaries and later Christian pastors oversaw the event. Thus, Musa Marafa earned early approbation for having "the white *malam*" name his son "Daniel" in an improvised dedication ceremony.[20] The mission seized upon the ritual as a moment to force men to commit their children to the church in the future—in effect claiming the child in advance for the Christian community. But this reinterpretation of the *bikin suna* undercut the crucial notion that committing to Christ was an individual choice.

The ritual eventually served to publicly stage some of the differences between Christian belief and surrounding religious practices. The role of destiny or chance in naming the child was eliminated—by 1945, the church had determined that the family would choose a name from the Bible because of its significance in the scriptures.[21] The *biki* became an occasion to preach from passages in the Bible that explained the child's name and commit the child to a Christian life worthy of that name. Finally, to demonstrate the lack of fear concerning the evil eye, Christians today publicly display the child in the doorway of the home of the parents and pronounce the name of the child out loud. The complex and ideologically slippery practice of slaughtering a ram was debated—Osborne put it on the agenda of an Church Elders Council meeting in 1946—but in the end the council determined that the attraction that meat distribution presented to kin, neighbors, and friends and its festive connotations made the ram an integral part of any *bikin suna*. It decided that Christians were not to permit a Muslim to slaughter the animal and were to emphasize that the slaughter was done for the pleasure of it (*don wasa*), not a form of sacrifice.[22] Having made such an argument about the nature of their own rams, Christian converts could hardly object to the meat distribution of their Muslim kin and neighbors. Despite the reservations of missionaries, church elders insisted that there was no sin in attending the naming ceremonies of Muslims.[23] Both missionaries and church elders micromanaged the matter of *bikin suna;* they were ever vigilant in case it should slip toward Islam or idolatry. One unfortunate Christian claimed to be the Malamin Almasihu (the Malam of the Savior), evidently attempting to carve out a niche for himself as the Christian counterpart of Muslim *malams* who are paid to oversee *bikin suna*. He named the child of a church member "Issa" (the Muslim name for Jesus), provoking such ire among the elders that he was placed in discipline. It was not appropriate, they opined, to name a child Jesus or Emmanuel in the way that Muslims name their children Mohammed.[24] This attempt to create a class of Christian *malamai* who would serve as paid specialists performing *bikin suna* for Christians was thus quickly squelched by the Church Elders Council.

This struggle over the *bikin suna* is interesting partly because many of the missionaries who joined SIM did not come from denominations that emphasized infant baptism. In evangelical Protestantism, the centrality of an individual public commitment to Christ as savior means that infant baptism verges upon heresy, and within Protestantism more broadly the status and meaning of infant baptism has been hotly debated. Within the Christian context of the United States, the notion of an individual's choice to be "reborn" is perhaps easier to reconcile with a rejection of infant baptism, since Christian models and ideas are readily available to most children in that setting without the dedication of the child to Christianity and a Christian upbringing through infant baptism. However, in a preemptive attempt to lay claim to the attentions of impressionable children before they become inculcated with Islam, the mission sacrificed the emphasis upon individual choice and commitment to Christ as it might have been understood in the sending countries of the missionaries. The mission went to great lengths to stake a claim to children who were young enough to be socialized into Christianity.

Horo was one weapon in this war to gain control of children. One of the earliest records of *horo* I can find for the Tsibiri community occurred in 1934, when the quarterly report for October to December notes,

"During this quarter we had to discipline another of the young Christian workers. Nanaya let Malams 'christen his first born child' and will be under discipline until Mr. Osborne's return."[25] In other words, as early as 1934 male members of the church were expected to deliver their children to the mission for upbringing. There is no discussion in any of the incidents I found in the church records of any recognition that the mother of the child might have some say in this issue. The mission in effect co-opted the paternal pattern in local practice, which held that a man could dispose of small children as he wished, particularly once they were weaned. Rather than support the notion that a mother should have control over the disposition of her children, regardless of her civil status as Christian or Muslim, the mission chose to support the principle of absolute patriarchal authority for its own ends.

The mission came to raise small children through a variety of means. One of the most important was the dedication of a child by converted men. In ordinary evangelical usage, the "dedication of a child" would simply imply that the parents had made a public declaration of their intention to raise the child in a Christian way. However, this public declaration took on a new meaning in this context of missionization in Niger. Christian men, whose wives might not be Christian, were expected to "dedicate" their children to the church, implying that the child (particularly if it was a girl) would be given to the missionaries at some point in the future to be raised in a proper Christian environment in a residential girls' home or boys' home. Missionaries made special requests of their prayer partners to pray that more such children would make their way into mission hands. In the case of the following request, the emphasis was upon access to impressionable girl children to shape them into brides for the young male converts now reaching the age of marriage:

> We thank the Lord for each of these little ones who are being taught in the Christian life at this early, impressionable age. In a special way do we feel the need for girls to be brought up under christian [sic] teaching in order that they may be the help to their future husbands which they ought to be. We want you to pray with us that the Lord will continue to send us girls, that they may help in the furtherance of the Gospel, after they have come to know the way of salvation.[26]

The exhortation to turn children over to the mission was so powerful that by 1945 church elders were asked to ponder whether it was appropriate to have church members dedicate their children to the church on the same day that they brought their semi-obligatory tithe, known in Hausa as *zakka*.[27] The elders determined that it might be better to separate the two "gifts"—the dedication of children would occur shortly after Christmas instead.[28] But the slippage toward objectifying children is rather striking here.

Fostering out one of one's children in the home of Muslim kin was one of the biggest sins within the Christian community. The mission insisted that children must be raised in a Christian environment. Yet local understandings of family and kinship encouraged the practice of sharing children with kin who were less fortunate in producing children. First-born children, in particular, were until quite recently often "given" to female kin of the father to raise as their own, both as a sign of respect and as a way to share the wealth of children—in much the same fashion that the chief's son, Isaka, was "given" to the mission. Patriarchy did not mean that some women did not benefit from the practice of fostering—they did, but they received foster children as a result of their influence on their male kin. Such children are known as *'yan ri'ko*, and girl children in particular are coveted by a man's female kin and wives to help with the tasks that fall to women—cooking, getting water and wood, minding infants, washing clothing and peddling cooked foods.

By the late 1940s, the missionaries and the church had begun to shun Christian men who shared their children. Reclaiming such children from relatives was extremely difficult and costly in social terms; the competing demands of mission and family for children led to serious ruptures between such men and the church on the one hand and between them and their non-Christian kin on the other.[29] It is worth noting, however, that there was no stigma about *receiving* children into a Christian house as *'yan ri'ko*. It was seen as a particularly virtuous act to bring pagan and Muslim children into the mission or Christian households to socialize them to Christian life. Here one sees the beginnings of a pattern of lack of reciprocity between Christians and Muslims that was to become a mark of intercommunal relations in the region.

But missionaries believed that even raising girl children in the homes of Christian men was risky, for such children would be subject to the influence of marginally Christian wives and superstitious grandmothers—the women who were so carefully excluded from church leadership. When the first generation of male converts had girl children, they were expected to turn them over to the mission to be raised and trained into Christian womanhood at the Soura girls' school, which was established in the early 1950s. When one male Bible school student failed to deliver his daughters to the new school he was told he would not be permitted to continue his own schooling unless he turned his newborn daughter over to the female missionaries at the school.[30] The level of coercion the mission was willing to invoke through the vehicle of *horo* and community pressure in order to foster children itself was quite striking, and it led to considerable bitterness among enlightened Christian men who did not see the value of the improvised girls' school and its domestic training curriculum. Some men suffered through humiliating *horo* because they had the temerity to send their daughters to the French-language public school instead.

The pattern that informs the mission's attitudes toward introducing new members to a household and taking members out of a household can be reduced to one precept: non-Christians are to be treated as an unwelcome contagion. A lone Christian male was not sufficiently strong to guard against the dangers of the Muslim or pagan women in his home. Therefore children should be taken out of such households. By the same logic, a young man who hopes to marry should not entertain marriage to a non-Christian woman. The children of such a union would be exposed to dangerous non-Christian contagion and their souls would be lost. The young man's marriage could not be "Christian" if his wife was not Christian. Therefore, Christian men could marry only Christian women if they wanted to remain part of the church. Because very few women and girls were attracted to the mission in the early years, it is not surprising that a severe demographic impasse resulted from this rigid logic. Young men could not marry at all, for there were no Christian brides.

It is worth underscoring how different this conception of conversion is from an understanding typical of most Muslim societies. Islamic expansion has often been enhanced by a far more relaxed attitude toward marriage and what constitutes a "good" Muslim household. Islam has regularly absorbed non-Muslim populations through marriage and concubinage. When non-Muslim women are brought into a household, so the reasoning goes, they will be exposed to their husband's superior understanding of God and will gradually learn proper religious practice from his sisters and mother (see e.g. Mack and Boyd 2000). A young Muslim man need face no impediment to marriage, therefore, for his own grasp of Islam and his mastery of the women of the household was understood to be sufficient to render the entire family Islamic. Muslims in Maradi would be as wary of fostering their children out into non-Muslim households as Christians were, but the presence of an adult Muslim male in the household was considered sufficient to guarantee that the children would be raised in an appropriate manner. There was no need to take the children out of the home because the mother was not fully Muslim. Whether reformist Muslims today would still acquiesce to this relatively tolerant logic is an interesting question. Reformist Muslim men are not shy about wooing Christian women in order to attract them back into the fold of the *umma*.

The Tsibiri church records reveal that many of the young men who converted early to Christianity suffered the consequences of this rigid conception of family and marriage for many years. Inevitably some were punished for "immorality" (presumably visiting prostitutes or divorced women) before eventually determining that if they were to marry they would have to take a Muslim bride. As soon as the church learned of any such engagement, the young men would be placed in *horo*.[31] Men who took non-Christian brides could not return to the church until their wives professed as Christians, and one hesitates to consider such a profession entirely "free" under the circumstances. In one instance in the early church in Zinder, the first "native Christian wedding" was not, as the disappointed missionary in charge hinted, entirely "Christian" in the evangelical sense. When the groom Abdullah chose a non-Christian woman, Zainu, as his bride, the missionaries told him that they would not marry them until she was a believer: "He got her to make a profession of faith in Christ, but she later admitted to us that she had only done it because she wanted to marry him."[32] Although some women were brought into the community in this manner, a steady trickle of formerly devoted men was lost to the church altogether when their wives or fiancées refused to convert. Such men abandoned Christianity, and some of them took several wives and established themselves as much-celebrated prodigal sons who had returned to the Muslim fold.

Regulating Women, Regulating Marriage

Attempts to gain access to children to socialize them early into Christianity ran parallel to efforts to regulate women's behavior in marriage. The mission had little leverage, given the very few women in the church at this point, so there seems to have been little impulse to actually discipline women who ran up against the mission's understanding of what was appropriate. But the Elder's Council was enjoined to begin defining Christian marriage. It decided that Christians should not marry too young. A young man should be eighteen and a young Christian woman should be seventeen at marriage.[33] Christians should choose partners for themselves. At this point, the clarity of the deliberations began to crumble, for a young man did not really have the right to choose a non-Christian bride. If his bride was not a Christian, the elders decided, he must draw her to the church and marry her only after she became a believer.

By June of 1945, it was clear to the elders that they needed to think things through further. The council decided that Christian women should not be secluded, as Muslim women in the region often were. The need to debate the issue suggests that at least some Christian men who had converted as married adults *did* keep their wives in seclusion. Seclusion, the council reasoned, was a "stumbling block" for women, for it would lead women to think that they were not trusted and that might lead them into "the trap of obsession," *tarkon jaraba*. The obliqueness of the council's language is intriguing: were women imagined to be likely to become obsessed with the desire for freedom? autonomy? sex with the men they never saw? The entire debate occurred in the absence of any female input—one suspects that the men's wives would have found some of this debate rather amusing. More pragmatically, though, the issue was about evangelism. Christian women were needed to evangelize to Muslim women in seclusion. The only way to reach such women, it turned out, was to have Christian women go to them.

Among the agenda items the elders did agree with the mission about was the question of *shan kunu*, the practice whereby a young bride went home to live with her kin to give birth to her child and remained there for many months to "drink milk," sometimes until the child was weaned at about two years of age. The elders found this practice to be a trap for men, something that "frequently leads to the destruction of a marriage."[34] The sense seemed to be that men would be tempted to have sex with other women if they did not have access to their wives. The local practice of abstinence until a child was weaned was therefore under direct assault both by the mission and by the elders of the church. A husband's sexual prerogatives were to be protected and the "unnatural" practice of abstinence brought to an end (cf. Hunt 1997). Of course, such abstinence is far easier to maintain if a household is polygynous. Therefore the fixation of both the mission and the elders on *shan kunu* resulted from concerns about the sustainability of monogamy under local practices about childrearing and birth spacing.

Osborne reported with some pleasure after a 1946 Christian wedding ceremony that the event provided the occasion for him to preach against four native customs:

1. A Christian does *not* "lock up" his wife.
2. At the birth of the first child the wife does *not* return to her mother's home until the child is a year or more old.
3. Christians do *not* give their children to relatives to bring up, but bring up their own children in the fear and admonition of the Lord.
4. The Christian wife does *not* leave her husband's home and return to her relatives after a quarrel.[35]

If in some ways the mission and the elders seemed to be joining forces to protect women from seclusion, the larger implications of their understanding of marriage as creating a conjugal unit that was cut off from a woman's family were potentially disempowering to women as wives. If a woman could not go home to her family to give birth or to put pressure on her husband when she was unhappy with her marriage, she had little or no leverage with which to prompt change and no control over birth spacing. Hausa women regularly turn to their kin for help in forwarding their interests in their marriages, for assistance in learning how to raise small children, and for spatial distance from the sexual demands of their husbands. A woman who chose to persist in such customs was not a Christian, according to Osborne and, to a lesser degree, the elders. Given the insistence upon the authority of husbands within evangelical Christianity, this left women with very little room to maneuver within their marriages. Divorce was so thoroughly rejected within this community that effectively a Christian wife had no recourse but to suffer her husband's ill-treatment in silence.

Other records show a consistent bias on the part of both the mission and the elders against customs that were advantageous to or simply pleasurable for women. At the 1954 regional missionary conference Pastor 'dan Nana was asked to report to regional mission authorities on a number of practices that missionaries in Niger found troubling. First among them was the drumming at weddings that was so popular among women young and old as an occasion to dance and flirt. 'Dan Nana was of the opinion that no real Christian would ever be a drummer, that this was not a suitable profession for any respectable person, whether Muslim or Christian. He felt that the drumming for young women and men at night was evil and should be eliminated—the suggestion seemed to be that it led to sexual impropriety. But drumming in the day for the bridegroom was acceptable, 'dan Nana said. The presence of a bride's girlfriends in the new home during the first week of marriage was also to be eliminated: "These friends live with the bride thus preventing her from living with her husband. They encourage evil thoughts in the mind of the bride and impose upon the hospitality of the home." But the practice of a groom's friends carrying him off to a male friend's house for a stay of several days "is considered harmless." Young men should no longer undergo the "washing of the groom" because of "evil words used in the ceremony." No women were consulted about what these practices might mean or what the loss to women would be in curtailing them.[36] The overall effect of the wholesale adoption of 'dan Nana's recommendations was to reduce the emotional and social bonds women reinforced at weddings and to rob the ceremony of much of its local symbolic content.

One side effect of the fact that the mission operated on both sides of the Niger-Nigeria border was that as missionaries crossed from one setting to the other, they picked up on variations in practice. Somehow practices "in the south" were always deemed to be superior to those in Maradi, with the unfortunate consequence that the highly conservative Islamic context of northern Nigeria had a tendency to be overlaid onto Christian practice in Niger. Thus, women were told by the Elders that Christian women should not paint the black marks known as *katambiri* on their faces or stain their teeth with tobacco leaves. The missionaries at the Tsibiri station also hoped to eliminate the practice among women of wearing bands of beads below the knee, known as *shege ka zo gona*, but here the council demurred. "Other decorations" beyond *katambiri* and tobacco stains, they averred, "are harmless."[37] The outward appearance of the Christian community was to be shaped through the control of women—no similar restrictions on male dress were to appear in the church records.

However, the single most striking issue the Tsibiri missionaries and the council oversaw that had implications for women was the policy concerning polygyny. A man who professed Christianity could become a full member of the community and take communion only through baptism. Only baptized men could become elders. But the elders would not approve the baptism of any man who had more than one wife. For men who had two wives at the moment of their profession of faith, this created an excruciating dilemma. In order to be "Christian," they had to divorce one of their wives; in principle, the second wife. This was a rather cruel requirement—the women themselves had no say over the status of marriages that were sometimes of long duration and relatively happy, marriages that had produced children and provided all parties with security and social standing. It is worth noting that a man's first wife is often a woman he has married to please his parents. It is his second and third wives that he marries for love. Sometimes later wives are married at the urging of a first wife who is lonely or would like more help running a complex and demanding household. It is not at all clear that it was a kindness to women to insist on monogamy under such circumstances. But in order to be full members of the church and to aspire to any kind of leadership within the church, men had to shed their second and subsequent wives. Here the right of women to choose their partners and the composition of their households was entirely eclipsed by the imperative of monogamy. The tale of Naino, which appeared in *The Sudan Witness*, is instructive in this regard:

> [Naino is] the eldest son of a member of the chief's family. His old father is a strict Moslem and has opposed his son's desire to follow Christ for years. Naino was a polygamist. He desired baptism long ago but the question of this second wife seemed insurmountable. He told her that in the new way of Christ which he was now following a man had only one wife, and he wished her to leave. She refused, knowing he was good to her. Finally, he removed the roof of her hut and told her she must go. His father meanwhile did all in his power to encourage her to remain. Finally Naino had no recourse but to take his first wife and children and move to another district, leaving the second wife. Not long after this she was married to another. Today Naino has a clear-cut testimony and is one of our brightest Christians. He has come through a time of serious testing and his faith and courage have been good throughout. (Osborne 1950, 2)

The unnamed second wife appears in the narrative only as an obstacle to conversion. Her remarriage after his departure—abandonment, one is tempted to say—is recounted in passive voice. She was not, evidently, given much choice in this issue of remarriage. The unilateral right of Muslim men to divorce their wives seems to have become a template for Christian men; they abandoned their second and third wives in a similarly unilateral fashion. The emotional or moral impact of this practice on the women is never discussed in mission publications such as *The Sudan Witness*.

In a similarly chilling narrative of shedding inconvenient second wives, we hear the tale of "pilgrim," a man who was exposed to Christianity at a mission hospital in Nigeria during his pilgrimage to Mecca. The man was moved to name one of his children through a Christian *bikin suna*, but the child died, "and the neighbors think it's because of the infidel's gospel." Although the narrative does not state it directly, the child seems to have been the offspring of his second wife; it was not until that child died that the man determines that the time had come to "release" his second wife. Relatives of the man's first wife were outraged at his conversion and took her away from him as well. After a period of ostracism his life improved: his first wife returned, her relatives became reconciled to his Christianity, and he became a full Christian (de la Haye 1953).

The delicacy with which this act of rejection is described in missionary writings is notable—the word "divorce" never appears. The wife is rather "released" or persuaded to recognize that in Christianity there is no such thing as a second wife. The legal status of such women is well worth pondering. Is she "really" divorced if, in her social setting, a divorce is something that is generally publicly recognized by Muslim scholars as a result of three statements by her husband repudiating her? Such women were left in a strange legal limbo. Was such a woman "really" divorced if there was no recognition of the divorce in civil society? How different is this "release" from the cavalier divorce Muslim men engaged in that the mission decried? And—and this is important—who has rights over any children the couple may have produced? In Maliki Islam, the *Christian* father would not have any rights over the children, but given the novelty and ambiguity of the situation, it is extremely unlikely that any of the men's wives were aware of this legal technicality. Somewhat out of keeping with Maliki law, ex-husbands in this region generally have a great deal of control over their children. It is likely that rejected wives simply assumed that in this case, as in others, the father had indisputable rights over the children. In this setting, the woman usually had custody of the children until they were weaned and a divorced woman could generally hope to retain girl children longer, sometimes until they were married. But given the desire of the Christians to claim as many children as possible to be raised by the mission, such a woman would need a great deal of support from her kin to protect herself from the loss of her children. The mission's impulse to take advantage of her vulnerable status as a single woman and urge her Christian husband to claim her children as "orphans" for it to raise would have been quite considerable.

The precise parentage of the children who made their way into the mission's boys' and girls' homes was rarely made clear, no doubt because their status as children of second and third wives was an embarrassment. Some of the children were "given" to the mission by parents who knew they were too ill or sickly to survive in their birth homes. However, it is striking that so many of the children who made their way to the boys' and girls' homes were the objects of a great deal of conflict. Although the mission and Christian men chose to refer to them as "orphans," they were rarely entirely lacking in kin. The tale of a student of the Soura girls' school named Mantai is instructive. She was entrusted to the mission by her Christian father before he died, and when she reached age fourteen in the late 1950s she was engaged to a young Christian man. Her Muslim mother reappeared before the wedding to reclaim her— ordinarily a Hausa bride is "given away" by her mother as much as by her father. When Mantai refused to leave with her mother (ostensibly to visit a sister who had just given birth), the embittered birth mother cried, "Go back to your white people! Were they the ones who gave birth to you? You do not love! I am through with you! You are no longer my daughter! I curse you!" For a Hausa parent to curse a child is no small matter—an index of how deeply wounded this mother was at the alienation of her daughter and the complete elimination of traditional female social and cultural ties from her daughter's marriage arrangements.[38] For young women, conversion to Christianity often meant a break with the networks of female kin and friends that would normally protect and sustain them.

This isolation and social vulnerability probably contributed to the growing cost of marriage to Christian girls. It appears that from relatively early in the development of the Maradi community, the traditional *sadaki*, or bridewealth payment, from the groom's family to that of the bride to seal the marriage was higher than was typical for a Muslim girl, and the accompanying trousseau a groom was expected to provide was also relatively costly compared with that of a Muslim bride. If a girl had little social network to protect her once married, and if marriage within the Christian community was virtually irrevocable, then Christian men would have to pay a much higher price to earn a young woman's commitment to marriage. The mission clearly felt that these demands were extractive, and Osborne had the issue of *sadaki* placed on the agenda in 1945. The payments, he implied, were a "problem" that the council needed to address. The council replied diplomatically through the vehicle of the Elder's Council minutes that although brides should not be treated as objects of exchange, the presentation of a *sadaki* payment was a good thing. The elders commented that it might be appropriate to set such payments even higher as a sign of recognition of Christian women's worth.[39] The elders also felt that a token of engagement was desirable. In other words, local Christians had no interest in eliminating or reducing the traditional exchanges that accompanied a marriage, despite the mission's perception that these amounted to selling the bride. Both Christian men and women were aware that Christian brides were precious and should not be given away in marriage unless the groom was prepared to make a substantial monetary commitment to her and her family. The *sadaki* payment would customarily in this region be given to her father. Other gifts would be given to her mother, and the trousseau— often the most substantial expense—would go to the bride herself. When the girl had been separated from her kin and raised in a mission girls' home sometimes a missionary would stand in as the girl's parent, receiving the *sadaki* and providing the countergifts that would typically be given by the bride's family to the groom's. In such cases, most missionaries were uncomfortable keeping the *sadaki* and generally gave it to the new couple to start their household. Young Christian men today continue to bemoan the extraordinary difficulty of beginning a Christian household given the high cost of securing a Christian bride.

Clearly the mission's attitudes toward both divorce and child fostering were rather inconsistent, not to say opportunistic. Divorce in a marriage between two Christians was virtually forbidden. The records suggest that only very rarely and reluctantly did missionaries or pastors concede that a Christian marriage was not sustainable, usually when the wife ran away and simply refused to return to her Christian husband. Thus, husbands who needed a woman to anchor a Christian home might eventually be permitted to turn to divorce as a solution so that they could remarry. However, Christian wives were always expected to suffer through a flawed marriage to a Christian man. Women were occasionally given church discipline for leaving an intolerable marriage, even in cases of physical violence or the husband's infidelity.

This reality has led to a situation in which Christian women in Maradi today are very reluctant to discuss their marital problems with pastors and elders of the church.[40] The church had and has, evidently, no remedy other than womanly patience and resignation. One quite striking difference between Christian marriage and Muslim marriage in this region is that Muslim marriages are quite brittle and a woman is likely to go through several marriages in her lifetime (Cooper 1997a), whereas a Christian bride will have, in principal, only one chance at marital happiness. Reformist Muslims often share evangelical Christians' repugnance for the fragility of marriage in the region and their sense that traditional marriage patterns among Hausa-speaking Muslims in the past were deeply flawed. If brittle marriage meant that men could "release" their wives at will and neglect their children, it also meant that woman had some hope of escape from unhappy circumstances. Christian women in Maradi have the benefit of far more secure marriages, but they have almost no way to leave a marriage should it fail.

But the early records of the Tsibiri and Zinder communities suggest that a woman who converted to Christianity whose husband was Muslim was often encouraged to find a way to divorce her husband if she could contribute to the resolution of the demographic impasse within the Christian community. An unmarried woman who could be drawn toward the church was a potential Christian bride—so long as she was likely to marry a Christian, her divorce was not seen to be an ethical or spiritual problem. The following tale from *The Sudan Witness* offers an example of how this logic worked in 1939. Tamu, a girl child fostered into the household of a woman (her aunt), was precisely the sort of child the mission saw as an appropriate object of reclamation. As David Osborne tells the tale, Tamu was married against her will by the aunt to an older man with a steady income (a trucker) whom she did not love. She fell in love with a Christian man of modest means, and when she rebelled against the marriage, her avaricious aunt and kin would not support her:

> Finally, missionaries and a kindly disposed government administrator combined efforts to bring relief from these unbearable conditions. It was decided that the girl must be released from the man, and he at once must receive the 300 francs he had paid for her. This was the official's order. So far so good. But the avaricious aunt still held the girl in her power, and the administrator would take no further steps to free her. Now began a battle between the forces of evil and those of good. (Osborne 1939, 13)

Eventually the persuasions of the "good" missionaries won out against the supposedly avaricious aunt, and the girl was handed over to the missionaries to be "cared for and taught in the things of Christ." She eventually converted and married the "poor" Christian man: Jadi Marafa, the 19-year-old aristocratic son of Tashibka—hardly a poor man, although his prospects within his class were modest. He was, of course, one of the young men who was to become an "elder" six years later in 1945. Characteristically, the missionary narrative entirely effaced the *sarauta* origins of the "characters" in their tales of redemption and quietly withheld the likelihood that Tamu's father was a member of the Christian community who had "given" his daughter to one of his sisters.

Jadi Marafa's recollections of his marriage reveal a far more complex picture and suggest that either the mission did not understand the difference between betrothal and marriage or chose to simplify the story significantly for readers. In his retelling, it is not the aunt who is the foster mother, but rather Mrs. Osborne, who had been "given" a girl to raise. Without consulting with the girl's kin, she arranged for the child to be married to the mission's protégé, Jadi. While the girl Tamu was, in the mission's understanding, betrothed to Jadi, he was sent off to Zinder for a lengthy period of work there for the mission. The life of a native evangelist was of necessity itinerant, and such young men rarely had the money or time to return home. When Tamu's mother saw the kind of life her daughter was headed toward, she decided she would violate the engagement agreement of the Osbornes. She accepted the engagement tokens of another promising man, a Kanuri truck driver whose travels would earn him good money and who could be counted on to return regularly to his bride, who could remain in Tsibiri near her kin. This was not a sign of avarice but rather, even in Jadi's recounting, a reasonable and even loving response to the readily anticipated problems of Christian marriage. In order to regain his fiancée, Jadi would have to outdo the Kanuri man's token of 300 francs.

Madame Osborne took the matter to the *commandant*, arguing that the girl did not want to marry the Kanuri man, she wanted to marry Jadi. She told the *commandant* that if the girl was to be married to the Kanuri man then she herself would need to be reimbursed for the cost of raising the child—a sum far in excess of the 300 francs the truck driver had paid to the mother already. Ultimately this reasoning won the day, and because the mother could not pay back the mission she lost the right to determine who the girl would marry. The Kanuri trucker was given back his engagement token and Tamu and Jadi were married in the first public wedding in Tsibiri (Marafa interview). Note that the mission, in recounting the tale, made it appear that some distant and avaricious aunt was trying to claim the child, when Jadi himself regarded the woman as the "mother" of his wife. The mission version of the story emphasizes the purported rights of the daughter to choose her husband, but in doing so it erases the mother's rights over her child, who was only sixteen.

The mission's ambiguous relationship to divorce and women's rights is particularly clear in the case of Zainabu and Abdallah. The couple was among the early Christian couples in Zinder, but Abdallah eventually reverted to Islam. The missionaries of the time, mistakenly believing that if they had married the couple they could also pronounce a divorce, rather high-handedly declared Zainabu to be released from her marriage to her Muslim spouse. She was quickly encouraged to remarry, and in

1944 she and another Christian man, 'dan Tafi, were married. Unhappily for Zainabu, she had little satisfaction in this marriage either. 'Dan Tafi took a mistress in Maradi and carried on rather openly and expensively with this unofficial second wife. Zainabu, having enjoyed the benefits of divorce in her previous marriage, found to her dismay that so long as 'dan Tafi could convince the missionaries that he was simply a sinful Christian, divorce would not be a remedy. Indeed, it appears that legally she had never been officially divorced from her first marriage, since the mission had no authority to issue a divorce—a fact that everyone quietly ignored. While 'dan Tafi's infidelity was quickly attributed to Zainabu's failure to satisfy him sexually (presumably through adherence to local practices related to child spacing and weaning), her choice to move out of their home and move into a disreputable neighborhood was regarded as a far greater sin.[41] Unable to either divorce or remarry, with no supportive kin to live with, ostracized by her church, and with no real means of earning a living beyond courtesanship (*karuwanci*), Zainabu had little recourse but to eventually return to 'dan Tafi and what was clearly a remarkably unhappy home. Little wonder, then, that Christian women quickly learned that a very sizable wedding settlement, particularly a large trousseau, would be an absolute prerequisite for a woman's security and sense of well-being in marriage. At the very least it would prevent her husband from acquiring an expensive mistress in the short term.

The Fragmentation of the Evangelical Community

SIM's work in Niger expanded beyond the Maradi region throughout the late 1940s and 1950s, often into areas that, like Maradi, offered contact with villages in which Islam had had less influence than in Zinder. To the west of Maradi, the region surrounding Dogondoutchi was particularly promising in this regard, for the Mawri population of the region spoke Hausa as a first language but had never been integrated into the Islamicized city-state structures of the Habe kingdoms. Populations from this region, sometimes known as Arewa, were curious about both Christianity and Islam. The mission worked at a station in Dogondoutchi in 1945 and discovered quite quickly that it was much easier there to make contacts with women and young boys than in Tsibiri and Zinder.[42] Competition with the rapid expansion of Islam and with the Catholic mission in Dogondoutchi encouraged the mission to put its energies into education in this region. SIM established both a boys' home and a girls' home in Dogondoutchi. Children raised in these homes came to the mission through a variety of avenues: drought conditions sometimes prompted parents to offer their children to the mission, early converts in the region sometimes dedicated their children to the mission, medical workers at the mission station in Guesheme might encourage a desperate parent to entrust a sickly child to the mission, and parents looking for an education for their children before the state expanded educational options after independence sometimes entrusted their children to the mission. The girls trained at the girls' home were encouraged to convert to Christianity and sometimes married young men from the Maradi region (as was the case in the marriage of Pastor Garba and Hajjiya Juma). As the Protestant community in Dogondoutchi slowly grew, male Christian converts from the older community in the Maradi region often served as visiting preachers or permanent evangelists. Without such native speakers preaching in the region, it is unlikely that the mission would have had much success.[43]

However, the histories of the two regions were quite different. Subethnic distinctions between different Hausa-speaking groups (Gobirawa/ Katsinawa versus Mawri/Arewa) could generate significant tensions over Christian practice. For example, in 1958, Naino, an evangelist raised and trained in the Maradi region, provoked considerable consternation when he had a naming ceremony for his newborn son. The head of the Dogondoutchi station, Benjamin Van Lierop, commented disapprovingly, "Our . . . Evangelist, who is from another district, had the poor sense to have a naming ceremony for his new born son with the killing of a ram as only Moslems do in our area but our Christians, who are mainly of pagan background, disapproved. The Lord undertook and a month later, one of our Christians, formerly a Moslem, did not want a 'naming ceremony' but brought the new baby to Church to be dedicated to the Lord, as we have always done in the past, thus breaking the unfortunate precedent set by the Evangelist which could have led to a lot of misunderstanding on the part of those who are still in darkness."[44] The controversy suggests that as Hausa-speakers who had never been Muslim converted to Christianity, they were very concerned to distinguish their practices from those of Muslims. Christians from Maradi, by contrast, had adapted the *bikin suna* naming ceremony and used it quite systematically to provide an occasion to reach out to Muslims and share their understanding of monotheism through a familiar vehicle.

As the Christian community in Niger expanded beyond the Maradi region, several differences began to become overlaid one upon another. Local circumstances and history meant that Christian practice varied from one region to the next. Ethnic differences coincided with age differences, status differences, and class differences, for the male converts from Dogondoutchi competing for positions of authority in the Protestant community were younger, poorer, and more likely to be commoners than the converts from Tsibiri and Maradi. The rancor between SIM and the Christian community of Maradi was less in evidence in Dogondoutchi. Men from the Maradi region and eastern Niger in general tended to attend the Bible school in Tsibiri for their more advanced training. Men from Dogondoutchi did attend the Tsibiri Bible School, but most circulated into SIM Bible training schools outside of Niger that were closer to western Niger.[45] Doctrinally, the training they received was identical, but Dogondoutchi's Christians were inevitably somewhat separate from the much larger and older core of Christians in Maradi and Tsibiri.

Some of the tensions over the role of younger men and the meaning of central rituals such as the naming ceremony have continued into the present. As the evangelical community has expanded and become ever more diverse in terms of ethnic composition, social origins, and educational attainments, competition between men for leadership of the community has led to the fragmentation of the community. The evangelical community today is centered in Maradi but has networks that reach all over the country. There is a small and rather conservative church in Zinder. There is a community in Dogondoutchi from among Mawri who speak Hausa as a first language but who have little of the overlay of Islam that has become pervasive in the southern parts of Maradi. Increased migration to Niamey has meant that a significant number of third-generation Christians with an education have jobs there as high-level functionaries, teachers and university professors, radio broadcasters, and so on. The wealthiest portion of the community has now established a significant church there while retaining strong family ties with Tsibiri and Maradi. Evangelical immigrants to Niger from other francophone countries also gravitate toward SIM's Centre Biblique (a training center and library) in the capital, where a French-language church has developed. The "community" of evangelical Christians has become extremely complex geographically, socially, and economically. There are evangelical churches scattered across Niger.

At independence, President Hamani Diori encouraged these scattered Protestant churches to form themselves into a legal entity to protect them if the mission suddenly had to pull out of Niger for political reasons. In 1960, a formal body to represent the churches independent of the mission was created, the Église Évangélique de la République du Niger. The first leader of the EERN was Ali 'dan Buzu, an educated member of the Tsibiri aristocracy who had been groomed by missionaries in Maradi for leadership (Ali 'dan Buzu, interviews, February 19, 2001, and February 20, 2001). As it was on the Church Elders Council, the leadership of this body was exclusively male and was dominated by Christians from the older community of the Maradi region. The EERN functioned alongside SIM for nearly two decades after independence, collaborating on development projects, organizing an African Missionary Society to send African evangelists into rural villages, and gradually taking over significant mission properties as SIM shed structures it no longer felt it should support so long as there was an independent church body that could more legitimately carry them forward. However, by the 1970s the EERN had become disillusioned with the limits of SIM's vision for the church and began to seek ties to ecumenical bodies globally in an effort to raise money to sponsor the kinds of educational and infrastructural initiatives that older Tsibiri converts had long criticized SIM for failing to deliver. Younger Dogondoutchi converts, often more faithful to SIM's evangelical priorities, attempted to seize the leadership of the churches. Tensions between the EERN leadership and the mission came to a head over the question of SIM's refusal to entertain church funding through groups affiliated with the World Council of Churches. In 1989, SIM formally dissolved its partnership relationship with the EERN.

Given the growing complexity of the evangelical community geographically, socially, and economically, it is not surprising that the local churches fragmented into a number of different organizations in 1989. The tensions over the funding of the churches' initiatives were overlaid on tensions between men of different generations, of different regional/ ethnic origins, of different social statuses, and of different dispositions toward evangelism as opposed to development. The EERN continues to exist; its conservative older leadership includes the aristocratic Tsibiri core, the early converts from Zinder, and the Katsinawa converts from Maradi town who were associated with Pastor Garba and his influential wife Hajjiya Garba. The first breakaway group is known as the UEEPN (Union des Églises Évangéliques Protestantes du Niger). This group is in some ways closer in evangelistic spirit to SIM than the older church and has rejected the EERN's ecumenical impulses. In an irony, because the EERN is the "formal" representative of the original church, the mission has had to deal far more often with the EERN than with the UEEPN. When the UEEPN originally broke away from the EERN in

1989, SIM chided the leaders of the new group for dividing the community, thereby undermining some of the potential there might have been to develop a shared agenda with the younger evangelical leaders of the Protestant community. Despite the mission's greater sympathy with these younger leaders, it has, as if in penance for the mistakes of the past, attempted to continue to work with the elderly leadership of the EERN. The leadership of the Union consists largely of middle-aged men who felt cut out of leadership positions by the EERN gerontocracy. One of the central leaders is a highly educated man who comes from Dogondoutchi, a region that has often been neglected because of its distance from the Maradi-Tsibiri core of the church. The emphasis Dogondoutchi converts place on the urgent need for Christians to distinguish themselves clearly and unambiguously from highly visible *bori* practitioners and Muslims has meant that the Protestants of that region are often very uncompromising in their rejection of all practices that might bridge the distance between them and the rest of the population. As in the past, tensions often focus on the question of whether naming ceremonies can be appropriately Christian. As more-recent converts they are often more zealous in their pursuit of converting others. UEEPN services are more lively than EERN services and have a far more mixed congregation ethnically and socially. The women's and youth choirs are important centers of activity in the churches, and they are willing to try out various kinds of instruments and dance movements. Drumming is an important part of what makes the services appealing. Church members tend to prefer the newer translation of the Bible, although there are relatively few copies in circulation to use. Pastors from Nigeria may be invited to lead the church and there is some slight tinge of the enthusiastic charismatic evangelicalism associated with the Pentecostal churches, although there is no speaking in tongues or faith healing.

A third group emerged in 1989, the "peacemakers" of Salama (Église Évangélique Salama du Niger). Some Christians tired rather quickly of the divisive breakup and competition between the EERN and the UEEPN when the community is so small and the resources to squabble over so modest. The Salama Christians made a point of refusing to take sides; they attempted to work toward some sort of reconciliation. This group is relatively small and has no real presence in Maradi, for it is associated more fully with Niamey, where the rancorous divisions between Dogondoutchi and Maradi probably make little or no sense. Their churches are quite similar to the UEEPN churches in practice.

Older men in the EERN are often highly critical of what they see as harmful innovations to the Hausa-language service that is characteristic of the UEEPN. They don't like drumming, which they argue is not suitable in a milieu in which some individuals are one step from the ignorance of *bori* drumming and Arna animal sacrifices. Dancing before the tabernacle may have been suitable for King David, whose people were already familiar with *adini*, or monotheism. But in Maradi such practices are dangerous, they argue (Ali 'dan Bouzou interview, February 20, 2001). Such criticisms reflect the acute self-consciousness of the early core of Christians in Niger. It is less that they worry that animists will confuse Christianity with traditional practices than that Muslims might confuse Christians with polytheists (*kafirai*). One leading pastor told me he would never send potential Muslim converts to a church with dancing and drumming because they would be too shocked that such a thing could go on in a place of prayer.

Debates therefore have more to do with anxiety about how Christians are perceived by others than with differences of belief among Christians. The preexisting social splits among the converts along a variety of lines—age, social class, region, ethnicity—have crystallized into conflicts over power and access to resources in the churches. Elderly men in particular claim for themselves the right to determine for others how they will practice their religion as modern Christians, something younger Christians (who have been trained in the importance of individual conviction) adamantly refuse. Younger Christians and those from outside the Tsibiri elite have less status to lose in pushing for more energetic evangelism that may attract social outcasts such as prostitutes from Nigeria and disinherited nomads. Furthermore, they did not suffer the worst of the abuses of the mission, and they are more willing to forgive and move on. Younger evangelical Christians are contributing to the growth of the Pentecostal churches; their forceful evangelism, dynamic services, and modern style is appealing to the churches. Much of the growth of Pentecostalism in Niger comes not from new converts to Christianity but from defections of evangelical Protestants raised in the older churches to this fresh new camp. Struggles over age, authority, the work of evangelism, and the symbolic meaning of Christian practices continue today in the competition between the evangelical and Pentecostal churches.

7

"An Extremely Dangerous Suspect":
From Vichy-Era Travails to Postwar Triumph

When the music changes, the dance changes.

—Hausa proverb

*B*y the late 1930s, SIM's persistent attempts to gain spiritual purchase in the Hausa-speaking region finally appeared to be showing results. In Nigeria, the mission had taken over the Kano and Katsina leper settlements from the government and had constructed a third settlement at Sokoto; the leprosy work was immediately "fruitful," making it likely that the mission would push to open further leprosaria and medical stations in Nigeria and Niger (Beacham 1940, 3). The translation work was also showing measurable results: 1,144 Hausa Bibles had been sold, in addition to 810 New Testaments, 32,283 readers, and 3,711 hymnbooks (Beacham 1939, 3). Plans to expand the mission's stations were afoot in 1940, despite the war in Europe, and the colonial government in Niger appeared to be receptive: "The Governor of Niger Colony was passing through Maradi and Mr. and Mrs. Osborne were able to have an informal interview with him. The Governor assured Mr. Osborne that the SIM could purchase a certain plot and house in Maradi, put up temporary buildings in Jiratawa, and that he was also willing to let us occupy Diapaga" (Kapp 1940, 19). There is something surreal in the cheerful reportage of the mission's publications of the early war period, suggesting that the mission staff of North Americans, Canadians, and a New Zealander was more than a little out of sync with the fears and preoccupations of most Europeans and the French.

The mission's oblivion to the impact of the war and its implications for continued evangelism was short lived, however. With the fall of France and the Franco-German Armistice of June 22, 1940, the political landscape in French West Africa was thrown into great confusion. Any effort to retake France from outside her borders, whether led from Britain or from North Africa, would be heavily reliant on the overseas territories for soldiers, matériel, food supplies, and moral support. It was entirely within the realm of possibility that Niger, along with the rest of the Afrique Occidentale Française (AOF), would rally to the Free French in support of de Gaulle. After the announcement of the armistice, some elements of the military in Niger rejected capitulation and envisaged joining Allied forces in Dakar or Nigeria (Akpo-Vaché 1996, 28).[1] By August 1940, Felix Éboué had decided to lend the weight of French Equatorial Africa (Afrique Équatoriale Francaise, or AEF) to the support of de Gaulle; if all of the AOF had followed suit, the bloc of African colonies would have become the backbone of the French resistance forces. As it happened, Gouverneur-General Pierre Boisson saw the rallying of the AEF in support of de Gaulle as a betrayal. For him, the primary duty of France's overseas administrators was to maintain the cohesion of the French empire and prevent any further erosion of France's position (Akpo-Vaché 1996, 37).

It would be unfair to label Boisson as pro-Nazi, although he would be vilified as such after the war. A veteran of World War I, he had little sympathy for Hitler's Germany, but, like many soldiers of his generation, he was deeply loyal to Maréchal Pétain (Akpo-Vaché 1996, 32). He was also wedded to a military hierarchy and incapable of imagining any kind of autonomous decision-making capacity within France's African territories. Pétain's understanding of the colonies, which he eventually referred to explicitly as the French "empire," was that they would be the guarantor of France's ultimate sovereignty and independence from Germany (48). So long as the overseas territories could be protected from German intrusion, they could serve as a conduit for American goods into France. The Vichy policy toward the AOF was to hold Germany at bay while attempting to sustain and cultivate economic links to the United States, which was at that point neutral (49). Anything that might cut off metropolitan France from the prestige and resources of the empire, then, was seen as a threat to the very survival of France as a sovereign nation. Boisson decided to back Pétain and forestall the emergence of an African bloc on July 6, 1940.

It was a complex and difficult decision to make and one that was necessarily tempered by the sense of embattlement the Allied pressure on the colonial territories fostered. In their haste to forestall Germany and Italy from taking Africa, the Allies made a bid to take Mers-el-Kebir and Dakar by force July 4th and 8th before the situation had fully crystallized, reinforcing French fears that the British were making a move to seize France's empire in Africa. Diplomatic efforts (which were often undertaken by British commercial agents) to persuade local administrators that they would be backed economically by Britain came off as attempts to "buy" supporters. In any case, once the bombardments had begun, informal discussions were moot (Akpo-Vaché 1996, 33–35). While many individual soldiers and administrators eventually made their way across the borders into British territory or the AEF to join the Allies, the AOF as a whole determined to support the government of Pétain at Vichy.

Thus, in the confused political currents of the time, it was the "*britanniques*" who appeared to be the most immediate threat to France's overseas empire. Despite Pierre Boisson's willingness to support Pétain, he took advantage of the AOF's distance from France to carve a path of relative autonomy from the excesses of the Vichy government toward Jews and Freemasons for as long as possible and obstructed any direct collaboration with the Germans. On the other hand, he regarded the liberal partisans of the Front Populaire and supporters of de Gaulle as threats to the political cohesion of the federation. As a result, the government of the period was increasingly authoritarian and resolutely conservative. Under these circumstances, any British subject would have come under heavy scrutiny, but those whose contacts, activities, and institutional ties linked them most closely with British territories in Africa were particularly suspect. Protestant missionaries, then, were closely watched, not because Boisson was particularly interested in religious matters but because British missionaries seemed to be natural conduits of information in likely sympathy with the expansionist interests of Great Britain as a colonial power.

While Boisson was himself neither an avid supporter of Vichy's cultural agenda nor pro-Nazi in orientation, local administrators far from Dakar had tremendous latitude to pursue the discriminatory policies the Vichy government authorized if they so chose. The Vichy government (both in France and abroad) advanced a pro-Catholic policy as part of a crusade to renew and purify France in the wake of what looked like the failure of the Front Populaire. This pro-Catholic tendency simply heightened the contradictions already present in the French colonial claims to republicanism in the context of empire. Because the missionaries of the Sudan Interior Mission came largely from English-speaking regions, the mission came to be seen as *"britannique"* in orientation and its personnel were regarded as potential spies with ties to neighboring British-held Nigeria. In reality, the largely North American personnel of the mission did sustain close ties with their SIM colleagues across the border, but they attempted to remain scrupulously neutral on political issues in order to continue their work.

Niger's Governor Maurice Émile Falvy, unlike Boisson, had a reputation for strong pro-German sentiments and collaborated vigorously with Vichy. Thus, in Niger, the mistrust of the *"britanniques"* was compounded by the pro-Catholic policies of the Pétain government, creating a climate that was particularly inauspicious for a Protestant mission such as SIM. And so it was that by November of 1942, David Osborne, who as a citizen of New Zealand held a British passport, was under detention in Niamey and relations between the mission and the colonial regime were at their lowest point ever. Osborne's detention and the subsequent efforts of a French Protestant, Pastor Keller, to act as intermediary on his behalf and on the behalf of other Protestant missions provide an occasion to consider the unenviable position of Protestant missionaries in this period: if they spoke out against the Vichy government, they would lose their ability to continue their missionary work; on the other hand, if they cooperated with the government they could be branded (as Keller later found) as collaborators with the German occupation.

It was a time of tremendous stress for the mission, but one with intriguing consequences. As potential Gaullists who possibly were in contest with the colonial regime (at least in the imagination of colonial administrators), SIM missionaries may have earned some undeserved sympathy from local Africans despite their repeated protests that they were entirely apolitical. However, the difficulties SIM missionaries experienced during the war are simply symptomatic of much broader issues that affected all of the French colonial territories. With the fall of France and the alignment of many Africans with the Free French, General de Gaulle recognized a need to address some of the injustices of the colonial system. In January of 1944, de Gaulle and Félix Éboué, the governor of AEF, convened a conference of colonial governors in Brazzaville to discuss potential political, social, and economic reforms. The conference was attended by colonial administrators, administrative advisors, officials from the commissariat of colonies, and members of the French Consultative Assembly in Algiers. This meeting, which became known as the Brazzaville Conference, opened the way for the representation of the

African colonies in the French legislature after the war, the abolition of much-hated dimensions of the penal code, and the adoption of reforms that would offer the colonies greater autonomy. While not all of the recommendations made at Brazzaville were adopted, the conference made it possible for Christians and missionaries represented by such men as Pastor Marcel Brun, a Frenchman who headed an association in the United States that raised funds for de Gaulle, to voice their frustrations over the way France had consistently thwarted the work of Protestant missions. Against the backdrop of the pro-Catholic policies of the Vichy government and the harassment of Protestants in the AOF, these complaints prompted the postwar de Gaulle administration to give close attention to redressing the perception that France had been unfair to Protestant missions. After the defeat of Germany, the French colonial government took a far more positive, albeit wary, attitude toward Protestant mission activity, opening the way for SIM to engage in much more medical and educational work than had been the case prior to the war.

One final issue emerges in a consideration of this period—that of the national and denominational identity of SIM as a mission. SIM had always seen itself as international and nondenominational. While on the whole its staff was made up of Protestants, there was no reason in principle that an appropriately evangelical Catholic or Orthodox Christian could not become a missionary so long as they passed a doctrinal test. Yet this apparent openness was perhaps somewhat illusory, given Andrew Walls's interesting observation that the notion of using such tests as a mark of membership in the fellowship of believers was in itself characteristically American (Walls 1990, 17). It was during the Vichy and early postwar periods that the Protestantism of the mission became most clearly marked and the staff was gradually identified as "American" rather than "European." Most important, however, the shifting national inflection of the "international" mission was to become central to its relations with the French administration. Because SIM regards itself as "international," the mission might not welcome a description that insisted too much upon its national character one way or the other. However, from its inception it was clearly Anglo-American in orientation and was staffed largely by North Americans (both U.S. and Canadian). Between 1930 and 1960, missionaries from many regions of the world joined in the effort, often from British Commonwealth areas such as Australia and New Zealand, but sometimes from Scandinavian countries and, in one case, from Armenia. Today missionaries from South Korea, France, and Switzerland round out the national profile of the missionaries in Niger.

Given the reality that the mission's staff was always mixed in terms of national origin, the question of its "national" affinities must become somewhat subjective.

This chapter heightens the relevance of this observation, for in the first stage of the conflict between the mission and the governor of Niger, it was the British passport of Osborne that contributed to Lieutenant-Governor Falvy's fears that the mission might betray France in the service of the British empire. Later, the accurate assessment that much of the money and staff of the mission could be linked to the United States rather than to Great Britain, in the context of de Gaulle's increasing mistrust of American intentions in Africa, led to the characterization of the mission in reports on the status of religion as "American." The mission was very much a part of the explosion of American evangelical activity that has characterized the twentieth-century wave of missionization (see Walls 1990). Andrew Walls's cautionary remarks, made over a decade ago when religion and American foreign policy were somewhat less clearly interrelated than they are today, are worth recalling: "A missionary's effectiveness, or even sincerity, will sometimes be measured by the extent to which the message preached is reflected in the nation from which he or she came; the higher that nation's visibility in the world, the more likely is this measure to be used. We do well to ponder that insofar as the missionary movement continues *as a separate* identifiable phenomenon, it is bound to be seen, for good or ill, as part of the United States presence overseas" (Walls 1990, 23). Whatever the mission's perception of its own internationalism today, it would do well to be exceedingly mindful of the national inflection others place upon it in an acrimonious global environment. Like it or not, SIM, like most evangelical missions, is seen by others today as "American" and will likely bear the political and personal costs and benefits of that association—whatever its own political orientation—in the years to come.

The Backdrop of the War and the Brazzaville Conference

The colony of Niger was a particularly vulnerable and sensitive site in Vichy's eyes, surrounded as it was by Chad (which had rallied to de Gaulle and the Free French), Italian Libya, and British Nigeria. It was also a strategically important source of vegetable oils, labor, and revenue. Finn Fuglestad notes that Niger's first military governor, who had been in harness since 1922, Général de Brigade Falvy, was "quickly dubbed von Falvy for his alleged pro-German sentiments" (Fuglestad 1983, 139). Falvy closed the border with Nigeria, stationed military units along the border to patrol and build trenches, and retooled Niger's state-controlled economy to provision North Africa and France. During this period, Falvy banned trade with Nigeria and the government made heavy demands on the local population by increasing taxes, requisitioning crops and animals, and extracting forced labor in its peanut fields. The atmosphere was heavy with intrigue and mistrust, as Falvy sent spies and *agents provocateurs* into neighboring countries and local chiefs vied with one another to exploit new opportunities and weaknesses (139–143). As Fuglestad notes, "Under the Vichy regime the Nigeriens were for the first time effectively reduced to a state not unlike slavery as the French organized the systematic plundering and looting of their country and its meagre resources" (144). When he first arrived in Niger, Falvy was concerned about the eighteen SIM missionaries, who had made "little progress in evangelization" and whose number "could not be justified simply for evangelism. The unrelenting surveillance they have been subjected to has not enabled us to discern any reprehensible behavior, but it is carried out with all the more care since most of these individuals are British nationals."[2] For the missionaries, this persistent scrutiny was extremely trying, and being cut off from mission health care facilities in Nigeria was, in several instances, to prove fatal. "Owing to the British blockade and a state of general suspicion and misunderstanding," Osborne reported in December of 1940, shortly after the death of his wife Drusille from an infected hand, "we with the rest of the workers in the Niger Colony have been almost entirely cut off from contact with Nigeria from last September. We are not allowed to cross the frontier. Supplies of European requirements are getting very low. No mail reaches us from the outside except an occasional letter via Cotonou. These take more than 2 months to reach us from Nigeria."[3]

Protestant Travails under Vichy

The entire war put tremendous strain on the struggling missionaries of the Sudan Interior Mission, as the death of Drusille Osborne in 1940 suggests. However, the brief period between the Allied landing on November 8, 1942, and de Gaulle's actual takeover of the AOF in June 1943 was particularly fraught. After the Allied landing, the Falvy administration's suspicions of "foreign" missionaries were heightened. SIM missionaries, cut off from news sources, were baffled by the increased surveillance under which they suddenly found themselves. After 1941, the colonial administration forced them to move to Maradi, where they could be watched more readily; it forbade any transborder activity that linked the missionaries to their co-workers in Nigeria; and it prevented them from "itinerating," or traveling in the region to evangelize (Beacham 1941b, 9). The missionaries found themselves permanently cut off from information and medical supplies; a number of children of missionaries died as a consequence (Ray de la Haye interview).

Mission publications of the period are oddly reticent about the difficulties the mission in Niger was having, doubtless to avoid further tensions with the French administration and to reassure potential American donors. In an annual report for 1941, Reverend Gordon Beacham, the director of the mission, remarked obliquely, "Many have been the difficulties with which we have had to contend. The conflict in Europe, which had spread to Africa during the past year, greatly increased transportation problems. Sinister forces in official circles threatened the very existence of our missionary activities, especially among children. A large part of our field is now amongst Moslems, who steadfastly and unitedly oppose every new effort to win converts from amongst them. We wondered how the war with its economic pressure would affect mission finances. Above all has been the constant 'counter-attacks' of Satan himself in the spiritual realm, blinding men's eyes, veiling their hearts, dragging down those who have made profession of faith in Christ, 'for we are not ignorant of his devices'" (Beacham 1941a, 1).

Under Vichy's watchful eye, the French administration made a sustained effort to learn something more about the activities of the Protestant missionaries for the first time, commissioning a study in 1941 that established that there were four stations in Niger, eighteen missionaries, six *collaborateurs indigenes*, and 250 converts.[4] Up until this time the beleaguered administrators of the region had shown little interest in the missionaries beyond expressing skepticism that they would succeed in converting any Muslims. So long as diplomatic relations between Niger and Nigeria were good, the regular suspicion expressed in colonial reports that the missionaries must be engaged in intelligence-gathering (given the seeming implausibility of converting the local population) simply meant that mission proposals to expand its activities were regularly rebuffed. With the break between France and Britain after the armistice, what had earlier seemed to be harmless information-gathering was regarded as a sinister threat to France's overseas empire. Suddenly the activities of the *"britanniques"* were subject to an intense scrutiny that was to become routine.

With limited supplies and little mobility, the mission appears to have placed more emphasis than in the past on preparing Hausa-language texts (Ogilvie 1942) and holding Bible conferences (de la Haye 1943). Conferences enabled the work of the mission to continue, for while the missionaries' movements were restricted, those of converts were not. The initiative of local Christians was at a premium. Both activities would have required collaboration and consultation with local African converts to a greater degree than the mission's previous emphasis on itinerant preaching had. Indeed, African converts seem to have played a central role in the survival of the mission, particularly in sustaining contacts with the much larger contingent of SIM missionaries across the border in Nigeria. Martha Wall, who was stationed in Nigeria at the time, recalls the arrival of 'dan Nana, by then an important figure in the Christian community in Niger, on one of his illicit forays across the border to collect and convey news: "Dan Nana, a Hausa Christian . . . had slipped through the lines, his mind crammed with messages to our mission family and with questions from the news-hungry isolated missionaries who valiantly kept at their labors for Christ. He had to memorize all the information that he carried back across that formidable border" (Wall 1960, 148). Hausa Christians probably played a larger role in the survival of the mission than is generally reflected in the published mission periodicals of the period. Akpo-Vaché's work on the Vichy period suggests that this may have been typical of a broader pattern; Africans performed much of the semi-illegal or clandestine work and were punished when caught far more severely than Europeans were (Akpo-Vaché 1996, 64, 108, 113, 122).

Pastor 'dan Nana's account of that period reveals the high degree of autonomy Africans had relative to the mission by that time, but it also reveals the ways in which missionaries took African labor and life for granted. When the missionaries were required to leave Jiratawa for Maradi, where they could be watched more closely, the mission had 'dan Nana return from Hisatau, where he was preaching and teaching, to take over the site. From the vantage point of the mission, "the Administration, having obliged the missionaries to leave their home [in Jiratawa], undertook to pay for a caretaker and 'Dan Nana fulfils this position and draws from the local official the sum of 21. per week."[5] Presumably as caretaker his duty was simply to maintain the physical facility. But in practice he was engaging in *aikin Allah*, the work of preaching for God, just as missionary Ray de la Haye had done previously. 'Dan Nana managed to sustain the station through gifts from the Tsibiri church, his modest government wages, trade in cotton, and farming. It was a source of some bitterness to him when he discovered later that because the government had classified him merely as a "*gardien,*" or guard, he could receive no benefits when he retired. From his perspective, if missionaries could retire with a pension after a lifetime of "God's work," why shouldn't he? Of course, missionaries never received government salaries in the first place. Yet even the most superficial survey of the Christian community near Jiratawa reveals that his work during that period was extremely important to the expansion of the church. Performing "God's work" had very different life consequences for "native evangelists" than it did for missionaries.

'Dan Nana was also called upon, as Wall suggests, to carry messages across the border to Nigeria. I asked him whether this wasn't risky:

> Oh yes! It was dangerous! They had said they wanted to give me a vehicle, a Land Rover, that I could use to act as if I were a trader. They'd give me trade goods, and I'd go over and get the news. So that's what we did, I'd bring it back to Malam Osborn, our leader. He cautioned me, "This is dangerous; if someone is caught in political spying they will kill him." (Pastor 'dan Nana interview, October 24, 2000)

So long as the information conveyed was not overtly political, one supposes, Osborne could comfort himself that he was not placing 'dan Nana at unwarranted risk. Despite the closure of the border, clandestine trade continued in Nigeria—indeed, France needed to permit some permeability to guarantee supplies of imported goods. The main function of the closure was to attempt to restrain exports of cattle, grain, and peanuts from Niger. Border guards did relatively little to prevent crossings at any distance from known administrative centers, contenting themselves with shaking down known "swindlers" on the main roadways and staking out the main cattle paths of Fulani where they crossed the border (Esperet 1942; Varenner 1942). While the system Osborne proposed proved workable for someone who knew the local terrain well, 'dan Nana adapted the plan to make it safer. He became well known to the border guards as an ordinary Hausa trader dealing in traditional medicines—a commodity that was of no interest to the government. The guards took little notice of him, for, as he put it, "as a black person they weren't at all afraid of me; I wasn't a European" ('dan Nana interview, October 24, 2000). Clearly the mission succeeded, through the offices of 'dan Nana, in maintaining occasional links with the mission offices in Nigeria. The French administration, whether because of paranoia or perspicuousness, suspected as much but was not able to prove one way or the other that the mission was maintaining such ties, nor did it understand through what mechanism the information was flowing. So convinced were they that the mission's evangelism was a facade that it seems never to have occurred to them that local Christians might be active as couriers.

The missives 'dan Nana memorized and carried were personal and intimate. The sole clue within the mission's own publications that any information had made its way out of the French territory came in early 1941, when the editor of *The Sudan Witness*, Phyllis Henderson, printed an obituary announcing the death of Drusille Osborne on October 11, 1940, of complications due to blood poisoning and pneumonia. *The Sudan Witness* was edited and printed in Nigeria, where the news that there was a medical emergency had arrived only some time after Mrs. Osborne's death. The announcement regretted that no word of her illness had been received until after her death and that Osborne's wired message requesting prayer had not arrived in time. The missionaries had had to rely on the French doctor rather than the mission's doctors in Nigeria, and the doctor had been unable to save her. It was only when missionaries in Nigeria received a verbal message through "a Christian man" that the news got through to her friends and relatives outside Niger that Mrs. Osborne had died. Clearly, being cut off from spiritual and moral support was extremely painful to the missionaries, quite aside from the logistical problems their isolation from their primary source of medical expertise, supplies, and finances presented: "The Mission has lost a noble worker, a French scholar, and one who was her husband's faithful helper in all matters pertaining to Mission and Government. French West Africa has lost one of its greatest benefactors, greater than any soldier who ever fell in battle" (SIM 1941, 4). Drusille Osborne, a French Canadian, had served as a critical intermediary between the administration and the mission, and it was not long before her absence would be keenly felt.

David Osborne was arrested and detained when the Allies landed in North Africa; his ordeal began in the absence of the mission's most valued intermediary with the French. Here is Ray de la Haye's account of Osborne's detention, highlighting the staff's sense of bewilderment and vulnerability:

> In November of 1942, Eisenhower made a three-point landing in Casablanca, Oran, and Algiers in North Africa. We didn't know anything about it, because the news that we were receiving was through Germany and all slanted, and we didn't know, in fact, [that] Germany was winning the war, we didn't know about

Russia, we didn't know about Guadalcanal and all that had happened down there. . . . [6] We were in Jiratawa, and south of the administration, so administrators came down there with some Senegalese soldiers [*tirailleurs sénégalais*, African countrymen in the colonial army who were not necessarily from Senegal] and told us to get out of there in a half an hour! Leave everything! They took our radio away, they took our Ford. . . . So here we were. So after, at the height of the war, when Eisenhower landed there in North Africa they came and took Mr. Osborne hostage, literally a hostage! Maradi of course was under the eye of the administration, but we were outside, seven or eight miles from Maradi, and they took Mr. Osborne and that was a sad situation, we didn't know what they were going to do to him, we didn't know where he went. And he was away about maybe three or four weeks. (Ray de la Haye interview)

Although the mistrust of foreign, particularly English-speaking, missionaries had a long and rather complex history, that mistrust seems to have reached an apex under Vichy that was epitomized in the detention of Pastor Osborne. An extract from an annual report for the colony of Côte d'Ivoire in 1940 gives a feel for the AOF administration's sense under Vichy that there was nothing to be gained in supporting "foreign" missions. In his report on mission activity the new administrator remarks, "In general my predecessor didn't feel that, under present circumstances, it was useful to allow foreign missions—which have access to significant means of propaganda—to grow in importance. In effect there is reason to fear that British missionaries will never think like the French while our national interests run up against those of their own country."[7] Several conscious strategies seem to have emerged from this mistrust. First, the administration denied the requests of "foreign"—meaning non-French, of course—missions to enter into new mission activities throughout the territories, particularly if they involved developing new properties. A terse but unambiguous telegram from Governor Falvy to his superiors in Dakar responding to the suggestion that more American missionaries be permitted to enter Niamey captures the tone of the moment: "Absolutely opposed to any new installation this nature Niger."[8] Second, Catholic missions were promoted wherever possible (despite the fact that their personnel was often "foreign," albeit French-speaking, as well). Vichy's unabashed preference for Catholic missions during this period was so egregious that it prompted many an outcry from Protestant mission groups and raised serious questions about the separation of church and state.[9] Third, the administration gave French Protestant personnel permission, indeed encouraged them, to enter the West African field.[10] And finally, the French created an oversight commission to handle all Protestant missions under the watchful eye of French Protestant leadership. The umbrella commission was known as the Missionary Federation of

French West Africa and was headed by a French pastor named Jean Keller of the Société des Missions Évangéliques de Paris.[11]

According to Virginia Thompson and Richard Adloff's study of French West Africa:

> In 1942 the Evangelical Mission of Paris took the initiative in organizing a Missionary Federation of French West Africa, which all but two of the Protestant missions in the Federation joined of their own accord shortly after the war. The Paris Mission not only helps its foreign colleagues acquire in France the linguistic and other training still necessitated by the French government's decrees, but one of its members stationed in Dakar represents the whole Missionary Federation in the latter's dealings with the administration. This organization gives unity to the work of Protestantism in French West Africa, smoothes relations between its missionaries and officials there, and, most important of all, imparts to it a supra-national character that has glossed over the many confusing sectarian and national differences which for years have hampered Protestant missionary work among Africans. (Thompson and Adloff 1957, 584–585)

This rather benign picture belies the quiet coercion involved in the French administration's encouragement of a Protestant uniformity that was to be directed by French interests. It is not at all clear that the federation was initiated by the Paris mission rather than by the Vichy government.

There were relatively few major French missions working in Africa. The Missionaries of Our Lady of Africa, better known as the Pères Blancs (White Fathers), had been founded in 1868 by the first Archbishop of Algiers, Cardinal Lavigerie. The White Fathers had given Catholic missionaries, who were generally much closer culturally to the French than Protestant missionaries, representation and visibility in Algeria, French Soudan, and the Great Lakes region in East Africa. Later the Redemptorists were active in French West Africa, eventually setting up schools in Niger. But at the time of World War II very little work was being done in the AOF by French Protestants. The Paris Evangelical Missionary Society, founded in 1866, was the single most important vehicle for evangelism in Africa by French Protestants; the Paris Mission, as it was known, had limited its work to the less Islamicized regions of Africa, principally in Gabon and Congo. Under the leadership of Alfred Boegner, the Paris Mission had, in the late 1880s, been a great supporter of colonial expansion in Africa, which Boegner saw as marking the "beginning of the age of missions" (Zorn 1993, 17). When the French administration began to feel a need for a Frenchman to act as go between with the protestant missionaries of other nationalities, it naturally turned to the leader of the Paris Mission, who at that time was Pastor Jean Keller.

The French administration commissioned Pastor Keller to make a trip in early 1942 to visit all ten of the foreign Protestant missions in the AOF and see whether they would be willing to accept him as liaison with the government of the AOF in Dakar. He also submitted a confidential report on what he had discovered about the various missions and their staffs on his *tournée*. Keller, as *délégué général des missions protestantes en AOF*, was to act as intermediary between the Vichy government and the "foreign" Protestant missionaries, at times attempting to protect the missionaries' interests, at others subtly advancing Vichy's vision of appropriate Protestant activity. "Foreign" missionaries faced an unpleasant quandary. Either they agreed to take advantage of Keller's offer to serve as intermediary, despite his unappealing pro-Vichy politics, or they would have to resign themselves for the foreseeable future to harassment that would render them far less effective as evangelists.

Ultimately, the Sudan Interior Mission found itself availing itself of Keller's services in the wake of a series of unpleasant incidents. The English-speaking missionaries in Niger seem to have had a number of disagreements with the administration over staffing and the like, but the most serious incident seems to have been precipitated by the French administration's displeasure at a publication in Hausa by Edward Morrow in which Morrow set passages from the Koran and the Bible alongside one another in an effort to convince Muslims of the superiority of Christianity. In February 1942, Berthet, the *directeur des Affaires politiques et administratives* for the colonies, wrote to approve of the governor of Niger's decision to seize the text, commenting that because of its lack of objectivity and imprecision, it seemed more likely to inflame passions than lead to conversions.

Incidents such as this seem to have led to a deterioration in the relations between SIM and Falvy to the degree that when Keller visited Niamey in May 1942, he was warned in advance by members of the colonial administration in Niamey that he should be very cautious around Osborne, who was characterized as "an extremely dangerous suspect."[12] The general impression within the administration that Osborne was not to be trusted was so powerful that when Jean Toby succeeded Falvy as governor of Niger late in 1942 he seems to have accepted wholeheartedly the notion that the mission was dangerous and its leader a spy. When Osborne failed to appear before Toby on the new governor's first *tournée* in the territory, Toby had him arrested.

How had Osborne come to be seen as "an extremely dangerous suspect"? The suspicions of the mission may have arisen out of the coincidence of the mission's requests to expand its operations in Niger with the outbreak of the war. Prior to the Vichy regime, the administration saw the activities of the mission during the war as relatively innocuous.[13] Indeed, the mission's shift from its unsuccessful efforts to convince the administration to permit the creation of vernacular language schools to a new approach that would replicate the success of the leprosy work in Nigeria seemed to be bearing fruit. The mission's proposal to build a leprosarium in Maradi had been vetted and approved, its request for a large tract of land and allocations for both patients and medical supplies had been granted, and its request that its medical personnel be permitted to practice despite their lack of certification in France had been approved on condition that they only do work on leprosy and the facility operate under the authority of the colonial medical services. As of June 13, 1940, the only tasks left were choosing an appropriate site and building the facility.[14] By June 22, however, France had declared an armistice with Germany, and by July 6, Gouverneur-Général Boisson had decided to prevent an African bloc from joining the Allies. From the vantage point of Niger's governor, Jean Rapenne, everything had changed and the situation was too uncertain to move forward with any such proposal. SIM seems nevertheless to have envisioned continuing as if nothing had changed. In response to a letter from Osborne dated August 2, 1940 (presumably proposing a suitable plot and a timetable for building), Rapenne rather gently replied "I have the honor of informing you that I most willingly authorize you to choose right away, in cooperation with the Commandant of Maradi, land that would be suitable for the eventual construction of a leprosarium. I nevertheless regret to inform you that I will not be able to make that land available to you without a formal request. The general situation having rather considerably changed since my letter of June 13th, it would be appropriate to postpone the project until the return of more favorable circumstances."[15] Rapenne's delicate suggestion that the situation was in flux provoked some ire from above as evidenced in the marginalia to the letter, which insisted that "the general situation has now returned to normal." From the point of view of Boisson and Dakar, Vichy backing was to be taken as definitive and administrative personnel should not suggest that there was any reason to be uncertain about the future. Shortly thereafter, Falvy, whose support of Vichy was unambiguous, replaced Rapenne as governor.

To Falvy, the mission's proposed expansion took on an increasingly sinister air; by 1941 the governor was characterizing the mission's expansion as "abnormal" given the small number of converts and the purported decrease in the spread of Islam.[16] The increasing mistrust of the mission resulted in alarmed telegram correspondence between Governor Falvy and the AOF commanders in Dakar: "Have distinct impression that at Maradi, where I just went, the English are in the process of organizing an intelligence center, particularly by means of the SUDAN MISSION. Indispensable that Zinder research office direct its efforts to this issue immediately."[17] The perception that the mission staff was largely British contributed to Falvy's paranoia concerning the mission: "More than ever the maintenance of so many pastors (18) is not justified by evangelism. Permanent surveillance has not enabled us to discover any reprehensible activities, but it continues with the greatest care because most of these persons are British nationals."[18] Falvy did little to disguise his distaste and mistrust for the mission from Osborne. In March of 1942, Falvy was replaced by Jean-François Toby, who seems to have inherited Falvy's mistrust of the missionaries. Osborne was detained in the first year of Toby's command.

The correspondence surrounding Osborne's detention in November of 1942 in the wake of the Allied landing in North Africa sheds much light on the mix of personality, cultural obtuseness, and wartime politics that entered into the escalation of mistrust that led to the incident and contributed to the tensions between the French administration and Protestant mission groups more generally. The most useful source for understanding the incident is a letter Osborne wrote to Governor Toby after his release protesting his detention and calling for a full investigation so that he could be exonerated. The letter is written in an uncharacteristically polished and formal French (rather different from the blunt and even presumptuous style of Osborne and Playfair's earlier request to build a leprosarium) that belies the frequent complaints of the administration that the foreign missionaries had little skill in French. But the formal veneer does not disguise the deep anger and resentment the relatively recently widowed Osborne evidently felt as a result of his detention and the espionage accusation.

December 12, 1942

Monsieur le Gouverneur:

Allow me the honor of presenting you with this letter pursuant to our conversation of November 30th in your office in Niamey, at which time you expressed your displeasure at my absence during your first visit to Maradi the 15th of June, 1942. I would ask that you permit me to explain in greater detail the circumstances surrounding this matter.

Governor Falvy had made a visit prior to your own during which he had evidently conveyed to his administration his desire that the missionaries not be notified of his arrival. Undoubtedly as a result of this the Mission was taken off the list of recipients for the circular announcing that visit. At the time of your aforementioned visit another circular was sent out to the Europeans but once again neither the Mission nor the name of any missionary was included on the recipients list. As a consequence, and in the knowledge of how General Falvy had handled the matter of his own movements, I came to the conclusion that the presence of the missionaries was not desired, and as a result I considered it an act of discretion to abstain myself from the public reception. On the day of your visit Mr. Kapp [a SIM missionary who was heading the work in Maradi] was in his office in Maradi, and in his conversation with the Commandant de Cercle did ask whether the Commandant thought that the Governor would want to see him. He responded that he would find out at the time of your arrival. That evening, the Commandant de Cercle sent a word to Mr. Kapp informing him that the Governor would see him the following day at 10 o'clock. Mr. Kapp kept that appointment, to which he had personally been invited. At the time of that meeting he conveyed to you how much I, as chief of the mission, lamented not being able to speak with you.

I believe that this explanation will demonstrate that under the circumstances I could not have acted in any other manner. Once again allow me to assure you that I had no intention of behaving disrespectfully. On the contrary, please believe that it is my sincere desire to show you a respect and devotion as deep as I have shown all the governors who have preceded you in the fifteen years of my residence in the colony.

After my arrest in Tibiri the 9th of November and my detention in Niamey, I think that it might be appropriate for me to set out my own attitude regarding the administration and more generally toward the French. I have been accused of spying and anti-French sentiments. I categorically and energetically deny these utterly groundless accusations. I defy anyone to provide proof of such allegations. I have never under any circumstances acted as a spy for Great Britain or any other country. Have I been anti-French? If that were so I would have left this territory, for the mission has neither the desire nor the ability to force me to remain against my will. In the colony I have always attempted to be respectful and amiable toward the French among whom I found myself. On three different occasions I have been to France, where I have spent a year overall. I have always strived to know more about France, its people and its language, as much for myself as for my work as director of our mission in Niger. Until her death in Tibiri in October of 1940 I was married to a French Canadian of purely French origins, and her death was an extraordinary blow to me and to the Sudan Interior Mission. I hope that all these reasons will make it possible for you to see that these accusations of espionage and anti-French feelings are in no way justified. I must protest once again and insist that these allegations are pure lies.

Allow me the honor, Monsieur le Gouverneur, of requesting that you order an investigation of this subject immediately, and as soon as my claims have been verified, as I am sure they will be, may I ask that you take whatever measures necessary to obliterate any traces of these accusations from my files. Far from being anti-French and acting in a manner that is prejudicial to the French Empire, I have the most ardent desire to see France re-established in her ancient glory and playing an important role among the great powers.

Please accept, Monsieur le Gouverneur, along with my anticipated thanks, the expression of my profound respect.

David Osborne.[19]

Osborne's letter suggests that relations with the administration were quite strained well before Toby's arrival and that, indeed, Falvy hoped to prevent the missionaries from discovering any information they could pass along to the British across the border. The mission was clearly in an awkward situation—the French administration was hardly welcoming and the mission personnel, whatever their real feelings about the Vichy government, felt unappreciated and misunderstood. Nevertheless the letter also suggests a certain obtuseness verging on arrogance on Osborne's part. Clearly with a new governor making the rounds it was appropriate for the head of the mission to introduce himself, whatever Falvy's practice might have been. Newton Kapp, the SIM missionary in Maradi, appears to have sensed this and made an overture that was accepted.[20] Given the poor relations he had with Falvy, Osborne's claim that he hoped to show as much respect to Toby as he had to the preceding governors probably didn't assuage Toby's fears.

If this scenario had played itself out in Maradi alone then we could simply conclude that personality issues had driven the incident and that with more tact Osborne might have evaded scrutiny. But all across the AOF, Protestant missions were finding themselves in hot water. Specific cultural dynamics and political tensions seem to have contributed to this broader pattern, well captured by Keller's study of "foreign" missions. In his report on his 1942 *tournée*, Keller suggested that as far as he could tell, the "attitude of the missions is correct" and that they did not in fact engage in politics. In a handful of incidents, individual missionaries engaged in activities in support of the Free French, resulting in the expulsion of a few missionary children from Guinea, the imprisonment of an African pastor in Guinea, and the imprisonment of one English pastor who helped some French citizens escape to a British colony. Of these incidents Keller remarked coolly, "It doesn't appear that one could argue that these foreigners have conducted themselves any worse than the French themselves."[21] In other words, Keller seemed to be arguing, foreign missionaries are no more likely to spy than the French who live in the colonies. So why, he asked, does the heightened suspicion of them persist?

First, he suggested, they were strangers. Furthermore, their Protestant emphasis on evangelism was unfamiliar to French administrators, who were more comfortable and more familiar with the Catholic emphasis on schooling exemplified in the work of Lavigerie and the Pères Blancs. The missionaries' evangelical zeal evidently wore thin when combined with their relatively weak skills in French. They also, he suggested, had a "*ténacité tout britannique*" derived from an undeserved sense of entitlement that was irksome to an administration that emphasized hierarchy and acquiescence to authority. I suspect that the "ténacité" in the case of SIM had to do with Osborne's rather unreasonable expectation that the mission could go forward with the building of the leprosarium— which was to be sited on the road to Nigeria and would have entailed bringing in more missionary staff—after the fall of France.[22] Keller argued that despite these cultural misunderstandings, the missionaries did preach submission to authority "in conformity with biblical teaching" and encouraged the payment of taxes. Despite the slow progress of the missions, their work did tend to support the kind of moral, personal, and familial development that was of the greatest interest for the *oeuvre civilisatrice* of France in those territories. As if to apologize for the Protestant missionaries' misguided emphasis on evangelism, Keller pointed out that the missions appeared to be in the process of rethinking whether they had missed out on opportunities to win the sympathy of the indigenous populations, presumably through education and medical work.

Keller intervened on Osborne's behalf, writing a letter to the director of security in Dakar in December 1942 that attested firsthand to Osborne's sympathy for France, his prayers for Marshal Pétain, and his commitment to a life consecrated to the religious work in French territory for which he felt a particular calling. Of Osborne's missteps, Keller remarked, "Perhaps he has committed a few blunders; he does not seem to have understood from the beginning the new situation created by the events of 1940 and has perhaps indisposed the administration for this reason. But that is not sufficient to justify his reputation as a dangerous man." In a subtle critique of the local administration that did not go unremarked in high places (it was underlined by the reader, presumably the director of security), Keller observed, "The fact that he is both Anglo-Saxon and Protestant is perhaps sufficient for some to justify a prejudicial attitude."[23]

One might wonder whether Keller, as a Protestant interested in advancing the work of Protestant missions, perhaps underplayed the Gaullist sympathies of the missionaries he visited. French Protestants in France had occasionally criticized Vichy policies, and some had entered the resistance movement.[24] Most French Protestants, however, remained loyal to Pétain despite their increasing discomfort with Vichy's treatment of the Jewish population and outrage over forced labor. By the time of the German occupation of the southern zone, disillusionment with the Vichy regime was high among Protestants. It is not clear that Protestants in Niger were any more inclined toward resistance than their French coreligionists. Akpo-Vaché suggests that no systematic resistance network existed in Niger, although individual Africans in Zinder, Maradi, and Birnin Koni did make unauthorized trips to Nigeria to meet with traditional and religious leaders. Even these individuals, who one might argue more plausibly resisted the Vichy regime, primarily conveyed only news and information on potential travel routes (Akpo-Vaché 1996, 122). Even assuming Pastor 'dan Nana qualified in this limited sense as a member of the resistance, this would seem rather slender evidence for the participation of the missionaries in a resistance movement.

However, my own interviews suggest that, at least in the case of SIM, Keller was in fact correct, for the evangelical missions so thoroughly placed evangelism before politics that the missionaries engaged in remarkably little activity that might be construed as resistance to Vichy. Unless one takes attempts to maintain information flows with the mission stations in Nigeria as itself a subversive activity, SIM missionaries in Niger did not really contribute to the resistance movement—these were hardly French resistance fighters. SIM missionaries were, in this, similar to their evangelical counterparts in France. Evangelical Protestants were not active within the resistance movement within France and historically had remained somewhat separate from the two umbrella organisms that brought together most Protestant denominations in France (initially the Union nationale des associations culturelles de l'Eglise réformée de France and later the Fédération Protestante de France) which were organized in the 1930s and were led by Pastor Marc Boegner. It was Boegner and his more liberal Protestant group that proved more active in the resistance movement than the conservative evangelical Protestants (Halls 1995, 103–105, 123–124, 193). Disengagement from politics is, of course, its own kind of political engagement. One could argue that in abstaining from politics or resistance to Vichy, the missionaries in a sense abetted the administration. Later on in the war, the Gaullists found themselves wondering why the "American" missions hadn't been more political, which is why the missionaries were subject to continued surveillance and suspicion. In a sense the Protestant missions in the AOF were destined to be under suspicion for the duration of the war no matter what they did.

So far as I can tell this was the end of the affair, for before Keller's next visit, the AOF fell to de Gaulle and the entire political landscape changed, once again, overnight.

Here is how Ray de la Haye experienced the change after the Allies took North and West Africa:

> Then suddenly, everything changed. The administration came out and said, You're free. You can go home, border's opened up. And it had, you see, Eisenhower had been successful in North Africa. And all of French West Africa, as it was known then, was free again, and de Gaulle came down to Dakar. And do you know who they [the local Hausa population] attributed it to? Mr. Osborne. He came back. Of course, they just about worshiped him. (de la Haye interview)

One of the ironies of Osborne's detention is that the local Christians, according to de la Haye, interpreted his persecution as a genuine sign of his resistance to Vichy and imagined that the coincidence of his return with the victory of the Allies in Africa was a sign of his access to divine power. This representation of innocent and credulous Africans is rather typical of the older generation of missionaries' storytelling style, but it is not borne out by my interviews with local Christians, who tended to downplay Osborne's brief detention and any heroism or martyrdom it might have implied. Nevertheless, a more-diffuse perception that the mission was part of the American liberation effort and de Gaulle's liberalizing movement may very well have served the mission well for a time.

By November of 1942, the status of the Vichy regime as nominally independent from Germany had been shattered when the Germans occupied the southern zone of France. When the Allies invaded France's North African empire on November 8, 1942, the Vichy government moved into a defensive posture that was particularly oppressive to anyone who might be construed as sympathetic to the Allies. It was only when the Gaullists took over North and West Africa in June 1943 that this difficult period of colonial rule began to fade. Falvy's successor, Governor Jean Toby, lifted the ban on trade with Nigeria and abolished the unpopular *champs administratifs*. Nevertheless, the colonial administration, whose personnel changed little under the shift of regime (as we shall see, Toby had served under the Vichy regime as well), continued to make heavy demands on the economy. Local chiefs were deposed if they failed to meet France's demands, as the Sarkin Katsina of Maradi, Dan Kollodo, discovered in 1944. Some would argue that France made even heavier demands on the AOF after 1943 supported the Allied cause (Manning 1988, 139).

What had changed substantially was France's sense of her own infallibility and the awareness among Africans that the myth of French grandeur had been destroyed. "In fact, the Vichy regime," as Fuglestad remarks, "by pushing the classic colonial system to its logical extreme so late in the day, had in a sense done the Africans a favour, that of thoroughly discrediting the system" (Fuglestad 1983, 145). Under the circumstances, Africans readily equated extraction of labor, wealth, and natural resources by colonial authorities in the absence of the right to self-government with Nazism. Roosevelt's Atlantic Charter seemed to augur an entirely new world order, one in which it was not clear that France would have a role alongside the great powers of the United States, Britain, and the USSR and one in which self-government would become the mark of legitimacy (Akpo-Vaché 1996, 192–193). If de Gaulle hoped to retain and shore up the support of colonialists within the African territories he would have to assuage their fears that he would deliver France's colonial territories up to others on a silver platter. Well before the territory of France had been taken back, de Gaulle had to begin to preempt any American criticism of French colonial rule. De Gaulle and France already owed the Africans, particularly the African soldiers who fought under him, a tremendous debt. De Gaulle convened the famous Brazzaville conference of 1944 in order to recognize the need for reform and to begin articulating a new colonial policy that, in principle, recognized African agency, input, and interests. "One striking feature of the conference," as William Cohen notes, "was that although it had been called to decide the future of French Africa, no Africans actively participated in its deliberations" (Cohen 1971, 166). The outcome of the conference was highly conservative: France explicitly rejected any plan for autonomy or self-government for African territories and articulated the continuing importance of France's paternalist role in the affairs of her empire. Despite its emphasis on the importance of traditional authorities, the conference's unwillingness to seriously entertain AEF governor Felix Eboué's proposal that indigenous institutions be respected is evident in the paternalist recommendation that polygyny be abolished and the continuing insistence on an educational policy that would lead to assimilation to French language and culture (167).

Although the political implications of the Brazzaville proposals were less revolutionary than one might have hoped, the paternalist emphasis on the social welfare of Africans did open the way for advances in the previously neglected realms of education and health care. With little financial means of implementing its social welfare proposals, and in view of the embarrassing record of the Vichy regime toward Protestant missions, it is perhaps not surprising that after the war French colonial administrators gave Protestant missions found them much more latitude to engage in "social mission" work than before. After decades of near-complete neglect of Protestant missions (they are barely in evidence in the colonial records prior to 1939),[25] the French administration began systematically collecting information both openly and covertly about their scope, personnel, activities, and potential. The impetus for this information-gathering was a need to keep close tabs on "the Americans." However, it was also the result of the attitude of greater openness toward Protestants and their missions that emerged out of the dynamics of the war and a need for a fuller grasp of their scope and needs. The Vichy regime's harassment of Protestant pastors and preferential treatment of Catholics left the postwar regime with the task of mending fences and restoring the luster of France's republican claims to religious neutrality. And de Gaulle owed a particular debt to his fervent (and well-endowed) supporters in the France Forever Association based in the United States, many of whom were Protestant (Beynon 1985). In France during the war, Protestant pastors and their congregations, notably under the leadership of Pastor Marc Boegner (head of the Fédération Protestante de France) had often been visible and active critics of the Vichy regime (Halls 1995). As the war drew to a close and as American finance and influence became increasingly important in Europe and elsewhere, de Gaulle found himself warily supporting the activities of Protestant missions, many of which had significant ties to the United States. As a consequence, a larger and more-developed network of Protestant converts, students, missionaries, and pastors emerged as decolonization drew closer. While this occasionally fractious network was not particularly visible in the party politics of the decolonization era, the colonial administration listened to its clamorous critiques of colonial policy and systematically investigated mission policy, marriage, the separation of church and state, and educational policy. One consequence, then, of Vichy's pro-

Catholic and xenophobic policies was that after the war "foreign" Protestant missions and their converts had a greater degree of influence and a broader scope of activity than they had before the war.

After de Gaulle took over the AOF, the SIM missionaries experienced a sea change in the administration's attitudes toward its activities. While it is clear that the surveillance of the missions continued, the obstruction of their expansion gradually faded until the administration seems even to have consciously relied on the networks, finances, personnel, and energy of the Protestant missions to promote a postwar explosion of educational and medical work. How much of this expansion resulted from the shifts the missions were already considering before the war and how much derived from Keller's influence is hard to determine. SIM had already committed itself to the Maradi leprosarium before Keller's intervention. In his visits to the Protestant missions, Keller encouraged mission work of a social nature and was happy to attribute the shift in attitude to the "penetration of our French mentality in the hearts of missions up to now rather closed to our influence."[26]

Struggles over Leadership

Keller was quick to claim credit for the Protestant missions' shifts in strategies and to suggest that Protestants could assist in France's civilizing mission. However, he was to discover that his wartime efforts to advance Protestant evangelism had a cost. At the time of the armistice, French Protestants had vacillated about whether to support Pétain or de Gaulle. Marc Boegner's son, Étienne Boegner, initially hoped to convince his father to join him in London to offer moral guidance to the Free French movement. Étienne Boegner later decided that it would be better for men with a moral vision to remain in France and attempt to modify the Vichy regime from within—which is the course his father did in the end pursue (Halls 1995, 153–154). Within France, many Protestants simultaneously backed the Allied cause and supported Pétain's program of moral renewal, which was symbolized by the replacement of the revolutionary watchword "liberté, égalité, fraternité" with the conservative national motto "travail, famille, patrie." Marc Boegner supported Pétain, albeit with increasing reluctance as the war progressed. After the war, such figures often found that their credentials were called into question by other Protestants, often expatriates in the United States, Great Britain, and the AEF who had backed de Gaulle as the tide began to turn in 1942. Foreign ministry files suggest that a subdued struggle

emerged to determine who would provide the leadership of the Fédération Protestante de France, particularly as the need for a liaison with
Protestants in the United States and Africa became evident to de Gaulle.
Protestants in the AEF were understandably reluctant to follow a leader
such as Keller, who had not rallied to de Gaulle during the war. Other
Protestants, even within the AOF, were quietly critical of Keller's energetic support of Marshal Pétain and Gouverneur-Général Pierre Boisson.[27]

When Keller's credentials came under scrutiny, the door was open
for another leader to emerge in the heroic figure of an army chaplain
who served the Free French troops, Pastor Marcel Brun. Brun had lived
in the United States for many years teaching at Swarthmore and heading
his own congregation in Philadelphia. Brun was active in the France
Forever association, which had lavishly funded de Gaulle through American philanthropic networks. After the fall of France, Brun had implicitly
supported de Gaulle by holding a much-publicized service of mourning
at the Église Française du Saint Sauveur in Philadelphia. Brun's activities
on behalf of French missionaries cut off from their mother churches
during the war immediately came up against the efforts of Étienne Boegner, who by this time had moved to North America, and the Fédération
Protestante de France (Keller's group), which was attempting to forge
alliances in the United States at the same time.

Brun's wartime credentials were impeccable, and de Gaulle invited
him to do a tour of inspection of missions in French Cameroun and the
AEF and to write a report on religious affairs to be presented to the
participants at the Brazzaville conference.[28] According to Brun, Pastor
Keller and Étienne Boegner attempted to hinder him at every step. Brun,
unlike Keller, was not a man to mince words. His open displeasure and
outspoken criticism of the process and outcome of the Brazzaville conference may have cost him the longer-term support of the French administration. Nevertheless, his detailed critiques and accusations of a
Catholic bias in the proceedings led to full-fledged studies intended to
help reformulate France's foreign policy in its colonies.

Brun lodged a series of specific complaints with Renée Pleven, de
Gaulle's commissioner of colonies, some that were related to the experience of Protestants in Africa and others that were broader in their
implications. Brun forthrightly objected to the emphasis on indissoluble
monogamous marriage in the Brazzaville proposals, which he pointed
out was inconsistent with Protestantism and in any case unrealistic in
Africa. He criticized the policy that required the exclusive use of French

in schools, a policy that treated indigenous languages as "foreign." The original intent of the policy, he argued, had been to promote French as the preferred metropolitan language, not to render local languages irrelevant. Insisting on instruction in French was unfair to Protestant missionaries (many of whom were not French and were not trained to teach in the French schooling system) and in any case inappropriate in Africa. Similarly, he pointed out, France's colonial health care infrastructure was so woefully underdeveloped that it made no sense to hobble missionary work in that arena.[29]

Given his caustic critique of French policy and his attacks on Étienne Boegner (who was popular with Pleven),[30] it is no surprise that Brun did not last long as the liaison between the Protestant missions and the de Gaulle administration. Yet the administration seems to have taken his complaints seriously enough to pursue them in a series of subsequent studies. There was a veritable explosion in interest in the missions after 1944, much of it in direct response to the issues Brun raised in the wake of the Vichy government's harassment of Protestant missions. Among the studies undertaken were the following: "Situation Juridique Comparée des Missions, 1944"; Enquête sur les Missions Religieuses" (1945); G. Monod, "Influence des Missions Protestantes en Afrique noire" (1945); and Christian Merlo, "Fondement juridique d'une politique missionaire positive" (1955).[31] These studies ranged broadly in attitude toward Protestant missions, from draft documents suggesting that France should interpret international treaties in such a way as to promote Catholic (French) missions over Protestant (foreign) missions, to G. Monod's claims that Protestant missions proved more attentive than Catholic missions to the social needs of Africans. While much of this material retains a tone of skepticism and wariness, it is clear that on the whole a far more positive, albeit opportunistic, attitude toward Protestant missions had emerged. The policy that was eventually formulated channeled the finances and energies of well-endowed missions toward more effective social intervention even as they contained the political influence of the Americans.

The American Invasion

As the foreign ministry began to gather intelligence on Protestant missions, it must have become increasingly clear that despite the frequent characterization of, for example, SIM in Niger as *britannique*," the staff was in fact heavily made up of Americans.[32] Foltz's report to the foreign ministry on the staffing of evangelical missions suggested that the overwhelming majority of evangelical missionaries were Americans. Ten of the thirty mission societies were American, and the 425 American missionaries in those societies far outnumbered the 177 French missionaries.[33] Reasonably enough, therefore, the English-speaking missionaries came to be seen as "Americans" rather than British in the latter part of the war and the early postwar period. Given de Gaulle's occasionally rocky relations with the United States, the presence of so many Americans may have been unsettling. Despite a greater sense of openness toward Protestant missions after the Allied victory in Africa, the covert surveillance of Protestant missions continued throughout the war, well after the Vichy regime's fall, and indeed intensified under de Gaulle.

Local administrators seem to have been more suspicious of the mission's activities than their superiors. When the governor remarked in his 1945 annual report to his superiors that he suspected that the missionaries were above all agents of the British and American governments, a more highly placed skeptic made the marginal note "There's nothing to support this."[34] The governor thwarted SIM's attempts to get permission to start a school[35] and, as if to find the evidence necessary to convince those in high places, seems to have intensified surveillance of the missionaries. In 1946, the *commandant* of the police in Niger submitted a secret report on missions in Niger that reveals that he went as far as intercepting the film the American missionaries were having developed.[36] In the face of a renewed growth in the mission staff after the war, the governor's skepticism concerning the true nature of the mission's activities continued: "The missionary zeal of the American pastors not being particularly active, *this invasion does leave one speculating about the true motives for their action.* They all remain under a discrete, but attentive, surveillance."[37] As late as 1947, the political officer was noting the peculiarities of the mission's typewriter, presumably so he could track the authors of anticolonial political tracts.[38]

Throughout all this surveillance there is no hint that any genuinely anti-French or anticolonial activity was ever uncovered. Perhaps once the apparatus of surveillance had been erected under Vichy it was difficult to resist the temptation to continue using it, even against one's allies, and perhaps the rather ingrained habit of seeing the missionaries as spies was equally seductive. However, this mistrust seems to have abated by 1948, when Governor Colombani remarked that although the Protestant missions seemed to be making little progress, their relations with the authorities were always "correct."[39] In this more relaxed climate, when one missionary in Zinder did engage in "inappropriate contacts with dubious political characters," the administration simply saw to it that "he was discretely brought to a better comprehension of his role."[40] By 1950, SIM had finally obtained approval to set up the first girls' home at Soura and had opened a dispensary in Galmi, suggesting that the "foreigners" were regarded as more or less harmless even by the local administration.[41] By 1951, the governor of Niger was eyeing the "tremendous financial means" of the mission more with bemused interest than with alarm.[42] The much-discussed leprosarium was finally approved in 1953 under Jean Toby, after Toby consulted with the relevant medical services and all agreed about the best location within the colony.[43]

G. Monod's 1945 study of foreign missions was quite explicit about its concern that France's emerging policy recognize and address the potential influence the United States could have through the vehicle of Protestant missions:

> On the level of ideology, it is clear that the United States, whose popular opinion has always been frankly anti-colonial, has used the occasion of the war and her emergence from isolationism to renew her vocation to educate the world. Political circumstances, the importance of the North American Council of Missions within the international organization of Protestant missions, the role of the Protestant church in American politics, all contribute to the emergence of a significant segment of popular opinion that judges French colonial policy severely, going so far as to characterize it as enslavement.[44]

While decrying the occasional overlay of religion and politics among some Protestant intellectuals, Monod suggested that most were not so much anti-French as pan-African and anti-European, largely as a result of the war experience. While he remained wary of potential American attempts to use humanitarian rhetoric to advance U.S. trade interests, and while he kept an alert eye on whether the ecumenical movement might advance an internationalism that undercut French culture, Monod argued that France needed to address the critical issue of how to educate Africans in order to emancipate them. In this urgent matter, Christian missions had an important role to play. Rather than oppose the Americans, whose power had been illustrated by the course of the war, France should attempt to channel their youthful energy:

> There is no question, as we've seen, of attempting to oppose the irresistible force of American messianism. . . . Rather, in working together with this movement, in cooperating with it, it seems that it might be possible to channel its sometimes incoherent flow, to act as guide and open the door so far as our interests will permit, in order to avoid its being broken open. The support we offer for American missions in French Africa, the good faith and spirit of solidarity that they will experience through this cooperation wherever we can provide it, will gain

for France the support of a broad portion of the American public and will enable our government to stand firm with greater freedom and confidence in those areas that are deemed contrary to French interests.[45]

And doors did indeed open, although France did not abandon its policy of insisting that schooling in the French territories be conducted in French. Nevertheless, the general climate of support for the Protestant missions enabled missions such as SIM to expand tremendously in the postwar period, opening a new era for both the missions and the populations they served and enabling the missions to forge close ties with the African elites that would eventually replace the colonial administration. Let me close, then, with Pastor Osborne's exhilarated description of the mission field after his release, blissfully ignorant, as he was, of the ongoing surveillance and suspicions of "the Americans," happy only that the mission could finally move forward. Free once again to travel, Osborne began to seek out new sites for the mission in June of 1944, and he wrote home to call for at least thirty more missionaries for the AOF: "Never have we known the French officials to show a more sympathetic and friendly attitude towards us and our work. God has wonderfully answered the many prayers sent up over a period of at least ten years for the creating of this very attitude and the opening of these very doors" (Osborne 1944, 6). Osborne had gone from being an extremely dangerous suspect to being an irresistible force of change, part of the postwar Africa that was taking shape, as Monod remarked, right before France's wary eyes.

8

Impasses in Vernacular Education, 1945–1995

Prosperity is the child of education.

—Hausa proverb

On a Sunday morning in Maladi, as we are walking up the street leading from the mission compound to the Seventeen Doors EERN Church, my Christian friends and I pass goats; a circle of boys crouched in the dust with their backs to us, lost in some imaginary world; the man who sells sandals; a woman frying *'kosai* beancakes with her little girl beside her—Muslim neighbors busy with their own Sunday routines. We form a gradually growing cluster of Christian women walking purposefully in carefully ironed Sunday clothes and modest head coverings, choir members distinguishing themselves by their matching Hausa-style outfits. Everyone is in good humor. We greet friends as they join our group from neighboring households, we salute folks we pass on the street, we hail the family of a functionary headed off to the church in his small Peugeot. Each of us is carrying a book, sometimes two—the Hausa Bible and a Hausa hymnbook. Choir members carry tattered notebooks full of handwritten songs. Closer to the church we pass a small neighborhood mosque, in front of which four or five Muslim men sit enjoying the shade of a little *rumfa* shelter and chatting, watching the world go by. "Good morning you all!" they call out cheerfully. "Good morning!" we reply. "Are you off to read?" they ask. "Yes," we respond. "Well, we'll see you later then." And off we go.

If the prime marker of being a Muslim in Maradi is taking part in prayer or *salla* five times a day, the prime marker of being a Christian, to the Muslim observer, is going off to "read." Within the local spiritual vernacular, Muslims "pray," Christians "read." A mosque is a *masallaci*, a house of prayer. A church, by contrast, is a *makaranta*, a place for reading and studying. This is not to say, of course, that Protestant Christians don't conceive of themselves as praying, but they do not use the same word as Muslims (*salla*), since that word has come to refer specifically to the five ritual prayers. Instead, they use a different Arabic loanword related to prayer (*sujada*). A Christian who has reverted to Islam is said by other Christians (in regretful tones) to have gone back to "praying." A Muslim who speaks of pagan ancestors might comment that they did not do *salla*. Thus, *salla* is the primary marker of Muslimness. Christians think of themselves not as "readers" but as "followers of Jesus." But the Muslim sees them as "people of the church" (*'yan ecclesia*) and the church is, above all, a place for reading. The Hausa word both Muslims and Christians in Maradi commonly use for a church is, interestingly, the same word as the word for school—*makaranta*. Muslims have schools too, *makarantar allo*, where small children learn to sound out and recite the Arabic of the Koran by writing the characters on little wooden boards known as *allo*. *Makaranta* is for children. But when a mature Muslim man heads off to pray with his fellow Muslim men in the mosque (for by and large women do not go to the mosques), he does not bring his Koran but rather his prayer mat, which a young son often carries on his head. Prayer and reading are temporally separate.

Yet in spite of the real importance of reading to Christian life and identity in Maradi, and despite the tremendous importance of missions to the expansion of western-style education in other parts of Africa (see Ayandele 1966; Oliver 1952/1970; Ajayi 1969), the appearance of the SIM mission in Niger did not lead to an explosion in schooling or to the creation of an educated Christian elite. At independence the mission could boast only of an agricultural school and a Bible school. After independence the mission developed a French-language Bible school in the capital and a single primary boarding school. It provided a correspondence course for theological training. All in all, it is a very modest record for eighty years' work, one that reflects the emphasis on pastoral development over elementary schooling in the mission's overall educational strategy: "Pastoral development is of highest priority for facilitating the development of the church. . . . The Mission does not look on Mission-operated general educational schools as a priority" (SIM Manual 1980, 49; quoted in Koley 1984, 12). Indeed, the most consistent and bitter reproach evangelical Christians level at the mission in Niger is that it failed utterly to provide access to the kind of schooling that Hausa-speakers fervently desired and expected for their children—the kind that would live up to the Hausa saying that "prosperity is the child of learning." SIM planted churches, but it failed to build schools.

Hausa-speaking Protestants in the Maradi region decry what they see as the void in their communities in terms of the deep theological training needed to generate respected religious leaders, the practical know-how required for the successful merchant or entrepreneur, or the fluency in French administrative culture that is invaluable to the aspiring civil servant or politician. A interview that was published in the mid-1990s with Gordan Evans, who was associate director of SIM in Niger at the time, suggests that the mission is deeply aware of the continuing desire of African converts for a Christian school system: "The churches want to recreate the system of Christian schools that the missions had created in the past that were later abandoned in favor of the national schools" (Charles and Keller 1994, 27). He went on to note that that SIM would like to assist them but does not want to open schools itself.

This comment is misleading in its generality, for it seems to suggest that at one point there was a "system" of schools in Niger that was later dismantled. In reality, SIM never made a serious effort to develop a formal educational system beyond its Bible schools in this particular setting. One can point to a single significant SIM institution for general education in the whole of Niger, the mission's primary boarding school in Tsibiri, which opened in 1966. Missionaries such as Evans, whatever they may think about the past, seem to recognize today that the "cruel lack" of spiritual, medical, and technical training within the national evangelical churches is one of the most serious problems Christians and missionaries in Niger face. If the mission had a single stunning failure that reverberated throughout its work in Niger, it was this one. How could such a failure have come about?

There are two rather different ways to account for this. The embittered Christian converts of an older generation I spoke to in Maradi point to the anti-intellectualism and racism of the early missionaries— by this reading, missionaries who despised education did everything they could to prevent Africans from becoming as well educated as themselves: "The earliest missionaries despised aristocracy, they despised wealth, and they despised education. You could say that they were hostile to all those things" (Pastor Cherif Yacouba interview). But missionaries who had worked in the region from the 1940s have a different explanation. They point ruefully to the enormous obstacles English-speaking missionaries faced in a French colony. The inflexibility of the colonial administration, they suggest, made it impossible to pursue the expansion of schooling as a systematic strategy of mission work. Some intimated that they suspected that the Catholic Church used its influence to prohibit other denominations from starting schools and clinics. Unlike SIM's work in the British colony of Nigeria, which took greater advantage of the potential that becoming part of the colonial educational infrastructure presented, SIM's educational work in Niger was stunted (according to this argument) by the lack of government cooperation, appropriate language skills, and the necessary certification. Yet even in Nigeria, the timing and geographical spread of the educational initiatives suggests strongly that the mission created primary and secondary schooling only with great misgivings and in response to persistent prompting from local Christians (Cox 2000; Turaki 1993).

Neither of these accounts entertains the likelihood that it was the specifically *fundamentalist* approach of the mission that rendered success in the domain of education impossible. At the heart of the failure to build schools was the incompatibility of two different belief systems— the republican assimilationism that undergirded France's colonial educational policy and the narrow fundamentalism of the American-led mission. While British Nigeria could somehow reconcile the contradiction of a secular government that relies on religious schools (in the same way, one supposes, that Britain reconciled monarchy with constitutional government and state religion with freedom of conscience), the educational system in Niger could not combine a secular republican government with religious educational structures. Critics of the mission tend to point across the border to Nigeria to suggest that SIM in Niger should have operated in the same way as missions did there, when in fact it could not. As former SIM director Ian Hay observes, "The British government in Nigeria worked hand in glove with non-government agencies in terms of the development of the education program. And our mission and many other missions were just given carte blanche to educate. . . . We had thousands of kids in schools, we had primary schools and secondary schools, and even in Bible training we had a seminary in Nigeria. Whereas it was much harder in the French territories to do that. And that level of education did not result" (Ian and June Hay interview).

The strongest proof that the French administration was not supportive of mission educational efforts is the relative failure of even Catholic missions to expand religious schooling on their own terms in the French Soudan during the same period (Benoist 1987). The Catholic mission in

Niger did not succeed in setting up modest primary schools in Niamey and Dogondoutchi until 1949, when the French administration began to become alarmed about the expansion of Islam into previously animist areas.[1] Once the Catholic Redemptorists gained a foothold in the domain of education, however, they expanded that work consistently and they have continued to maintain their schools into the present. By contrast, SIM's fundamentalism guaranteed that none of the pragmatic compromises that eventually made some limited success in schooling possible for Catholics were ever made in Niger. Because of its willingness to cooperate with the colonial government, the Catholic church at length was able to create a network of schools in Niger, including one of the country's most highly regarded secondary schools, the Collège de Mariama in Niamey. But the schools were very much subject to state regulation and followed a strictly secular curriculum. The language of instruction was French, of course. The Catholic church regarded the creation of schools as an act of charity and a means of entrée into local communities, not a mode of direct proselytization in itself (Berthelot 1997). Not incidentally, those schools have consistently provided the highest-quality academic instruction in the country. It is, indeed, a pity that there are not more of them.

France's disposition toward religious education had long been deeply ambivalent. Even within France, the relationship between religious schooling—which was associated with the Catholic clergy—and public education vacillated wildly over a relatively short period of time. The French Revolution abolished the church's monopoly on education, but by the time of Napoleon I, religion was seen as an essential part of public education and order, to be carefully controlled by the state through the university. During the restoration, the religious orders hoped to wrest control of education from the university (which had the right to oversee staffing and curriculum). By the Third Republic, church and university tensions had become so pervasive that an alternative strategy that endorsed freedom and neutrality in public schooling had emerged. By 1904, the religious orders were forbidden to teach altogether. But the threat to the public welfare World War I represented led to a renewed *"union sacrée"* between church and state and schools were once again entrusted to the holy orders. With the championing of Catholicism under Vichy, the *écoles normales* were closed and private religious schools received state subventions. After World War II, French administrators responded to African parents' demand for education by supporting the construction of more schools and the hiring of more teachers, resulting in a huge expansion of schooling in the years leading up to independence (Manning 1988, 169). One way to meet this demand was to support the mission schools but to find ways of doing so that would reduce the danger of too close of an alliance between the secular state and the Catholic church. The solution was to provide a range of kinds of subsidies to religious schools. So long as private schools submitted to state regulation they could receive grants. This principle was gradually elaborated but was not fully formalized until 1959, when a law known as the *loi Debré* was passed. Under this law, schools could receive grants to help pay salaries and benefits for teachers under a *"contrat simple."* A closer association with the state that implied closer state supervision through a *"contrat d'association"* enabled schools to receive assistance per number of students as well, and staff became direct employees of the state (Erny 1982).

Obviously, if France was not certain how to resolve the relationship between the clergy and the need for public education within the metropole, the question of how to handle education in a largely Muslim milieu under colonial domination was even more difficult. In the nineteenth century, the Catholic church had a monopoly on education, and indeed its teaching staff was paid by the French government. But by the early decades of the twentieth century, France had begun to develop the conception of lay education with strong state oversight. Even so, it remained difficult to disentangle the strands of French *"civilisation"* in the name of which colonization occurred. To what degree was Christian training a necessary element in the evolution toward "civilization"? France could not impose Christian schooling on a Muslim population without generating deep resentment and fomenting rebellion. Furthermore, to be too supportive of missions could expose a colonial administrator to accusations of proclericalism by competitors for his position whenever the political winds might shift. The legal status of missions was ambiguous enough during World War I that it was relatively easy for administrators to sidestep these contentious issues by denying missions permission to operate. In French Soudan, the upshot of this for the Catholic missions was that the modest network of schools created by Catholic orders were deliberately sabotaged through competition with newly created public schools in the period 1906–1914 (Benoist 1987, 209).

The close of the war changed the political landscape considerably, for the Treaty of Saint-Germain (September 1, 1919) obligated signatory powers to give missions of all nationalities and denominations equal access to the African colonial territories in the name of "progress and civilization." Having consistently thwarted French Catholic missions in its Muslim territories, France faced the unappealing prospect of having now to support an invasion of foreign Protestant missions, particularly those from the United States (Benoist 1987, 256, 281). France's solution was to quickly draw up regulations concerning schooling that would enable it to control the activities of any missions that might attempt to enter its territories. By September 3, 1920, a *dépêche* had gone out confirming that within the colonies the language of instruction in schools would be French, as it was in the metropole (256). A February 14, 1922, *décret* further established that no private schooling could be administered without permission. Authorization would require adherence to official educational programs, exclusive use of the French language, formal record-keeping, and submission to official inspections. All personnel would need to have diplomas from officially certified schools. "Private education," the *décret* explained, "has the same function as official education and must employ the same instruction methods. Its essential goal is to teach the French language, to give students the basic elements of a general education, to strengthen and refine character, and to enhance the sense of loyalty toward France" (281, author's translation).

For Catholic missionaries (not all of whom were French) the requirement that schooling be conducted in French in the service of French culture was unwelcome—missions had found that their students were regularly absorbed into colonial employment before their spiritual training could be perfected. Catholic missions (like the Protestant missions) on the whole preferred vernacular instruction. However, it was the requirement that all staff have official teaching certification that was even more difficult to surmount, for most male Catholic missionaries had religious rather than secular training (176–177). The Catholic educational system came, as a result, to rely heavily on teaching staff from female missionaries with a stronger lay scholarly tradition, such as the Congrégation des Soeurs Blanches. In Niger as well, it was this feminine order that staffed the modest Catholic school infrastructure.

It can hardly be argued that Catholic missions found it easy to establish schools or that those schools conformed to their own ideal vision of Catholic schooling. It is not surprising, then, that the network of Catholic schools in Niger at independence was quite modest, consisting of an *orphelinat* (a residential school originally conceived for *métis* orphans) in Maradi, a primary school in Dogondoutchi, and a *collège* (the equivalent of a junior high school in the United States) in Niamey. To the degree that the French colonial administration could be said to have supported mission schooling, it preferred French Catholic missions to those from the Britain and United States. This tendency was most keenly felt by non-French missions during the Vichy period, when grants and subventions were directed exclusively to Catholic missions.

After World War II, the situation underwent a sea change, for missions of all kinds were given much more latitude to operate in the colonies, particularly in the domains of medicine and other social services. However, France's fundamental commitment to French-language instruction with strong state oversight for its general education program remained. SIM's insistence on vernacular instruction and the failure of its "foreign" (meaning non-French) personnel to demonstrate competency through the acquisition of a French *diplôme* meant that even after the war, administrators in Niger deliberately thwarted the mission's efforts to set up schools.[2] To the outside observer who is neither wedded to the French vision of assimilation nor committed to the mission's vision of a vernacular church of Christian farmers, this dialogue of the deaf has had tragic implications. One can trace the impact in any number of domains, but the consequences are perhaps most stark in the realm of health care delivery. At a time when the French administration was desperate for female personnel who were literate in French to help staff its overwhelmed medical infrastructure, the mission was punishing students who aspired to speak French and teaching girls to sing songs in Hausa. It did everything within its power to prevent the emergence of the kind of self-assured and "modern" francophone nurses who sported western suits that Nancy Rose Hunt describes in the Congo (Hunt 1999). For its part, the French administration refused to yield enough ground to accommodate an intermediary class of laborers who were literate in local languages to fill the gap, as occurred in Nigeria. Both the administration and the mission held rigidly and stubbornly to self-serving conceptions of education that were deleterious to the well-being of the Nigérien population in the long term. The outcome is that Niger has one of the least-developed medical systems in the world today.

Nevertheless, to fully appreciate the educational impasse that developed for SIM in Niger, we will need to back up and explore the story of how the mission came to the region in the first place, how its fundamentalist philosophy shaped its missionizing strategies, and how a community of readers and believers came into being in the unlikely setting of Tsibiri, Niger.

"It shall not return unto me void": SIM's Conception of Education in "the Word"

In order to understand how a mission committed to "the Word" could neglect education, some perspective on the mission's peculiar conception of what it would mean to become literate in the Bible and skilled in conveying it to others can be gained from reflections on what is known as the "Wordless Book." Despite the importance in Protestantism of direct access to "the Word" through the vernacular Bible, SIM and other evangelical missions maintained something of a mystical understanding of the power of biblical verses to act on human hearts in the world. Missionaries spoke of "giving" verses to individuals who would be transformed by the experience of memorizing and repeating those verses. One of the most important inspirational passages in the Bible for SIM missionaries of the era was Isaiah 55:10–11: "For as the rain cometh down, and the snow from heaven, and returneth not thither, but watereth the earth, and maketh it bring forth and bud, that it may give seed to the sower, and bread to the eater: So shall my word be that goeth forth out of my mouth: it shall not return unto me void, but it shall accomplish that which I please, and it shall prosper in the thing whereto I sent it." Missionaries took this to mean that even if "the Word" were not fully understood by those who received it or not acted on immediately, the power of God's word through verse memorization and oral repetition would act on the recipients and on the world around them to open their hearts to Christianity. Accordingly, the memorization and repetition of Bible verses was regarded as an important activity. One mnemonic device to help the illiterate to recall such verses was a booklet of paper or felt known as the "Wordless Book."

Adapted from Sunday school lessons for children in the United States, the booklet had no print in it at all, but rather four pages colored black (for sin), red (for the redeeming blood of Christ), white (for purity), and gold (for heaven): "By means of colored pages . . . the simple Gospel truth can be 'read' by people who have never learned any alphabet" (Wall 1960, 209). In order to keep this souvenir booklet, recipients had to memorize and recite perfectly passages of the Hausa Bible that were appropriate to each color in the "book"; these verses would be chosen by the missionary. Thus, for the red page a potential convert working with nurse Martha Wall was induced to memorize the line, "Repent ye therefore, and be converted, that your sins may be blotted out" (209). Here is teacher Rita Salls's description of how the booklet was used:

Well usually we began with the yellow or gold page, and talked about heaven. . . . And then we read them verses to make sure they knew we were reading from the Bible, and said that God said that only those whose names were in the book of Life could get in, and that there was no sin in heaven. So then you go to the black page, which is the first one . . . and you talk about what sin is, because their idea of sin, of course, and ours are two different things. To the Muslims sin is not fasting, not praying, not going to Mecca, not giving alms, and so forth. . . . And then we talked about sacrifice and how God said that only by the shedding of blood, so we go to the red page, and only with the shedding. . . . [we explained] that blood of bulls and goats was not sufficient, and that was why God sent his Son. And so then you cover up the black page with the red one and you say, "This is what God does." And then the next one is the white one, and you go into cleansing and forgiveness. . . . And you go back to the gold one and you tell them . . . that now, if they have forgiveness then they will not be left out of God's house. (Rita Salls interview)

The Wordless Book became a staple of SIM evangelism and captures the way that the priority of God's Word in SIM's fundamentalism had the odd effect of reducing the importance of the more-conventional Protestant understanding of individual *interpretation* of the Bible. One did not, in effect, need the printed word at all, at least not at first. The recitation of powerful words probably resonated with local practices around both Arna ritual (which involves the repetition of powerful incantations to local spirits) and Muslim *boka* healer practices (in which written charms and potions derived from ink render the potency of the Koran active in the affairs of humans in this world). A visitor who had been cured "miraculously" through the medicines proffered by missionaries would take these "incantations" back to his or her village and repeat them. To unschooled local populations, the emphasis on the power of the oral word represented in a "book" might not have seemed so unfamiliar. Much of the mission's approach to education—an emphasis on memorization, moral lessons around biblical stories and personages, lessons adapted for understanding at the level of children, and the teaching of humble practical skills—follows from this central understanding of "the Word" and the mission's rejection of "worldly wisdom." Becoming reborn in Christianity was not the rational outcome of deep reflection on the Bible; rather, it would occur with the intervention of the Holy Spirit through the "foolishness of preaching" celebrated in I Corinthians 1:19, 21: "For it is written, I will destroy the wisdom of the wise. . . . It pleased God by the foolishness of preaching to save them that believe."

The following description of schooling directed at children offers a glimpse at the ideology and style of the SIM's schooling before the

French administration intervened and closed the loosely structured vernacular-language mission school at Tsibiri because it did not meet government standards of teaching accreditation and curriculum.

> A hymn and prayer start the day. Then comes recitation of memorized passages of the Word of God. Then reading, writing and arithmetic, hygiene, all are used to help the children, and to guide them into a real knowledge of the Lord Jesus Christ. There are countless interruptions. Discipline is meted out for these uninhibited youngsters. As we talk of the fundamentals of hygiene, two rows of hands are extended for inspection. . . . We tell [these children] of the Lord who wants them to have "clean hands and a pure heart" and it is only possible with the cleansing blood of Jesus Christ. In this and many other ways we can present the claims of Christ to these young ones of Africa. (Salls 1949, 2)

The lesson was so steeped with Christian edification that it is not entirely clear what the children would have made of the "hygiene" lesson in itself. Clearly such an education, which was entirely devoid of practical training in French or in literacy beyond the vernacular Bible, was of little use to the colonial administration, which by the 1940s had begun establishing more government schools that were open to all children with a view toward creating a cadre of French-speaking functionaries to assist in governing the colony.

SIM replaced this early school, designed for young children, with a Bible school, which the missionaries felt was necessary to train adult evangelists, without whom preaching in the rural areas would not be possible. The mission seemed to struggle with the degree to which it should emphasize the work of native evangelists. For while spontaneous evangelism demonstrated the vigor of the emerging church and therefore the success of the mission, it undercut somewhat the ongoing promotional pleas for "more men" from the western world to further the urgent work of missionization. In unguarded moments, the mission might refer accurately enough to such African preachers as "missionaries." But they needed to maintain a distinction and hierarchy between western "missionaries" (white men) and "native evangelists" (African men), not least because once the mission actually hired African evangelists the enormous differences in living expenses, benefits (particularly for health and retirement), and other resources had to be justified in some way. The crisis in the mission's self-conception only deepened—it had white women laborers in the social services it devalued and it had African male evangelists whose skills belied the need for mission preachers in the classical mold. Where were the (white) men prefigured in the earlier martial imagery of the mission, the men who would preach upright in the market-place, arm raised to heaven, Bible in hand, "giving the Word"?

The solution was to emphasize the mission's ongoing need for (white) male missionaries to train the growing number of African (male) converts so they could become better evangelists. The gradually evolving mission strategy, which was not fully articulated until the end of the 1930s, was to generate converts, have them begin a church, and then train them to carry forward evangelization: "African evangelists may go and preach anywhere. These are the men who are being used in hammering at the bastions of Mohammedanism" (SIM ca. 1950). It was not until 1946 (eighteen years after arriving in the Tsibiri region) that the mission began to make serious plans to develop a Bible school to train male African evangelists to become the means through which the mission would extend its reach to the local populations (Osborne 1946, 9). The claim of the mission was that this had been long in the planning and that the French administration had impeded the implementation of the school: "For some years, money had been on hand to build a Bible School. Every time application was made, the government had refused permission for such a school. The reasons varied. Sometimes they were seemingly logical objections—often the flimsy quality of the excuses was as apparent as it was disheartening. Yet at last all conditions had been met. The permit was won by patience and diplomacy and much prayer" (Wall 1960, 223).

But by the late 1940s the mission could no longer ignore the deeply felt need for education among the Christian community. It faced some confusion about how to meet that need with a mixed clientele, a relatively small mission staff, and an ideology that resisted secular education tenaciously. It could not readily compete with the government schools, and in any case some of the converts were already adults. The Bible school was a way of offering modest education without compromising the mission's core fundamentalist convictions. The Tsibiri Bible School was inaugurated in 1947; the teaching would be in Hausa, but the teachers were French-speaking missionaries who had met the French requirements for certification. In all, the school graduated thirteen students before SIM closed the school in the mid-1950s to shift its energies to younger students.

It is no surprise that the French administration was reluctant to approve SIM's Bible schools; the proposed program was very narrow, instruction was done in vernacular Hausa rather than in French, and the educators had no commitment to shaping French subjects for colonial rule. SIM was not interested in developing a broad-based French-language primary school that would lead to secondary and higher education, the kind of school the French administration might have approved. The mission had no expectation that any SIM schooling would be geared to train evangelists to become missionaries on a par with the white missionaries. The school SIM envisioned was to be taught entirely in the Hausa vernacular with a strict view toward training simple men to carry "the Word" to their "unreached" kindred and neighbors in the Sudanic belt. In Nigeria, the mission's strategy of promoting early education in the vernacular was suited to the British philosophy of governance, and the mission had greater success there in developing primary schools and Bible schools with an emphasis on Christian education. It was possible to become literate in the vernacular there and go on to a successful career as a chief, for example. In Niger, the French colonial educational philosophy, which emphasized literacy in French through a secular curriculum, made it extremely difficult for the mission to reconcile its own vision of education with that of the colonial administration or the aspirations of the converts. Those of the chiefly class in Niger increasingly found that the French administration preferred to work with men who were literate in French. The mission's insistence on vernacular education set itself up for increasing tension with its most influential converts.

Because the mission emphasized material asceticism and a rejection of worldly power, its resources for running the school were modest and its expectations of the students included manual labor for the upkeep of the school and to feed the student body through farm work. Students were expected to move away from their homes and live at the school with their wives for four years or more. The curriculum was narrow both in terms of what it provided for the deeply reflective Christian and in terms of what it might have offered an adult who craved an education suited to a challenging political and economic environment under French rule. Simply taking its theological training into account, it is striking that the approach envisioned no training in the biblical languages or in biblical criticism (SIM ca. 1950, 12). Serious and respectful engagement with Muslims would have entailed an introduction to Arabic and the Koran. Of course, any such training would have required the students to have access to English- or French-language materials as well, since little would be available in Hausa, and so training in either French or English would be a necessary prerequisite to deeper theological training. From a more worldly perspective, the schools offered no training in the official language of administration, no schooling in the history of France or the

AOF, and very little that would be useful for a life in civil service or commerce. Despite the overblown language of the fund-raising materials ("to speak of the curriculum is to reveal the well balanced training for the prospective pastors and evangelists," 11), it was an extremely narrow curriculum that required only rudimentary prior training in Hausa-language literacy.

SIM had always hoped that it could generate the means to expand native evangelism through revenues raised by the local churches. The ideal would be for the expansion of evangelism to be self-supporting: the local churches and populations would, of their own accord, raise the necessary funds to train and send forth their own evangelists. The mission's job was to foster churches, which would then go forth to carry forward the "great commission." Thus, when the schools were created, the mission had only modest funding for them, and in its fund-raising materials, the mission broached the question of outside support for students only with caution: "It has been proven as unwise to submit the name of any particular student to a supporter of the Bible Training Schools. Since many of the students are not supported from the homeland, it immediately causes a division where one knows a group in the homeland provides for his training" (SIM ca. 1950, 15). Students at SIM and the later SIM-derived schools were expected to raise money for the training, do farmwork to cover food expenses, and "do other labour to cut down expenses normally paid to labourers on a mission station" (13).

Immediately, the deep divisions within the Tsibiri community emerged as segments of the student body disdained the manual labor that was seen to be more fit for others and bristled at the lack of consultation evidenced in the structure of the school and the conception of the educational program. These tensions were played out regularly in animosities over who would perform what labor, over who would have access to treatment in the dispensary, and in heated soccer matches, with the converts taking sides in proxy battles over the mission's approach. Members of the *sarauta* courtly class would not normally have taken part in such undignified physical labor. The anger and bitterness underlying these tensions took the missionaries entirely by surprise. The early malaise in the community resulted in a growing vigilance among the missionaries about any signs of "pride" among the converts and a mistrust of the judgment and spiritual maturity of the converts. SIM missionaries of the 1930s and 1940s tended to associate the sin of pride or self-righteousness with Muslims in their writings (Morrow 1934; Jackson 1935). Director Gordon Beacham, in discussing SIM's educational philosophy, suggested that western secular education was dangerous and would prevent Africans from becoming truly "civilized" (Beacham 1941a, 9). Western education was distracting and tempted Africans to aspire to a western lifestyle. The missionaries of that era worked to expunge any signs of pride from converts. Among the most important manifestations of pride was a convert's aspiration to speak English or French rather than Hausa; students of the mission who were caught speaking anything other than Hausa were punished by having a tablet of Nivaquine (a bitter-tasting prophylactic against malaria) put in their mouths.

The significance of struggles to control the purported pridefulness of the independent-minded converts was not fully impressed upon me until I had a rather unsettling experience as I was discussing the Bible school and agricultural school with one former student and worker. We were looking at old photographs dating from the early days of the church and the Bible school. In my previous research, looking at old photographs with informants had been a pleasant and fruitful way of finding common ground in thinking about the past. I was startled to discover that the photographs I found rather charming of early Bible school students dressed in shorts and worn shirts were humiliating and upsetting to the man I was talking to, an extremely dignified pastor who, like many Christian men, regularly dresses in the same kind of modest clothing a Muslim scholar would wear. It took me some time to understand why these photographs were so distressing. They recalled a time when the missionaries would distribute secondhand clothes to the mission "boys." Before they allowed the converts to wear the clothes, the missionaries would rip out the collars, cut the sleeves short, and cut off the legs of slacks so that the adult students had to go bare legged, something no dignified Muslim man would ever do, except perhaps to work in his fields. Male students and employees of the Bible school (and later the farm school) were humiliated and infantilized in a systematic fashion; the scars of that humiliation are far from being healed. The missionaries marked their students as visibly different from both their Muslim neighbors and from themselves, humbling them in advance so that they would not be overtaken by "pride."

The missionaries dismissed the notion that there were flaws in the conception of the school and in the mission's language policies, for any discontentment could be placed at the door of Satan. "The Devil does not sit idly by and let a Bible School run a smooth course," SIM deputation secretary Reverend Carl Tanis declared during a visit from the United States, according to Martha Wall. "You'll have discipline problems you never dreamed of; your health will be attacked. You must remember that there is nothing Satan hates and fears more than a training school for evangelists" (Wall 1960, 225). In an overview of SIM activities in Niger in the 1940s, retired missionary Alberta Simms suggests that the high personal cost to missionaries of the mission's work during the last half of the 1940s in illnesses, deaths, and permanent disabilities was the direct result of such an encounter with Satan (Simms 1992).

Important as it might be to train African evangelists, the central belief of SIM missionaries that the end of time was at hand and that the souls of pagans and Muslims were daily being lost to eternity meant that the urgent need to evangelize took precedence over longer-term planning for the education of the growing Hausa-language church in Niger. Missionaries who were motivated by the belief that they would be devoting their lives to personally saving the souls of individual Muslims and pagans took little interest in instructing and mentoring those who had already been converted to Christianity. The dynamism of the mission was (and still is) largely derived from the vision and commitment of individual missionaries, who had tremendous latitude to champion particular projects rather than submit to long-term planning and oversight. While missionaries yielded to decisions of a central board, once in the field they were very much on their own and could continue or discontinue the work of other colleagues who left the field as they chose. As the costs of this short-sighted approach became all too evident, many missionaries lamented their earlier neglect of "discipling." Interest in the Tsibiri Bible School flagged when the missionary most closely associated with it moved on to work in translation and radio; the mission shifted its energies to two educational establishments targeted at children rather than the adult converts. The ill-fated Tsibiri Bible School was one in a series of institutions the mission began and then dropped just as capriciously as it had begun them with little or no consultation with the local church.

The mission's strategy by the 1950s was to establish schools for rural boys from villages without schools and girls who were of little interest to the government. This approach was in many ways made possible by the mission's takeover of the Tsibiri dispensary from the government at the close of World War II, for this extremely popular medical work attracted marginal children to the mission from distant households that would otherwise have despaired of keeping their children alive. In 1953, District Superintendent Newton Kapp claimed in a jubilee-year reflection on SIM's activities that "five years ago our Africans cared little for education. . . . The Government Administration is conscious that the masses have to be educated. Will the Mission lag behind in its educational endeavours? We have started a Girls' School in Maradi, as the greatest need has been to provide Christian wives for our converts. The future of our believers is in creating Christian homes" (Kapp 1953, 20). This was part of a broader SIM strategy throughout its mission fields to raise girl children who would "blossom and bloom into Christian girlhood and womanhood. In turn they marry Christian men, set up Christian homes, and bring up their children in the nurture and admonition of the Lord!" (SIM 1955).

In 1951, missionary Rita Salls began a girls home to serve children from the Maradi region. The school was located in the small village of Soura midway between Maradi and Tsibiri. By 1954 it had "29 girls, ages 3 to 15 years, 3 small boys awaiting opening of a Boys' Home, and 2 babies who were orphaned within a few days of birth and would have died except for the missionaries' willingness to receive them" (Kapp 1955, 2). The mission hoped to open a boys' home but awaited access to enough land for the students to support themselves through farming. That year the Bible school for older students had graduated six students: "At last there will be men available to go to the distant villages and reach those who are still in darkness" (2).

The girls' homes were explicitly conceived as schools for teaching housekeeping skills (écoles ménagères) rather than literacy skills and the government held them to a far lower standard than the primary schools. Indeed, such schools were approved only because they could be categorized as the "écoles de catechisme" that were parallel to the supplementary religious classes Catholics offered outside of the regular schoolday.[3] Training did not need to be in French, there was no need to strictly adhere to secular education, and there was no expectation that conventional academic subjects would be taught. The schools were, after all, preparing girls to become good wives, not useful functionaries. But because these schools were not formally recognized as part of the school system, they could not receive government subventions. Once they were approved, the administration more or less forgot them and did not trouble to inspect them as they did the academically oriented schools Catholics set up.

Verna Dorset's coloring book to promote the Dogondoutchi home offers a rather full glimpse of the workaday life of the girls' homes, revealing how little emphasis was placed on reading, writing, and other literate arts: "After morning chores were completed, there was three hours of learnin'—The Three R's—hygiene—history—Bible with study books and Bible memory. They were quick to respond to the salvation message" (Dorset 1963). The document, published in 1963 to commemorate the ten years the Dogondoutchi home had been in operation, reveals the mission's undisguised resentment at a government requirement that the mission send ten of the girls to obtain a more rounded education at the secular state school, for that education made it more difficult for it to oversee the activities it regarded as more relevant to the training of a Christian wife. Much of the children's time and effort was devoted to simply keeping the home operating. Indeed, at a similar school in Oro (Nigeria) that the later schools were modeled on, the mission's philosophy was to avoid instilling any taste for the foreign or novel in the girls: "We did not want our girls to go out feeling proud and superior to their less fortunate sisters. This would hinder their testimony" (Bulifant ca. 1938, 10). The introduction of French was regarded as just the sort of foreign influence that would turn the girls and make them "proud." What time was devoted to schooling went heavily toward memorization of songs and Bible verses and to Bible study (indeed, the only image in the book that shows the students in a classroom bears the caption "Bible Class"). Graduation was explicitly equated with marriage: "Blouses, skirts, and pillows were adorned with varied appliqué, using up every scrap. It was difficult to distinguish the hand-sewn from those done by machine. Their completed items were stored in their 'hope chests' until their 'graduation' (marriage)" (Dorset 1963). Even as students, the girls were expected to take part in evangelization. When a girl could read in Hausa, the mission felt that her schooling was a success, so long as she was eventually baptized and found a Christian husband.

The conditions under which such schools operated were challenging, for the girls were of differing ages and experiences and were permitted by their families to stay for unpredictable periods of time before being taken off for marriage. In a 1959 letter to her prayer supporters, Rita Salls reported:

> Our family has now increased to number 38; and as we look at the home circumstances of each of these children, we catch a glimpse of the moral and spiritual poverty of Moslem Africa. Thirteen of them have lost their mothers, two are illegitimate and fourteen come from broken homes. . . . The heartbreaking fact is that eight children come from homes that at one time professed Christianity but no longer do so. And some of these are even among the broken homes today. Ten children either come from Christian homes or were being brought up by Christian relatives.[4]

The girls were either the offspring of early commoner converts such as 'dan Nana or they were "orphans" whose kin hovered ambiguously off-stage (widowed fathers, biological mothers of illegitimate children, divorced mothers). Some were children of families that were not interested in attempting to raise them, at least so long as they were unwell or uncooperative. The mission began to attract enough women converts to balance the growing population of young male converts only after the French government turned over its large dispensary in Tsibiri at the close of World War II. The success its staff of female missionary nurses had in treating an enormous range of illnesses created the conditions for attracting a number of girl children who would otherwise have been abandoned because they were ill or crippled (Rita Salls interview). In Dogondoutchi, some of the girls were offered to the school during a serious famine (Dorset 1963). To be fair to the mission, it is important to underscore that it is not at all clear that such girls would have received any education at all or indeed that they would have lived very long if the mission had not been willing to establish the girls' homes. The discipline problems referred to repeatedly may in part reflect the reality that the mission was schooling some children who had, in effect, been rejected by their relatives.

The graduates of the school recalled working twice as hard on Saturday so that on Sunday they wouldn't have any work to do. Then they would sing hymns the missionaries had taught them that had been translated into Hausa. What about evangelizing, I wondered? One woman reported that when it became clear that things went better without the missionaries, the girls went out without them in the company of Halima, the housemother. They'd go and visit in all the villages nearby. The Muslims never chased them away—they'd bring out mats to show hospitality and the girls would start by singing. The girls preferred their own songs in this setting, new songs they had learned from Hausa-speaking Christians from Nigeria or songs they had made up themselves. They also used the Wordless Book. The Christians in the villages surrounding Soura, she insisted, converted as a result of evangelism by the students of the girls' home.[5]

Veterans of the girls' school who still live in the Maradi region with whom I talked spoke of it with great fondness. I visited the site of the school with a number of the graduates, who are now middle-aged women, while they recounted their experiences in what ended up being a kind of impromptu homecoming. The church in Soura is in fact their old schoolroom, with the blackboard still intact, a concrete symbol of the *makaranta* (church) that was in fact the *makaranta* (school). Dorm life was an adventure, and the work to keep up the school was not so different from what they would have experienced at home. Darker recollections involved discipline, such as being locked in a windowless room as a punishment or being spanked. But even these memories were recounted with some humor, suggesting an acceptance that the discipline was justified although perhaps the means were unwelcome. Other challenges involved the substantial distance some of the girls eventually had to walk to attend the government school in Maradi, meeting the challenges of seasonal floods and the serious infections they got from insects (probably Guinea worm) in the river that made it even more difficult to walk. I had chosen to discuss the school with the women while we were on the site because it seemed likely to trigger many memories, and on the whole those memories were very positive ones.

Although most of the female graduates' assessments of the school were highly positive, the male reaction to the school was one of utter rejection. Men in the emerging Christian community saw the curriculum as devoid of intellectual content in a context in which literacy in French was becoming more and more important. While many of the early students in the school came from the commoner family of 'dan Nana and from villages in which he evangelized, the leader of the aristocratic converts in Tsibiri at the time, Pastor Cherif Yacouba, eschewed the school altogether; he sent his children to the government schools in Maradi and Tsibiri and urged others to do so as well. Cherif was part of what one might think of as a third wave or generation of *sarauta* converts (the early 1930s first wave included Ta Shubka, Musa Marafa, and Abdou while the second in the later 1930s included Jadi Marafa and Barmo Abdou) that emerged in the mid-1950s, a cohort including such men as Malam Kashalu, Maman Na Kwadege, and Shekari. These men were far more conscious of the urgency of successfully engaging with the larger francophone context in which they sought influence and work as independence loomed on the horizon. When chastised for his "pride" by the missionaries for refusing to send his girls to Soura, he replied, "This is not pride [*girman kai*]; I would rather my children to be with me, where I work, so they can learn by seeing. If I go somewhere they will go with me" (Yacouba interview). He chose to send them to public schools and teach them Christian values at home with his Christian wife, Dela, who was an influential member of the early community. Not incidentally, his children went on to attain advanced degrees and prominent careers in Niger and Europe. The pastor himself had not received a French education, since his father did not want to send his only son to the French school. Pastor Cherif wanted his own children to receive such an education and unsuccessfully pushed the mission to help him acquire one himself. Speaking in Hausa he recalled:

I said, "I don't want my children to lack an education." . . . I said, "You must teach me French." Some people, they said, "No, that's not why we brought you here, we brought you here to teach about God." I said, "Fine. . . . But one day soon, if you don't speak French you won't be able to preach." So, you see that day has come. Whatever you say, if you say it in Hausa, it isn't seen as being *valable* [Fr.; worthy of attention]. (Yacouba interview)

The resentment of men of this generation toward the mission for its failure to help Christians become educated deepened as they saw the difference between the choices missionaries made for their own children and the kind of education SIM seemed to feel was adequate for the converts: "The missionaries that I spent time with, they sent their own children to Nigeria to go to school. We had grown up with and raised those children, and they went down there to learn and the missionaries kept us here and taught us how to grow corn, sorghum, whatever, but they'd send their own children to Nigeria. . . . They'd be teaching us how to grow corn and take care of crockery" (Yacouba interview). The missionary children, who were generally fluent in Hausa and very much a part of the daily landscape of the converts, could easily enough have studied in Hausa with the other Christian children, he reasoned. The fact that they did not was deeply telling. Hausa-language instruction, he determined, was in fact inadequate, and the missionaries knew that. Cherif's and other older men's assessments of the songs and Bible verses the mission taught the girls at Soura and Dogondoutchi to parrot were scathing (e.g., Ali 'dan Buzu interview, February 19, 2001).

The overwhelming sense of men of this second generation of converts was not just that the "Americans" of the mission had failed to establish suitable schools but that they had done so deliberately (Yacouba interview; 'dan Buzu interview, February 19, 2001). The adjective "American" had come to be used by local Christians to characterize the most narrow minded and recalcitrant of the missionaries (regardless, in fact, of their national origins), who systematically worked to humiliate the converts and keep them in their place.

From Bible School to Farm School and Back Again

When the short-lived Bible school closed, the mission determined that the graduates would go to evangelize in small "unreached" villages such as Hisatau, Dargi, and Tamroro. It assigned the evangelists to different territories, by this account, without consulting the Christians. Barmo, as it happened, found this period of evangelizing exciting and enjoyed recounting his approach to me. They would gather the village leaders and the commoners and they'd announce that there would be preaching. Dargi was a strongly Muslim region at the time, but he commented that in those days the Muslim scholars didn't give him a hard time at all, it was all "play and laughter," for since they were native Hausa-speakers no one was afraid of them. One even has the sense that there was considerable collaboration and consultation between him and the community leaders he approached for access: "We'd go to the head of the village and they'd give us advice, come at this time, do this, do that." The happy tenor of his description of life in Dargi and Tamroro performing "God's work" by preaching contrasted sharply with his comment on the next stage of his life, which was notably lacking in collaboration and consultation: "That was that, then they brought me back here to Maza Tsaye, together with Ockers" to help build the new boys' home (Barmo Abdou interview). Similarly, the mission enjoined 'dan Nana to return to Soura to run the girls' home. 'Dan Nana helped supervise the children, but one of his primary tasks was simply to grow grain for the school.

The boys' home, or farm school, which was founded in 1957, was closely associated with John Ockers, a former Chicago clothing salesman. Like the school at Soura, the farm school was designed to house the as-yet-unsaved boys who gravitated to the mission from Muslim and Arna households under one form of stress or another. These children were routinely referred to as "orphans," although most had families in the region. Before the farm school had even opened, the mission had thirty children in mind—these were the children of peasant farmers who hoped to secure an education for their children, parents who would be drawn to the school in part because it appeared to offer skills in farming that would be neglected in the government school. The school was permitted to operate using vernacular languages; it emphasized manual skills and Bible training, a kind of Bible school in miniature for younger boys. The administration had always favored such practical technical education, and so for once the mission's aims and those of the government were in accord. There would be sewing (and songs) for the girls, and plowing (and prayer) for the boys, activities that struck the French administration as "suitable" for the general population of Niger.[6]

Barmo's sense of frustration at not being consulted and being abruptly moved to Maza Tsaye was echoed in numerous other interviews I conducted with the native evangelists of that generation. Rather than trust these men and their wives to establish a flourishing Christian community, the mission peremptorily brought the men back to a small village near

Maradi where the mission had acquired large tracts of farmland. The men were expected to perform maintenance tasks, preach, and teach the students about farming, in particular how use an ox-drawn plow. This kind of school bore no relationship to the kind of education the Christian community envisioned.

Members of the Tsibiri *sarauta* class did not farm directly themselves, although they managed large tracts of farmland and relied on an agricultural economy. The notion that such converts would best serve the advancement of Christianity by being forced to teach farming was eccentric at best. The less-charitable interpretation is that the mission chose to deliberately humiliate these men, who had become independent and influential and who were showing signs of too much "pride." Barmo commented that he worked "a long time" with Ockers, then went off to oversee a partially government-sponsored animal research center at Kegel as a result of his experience with using oxen and his links with one of the aristocratic families that underwrote the scheme. This activity, which involved managing large sums of money, served as a confidence-building bridge that enabled him to get out of working at the farm school, which he clearly found unpleasant. Barmo later went on to preach and do "God's work" (*aikin Ubangiji*) in Nigeria. His language suggests that he did not see working at the farm school as "God's work."

Ockers's approach was a new endeavor for the mission; for the first time SIM was bringing technical training to the population of Niger. However, in other ways the school simply carried forward an earlier philosophy: the local populations were to be trained to be simple Christians whose general position in life would not be altered by the education provided. The mission envisioned the school as an alternative to the public schools that produced white-collar workers for government service. The SIM school would produce Christian farmers, men who would remain in their villages of origin to exemplify Christian life and anchor Christian churches. Ockers did not have significant training in agricultural techniques before he joined the mission, but he learned techniques from United States Information Service (USIS) materials:

A former Chicago clothing salesman who considers himself "least qualified" for such a project, John began by planting 25 acres of peanuts, using his Jeep station wagon as a tractor, followed by boys using "new-fangled" oxen-drawn implements. . . . The staunchest Muslim soon found it hard not to respect—and listen to—the Christian missionary who could increase the yield of a millet field from 75 bundles to 325. "The results of the School have been an astonishment to government leaders, technicians, and all the common people," says John. (Lovering 1963, 8–9)

True to its original approach, the mission was not interested in improved agriculture for its own sake or merely to improve the lives of Africans but saw it as a way to attract converts: "'We repudiate the "social gospel" which ignores the saving Christ,' he states plainly. 'All our activities are part of the plan to fulfill the passion of our lives—evangelization'" (Lovering 1963, 9). The notion that Ockers was able to produce nearly miraculous improvements in yields through good old-fashioned American know-how reinforced the mission's commitment to a conception of paternalistic (white) male evangelism. The land the government of Niger made available to the mission at Maza Tsaye outside Maradi soon became an impressive farm with a modern windmill to irrigate fruit trees, imported tractors, animal traction equipment, and a great deal of unpaid labor in the form of the sizable student body. The school imported improved milk cows, developed a seed improvement scheme in conjunction with the government, and dug a number of wells (SIM 1982, 6).

The technical skills the school was meant to impart, however, could not readily be carried back to villages, for the kind of equipment available to a Chicago man who could raise funds for expensive materials at churches in the United States was simply beyond the practical reach of the students. Bible school graduates who were dragooned into working at the farm school doubted very much that the training Ockers offered was of much practical value in the long run. While Ockers managed to adapt traction equipment so that donkeys could use it and set up an *atelier* to teach young men how to weld farm equipment to sell and raise money for the school, many of the men who worked under him were deeply disillusioned by the work. Ockers's tight control of access to equipment and training meant that only those few who met the mission's rigid moral standards were permitted to acquire the animals and equipment necessary to use the methods taught, alienating many Christians from the school and from him in particular. In effect, Ockers's control of the technical materials gave him a particularly potent weapon in the battle to "discipline" Christians into a conservative fundamentalist vision of Christianity. The bleak view of the school among Christian converts was that students professed Christianity to gain access to schooling and equipment only to revert to Islam and take white-collar jobs with the Ministry of Agriculture upon graduation or they diligently learned techniques that they would of necessity abandon once they returned as impoverished peasants to their home villages ('dan Buzu interview, February 20, 2001).

It is not surprising that the Muslim students that were attracted to the school were interested in social advancement through education and had far less interest in Ockers's vision of progressive Christian farmers. One of the students who converted to Christianity, Malam Ibrahim, suggested that it was only later, after deeper exposure to Christianity in Tsibiri, that he really became committed. His eight brothers did not convert, although their father sent them all to Maza Tsaye for schooling. Long exposure to missionaries and Christians was required for conversion; the schooling alone would not have had the same effect (Malam Ibrahim 'dan Jima interview).

Other converts were diplomatic in their assessment of the positive effects of the schools. One pastor I interviewed suggested that although only a handful of conversions resulted from the various agricultural training efforts of the mission at Kegel, Danja, Maza Tsaye, and Aguié over the years, the effect of the training did alter how people in the region farmed. Everyone began using animal traction and fertilizers. So in that way, he averred, it was a big success. Before SIM's interventions there were no people using ox-drawn plows; now it is commonplace throughout the region. But in terms of converts, he could think of only a handful, something on the order of four or five along with their children. Most of the students who converted at the farm school turned back to Islam or *arnanci* (spirit worship) later (Pastor Ayyuba Lawali interview).

It is an irony that at this point the mission came full circle. Having closed the Tsibiri Bible School in the mid-1950s in favor of a focus on younger students at the farm school at Maza Tsaye (an initiative that was very popular with the government of Niger), the mission came to feel that the farm school was not having the desired effect of producing converts to Christianity. Finding that adult Christians, some of whom were illiterate, still had an interest in a Bible school, the mission decided to reopen the Bible school, this time in Aguié rather than Tsibiri. The farm school would be gradually transformed into a literacy training center for aspiring preachers, a place where adult men supporting themselves through farming at Maza Tsaye would gain enough literacy skills to go on to the the Aguié school to become certified as preachers. As an SIM publication explained the problems with the farm school and the rationale for the shift, "The goal of the school is to produce farmer-evangelists, not just farmers. The staff soon learned, however, that most students were young fellows who were more interested in getting an education than in farming or evangelizing. They had to do some heavy pruning of the enrolment system. Now, applicants must be at least 17 years old, Christian, and committed to reaching others with the gospel" (SIM 1982, 60). Conveying "improved" techniques to Nigériens became less important—the farming was largely a means of supporting the student body. The shift in attitude is signaled in a jaded comment by a missionary concerning the intensive farming seminars the school offered to evangelists: "They're farming anyway. . . . They might as well do it right" (60). The more promising aspiring preachers would be sent on to Aguié for further training, which by this point included some training in the French language. The question of who would be permitted to obtain this coveted instruction became highly contentious, leading to further friction among Christian converts and between the church and the mission.

When men were chosen for the Bible school their wives were expected to accompany them to the school and to attend special classes for the wives. Entire families moved together to reside at the school. But the wives of male Bible school students found it all but impossible to get anything out of the training the school offered. Wives of the men chosen to go to the Aguié Bible school recalled this as an extremely difficult life. Families with little in common from all over the country had to work together in a limited amount of space. Women found that they had a quadruple workload—coping with the unfamiliar routines of schoolwork, carrying on conventional farming on the family plot, finding ways to farm collectively on the women's plot, and of course continuing to maintain a household (cooking, raising children, and collecting firewood and water). The wives of the male students found it difficult to handle conflicts between their own children and those of other women, who might not speak the same language and could have very different ideas about discipline (A'i Masoyi interview). The women did not have fond memories of this experience and it is not at all clear that they felt that the training they received served them well. Men stressed the academic challenges they faced given their limited prior preparation and the intense competition for a limited number of places among individuals who hoped to become respected preachers through the training. Since becoming an elder was contingent on proving to the mission that one was properly conversant with the Bible, there was more at issue than simply becoming a preacher. To be a fully recognized adult within the church, one had to prove oneself in the Bible school.

Despite the intensity of this shared experience, no one (male or fe-

"Women of the Bible school, preparing food outside."
Courtesy of SIMIA (NR 150), photographed by
Genevieve Swanson, 1983.

male) described this experience as an occasion for the formation of a
sense of *esprit de corps*. Whatever the strengths and weaknesses of SIM's
network of Bible schools, all of the major leaders of the evangelical
churches in Niger (there are now four competing associations of
churches) went through it. Thus, the Bible schools served not only as
sites for training evangelists; they were central to determining who would
become pastors and ultimately who could become a leader within the
evangelical community. The students came from different regions of
the country, their class backgrounds conflicted in the larger society, and
the ethnic groups they represented had sometimes been at war with each
other in the past. These tensions and competition between students were
eventually played out in the fragmentation of the evangelical churches
into numerous different associations at the national level. Rather than
becoming a force for Christian solidarity, Bible school graduates fed into
existing tensions and contributed to the remarkably fractured character
of the evangelical churches today.

A Moral Education: Lessons from the Tsibiri
Primary School

One carefree morning, at my enthusiastic insistence, my assistant
Ayyuba and I took a bush taxi from Maradi to Tsibiri to visit his old
alma mater, the Tsibiri Primary School that SIM established in 1966.
The school sits on a hill slightly above the town overlooking fields on
one side and the outskirts of Tsibiri on the other. At the edge of the
school property is a melancholy cemetery that gives evidence of the tremendous personal price many missionaries were willing to pay in order
to fulfill the "great commission" in Niger. The graves of many missionaries and their children rest within a few feet of the sign marking the
entrance to the primary school. As we walked the grounds, Ayyuba rem-
inisced about how hard it was to draw water from the deep well, about
the lousy food, and about the valuable Christian training he felt he received at a time when missionaries still ran the school, which is now run
by the EERN. Increasingly pensive, he recalled being punished for eating
fruit from the fruit trees when he was hungry. Clusters of small children
huddled around food pails eating their lunch and watching us warily as
we passed. Do you know them, I asked? No, he said, it's all children of
Muslim families now. We explored the depressingly dilapidated dorms,
whose light fixtures had been torn out, leaving the hanging entrails of
wiring. Children's modest bedding lay scattered on the dingy floor. In
the main school building, supercilious teachers, all of whom were male,
greeted us coolly. As we made our way out to explore the modest garden,
the budget manager pointedly told me that Ayyuba's younger brother's
school fees had not been paid. We continued on our way in embarrassed
silence. Our happy-go-lucky expedition had gradually turned somber.
Later, as partial compensation to Ayyuba for the many ways he had assisted me, I helped his parents meet the school fees, knowing that no
one had the money for the youngster to finish out the year. But given
all that we both eventually came to know about the school, it was hard
for us not to have some misgivings. What should have been cause for
celebration gave rise primarily to unease.

Whereas under the French, a religious school conducted in English
by American missionaries would have been unthinkable, after independence the Nigérien government was far more open to investment in
infrastructure of all kinds. Like so many SIM initiatives, this school was
primarily the brainchild of one missionary, a Canadian woman named

Gwen Van Lierop. From the perspective of local Christians, Van Lierop championed the school by seeking out funding on her own, in spite of the objections of the mission, and was responsible for paying the school fees of many Tsibiri Primary School students (Malam Saley interview; 'dan Buzu interview, February 20, 2001).

Rather than establish a day school in a major urban center such as Maradi or Niamey, Van Lierop, mission staff, and local church leaders decided to create a coeducational primary boarding school. This was a major decision that was to have long-term ramifications for the school. In my view, it was a serious mistake to establish a residential school rather than a day school. During the period I was able to document (1967 through 1995), the school never had sufficient means to cover the very substantial expense of running a boarding school; it is clear that today the school continues in a state of constant crisis. The lack of sufficient funding to run such a school had profound implications for the pedagogical and moral mission of the institution. So long as the mission oversaw the school, these problems could be held more or less in check. However, once the school was transferred to the EERN churches without sufficient resources to run it properly, it fell into steep academic decline.

When it was first created, the school was intended to serve the children of the converted Christians, many of whom were evangelists working in remote villages with little access to schools. These evangelists worked with very little pay and subsisted, like other villagers, on farming. Initially, then, the student body was heavily made up of Christian children from modest backgrounds whose parents aspired to give them a more thorough education than their own in a suitably Christian environment. Once the school was there, however, missionaries and churches used it as a way to draw the disadvantaged children who fell into their orbit into Christianity—sometimes these were the children of parents being treated for leprosy at the Danja Leprosarium, for example. Later, however, after the language of instruction shifted from English to French, non-Christian families with sufficient means began sending their children to the school after they had failed out of the public schools. The student body was increasingly made up of paying *"redoublants,"* students who had to repeat a grade and had little interest in the Christian dimension of the school. The school accepted higher and higher proportions of such relatively weak students, and the overall quality of the student body declined over time and the Christian character of the school was diluted. It was hard for the school to acknowledge the reality of its shifting student body, but it was even harder to turn down paying students given the perilous financial condition of the school.

Why was a residential school deemed necessary? Itinerant evangelists in distant villages could leave their children with the school knowing that they would receive a Christian upbringing. In some ways this was quite similar to the way missionaries handled their own children's schooling during the 1960s; many missionary children were educated in special boarding schools such as Kent Academy and Hillcrest in Nigeria and Gowan's Home for Missionaries' Children in Collingwood, Canada. Evangelists were simply mimicking the family style of SIM missionaries of the time in advocating the creation of a boarding school.

Minutes of planning meetings for the development of the school show that missionaries and converts wanted to create a Christian environment in which biblical teachings were reinforced through practice outside the classroom. Classes in Bible study and secular subjects were not in themselves seen to be sufficient. Children would put Christianity into practice in their hygiene, in their relations with one another, in their evangelism to their neighbors, and in their approach to subjects such as history and science.[7] In many ways, the most important aspect of the school from the point of view of Christian parents and missionaries was the moral training that would be provided by the supervisors of the children rather than the teachers:

> Mister Ockers reminded us that this position is the one with the most responsibility in the school because it is the "raison d'être" of the school, that is to teach children "discipline" regarding God's Word in how they live, not just in class. The ones who will oversee the children will be parents in God's name, to explain God's ways, and to draw the children to God, to lead them along in his path. Everyone agreed to this speech.[8]

At first, teaching was conducted in English and the staff was made up largely of anglophone missionaries. The school was closely linked with the English-language mission schools SIM had established in Nigeria. Students who succeeded in Tsibiri went on to higher levels in Nigeria. At the end of their studies they would be fluent in English and would have an education that was recognized within the anglophone system. The supervision of the children was in the hands of trusted local pastors and their wives. For many years, from the opening of the school until his death in 1982, Pastor Maman Kouloungou was an anchor for a shifting staff and student body, serving the school in a variety of capacities, primarily as a supervisor of the male children.

During the period when the language of instruction was English, the results obtained by students appear to have been rather good. Graduates of the school I spoke to from that era were proud of the school and felt it had served them well. Some were dismayed by the school's decline and hoped to somehow revive the school through an alumni association, but they were not convinced that a boarding school in Tsibiri would work. They spoke of trying to establish a new primary day school in Maradi. Parents of these alumni on the whole also had positive reports. One woman maintained that the English-language schooling her children got at the Tsibiri school served them well so long as they planned ahead. They needed to find their way into the Nigerian school system. People who didn't plan ahead ended up with something they couldn't use in Niger. Her older children all went to the school and went on to obtain desirable jobs teaching English in Niger.[9]

Many of the older men of the church, on the other hand, who had long urged the mission to create French-language primary schools, insisted that the English-language era of the school was a terrible mistake. The children obtained schooling that was of no relevance in Niger, had difficulty continuing into secondary school without assistance to pay for board in schools in Nigeria, and then could not find jobs because their educational achievements and networks were not recognized in Niger. It is presumably in part because of the persistent objections of these men that the school eventually shifted from English-language instruction to French. Discontentment on the part of Christian parents with a curriculum that seemed to guarantee that their children would spend much of their lives in Nigeria meant that the number of Christian children enrolled in the school was not always as high as the mission had hoped. The school came to function more and more as a place to gain access to Muslim students who might be attracted to Christianity rather than a place to foster Christian community and discipleship. In 1973–1974, the school shifted to the French-language program, but it still taught English and Bible study for an hour before regular school time. Students would still have the benefit of access to English; with the addition of intensive English for the older students, there was the potential to continue study in the SIM schools in Nigeria. The first students sat for the exam to enter secondary school in the public school system of Niger in 1979.[10]

However, the shift to French-language instruction required a massive shift in staffing and the hiring of teachers who were not missionaries. These teachers had to be paid at the standard government salary rate and had to be recruited from among the small number of evangelical Christians in French-speaking countries. For a school that was already running at a loss, this was a major burden to take on. For the first time, the school council entertained hiring Catholic staff, finding that it was difficult to meet its need for teachers within the modestly educated evangelical community.[11] In contrast, the mission did not have great difficulty finding suitable supervisors for the dorms. But once it had to find both certified francophone teachers with suitable religious beliefs and supervisory staff for the Christian upbringing of the children in the dorms on the other, it faced constant crises in staffing.

It is clear that within a decade of its opening, the school was a subject of intense debate within the Christian community and was regarded at best with ambivalence by the mission. Because it operated regularly at a loss, it was a drain on mission finances. This was a significant problem for a mission that emphasized that all institutions generated by missionaries had to be self-supporting. As the school admitted more students who could actually meet the fees, its Christian character became diluted and the standard of preparation of the students declined. John Ockers, who was a member of the council that oversaw the school from its inception, reported in a mission newsletter in 1979:

> Different people look at Tsibiri School through different glasses: District Superintendents [of the mission] may look at it as a perpetual headache of palavers; some folks look at it as an institutional evil; the school committee and PTO perhaps view it as a financial enigma; many missionaries and many nationals view it as a great place to send a kid to learn about Jesus who at home is effectively squelched by muslim parents, relatives and muslim priests [sic]. (Ockers quoted in Koley 1984, 14)

The fall of Diori Hamani in a coup d'etat in 1974 considerably altered the conditions in which the mission operated the school. The military regime of Seyni Kountché sought legitimacy through a strong antiwestern and pro-Islamic stance. SIM began to be concerned that its ability to continue operations in Niger was at risk because laws were passed banning foreigners from participating in the economy in a broad range of positions (Koley 1984, 25). The government instituted policies that mandated that expatriate employees be replaced by Nigériens and encouraged practical training in agriculture in an effort to focus on ordinary farmers suffering from the extended drought. Kountché aimed to alter the culture of schooling in Niger to orient students to rural life and farming rather than urban white-collar employment as the ability of the government to absorb school-leavers declined and urban centers became sites of student unrest. In addition to the regular courses, the school was now expected to offer practical training in gardening and nutrition with no increase in its revenues.

The mission hoped to effect a transfer of the school to the national Christians in view of the danger that the mission would suddenly be excluded from schooling altogether. Diori Hamani had encouraged the national Christians to create a suitable corporate body to receive many mission institutions not long after independence, and it was in this context that the Église Évangélique de la République du Niger was created. It was headed by many of the men who had been trained in the mission's Bible schools. The transfer of some mission properties had already occurred under Diori, including the farm school and the Bible school at Aguié. In the 1970s, the mission began to put more and more of its own energies into medical facilities and relief and development work. It had neglected formal academic training for the Christian community for many years, and there was no one suitable to run the Tsibiri Primary School. There was no one trained to handle the complex and vexatious problem of the finances of the school, there was no one trained in educational management to oversee the school, and the teaching staff was young and inexperienced. When Pastor Kouloungou died in 1982 just as the mission was poised to turn management of the school over to him, plans to transfer the school had to be put on hold. It was not until 1990 that the government formally recognized the transfer of the school from SIM to the EERN. Even with eight years to manage the transfer, the school still did not have suitable personnel to handle the budget and was having great difficulty finding suitable supervisory staff to oversee the dorms, particularly for the girls.

While the EERN establishment resented the mission's oversight of the curriculum and occupation of staff positions coveted by educated Christians, it did not want to take on the cost of running the school itself. SIM proposed that the EERN seek out further support for the school while recognizing that the mission's engagement would be ending soon.[12] In the meantime, one of the leaders of the church who had spent a great deal of time in Europe managed to find an outside donor, the Lutolf family of Switzerland, that was willing to provide the school with substantial financial support ('dan Buzu interview, February 20, 2001). The transfer of the school was finally made in 1990.

SIM's sense of urgency about ridding itself of the school, however, was not simply due to the financial encumbrance it represented. The school raised "certain concerns" among the senior missionaries who were familiar with a series of disturbing events that had transpired there.[13] The documentable incidents were for the most part structurally similar: male teaching staff were alleged to have engaged in sexual improprieties with female students. Either the supervisory staff ignored students' complaints because they could not believe the "lies" the students were telling about the teachers or male administrators brushed off the female supervisory staff's complaints about the teachers' behavior. The pattern showed a serious lack of authority over the male teaching staff. In most cases like these, rather than investigate the accusation or discipline the teacher, the authorities determined that the girl was "deficient" and sent her away.[14] Nigérien educational culture, unfortunately, does tolerate a certain amount of sexual activity between secondary school students and male teachers. However, because the school was a residential school for *primary* rather than secondary students—all of whom are under sixteen— the students were perhaps more vulnerable to the depredations of teachers than is normally the case in Niger. Primary schools are not generally boarding schools (although there are some primary boarding schools for the children of nomads). The combination of marginal and weak students who were hoping for a second chance at school, teachers whose salaries were regularly unpaid, and a lack of disciplinary oversight of teachers made for an environment that was particularly conducive to the sexual harassment of students.

The mission seemed incapable of coming up with a reasonable way to clarify sexual boundaries for the teaching staff or establish a clear hierarchy for discipline. In many ways, the supervisory staff for the dorms were like servants: they oversaw things such as cooking and cleaning and the general cleanliness of the children. They were paid less than the teachers, they had limited education themselves, and their duties regularly increased as the financial condition of the school declined. Eventually, the supervisor of the girls' dorm, for example, was expected to be the cook as well; later, teaching sewing was added to her duties. Married couples who shared the job had to split a single salary. It was not reasonable to expect such employees to discipline educated male teachers. The school's directors, who might have provided the discipline, seem to have had more sympathy with the teachers than with the supervisory staff and the students. Whatever was the case, no clear line of authority was established in the wake of these incidents. Later, in drawing up school rules, SIM did not raise the question of appropriate relations between students and faculty as a responsibility of the academic director and faculty. Rather, what follows was buried in the rules governing the responsibilities of the woman overseeing the girls:

> Unmarried teachers should not under any circumstances solicit services of any kind from the girls entrusted to the school and they should be vigilant about their own comportment: no appearance of familiarity is permitted and no gifts should be either given or received. It is recommended that each day be begun with the reading of a text from the Bible and a prayer.[15]

In other words, it was implicitly the duty of the girls' dorm mother to see to it that the unmarried male teachers did not compromise the girls, and one way to do that was to make sure the girls began the day with prayer. Another was to spy on the girls to see whether they were receiving gifts. No one seems to have worried much about the behavior of married men or about whether the boys might be subject to sexual abuse as well. Placing this burden on the dorm mother and the girls displaced responsibility from the male teachers and the school's academic director. This was a particularly perilous solution, since finding a woman to oversee the girls was often difficult and personnel were sometimes secured only at the last moment.[16] In the 1980s, the school's academic performance slid precipitously. By 1988, only four out of thirty-four candidates qualified for the *certificat d'études primaires* (which was a prerequisite for secondary school); all of the students who passed were boys.[17] This is in striking contrast with earlier results: in 1979, fourteen students took the exam and ten passed; seven earned scholarships to go on to secondary schools (Koley 1984, 18).

Once the school became the responsibility of the EERN, it became clear that the churches simply were not in a position to contribute substantially to the functioning of the school.[18] Without the financial assistance of the Lutolf family, the school would have closed immediately. The financial troubles of the school led to rather predictable suspicions that somehow someone was embezzling the money to run it. A quick glance at the enormous difference between the expenses of the school and its income suggests that there is no particular reason to assume that someone was stealing money—without SIM to cover the deficit caused by the failure of parents to pay the school fees, the pain of operating in the red had to be absorbed somehow.

The school's problems only became more acute after 1990. The government of Niger had been in economic crisis since 1990, and the modest government subventions that had contributed to the running of the school in the past had also dried out. By 1992, there is some suggestion in the documents that the students were not being fed adequately, despite assistance from the World Food Programme. The Christian bookstore in town refused to allow the school to continue buying supplies on credit. Classes were too large, the staff was not professionally trained, there were only enough texts for the teachers so that lessons had to be copied onto the blackboard, and the tuition payments of parents were irregular at best.[19] The rather unfortunate solution to the economic deficit seems to have been to fail to pay the teachers their salaries for months at a time. The demoralized staff, prepared to believe that the director and budget officer were not serving their best interests, tended to turn to the EERN with their grievances rather than address them to the director of the school.[20]

In this climate, it is hard to see how anyone could expect modestly schooled female dorm staff to discipline the unpaid and resentful educated male teachers effectively. During the school year of 1993–1994 another crisis occurred. The housemother for the girls accused one of the teachers of attempting to rape one of the students. Other girls came forward to allege that this was the second time the teacher had attempted a rape. It was noted that two of the female students seemed to visit his room regularly. The director reported all of this to the president of the EERN, stating finally, "The Director has given [the teacher] a severe warning against such activities, extremely blameworthy in a teacher, an educator of Christian youth."[21] Evidently the word of the housemother and the student were not deemed sufficient to justify suspending or firing the teacher immediately.

Whatever the truth of any single allegation, it is clear that the school has failed utterly to meet its original charge to raise children in a conservative Christian environment, one in which Christian precepts would be exemplified and enacted through daily activity, service, and evangelism. Beyond making it possible for some failing students to have a second chance in school, it is hard to see how this establishment is contributing to education in Niger, to the aspirations of the Christian families, or to the original imperative of the evangelical community to foster a missionary consciousness among its converts. The Tsibiri Primary School failed on both academic and moral grounds, and given its appalling reputation today, it is hard to see how it can be redeemed.

The lesson SIM personnel often take from this is that it is not a good idea to support fixed institutions and educational infrastructure. However, there was no real reason why the school had to be a boarding school. If the students had been housed with Christian families for a minimal boarding fee in Maradi, they could have received a high-quality education in a day school while conceivably benefiting from the kind of exemplary Christian environment itinerant pastors hoped their children would be raised in. Many rural children were raised in the household of Pastor Garba and other Christian families in just such a manner so that they could attend the public schools in Maradi. The strategy of evangelism through fostering was, indeed, one of the most important ways the Christian community expanded in Maradi. The notion that only through boarding schools can children go to school away from their home villages is an odd one that bears little relationship to realities on the ground in Niger—extended social networks, for better or for worse, regularly absorb children for the sake of schooling far from home. Such children would not be immune to sexual harassment or exploitation of their labor, but were such abuses to occur they would be neither systematic nor the fault of the school itself.

Given the outcome of this experiment, it is unlikely that the SIM mission will ever entertain establishing primary schools in Niger again. The EERN may have an ongoing interest in creating a network of Christian private schools, but the poor oversight of the school now means that those few Christians who are enthusiastic about private schooling would be unlikely to entrust their contributions to the EERN. It is far more likely they would set up independent corporations of interested donors and build schools on a rather modest scale staffed by trusted friends, family members, and colleagues. Because the public school system in Niger is in a state of collapse, private schools may very well be the only way forward for the children of Niger. One way or another, Christians in Niger and donors abroad will need to reflect deeply about how best to meet the educational needs of these children in a context in which private Islamic schools are very much on the rise and the most powerful international lenders are hostile to public-sector expansion. Private Islamic schools (which are less subject to strikes than the public schools) are undoubtedly the best solution for most Nigérien families that can afford them at the present moment. Whether such schools could ever serve the Christian community well is a question the mission has studiously avoided answering. The question of the relationship of churches to schools in Niger remains urgent and unresolved.

9

Handmaid to the Gospel:
SIM's Medical Work in Niger, 1944–1975

*"The tall one, Father of Kero, Rushing off to
'Dan Issa [to preach]"*

—Epithet of praise (*kirari*) for Jim Lucas,
who built the hospital at Galmi and
originally oversaw the Danja Leprosarium

Of Nurses and Evangelists, Successes and Failures

When Adamu Na Mamayo was a young man in Nigeria tending his
father's cattle, he was encouraged to pursue Koranic learning as his father, a Fulani Muslim scholar, had done. He was eighteen and well
trained in Islam when his family discovered that he was showing symptoms of *kurtu*, or leprosy. They sent him to a SIM leprosarium in Nigeria
for treatment in the early 1950s. As the son of a Muslim scholar, he was
not at all inclined to listen to the preaching of the missionaries. But he
had to stay at the leprosarium for several years, for at that time treatments of leprosy (Hansen's Disease) had limited efficacy. Like many
Hansen's Disease patients, he tolerated the ineffective treatments because
the mission was quite effective at treating the symptoms and side effects
of the disease, such as cuts, burns, and loss of the use of hands and feet.
The mission could also provide useful documentation when the disease
had ceased to be contagious, enabling the patient to travel. Missionaries
also had a great deal of experience with the disease; they knew that it
was not highly contagious and as a result treated patients with humanity.[1]
Adamu lived in a kind of village with other patients, farming to earn

his keep and becoming accustomed to the Christianized routines of the leprosarium. In time he came to enjoy hearing the missionaries recount in Hausa some of the familiar stories in the Abrahamic tradition, particularly the story of Noah. He found that he wanted to know more about some of these stories and began to read the Hausa Bible in secret. He hid his new interest from his family and quietly questioned Muslim scholars about the new Christian perspective he was gaining on Jesus and the prophets. During his long stay at the leprosarium, he fell in love with another patient, a young Hausa woman from the Maradi region. By the time he was cleared to leave the leprosarium after five years he and his Hausa bride were crypto-Christians. He went home with a Bible, which he did not hide, but he was not ready to confront his father directly. Reluctant to tell his family of his conversion, he persuaded the mission to support him for further biblical training in a SIM Bible school in Malumfashi so that he would be fully equipped to counter the arguments of his scholarly kin. Eventually he did go home when he was about twenty-five and openly profess his Christianity. "Oh no," cried his mother, "there will be no one to bury you!" His father died six months later. In Nigeria, his kinfolk and Muslim neighbors refused to eat with him. It was clear that he no longer had a viable community. Eventually, in 1977, the mission encouraged Adamu to move to the Maradi region with his Nigérien bride to serve as a preacher in the SIM leprosarium in Danja. Adamu came to Niger to live near his wife's family and raised his own children in the more congenial setting of the Maradi region, where Muslims and Christians have traditionally had a less fraught relationship with one another.

Scholarly work on health and missions in Africa often focuses on curing and the body, western conceptions of medicine, and the violence of western medical intrusions. These are important issues, yet in this case it was precisely the failure of the mission to provide a quick and effective cure for Hansen's Disease that ensured the conditions that gave Pastor Adamu long exposure to Christianity, habituation to Christian routines, and the possibility of creating a family and earning an income as a preacher. SIM's medical interventions in this region begin with this paradox—that it was the inadequacy of "scientific" treatments for leprosy that made leprosaria particularly fruitful sites for evangelism before the widespread use of sulfone-based antibiotics in the mid-1950s (on the gradual adoption of the use of antibiotics, see Silla 1998, 106–115). Once SIM had a broader network of medical installations and relatively effective treatment options for a variety of medical conditions, the value of medical evangelism declined, for patients came for shorter periods of time and were less likely to become acculturated to Christianity in quite the manner that Adamu and his wife did. SIM in Niger came to have a rather ambivalent relationship to its medical work, for the more effective it was in medical terms, the less useful it became as a vehicle for evangelism. Unfamiliar treatments that could effect near-miraculous cures (as in the case of cataract surgery restoring vision) might attract attention for the mission. But a recognition of the efficacy of western medicine did not translate directly into conversion or the rejection of older spiritual and therapeutic beliefs.

Recent work in medical history has not painted a particularly flattering picture of the effects of western scientific medicine in Africa. It is now more clear than it was in the past that some of the interventions carried out in the name of health under colonial rule were not just oppressive and deeply resented—they actually contributed to the spread of the very diseases that superior civilization and "scientific" approaches were supposed to vanquish. Rather than curing or simply palliating diseases such as sleeping sickness, colonial interventions sometimes created conditions that guaranteed the spread of serious contagions. At the same time, the allocation of energy and resources to such scourges as sleeping sickness, leprosy, yellow fever, smallpox, and meningitis meant that social and political conditions that contributed to ill health were neglected or ignored (Lyons 1992). In view of that reality, one might take cold comfort in the utter neglect of any kind of medical intervention whatsoever in colonial Niger. There was so little medical work in Niger under colonial rule that perhaps the best that can be said of it is that it can't have done much harm.[2]

Where the demand for labor in other colonies in a sense constrained the government to take an interest in the health of its potential labor pool, Niger was never regarded as a promising source of labor. Instead, the region was a source of grain, livestock, and eventually peanuts. The administration neglected diseases such as leprosy that had little impact on the white population, and it was too preoccupied with political control, tax collection, and peanut and cattle production to care very much about the general health of the local population.[3] The system was so rudimentary and so little oriented to the needs of the indigenous population that the capital of Niamey did not have any hospital beds designated for African subjects until 1948.[4] Given the weakness of the infrastructure it inherited at independence, it is not surprising that Niger regularly appears in United Nations and World Bank publications as having some of the worst living conditions in the world (second only to war-ravaged Sierra Leone).

SIM's post-Brazzaville entry into medical work in Niger to redress this void had a scattershot quality for three reasons. First, France's distaste for the contamination of secular government by cooperation with religious institutions meant that the kind of hand-in-glove relationship between missions and state that emerged in its most extreme form in the Congo was never in evidence in Niger (cf. Hunt 1997). France's health interventions tended toward mass vaccination campaigns and the forced removal of towns to more-salubrious locations; the military dimension of these interventions was more than metaphoric (Bado 1996). Without an overarching vision of health care from the state (both during the colonial era and after), the mission was left more or less to its own devices. If it proposed something that interested the government, it would probably be approved, but beyond that there was little cooperation between the mission and the state.

Second, SIM never developed a larger philosophy about the significance of its health care interventions because the funding and enthusiasm for any project was largely spearheaded by particular individuals who raised funding for their work from their own personal networks of supporters at home. It never articulated a commitment to sustain a medical infrastructure or cultivate and pay a medical staff as an end in itself. To do so would have implied an entirely different system of financing for mission work that would have been closer to that of the older denominational missions. In other words, the mission as an institution would have had to raise money for medical work as its defining function and then hire appropriate staff to serve in its facilities. The notion of being called to service would have been lost, and the sense that individual missionary work was financed "by prayer" would have had to have been abandoned.

Finally, almost from its inception as a mission, SIM was ambivalent about the relationship between prayer and healing. The three initial founders had been trained by Reverend Albert B. Simpson at the Missionary Training College in New York (later known as Nyack College) to believe that there was a lost world in need of saving and that divine healing through fervent prayer would assist the missionary in the field (Turaki 1993, 38–39). The conviction that they were God's anointed servants and that God would therefore protect them from illness was permanently shaken when two of the three (Gowans and Kent) died almost immediately (53–54, 57). Early losses among SIM missionaries in the face of the health challenges West Africa posed had a humbling effect.[5] The faith missions had emphasized the power of prayer and SIM insisted that God would meet its workers' financial needs if those with genuine faith practiced "definite prayer" (80), and this recognition of prayer's limits was unsettling and occasioned much soul-searching on Rowland Bingham's part. After two decades of tremendous losses among its ranks, SIM finally began to have greater success keeping missionaries in the field because of a number of advances in tropical medicine, prompting Bingham to remark, "It can be seen what a tremendous debt we owe to medical science" (Bingham 1943, 31). SIM's ongoing discomfort with Pentecostalism has partly to do with its reluctant but pragmatic recognition, born of painful experience, that sometimes prayer is not enough.[6]

Bingham wrote regularly on the subject of faith healing as editor of the *Evangelical Christian* magazine, writings that were gathered together and published in his popular book *The Bible and the Body: Healing in the Scriptures* (1921/1952). The book offered a biblical basis for a position *against* divine healing as a response to the Christian Alliance and Christian Science movements of the late nineteenth and early twentieth centuries. He responded to the claim that "all sickness is of the devil" and the notion that sickness is due to sin with the argument that although human illness followed from the fall from innocence, the particular illnesses of individuals could not always be attributed to moral lapses: "There is a tremendous amount of sickness in the world to-day which has no direct connection with sin, and, as far as the individual sufferer is concerned, is due to no breach of the Moral Law" (28). The faith healing movement tended to imply that the use of any means beyond prayer revealed a lack of faith in God. For adherents of the faith healing movement, Christ's atonement for human sin guaranteed that prayer would effect a cure for any human illness, a line of thinking captured in the phrase "Divine healing is in the Atonement."

Bingham used a close reading of the central biblical passages of the faith healing movement to argue instead that God "has chosen to use means and to guide in their right selection for the healing and health of his people" (31). God as healer had provided, through "the Great healing Covenant," six ways to bring humans into health beyond prayer—sanitation, sterilization, quarantine, hygiene, exercise, and rest. Only when moral lapses were the source of illness would prayer be an effective cure: "Sickness needs no atonement, but sin does: and where sickness is caused by sin, the atoning sacrifice is essential for the forgiveness of sins" (37).

It is interesting to note that Bingham believed that leprosy, as the "one incurable disease" medical science faced, must constitute one of the few examples of disease caused by "spiritual uncleanness and sin" (39–45). Many of the cases of miraculous healing in the Bible involved cases of leprosy. Thus, although the mission Bingham founded rejected faith healing on the whole and was open to the use of rational medical science as an appropriate and indeed godly "means" to bring about health, in its attitude toward leprosy it promoted (at least until the early 1950s) the belief that prayer and repentance might have a kind of efficacy in the face of the sin that produced the disease. The possibility that prayer might indeed have an efficacy beyond the "means" God had provided through science in the case of leprosy may well have contributed to the mission's sense that leprosaria were particularly appropriate sites of medical intervention for an evangelical mission.

After 1920, SIM's understanding of the relationship between prayer and healing was, therefore, shifting and ambivalent. SIM proceeded gingerly in medical work, occasionally claiming medical successes as signs of spiritual breakthrough and God's miraculous action in the world but also carefully skirting the daunting question of how to understand the many heartrending failures this kind of "physical ministry" would inevitably entail. Its emphasis on evangelism over health care relieved the mission of responsibility for measuring its success in terms of its effectiveness in healing the population, whether through science or through prayer. Station records recorded incidents of "treatment" for ailments and counted converts, but the mission made no attempt to keep track of treatment outcomes in the prewar period (SIM 1932, 31–32).

Nevertheless, by the time of Niger's independence, SIM had built a leprosarium at Danja and the best hospital in Niger at Galmi and had dispensaries staffed with qualified nurses scattered across the country. The mission's links with the highly developed mission health care infrastructure in Nigeria also meant that Nigérien patients could be referred to the Kano Eye Hospital and other such facilities and mission staff could benefit from medical training with qualified and experienced doctors without having to leave West Africa. SIM missionaries set about filling the tremendous vacuum created by the French administration's years of neglect with characteristic vigor and enthusiasm, becoming for a time the backbone of the medical infrastructure of Niger. SIM's rather heroic medical work is something about which it should be justifiably proud, and during this period (which lasted from 1944 through about 1975), President Diori Hamani honored Dr. Burt Long and three nurses, field director Newton Kapp, and his wife Doris Kapp with National Orders in appreciation for their service to the newly independent country (Fuller 1967, 124–125; Lovering 1966). As the epigraph for this chapter suggests, the medical work was on the whole deeply valued by local populations, producing goodwill for the mission and intimate relationships between the local population and individual missionaries.

This movement into social services was an extraordinary departure from the original impulse of the independent premillennial evangelical mission movement. All evangelical missionaries had mixed feelings about medical work and its potential material distractions from evangelism and the spirit, and debates about medical mission work are almost as old as evangelism itself (see Beidelman 1982, 109–112; Comaroff and Comaroff 1997, 323–329). However, the faith missions, brash latecomers to the mission endeavor, entered such debates with the assurance of those who have little practical experience.

As Dana Robert has argued, premillennial mission theorists felt that "proclamation of the gospel took precedence over such traditional missionary activity as education and medicine," and it was this conviction that led to the creation of independent mission boards and the faith mission movement (Robert 1990, 32). Evangelical mission theorist A. J. Gordon of the American Baptist Missionary Union, for example, "explicitly rejected educational, industrial, or other 'civilizing' forms of mission work as not only unnecessary forms of mission but as undesirable. For example, not only did higher education not bring the unsaved to Jesus Christ, but western education prevented them from becoming Christian" (41; see also Austin 1990, 55, on Henry Frost of the China Inland Mission).

The gradualism implied in providing education and social services to win converts slowly to salvation ran very much counter to the original premillennialism of the faith mission movement. Once the student volunteer movement of the 1880s had gathered force and the century had turned (with no Second Coming), the well-known watchword "the evangelization of the world in this generation" lost some of its premillennial content while retaining its eschatological urgency (Robert 1990, 38). The institutionalization of the movement in the 1920s became, in a sense, the triumphant paradigm through which mission work would proceed. Eventually it became possible, for some at least, to contemplate using physical institutions to enact urgently needed spiritual change while retaining both an antipathy for secular education outside the evangelical subcultural milieu and deep misgivings about the social and material aspirations of potential converts. The approach did not, however, imply that a life of service or an ethos of charity should take precedence over verbal witness for Christ. Medical and educational work would be, as David Osborne carefully noted at the time, "handmaids to the Gospel" (Osborne 1946, 9).[7]

The shift toward "physical ministries" that characterized the mission's work, particularly during the 1950s and 1960s, was the outcome of a complex array of factors, including the resistance of Muslims to evangelism, the growing proportion of female missionaries, the opening up of new possibilities in the wake of the Brazzaville conference, and a softening and humanization of "the Muslim" in comparison with other perceived evils in the Cold War era. The mission associated the shift in the tenor and audience of its evangelism strongly with the demographic shift in the mission staff: "One of the results of mission stations being 'manned' by women (because male missionaries are not coming to the work in sufficient numbers) is that more attention is given on these stations to the African women and children" (Kirk 1950, 7). Indeed, the image of the mission that was conveyed through its periodicals changed substantially as single women missionaries, often nurses and teachers, contributed articles that reflected on work in the mission fields. Articles about medical work easily overshadowed the reportage on translation work, Bible schools, and itinerant preaching, the former mainstays of the mission. Little wonder, then, that some of the older missionaries who were wedded to the more masculine image of the pioneer evangelist in the wilderness fretted that not enough men were working and too little old-fashioned preaching was occurring.

Conflicting Priorities: Colonial Perceptions of Niger's Medical Needs

SIM first began to take an interest in medical work in Niger as a result of the extraordinary success of the leprosaria the mission inherited from the colonial administration in Nigeria in 1937 in producing committed converts. However, the mission in Niger quickly found that it was at odds with the French administration over the medical priorities of the colony. One reason colonial administration mistrusted Osborne and his efforts to obtain permission for medical work may have been that leprosy did not seem at all obvious as a primary medical target in a colony as lacking in facilities as Niger. From very early on, the colonial medical staff expressed far greater concern about venereal diseases, particularly

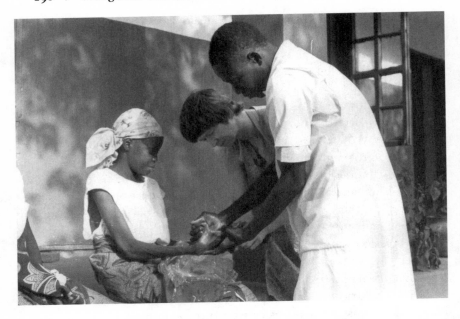

"Maradi Leprosarium. Pat Morgan examining 'wax treatment' for disfigured hands." Courtesy of SIMIA (NR 70), photographed by Derek Frost, 1984.

syphilis, which appeared to be a serious problem in the region.[8] Vaughan's work suggests that early colonial medical understandings of syphilis was murky at best; the difference between endemic and venereal syphilis was poorly understood and the disease was in any case often confused with yaws (Vaughan 1991, 137–138; see also Bado 1996). Whether syphilis was indeed the rampant problem medical reports portrayed is difficult to know. But it is clear that the colonial administration identified this, rather than leprosy, as a high priority.

At the level of the AOF as a whole, the medical services were preoccupied with major life-threatening epidemics that included plague, smallpox, yellow fever, and meningitis. Diseases that, while contagious, were primarily characterized by their slow debilitating effects rather than by mortality were of less concern. Unlike the British, who tended to treat leprosy as a dangerous epidemic, the French medical establishment regarded it largely as a debilitating rather than a fatal disease, an assessment that shaped the strategy regarding its treatment.[9] Maradi was particularly susceptible to epidemics of all kinds (including leprosy) because it lay on the critical north-south corridor of trade, labor migration, and pastoral movement between Niger and Nigeria.[10] In an allied development, the growth of trade, male labor migration, and urbanization caused colonial administrators to express alarm about a perceived rise in alcoholism in Maradi.[11]

It was not until 1936 that any colonial administrator in the Maradi region became concerned enough about leprosy to mention it explicitly, and one suspects that this may have been prompted by a particularly scathing commentary by the Service de la Lèpre in Bamako in the preceding year.[12] Later *rapports de tournée* continued to note scattered cases, which were often associated with blindness, but leprosy never was an overriding concern for colonial administrators of the region and in general their hope was that it would die out on its own.[13] Of course it may simply have been the case that local populations hid Hansen's patients or sent them to the mission-run leprosaria in Nigeria, a strategy that was possible by the late 1930s. In the mid-1920s, the French government initiated a new policy in response to its perception that the African population was in decline. Its solution was to work to eradicate major contagious diseases, a plan that generated many rules and regulations and a handful of research institutes, such as the Institute Central de la Lèpre in Bamako. But it is not at all clear that these territory-wide endeavors had much impact on the perceptions or activities of administrators in Niger in general or Maradi in particular (Bado 1996, 246, 255, 284, 355, 428).

Thus, by 1940, the year in which Osborne's proposal to build a leprosarium in Maradi was briefly approved and then abruptly set aside "until the return of more favorable circumstances," the medical report for Niger notes that the hospital in Maradi had treated thirty-three leprosy patients and had discerned ninety-five cases in the region as a whole; by comparison, it treated 944 cases of smallpox and 626 cases of malaria.[14] It is easy to imagine that Niger's administrators found Osborne's insistence upon a leprosarium perplexing and perhaps even suspiciously wrong-headed. This was a medical intervention that could be put off without great human or health costs, or so it probably seemed to the French administration at the time. And indeed, SIM's interest in leprosaria was evangelical rather than medical—missionaries such as Osborne with at best superficial medical training could hardly have had any real sense of the medical priorities of the region. They simply knew that the SIM leprosaria in Nigeria had proven to be marvelous sources of converts and native evangelists. Following Bingham, they were disposed to believe that leprosy, unlike some other forms of human suffering, fell into the realm of illness caused by sin and curable through repentance and conversion.

The French colonial administration's first move in Niger to begin to make amends for the unpleasantness of the Vichy period did not revive the moribund issue of the leprosarium; instead, it transferred an existing government dispensary in Tsibiri to the care of the mission in 1944. With the need to mobilize all available medical personal in the service of the war effort, such a transfer of costs and personnel undoubtedly served all parties well:

> In 1944 the Government turned over to us the use of their large dispensary at Tsibiri. Since then we have had a registered nurse in charge, caring for an ever-increasing medical work which in addition to bringing physical relief to thousands is a wonderful handmaid to the Gospel in that souls are being saved through it. (Osborne 1946, 9)

This was an extremely important development, for it gave the mission access to populations it would not otherwise have been able to reach and produced committed Christians who then went on to become evangelists themselves. These facilities were generally overseen by female missionary nurses, although the mission hoped to have more male medical staff and regularly underplayed the role of women as full-fledged missionaries in their own right. It regularly reiterated the danger and unsuitability of such work for women in an attempt to shame American men into entering the medical work of the mission: "Surely the fight in Satan's territory is a man's as much as Korea, and God's command as firm as that of the United States military" (Troup 1956, 6). Yet it was the feminization of the mission's work that enabled it to attract a broader base of converts that included women and children and that would enable the Christian community to grow in a more organic fashion through marriage, childbirth, and child fostering. The success of such a strategy would require concurrent efforts in health and education and a significant degree of confidence that the indigenous Christian community would take up evangelical outreach. In the 1950s and early 1960s just such a synergy was operating in the Maradi region; this was a period of tremendous growth in the church despite growing tensions between the mission and the church over vernacular education.

High and Eternal Spiritual Dividends

Martha Wall's 1960 memoir, *Splinters from an African Log*, can be read as a rejoinder to the perception in some faith mission circles that a shift to medical ministry constituted a betrayal of SIM's original mandate. Through her eyes, medical work emerges as an effective strategy of evangelism that was particularly apt for Muslims: the investment in permanent infrastructure became a reasonable and indeed cost-effective means of carrying the evangelical work forward in her memoir. With a rather unabashed American penchant for financial metaphors, Wall regularly argued in mission publications for the importance of investing in medical work for spiritual ends: "Because the dispensing of these drugs is used only as the means of gaining hearers of the Gospel of Christ, the money—and lives—invested for this cause will bring high and eternal spiritual dividends" (Wall 1953b, 6). SIM never promoted medical work with the sense that relieving suffering or promoting health was an end in itself. It would be hard in such a setting to provide medical care simply out of Christian love and kindness in the spirit of charity or the desire to nurture a Christian civilization that characterized much of the medical work of Catholic missions and the denominational missions.

The defensiveness of Wall's book reveals an ongoing perception that "real" mission work involves "giving the Word" to "unreached" people in difficult and dangerous settings—the itinerant preaching of the older model of evangelical revival. Indeed, the most triumphant part of the memoir is Wall's closing description of her dangerous preaching adventure in a remote village where one former patient had long ago asked for a missionary to come teach. Dismayed to discover that this precious contact had since died, she set off intrepidly during the rainy season, only to become ill; she had to be evacuated with great drama. The pioneer preacher prevails within Wall's narrative as the highest role of the missionary. The function of her story is to impress upon the reader the urgent need for more (white) men to come to African to perform this romantic and dangerous work that was so unsuitable for women:

> Here is the tragedy of missions. Men—sincere, zealous, red-blooded young men—are competing for a place to serve Christ in their homeland, *but this old maigari had died, pleading for more knowledge of the way of Christ!* I could have wept. I might go now to teach them what I could in ten days, but for frontier work, for trekking, for establishing churches or training leadership for a Christian community, God has never intended to use women. It is man's work—a work that demands strong sinews in arm and soul. (Wall 1960, 278; emphasis in original)

In fact, African evangelists were already serving the village in question, so the sense of urgency she conveys is quite artificial. The fact that Wall herself, the greatest defender of the mission's medical work, succumbs to the allure of the romantic image of the pioneer missionary simply underscores how deeply ingrained it was and how profoundly gendered and raced it was.

The mission's movement into its strikingly successful but strangely devalued medical work seems to have been reinforced by an awareness of early converts that this would prove a more promising avenue than itinerant evangelism alone. Pastor 'dan Nana, who was by that time quite experienced as an evangelist (having regularly visited the very village Martha Wall set out to save), figured prominently in missionary Rita Salls's memories of why the thrust of the mission enterprise shifted to a greater emphasis on social services, medical care, and education: "Pastor 'dan Nana used to say, 'With the Muslims, talking about love is never going to do it. They have to see it. You have to demonstrate it'" (Rita Salls interview).

Note that Pastor 'dan Nana was advocating a sense of "love" as service that was very different from the inflammatory rhetoric we saw in the contemporary sermons on "love" analyzed in chapter two. Evangelical converts emphasized the sense of love as human kindness toward other humans that some of the early missionaries to the Maradi region tended to lose sight of in their emphasis on evangelism over "the social gospel" (Lovering 1963, 9). Pastor 'dan Nana's sense of "love" differs from both the earlier generation of missionaries and his contemporary Pentecostal colleagues. This new approach, however, was accompanied by a corresponding shift in the demography in the mission. With many men mobilized during World War II and later during the Korean War, it is perhaps not surprising that female missionaries took up the slack in greater numbers than in the past. Despite the danger of travel in wartime, women were willing to take up the challenge, indeed the adventure, of launching careers as missionaries; they were part of a postwar shift in attitude in American culture toward women's work outside the home (Kessler-Harris 1982). Medical work that could be done by trained nurses was a particularly promising avenue for both the mission as a whole and individual women to pursue. As demobilized men returned after the war, the movement of skilled women into mission work, if anything, accelerated. Rather than remain at home and fight for equal wages or continued access to jobs and promotion, such women sidestepped the ideological complexities of wage labor by becoming missionaries. This option was made possible by a recognition within evangelicalism of women's duty to take up a "prophetic" (rather than priestly) role in obedience to the "great commission." Rather than preaching, however, postwar female missionaries served as teachers and nurses. Mission work enabled newly confident evangelical women to simultaneously adhere to an ethic of submission and engage in an act of self-assertion that cannot be readily equated with feminism (Tucker 1990, 264).[15] Thus, rather than pursuing a promising medical career in the United States, nurse Martha Wall became a selfless missionary: "I had exchanged my own way for Christ's, and found even then that I had chosen well" (Wall 1960, 96). Many of these women remained single for their entire careers. Rather than marry and bear children themselves, they devoted their attentions to the patients and students they often referred to as their "family" (see, e.g., Walls 1960, 183).

"Peaceful Invasion"

The banner headline above the spread of photographs in *The Sudan Witness* to celebrate the opening of the Katsina Leper Settlement in 1937 when the colonial government of Nigeria handed it over to SIM described it as a "peaceful invasion."[16] It was a highly feminine missionary army that entered into medical work in the late 1930s. In effect, SIM was permitted to take over the government leprosaria in Kano and Katsina (in Nigeria) because medical experts no longer believed them to be effective means of countering the disease and because colonial doctors could no longer find a justification for coercive methods of segregating sufferers in the absence of any effective treatment (Bado 1996, 163, 222). The leprosarium in Danja, Niger, opened later, in 1954. The colonial leprosaria had, in reality, simply served as asylums or prisons. How one would describe them depends somewhat on whether one argues that the inmates had been rejected by local populations or imprisoned by colonial authorities. Some combination of the two seems to have been at work in the case of Katsina, where the emir, as representative of the colonial state, was quite supportive of the effort to cloister lepers (Cox 1938). SIM understandably did not choose to emphasize the likely coercion involved in "recruiting" the leprosy patients it had inherited. Wall nevertheless obliquely acknowledges the reality that the patients did not come of their own free will in her memoir as she describes her initial experiences at the leprosarium in Katsina: "The settlement had been, during those first years, more an asylum for beggars and cripples than an institution of healing. The hopelessly crippled and the outcasts had been driven from their homes or the market places to find a haven of refuge" (Wall 1960, 90).

Because there was no cure at the time and the treatments the mission could offer were at best palliative and at worst experimental, missionaries readily attributed improvement in condition to spiritual transformation (95). If the British colonial government of Nigeria was happy enough to permit missions to take over the unpleasant task of treating leprosy, missions for their part were interested in such work because of the potential it offered for evangelization. As Yusufu Turaki points out, the terms of agreement under which missions were given control of leprosaria in 1937 in principle stipulated that there should be no proselytization. But missions such as SIM were unambiguous about their position "regarding the preaching of the Gospel and evangelization in the leper settlements: 'No evangelism, no leprosy work'" (Turaki 1993, 180). In the end, the anti-proselytization clause on "Religion in the Leper Settlements" was never enforced because the colonial administration needed the humanitarian services the missions were willing to offer. Later, as the mission began medical work in Niger, a similar tacit agreement to turn a blind eye to the open evangelism occurring at SIM facilities obtained. It was violated briefly only once by a scrupulously secularist medical inspector in the mid-1950s (Kapp 1955).

Until the 1950s, existing treatments, which consisted of intramuscular injections of various oils (in the case of Katsina, hydnocarpus oil was used), produced no immediate and dramatic effects. Patients were constrained to remain in the leprosaria for extremely long periods of time—often from five to twelve years—before being allowed to leave symptom-free. The improved nutrition and close attention to secondary effects of the disease (including tropical ulcers, loss of limbs, and eye problems) patients received at the centers ensured that in balance their overall health did tend to improve; the palliative effect of the care at leprosaria created a modest attraction to the centers and an inducement to remain at the sites. These long sojourns at leprosaria meant that a kind of Christian community life could become normative and individuals could be socialized into Christianity through repetition and habit. Mission leprosaria regularly mimicked African village life, with circles of huts, elders to regulate disputes and structure activities, and the possibility of engaging in productive activities (farming and crafts) (see, e.g., Wall 1960, 87; Shankar 2003).

The shadow of colonial coercion hovered over the mission's leprosy work in Nigeria from 1937 to 1955. Wall's attempt to set up a crèche for children who had not been infected with the disease was met with initial reluctance: "Word had gotten around camp that the white doctor was planning to take their babies away by force" (Wall 1960, 102). The struggle over control of "orphans" raised in the mission's boys' and girls' homes suggests that these fears were not utterly irrational—once children came under the charge of the mission, it became more difficult for parents, particularly mothers, to regain authority over them. The mission's strategy of demanding repayment for the cost of raising such children when they were reclaimed would have effectively prevented most parents from attempting to confront the mission. Leprosaria across Africa regularly attempted to disrupt the "promiscuousness" that was argued to spread the disease by forcibly cutting patients off from their spouses, children, and other kin (see Vaughan 1991, 86). In leprosaria built by the mission (rather than the government) it was standard policy to take newborn infants from their mothers before contact could lead to infection. It was only fear of losing patients to "ignorance and prejudice" that prompted Wall to reassure her patients that they were welcome to bring their children daily in exchange for a nourishing meal, clothing, recreation, and the occasional bath (Wall 1960, 98–99). Wall's crèche was an occasion to inculcate in potential converts an understanding of hygiene and cleanliness that associated purity and health with white dresses and showers on the one hand and the blood of Christ on the other (102). The long residence of adult patients gave missionaries unprecedented access to the impressionable children who often accompanied them. These children would hear Bible stores and learn to read in Hausa at the feet of female missionaries and native evangelists while their parents were undergoing treatment.

All missionary medical facilities required the patients to routinely submit to "a Gospel message" before receiving daily treatment since "the purpose behind all medical service is primarily to draw these people, who might otherwise not be contacted for Christ, to listen to the message of His salvation" (Wall 1960, 80). SIM missionaries took so much for granted that their medical work provided an occasion for evangelism that they were frankly baffled when, for a brief moment in the 1950s, the French colonial government in Niger prohibited them from preaching in the Tsibiri dispensary (Kapp 1955, 2; Liz Chisholm interview, November 16, 1990). If missionary personnel were not interested in medical work unless it made evangelism possible, it also followed that patients were not to receive treatment unless they had submitted to evangelism (Burt Long interview, November 26, 1986). Preaching in SIM medical facilities was largely done by native evangelists, such as Pastor Adamu, who were native Hausa-speakers. Mission studies of converts revealed that repeated exposure to the gospel over long periods of time was a

"Evangelist at Galmi Hospital." Courtesy of SIMIA
(NR 32), photographed by Olin Kinney, 1971.

necessary component of conversion; the daily gospel service prior to receiving treatment was a central part of how patients at leprosaria eventually came to convert (Chuck Forster interview).

In a kind of medical parallel to the use of *boro* in controlling the behavior of church members, the mission instituted a variety of mechanisms in an attempt to expose patients consistently to the gospel and to constrain them to adhere to the mission's schedule of treatments. For example, the Maradi leprosarium for a time fined patients who failed to follow the leprosarium's moral expectations or who were tardy for treatment.[17] Concern that this system invited abuse by the staff (who posed regular disciplinary challenges of another order), the mission later developed explicit rules that dictated behavior (they determined where different patients could reside, controlled their sexual behavior, established whether they could or could not marry or divorce, and prohibited drinking, drumming, and alcohol) and were linked to a system of demerits. Those who did not follow the rules could be expelled.[18]

Such puritanical rules were not always easy to enforce. Residential arrangements simultaneously reduced the possible spread of contagion and reinforced Christian conceptions of chastity and gender norms. Young men and women were sequestered in separate dorms that were carefully policed; men and women were expected to engage in different kinds of activities in their separate spheres during the day. The carefully segregated dorms and daily routines reiterated a dimly articulated sense that leprosy, the symptoms of which resembled those of some venereal diseases, was associated with sexual license outside of proper marriage. Adultery was so serious an infraction that patients who were determined to have committed adultery lost all "credits" and could be treated only on an outpatient basis.[19] Women's movements were particularly constrained—they were not to walk around after sunset except to go to the church or to school.[20] One mission employee who chaperoned the patients found that leprosy patients did not always welcome such policing: "The *kutare* [lepers] said I was bothering them and they chased me away" (Malam Kashalu interview). Many patients who, like Adamu, had been reviled in the outside world, formed romantic attachments with other patients at the leprosaria; it is easy to understand why overly intrusive supervision would be perceived as unkind and degrading.

Christian understandings of monogamous marriage were modeled by missionary and African staff and encouraged among the patients. Muslim residents who married Christian spouses found themselves in an even more socially precarious situation than the one their disease created for them. Because Muslim relatives generally disapproved of marriages to Christians, the mission often stood in a parental role while the residents of the leprosarium became the congregation and community. Weddings sponsored by the missionaries took on an entirely new format that emphasized the promises of the couple to one another over the more familiar stress on ties among a broader network of kinfolk. Male patients were expected to contribute to their own support through farming on land offered by the mission. Even the farming practices of the leprosarium at Danja were marked by the methods and equipment the mission associated with the "modern" techniques of a Christian farmer. These techniques, in Niger at any rate, included the use of animal traction (to assist patients whose strength had been diminished by the disease), a practice that was accompanied by ancillary beliefs that wives should not be "made" to farm and therefore did not need plots of their own. While men farmed, women were taught to sew and maintain a hygienic Christian home.

The entire community marked major events in the Christian calendar; this became a way of alleviating the boredom of routine. The celebration of Christmas in particular was an important moment in the year. Leprosarium feasts at Christmas, to which the neighboring Muslims were invited, were replicated later by former patients in their home villages as a way to introduce Christianity in a welcoming manner that ran parallel to the *salla* feasts of Muslims at the two great festivals. In other words, committing to sustained treatment meant being submitted to a Christianized habitus over a relatively long period of time and finding community among participants in a distinctive belief system. Little wonder, then, than many patients and their children eventually became Christians without ever being able to identify a specific moment or event that led to their spiritual transformation.

Vaughan argues that missions worked to teach such patients to take on the identity of "lepers" (Vaughan 1991, 86) outside and beyond pagan society. Although colonial governments, particularly in East and Central Africa, tended to understand disease as related to detribalization, missions, she suggests, had the opposite understanding of the causation of disease. In the mission worldview, it was the contamination of "pagan" practice that led to disease, and it was the duty of the missionary to erase pagan superstition and replace it with Christian family life (86). SIM had a rather different understanding of the relationship of Christianity to traditional life. The ideal Christian was to remain *vernacular* in character—he or she should not take on western language and dress, nor should he or she aspire to the kind of education, housing, or lifestyle that the missionaries enjoyed. Christian converts were to return to their places of origin, farm, and carry forward a vernacularized Christianity.

SIM's hope was that its former leprosy patients would return to their traditional homes and carry "the Word" as native evangelists. If to be a born-again Christian was to be an evangelist, then above all else what the mission hoped to produce through its leprosy work was committed evangelical Christians. The mission capitalized on the sacralized image of the leper restored to health through Christ's miraculous intervention in the New Testament and encouraged former patients to become the kinds of "Samaritan" witnesses to "the Word" described in the healing of the ten lepers in the Gospel of Luke: "And one of them, when he saw that he was healed, turned back, and with a loud voice glorified God, and fell down on his face at his feet, giving him thanks: and he was a Samaritan. . . . And [Jesus] said unto him, Arise, go thy way: thy faith hath made thee whole" (Luke 17:15, 16, 19).

It was not sufficient to forge an identity as a leper or even an identity as a product of a miraculous cure. The leprosy sufferer was to become the witnessing Samaritan, someone who would return to his or her own people to carry forward the work of Christian evangelism. God had, in effect, created the lepers precisely to become native evangelists to their own people. With his customary hyperbole, Dr. A. P. Stirrett captured some of the excitement the mission's shift into medical work elicited precisely because cured leprosy patients would become Christian witnesses to the curing power of "the Word" in the vernacular tongues: "Yes, I believe that these leper colonies will prove a key to the evangelization of the Hausa nation, and then this Hausa nation, evangelized, will prove to be the key to the evangelization of the many more millions outside" (Stirrett 1937, 4–5). SIM never intended to create exceptional spaces and unique identities isolated from an impure traditional world but rather hoped to send former patients back into their ethnic homelands (in a kind of reverse contagion) to carry the seeds of Christianity.

A Window on the Work: The Tsibiri Dispensary

Patients were to become carriers of the word of Christ and native nurses were to remain properly humble Christian evangelists, but the work and experience of the medical missionary staff in the mission's developing medical infrastructure was upheld as dangerous and heroic. There was an important performative dimension to such work, for not only were medical missionaries sent to heal Africans, they were also to play the role of the western Christian blessed by God with superior scientific knowledge and moral training. Africans were to remain vernacular, but missionaries were marked as knowers of western medicine and science, the holders of answers. In fact, so rapid was the mission's expansion into medical work and so urgent was the need for missionaries to handle the growing work in the dispensaries, hospitals, and leprosaria that medical workers often had little time to master local vernacular languages (Wall 1960, 66–67; Chisholm interview, August 12, 1997). While medical staff were expected to evangelize, in practice their language skills were sometimes so rudimentary that the most they could hope to do was read out loud haltingly from the Hausa Bible (Wall 1960, 79).

The development of recordings of the Gospels in African languages after 1942, which SIM heralded as a "significant event in gospel outreach in Africa," facilitated this approach to evangelism; specialist missionaries could substitute recordings for mastery of local languages (SIM 1971). The mission staff began to subtly differentiate between fluent Hausa-speakers, who were often senior male missionaries who could preach (men who taught farming and women who worked with women and small children, for example, often acquired impressive language skills) and those generally female newcomers whose scientific know-how prevented them from engaging in the broader range of social interactions with local populations necessary to gain fluency.

Indigenous therapeutic systems that were to be rejected were marked by their occult and hidden quality—"heathen potions and Mohammedan charms." By contrast, the work of western medical missionaries needed to appear to be utterly open and transparent (Chisholm 1954, 4). Martha Wall used the opaque and "imprisoning" compound walls of Hausaland as a metaphor for constraints of Islam that contrasted with the openness and light of Christianity (Wall 1960, 104–121). Ironically, the transparency of scientific missionary medicine was somewhat occluded by the separation of preaching from curing, speech from action, and science from religion. Those who cured were not in a position to articulate how they did so or what it might mean. They were simply carriers of the power of western medicine. For some missionaries with only rudimentary medical training who stood in for absent nurses, maintaining this all-knowing stance was difficult: "My lack of knowledge was devastating. Never had I faced such an impossible task! Never did I find it so difficult to believe the Lord's assignment as I did then" (Simms 1992).

For medical missionaries, the task was not simply to cure patients but to use western medicine to reveal the sinful failing of indigenous beliefs. And here SIM walked a rather fine line, for unlike the nineteenth-century missions that equated western civilization with Christianity or the government doctor who equated civilization with science, SIM rejected indigenous religion while attempting to foster the emergence of a kind of vernacular Christian life. Rebirth did not require assimilation to western life—indeed, in some senses it precluded it. The challenge would be to convince patients to convert to Christianity without prompting them to abandon the simple peasant aspirations of their parents and grandparents.

They should not become too enamored with western science or European languages. Indeed, to become too attracted to the tools of upward mobility was itself a sin, a sign of pride. There was a limit to just how transparent mission medicine would be. The mission was clearly reluctant to transfer medical knowledge to the local population; it did not begin to establish training centers for nurses in Nigeria until the last half of the 1950s (Turaki 1993, 171). Even those rare Africans who were singled out for more-advanced medical training were expected to take up the double and sometimes unwelcome burden of mastering both medicine and evangelism, and they were closely watched for signs of "pride" (Ali 'dan Buzu interview, February 9, 2001).

Routines at the Tsibiri dispensary, as elsewhere, were organized to maximize the potential for patients to hear the gospel. Like the leprosaria, the dispensaries always began the day with a sermon. Because of the limited linguistic skills of the medical missionaries, these presentations were often given by African staff, and eventually medical facilities had trained pastors whose primary responsibility was to take over the evangelical work from the missionaries, as in this depiction of a native evangelist's preaching by Martha Wall:

> "You women who are about to give birth to a child," Umaru said. . . . "Do you say that your child has life?" Any woman who had experienced the last months of pregnancy knew what Umaru was talking about, and there was a general hum of assent. . . . "Yet if that movement ceased before you came to birth," continued Umaru, "and the baby did not breathe after it was born, would you not say that the infant had never lived?" Again there was general assent. "You who say you are alive and think you are but are moving about in the darkness of your ignorance and sin are as this unborn babe." (Wall 1960, 175–176)

Providing prenatal and postnatal care to women and their infants was obviously a particularly promising avenue for guaranteeing repeated exposure to the gospel in a setting that illustrated the emphasis on nurturing love in Christianity and opened the way to speak about rebirth. Beyond such carefully tailored sermons, patients were also ministered to during the rest period after the clinic was closed: "We gathered our family every afternoon for an informal visit. We could lead our patients to chat about our faith; we taught them Scripture portions; we answered questions. . . . Many of these patients remained for a month. A few remained as long as six months. All this time they were absorbing the simple tenets of the Christian faith under the most favorable conditions" (183).

Patients who were suffering from more intractable or dramatically disfiguring diseases were also particularly likely to find the mission's interventions (medical and moral) compelling. Similarly, the East African missionaries Vaughan studied noted, " 'Ulcers have one great recommendation from the Mission point of view—they take a long time to cure'" (Vaughan 1991, 61). The mission's policy of never giving patients more medicine than they could safely consume at one time also ensured that they would remain at the site until their treatment was finished instead of returning home for their convalescence (Wall 1960, 189). At Galmi Hospital, patients were required to stay for two weeks regardless of the treatment so that they could be subjected to a systematic exposition of Christianity (Long interview, November 26, 1986).

Medicine and *Magani*

The mission anticipated that sustained exposure to the gospel at medical facilities would plant the seed of Christianity. But it also expected the healing power of western biomedicine to convince patients of the superiority of the missionary understanding of disease and therapeutics. It came as something of a shock to discover that the success of western biomedicine did not immediately annihilate prior spiritual and therapeutic systems. Mission medicine could blur into what Bado refers to as empirical-metaphysical medicine (Bado 1996, 10), or traditional medicine. Traditional medical practices in the region are known broadly as *magani*, a term that encompasses remedies of all kinds, including potions, charms, spells, and oral incantations. *Magani* can be prepared by specialists of various kinds, including *bokaye* (traditional healers) and Muslim scholars. *Magani* can also include written charms (*layya*) in the case of *bokaye* and potions made from the ink of Koranic writing (*rubutu*) in the case of *malams*. The blurring of mission medicine into *magani* is suggested in an anecdote that is something of a stock missionary story, related by nurse Liz Chisholm about the challenges of treating patients at the Tsibiri dispensary:

> And one fellow, we used to cut up any cardboard paper that we had to make cards, so we'd have a record of who it was, and we could record it in our record book so we'd know who came. And we'd write on it the medications they were getting. Well, this fellow came back and he didn't have the card anymore. What happened to the card? "Well, I took it, and I feel a lot better!" (Chisholm interview, November 16, 1990)

Some of the practices the mission engaged in that Martha Wall described in her memoir may have inadvertently fed into the magical expectations of the patients: the times of day when patients should take a dose of their medicine were calibrated to the Muslim prayer times (1960, 190); resting patients were encouraged to memorize passages from the Bible while turning the blank pages of the Wordless Book—a mysterious process of incantation that may or may not have been associated in their minds with curing (208–209); and evening entertainment consisted of listening to gospel songs and messages from "the magic black box" of the ubiquitous phonograph (216).

The magical curative properties of sacred words, long familiar in this region through the local practice of "drinking" Islamic texts to effect cures, would have readily transferred to the use of Christian texts in a similar manner, regardless of Bingham's rejection of faith healing. Alberta Simms commented that at the end of a long process of analysis, it sometimes became clear that it was this variety of *magani* that the patient desired:

> Some patients, after a few days' acquaintance with us, reveal the real reason for their coming as they lean through that window to whisper, "Won't you give me medicine that will bring back my husband's love?" (Simms 1949, 21)

Diagnosis was undoubtedly complicated by the exclusivity of western medicine. Patients who attributed their problems to the spirit world would be told they had to *choose* between the *magani* of the *boka* (referred to by missionaries as "witch doctors") and the *magani* of the dispensary. Distinguishing symptoms of disease from the effects of local medicines could be difficult. One nurse observed that local medicines could in fact have pharmacological properties that had real effects—it was difficult to know what to prescribe and how much when patients were taking western medicines in combination with herbs and other local substances. The problem wasn't that all local medicine was empty or ineffective, it was that they were used according to different assessments of symptoms, etiologies, and typologies of disease. Western medicine was difficult to apply in such a context, and missionaries encouraged patients to abandon all other medical treatments, which they uniformly treated rhetorically as forms of superstition and witchcraft, despite their occasional efficacy.

This exclusivity was quite different from the spirit of other healing regimes in the region, which could be appealed to in overlapping and complementary fashion. Renouncing the use of other modes of healing would have felt like a great sacrifice to many in a setting where there were so few effective medical options in place and when many of their most acutely felt needs were emotional and social rather than narrowly biological (Chisholm interview, November 14, 1990; Malam Sabo interview). Knowing that the missionaries would chide them for drawing on competing health treatments, patients would be reluctant to reveal in full what regime they had been following prior to coming to the hospital or dispensary.

Given biomedicine's jealous exclusivity, why did patients seek it in the first place when there were other therapeutic options? It is possible that existing therapeutic options were unable to keep pace with the rapid expansion of epidemic diseases set in train by the great mobility of the colonial period. Rapid population growth in urban centers in the absence of clean sources of water meant that diarrhea was a serious problem from 1945 to 1960, particularly during the rainy season. The location of villages in river valleys where the *fadama* soil (rich soil near river valleys and lakes that flood during the rainy season) was located meant that malaria was endemic. It continues to be the single most challenging health issue for the population overall. By the time of SIM's interventions in Niger, modestly effective treatments for a variety of pressing conditions (yaws, leprosy, eye ailments, malaria, diarrhea) were coming into use, making the *magani* of the dispensary competitive with that of the *boka*. Government-sponsored vaccination campaigns gave missionary medicine the powerful image of the needle (or *alura* in Hausa), which resonated deeply with Hausa conceptions that diseases were transferred and could be treated through the skin. The effectiveness of some of those campaigns undoubtedly contributed to both the sense of potency and the mystique of western medicine.

However, mission nurses and doctors were never to my knowledge specialists in mental or emotional illnesses (the art of emotional and social equilibrium). There is very little mention in the mission's writings of psychiatric problems at all, although where they do appear they tend to be seen as "demonic."[21] Missionaries regularly refer to *bori* dances as events that involve "the very presence of the Evil One" (Ray de la Haye interview), so it is unlikely that women or *bori* practitioners in general would openly refer to their practices in the presence of the mission medical staff. Whether one regards spirits as real or not, demonic or not, any therapeutic system that simply ignores the pervasiveness of the spirit world in Maradi and Dogondoutchi is destined to be of limited importance.[22] Adeline Masquelier's work with *bori* adepts in Dogondoutchi reveals a vivid world that western biomedicine was powerless to address in the narrative performances of her informants:

> Many 'yan bori who described the circumstances of their involvement with the bori to me often determined that their afflictions were caused by spirits. They realized this when the likita (biomedical practitioner) could not find anything wrong with them even though they were on the brink of death. . . . The illness was their responsibility, and so was the cure, provided the afflicted agreed to become involved in the bori. (Masquelier 2001, 79)

Rather than directly confront the lived experience of the spirit world of Hausa, the mission seems to have studiously ignored it. To tell people who know from their intimate bodily experience that they are suffering from the jealous affections of a spirit, either that there are no spirits (which is not, so far as I can tell, the position of most missionaries) or that the spirits must be rejected as hateful demons (the more common position) would have seemed utterly preposterous to many. Missionaries too readily equated *bori* spirit possession with evil sorcery and could be thoroughly credulous in the face of stories about the powers of black magic to kill and injure (Carpenter 1959, 4). As Masquelier notes, most Muslim scholars concede the existence of such spirits, although they too tend to see them as the work of Satan. Like most strict Muslims, the best the mission could have hoped for would have been to exorcize them. This would have flown very much in the face of Hausa understandings of spirit possession: as a *gado*, or heritage, it is both a blessing and a burden. Like most inheritances, it is a source of wealth and sorrow, something to be managed with care and wisdom. Without a strong faith healing tradition or a consistent appeal to the power of the Holy Spirit (approaches that have characterized the Pentecostal missions), SIM seems to have been at a loss about how to counter the appeal of *bori*.[23] In the many self-congratulatory writings of the mission I examined, I saw no evidence that it had success in effecting lasting exorcisms through which the longer-term health of the individual was restored. Thus, while Muslim practitioners in Kano and Pentecostal ministers in Niger more recently might make a systematic ministry of exorcism, SIM never went that route. But evidence exists that conversion to Christianity was itself a source of profound emotional disruption for some (Osborne 1945, 10).

Many of the early converts to Christianity in Tsibiri eventually reverted to their earlier practices for reasons that missionaries tend to attribute to the designs of Satan or the immaturity of their faith. But returning to *bori* also was related to the failure of the mission to provide fully effective alternatives to the practices that had sustained people in the past. As the mission expanded its work in the medical domain, it found that it was unable to erase these competing practices and that in the desperate war-hospital atmosphere of most medical stations—which was quite different from the temperate communal life of the leprosaria—conversions were few and far between. The mission's disillusionment with medical work resulted in part from the emergency conditions in which it generally worked, which I shall discuss in a moment, but it also stemmed from the clear failure of mission medicine to supplant therapeutic systems based on beliefs that were antithetical to fundamentalist Christianity.

The medical mission's lack of focus on fertility also contributed to the ongoing significance of *bori*. Treating problems related to women, fertility, and reproduction, perhaps partly because of the lack of any serious development of midwifery as a local therapeutic specialty, has traditionally been seen as the domain of the *bori* spirit cult, although *bori* membership is by no means limited to women.[24] *Bori* is, as Adeline Masquelier elegantly demonstrates, a medium through which individuals, particularly women, experience, interpret, and act on their world (Masquelier 2001). The highly resonant phrase "*bori* is women's war" captures the many different ways in which women may feel embattled and turn for support and empowerment to spirit possession.[25] Women's deep concern with fertility and reproduction is addressed more directly through *bori* than through any other therapeutic options available to them.

Since it would soon have been clear that the mission's facilities had nothing to offer in the way of *magani* for matters of the heart either, perhaps the mission's inability to compete with the areas in which *bori* specialized meant that the two therapeutic systems coexisted relatively comfortably despite the exclusivity of mission medicine.[26] The continuing openness of Arna to Christian evangelism when Muslims were warned to avoid missionaries suggests that there wasn't a perception among those Hausa-speakers who had never converted to Islam that medicine purveyed by Christians posed a threat to their own belief system. Arna practitioners would have had the capacity to handle the Christian God as the creator spirit Ubangjiji if they were so inclined, even if only temporarily. *Bori* practice, with its expansive and absorptive pantheon of supernatural but immanent spirits, could at least entertain the Christian God as simply another invisible force. In other words, for non-Muslims and culturally hybrid Muslims, making use of Christian facilities does not seem to have implied a disenchantment with other therapeutic options. But for the traditionalist Muslim scholar accustomed to having a monopoly on access to the healing powers of a monotheistic God through the sacred words of the Koran, mission medicine does seem to have presented a challenge.

The medical practices of Hausa-speakers continue to be rich, varied, and constantly evolving as new practices are absorbed from other regions and as therapists from *malams* to *bokaye* develop new treatments for the constantly shifting conditions of modernity (for a particularly interesting treatment of this in the context of spirit possession, see O'Brien 2000). Therapeutic practices that blend medieval Islamic humoral understandings of the body; empirical experience using grasses, herbs, and other substances; the management of the powers of unseen spirits; and a system that honors highly local deities for broader communal well-being are interwoven and resonate with one another. Some treatments are remarkably ordinary, and their very ordinariness must have made most patients reluctant to abandon them and skeptical of the mission's rejection of all local practice. Other local therapeutic practices are more specialized, although in general the Hausa do not have the kinds of *nganga*, or "witch doctors," that are usually depicted as the competitors to western medicine in eastern and southern Africa.[27]

Given the breadth, plurality, and occasional hybridity of Hausa approaches to restoring *lafiya*, or well-being, and given the general attitude among Hausa that the consumer should try a variety of options of different kinds, it is not surprising that Hausa-speakers were willing to test out the wares of the mission dispensary, nor is it surprising that one major impediment to conversion was an aversion to the notion of medical exclusivity the missionaries purveyed. As Adeline Masquelier observes, "Few individuals understand biomedicine as a stable and bounded domain of health care that operates in isolation from other therapies" (2001, 92).

Unlike traditionalist Muslim scholars, the *bori* adepts and Arna priests do not appear to have felt particularly threatened by this alternative therapeutic system—all of the tales of rumor and resistance I encountered could be traced to Muslim *malams* (who cast missionaries as sorcerers and soul-eaters), not Arna or *bori* (Jadi Marafa interview; Wall 1952, 9). Yet Christians and missionaries see Christianity as utterly incompatible with *bori*, so no practicing Christian would ever admit to taking part in *bori* or to consulting a *boka*. Any Protestant known to be consulting *boka*, *bori*, or *malamai* would immediately be placed under church discipline, and from the onset of the community, this prohibition was absolutely clear. Most Protestants today maintain careful distance from relatives who take part in *bori* and are acutely embarrassed if neighbors and fellow congregants discover that one of their family members practices *bori*.[28] Both Tsibiri and Dogondoutchi are major centers of *bori* in Niger, making both towns ripe prospects for converts who hope to redress the ridicule and contempt of Islam for the *jahilci* (pagan ignorance) of *bori* without capitulating to its unwelcome hegemony. Zeb Zabriskie offered this observation about the reception of missionaries in Dogondoutchi: "Moslem teachers are intensifying their efforts to get more children into their own schools, and are pointing out that all who follow Christ are infidels. The pagans, on the other hand, generally welcome the missionaries. Even though they do not accept their message, that message gives them ammunition to hurl back at the Mohammedans, and while this conflict goes on, the way of salvation is explained to all, old and young, pagan and Moslem" (Zabriskie 1947, 11). Something of this kind occurred in Sudan, where long after the departure of the SIM missionaries in 1964 there was an explosion of conversion to Christianity in rejection of the oppressiveness of state-imposed Islam (James 1988, 24, 264).

"A Continuous Disaster Area": The Case of Galmi Hospital

The mission's longer-term engagement with medical work, then, was frustrating in part because local populations rejected the exclusive claims of western medicine and were not particularly inclined to convert to a religion that would have required abandoning a broad spectrum of therapeutic options. But the extraordinarily impoverished state of Niger's medical infrastructure also meant that any medical facility that existed faced a constant flow of emergency cases and patients far too ill to discuss theological matters. Working in such settings was like setting up in a "continuous disaster area" (Lovering 1966, 3). Rather than discuss in detail all of SIM's facilities I will focus on the jewel in its crown, the hospital at Galmi, which offers a glimpse of the very real generosity of mission medical workers and at the same time helps us understand why building medical infrastructure is no longer a primary goal of the mission in Niger.

Although Nigériens looked on early colonial medical facilities, which were often staffed with military doctors, with mistrust and skepticism, they received the mission's medical work with great enthusiasm very quickly. SIM's work expanded into ever larger and more ambitious facilities, culminating in the establishment of the hospital at Galmi. Galmi Hospital was built, as former SIM director Ian Hay aptly put it, at "really the end of nowhere" (Ian and June Hay interview). Initially it was simply to be another dispensary, and when David Osborne, Newton Kapp, and Jim Lucas went out together with a young Tsibiri convert named Ali 'dan Buzu to stake out a site in a village called Dogarawa, they intended to set up a new station along an imagined line that would eventually form a necklace of stations around the farming belt along the southern rim of Niger. They found that the local chief, who was Muslim, was not receptive to the idea of a Christian dispensary in Dogarawa, and the district officer of Birnin Konni told them to choose a plot farther along the road, with the obstructive stipulation that they couldn't take over any arable farmland, which was, as Zeb Zabriskie remarked, "a pretty big order" (Zeb Zabriskie interview).

In the end they choose a rocky outcropping known as Galmi. There was little water there, there was only a very tiny village, there was, in fact, nothing to recommend it as a site: "There was nothing there, I tell you, there wasn't even water! It was dry!" ('dan Buzu interview, February 9, 2001). As Ali 'dan Buzu tells the story, he and Jim Lucas camped out under their truck at this unlikely site. From this makeshift base, they hired workers, bought building materials, and began the work of creating a station ex nihilo. Because there was no missionary for the facility, 'dan Buzu, who had been a dispensary worker in Tsibiri and was being cultivated by the mission to be a medical worker, was the first person to dispense medicine there. Later, when a Canadian woman came to take over the dispensary, he was sent back to Tsibiri. Very soon thereafter, in 1950, Dr. Burt Long, whose name is virtually synonymous with the founding of Galmi Hospital, arrived.

The facility grew rapidly and eventually became home to the largest number of missionaries in Niger, in effect becoming a kind of missionary village that was heavily populated by single women. Because there was no town nearby, missionaries had to create a social world of their own. "The life was the hospital compound, the work, and what you made out of it" (Brown 1993, 34). Missionaries were quite cut off from the world of Nigériens despite their constant contact with patients, and they had to learn to work well with one another.

This isolated medical facility became a key element of the medical system of Niger, and it handled many of the more complex and risky cases from elsewhere in the country:

This was opened in 1950 by Dr. Burt Long, and is one of the only three hospitals in the country. The other two are government. In the land which the United Nations lists as having the lowest doctor-population ration in the world (1 doctor to 96,000 people, contrasted with the USA's 1 to 790), Galmi has no choice but to be a down-to-earth, no-nonsense institution that dispenses medicine as though it were going out of style. . . . "This place has so many patients," comments Jim VerLee, "you'd think it was the evacuation center for a continuous disaster area." (Lovering 1966, 3)

Echoing VerLee's language of catastrophe, Harold Fuller characterized the hospital as operating "like a battlefield clinic" (Fuller 1967, 124). As Fuller and VerLee's comments suggest, the medical demands of work at Galmi rapidly outpaced its capacity to engage in evangelism. While the number of patients the hospital handled never stopped growing, the infrastructure of the hospital remained quite spare: as late as 1972, the road to the capital was still largely unpaved, there was electricity only in the evening, the staff used kerosene refrigerators, and there was only one vehicle. By 1982, the hospital had 120 beds, an outpatient department that saw 200–300 patients a day. It included an obstetrical unit, an ambulatory unit for 80 patients, a TB unit, and an under-five clinic that handled 150–180 children a day. The hospital also trained local "barefoot doctors," who were equipped to provide basic health care to local villagers. Dr. Jim Ceton conveys something of the frustration SIM's medical staff felt as they addressed the extraordinary medical needs of Niger when their fundamentalist convictions taught that evangelism *ought* to take precedence:

When we came back here after furlough, I was full of enthusiasm and plans for involvement in evangelism and helping establish the church. My wife, Mary Lou, and I were determined not to let the demands of our medical work sap all our energies. The obvious answer was to say "no" more often to less urgent medical needs, so there would be a better balance between physical and spiritual work. That sounds good on a quiet day off, but there are times when it is hard to say "no." . . . [He then describes an evening when he was recalled to work to handle a prolapsed umbilical cord, a man with an intestinal tumor, a woman who had been in labor for two days, children with fevers and broken bones, and victims of a truck accident.] . . . It was 1:30 am by the time it was all over. The same basic story can be told by many missionaries. How *can* you say "no"? (Ceton 1982, 7)

Outpatient services at the hospital followed the same pattern as the dispensaries and the leprosarium: patients were captive audiences as they waited for treatment. Missionary Wendy Brown, who spent a month recovering from an illness in the late 1980s, described the outpatient clinic at Galmi from the vantage point of both a missionary and a patient:

> [The clinic was] thronged with people and my spirit was lifted as I saw the Christian murals and accompanying scripture texts depicting such things as man shackled by sin and the release of this bondage in the work of the cross. Either tapes were played or an African preached the gospel as people sat in the queue for the doctor, patiently waiting to be seen and unable to avoid hearing the Good News. (Brown 1993, 35)

Yet despite some commonalities, Galmi was never really comparable to mission leprosaria or to dispensaries located in villages. Even the medical services that targeted women and children and had proven so central to the emergence of the Christian community in Tsibiri became highly institutional and impersonal in such a setting because as a hospital Galmi handled mostly emergency cases. Since the high fatality rates in emergency cases weakened confidence in the hospital, maternal care was slow to develop. Margaret Hayes was brought in to Galmi in the early 1980s to upgrade its obstetrics unit, and in order to do so she trained three "semiliterate" local women to become "aides" to assist her and the one Nigérien midwife on the staff. Together the five women handled some cases "so terrible they [would be] considered Middle Ages stuff" in conventional textbooks (Hayes 1982, 7).[29]

The hospital setting was difficult for missionaries accustomed to medical work in advanced settings. Wendy Brown reflects on the strain put on fellow missionaries:

> The nurses had to cover for each other when sick . . . and worked long hours with the added pressure of making decisions that would probably be made by doctors back home. . . . I glimpsed the emotional strain the nurses were under as they struggled to come to terms with deaths that would not have occurred in their home country. (Brown 1993, 35)

Here, as elsewhere, local evangelists had to take up the greater portion of the task of actually preaching the gospel, and the missionaries came to rely on recordings to supplement the evangelical work. Native evangelist Pastor Mahamane Souley, whose job for a time was to provide religious discussions at the bedside of patients at the hospital at Galmi, found his work to be extremely intimate, quite different, and far more demanding than preaching in the waiting rooms of dispensaries and the leprosarium (Pastor Mahamane Souley interview). One-to-one encounters of this kind with patients facing life-threatening illnesses or in great pain from surgery would, one can imagine, require a kind of maturity, discretion, and compassion that is of a different order from what a young dispensary worker or nurse's aid could offer in an off-the-cuff sermon to pregnant women or to stalwart leprosy sufferers. Evangelizing in such a setting proved to be emotionally draining in ways that hospital assistants (who were traditionally hired from among the Christian population) were simply unwilling to endure without extra pay. This was real work, God's work, and it was unreasonable to expect overtaxed African staff to take it on in addition to their other duties without compensation. The mission found that only native evangelists and the missionaries (effectively the nurses) were willing to take on such demanding evangelism, which compounded what was already a very difficult burden and generated tensions between missionaries and Nigérien hospital personnel. As labor unions grew in political significance in the postcolonial period, labor disputes became endemic at SIM medical facilities, calling into question the notion that all workers should be fueled by the "great commission" rather than by material concerns.

In principle, the mission could gain contact with many more Nigériens at the hospital than it could ever hope to encounter through itinerant preaching or by creating stations in villages: "Look at the people streaming in—missionaries just couldn't get out to reach them all where they live!" enthused SIM's Canada Area Representative Harry Percy during a visit in 1966 (Fuller 1967, 124). But because of the number of patients the hospital handled, it wasn't feasible to encourage them to stay for the long periods of time that were necessary to prompt conversion, nor was it possible to follow up on patients after they returned home. Many patients were so ill that the rare converts were unlikely to survive long enough to found churches themselves, although missionaries might take comfort in saving individual souls (Long interview, November 26, 1986). Because the hospital was a kind of oasis in the wilderness, it was difficult to forge the kinds of friendships with local people that might have fostered more-enduring relations. Patients did not remain long enough to become close to the missionaries, and there were very few lasting conversions on the site itself. The hospital's forbidding, dry, and windy location did little to ease the burden of the work. Growing labor tensions between the mission and the hospital staff have made work conditions at the hospital in recent years quite unpleasant. Galmi, despite its undeniable importance as a hospital, has come to represent the limitations of evangelism through fixed infrastructure in Niger.

SIM has never aspired to separate its medical work from evangelism, and as a result has taken little pride or pleasure in medical work for its own sake. The mission's efforts to evangelize at health facilities were highly successful among leprosy and eye patients but were less productive among other kinds of patients. The qualified enthusiasm of Superintendent Newton Kapp in 1955 about the fact that there had been "several genuine conversions" at Galmi Hospital after four years of operation (at a time when "in a week's period there were fifty major operations performed recently") hints that many conversions were not so genuine. It also suggests an anxiety that the demanding medical work was proving less *evangelical* than one might have hoped (Kapp 1955, 2). It is an irony that the better treatments for leprosy became, the less effective medical centers were at bringing about conversions. The period required for a cure shifted from a stay of up to fifteen years before the development of effective sulfone treatments to a stay of six months to a year under current treatments developed in the 1980s (Adamu Na Mamayo interview; Charles 1994, 6). By the 1970s, many patients could be treated on an outpatient basis.

Furthermore, as confidence in western medicine grew, patients came in sooner rather than later for treatment for problems such as tropical ulcers, which meant that they did not have to stay nearly as long to be cured (Chisholm interview, November 14, 1990). As the "fruits" of the medical ministry began to diminish with the improvement and gradual acceptance of western medicine, the mission became overwhelmed with the enormity of the essentially humanitarian task it had taken on in its hospitals and dispensaries. The medical work was so taxing in terms of time, cost, and energy that the evangelical rationale for the work became less and less clear. The cures of western medicine alone did not automatically prompt a rejection of prior spiritual beliefs and practices, and doctors and nurses simply did not have either the opportunity or the linguistic skills to effectively evangelize.

The mission found that it had tremendous difficulty meeting the staffing needs of its medical facilities, particularly its hospitals. From a peak of 1,318 SIM missionaries in all of its stations in Africa in 1960, the size of the mission dropped for the next two decades to 1,140 in 1980, presumably due to the uncertainties and shifting perceptions of cultural imperialism in the immediate post-independence environment and competition from other forms of service ("Statistical History, 1970–1991"). This difficulty was aggravated by the toll that exposure to an extraordinary and sometimes unparalleled spectrum of illnesses could take on the staff that chose to take up such work.[30] By the late 1970s, the ravages of the Sahel drought were bringing urgent needs to the mission's medical staff that could not really be addressed through medical facilities alone (SIM 1976). While the female staff was taking extraordinary risks in medical work, evangelically inclined men eschewed the mission field because it was perceived to be too "effeminate" and not challenging enough (SIM 1961). As the appeal of this work for men appeared to have declined, and as women shifted to other forms of social work, staffing issues became ever more acute.

Funding infrastructure with extremely high overhead for buildings, medicines, and equipment was also a problem for the mission. Many evangelical contributors were, as Martha Wall's memoir suggests, far more willing to fund missionaries and preaching than to pay for buildings and medicine. As a result, individual missionaries at particular medical sites built ties with other Christian organizations that could help cover buildings and other costs. That is how the dispensary at Guesheme was expanded to include cutting-edge facilities for eye treatment and a modern maternity ward. But alliances with other Christian organizations that were less clearly evangelical in character exposed the mission to attack from fundamentalist purists, creating ruptures between mission and missionaries, converts and medical workers, SIM and other fundamentalist mission workers in Niger (notably the Baptists, who had a growing presence in Niamey). The funding of the Guesheme dispensary became something of a flashpoint for debates about the function of medical mission work that contributed to both the fragmentation of the Christian church and the mission's disenchantment with medical evangelism ('dan Buzu interview, February 19, 2001). Shortly after the expansion of the dispensary, the mission began to retreat entirely from the Guesheme facility, ceding it to the government health services.

As if these issues were not already enough, in the independence and post-independence period, the possibility that the independent government of Niger would seize control of the entire medical edifice seemed all too real.[31] A nationalist sentiment that all major structures and positions should be "indigenized" was very much in the air; the expatriate African population (which was largely from Dahomey) that had staffed the public school system and much of the Catholic school system was expelled in 1963 (for a Catholic view of this period, see Berthelot 1997, 111–115). The expulsion of SIM's missionaries from Sudan in 1964 (James 1988, 15) contributed to a feeling of uncertainty throughout the mission that was felt particularly acutely in Muslim regions. Diori Hamani encouraged the evangelical Christian community to establish an independent corporate identity so that someone could take over the mission's properties if it ever had to pull out suddenly ('dan Buzu interview, February 9, 2001), which is why the EERN came into being in 1964.[32] Other missions sometimes handled nationalization of their schools and medical infrastructure by permitting missionaries to stay on as staff under various negotiated arrangements, but it is hard to see how such arrangements could have worked for SIM, given its funding structure and fundamentalist ideology. The mission had little reason to be optimistic about the government's support in the face of strong nationalist sentiment, despite warm relations with Diori Hamani. Oumarou Youssoufou, who ought to have been sympathetic as one of SIM's former students (he was one of Pastor Garba's protégées, a rare success story who had gone on to become first secretary at the Niger embassy in Washington) was openly critical of what he regarded as the mission's antiquated style of "master-servant relationship" in the postcolonial environment, pointedly suggesting that Peace Corps volunteers were more open and more understanding (SIM 1972). In any case, the government had a strong and growing interest in finding positions for the growing number of educated Nigériens who came to see a guaranteed job with the government as an entitlement that was linked to successful completion of schooling.

Rather than struggle to sustain its medical work under such difficult and potentially compromised circumstances the mission began to emphasize relief and development work in rural areas that was similar to the work of secular NGOs and the U.S. Peace Corps, instead of expansion of its traditional medical work on sites that could become isolated mission enclaves. Disillusioned with the limited success in producing conversions at medical sites beyond the leprosaria, stymied by the problem of how to fund fixed facilities without drawing on ecumenical or secular funding that would emphasize health over evangelism, and appalled with the labor activism it was facing from its increasingly restive and assertive (but sometimes poorly qualified) Nigérien staff, the mission began gradually to shed itself of its dispensaries by turning them over to the state more or less of its own accord.[33] Unfortunately, from the vantage point of the Christian community and the EERN, SIM had never generated a cadre of educated Christians that was equipped to run the dispensaries or funding sources sufficient to the task of sustaining these sites as Christian facilities. For its part, the Nigérien government wanted to be able to make use of the facilities and to staff them with its own personnel. SIM's approach was simply to turn the network of buildings and indigenous staff over to the government directly and walk away. The mission supported the sophisticated facility at Guesheme, for example, until 1976, when it stopped staffing the dispensary with missionaries. It cut off its remaining financial support to the station in 1982; a significant reduction in services available to the local population was the predictable result ("Le Dispensaire, l'état et les missionaires").

The local population and Christian converts experienced the mission's ceding of its dispensaries, including the facility at Tsibiri, as an abrupt abandonment. Nigérien Christians had something of a proprietary interest in the medical facilities, having, like Ali 'dan Buzu, worked to obtain permission to build them, labored to construct them, raised money to equip them, and staffed them when there were no missionaries to take up the work. On the whole, Protestants in Niger were proud of the medical work of the mission and their own contributions to that work. In their view, it was not entirely clear that such facilities were the mission's to give away to the government. In any case, since the EERN did not have either the resources or the staff to sustain these clinics, the medical infrastructure SIM released naturally became the property of the Nigérien government's Service de santé. Ali 'dan Buzu, one of the few early converts the mission trained to take up medical work, saw the mission's changeable behavior as capricious and even destructive: "*Whoosh!* They are like a wildfire, they come blazing like that *whoooooh*, and then two years later, that's it. Burnt out. They've taken off and abandoned what they started" ('dan Buzu interview, February 19, 2001).

Beginning in the late 1970s, the mission shifted its restless energies into domains that could be less readily seized by an imagined "socialist" or "nationalist" state and in which it hoped to have more success in converting "unreached" nomadic Nigériens (particularly the highly romanticized Fulani and Tuareg), those who were hardest hit by the Sahel drought. As the emphasis shifted away from medical work that was fixed spatially in the southern zone populated by sedentary farmers, a revitalized sense of mobility and possibility emerged—mission publications increasingly featured the desert regions of the north of the country and the bustling capital of Niamey. With this change in philosophy came another shift in the mission's demography. Within the United States, the center of gravity of fundamentalist Christianity had shifted from the urban north (Chicago and Boston and, in Canada, Toronto) to the south (SIM headquarters gradually migrated from Toronto to Cedar Grove, New Jersey, and finally to Charlotte, North Carolina), encompassing the more conservative elements of the Southern Baptist Convention. The racial conflict, sexual license, and moral confusion of the United States in the 1960s and 1970s prompted evangelical Christians to articulate ever narrower understandings of sexual hierarchy in a desperate attempt to reinstate some kind of social order. In such a climate the appeal of mission work for single evangelical women seems to have declined as some dispensationalists decried women's greater prominence in public life and in the labor force as a sign of the end times. The antifeminist backlash also contributed to the retreat of some fundamentalist women into the home and childrearing despite the emergence of prominent women leaders of the movement who, paradoxically, succeeded in evading such restrictions themselves in the name of service to God (for a good overview of this shift, see Lindley 1996, 345–355; for the broader context of U.S. women's labor-force participation, see Kessler-Harris 1982).

In the decades since 1980, more married couples, albeit by a slender majority, have been drawn to SIM mission work and fewer single women have entered with a view toward a long-term career as missionaries, perhaps because secular options such as the Peace Corps have become more appealing to service-oriented single women. Single men, as in the past, have not been attracted to mission work. Married mission women increasingly devote themselves to schooling their children at home instead of sending their children to boarding homes—part of a rhetoric of "family values" that has overtaken the American fundamentalist movement. The entire tone of the mission had changed once again—it was in effect remasculinized by the mid-1980s. By 1986, SIM had recovered, and it continued to grow in size from that time on; although it still seems to be the case that there are roughly two women to every man ("Statistical History, 1970–1991"; Ian and June Hay interview). While the mission continues to run the leprosarium at Danja and the hospital at Galmi (in what seems to an outsider to be a rather demoralized fashion), many observers predict that the mission will not retain those extraordinarily demanding and "unprofitable" institutions very much longer; it is moving into other areas.

There is one medical initiative in which it seems to me probable that SIM will maintain a significant and growing presence, and that is in the area of AIDS treatment and prevention. Both Danja and Galmi handle AIDS cases today, and in Niamey the mission sponsors an AIDS awareness program. Migration to better labor markets has become a necessary life stage for many men in Niger, and circulation to such centers as Abidjan and Lagos has become much more common in the past twenty years. The growing mobility of men is associated with the gradually increasing visibility of AIDS in Niger. AIDS has, from the vantage point of evangelism, many of the same qualities leprosy had in the past—it is socially stigmatized, it requires regular appearance at medical facilities, treatment may occur over many years, it has implications for sexual behavior and family life, and it invites deep reflection on the ravages of sin and death. There is as yet no cure and the government of Niger cannot hope to adequately address this public health problem alone. Although in the era of political correctness, missionaries may not say so openly, evangelical Christians generally associate AIDS with sinfulness. As Gordan Evans remarked in an interview published in 1994 in which he pointed to AIDS work as one of the new fields for the mission in Niger, "These are the lepers of our times" (Charles 1994, 24, author's translation).

10

The Tree of Life:
Regenerating and Gendering the Garden after the Fall, 1975–2000

> *The gospel is a very potent change agent, but we must remember that we do not use the gospel to accomplish a "greater purpose," i.e. development, but rather we realize that the process of transformation brought about by conversion is development in the ultimate sense.*

> —J. Matthews, "Annual Project Progress Report, April 1998–March 1999"

I was invited to visit some of the villages in which SIM has worked in the areas of agro-forestry and rural development by an impressive Maradi celebrity named Ibrahim Yahaya, popularly known as Jaho. Jaho hosts SIM's weekly development radio show on Radio Anfani. The show airs live at noon when people are at home preparing the midday meal and is rebroadcast in the late afternoon when people are listening to the radio in the cool of the day. Jaho tells jokes, interviews local farmers, visits a broad array of development projects, and generally acts to encourage deeply discouraged farmers in an engaging and jovial manner. The show is much appreciated by the government, by Peace Corps volunteers, and by ordinary farmers. Nothing in the program has specific religious content but it does create a great deal of goodwill for the SIM mission. Jaho's voice and impressive person (he is tall and when he is at public events he dresses with great flair in traditional Hausa garb) are readily recognized by people throughout the region; he is associated not with Christianity but with modernity and development. Having worked for many years for SIM in the realms of reforestation, development, and relief, he is well known and has received awards from the government of Niger in recognition of his contributions to development (Rinaudo 1994b). Because of his Fulani family background and his long familiarity with Hausa-speaking farmers, he has proven an indispensable intermediary in mediating the sometimes-violent conflicts between pastoralists and farmers in the region (Rinaudo 1995). This is a man who loves his job, loves trees, and feels passionately about the importance of SIM's work in development.

On the way to the project villages, we passed by his house near the Danja leprosarium to pay a visit to his wife. Painted on the outside wall of his home is a charming life-size mural of a tree, above which are the words *L'arbre, c'est la vie* ("Trees are life"). Trees, with their biblical resonances of the garden before the fall and their long association with Paradise, bear a symbolic weight that resonates among both Muslims and Christians. The mural reflects the sentiment that motivated SIM's rural development work for many years and one that was very much in sympathy with the national government's environmental policies, which are captured performatively in annual tree-planting events. He commented with some acerbity that recently a SIM missionary visiting his home remarked, upon seeing the mural, that it should have read, *Dieu, c'est la vie* ("God is life").

SIM's ambivalence about development is nicely captured in this interchange. Development work has often been driven by something akin to evangelical fervor—the commitment of those who feel they have the answer that will save the ignorant African farmer. The adoption of development initiatives (such as planting trees) is treated as a mark of a kind of civic virtue. But that secular fervor and the inevitable emphasis in development on relatively long-term physical goals are in tension with SIM's historical commitment to the immediacy of spiritual transformation—it is rebirth in Jesus Christ that will save the people of Niger, with or without trees. Indeed, SIM believes that without spiritual change there can be no real improvement in physical conditions: "Development ministries are incomplete if they do not address both the spiritual and physical needs of man" (Rinaudo 1988b, 6). Trees, stoves, and woodlots are outward markers of Christian love to Muslims, but in themselves they are not (eternal) Life (Lovering 1985, 2). Only when farmers are transformed spiritually will their gardens begin to thrive.

This same tension between physical and spiritual goals informed SIM's medical work in the 1950s and 1960s, and it is perhaps surprising to find it reappearing, apparently unresolved, later and in another domain. A few questions come to mind. How did SIM, which was already wary of physical ministries by the 1970s, become so deeply engaged in relief and development work? How did it conceptualize such work in order to relieve the unproductive binary tension that had begun to plague the medical work? And why, having become so engaged, would more-recent SIM missionaries—who in principle are committed to a less binary understanding of body and spirit under the banner of "holistic development" or "wholistic ministry"—nevertheless continue to view development commitments with an ambivalent critical eye?

SIM's interventions in the realm of relief and development have taken two major forms: an emphasis on tree-planting to address the perceived degradation of the landscape and a food-for-work program designed to ensure that those most in need during periods of stress—women and children—receive food aid. I will discuss the mission's emphasis on trees first—the regeneration of the Garden. I will then turn to the question of how relief and development work has been conceptualized, focusing in particular on the gender and property implications of the mission's approach. A number of ironies and contradictions will emerge: SIM itself contributed to the destruction of the tree cover in the region through its promotion of animal traction; SIM's *relief* work was and is in considerable tension with its interventions into *development*; and, perhaps most important, the mission's lack of understanding of access to land, intrahousehold dynamics, and gender relations has meant that it has both failed to protect the interests of its Christian converts and has missed opportunities to promote its technical packages more effectively. It has largely ignored the profound implications of its technical promotions for gender relations. It has also been blind to the ways in which its own conceptions of property have had powerful implications for political dynamics in the villages in which it works. Because the mission has always viewed itself as apolitical, it has regularly failed to understand that farming is micropolitics at its finest—it is not plausible to intervene into an agro-pastoral regime without engaging with the political processes through which land access is defined, labor rights are organized, and market processes are mediated. Micropolitical processes ultimately engage larger national politics—a problem the mission consistently refuses to address. Faced with an insistence (which is buried in technical packages) on conceptions of land and trees as private property, villagers have operationalized those conceptions in the only way that is readily imaginable in the local context: through reference to Islamic law. It is an irony that the mission has effectively done much to promote Islamic conceptions of law, marriage, and property in the region.

Of Ox Plows and Trees

Jaho's *L'arbre, c'est la vie* mural bears the traces of the history of SIM's entry into development work via reforestation, for the earliest efforts at what might be thought of as relief and development today (rather than simply the technical education offered by the boys' home farm school) were initiated by Zeb Zabriskie during the Sahel drought of the 1970s. As the prolonged drought prompted SIM's Maradi station to distribute food aid, the mission and the independent church began, under Zabriskie and Pastor 'dan Nana, to promote reforestation through the construction of windbreaks as a parallel program (Isch 1989, 3). The idea, which was very common at the time, was to stop the encroachment of the desert by planting trees. While the mission and church cooperated in this venture, it is quite clear that the mission masterminded the effort while the missions redirected local evangelists out of their regular preaching and into this new approach to outreach. In SIM's view, this development project was about teaching the improvident African farmer the importance of trees in order to protect the land. Thus, SIM's initial conception of "development" was reforestation. Despite its elaboration of a plethora of other "project components," the most consistent characteristic of SIM's development philosophy over several decades has been its focus on trees. SIM's initial conception of reforestation as the planting of a band of trees to halt the spread of the desert revealed a lack of knowledge of the history of the explosion of peanut farming in traditionally pastoral areas that had insufficient rainfall to support farming in normal years. Most NGOs at the time had equally facile understandings of the problems of drought and desertification and made equally ad hoc responses in the form of food aid combined with reforestation efforts.

Just as those evangelists who in an earlier moment had been drawn out of preaching and into the mission's boys' and girls' homes expressed resentment at giving up what they regarded as fruitful evangelical work in order to pursue the mission's priorities, some of the Bible school and farm school men who were yet again diverted from their evangelical work into the new emphasis on relief and development felt that this was a terrible mistake. It was one thing to promote "modern" agriculture under

Ockers, an activity that gave Christianity a certain luster. Food for work was another enterprise altogether, one that degraded the associations that came with Christianity. Things began to go wrong, one such pastor remarked, when Muslims began to say that we were giving people food to become Christians: "You see, the business started [during the famine relief], we are still suffering from that. Because, people say, they gave the country aid before, so now what are we doing now? Those of us who are close to the Europeans, they are always coming to us to get help, they say the whites gave us money, it's nothing but trouble. That's what ruined everything" (Pastor 'dan Nana interview, October 24, 2000). Many felt that Christianity had become monetized through the exchange of tree-planting or livestock-handling for food in a context in which some desperate farmers and pastoralists felt constrained to convert to remain in the good graces of the mission. And many within the Christian community felt that this was the beginning of the decline of the growth and standing of the local evangelical church.

While many men who were trained through the mission's agroforestry work retain a deep love of trees, farming, and the animals they learned to care for, their ambivalence about the development component of the mission's activities is palpable. In part that ambivalence is due to a sense that Christianity was thereby devalorized—taking on the mission's teachings was a sign of poverty and desperation rather than a sign of choice and modernity. The higher calling of God's work, preaching the gospel, was reduced to food for work. In such a mercenary understanding of conversion, there is never a large enough sum to entirely compensate for selling one's soul—the desire to get something more is always escalating, and that grasping attitude is infectious. Indeed, if those who have not converted can be bought with grain and cattle, why shouldn't those native Christians who work to evangelize among them benefit as well? Missionary misgivings about the effects of relief aid in Maradi seem to confirm the impression among Christians that such aid significantly altered relations between the local population and the mission (Stilwell 1989, 102).

There is a certain irony to the mission's promotion of trees, which began in the late 1970s, one that so far as I can tell SIM does not appreciate but would have been all too obvious to the older Christians who cooperated through the EERN with the mission's development efforts. SIM's long commitment to teaching "modern" agricultural methods at the farm school from the 1950s had contributed to the destruction of many of the trees in the region and the extension of agriculture into the northern zones. In the early years, of course, the discourse was one of "modernization" rather than one of "development." To sustain a successful Christian community, it was believed, Christians had to have the means to support themselves. To induce others to convert to Christianity, Christian farmers would need something striking to attract the attention of proud and skeptical neighbors. What could be more impressive to the Hausa farmer than stunning increases in crop yields? (Lovering 1963, 8–9)

SIM's farm school became a model for government efforts to improve agricultural production, and there has long been a flow of SIM agricultural trainees into the government services, in particular into the Service d'élévage, which is in charge of improved animal husbandry for plowing. Working over several decades toward the same goals of promoting animal traction, improved seed varieties, the use of chemical fertilizers, and major cash crops—particularly peanuts—the government services and the mission at length succeeded in making plow agriculture the norm in the region, regardless of whether it was suited to the soils, the incomes, or the plot sizes of Maradi's farmers.[1] Much of what both the government and the farm school promoted was simply impractical and unsustainable for most farmers. Improved seeds, fertilizers, and insecticides were too expensive without subsidies—it was not until the Kountché regime provided such subsidies that farmers began to adopt these techniques.[2] Beginning in 1976, state subsidies for inputs and equipment made it possible for farmers to begin experimenting with using fertilizer, a range of short- and long-cycle millet seeds, and ox-drawn plows and seeders. In the Maradi region, the multinational Projet de Développement Rural de Maradi (PDRM) simultaneously promoted and studied this ambitious attempt to transform Maradi's agriculture.[3] The technologies and strategies that the farm school had promoted from the mid-1960s were very much in keeping with the state's new approach, and farm school staff and graduates often found employment in the burgeoning business of promoting improved techniques and animal traction (Barmo Abdou interview; Malam Lawali interview; Malam Ibrahim 'dan Jima interview).

The mission's farm school training had encouraged students to clear large tracts of land, plow them with ox-drawn plows, seed them with a single crop—either millet or peanuts—and use chemical inputs such as fertilizers. The Projet de Développement Rural de Maradi promoted by Niger's military government picked up on many of these same components and taught them to farmers in a technical "package." Where in the past farmers had generally intercropped several different crops on the

John Ockers at the farm school with tractor and windmill.
Courtesy of SIMIA, *Africa Now* 18 (1963): 8.

same field (generally beans or peanuts together with millet or sorghum), these technical packages were designed to maximize output of a single crop and were poorly suited to multicropping. In order to earn cash to meet the tax demands of colonial and postcolonial governments, farmers tended to plant more and more peanuts.

However, monocropping of peanuts made farmers extraordinarily vulnerable to fluctuating market prices, drought, and disease. Farmers at length made their own choices about what to use and what to reject— millet replaced peanuts as a cash crop in the 1980s and was later supplemented by cowpeas in the 1990s. Rather than use the new equipment to work the dune land necessary for peanut production, some farmers began to use it to work the heavy clay soils of the valley, producing dry-season vegetables and fruit in areas where there was an urban outlet. The single component of the technical packages taught by the mission that was widely adopted in the region, according to the many pastors and evangelists I spoke to who were involved with the farm school, was the use of ox-drawn plows. If SIM succeeded in anything, it succeeded in popularizing *noman shanu* (farming with cattle).

Clearing the land for plowing using animal traction contributed to the denuding of the landscape, the parching of the soil, and the destruction of natural insect habitat necessary to sustain the quality of the land. It also made it possible for farmers to make up in area under production what they lost in yields per acre as they worked unsuitable or exhausted land. Opportunistic urban merchants could also use such techniques to clear and lay claim to large tracts of farmland near the city of Maradi with a canny eye toward land speculation rather than farm profits. Farmers regularly associate soil erosion and exhaustion with the use of the plow in Luxereau and Roussel's study of ecological and social change in Niger (1997, 46, 66, 115, 156). As the population grew and farmers (and urban merchants and functionaries) took over more and more of the remaining bush land, very few of the indigenous trees survived. Farmers, who are accustomed to seeing trees as gifts of Allah and not as something to be consciously planted, had few indigenous resources at hand to restore the damage. Within the local system of land tenure, adult trees are a mark of *daji*—land that is as yet unclaimed. It is by cutting down trees that an individual lays claim to bush land. In and of itself such an approach to land use need not be especially destructive if there is enough land for periodic fallow periods and if the roots of the trees that are cut for crop planting remain undamaged. But local arable land has been completely overtaken by farming and it is no longer possible to fallow over fields. This, combined with the "modern" practice of removing tree roots as well as tree growth, has caused severe stress on local farmlands.

The promotion of animal traction had other significant social effects. As land use became increasingly individualized and as technical elements were promoted that focused on male heads of households and ignored women's long-standing roles in agriculture and livestock-raising, the women of the Maradi region, who had always been active farmers in the past, were increasingly marginalized from new techniques of production (see Cooper 1997a). SIM's farm school and Bible schools provided the template for the training offered to farmers—they set a pattern that was reiterated in the training offered later by the government agricultural services and the PDRM. In SIM establishments, the student was always assumed to be an adult married man whose wife would simply accompany him; she was never conceived of as a farmer. The men would become pastors, learn "modern" farming techniques involving animal traction, and become the visible backbone of the church. "Wives" were offered rudimentary literacy training along with the stereotypically feminine subjects of hygiene, health, and nutrition training. In practice, their duty would be to cook, clean, and tend the children while their husbands were in school. They might be handmaids in evangelism, but they would not be farmers. Little wonder, then, that Christian couples perceived an appropriate Christian farming household to be one in which husbands did the farming while wives attended to domestic tasks. Christians trained in animal traction techniques then carried this model into other secular settings. It is no coincidence that SIM trainees were often hired to staff later efforts to popularize the plow.

Tony Rinaudo, who began work with SIM in the early 1980s, was one of the few missionaries who was openly critical of the "modern" approach and its environmental effects. But he did not acknowledge SIM's earlier involvement in propagating that approach and did not recognize its gender implications. Describing the work of the program he oversaw in the 1990s, he remarked:

> The type of development work that we do, and the thing that's had the biggest effect in the areas in which we're working, is natural regeneration of trees that are already in the fields. Through the last twenty to thirty years farmers have been taught to completely chop out any woody materials in order to be "good modern farmers." Then they can use oxen and plows. They can plow and sow in straight rows. They can apply fertilizer and all that. It's been disastrous for Niger because of the climate that we have here. (Rinaudo 1994a)

In the early 1980s, after many years of cooperating with the government to promote a package of "modern" techniques, including animal traction, the mission decided to leave the animal traction component to the government, since the "objective" of making the population aware of the advantages of animal traction had been "achieved" (Isch 1989b, 14; Rinaudo and Evans 1999, 24). Among the reasons it abandoned the "modernization" approach was a keen sense that the students who had learned such techniques at the farm school and the Bible schools were not in a position to transfer their learning to the villagers among whom they farmed later: "The school provides opportunities and equipment that are not available in the village, so that when it comes to reproducing what is done at the school the students don't find the same means in the village. They therefore can't really show villagers what they have learned at the school" (Isch 1989b, 29). Farm school graduates did, however, find an appreciative audience for their learning in development projects and government services.

Without ever openly repudiating the earlier approach, SIM mission-aries quietly shifted energy away from promoting "modern" inputs to elaborate instead on various efforts begun over the years to promote reforestation, an emphasis that reflected its growing concern about en-vironmental degradation. In conjunction with Christian evangelists trained through the Bible schools and the farm school who worked on behalf of the EERN, they developed an array of project elements. Thus, in addition to windbreaks (which SIM missionaries had promoted from the mid-1970s) and tree nurseries to raise wood for sale (which they had promoted from the early 1980s), the mission began in 1983 to promote natural tree regeneration and "improved" stoves that were designed to reduce the demand for firewood. The emphasis on tree-planting also called for substantial amounts of water, so well-digging entered the rep-ertoire in 1984, along with a handful of elements that were intended to improve food security, such as the reintroduction of manioc as a staple food crop (from 1983) and poultry-raising (from 1984). The food-for-work program of the late 1980s brought an additional component that emphasized dry-season gardening either near a well or in the river valley, in many ways simply expanding on the earlier promotion of tree nurs-eries.

At the heart of the mission's new approach was a strong emphasis on agro-forestry. However, promoting trees was far more complex than the mission imagined. If clearing trees is part of how one establishes rights to that land, it is also true that planting a tree can be a way to stake a claim to land—trees sometimes mark the borders of land and they may demarcate the terrain where animals are not welcome during the planting season. Keenly aware that planting trees is also a way of establishing rights to land, farmers during the 1970s surreptitiously uprooted trees planted for the state out of civic duty during the *fête de l'arbre* (national tree-planting day) for fear that they were part of a larger strategy of the Diori regime to appropriate their land as "vacant forest" under an un-popular 1974 law. In other words (as one judge commented to me), *icce na yin 'kunya* (trees are a source of divisiveness and shame) because they are so often at the heart of disputes between individuals. Trees are the issue in debates over who cleared land first, who is intruding into some-one else's fields, whether land is bush or fallow, and whether or not land is available for pasture.

Nevertheless, SIM promoted tree-planting with a zeal akin to the piety with which recycling is promoted among American schoolchildren, as if by planting trees, past sins could be absolved and a reborn commitment to the environment established, despite the broader realities within which the practice was embedded. The kinds of trees that have been promoted have shifted over time (from eucalyptus to Australian acacia to baobab and, most recently, to the managed regeneration of trees that naturally occur in fields), but in the judgment of SIM missionaries, it was the tree that would be the source of life—not cash, labor migration, education, gender equity, or any of a wide range of imaginable life-saving strategies.

"Religion that God our Father accepts as pure and faultless": Famine Relief

SIM's entry into relief and development occurred more as an emotional and moral response to the tragedy of the Sahel drought than as a conscious approach to development or evangelism. As former SIM director Ian Hay remarked, reflecting on the Sahel drought and the later 1984 drought, "It wasn't that we had some great strategy to start a relief and development kind of program. For instance, in Maradi, they woke up at the station there looking out at the field, and there were some Fulani, and then there were some more, and some more, and before long there were 5,000 people out there, all of them starving. I mean they had lost their animals, they had lost everything. Well, what do you do when you're having lunch there and there are 5,000 people out there starving?" (Ian Hay interview). The mission first intervened in the local economy through the farm school as a strategy for reaching young male children when it was largely blocked from opening formal educational institutions; its entry into relief work was far more spontaneous.

Very little documentation of the earliest relief efforts remains, so desperate was the moment and so inexperienced and overstressed were the personnel (Isch 1989b). But it is clear that in the last half of the 1970s the mission contributed to the distribution of relief grain in the Maradi region and began in a modest way to promote other activities related to desertification. At first the mission simply purchased grain with existing funds. Later it raised funds to cover the food distribution through its donor networks. The more institutionalized its relief program and development interventions became, the more it relied upon collaboration with secular funding agencies such as the Canadian government's International Development Agency (CIDA). In some ways it might seem strange, given Ian Hay's description of the experience of suddenly facing thousands of starving refugees, to ask how the mission justified its entry into such work. Helping the hungry seemed to be, in some rather obvious way, the Christian thing to do. The urgent need to promote "the Word" had to have seemed difficult to insist upon in the face of the urgent need to save people's lives. The biblical justification for the mission's relief work was not hard to find and it was indeed only later (in the late 1980s, so far as I can tell) that anyone felt called upon to find specific scriptural grounds for giving out emergency relief food. It seems to me that it was in fact in the context of the mission's growing involvement in development work that the interest in seeking out a biblical basis crystallized. It is interesting, though, that the mandate of the texts the mission turned to to justify relief and development work is quite narrow. The point that emerges immediately is that it is far easier to justify relief work biblically than it is to come up with a coherent scriptural mandate for intervention in the realm of development.

Two concrete biblical references missionaries cite with reference to relief are Deuteronomy 14:28–29 (the commandment to tithe income in order that "the stranger, and the fatherless, and the widow, which are within thy gates, shall come, and shall eat and be satisfied") and James 1:27 ("Religion that God our Father accepts as pure and faultless is this: to look after orphans and widows in their distress"; New International Version).[4] The Judeo-Christian tradition does not just exhort its adherents to feed those in need, particularly widows and children; it commands them to do so. The fact that "the stranger" is omitted from James's reiteration of the commandment suggests that with the advent of Christianity, there was some slippage away from protection of exiles and refugees (the more masculine images) toward caring for vulnerable women and children. When missionaries were faced with a field full of starving women and children, it was not difficult to know the right thing to do—supply food. And that is what SIM did in the drought of 1984:

> Three relief camps were established in Maradi and were inhabited by terribly destitute, ill, and hopeless persons, mostly women and children. The largest camp near Maradi station consisted of 5,500 people at peak. A second camp was comprised of 350 extremely malnourished children who were given high protein rations daily. These two camps received seven and a half tons of food weekly. Buzu people made up the third camp and received one and a half tons per week. (Stilwell 1989, 2)

The food distribution took place on an impressive scale and caused substantial numbers of people to move to refugee villages:

Most of the people lived in crude huts made of millet stalks. Many had walked one hundred kilometers and more to seek aid. Allotments of beans, milk, oil, sorghum, and millet were distributed weekly. Grain distribution was expanded to include people up to thirty kilometers away. A total of 11,500 people received weekly rations. In all, the food given out here equalled 1,879 tons over a twelve month period. (Stillwell 1989, 2)

By the 1984 drought, the Niger government had determined that it wanted to control food aid distribution so that it did not promote dependency or refugee camps. Alarmed at such large population displacements, the government insisted that if the mission was to continue to give food aid it should do so through food-for-work projects in rural villages rather than through food handouts. The Kountché regime aimed to encourage rural development in order to prevent large relief camps outside major urban centers and to slow rural-to-urban migration. To accommodate the government's preferences, SIM embarked on a food-for-work program through which households that remained in the villages could obtain food rations if they planted and protected trees, made a vegetable garden, and made an "improved" stove (Isch 1989b, 19). Food for work in villages to the north and south of Maradi involved some 35,700 people. Farmers there "were educated in the values of reforestation," while at Soura, where some 1,200 nomadic Fulani gathered, pastoralists were "encouraged to try Dry Season gardening." They dug shallow wells and were given food to supplement the unfamiliar crops they grew, which included wheat, corn, beans, potatoes, sweet potatoes, lettuce, and cassava (Stilwell 1989, 3).

While the logic behind this and subsequent programs that were promoted throughout the 1980s and 1990s seemed reasonable, observers were regularly troubled at the pretense that villagers could "choose" to participate in the program when they were starving. As Stilwell notes of the food-for-work program in Maradi, "Many people were simply unable to contribute any work due to illness and weakened physical condition" (1989, 3). Project activities seemed to belong to those distributing the aid, not the villagers and refugees, so it was not entirely clear that the program could effectively promote independence. And it was difficult to know how to distinguish those with genuine need from those who were simply opportunistically seeking subsidized grain (Rinaudo 1997c). As a rule, as the relief program became more closely integrated into the mission's other ongoing development efforts, farmers in food-for-work villages were required to engage in an array of project activities in order to

"Women line up with their children as they wait to gather their rations of grain." Courtesy of SIMIA (NR 203), photographed by Tony Rinaudo, 1985.

earn the right to a 50 percent subsidy in grain purchases rather than a direct grain allocation (Rinaudo 1997a). SIM's various development activities were dubbed the "Maradi Integrated Development Project," or MIDP, and were gradually expanded to include many villages in the region. In some ways, the government-mandated need for a food-for-work dimension to the distribution of relief food drove the project in its early years, and various components were added with little overarching philosophy to guide staff in its increasing engagement with development.

The food aid dimension was clearly part of the appeal of becoming a SIM project village; villagers in project villages could receive subsidies in exchange for work "for" the mission that included planting trees, making compost, and digging holes known as *zai* in fields to create concentrated regeneration zones for composting and seeding. But that did not necessarily mean that villagers were interested in performing such work for themselves. Indeed, in come cases, the food aid may have created a sense that it was not necessary to invest undue labor in dry-season farms since the mission would intervene if necessary with grain. Luxereau and Roussel found that the head of one village declined to plant his rather profitable dry-season vegetable garden after meeting his social expenses because he knew he had grain reserves from the previous year and was certain that he could benefit from food aid "from a religious mission" if necessary; that mission was undoubtedly SIM (Luxereau and Roussel 1997, 170n8). It is no surprise that the number of SIM's target villages mushroomed from 6 in the early 1970s to 124 villages by the time of the 1998 famine (Rinaudo and Evans 1999, 7). "Food aid," remarks a SIM manual, "has certainly played a decisive role in the shaping of MIDP" (10).

Even when such programs were in place to discourage emigration from the rural areas, many destitute women and children nevertheless continued to make their way to Maradi, where they might receive help from the mission. Thus, in 1994 1,500 women in Maradi and 400 malnourished children sought assistance (Rinaudo 1994b). A similar number arrived in 1997:

> Most of the 1,300 people being helped in Maradi with a food for work program are women who have been widowed, divorced, or abandoned by their husbands. Each person being helped has their own garden plot for raising vegetables and work for grain is provided twice per month. Over forty malnourished children mainly from this group receive special meals three days per week as well as take home rations. Those being helped are also being taught basic hygiene, nutrition and other skills. (Rinaudo 1997a)

For those who most closely resembled the destitute orphan and widow depicted in Deuteronomy and James, the logic of the food-for-work programs was far from obvious. What did it mean to require women to work in gardens owned by the mission on river valley land that bore no relationship to the parched land in the villages they had fled? Was this really "sustainable" and "independent"? If they had no land in their villages, would they ever return? Was there an appropriate way to address the development needs of women if they were now effectively urban? Some of the women were clearly permanent immigrants to the city; they had been abandoned by husbands who had left in search of work and food and showed no signs of returning (Rinuado 1997a). Similar questions could be asked of the gardening activities SIM promoted for the refugee pastoralists. How could dry-season gardening techniques to grow high-value vegetables on expensive urban land be useful to nomads with no land? Would such gardening be a viable alternative in an area without a nearby urban outlet for the products? Thus, the "relief" SIM offered that appeared to be closest to the spirit of Christian charity was the least consistent with the government's emphasis on village-based rural development designed to discourage refugee camps and migration to the city. The project staff began to be concerned about the annual recurrence of its food-for-work program in the urban center of Maradi:

> MIDP is concerned that a large and permanent contingent of unemployed women remains in Maradi. Although harvests were very good this year, most of the women helped in the food for work program do not have any farm land. For these people, famine is an every year occurrence. We are not prepared to carry out relief work every year, nevertheless these people will be here asking for food next year. MIDP staff are currently discussing this problem, but we do not foresee any solution. (Rinaudo 1998a)

The growing and rather visible contingent of desperate women attracted to SIM in Maradi was also increasingly in tension with the sentiment of Muslim purists that single women should not be encouraged to make an independent life in the city but should rather find husbands. The mission's relief work that focused on single women could be seen by Islamists as undermining an ideal of female dependency in marriage. In the opening chapter of the book we saw that this sentiment is neither fleeting nor insubstantial—it has led to violence in the past and is likely to do so again in the future.

Lori Hartmann-Mahmud found that this sentiment was echoed by many married rural women in the Maradi region, who had little interest in the kinds of programs urban women's groups proposed to provide single women with security and autonomy. They were more interested in development interventions that would improve the ability of husbands and wives to work together cooperatively in supporting their households. Summarizing the reflections of one relatively well-off woman, she notes:

> She really stressed that one should help married women. . . . If single women are helped then that norm of not marrying will start to be accepted. She is very much against that. Women should be encouraged within their household. Don't be too quick to encourage divorced women only. That may lead to an impression that it is better to be single—and that is not good. "If you help single women, married women will not be patient. They will see that the other has succeeded on her own, and she will be quick to leave the marriage." (Hartmann-Mahmud 2000, 324)

Such sentiments may be reactionary—this woman, who had been to Mecca, was in the luxurious position of being able to sit in judgment on her less-fortunate sisters. But they may also reflect a real need for NGOs and governments to focus attention on how to help stressed couples cope together. When women who are left to manage land they do not own find that their husbands who leave to "eat the dry season" never return, their access to land in their marital villages rapidly deteriorates and they will probably seek help in the city, as was the case for A'i Mai Muni (A'i Mai Muni interview). If they are lucky, as she was, they will become integrated into city life somehow. She became a member of the Christian community gradually after working one of the SIM gardens, and her daughter found work with one of the missionaries. The question is whether such women would be better served by programs that made it less likely that the couple would be permanently separated in the first place.

Obviously, for such an outcome, rural development strategies would have to be targeted with a careful eye for the needs and problems of married rural women as well as the intrahousehold dynamics that most impinge on the success of the household as a whole. How can husbands cooperate with wives to minimize women's labor demands, maximize their access to income, and ensure the security of the household's claims to land if she must manage the farm while he is away? How can women cooperate with their husbands to reduce the need for off-farm income, minimize expenses, and make it more likely that he would be in a position to return for the farming season? Husbands and wives do in fact cooperate sometimes; women sometimes pasture their small ruminants in men's fields (an exchange of crop residue for manure), for example, and households sometimes invest in labor-saving expenditures such as grain-milling services that free up women's time for food trade (an investment of male cash so that women's savings can be used to purchase small ruminants to benefit the family as a whole). The recognition that development interventions that targeted women alone rather than households were not addressing the realities of rural women's needs prompted the international humanitarian aid organization CARE to name one of its most recent gender-equity projects in the Maradi region as Tatalin Arzikin Gida (Tending to the Household's Resources). Meeting women's needs would require reflections among and between men and women on how to successfully secure all of the household's resources for the general well-being of the family and village (CARE 2000). A successful household depends on the contributions of many members, despite the pattern of individualization and fragmentation of the land in the region. This was one of the striking discoveries of David Rain's study of migration in Maradi—the more densely populated villages and the larger households with a population that flows in and out are successful (Rain 1999), very much to the contrary of the antinatalist instincts and antimigration impulses of Malthusian policymakers.[5] Keeping households together, not so much through prevention of labor migration as through broader strategies of cooperation, is very much at the heart of rural success. It is not obvious that single women's autonomy in the city is consistent with what villagers know about what makes a healthy village and household work. Someone has to secure cash for the farm, and those people have to want to come back, and someone has to be at home to patiently mind the farm until the migrant returns.

Clearly SIM's intervention into famine relief threw it into a broad range of extremely complex issues. While the "pure and faultless" activity of feeding widows and orphans might at first have seemed rather straightforward, the mission soon found itself engaging in demanding and perplexing development problems. Despite the growing ambiguity and complexity of its work, a strong consensus continues among SIM missionaries that emergency aid is appropriate and relevant. When SIM launched a major assessment of its relief work in 1989 that included a survey of its missionary staff across the globe, it found that missionaries quite overwhelmingly supported such work (Stilwell 1989, 108). However, the survey found that there was much less consensus about "physical ministries" more broadly, which would include both the health care interventions discussed in the preceding chapter and rural development more broadly. The report notes, "There is a noticeable difference among SIM missionaries regarding their opinions about the role of more long-term, development-type of ministries. . . . Some SIMers see development ministries as being outside of the scope of the SIM spiritual mandate and best left to other organizations. . . . Many SIM field missionaries find themselves in a situation where they regularly observe chronic physical need, see the necessity for long-term development-oriented solutions, but don't know if SIM can become involved in addressing the needs without compromising the SIM purpose and goals" (109).

In other words, missionaries did not find it difficult to justify relief work, despite their reservations about physical ministries, but they felt that longer-term development work would be harder to justify. There are a number of ironies to this. The first is that SIM mission workers in Niger constituted a significant number of the missionaries who had reservations about the appropriateness of relief work (Stilwell 1989, 63). The more deeply workers were involved in relief work, it seems, the less convinced they were of its efficacy. But this was not, I think, because they did not espouse "physical ministries"—to the contrary, their frustrations with relief work had led them to feel that only longer-term interventions would get to the root problems the population faced (103). Relief aid could, in fact, undermine the population's ability to commit to serious development work and undercut the mission's evangelical efforts by giving the appearance that it was seeking "rice Christians" (102). Administering such massive programs made it all but impossible to continue other urgent activities to protect and promote the well-being of the local populations and to come to a deeper understanding of the technical issues and social problems of the area. The preponderance of medical personnel in Niger probably contributes to this longer view and sense of realism about what relief aid can and cannot accomplish. Missionaries in fields that were not directly involved in relief work were more likely to see relief work positively; they had not watched grain disappear into the black market or experienced the painful struggles between the mission and local churches over control of valuable goods (100). They were not faced with the annual recurrence of food-for-work programs even in years when the harvests were good.

The Problem of "Engaging Farmers" and "Involving Women"

Having been drawn willy-nilly into development work as a result of the twin desires to restore the deforested garden and feed deserving widows and orphans, the mission faced the challenge of persuading "degenerate" farmers and "deserving" women to "engage in development" as the mission conceived it. But the mission's attempts at reforestation were still conceived as a response to the failures of "traditional methods" rather than through the lens of far more complex political and economic realities that were nothing if not modern. As a result, the project experienced some rather spectacular failures. Not long after the shift away from promoting modern inputs toward reforestation, the entire project was thrown into a state of crisis by the 1984–1985 drought. "It was in this tragic context," the 1989 evaluation of the project remarked, "that the project activities experienced a kind of collapse" (Isch 1989b, 18). Half of the windbreaks planted in 1983 died, the "improved" stoves introduced that year were not being used the subsequent year, and the manioc didn't produce well. Very little that the mission promoted had any immediate resonance for villagers, whose little remaining energy was directed elsewhere. In adopting project elements, villagers had simply been pleasing project staff, and in a crisis year, such politeness was abandoned. The linkage of food for work with project elements further undermined local engagement and initiative, for there seemed to be little reason to devote energy to the activities the project promoted without getting something in exchange. Thus, the tree nurseries and windbreaks villagers planted regularly as part of food-for-work programs just as regularly died for lack of watering once the program was finished. Successive years of food crisis and food-for-work programs have only exacerbated this problem, particularly in project villages added to the mission's roster during and after the 1984 drought.

SIM now takes the attitude that one of the challenges of working in Niger is what it perceives as the belief of many farmers that development is a kind of industry and that development workers' salaries are a function of how much "output" farmers produce in the form of visible conformity to project requirements. By this logic, when farmers perform work under the guidance of a "project"(even on their own lands), it is in fact the development promoters who benefit, not the farmers. The mission is aware that Nigériens may feel very little engagement with the proposed elements themselves (Rinaudo and Evans 1999, 7). The mission's assessment of the source of its difficulties in forging constructive relations with farmers resonates with Kari Bergstrom's observations of dynamics between villagers in the Maradi region and other development NGOs. Farmers in the two villages she studied

> tend to see their relationships with development projects such as CARE and UNICEF in terms of . . . hierarchical relationships (i.e. colonial administration, state, royalty, and wealthy traders) that they are familiar with. The notion of altruistic intervention with the goal of empowerment and self-sufficiency, which is key to how UNICEF and CARE see themselves today, is not well understood locally. . . . Instead, many tend to see CARE and UNICEF as institutions looking for workers in order to make their projects successful for reasons of self interest. (Bergstrom 2005, 19)

Farmers in the region are not only skeptical of development interventions but may even see development promoters (and missionaries in particular) as rather parasitic. In response, missionaries decided to take the word "project" out of the MIDP title; they now refer to it instead as a "program" to reduce the perception that its development interventions could be thought of as a machine for generating cash for the mission and handouts for grasping villagers (Rinaudo 1997a).

While the mission tends to regard this attitude to projects as a by-product of the incompatibility of food relief and handouts with real development (a reasonable enough conclusion that is shared by many NGOs), some attention to the specific kinds of "outputs" it has pushed farmers and rural women to produce sheds light on the deep mistrust many have evidently begun to feel toward government and NGO interventions. Luxereau and Roussel's work, which focuses on tree-planting (the most salient example of SIM's agro-forestry emphasis), reveals that some of the exotic trees promoted in the Maradi region have proven undesirable from the point of view of farmers. *Prosopis juliflora*, which has been promoted by nurseries in Madawa as live fencing, is known in Hausa as *tsakwasaran Madawa*, or "the viper of Madawa," because its thorns cause serious inflammation. Once it is planted it is very difficult (and painful) for a farmer to get rid of it. It is not entirely clear, in such a case, that he or she can choose to abandon it. The eucalyptus tree (*Eucalyptus camaldulensis*) so vigorously promoted as a fast-growing source of wood has proven to compete with the crops in fields alongside it because it consumes so much water. Farmers say that it is a very "hot" tree, but once it is planted they no longer legally have the right to uproot it and can only hope that it will die on its own if they neglect it (Luxereau and Roussel 1997, 107–108, 124n11). The Australian acacia (*Acacia holosericea*, SIM's signature tree because the mission introduced it into Niger) was promoted as both a fast-growing woody species and a source of extra protein. However, transforming its seeds into edible flour requires substantial specialized knowledge and considerable labor. Its roots compete with other plants for water, making it an inappropriate choice for land that is close to millet fields. Unfortunately, it was generally promoted in the context of windbreaks next to fields. Because the seeds of local varieties of acacia are poisonous, this intervention is dangerous without sufficient training in how to recognize different species and how to treat the seeds. The promised market for acacia flour rarely materialized (Rinaudo and Evans 1999, 50–51).

Little wonder that farmers hesitate before planting trees if they cannot discreetly uproot them should they decide they don't like the outcome (the government imposes draconian punishments on those who destroy tree cover). When farmers can *choose* what to plant and where, they often prefer the neem (which was introduced from India), which is much appreciated for its shade, or, more recently, the sturdy baobab, which provides edible leaves (Luxereau and Roussel 1997, 108, 127; Matthews 1999b). Often farmers seem to prefer to plant trees in their compounds (where they can decide privately how to proceed, protect the fruit and leaves, and water at their convenience) rather than in their fields. This pattern of planting trees and protecting any seedlings that grow on their own close to human settlements resonates with Fairhead and Leach's paradigm-altering work on the forest-savanna mosaic—African farmers have historically generated forested areas in the proximity of settlements, not simply depleted them (1996). None of these preferences were predicted by development planners—these patterns were very much an outcome of farmer choices. Farmers with decades of intimate and often painful experience with trees that have presented as many problems as solutions might very reasonably feel that they have been gullible in the past. They might also legitimately note that all this conspicuous tree promotion has served to attract international aid to the government and donations to NGOs but has had very mixed consequences for the target communities. The mission's success in promoting tree-planting over two decades has been remarkably modest, prompting a recent evaluation to encourage MIDP to "reassess" its commitment to this approach (Evans 1999, 55).

Other components of SIM's gradually emerging "holistic development" program have been slow to take root for similar reasons, particularly those appendages added belatedly to "include women" in development. Despite its long-standing promotion of trees, one SIM evaluation found that when villagers were asked what could be done about deforestation, men replied that they could plant new trees and protect those that exist. Women, who are charged with finding firewood on a daily basis, feigned ignorance about any solution to the problem of deforestation (Isch 1989b, 28). From the vantage point of women, trees planted or protected by men on men's fields had little relevance to their own immediate experience of the loss of trees and wood. The separation of husbands' and wives' property in local farming practice meant that targeting male heads of households did not necessarily mean that women in such households had access to the wood their husbands produced. Protecting bush trees any further would hardly serve women's interests, since they relied on such trees as a source of firewood in the absence of their own trees. The mission's early promotion of trees never really addressed the critical reality that women, who are great consumers of wood, were not on the whole in a position to either participate in or benefit from these interventions. Either the land or the trees (or ideally both) had to belong to the women. But nothing in the mission's approach addressed the problem of women's lack of access to resources such as land and trees. To the contrary, much of the impact of project interventions reduced women's access to land or to trees as a collective resource;

instead, land became an increasingly privatized and masculinized form of wealth.

Rather than reflect deeply on the labor and land issues that have made the reforestation efforts appear to have nothing whatsoever to do with women, the mission, like many NGOs, decided to promote "improved" stoves and poultry-raising. Attempts to introduce poultry have almost always ended up benefiting men, and the mission has done little research to determine why that might be. Undoubtedly the gender of the staff that promotes such interventions (which is largely male) has something to do with this impasse. SIM, rather shockingly, has no local Hausa-speaking women to act as extension agents, although it has occasionally had female missionaries who were committed to the MIDP. The start-up costs and recurrent costs (particularly the cost of necessary vaccinations) may also be a factor that inhibits women from taking up poultry-raising—it is an enterprise that requires capital and feed at the outset. Given women's long-standing interest in small ruminants, it is perplexing that no attention has ever been focused on goats and sheep in an effort to reach women—they are less problematic to raise than disease-prone poultry, they are harder to steal, and they are less subject to immediate consumption when guests appear. But they are not "new" and therefore, perhaps, less interesting to SIM with its tendency to seek visible signs of local transformation.

The few women missionaries who have worked with the rather masculine project over the years have tended to be devoted instead to promoting "improved" stoves. It is quite clear to me that local women do not see such stoves as an improvement at all—no development intervention that has promoted these inconvenient and fragile clay stoves has, to my knowledge, been a success. They are easily damaged, difficult to adapt to local cookware, and, most important, they can't be moved. Women like to set up their cooking wherever the rain, shade, breezes, child care, and entrepreneurial needs dictate—fixing a clay stove in one location is entirely incompatible with their needs. Because women can be divorced at will by their Muslim husbands, fixed property in the form of molded clay stoves is not particularly desirable—if they have to leave the home they cannot take the stoves with them. There is a certain Puritanism in insisting that women build and use such "modern" wood-saving stoves when the demands on their time and energy are already so high and when far more convenient and relatively fuel-efficient portable metal stoves are readily available on the market. Husbands might reasonably be expected to save money to purchase such stoves for their wives as gifts as part of a general household approach to reducing fuel use and saving labor, but that wouldn't be "involving" women enough because it wouldn't require their labor. Husbands are unlikely to expend income on such stoves so long as women manage to scare up enough firewood to cook over a traditional stove for free. Rather than examine its own motives, dynamics within households, or the preferences and constraints of women, the local mission staff has tended to content itself with attributing the lack of enthusiasm for "improved" stoves to the power of "tradition" in women's lives: "Whatever the real advantages, whenever tradition has the upper hand, people refuse to become involved" (Isch 1989b, 32, author's translation). Reference to tradition thus absolves the staff of any responsibility for failed project components, particularly those that involve women.[6]

A more recent effort to "involve" women has focused on health care initiatives since about 1995—rather belatedly in the context of the usual rhetoric of "holistic development." To an outsider, the various health schemes are quite peculiar. Women are encouraged to use and process the seeds of the Australian acacia as a high-protein food supplement— suddenly it becomes clear that in order for this agro-forestry "component" to function, it is women who will be expected to contribute their labor to the processing of the seeds. One wonders whether the women were consulted when the trees were planted and who "owns" the processed seed flour. As it happens, this work is extremely labor intensive— it is hard to see how this would be an appealing activity unless the woman could gain some income from it (but there is no market for the flour) or the household was so stressed in a famine year that there was little choice. As an intervention "for" women, it seems problematic, to say the least.

Another of MIDP's perplexing approaches to health care promotion is its practice of encouraging project villages to create a "health committee." Because the missionaries promoting health for MIDP have always been women, the health committees are inevitably seen to be women's affairs. The women who make up the health committees are then trained in such topics as basic measures to prevent diseases, hygiene, nutrition, the benefits of colostrum, the importance of immunizations, rudimentary medical treatments, and when to send an ill person to the hospital. SIM missionaries expect these female village health workers to visit the homes of other villagers regularly and teach them what they had learned and carry the information to other villages. It is a rather evangelical model, if you will. The problem is that the mission never included any means of paying the "village health workers" either for the time committed to learning or the time they would be expected to devote to "sharing" what they had been taught. It is as if the mission imagined that there were villagers with no other demands on their time who can afford to volunteer health services as a kind of civic charity (Rinaudo and Evans 1999, 66–67). This is, of course, rather bizarre given that most development agencies agree that women's time is already under tremendous pressure (see, e.g., CARE 2000, 49, which estimates that women work eighteen hours per day regardless of the season).

Once again, rather than successfully reducing women's workload or compensating them for their labor by promoting some kind of income-generating activity, the mission seemed instead to be envisioning placing new demands on their time. In noting the discontentment of villagers with this arrangement and their "lack of motivation," the project reports remark, "We feel the only way to create a sustainable development movement is to find true volunteers who are motivated to see change in their own community" (Matthews 1999a). Outside evaluations regularly pointed out to the Maradi mission staff the flaws in its notion of volunteerism, to the point that one recent evaluation from the central office of SIM in Canada has a rather exasperated air: "This evaluation is not the first to question the MIDP's expectations concerning social responsibility and volunteerism. The independent 1996 de Campos evaluation asserted that promotion of committees and discussion groups pertaining to mutually beneficial social and community aspects of life do not reflect a realistic understanding of the Hausa socio-cultural environment" (Evans 1999, 40).

Far more popular both with MIDP villages and villages throughout the Maradi region is a movement among development institutions to promote small dry-season gardens of indigenous plants within women's compounds as a way to compensate them for the loss of nutritious and naturally occurring plants in fields as mechanized weeding has become popular in men's fields. Women are encouraged to collect local seeds so they can plant popular native vegetables to eat and dry in the protected space of the compound. Dried leaves are sometimes also marketable, and women can often sell the highly nutritious cooked vegetables to earn cash (Charlamagne 1996; Rinaudo 1995). These *kayan miya* (things for making sauce) gardens show more promise than the "health" interventions promoted by the mission, largely because they treat women as cultivators and entrepreneurs rather than as "naturally" altruistic guardians of the health of others.

As this quick survey of interventions "involving" women shows, one regular shortcoming of the mission's rural development work has been a failure to consider the cost of the labor it expected project villagers to commit to various project components. As a result, farmers have been reluctant to take on some of the more labor-intensive SIM project components (farmers have been notoriously disinclined to take up the digging of *zai* holes to regenerate land, for example). Despite their disinclination to plant new trees, given how unpredictable, time consuming, and contentious trees can prove to be, farmers do value the benefits of trees. Farmer managed natural regeneration (FMNR), a set of techniques farmers can use to encourage the regeneration of growth on tree stumps already existing on their farms, has become the keystone of MIDP agroforestry efforts of late precisely because of its popularity with farmers. They recognize its utility and welcome the reintroduction of trees into an agro-pastoral system that is increasingly practiced under individual land tenure arrangements. It was only after several decades of work to promote tree nurseries, windbreaks, and planting trees in fields that SIM workers began to emphasize protecting and regenerating existing trees, a practice that farmers seized upon enthusiastically partly because it was far less politically problematic than *planting* trees. When the land is individually owned in freehold, the trees on it can become valuable sources of wood for the owner to use or sell. The trees themselves protect the soil. Observers of local agricultural practice all seem to agree that local tree management has begun to improve dramatically as farming practices in the Maradi region intensify and freehold tenure wins the day (see, for example, Mousa 2000; Mahamane 2001; Awaiss 2000). At the heart of the transformations in the region, then, has been a major shift in the understanding of property, to which we must now turn.

Scripturalizing the Whole: Gender, Property Rights, and the Eighth Commandment

Trees are part of a broader cosmology that has been profoundly disrupted by the occupation of all available farm land and the shift toward individual property in the region. One could argue that the loss of tree cover in the region is part of a massive desacralization of the landscape that began in the 1970s and was made possible technologically through the promotion of the plow (largely by "Europeans") and ideologically through the promotion of Islamic law (by Muslims and the state)—a massive act of conquest by the monotheists. Luxereau and Roussel found that the very few remaining stands of trees in the Maradi and Dogondoutchi region were frequently protected because they were understood to be the homes of local spirits (1997, 39–41, 101, 106, 108, 123). Where there are significant and varied stands of trees, there is a corresponding sociological variation in the religious practices of the local population. Of course, adopting western methods of agriculture did not mean the rapid expansion of Christianity, for adopting techniques was far easier than adopting Christian monotheism. But Islam, which had been present in the region for centuries, was a familiar legal and ideological resource that could be drawn on to justify increasingly individualized labor and land arrangements. Islam therefore expanded like wildfire under particularly congenial circumstances beginning in the 1970s—a process that was already well under way during the colonial period. The aggressive clearing of land occurred in conjunction with the expansion of an Islamic understanding of property as individually heritable and of land and trees as devoid of spiritual content.

In an ironic twist, some of the development proponents at the mission are now struggling to resacralize the realm of the natural world by promoting trees and a sense of stewardship over creation. This line of thought argues that by taking part in the whole of creation responsibly, humans can become transformed spiritually. This will enable them to become better stewards of nature: "Rural development is a valid expression of the Gospel. And the principle objective of SIM is to recover the total person by enabling people and communities to realize their potential and to see their lives transformed by God's designs through an improved management of the resources at their disposal" (Rinaudo and Evans 1999, 5, quoting a 1993 SIM community development manual). Something like this is suggested in the mission's confused references to "holistic development" and "spiritual wholism." However, it is never quite clear what these oft-repeated terms mean. "Holism" is intended to be a theory that emphasizes the interdependence of organic elements. "Wholism" implies thinking about the sum of a number of discrete parts. Is it the body and spirit that are to be seen as a whole? Or is it humans and nature? Are they organic wholes? Or are they simply discrete parts of a single whole? Is "holistic development" simply an approach to development, one that encompasses both bodily and spiritual needs, which nevertheless remain separable? Or does "spiritual wholism" imply that body and soul are part of an indissoluble and complex whole that is greater than the sum of the parts (body and soul, humans and nature)? The slippage in spelling between the two terms is symbolic of the conceptual confusion of those who promote this approach.

Also in evidence in rather subdued form is the more complex and implicitly political understanding that is common in many secular NGOs of holistic development as an integrated approach that recognizes that a community's needs in a range of different domains may be interconnected (health affects the ability to do work, insufficient nutrition may contribute to health problems, environmental issues may dictate choices about what food to produce, political concerns may contribute to environmental problems). This notion of "integrated" development emerged partly in recognition that sometimes a single expensive intervention dictated by the state (such as the irrigated perimeters initiated in Niger) will not really resolve the tangle of problems a village faces and may indeed exacerbate them. While the understanding of "holistic development" as addressing a complex set of linked problems does appear in some SIM documents, the relationship of this approach to the spiritual issues discussed above is never articulated: "The project aims to be 'integrated' and 'holistic,' not to attack a single problem but to attend to the principal underlying problems that hinder people (poverty, illness, ignorance and civic inertia, spiritual and cultural tabus [sic])" (Rinaudo and Evans 1999, 6). Despite the glancing reference to "civic" concerns, SIM resolutely avoided the more-politicized dimensions of such an understanding because it felt that the politicized nature of the actions of secular NGOs detracted attention from the more important issue of spiritual transformation. The mission's muddled attempt to bridge the physical-spiritual binary faces yet another challenge in the legacy of the *fête de l'arbre*. Because the national government required schoolchildren and farmers to plant trees as a sign of loyalty to the government, tree-planting now has a secular civic content. Tree-planting may be patriotic, but it is not seen as a particularly spiritual activity. In other words, in Niger, tree-planting is often a form of worldly political engagement rather than a manifestation of a spiritual commitment or an approach to a complex whole through attention to numerous interdependent elements. Having contributed to the generation of a kind of spiritual sterility to the landscape, the mission is now facing an uphill battle in its efforts to reinject Spirit into agro-pastoral pursuits and development.

SIM entered first into "modernization" of agriculture and later into reforestation with little understanding of how complex these interventions would be. The mission never anticipated that its efforts in the realm of development would contribute to the expansion of Islamic law and to the spread of the cachet and practical utility of becoming a Muslim. Pressed to find a scriptural basis for development work beyond tithing to support widows and orphans, evangelical missionaries seem to have found their mandate almost exclusively in a handful of Old Testament passages with little practical import.[7] SIM missionary writings on development turn rather predictably to Genesis 1:26–31, in which Adam, who was made in the image of God, is given dominion over creation, as in an article by MIDP director Joel Matthews:

> As faithful caretakers, we are to lovingly restore and tend the royal garden for our Master, knowing that it all belongs to him. We are keenly aware that God created mankind in his own image and has given us dominion over his creation (Gen. 1:27–31). (Mathews 1999, 298)

Genesis could be used to support responsibility and an attitude of protective caretaking of the natural world. However, the mission has regularly emphasized the belief that humans have a special status within creation and a duty to oversee and render profitable the created world. As any good critic of Enlightenment thinking will note, this is a rather species-centric view of the world and one in which humans have a duty to control and dominate nature. Indeed, Matthews notes the historic affinity of just such a vision of nature with a version of capitalism he rejects as un-Christian (293). Yet this passage is just as likely to inspire rampant capitalist extraction as it is to inspire sustainable development. Indeed, one could see in this passage the seeds of the dualism that led to the objectification of the natural world in the service of science, civilization, and capital.

Perhaps other passages that are more closely related to agriculture and husbandry would be more helpful. SIM missionaries cite a rare passage that offers specific guidance in the realm of agriculture—Exodus 23:10–12, which establishes the seven-year fallow period and a day of rest (cited in Isch n.d.). However, since farmers in the Maradi region and much of the world already had practiced fallowing it is hard to see how this "godly principle" offers much that is new. Muslims who rest on Friday are unlikely to find that keeping the Sabbath is an unfamiliar departure from previous practice.

The one "godly principle" that appears in evangelical reflections on "wholistic" or "holistic" development that has specific and rather radical practical implications is Exodus 20:15—"Thou shalt not steal." When one turns to the biblical passages SIM's development personnel cite to justify and guide its interventions in development work, one finds, oddly, that it all boils down to the eighth commandment. How does this modest and seemingly commonsensical commandment offer guidance in development? It is the foundation of western Christian arguments for the notion of private property. And this is where SIM's technical promotions join forces with the expansion of Islam, for in mission writings any conception of use rights that is not consistent with individual freehold tenure is understood to entail "stealing." In SIM thought, wholism becomes the rectification of another culture's flawed understandings of justice.

"Culture," declares the MIDP technical manual, "is one of the most significant factors working against broader adoption of FMNR" (Rinaudo and Evans 1999, 35). Primary among the "cultural" factors the project has in mind are a "lack of respect for agricultural property (e.g. free access for everyone and no law protecting trees, even if they are left growing on purpose)." In reality, the notion that there should be a kind of understanding of "agricultural property" that excludes free access and regards trees as part of the land rather than as a separate form of wealth is not simply a shift in "culture," it is a radical reworking of understandings of property. The mission chose to see a regime of communal ownership of trees as a "lack of respect"—an absence of an understanding of justice. But in fact, from the perspective of the women who are increasingly excluded from access to land, providing communal access to firewood is doing justice. A determination that trees should be seen as private property might be seen, from their perspective, as unjust.

But from within the mission's way of defining its biblical mandate, its task was to teach people that communal rights are in fact a form of stealing. Once SIM announced that communal tenure was a form of theft, it began to cast any reluctance on the part of farmers to "prosecute" such "theft" as an irrational "taboo." Any other way of understanding fairness or justice, evidently, is not an alternative system of justice but rather a devolution—a falling away—from the proper relation of man to man and man to environment as dictated by God's law. Unable to see local arbitrators as upholding a legitimate local understanding of justice and fairness, the missionaries criticized local chiefs for failing to impose appropriate consequences for "theft": "for example when a chief doesn't defend those who have worked hard to protect their trees when wood is stolen and don't punish the guilty parties" (Rinaudo and Evans 1999, 35). In its formulation of the problems it faces, the mission sees local culture as unreasonable and unfair. Its job, then, is to encourage villagers to abandon irrational "customs." But a more honest appraisal of the mission's approach would concede that the mission is in the business of modifying property rights and the local conception of land tenure—obviously an extremely political (and not merely cultural) agenda.

Thus, from the perspective of the mission, if a woman cuts branches

from a tree on her neighbor's land for firewood, she is stealing. If someone uses his neighbor's crop residues to feed his livestock, he is stealing.
If a pastoralist follows a familiar pathway to the water and tramples the
portion of a farmer's crop that intrudes into the cattle corridor, the pastoralist has damaged private property and should be punished. The mission encourages farmers to leave their millet stalks on their fields to help
protect their land from wind erosion and tells them that they should cut
the stalks into small pieces to prevent their neighbors from "stealing"
the straw. This rather flat conception of theft, property, and morality
permeates other domains of mission thinking. For example, when I explained to one female missionary nurse that women often use the "chop
money" their husbands give them as capital to set up a food trade and
then use the cooked foods they sell along with their profits to contribute
to food for the family she was scandalized, for to her this appeared to
be "stealing," even though the capital was restored and family well-being
as a whole was enhanced. She found it difficult to grasp the notion that
resources might have multiple uses and owners.

Note that the recasting of property relations the mission promotes
consistently undermines the communal use rights that married women
rely on. As a general rule, married women's only access to land and trees
in their marital villages is through local practices that protect use rights
rather than inheritance or ownership rights. This is particularly ironic,
since when it comes to labor, the mission has consistently taken the
position that women ought to be willing to contribute their time and
energy to the well-being of the community; the village health work is a
good example. It expects women to be naturally altruistic. But when it
comes to *land,* the mission suddenly abandons the notion of communal
well-being as a departure from God's law. It believes that men are naturally individual stewards of their private domains.

Of course, women can benefit from the privatization of property. A
woman who inherits land from her father in her natal village, say, or a
woman who succeeds in purchasing a plot of land near her husband's
land is in a position to benefit from the conceptions of private property
the mission promotes. Indeed, the only hint in MIDP documents that
women are enthusiastically taking up tree management occurs in a context in which women own the trees:

> On recent farm visits it was interesting to note the increasing level of women's
> participation. Most striking was their adoption of FMNR. In Niger, not including
> women in project planning has made them the biggest cause of failure of FMNR[:]
> because they are major consumers of wood they have indiscriminately harvested
> trees deliberately *left by male farmers.* In the MIDP villages women have started

to manage *their own trees* to the point of meeting household needs for firewood and fencing. (Rinaudo 1995; emphasis added)

Rinaudo doesn't elaborate on the difference between men's trees and women's trees or on the critical question of how women had come to see particular trees as "their own." Until twenty years ago, a wife in this region could expect to be loaned a plot of land known as a *gamana* by her husband. Anything she grew on that plot in her free time was hers to dispose of as she wished. Women then, had recognized use rights to land and a right to control the portion of the crop they produced on their own. Women's use rights to certain assets of the farming household have a precedent in the region, although those rights have eroded in recent years. Few women in the region have *gamana* plots today. Whether the trees Rinaudo discusses were on the land of women's husbands which women had recognized rights to use and therefore an interest in managing or the trees were on land owned by women themselves is not clear—these would be interesting issues to know more about if one hoped to reproduce the phenomenon elsewhere. The question would be whether it is useful to promote an understanding of farm property as shared marital property so that women have rights to wood on that land or whether some modification of preexisting usufruct rights (parallel to women's previously accepted use rights to *gamana* land) is at issue. The latter is, I think, a great deal more likely than the former given the fragility of marriage in the region and the normative assumption that when a couple divorces a woman takes her cookware and other such moveable property but the husband gets everything else (land, equipment, cattle, and sometimes even the small ruminants she raises), regardless of how much her labor and income have contributed to the well-being of the household. It is also possible that Rinaudo witnessed the handful of older women who, because they married cousins in their natal villages, are benefiting from their newfound potential to inherit land from their fathers under Muslim law, land that they can use while they live in the same village as their husbands. Regeneration and tree-planting will be successful development endeavors only if women are in a position to own and/or have the use of the wood from protected trees. Conceiving of women as the dependents of their husbands has not been helpful in protecting women's access to land and trees.

Since the mid-1990s, individual appropriation of an array of resources that had previously seen as open to all has become more and more common in the region. Specific trees are sometimes marked now to make sure that everyone understand those trees are private property, and local practices about how much of a tree can be cut by non-owners are changing. Damage to trees by pastoralists' animals now are treated as a form of property damage (Luxereau and Roussel 1997, 125). Individuals protect certain rare trees and plants needed for making local medicines. One of SIM's project villages, Garin Magaji, regularly appears in Luxereau and Roussel's study as a site where property arrangements are shifting visibly. SIM's years of promoting its vision of "justice" and the "proper" understanding of property seem to be bearing fruit. As Rinaudo reported in 1998:

> One of the villages (Dogon Baushe) is beginning to show change in [the] area [of "stealing" wood from regenerated trees]. Previously, farmers were not able to conserve trees on their farms due to theft. This situation dates back to as far as people can remember. Recently, however, people have been leaving more and more trees on their farms. When we inquired as to the reason we found that our presence has pressured some land use policy revision. From what farmers said it started a few years ago when we were pushing natural regeneration. Certain species, if they were above a certain size, would not be stolen (the highest valued species) from the farms. The reason why was because people knew from experience that if they stole wood there would be an investigation supported by the chief. As thieves left off stealing these species, gradually the farmers began regenerating other lesser valued species. When these were stolen they were also investigated. Today, it seems, farmers are feeling more secure about their farms and consequently, more trees are being regenerated. (Rinaudo 1998b)

In effect, this "apolitical" mission has succeeded in promoting the criminalization of behaviors that were accepted within previous conceptions of communal use of trees. The resulting success of farmer managed natural regeneration in the Maradi region is, of course, something the mission is proud of, and indeed it is hard not to applaud the improved protection to trees in the region. However, the larger questions of whether an "apolitical" mission should intrude into local property conceptions at all, whether it has done so in ways that protect women's interests, and whether such intrusions have had the ironic effect of promoting Islamic conceptions of law (and consequently Islam) in the region are left altogether unanswered. Whether and how to modify land tenure practices in rural areas is a matter of heated debate among Nigériens. Each attempt by the Nigérien government at producing a modified legal code to regulate land, livestock, and inheritance practices in rural areas provokes intense scrutiny by a host of interested parties: women's groups, Muslim groups, traditional leaders. Everyone is acutely aware that any formalization or reformulation of land tenure practices will likely have an impact on women's access to land and their prospects for autonomy. Women's groups hope to enforce women's rights to inheritance, traditional leaders hope to protect the status quo, Muslim groups want to prevent anything that would undermine husbands' authority over their wives or encourage women to reverse the expansion of seclusion. But because the mission has naturalized and sacralized its conception of justice and has resolutely failed to train and hire female staff, it operates in a kind of vacuum, neither engaging directly with larger political debates nor inspecting closely how its interventions affect micropolitics within villages and households.

11

Ça bouge:
Hausa Christian Practice in a Muslim Milieu

Two jokes:

Some Hausa were visiting some European Christians for the first time and were very unfamiliar with their habits and customs. So the leader of the Hausa was keeping an eye on his companions and noticed that they kept making mistakes and doing uncouth things as they were eating and so on. The Europeans shut their eyes and they were praying, but the Hausa didn't understand what they were saying or doing. They did notice that at the end of each sentence the Europeans went *"uh huh,"* and at the very end they said [in English] *"In Jesus' name, Amen."* Now the Hausa and the Europeans didn't understand one another's languages, except for the leader of the Hausa. So he said to the Europeans, "Now we are going to pray." And the Europeans said [in English] *"That is good, that is good!"* So the Hausa copied the Europeans, and they clasped their hands and they shut their eyes. While they did that, the leader of the Hausa said to them in their own language, "Now here are the things you are to do: when they give you food you will eat it with a fork," and the Hausa said *"uh huh."* And he said "And this cloth is for wiping your hands," and the Hausa said *"uh huh."* "And when you sneeze you cover your mouth," and the Hausa said *"uh huh."* And when he had run out of things he needed to convey to them he said *"In Jesus' name"* and they all said together *"Amen"* and the Europeans said, *"That is good, that is good."*

There was a Hausa jokester and he was with some Europeans who couldn't really say Hausa right, so he was teaching them how to say some songs and prayers in Hausa. They had a hard time saying God's name, *"Ubangiji,"* so they practiced and practiced, but the best they could do was *"na ji, uba"* [I hear, Father]. So he said, "That's o.k." So he taught them a prayer about hearing God's word, *"Ubangiji Yesu, na ji Ubana"* ["Lord Jesus, I hear my Father"] and they practiced and practiced. Then, when they were ready, they went to church, and the time came to say their new prayer. And everyone was very surprised to hear them cursing *"Ubangiji Yesu, na ci ubaka!"* ["Lord Jesus, I eat your father"—a very offensive profanity in Hausa]

We were all sitting up late into the night waiting for the women's group from Kano to come for its visit. After a week of fear, anger, and sorrow because of the riots in which the mission compound and church were burned; after the acute disappointment of hearing that the Kano women were not coming despite all our careful work to prepare songs and dances, clean the church compound, and assemble expensive foods and cooking utensils; after all that, we needed some humor. One of the church men had gone to Kano to try to persuade the women to come despite the news of religious violence in Maradi; he was to tell them that all was quiet and that they should come, that we needed the fellowship. But he had left hours ago and it would be longer still before he returned. "Come on," the women coaxed the best comedienne among the group, "come on, tell us a joke." And so she did, and the jokes she performed with marvelous voices and extravagant gestures were bold and bawdy and irreverent. They were Hausa to the core. We laughed long and hard, and it felt good. These, I knew, were not jokes you would tell to an American evangelical missionary. But, it turns out, they are jokes you can tell to an evangelical Christian in Niger. Never was I so acutely conscious that these Christians were by no means carbon copies of the missionaries either in their beliefs or in their practices.

I don't know that all Christians would have been amused; the setting was highly gendered and the participants were commoners, or *tallakawa*, not dignified *sarauta*, courtly class Hausa. The jokes were shared in Hausa among older women who were not particularly well educated, many of whom work regularly in the homes of English-speaking missionaries. And the circumstances were unusual—we needed to break the tension desperately. But these were undeniably Christian Hausa jokes—they wouldn't have made sense to a Muslim and they wouldn't have been funny to a missionary. The ever-shifting space of Christian practice in

Niger that oscillates ambivalently between the hegemonic assumption that to be Hausa is to be Muslim and the missionary insistence that to be Christian is to be an evangelical fundamentalist. Being a Protestant Christian in Niger means more than adopting a certain set of beliefs or attending a certain church. It means seeking out and sustaining a community in which one can tell such jokes and they will be appreciated. It means celebrating playfully the knowledge that it was the Hausa who taught the hapless missionaries the language of belief, not the reverse. It also means enjoying the secret knowledge shared by Hausa Christians that the social practices of the early missionaries (and of their current employers)—the eating habits, the dress style, the anglophone performance of piety—are not the same thing as Christianity itself. It means finding common cause with other Christians in the face of the overweening attitude of superiority of "Europeans." It also means drawing from the deep well of the mimetic arts at the core of Hausa popular culture. These jokes are in a sense exorcized Christian counterparts to the "horrific comedy" of spirit possession—ways of simultaneously appropriating and taming the Otherness of powerful and dangerous strangers such as European soldiers and American missionaries (Stoller 1995, 7).

I think it would be a mistake to see these jokes at the expense of the western missionary (for the Hausa, "European" includes Americans, Canadians, Australians . . . and, not incidentally, me as a researcher) as signs of contempt or hatred. Telling the joke requires taking on the part of the missionary, becoming, for a moment, embodied as the object of ridicule. Indeed, in the second joke it is the comedian herself who commits something close to blasphemy in recalling the history of how missionaries acquired language skills. These jokes have the classic contours of a "my mother" joke. I get to poke fun at my mother—or even more boldly in this case, Our Father—but if you (who are an outsider) were to make the same joke at my mother/Father's expense it would not be humor but insult, cause for offense and potentially for violence. After the rioting in Maradi, who *could* one make fun of? To make fun of one's Muslim kin and neighbors at such a time would not be funny—there was precious little that was funny about the riots and the intercommunal resentments they so starkly revealed. The Christian thing to do, the nonviolent thing to do at a time when turning the other cheek takes a certain amount of effort, is to turn one's humor inward to a safer target, one that reinforces one's sense of community and restores a reassuring sense of the familiar. Perhaps paradoxically, to me these are very affectionate jokes, told at a moment when the attack on the mission had left Christians feeling a bit more inclined than usual to reclaim the missionaries as their spiritual parents, suitable subjects of affectionate teasing. There is nothing so Hausa as using *wasa*, or playful joking between groups that tend to be in some kind of in regular competition with one another, to defuse tension and generate a sense of common interest.

Christianity in Maradi is faced with an irresolvable quandary. Christians consciously and unconsciously emphasize commonalities between their beliefs and practices and those of traditionalist Muslims, reformist Muslims, and Arna so that there will be a "bridge" to others that will make conversion imaginable and coexistence conceivable. They go to the naming ceremonies of their Muslim friends and relatives, for example, or to the weddings of rural Arna kin. But if there was no real difference between Christianity and Islam or between Christianity and spirit practice, there would be no impetus to convert. It is particularly important not to give Muslims the impression that conversion to Christianity is in reality reversion to the paganism and ignorance of Arna/*bori* practice. So one must also emphasize differences and insist that they are *critical* differences. These differences have a bearing on salvation. Christians may refuse to eat the meat at a Muslim friend's naming ceremony—a serious affront—to illustrate a rejection of animal sacrifice. The Christian thereby implies that in fact the Muslim is engaging in paganism—worse, in satanic worship. Suddenly it looks as if it might have been more polite to skip the naming ceremony in the first place, and indeed many Pentecostal Christians would insist that this is the better choice, for seemingly innocent "customs" such as jumping a certain number of times across a slaughtered animal are implicit covenants with the devil. This emphasis on distinguishing differences can be alienating and estranging. And so it is that Christian practice in Niger oscillates constantly between poles of attraction and repulsion, commonality and difference, ever mindful of the disdain of Muslims, the criticisms of other Christians, and the judgments of missionaries.

Under the circumstances it would be perilous to try to describe a single set of practices and pronounce them to be the sum of Christianity among Hausa-speakers in Niger. Instead I will attempt to trace some of the major issues that seem to me to mark the points around which evangelical Christians engage in performative debate. I have used three strategies in sketching out this space of oscillation. The first explores how evangelical Christians talk about the differences between Christianity and Islam. The second traces the process through which one becomes recognized as Christian within the Christian community. And finally I attempt to note the difference between the many normative claims Christians made to me about what characterizes Christian community and family life and the realities that emerged in interviews, conversations, and observations of many Christian families of different social backgrounds and in different settings. The chapter draws on the songs Christian women sing, the rituals Christians engage in, and the strategies men and women use in evangelizing.

Christianity in Maradi, of course, includes more than simply native Hausa-speakers, and the Christianity of the evangelical churches is not entirely representative of the more Pentecostal strains of Christianity now spreading like wildfire in the region. Furthermore, the growing presence of Hausa-speaking Christians of other ethnic backgrounds in the Christian church in Niger has generated many strains, and some of the debates about just what constitutes Christianity developed as native Hausa-speakers watched the emergence of practices that differed considerably from their own, often with the blessings of the new generations of missionaries of SIM or under the guidance of Nigeria-inspired Pentecostalism. Still bearing the animus that arose from the cultural violence done to the early Christians by early missionaries whose understanding of appropriate Christian behavior was narrow and puritanical, some Hausa Christians find these new converts mystifying. The newly culturally sensitive missionaries, for their part, see these critical evangelical Hausa Christians as ethnocentric for attempting to impose Hausa norms on Tuareg and Fulani churches. The burden of church/mission history continues to create ever-evolving tensions and misunderstandings.

"What are the obligatory acts in which Christians must engage?"

How have the central assumptions of Islamic practice in this region of Hausaland shaped how Christians present themselves and how have they come to understand what appropriate Christian practice might be? Because most Hausa-speaking Muslims do not have direct access to sacred texts written in Arabic, much debate about Islam in West Africa has centered not around exegesis but rather around the particulars of ritual performance. Debates about praxis are central to religious discourse in this region. This emphasis on practice makes itself felt within Hausa evangelical Christianity in two ways. First, Hausa Christians participate in broadly held Hausa understandings of the sacred that are deeply colored by Islam and very much taken for granted.[1] Second, Hausa evangelical Christians consciously distinguish themselves from Muslims through a variety of specifically Christian adaptations to or refusals of Muslim practices.

I was very struck by this dynamic in the course of a seminar on evangelization to Hausa women the EERN sponsored in Maradi in February 2001. Women from a variety of churches in the region, both rural and urban, traveled to Maradi to take part in the first conference of this kind to be held in Niger. Hence a rather broad cross-section of women from the evangelical and Pentecostal communities had gathered to discuss how best to present Christianity to their female relatives, neighbors, and friends who are Muslim. A missionary theologian at the Bible school who was from the United States (who was working at the invitation of the rather ecumenically inclined EERN rather than for SIM), a specialist in Islam named Barbara Kapenga, presented the general outline of the beliefs and practices of Islam, describing the five obligatory acts that are the pillars of Islam (statement of belief, or *shahada*; regularized laudatory prayer, or *salat*; tithing, or *zakkat*; fasting and abstinence during the month of Ramadan, known in Hausa as *azumi*; and, if one has the means, performing the collective pilgrimage to Mecca, known as the *hajj*). She noted that there are parallel acts that Muslims also engage in that are not obligatory: in addition to *salat* one can go on to perform *addu'a*, individualized invocations to God; in addition to tithing, one can offer alms to the poor, known as *sadaka*; and one can perform a private pilgrimage to Mecca, known as *umra*. She devoted a fair amount of time to what Muslims understand to be obligatory. She then asked the audience to break into small discussion groups to reflect on a number of questions that she noted are commonly asked by Muslims, the first of which was "What are the obligatory acts in which Christians must engage?"

I was startled by how different the answers the groups presented were from what I expected, prompting me to examine why I had expected anything in particular. My own personal response would be to say that Christians don't have the kinds of ritual obligations that Muslims have— it is not works but faith that guarantees salvation. This is obviously a rather Protestant reading of Christianity. Having been raised as a Catholic, I have a deep appreciation for ritual, for the sense of obligation it can entail, and for the pleasurable deepening of the rhythms of life it can provide. I now adhere to a rather idiosyncratic brand of Christianity in which an appreciation for the possibilities of ritual is eclipsed by skepticism about institutionalized religion that guarantees that I rarely give any evidence of my beliefs through any outward show of practice. So my own response would have reflected this itinerary away from obligation and toward individual belief, skirting gingerly around the issue of just what "faith" and "salvation" might consist of. Probably my own favorite passage from the gospels is one that in many ways relieves me of any sense of obligation toward the rules and rituals of institutional religion. It is Jesus' answer to the contentious question about which of the laws it is the most important to keep: "Thou shalt love the Lord thy God with all thy heart, and with all thy soul, and with all thy mind. This is the first and great commandment. And the second is like unto it, Thou shalt love thy neighbour as thyself. On these two commandments hang all the law and the prophets" (Matthew 22:37–40). The emphasis on love above all else in the gospels is probably what disposes me to continue to think of myself as a Christian despite considerable evidence to the contrary.

The older generation of missionaries I had been interviewing to learn about the early history of the mission has quite different beliefs from my own. They would, I think, emphasize that faith in Jesus is the assurance of salvation—this is what it means to be reborn. Their belief that salvation is *exclusively* available through the acceptance of Jesus Christ as Savior fuels their evangelical impulse. What "love" means for contemporary Pentecostal preachers is, as we have seen, quite particular. My own beliefs are far more ecumenical. Indeed, my historicized approach and my liberal impulse to be very expansive in interpreting just what "salvation" might mean would not, it is safe to say, be seen by evangelical Christians as truly Christian. Having known Muslims, for example, who seem to me to love Allah with all their hearts and to love their neighbors as themselves, I am not overly worried about their salvation.

Evangelical missionaries at SIM have a far more literal approach to the scriptures and make no distinction between the authority or contemporary utility of one passage over another (beyond excluding the Apocrypha). Theirs is a heavily Pauline interpretation of Christianity, one I do not share in part because I don't see the epistles as having anything like the sustaining lessons for contemporary Christians found in the parables in the gospels. For them, there is a certain *obligation* for true believers to share the word of God with those who are not Christians in order to save their souls. At its limit, their belief implies that to be a

Christian is to be a missionary. There are no ritual obligations, and true belief simply implies faith in Jesus as Savior and regular reliance on God's intervention as a result of prayer and Bible study.

It was interesting to me that the women at the conference all approached the question of obligation with the attitude that in fact Christianity *does* entail obligatory acts (*ayyuka wajibai*). Although the participants included some women from Pentecostal churches and a larger number of women from the various evangelical churches (EERN and UEEPN alike), no one dissented from this view. Although the different discussion groups used slightly different language and ordered their responses in a variety of ways, their presentations to the whole assembly were remarkably consistent. The obligations of the Christian are as follows: profession of faith (*ban gaskiya*), prayer (*addu'a*), tithing (*zakkat*), fasting (*azumi*), preaching (*wa'azi*), love ('*kauna*), and fellowship (*zummunci*). It seemed to me that although the women who had higher training in evangelical schools emphasized love, it was embedded in the list and did not have any particular priority. None of the groups presented *ban gaskiya*, or faith, as different from *ayyuka*, or works, although somewhat later a male Hausa, Pastor Lawali, who had had higher theological training, did gently suggest that so long as Christians had faith, they did not need works. But clearly the more popular perception and practice among devoted Christian women—who are of course charged with socializing children into Christianity—is rather different. Indeed, one can draw a series of parallels between the obligatory acts of Hausa Muslims and obligatory acts as popularly perceived by Protestant Hausa Christians:

Muslims

Kalma Shahada
Statement of the Arabic formula whereby an individual acknowledges that he or she is a Muslim: there is no God but Allah and Mohammed is his prophet.

Salla
The five daily prayers of Muslims that praise God, more or less synchronized so that all in the community pray uniformly at the same time.

Christians

Ban Gaskiya
Faith, trust; to publicly announce one's acceptance of Christ as Savior.

Addu'a
The word Christians use for any prayer other than the ritual prayer of Muslims. Such prayer generally contains praise of God, thanks for what God has provided, and requests or invocations. *Addu'a* can be performed at any time and can be individual or collective.

Zakkat
Tithing a percentage of one's wealth annually for the good of the entire community

Zakkat/Baiko
Regular giving for the benefit of one's church. The giving is irregular and imprecise but constitutes a substantial proportion of a Christian's income.

Azumi
Collective fasting and from sunrise to sunset during the month of Ramadan.

Azumi
Occasional and voluntary individual or collective fasting to enhance prayer and reflection to address a specific problem or concern.

Hajj
Pilgrimage to Mecca for those who have the means during the month of Zulhaji, the twelfth month of the Muslim calendar.

Pilgrimage
No one suggested that Christians have an obligatory pilgrimage, although West African Christians do visit Jerusalem and the Holy Lands. Christian women who have been to Jerusalem are referred to as Hajjiya, the term used to describe a Muslim woman who has been on pilgrimage to Mecca.

Nuna 'kauna
To show love to others.

Zummunci
To take part in Christian fellowship.

Shaida bishara; wa'azi
Giving witness to the good news of salvation through Jesus; preaching.

A number of features of this list emerge upon closer inspection. Protestant Christians see themselves as performing many of the same acts as Muslims. However, because they don't do those acts at prescribed times and collectively, they understand themselves to engage in acts of devotion more freely, more often, and with less ostentation than Muslims do. For example, one relatively well-educated woman noted that while Muslims have five required times for prayer, when Christians pray, their prayer is perpetual: "I can be walking down the street and be praying," she observed. And indeed my own experience with Christians suggests that this is not much of an exaggeration: I haven't yet done an interview, attended a meeting, or visited a home when prayer wasn't called for. Thus, Hausa evangelical Christians have the sense that you don't confine prayer to artificial times and that it is appropriate at all occasions. Their insistence that their devotion is fuller than the prayer of Muslims is perhaps a reaction against the common Muslim perception that Christian practice is not as exacting (and therefore not as meritorious) as Muslim practice because Christians go to church only on Sunday. Of course, for Christians to lay a claim to more-constant devotion, they must overlook *zikiri*, the more or less constant Sufi prayer in remembrance of God.

Two elements of this parallelism between Islam and Christianity converge in an emphasis among Christians on early morning prayer. It is clear to me from observations and conversation that the more-devoted Hausa Christians of Maradi rise at the same time Muslims do for the early prayer call. They wash their faces carefully—particular emphasis is given to washing one's eyes on waking. Where Muslim ablutions tend to dwell more on the ears, nose, and mouth, Christian imagery that emphasizes vision as the highest form of knowing and blindness as ignorance may account for this focus on the eyes. Having opened their eyes entirely and erased the sleep from them, Christians gather as a family for prayer before beginning the day's activities. It is interesting that now that they are fully awake they pray with their eyes shut, to block out the distractions of the world. Muslims often find the Christian practice of praying with the eyes closed rather odd, but Christians readily account for it by suggesting that prayer with the eyes open is less respectful, more worldly. This theme of early washing and family prayer emerged regularly in conversation and was standard fare in the skits Christians put on for their church gatherings to explore problems in Christian life. In important ways, Christian practice shares in the life rhythms, understandings of piety as related to cleanliness, and collective, albeit familial, prayer so valued by Hausa Muslims, but with interesting and distinctive variations.

I am reminded of Peel's observation that in translating the Christian concept of "holiness" into Yoruba, Crowder settled on a term which imported "a complex of meanings—holiness, purity, ritual cleansing, and so forth—that were strongly emphasized by Muslims in relation to their own faith" (Peel 2000, 197). In a similar fashion, evangelical Hausa Christianity seems to have imported from their Muslim neighbors an understanding of holiness as ritual purity and cleanliness. The mark of a Christian wife is her attention to keeping a Christian house: one that is clean and orderly. But although missionaries of an earlier era suggested that cleanliness is next to godliness, the later evangelical wave was not necessarily interested in transforming Africans into tidy Europeanized Christians. For instance, none of the Nonconformist emphasis on particular patterns of building and order is evident in SIM's approach (cf.

Comaroff and Comaroff 1997, 274–322). This emphasis on cleanliness seems to derive at least in part from evangelical Hausa Christianity's emergence within a milieu overshadowed by Islamic practice. Cleanliness becomes less a mark of acceptance of the civilized practices of Christianity than evidence of participation in a broader Hausa deference to ritual purity in honor of Allah.[2] Christians simply go a step farther than Muslims in a competition for sanctity and piety; they make cleanliness something that does more than simply precede prayer or mark the end of a period of impurity. It is a constant requirement for those with Christian faith.

This emphasis on cleanliness can thus be turned on Muslims to suggest that they are not actually pure before God. For example, traditionalist Muslims in the region often seek out the help of a Muslim scholar when they need help resolving a social or physical problem. The scholar will write an appropriate passage from the Koran on a wooden board and then the supplicant will drink the water used to wash the words from the board. This common practice, known as *rubutu*, is among the practices reformist Muslims criticize. When I asked Christians whether they knew anyone who had had recourse to *rubutu* when other remedies had failed to resolve their problems, the most common answer was that no, that Christians don't drink *rubutu* because it is "dirty." Obviously this doesn't mean that in private Christians have never been known to seek out *rubutu*, but it does expose some of the grounds on which Christians and Muslims compete.

There has been a long verbal struggle between Christianity and Islam in Hausaland over who gets to lay claim to the central Arabic term for prayer, *salla*. It is sufficient to remark of someone that he or she does *salla* to convey that the individual in question is a Muslim. However, in Arabic, the term has a broader usage and could be used to describe Christian prayer. Since Hausa Muslims have monopolized the term *salla*, Christians have had to make use of other words to refer to their prayer. They gravitated toward the Arabic lexicon of prayer in their search for an alternative. The supplicatory prayer Muslims offer after their *salla*, often to pray to God for assistance in the face of a particular difficulty such as drought, is known as *addu'a*. Christians have come to use this term to describe their own prayer, whether it is prayer in praise of God, prayer in thanksgiving, or prayer invoking God's aid. Semantically, the word "*addu'a*" seems not terribly distant from "*ro'ko*," but its Arabic origin gives the word a sanctity that provides useful spiritual capital.[3]

Given the linguistic divide here, where Muslim prayer is *salat* and

Christian prayer is *addu'a,* misconceptions inevitably abound. Hausa Muslims imagine that collective Christian prayer consists only of prayer to make requests (so when they see Christians say grace before a meal they suppose that Christians are in fact praying to the food itself), while Hausa Christians see Muslim prayer as highly formalized and depersonalized. The understanding of prayer as praise and thanksgiving that is so important to most Christians is lost in the term "*addu'a,*" which refers to requests made to God. Thus, Christian prayer appears to the non-Christian to be insufficiently respectful because the word "*addu'a*" doesn't suggest praise and thanksgiving. On the other hand, Christians tend to find the tendency of Muslim women (who pray at home rather than in the mosque) to perform *salla* with their eyes open in the midst of all manner of tumult (radio, conversation, children crying) to be empty. In a final odd twist to the vocabulary of prayer, when Christians want to convey the sense of joining together for the *collective* reverence to God they share on Sundays, they use the term "*sujada,*" which more properly refers to the prostrations Muslims do when they touch their foreheads to the ground in obeisance to God. But it is precisely this act of prostration that Christians regard as the outward mark of empty ritualism verging on idolatry in Islam. When Christians do make jokes about Muslims, the habit some Muslim men have of abstaining from wiping away the dust that sticks to their foreheads after doing prostrations is a popular target of ridicule. It is, after all, dirty.

Thus, while Christians maintain careful parallels between their acts of devotion and those of Islam, they are constrained by a certain kind of spiritual competitiveness to develop ways of distinguishing their acts from those of Muslims. If wealthy Muslims make a collective pilgrimage to Mecca, fortunate Christians make a voluntary individual trip to Jerusalem instead, earning the title "Hajjiya" if they are women. Where Muslims in principle give a set portion of their annual wealth to the community, Christians make regular voluntary gifts more commonly known as *baiko* to their churches. If Hausa Muslim women veil and increasingly take on a form of *burka* known locally as *hijabi,* Hausa evangelical Christians often argue that Paul teaches that it is "obligatory" for Christian women to cover their heads. Yet Hausa Christian women are not attempting to "pass" as Muslims, for the print on the cloth they wear often carries Biblical verses and Christian symbols that make it entirely clear that the wearer is Christian. Christians and Muslims agree that smoking and drinking are ungodly. While young Hausa Muslim men do nevertheless regularly smoke, I've never seen a practicing Christian in Maradi smoke.

In other words, there are quite a few parallels between Christian and Muslim practices that prompt me to suggest that there are specifically *Hausa* dimensions to evangelical Christian praxis in Maradi and that those elements reveal an agonistic acquiescence to traditional Hausa Islamic assumptions about spirituality. Both Christians and Muslims reject the practices of the Arna, despite a broadly shared Hausa belief in the existence and power of spirits.

But there is one element on the list of evangelical Christian "obligations" I have drawn up that is specifically evangelical rather than Hausa. That is the inclusion of *wa'azi*, or evangelization, among the obligatory works of Christians. This duty is honored more in the breach than the observance among Hausa evangelical Christians in my experience, but nevertheless it is a legacy of the evangelical outlook of SIM. Christian women remind themselves and others in their congregations of this obligation regularly through song, as if they were in danger of forgetting:

Always, always we keep preaching the Good News
The end of the world comes and people have no humility
They are not obedient to the love of God
They don't know that judgment day will come and they will give an accounting . . .
We followers [of Jesus] let us not ignore our duty to preach the good news of Lord Jesus

The commitment to evangelization, however lackluster, distinguishes evangelical and Pentecostal Christians quite markedly from local Catholics. Catholics regard the evangelical impulse of Protestant Christians as culturally inappropriate and feel that it invites conflict with Muslims. When violence is visited on the evangelical community, both Catholic and Muslim Hausa-speakers may murmur sympathetically, but they tend to shrug and remark, "Well, they have been preaching" in a tone that suggests that "they" had it coming.

Social Capital and Spiritual Nonconvertibility

Evangelical Christians in Maradi inhabit a world imbued with Islam and they must navigate urban terrain in which status, power, and authority all derive from access to Islamic capital that is banked through collective acts of devotion. In order to take part in that world, they have had to find ways to participate in the kinds of social exchange that are valued and recognized by their Muslim kin and neighbors. Literacy in a sacred text is potentially a tremendous form of cultural capital for Christians, but gaining that literacy has been the product of years of struggle, revision, and compromise. Because Muslims recognize Jesus as one of the prophets, they are willing to entertain the possibility that the gospels are a sacred (but potentially corrupted) text. It is interesting, therefore, that relatively scholarly Muslims often consult with Christians about what might be contained in that text (the Linjila), and this opens a door for Christians and Muslims to share in the "religion of the book." Evangelical Christians believe that faith in Jesus is the only way to salvation, however. While Muslims accept some elements of Christianity and imagine that there might be something to be learned from Christian holy texts, evangelical Christians reject Mohammed's claim to be a prophet and do not look to the Koran for spiritual enlightenment. Evangelical Christians feel that they have something to "give" Muslims, but they refuse to receive anything in return. Evangelical Christianity is exclusive rather than inclusive in its attitude toward other religious practices. Evangelical Christians' rejection of the spiritual and social capital of Muslims makes it rather difficult for them to function within the same social milieu.

The tendency of evangelical Christians to reject anything that is Islamic feeds a pattern of nonreciprocation. Gifts and exchanges are extremely important in Hausa culture as a means of cementing social ties, reducing tensions, and creating a sense of goodwill. Gifts of food, for example, are an important way of establishing a sense of neighborliness, or *zummunci*. Muslim food prohibitions complicate this kind of sharing a good deal, for many Muslims in Maradi fear that anything cooked in a Christian household might not be permissible to eat. But Christians may decline to accept offerings of food at celebrations of major life events for a Muslim neighbor or family member for fear that to accept it is to enter into an implicit compact with the devil. Or if a Christian accepts such a gift, he or she may be at a loss to know how to reciprocate. Marriage is another realm in which Christians and Muslims have difficulty nurturing social ties. Muslim men may attempt to marry Christian women in the hope of converting them, but Christian women cannot marry Muslim men without leaving their community. A Christian man who hopes to marry a Muslim woman will be also ostracized from his church.

For close to a century, however, Hausa Christians and Muslims in Maradi have lived alongside one another relatively peacefully. There are a number of reasons for this, with contradictory implications. Of the "duties" Hausa Christians enumerated—the one that is most strikingly distinct from Hausa Muslim ritual—is the commitment to show love, a commitment that is captured in many Hausa Christian songs:

If you don't love your brothers and sisters
You don't truly have Jesus in your heart
Jesus said we must love one another
For love is the greatest [commandment]

SIM missionaries, who have historically (as we have seen repeatedly) had a more literal understanding of evangelism as "giving the Word," or preaching, often miss the more affective and performative ways in which Hausa Christians enact the duty to "give witness." Christian women do participate in the major life events of their Muslim kin and neighbors, offering the same kinds of wedding gifts to the bride or mother that any Muslim woman would (cloth, kola nuts, cash, kitchenware). They go to great lengths to visit ill neighbors, whether Muslim or Christian, and offer help with minding their children or advice on how to treat the ailment. They offer children in the neighborhood free snacks when they are frying treats for sale even though it sometimes means they will not make a profit. And so I imagine that this gentle and loving approach to their Hausa Muslim neighbors has, in the past, contributed to feelings of sympathy and commonality.

However, their sense of marginality and vulnerability also causes Christians to emphasize their participation in a specifically Christian community typified by the kind of gatherings where the jokes recounted above are heard. The women's group in most churches is known as the Zummuntar Mata, and in a rare borrowing from English, Hausa-speaking Christians in Niger sometimes refer to such gatherings using the term "women's fellowship." Since *zummunci* (friendship) can be something shared with Muslims, it seems that the English term "fellowship" captures a specifically Christian form of sociability enjoyed by the "followers of Jesus." The exhortations to show love and evangelize would seem to invite a great deal of interaction with Muslims, but in practice many Christians keep more or less to themselves out of fear or indifference. They devote the greater part of their time, energy, and income to activities with other Christians and direct most of their gifts to building their churches and assisting other Christians.

It seems to me that evangelical Hausa Christianity is somewhat shackled by its efforts to meet and counter the hostile gaze of an imagined

Muslim audience by converting its own practice into forms that are calculated to placate Muslims. In spite of the extraordinary vitality of the women's groups in the churches, I was told that women should not be made pastors because Muslims would see and disapprove because women don't preach in mosques. The fundamentalism of SIM partly explains this rejection of leadership roles for women, but Hausa Christians have been known to part ways with the mission on other issues, most notably sources of funding associated with the relatively liberal World Council of Churches. Pentecostal churches seem to be a good deal more open to the possibility of women occupying leadership roles, although in Maradi none of the Pentecostal churches had a female pastor.

The evangelical churches have also splintered over such issues as whether drumming and dance are admissible in the churches, given the fact that Muslims regard such activities as inappropriate for the mosque. Older church leaders in Maradi regularly spoil the fun of the youth group's music festivals by loudly proclaiming that these typically Hausa dance and music competitions are sinful. As a result, they are losing some of their younger members to the newer and highly kinetic Pentecostal churches that make no concessions to Muslim perception—although they might be even more critical of the dangers of dance. In many ways, the boundaries of evangelical Christian practice have been set in advance by Muslim perceptions of spiritual practice. By contrast, Pentecostal Christianity today actively rejects Islam as satanic and does little to placate Muslim sensibilities. One reason the Pentecostal movement has taken off in Niger may be that younger Christians and rural Christians from villages with less exposure to Islam see no particular reason to continue this tradition of mirroring Islam in order to outperform it. Pentecostal churches devote much more energy to evangelization than do the "evangelical" churches, and they are unabashed in their use of electric instruments, loud drums, and outspoken sermons amplified so that the entire neighborhood can hear. The traditionally evangelical churches are hampered by their constant attention to what Muslims might think of Christianity. The Pentecostal churches march, quite literally, to a different drummer.

One of the most striking Muslim attitudes that has affected evangelical praxis is a hostility to Hausa spirit veneration. Despite a contempt for *kafirci*, traditionalist Islam in the region imported some elements of Arna belief into what became a highly textured accretion of largely urban religious practices. But in a bid to be more pious than the most monotheistic of Muslims, evangelical missionaries rejected all Arna practices, and historically SIM did little to either address or recognize the demands of the spirit world. As a result, the evangelical community that has emerged has missed the opportunity to convert the energy devoted to spirit veneration into something more like reverence for the Holy Spirit. This is the type of daring move that the Pentecostal churches have been willing to make and that, I would argue, has contributed to their success. It is impossible to say whether this has been a conscious strategy. Rural Hausa in regions relatively untouched by Islam have been quite drawn to Pentecostalism, which drives out spirit possession with the indwelling of the Holy Spirit, replaces *bori* dancing with speaking in tongues, and displaces all-night spirit-possession dances with long evening services in which a heightened state is achieved through loud and repetitive music. Precisely because Pentecostalism takes the spirit world extremely seriously as the source of constraints on the success of the convert, the community, and the nation, it is more attuned to the sensibilities of rural Arna. Rather than simply domesticate or ignore spirit practices, it actively works to counter them—to exorcize them. Similarly, it works to excise all Islamic practices, not to placate Islam. However, if Pentecostalism is highly effective in terms of evangelization, it also tends to inflame Muslim resentments even more than evangelicalism, as we saw in the opening chapters of this book.

Christians, then, engage in the local social economy in a complex and contradictory fashion. They have a long history of drawing on Islamic terminology, partly because of the reliance on Muslim "middle figures" in their translation of Christianity into Hausa. They also have mirrored and amplified many Hausa spiritual practices in their own Christian praxis. Yet they have disrupted the local social economy by refusing both Muslim and Arna social capital. The spirit of toleration and borrowing that had long been a hallmark of religious practice in this region (in contrast with Hausa-speaking northern Nigeria) seems to have become a thing of the past, while religious friction is very much on the increase. As Niger's economy and political crisis deepens I only hope that the deeply held indigenous Hausa value of *zummunci*—the honey-sweet quality of mutual sociability—which predated both Islam and Christianity in the region, is powerful enough to withstand what the rumblings of religious upheaval would seem to foreshadow.

Zummunci and the Zummuntar Mata

A Christian service in Maradi of a Sunday is a very different thing from a Friday Mosque service, despite the shadow of Islamic practice that tends to hover over Christian praxis in this region. The most striking difference is the presence of women and girls. Mosque services in Maradi are still almost exclusively masculine affairs, despite the efforts of reformists to demarcate sections of mosques for women. Young men carry their fathers' prayer mats and become acculturated to masculine practice, but girls and women pray in the home. The gender segregation during prayer is very striking. Given this reality, women's prayer has a catch-as-catch-can quality on Friday, as it does on most days of the week. Women must perform their ablutions and prayers in settings that are noisy and distracting. This stands in contrast to men's practice of prayer; the entire religious community sets aside a particular space and time of respite from worldly concerns so men can pray. Some women manage to retreat to a quiet corner, but there is undeniably a difference in the experience of *salla* for women and men; for women, it is less associated with collective times and spaces, it is often performed alone, and it is imbued with the distractions of daily life.

By contrast, when one enters a church compound in Maradi prior to a Sunday service, one finds men and women, girls and boys, babies and elders. While there is marked separation according to age and gender, everyone shares the same time and space for collective prayer, or *sujada*. Sunday service is not just an occasion for prayer and a sermon. Before the service it is not unusual for men to gather for a Bible study. Older women may gather to practice songs. Elders may hold a business meeting after the service. Younger unmarried Christians linger to flirt and comment on the news of national life. During the service itself there is always a very lengthy period of announcements, for the business of reporting on community life is carried on during the service (donations, trips to visit other churches, illnesses, weddings, naming ceremonies, formal name changes), in part because there is no way to produce and distribute a community newsletter. One has a strong sense of a diverse community that is constantly at work to revitalize itself.

In the church I tend to frequent, men sit on benches on the left, women sit on benches on the right, youth sit on less comfortable benches without backs in the middle, and small children sit on the floor in front of them. The children leave the building partway into the service for Sunday school under the trees. The elders sit facing the congregation on the side of the men (for they are all men). The women's fellowship group, or Zummuntar Mata (in which I participate), which is in principle exclusively for older married women, generally sits facing the women or at the front of the women's side of the church. If there is a "*kwaya*," or youth choir (which is open to younger men and women who may or may not be married), it may sit facing the men but toward the youth section in the middle. The pastor will rise from among the chairs of the elders to offer the sermon. After the service the older men, whose dress style is often indistinguishable from that of Muslim men, exit through a door to the left and gather to joke, share news, and enjoy the shade of a tree. Older women, particularly those wearing the matching Hausa-style outfits of the women's choir, leave through a door to the right and socialize with one another in Hausa under another shade tree. Younger men and women, dressed in relatively western-style outfits that feature blouses worn with narrow skirts or slacks and heels for women and locally tailored suits for men, leave through the "main" door and chat in French and Hausa as their small children scamper and play in the forecourt. In this way a young woman can gracefully avoid spending much time with her mother-in-law and sons can find some distance from their sometimes-overbearing fathers.

But the shape and flavor of a contemporary Hausa-language church service has developed over time and has taken on a particularly self-confident and autonomous form only since about 1990 as missionaries and Christians worship in separate settings more often. In the late 1980s, Hausa sermons were translated during the service into English for non-Hausa-speaking missionaries in the congregation. One consequence of SIM's movement toward evangelizing among groups beyond the Hausa in Niger since the 1970s has been its growing awareness of just what was and wasn't "Hausa" about practice in Maradi. By the 1970s, the mission was engaging in some deeper reflection on how to heal some of the rifts between the mission and the church and how to help the seemingly moribund indigenous church become more autonomous, more organic, and more vital. In a study of SIM-derived churches made in 1979, missionary Bill Lyons observed that non-Christians in Niger thought of the gospel as "*abin Nasara*" ("a thing of the European Christians") or "*sallah Turawa*" ("the European style of prayer"). This was probably due to many factors, not least of which was the reality that most Niger Christians were employed in one way or another by the mission. Chapels on mission compounds were often the only sites for Sunday worship. He reported some unwelcome realities rather bluntly:

> I feel that the Hausa worship service is very dead, very boring. . . . Why? The song service is a major cause. The tunes are almost all borrowed from Western hymns. They are sung too slow. The people do not identify these as an expression of the Hausa culture. For the illiterate, there is very little chance to participate. I think that we need to eventually discard the hymnbook and write some hymns

Maradi woman on the way to church. Courtesy of SIMIA (NR 46), photographed by Kerry Lovering, 1982.

in the form where the leader sings a bar, the congregation responds. . . . Also, why cannot the major musical instrument of the Hausas be used, the drum? (Lyons 1979)

SIM was historically quite ambivalent about drawing on indigenous musical traditions, despite the desire of some more musically inclined missionaries such as Ray de la Haye to draw on local melodies and drums. When de la Haye began improvising in this direction in the 1940s and early 1950s he was sharply informed by SIM's Western Sudan field director that this was not appropriate, for the prior histories of those melodies were often "satanic" and there might be inappropriate associations (Ray de la Haye interview). Songs in Hausa to Hausa melodies would in the end have to be developed by the Christian community itself.

Lyon's suggestion that the Hausa worship service might benefit from some changes tending toward indigenization had rather interesting gender implications, for my discussions with Christian women make it quite clear to me that they had been singing their own songs using Hausa-style melodies at least from the 1950s. That those songs had never been recognized in the formal church service when even the missionaries found the service boring bespeaks a stranglehold by the male converts on the worship service. Men over 50, who tend to dominate the leadership of the churches, had nothing but contempt for the kinds of vernacular songs modestly educated women circulated among themselves. When women of the Soura girls' home went out to evangelize on their own without the missionaries, they sang their own songs rather than the dead hymns from the hymnal, for they knew that their songs were more engaging and effective.[4] It was their songs that graced some of the earliest baptism ceremonies.

Indigenization of the service in the late 1970s in effect opened the way for women (and later young people) to have a more prominent and recognized role in the church—they got to face the congregation like the elders and there would be a moment for them to express their own understanding of Christianity through song. Because only men were permitted to become pastors, men dominated the actual sermons. Illiterate women were not called upon to do the readings. But women were central to the generation of Hausa Christian music. They had long used percussion to accompany any music they found moving, even the classical music missionaries occasionally played on the magic black box of the phonograph. Women took pleasure in taking images from the Bible and rendering them into song, precisely because so many of them could not read well. The songs then became a kind of *aide-mémoire* through which biblical teachings could be retained.

When I was observing the conference on evangelization to Muslim women, I was struck by the fact that when the older or less-educated women wanted to recall a passage that seemed to them to be relevant to the debates, they used the songs as mnemonic devices, as a kind of index to the portions of the Bible that most mattered to them. In this way, women both retain access to key portions of the Scriptures and pass them along to their children, who hear the songs their mothers sing. Here, for example, is a song that tags Philippians 3:10, "That I may know him, and the power of his resurrection, and the fellowship of his sufferings, being made conformable unto his death"; in which the chapter and verse numbers are embedded in the lyrics:

> In Philippians chapter three verse ten
> Here it says I should know him and his power
> That I know Jesus is my Savior, I should know him and the power of his res-
> urrection

In another song, the signs of the Second Coming (which is never far from the minds of evangelical Christians) are indexed: "The book of Matthew Chapter Twenty-four, that is the mirror, that is the mirror for followers [of Jesus] of the final days." The song then reports the various signs evangelical Christians regularly list verbatim (often at breakneck pace) as they appear in Matthew: "Nation shall rise against nation, and kingdom against kingdom: and there shall be famines, and pestilences, and earthquakes, in diverse places." (Matthew 24:7). By singing such songs to themselves, women were able to recall the correct passage in the Bible, which they might then consult directly.

Women seek passages that shed light on women's roles in the Bible. Because there are relatively few references to women in the New Testament, they turn eagerly to stories in the Old Testament for images and models of ideal feminine behavior and for consolation in the face of the typical trials of womanhood in this setting. For example, they turn to the story of Hannah, whose failure to bear a child caused her to suffer bitterly from the contempt of her co-wife. She went before God and prayed for a son whom she would dedicate to God's service, and her prayer was answered. And so, as the song reports, she named the child Samuel, or "I asked the Lord for a child." The Hausa version of her name, Hannatu, is quite popular among Christians, and the song records her tale of trial and triumph without criticism of either polygyny or the local imperative that women bear male children. In the workshop on evangelism, it was clear that Christian women wanted to convey to Muslims how Christianity valorizes women and their own experience of a strong community among Christian women. Thus, they turned to a song that praises Ruth for her loyalty to her mother-in-law Naomi after the death of her husband: "Let us love as Ruth loved."

After women's "traditional" Christian songs had been introduced into the services in the 1970s through the Zummuntar Mata groups, more-fashionable and modern youth *kwaya* songs began to emerge. In the 1980s, these became outlets for leadership roles for younger men, who directed the choirs, and for younger women, who developed updated songs on themes their mothers might not relate to. These younger men and women often had more secular education than their parents, and this difference became evident in the songs they produced, which tend to feature French and English over Hausa. The songs these groups sing today tend to display a greater dynamic range and theatricality than the women's songs—the youth choirs offer dramatic performances that include gestures and synchronized arm and leg movements and, occasionally, elaborate choir uniforms (one uniform consisted of purple robes and purple mortarboards, as if the *kwaya* had just graduated from an American college). The songs feature elements of modern life such as western musical instruments and telephones. They are not necessarily more polished musically or more theologically sophisticated than the women's songs, and indeed confusion about just what the French lyrics are and how to pronounce them can take up a considerable amount of practice time. One such song resolves that problem with a particularly simple response:

> Leader: *Les trompettes de Dieux nous emporteront*
> Response: *Pararara, pararara, pararara*

The women's groups are often led by women who have many years' experience playing local instruments; their performances contrast with the occasionally painful performances of younger men on "modern" instruments for which they have little training.[5]

Neither group, to my mind, engages in particularly deep theological reflection through song, and since many of the songs are thirty to forty years old (women save and recycle the lyrics to songs that have been carefully written down by hand over many years), I don't think this superficiality is particularly new. On the whole, the images and metaphors are strictly borrowed from the text of the Bible. Where the text deviates from the Bible, it is simply to fit the meter of the line or to simplify the vocabulary.[6] Choruses provide occasions to include clapping and gestures. Biblical tales that are particularly relevant to evangelical thinking and to evangelism to Muslims, such as the story of Noah and the flood and the sacrifice of Abraham, are common themes in songs. By casting familiar biblical stories in vivid local detail, the songs sometimes provide a humane window onto what might otherwise be distant stories in the Bible. This song reflecting on Abraham's trip to Mount Moriah with his son Isaac (whom Abraham intends to offer in sacrifice to God), for example, emphasizes Isaac's childish innocence in a chorus that is repeated six times:

> Isaac said, Daddy,
> There's the wood and the fire
> But where is the ram to be sacrificed?
> His father said, Son
> God will prepare in advance a ram to sacrifice.[7]

Songs thus shed light on local framings of familiar themes. And women's roles as mothers and wives tend to color their ways of reading the Bible. For example, one popular women's song simultaneously recognizes the traditional Christian view of women as the source of sin and the Fall, and reiterates the supremacy of those women who have borne children, for they thereby accept gracefully their punishment from God. Since only married women with children can be in the Zummuntar Mata group, the refrain, "Come!" is simultaneously inclusive and exclusive:

> God loves us
> But our misfortune as women
> Because we have sinned, that is why God
> Has punished us with the pain of childbirth
> Women (Come!)
> We women of this world who have children (Come!)
> God is calling (Come!), let us prepare now to receive
> The punishment that is within us, [which is] why God said
> With difficulty would we bear children (Come!)

If such a song deliberately excludes women who have not borne children, it nevertheless creates a ground of common experience around which Christian women can generate a sense of community and valorize the contributions of women to Christian life. Women's choice to submit to the pain of childbirth becomes the paradigmatic act of submission to God's will.

The growth of such musical groups encourages greater circulation and cooperation among and between Hausa-speaking churches on both sides of the Niger-Nigeria border. The circulation of women's groups is an important way in which Christians in Niger sustain contact with the more-developed Christian communities in Nigeria. Songs cross the border, are borrowed and adapted, and make their way back again. Women's groups compete to see which can perform the most new verses to a song, and group members wear matching outfits they refer to as "uniforms," as if the groups were sports teams. In other words, the women's groups do not simply perform for their churches—they take part in a much broader community of Christian women who simultaneously share the gift of music and compete with one another. This is very much in the spirit of *wasa*, playful competition, for in this way social tensions are both recognized and defused. For many marginally literate women, the primary occasion for writing is to record songs in a notebook so that they can learn the words. After the Bible, a woman's tattered collection of handwritten songs is likely to be her most valued text.

But the lack of other, more intellectually demanding forums for women probably leaves more-educated women feeling rootless and slightly alienated. Educated women of my own age, who generally were not members of either the women's group or the *kwaya*, might approach me after a service and speak in French, expressing some muted surprise and puzzlement that I found the time-consuming and socially conservative Zummuntar Mata group worthwhile. But I was not the only well-educated "stranger" who found the women's group a reassuring and agreeable source of social contact, for educated Zerma and Fulani women seemed, like me, fairly willing to take advantage of the ready social entrée the women's fellowship group could provide them in an alien milieu.

Creating a sense of fellowship, or *zummunci*, requires constant work and effort to overcome potential differences:

> Let us shake hands together in friendship
> Let us shake hands together in love
> Let us reject all of our differences
> Love of God has brought us together . . .
> As Christians we are all the same
> Let us reject all of our disagreements
> And all insults and jealousy amongst us

While the schism between the evangelical churches in Niger that began in 1989 has created ruptures, the women's groups work tirelessly to bridge those ruptures—visiting one another when someone is sick, attending naming ceremonies, and sharing songs at various women's meetings that encompass more than one church. There is absolutely nothing comparable among the mature adult men. Men don't have cross-church Bible study groups, for example. Adult men seem to see songs as childish and backward, and there is a condescension in their manner when they address the women and the youth groups. At the same time, there is a subdued air of jealousy among the men about the fact that the women have such a lively social life through the churches, one that offers a strong pretext for spending time outside the home and provides them with another important role (despite the Zummuntar Mata's constant reinscription of the values of wife as child-bearer and homemaker). Men comment quite regularly in jest that they should create a men's group.

Muslim and Christian women share an understanding that a song can be a kind of spiritual offering, so it is not surprising that this particular activity flourishes among Hausa-speaking Christian women or that men might find it somewhat threatening. As one song declares, "I thank God that he gave me the gift of making songs." Women also see singing songs as their own form of preaching. A particularly good women's choir might even generate a cassette tape of its best songs to raise money for a particular project or event, mimicking the taped sermons of Christian pastors and Muslim scholars. As if to respond to the possible criticisms of the older men who see songs and drumming as inappropriate in a Muslim context—the same men who discourage women from becoming preachers—women index in song the psalms that endorse so unambiguously this mode of prayer and praise: "In Psalm Thirty-Three, starting with the first line we will sing a song, all the way to the eleventh, let us learn how to praise."

The women's activities are critical to sustaining a broader sense of Christian community and maintaining networks that counter the divisions among the men who compete for authority in the church. While men devote a great deal of energy to criticizing one another and the mission, women are far more interested in generating positive social interactions. Some of the women's sense of the importance of the sustaining work of *zummunci* seems to have rubbed off on the younger generation of men, whose youth groups show a similar interest in moving forward in a common spirit rather than dwelling on the injuries and injustices of the past. This does not mean that women and younger men are not aware of or interested in class, ethnic, racial, and regional differences—their songs suggest that they are acutely aware of the tensions

created by those differences and it is competition between different singing groups that serves to generate a sense of common identity as Christians. Once again the playful recognition of difference—*wasa*—is part of
how the social wounds are healed.

Beyond Baptism: The Complex Process of Conversion

Given the importance of ritual washing in Maradi, local populations,
particularly Muslims, often see the Christian practice of baptism as the
key marker of an irreversible conversion to Christianity—an apostasy
(Kapp 1939, 9).[8] Baptisms have been celebrated by the missionaries in
their writings over the years as the clearest mark of the number of conversions they have brought about through their work. Since, as Roland
Oliver wryly pointed out in one of the first studies of missions in Africa,
"the evangelical subscriber paid and prayed for 'conversions,'" (Oliver
1952/1970, 25) neither SIM nor the mission's supporters counted the
establishment of mission stations or social service infrastructure alone as
marks of success. Success could only be measured in conversions, and
conversions were most readily counted through the proxy of baptism.

SIM did not promote infant baptism, of course, but instead encouraged public testimony by adults followed by immersion, which took place
after the missionaries at the station in question felt confident that the
candidate understood the meaning of conversion. Without a moment of
public testimony before the Christian congregation, the individual's adherence to Christianity is only partial or incomplete, as one woman
pointedly indicated to me as if to remind me that my participation in the
Zummuntar Mata did not translate into full membership in the Christian
community.

But baptism is in fact a rather rough index of who is and isn't a
Christian, since the prerequisites for baptism, as we have seen, required
polygynous men to shed their supernumerary wives. Not everyone who
left Islam ultimately was baptized, for it was not practical. Furthermore,
key moments of inward change could occur both before and after a formal baptism had occurred. Among the Christians I interviewed, a range
of central events surfaced in the narratives of conversion that marked
important moments of change: for most Muslims, the choice to stop
praying with other Muslims was a key decision; choosing not to fast was
another public moment of rupture. For Arna, ceasing to make beer in
order to call a *gayya* (a party called to work together in the host's fields

in exchange for beer) often marked an important break. For members of the *sarauta* class, choosing to reject the offer of a titled office that would have entailed making sacrifices was an important ratification of commitment to Christianity. For one man, his success in giving up smoking with the help of prayers of support from his church marked his final break with his former life and habits; for his wife, it was the moment when she threw out the charms protecting her babies that marked her real choice to depend on God alone. And within established communities there are distinctions between individuals who have professed publicly, those who have been baptized, those who are welcome to partake of communion, and those who are recognized as preachers and elders. Conversion entails far more than baptism.

By 1960 or so, some of the SIM missionaries had become more sensitive to the problems that the rigid insistence that polygynous men shed their wives created and had become more sympathetic to the polygynous men and their vulnerable wives and children. Martha Wall developed something of an intermediate position in her outreach at Garin Magaji as she drew up a list of the members of the Christian church there: "I had planned to approach the matter of polygamy very carefully as it is not a matter essential to salvation, though it is one of the greatest and saddest problems of establishing a church in this land. . . . I told Madugu that his having several wives could not keep him from eternal life, though it would exclude him from church fellowship" (Wall 1960, 289). She found that some of the hostility of women to Christianity, not astonishingly, was due to their resentment of the religion "that threatened to break up their home" (290). Wall's solution was to make a distinction between her book, which listed members of the Christian church, and the Book of Life, in which she was confident that Madugu was listed among the redeemed (289).

SIM policy in the mid-1980s had not resolved this difficulty, despite the growing sensitivity of missionaries on the ground. The mission continued to support the position that the Bible teaches monogamy but that a polygynous convert in an area where there was an existing church must listen to the Holy Spirit and abide by the teachings of the local church— in this case the EERN. SIM did not insist that baptism would be appropriate in such a case; it left that decision to the church. Nevertheless, the mission seemed to be increasingly staking out a position that was distinct from that of the EERN, which was to make its own decision about how to handle polygyny among converts. Where there was as yet no organized church in those new areas into which the mission had begun evangelization among Fulani and Tuareg populations, the mission took the decision to stake out a middle position. Someone who has already converted to Christianity could not become polygamous subsequently. But "if, because of the specific problems of [the] first generation of Christians in a polygynous society, a believer who has several wives is baptized . . . he should not become an elder of the church, in keeping with the scriptural teachings of Titus 1:6 and Timothy 3:2."[9] In practice it does not seem that the mission acted on this proposed middle position, undoubtedly because of fierce opposition from the EERN.

The schism among the churches in 1989 brought unexpected opportunities to redefine what constituted membership in the Christian community. The EERN had an established policy against baptizing men with more than one wife. The possibility that individuals could choose among the different factions of the SIM-related churches or choose to join a Pentecostal church put pressure on missionaries and pastors to rethink this rather inhumane policy, as Daniel Paternoster noted in a report on a baptism held in 1993 among Fulani near Tassa Ibrahim:

> The opportunity to publicly identify with Christ in baptism had come. Some had waited over five years out of respect for an established church policy against baptizing men with more than one wife. Changes in the church situation convinced them now was the time to go ahead. . . . This baptism was a public expression of an inward change, a statement of repentance and identification with Christ in dying to self, burying the past and rising to new life in Christ. Eighty-seven men, women and children made that profession that day. (Paternoster 1994)

This highly celebrated event was held in cooperation with one of the Pentecostal missionaries in the region, who filmed the baptism, and a Pentecostal pastor. When Paternoster and his SIM colleague announced that the baptism was done "in Jesus' name" in characteristic evangelical fashion, the Pentecostal pastor corrected them, announcing that the baptisms were done "in the name of the Father, the Son, and the Holy Ghost." Pentecostalism and the schisms within the evangelical community contributed to the formation of a Fulani church that would look, sound, and feel rather different from that of the Hausa Christians in Maradi.

However, the policy that a polygynous man can be baptized but may not serve as a church elder or a deacon (following I Timothy 3:2 and 3:12; see Echert 1993, 14) because he has not shown his "maturity" still privileges monogamous men over polygynous men and still offers an inducement to divorce. This policy makes it difficult to form a working church in newly evangelized regions, where there simply may be no men who are eligible to serve as elders. Churches then are entirely subject to the leadership of sedentary Fulani who have acculturated to Hausa life or to the Hausa leaders of the established churches. Wodaabe Christians are then "second class" Christians with little autonomy, cultural or otherwise (Burt 1994, 5). Missionaries who work in these kinds of frontier areas are quite divided over this issue, whatever the formal SIM position may be. Tuareg and Fulani churches that take the decision to permit polygynous men to be elders would be seen as renegade sects by SIM and would receive little support from the very missionaries who should, in principle, help them to "mature."

However, my own observations of Christian families in Maradi suggest that in fact a kind of underrecognized polygyny exists in Maradi among Christian men acculturated to Hausa life who were not polygynous at the time of their baptisms. It takes a rather particular form, for when a Christian man marries a Christian woman in a public wedding, the assumption of all parties is that this will be a monogamous household, fashioned after the pairing of Adam and Eve—there is no overt challenge to the notion that Christianity entails monogamy. However, the imperative to produce children is extraordinarily strong in Maradi, for Christians as for Muslims. A man who fails to produce children and does nothing about it may be accused by others—including Christians—of being a homosexual. Homophobia is extreme among Christians in Maradi, the dual legacy of a Muslim environment and the teachings of fundamentalist missionaries. A Muslim man who loved his first wife would simply take a second wife in the hope of having children. Yet if a Christian couple does not have children within several years, there seems to be no acceptable remedy within Christian orthodoxy. The couple is not to divorce. I know of no married couples that were divorced and then remained Christian—it simply is not done, despite the high incidence of divorce among Protestant Christians in the west. The only pattern I can discern among Christian couples who break up is that the man has left Christianity and in effect has taken the Muslim male prerogative to repudiate his wife. This is not uncommon, although Christians in Maradi do not like to admit it openly. Such men then go on to take Muslim wives and lovers and leave the Christian community altogether. Their ex-wives either carry on as if they were widows or eventually leave the Christian fold.

The other solution is for the Christian man to take a second wife in a Muslim ceremony while retaining his Christian wife and continuing to take part in the Christian community. While this solution is frowned upon, in practice it does occur. The Muslim wife, who will live apart in her own home, then becomes simply a means whereby the man can produce offspring, who are raised as Christians although their unorthodox backgrounds mean that they are likely to be shipped off to school or fostered among Christians at a distance where they are less visible. The Christian wife goes about her business as before and has the monopoly on the husband's public displays of familial life. No one expects the Muslim wife to either take part in Christian life or to convert—indeed, if she did so, that would create something of a quandary. These men may be prominent members of the Christian community and have in no way rejected their avowed commitment to Christian beliefs. They cannot, it is true, continue as preachers or as recognized elders, but that does not mean they are not influential within their churches. When missionaries mention such men, they will say that they "fell away" and are no longer Christians, as if the men had reverted to Islam. But that is not how they see themselves, nor is it how local Christians view them, however scandalized they might be.

Some of this malleability at the level of practice is possible because the church is no longer under the control of the mission. Before the churches became formally independent from the mission in 1960, missionaries could exclude individuals from a congregation and they could see that "discipline" was given to Christians who did not live up to their expectations. From 1960 to 1989, the EERN could discipline its members if it chose to, and church elders did sometimes use *horo* to discipline members. But after the fragmentation of the church in 1989, there was no real way to effect "discipline," or *horo*. An individual who is rejected from one congregation will simply seek out another, which will be quite happy to see its flock increase. So far as I can tell, the notion of church discipline has been largely abandoned in recent years. Many Christians in Maradi have bitter tales to tell of *horo* that they felt was unjustly placed on them, and many of those tales, which admittedly were told by interested parties, do suggest that "discipline" has been intemperately applied. As one older pastor pointedly remarked, the sins of the missionaries such as arrogance or worldliness were never subject to *horo* (Pastor 'dan Nana interview, November 3, 2000), so from the very outset there was a lack of reciprocity—those who could impose *horo* did not themselves always show restraint or Christian behavior. In a striking image, one man said that *laifi tudu ne* (sin is a mountain) on which one stands to see the faults of others; making such intrusive judgments is itself implicitly a kind of sinfulness.[10]

To offer an example of the intrusions into private family life that are so resented, one woman whose husband was regularly seeing a *karuwa* (a Hausa woman who provides entertainment and sexual services to men) was forbidden to attend church for several months because she fought with him over the issue instead of displaying the womanly virtue of patience, or *hakuri*. When he eventually left her and the church entirely for the *karuwa*, she began to go back to church, but the incident left her deeply scarred and she does not, under any circumstances, consult with male pastors about her emotional life or her needs as a single woman. By imposing *horo* for failings that were not really significant—a youthful experiment with beer, a moment of flamboyant dress, a marital spat—the mission and the churches eventually made it less possible to effectively convey disapprobation for behavior that was more clearly incompatible with Christianity. For women, this means that they are charged with keeping peace in homes that are sometimes burdened with rather substantial problems:

> Here is some good advice, women, listen well
> How we can have a peaceful home
> Let us be patient so that we don't give Satan any opportunities
> Let us prevent our homes from becoming a resting place for Satan
> Women, let us cease causing disagreements in our homes
> So that we can prevail upon our men to come to Jesus
> Goodness, women, leave off quarrelsomeness in your home
> Don't let us be beautiful outside the home but unlovely at home
> Disobedience has been the work of Satan from the beginning

Obviously the latitude Christian men seem to permit themselves in their practice of Christianity is not readily available to Christian women, who are to be obedient to their husbands even when those men have "strayed from Jesus." That women sing such songs of exhortation to one another suggests that it is not particularly easy to avoid "quarrelsomeness."

Performing Christianity

Christians of this region have developed a series of public practices that simultaneously resonate with Muslim practice, perform the nature of Christianity as a distinctive belief system, and serve as modes of evangelism. These events take advantage of the reality that in Niger, any unusual event will draw a large crowd of young and curious onlookers. Probably the most striking of these adaptations is the *bikin suna*, or naming ceremony. Muslim families hold a ceremony outside the father's home eight days after the birth of a child. Muslim scholars will be invited as well as friends, neighbors, and kin. The ceremony occurs very early in the morning before the work of the day has begun. Women gather inside the compound, crowding the mother and baby in a room decorated with heavy wall hangings and smoky with incense. Men sit on mats in front of the home, and it is they who actually listen to the speech of a Muslim scholar who will choose a name. When the women hear the news that the name has been chose, they ululate noisily. Afterward, everyone will share a meal together and a ram will be sacrificed as alms and the meat will be distributed. Muslim men regard the purchase of such a ram as an absolutely necessary expense and will borrow money at high rates of interest to meet this social obligation.

The evangelical Christian variant on this serves a function somewhat akin to infant baptism. The men gather outside the home of the couple, the women inside, and the *bikin suna* is carried out early in the morning. At first the event seems indistinguishable from a Muslim ceremony. But the naming event among Muslims occurs very quickly, and in reality the name that is chosen has little social significance because most Muslim women have a taboo against using the formal name for fear that it will bring bad luck to the child. So in practice the child will almost never be referred to by his or her formal name. Christians have a very different relationship to the name itself. The parents choose a biblical name themselves, and they invite a pastor to offer a sermon that reflects on the meaning of that name for the Christian community. The child is not kept hidden inside the compound but is brought out to the doorway and joyously displayed to the crowd, as if to demonstrate a lack of fear of the evil eye—the Christian God will protect this child. When describing the difference between Christian and Muslim *bikin suna*, Christians never fail to note that the child is brought out for public viewing. The display is one way of establishing the community's claim on the child. In effect, Christians use the name as an occasion to preach to the Muslim kin, neighbors, and curious onlookers about some key values and key texts of Christianity and something about the nature of Christian community. Because public preaching to evangelize is not permitted but naming ceremonies cannot be forbidden, these ceremonies have become one of the most important ways that the Christian community reaches beyond the walls of the church: "A large captive audience is exposed to nothing less than a full gospel message taking up to an hour. This is a culturally acceptable way in a country which doesn't allow open proclamation in other circumstances" (Isch 1989a, 3). Pentecostal Christians are somewhat anxious about this ritual, in which they also participate, for fear that its Islamic and pre-Islamic history may offer precisely the kind of "opening" demons seize on to inhibit the success of the child in the future.

Christian weddings also have a rather significant performative dimension, although the practice of holding such weddings in a church reduces the likelihood that a Muslim audience can be drawn. The weddings I have seen, however, were deliberately held outside in the church courtyard to accommodate the crowd rather than inside the church building, and many Muslims did in fact attend. A Muslim wedding in Maradi does not entail the public appearance of the bride and groom together at the actual religious ceremony—this is an event that involves the groom and the male kin of the bride and groom, and indeed sometimes the bride and groom are not even in the same village or country at the time of the formal ceremony. For Christians, the couple itself is at the center of the ceremony. Their parents may or may not even be present—in the earliest weddings of converts it was often a missionary who more or less stood in as parent. When Christians describe the difference between their weddings and a Muslim ceremony, they comment that a Christian ceremony is one in which there are questions. By this they mean that for Muslims the public consent of both bride and groom are not necessary, and indeed given the youth of the bride in many cases (Muslim girls may marry as young as thirteen, and in exceptional cases even younger), it would be difficult to stage "consent" in any convincing manner. Some of the traditional ceremonies, which are now falling into decline, would even require the bride to attempt to run away (in play?) until the groom gives her and her girlfriends small gifts. For Christians it is this public response to the questions "Do you take this man? . . . Do you take this woman?" that is absolutely distinctive. It highlights women's choice in marriage and the sense that Christian marriage entails the creation of a couple and that that couple in marrying enters as full adults into a broad community—their marriages are not simply marriages between two families. The public pairing is related to the emphasis on monogamy—this is a choice of the one partner for life patterned after God's creation of Eve to be Adam's helpmeet. There will be no other members of this marriage. One can easily understand why, when men violate their Christian monogamy, they cannot do so with a second Christian marriage.

Today weddings may involve white gowns and veils, but in contrast to the focus on the beauty of the bride alone in many western bridal photographs, photographs of weddings in Maradi almost always include both the bride and groom in the frame, once again focusing on the couple. Sometimes the bride and groom wear matching outfits made from the same kind of cloth. Although the dress and the ceremony proper are distinctive to Christianity, the feast following the ceremony would be familiar to most Muslims. After the ceremony, a dish with meat will be offered, drinks will be served, and everyone will sit down on mats together to eat, men and women discretely separate. There will be much laughing and joking.

In my previous work among Muslim women, I devoted considerable attention to the importance of the exchange of wedding gifts. The high rate of divorce among Muslims and the competition between co-wives has historically meant that Muslim brides expect substantial gifts from their husbands, formerly known as "gifts for the room" but more recently featuring a "valise"—a suitcase full of expensive clothing and other goods. These gifts may then become important capital and savings for her and her children in times of stress (Cooper 1997a). In principle, the fact that evangelical Christians do not practice divorce and are not polygynous should ensure that wedding gifts for the bride have less importance than among Muslims. The antimaterialism of the fundamentalist SIM missionaries would also seem to imply an aversion to any acquisitive aspect of something as central to Christian life as marriage. In practice, however, weddings among Hausa-speaking Christians also involve considerable gift exchange—many of the same stages of gift exchange will occur, from the modest gifts a groom offers a bride's parents to signal his interest in her to the gifts of female relatives to the bride and groom to the sizable suitcase full of expensive cloth and other gifts the groom must give his new wife. For all the differences between Christian and Muslim ceremonies, this element of commonality is rather striking. But because there is no *sadaki*—no ritual gift from the groom to the bride's family that formally seals the marriage—the countervailing return gifts from the bride's family seem to take on less importance. Both men and women within the Christian community agree that Christian weddings are very expensive in comparison with Muslim weddings and that the primary expense is the "valise." Young men find this requirement quite onerous and push, along with their fathers, for some kind of cap on the wedding expenses. Older women strenuously resist any such adjustment to local practice when it touches on their own daughters, although they agree that the expenses are high and that in principle there should be some cap.

Why are Christian brides so demanding? This may in part be a simple matter of supply and demand. Christian families are limited in number and most young men want their children to be raised by a Christian mother. They don't simply want a marital household; they want a Christian one. Because there is a finite number of Christian women and because Christian girls never marry before the age of fifteen, which is relatively high for the region, there are fewer potential brides to choose from. The number of men in this community has always exceeded the number of women, for the simple reason that Muslim men are far more likely to be exposed to Christianity and to convert than are Muslim women. Such men must compete with young men raised within the Christian community for the limited numbers of Christian girls, and the tendency of these girls to go to school and to wait until they have finished schooling to marry makes them quite desirable as brides.

But it is also possible that it is precisely because Christian women only have one chance at marriage that they hope to extract as much from that solitary moment of leverage as they possibly can. They will never have another opportunity to acquire moveable wealth on this scale. And their mothers will have only one opportunity to test the willingness of the groom to meet the needs of the bride and to show respect for his mother-in-law. Women whose husbands leave the Christian church or join the small but rather important set of polygynous Christian men are marooned in marriages they cannot themselves repudiate. They cannot remarry. They may have to rely on this body of goods until their children are old enough to support them, a rather humiliating prospect. Because at present Christians do not generally use the courts to regulate disputes, there is no mechanism through which a woman can claim half of the conjugal property if a marriage collapses. Women have no other form of insurance against the unpleasant possibility that their marriage will depart from the Christian ideal. Because in the past both the mission and the church have resolutely ignored the legal dimensions of property rights, women have no recourse but to secure the greatest protections they can at the outset of a marriage. Setting the cost of marriage as high as possible makes it less likely that a groom will seek a second wife at any time in the near future, and it also means that if he ever does choose to do so he will be unlikely to expend as much in that marriage as in the first, establishing the primacy of the first, Christian, wife in a monetary way.

From the perspective of a young couple attempting to set up house together, the insistence of the mother of the bride on these wedding gifts can seem an unbearable burden, for it locks the wealth of the groom, often a modestly employed urban dweller, into forms that don't necessarily serve the couple as a whole particularly well. They may hope to buy land to build a house, for example. But because in practice there is no real way for husbands and wives to be co-owners of all the marital property—all property in effect ends up belonging to the groom—older women are reluctant to let their daughters become vulnerable in this way. So despite the public performance of difference in the ceremony itself, the surrounding marriage customs hint at a certain unease within Christian marriages on the part of women. Although men and missionaries regard this extractive impulse by older women as a backward custom, evidence of women's poor absorption of the deeper values of Christianity, a more useful response would be to pay closer attention to the legal implications of property and begin to establish the legal precedent for women's ownership of half of the conjugal property if the monogamous character of the marriage is violated. Patience, the only remedy a woman is enjoined to pursue at the moment, will not reduce the cost of marriage payments.

Evangelical Christian practice in Maradi is shaped in substantive ways by the consciousness that Christianity is in competition with Islam and must constantly prove itself in terms that are legible to Muslims. But the specific logics of monogamous marriage and conversion have generated a variety of practices that are distinctively Christian and bear strong traces of the turbulent relationship between evangelical missionaries and relatively tolerant and adaptive Hausa Christians. Within this community, the generation of a sense of community has in many ways fallen to women and their lively fellowship groups, without which it is difficult to imagine the contemporary churches surviving. Christian practice in Niger continues to oscillate, to move and play, in the spirit of *wasa*, between the contradictory poles of faith and works, fundamental difference and adaptive absorption, masculine authority and feminine resilience, and the commanding presence of Islamic hegemony and the appealing call for a distinctive Christianity.

Epilogue:
SIM's Successors and the Pentecostal Explosion

$\mathcal{I}$t is commonplace today to view the explosion of Pentecostalism in the past twenty years as a new and distinctive phenomenon. Certainly it has a number of features that are strikingly different from the evangelical Christianity SIM introduced into the region. However, despite the emphasis within Pentecostalism upon a distinct rupture with one's past, as a historian I can't help but be struck by how the Pentecostal explosion is an organic and in some ways logical outcome of the successes and failures of SIM (on the one hand) and of false promise of development discourses in one of the most marginal of spaces on the globe (on the other). When SIM's agropastoral efforts of the mid-1970s drew it ever more deeply into relief and development work, missionaries chose to target parts of the region that had not already been affected by the medical work and in particular that could not be reached through the successful leprosarium at Danja. Focusing upon the north not only opened a way to work with nomads, it also enabled the mission to work in a sustained fashion with Arna Hausa-speaking populations who evangelists say "have no religion whatsoever, only sacrifice."[1] Since the 1980s, Christian evangelists in the region have also tended to look north, where the influence of Islam emanating from Nigeria is attenuated. During the two decades in which the mission worked closely in this region it had relatively little success drawing converts; some missionaries felt that the area was so strongly overtaken by satanic demons through Arna sacrifice and *bori* spirit possession that it was not much more promising than the areas that were strongly Muslim.

In the late 1990s the mission began to reduce its relief and development work in Niger because of political instability, the departure of Tony Rinaudo from the mission, and reduced contributions to mission efforts. Many local Christians felt that this was yet another example of how the mission unilaterally chose to abandon various institutions without much consultation with its national employees or the local church. Some in the mission and the local churches felt that the relief and development phase of the mission's work was a failure. The sizable staff that was laid off and the reduced visibility of the mission in rural areas was noted with bitterness by those affected. However, if one steps back and looks at the larger picture, it is less clear that SIM's relatively lengthy commitment to Arewa met with no success. The staff that was laid off shifted to other kinds of work where they used many of the skills, social networks, and strategies they had acquired while working for SIM. Some found employment doing development work in one of the most extravagantly funded of the evangelical Christian missions, World Vision. Others became engaged in contributing in a variety of ways to the Campus Crusades of Christ effort (in conjunction with the EERN) to show the film *Jesus* (a 1979 film rendition of the entire Gospel of Mark dubbed into Hausa and other local languages) in villages throughout the region. Yet others found a more congenial home in the emerging Pentecostal churches, taking their interest and social commitments in Arewa with them. The net result of the ongoing work of the successor institutions to SIM is an extraordinary explosion of conversions to Pentecostal Christianity in the Arewa region today.

It was in reflecting upon how Campus Crusades shows the *Jesus* film that I came to the conclusion that the growth of Pentecostalism cannot be understood without knowledge of the history of SIM's evangelicalism. I had asked if I could come along with Pastor Ayyuba Lawali of Campus Crusades for Christ for a showing so that I could find out more about this controversial yet highly successful contemporary strategy of evangelization. I knew that in some parts of Africa the film showings had been the occasion for riots and other violence; before I had met Pastor Ayyuba I thought of the film evangelism as unnecessarily confrontational, part of a range of aggressive activities Pentecostal and evangelical Christians engage in that infuriate Muslims and are therefore culturally insensitive. I was somewhat surprised to discover that I *liked* this gentle and good-humored pastor very much. Coming himself from an Arna background, he had converted to Christianity only after spending nine years in treatment at the Danja leprosarium. He still bears the marks of the debilitating side effects of leprosy. After training at the SIM Bible school, he went on to become a preacher in the region surrounding the leprosarium. It was only relatively recently that he had begun work with Campus Crusades showing the *Jesus* film.

To his mind it is easier to reach people today than in the past, for there is a "yearning to seek out the news" among Arna and Muslim alike that didn't exist in the past. People want to learn more about Christianity, whether they are favorably disposed to it or not. Ordinary Muslims have deeper learning today and so they know that there was a "prophet" named Jesus, and they are curious to hear what Christians have to say about him. Arna, who are increasingly under assault from an over-whelmingly Muslim milieu, find in Christianity an alternative to the name-calling of Muslim neighbors. Showing the film is the most straight-forward way of sharing the gospel with illiterate people. Rather than interpret Christianity himself or argue with Islam, he noted, he lets the film speak for itself. No one is compelled to watch, no one is required to agree with its depiction of Jesus (Pastor Ayyuba Lawali interview).

Pastor Ayyuba's explanation for why he shows the *Jesus* film resonated a great deal with SIM missionary Chuck Forster's recollections of show-ing filmstrips in Niger during the 1970s. The mission learned very quickly that providing entertainment for local populations was an ex-tremely effective way of reaching otherwise wary and suspicious audi-ences. Early missionaries used old-fashioned phonographs and gospel re-cordings to attract listeners, missionary Ray de la Haye was well known in the region for playing wind instruments to attract a crowd, and singing in marketplaces was another way to draw an audience. Using entertaining audiovisuals to attract audiences was therefore one of many techniques SIM used, and it had become commonplace in the region well before Campus Crusades began showing the *Jesus* film. Chuck Forster would combine segments on the Old and New Testaments with a filmstrip of one of many extremely popular animal morality tales written by "Jungle Doctor" Paul White. The images would be projected onto a simple screen. Showings on Friday night in Maradi town might attract hundreds of viewers, including Muslim scholars and their *almajirai* students. When he eventually had to set aside the filmstrip ministry (which he nicknamed "the Gospel Trap" because it was so popular with non-Christians) in order to attend to administrative duties, disappointed viewers exclaimed, "That's not very generous of you, we gotten accustomed to this and now you're abandoning it!" (Chuck Forster interview; author's translation).

As I set off with Pastor Ayyuba's team one late afternoon I couldn't help but be struck, then, by how deeply indebted this "competing" effort was to SIM's previous engagement with the region. The preacher had been converted and trained by the mission, the vehicle being used was rented from the mission, the driver was one of SIM's most experienced development workers, and the goodwill of audiences in search of entertainment had been cultivated through the work of missionaries such as Forster. On their first attempt, the crew targeted a village they had made some kind of previous arrangement to visit that was within view of the main paved road out of Maradi heading north. As we pulled up before the home of the village head, there was a distinct chill in our reception. The signs of *'yan izala* reformist Islamic influence were everywhere, from the numerous small mosques to the *hijabi* veils worn by the tiniest little girls of the village. The village head, we were told, was in his fields and would not be back for a long time. Fine, the Campus Crusade workers said affably, we'll wait.

We were not invited to join the Muslim men on their mats under the *rumfa* shelter, so we sat apart on a well-worn log that seemed to serve as a village meeting place. Small children watched us warily as the evangelists murmured among themselves about villages that it would make sense to target in the future, better prospects further off the paved road where the influence of Maradi and Muslim evangelism would be less acutely felt. The network of villages that several of them had previously visited for SIM's Maradi Integrated Development Project was clearly the map they were following in their work—these were more promising sites than the present village, for they were in the Arna belt. The men swapped tales about their previous development work in that area, gave detailed instructions to one another about how to find promising villages, and talked excitedly about the effect of sustained work with such villages. Eventually the village head, a middle-aged man in the garb of a prosperous Muslim trader (not of someone returning from the fields) returned well after nightfall and told us firmly that they were not interested in the showing, that they didn't like that kind of trouble here. Fine, fine, the team members said without rancor. And we climbed back into the truck and made our way out of the labyrinth of the village in the dark. This, they said, was not an uncommon occurrence, but neither was it the norm. Generally, they suggested, people are pretty excited to see them.

And indeed, that seemed to be the case on our second attempt some nights later. We drove farther into the bush off the main road to the east of Maradi. The village was small and unassuming, busy with its agricultural tasks. We arrived a bit before sunset and sought out the village head. This man was more the rustic farmer than the leader of the other village and seemed a bit puzzled about what to make of us. He said, "Well, I don't know what to do for you," perhaps concerned that he would be expected to compel people to watch this Christian film. Pastor Ayyuba laughed gently and said, "You don't have to do anything. Just show us an open area where we can set up to show the film and we'll do the rest." We were shown to the edge of the village where a path led toward the bush; in the distance, village women were busy collecting firewood. Noting quietly among themselves that the field seemed to be a public latrine, the team instead paced out the size of the cul-de-sac where the last of the village streets gave way to the paths into the bush through the open field. Agreeing that this cul-de-sac would serve their purposes admirably, the men began work setting up the projection screen.

As his fellow workers did the physical labor he himself could not do because of the enduring debilitating effects of leprosy, Pastor Ayyuba remarked to me, "Really you don't have to do any advertising, because village people are so curious watching you set up that before you know it the whole village is there staring at you." Before long, a large number of children were watching us with wide-eyed curiosity. In a village with no electricity and little access to town, this hum of activity was a welcome form of entertainment. The two-sided screen the men hoisted like a sail was ingenious, a sheer cloth stretched across a set of interlocking poles held up with taut guylines. Speakers were attached to the two poles, and the projector, generator, and sound equipment were set some sixteen paces back with a microphone for Pastor Ayyuba. This was a low-tech masterpiece of American ingenuity.

By the time they were through there was a sizable crowd, and Pastor Ayyuba began to explain to them what the team was doing. They would be showing a film about Jesus Christ, from his birth from the Virgin Mary to his death. He did not refer to Jesus as prophet (*Annabi Issa*) but rather as Savior (*Almasihu*). The term he used to refer to Mary (*budurwa*) is one Hausa-speakers use quite regularly for unmarried girls of about ten to twelve who are understood to be sexually inactive. The question of Mary's virginity is one of the occasional points of contention between Christians and Muslims. While he made no attempt to mask the difference between how a Christian talks about Jesus and how a Muslim does, his style was easygoing and homey. His description made it seem as if watching the movie might be fun. Then, with his winning down-to-earth style, he remarked humorously, "No one can listen to preaching on an empty stomach, now can they? So you all go home now and eat your dinner. And people who want to pray the last Muslim prayer (*lisha*), they should go ahead and do that too. We'll wait, we won't start until after *lisha*." This open and relaxed invitation left the timing and audience for the showing entirely up to the villagers. If none of the men ever returned to say that *lisha* had been finished, there couldn't really be a showing. If no one chose to return after dinner, there would be no audience. Pastor Ayyuba and his team relaxed confidently as the sky grew dark and the brilliant stars of the rural sky appeared.

Eventually the children returned, and then the men, and, a good bit later, the women. The children were invited to take the best seats in front of the screen. The men sat under the trees behind the children on benches and chairs they brought from home. Women gathered on the other side of the double-sided screen, comfortably distant from the men. They could see the mirror image of the film, but the credits would be impossible to read. But since few of them could read anyway, that didn't much matter. They could make as much noise as they wanted, commenting on the film, on Jesus, on Mary, and so on without troubling the men and children or provoking rebuke. It was the ideal arrangement, for the number of women grew as they finished up their evening chores. The women were therefore noisily busy greeting one another and catching up on the "plot" well into the movie.

Watching the film in a rural village in the middle of nowhere brought home for me just how real the *world* of the gospels is to people in Niger. If one sets aside the soulful blue eyes of the white actor playing Jesus, then the long robes of the men, the sheep and shepherds, the women bearing water, the demons and illnesses, the desert landscape, the imperial politics, all are utterly familiar to such an audience. There is nothing quaint or old-fashioned about what occurs in this film to the average rural dweller in Niger, where young girls get pregnant unexpectedly, people are taken over by spirits, jealous religious authorities attempt to undermine those who disagree with them, taxes are unfair, and state power is brought to bear in contexts in which it is hard to see the justice. It suddenly seemed to me that such an audience has a more immediate understanding of the world of the gospel than those of us in highly developed secular lands. Spirits are very real. Jealousy has malignant consequences. The audience's reactions were interesting—at first the young men seemed to have come prepared to feel contempt for Jesus, and they laughed in an irrelevant early scene when the actor tripped slightly. But the man depicted in the film was a man who met needs that any of these villagers would know all too well. He fed the hungry, he defended the poor, he healed the sick, he drove out the demons of the possessed. This was, if nothing else, a very generous and powerful man. By the end of the film the mood of the audience had changed—not only did people seem to respect this man a great deal, they did not want him to be dead.

What they took from the story is another matter that would be much harder to determine. It seemed possible to me that many did not see him as God but rather as a really good doctor or *boka* (traditional healer). The notion that there is such a thing as a fatal illness didn't seem to be part of the audience's general understanding of illness and death. If you survive an illness it can't have been fatal, so there's no *miracle* there. Pastor Ayyuba went to some pains to explain that the sick *would have died* but that Jesus brought them back to life. Later it wasn't clear to me that everyone in the audience understood that (from within the understanding of the film) the crucifixion was unjust. People were noisily speculating about what crime Jesus had done to be crucified. Again Pastor Ayyuba had to intervene to explain that Jesus didn't do anything wrong, indeed he was without sin; it was the prompting of the priests that led to his death. If the film very effectively conveys a positive image of Jesus and makes his world seem anything but foreign (no mean feat when Christianity is equated with the west by contentious Muslims), it would take considerably more than this film alone to provoke a conversion. Pastor Ayyuba gave out booklets (which are readily available through publishing houses in Nigeria, many of them Pentecostal in orientation) to many eager hands, but this, presumably, would only be a beginning.

And this is where the network of Pentecostal preachers of the newer missions such as Vie Abondante comes in. Once a village has some interest in learning more, Pastor Ayyuba attempts to link it up with whatever Christian preacher and congregation is closest. Thus, the film team and the preachers who are active in the region continuously share information. Because Vie Abondante is training its own pastors and brings in pastors from Nigeria, it has far broader coverage in the region than SIM and the financially strapped EERN, which nevertheless supports 55 evangelists. But the villages that have been receptive and the social networks that have been used to tap into them come out of previous work done by SIM staff and converts. SIM regards the activities of the competing Pentecostal missions with barely disguised resentment, despite friendships on an individual level between SIM and Vie Abondante staff. Where Vie Abondante or Assemblies of God staff can afford to comment philosophically that competition is good (which is a very neoliberal

American understanding of the spiritual economy), SIM and the evangelical churches are not entirely pleased with the activities of these parvenus in their back yard. SIM nevertheless continues to provide logistical support for showing the *Jesus* film and resigns itself to the advance in Pentecostalism that the Campus Crusades activities set in train.

American fundamentalism has long had an ambivalent relationship to Pentecostalism. In terms of doctrine, there is little to separate most evangelicals from their Pentecostal co-religionists. However, fundamentalists held Pentecostalism at arm's length because of a skepticism about faith healing, a distrust of the authenticity of speaking in tongues and other such signs of the Holy Spirit, and an understanding of the unfolding of time that places the kinds of spectacular miracles of the gospels in a past "dispensation" of God's will at the time of Jesus and the early church. Certainly the relatively ascetic disposition of SIM, which aimed to generate modest vernacular Christians rather than flashy westernized converts is very much at odds with the gospel of prosperity the Pentecostal movement offers. The "by prayer" mission simply believed that prayer would provide the means for evangelism to go forward—it made no grand claims that prayer would bring personal wealth or that it would guarantee physical healing. Gradually, though, charismatic leaders in the United States have gained greater and greater credibility and stature. Televangelism has made prayer healing, enthusiastic charismatic preachers, and a far more emotional variety of prayer staples of the evangelical diet. Charismatic Christianity is now, as it were, part of the evangelical mainstream.

Some retired SIM missionaries now express some regret that they did not take the power of the Holy Spirit as seriously as they might have—"you can dispensationalize history," one woman remarked dryly, "but you can't dispensationalize God."[2] The mission, they now feel, might have thought more imaginatively about driving out demons, prayer healing, and open emotionalism and confession than it did when they were in the field. This regret reflects, I think, a shift in attitude that has as much to do with changes in the United States as with experience in the field. Enthusiastic fund-raising and an active engagement with mission work have meant that over the past fifteen to twenty years a conventional evangelical mission such as SIM finds itself more and more in competition with Pentecostal preachers whose combination of high spirits and ample economic means have given them much more scope and visibility. At the same time, more Christians in the United States are drawn to an understanding of mission as development work that should mirror and compete with more-secular institutions such as the Peace Corps and Oxfam. SIM leaders are acutely aware that dollars that once would have come to them are now going either to World Vision, which devotes itself to development, or to the relatively decentralized Pentecostal missions.

The effect of these developments on the Maradi region has been interesting to watch, for the interconnections among and between the different Christian agents working to convert Muslims in the region are many and multidirectional. One can now trace the contours of a Christian sector of the economy. Areas to which SIM and later the formal evangelical EERN churches have not been able to send a pastor are finding that they can meet their needs by recruiting someone, often Pentecostal, from Nigeria. Staff trained by SIM to read Hausa are hired because of those literacy skills by CARE (now only nominally Christian in orientation). Evangelical and Pentecostal Christians work alongside one another in World Vision (the most prominent of the well-endowed Christian NGOs at the moment). Families cross a variety of lines with little friction: a woman who works for the EERN may have a daughter who teaches literacy and sewing to women for Vie Abondante. The younger generation of Christians, it seems to me, are fluid and experimental and most of all happy to work wherever they can find employment. Many are better educated than their parents because they attended the public schools. They are open to both Pentecostalism and development work in ways their parents (who were trained by SIM to view both with skepticism) are not. Many younger Christians work for NGOs rather than following the path of their parents to become pastors and evangelists, but they still regard themselves as doing "God's work." The expansion of Pentecostalism is in many ways an outcome of the long work of evangelical missionaries in the region, who laid the groundwork for what they now experience as a competing and rather threatening style of Christianity. They rendered Christianity plausible within the local landscape—Pentecostalism simply took that plausibility and made the power of the Holy Spirit and of demonic powers a prominent part of that familiar world.

But the appeal of Pentecostalism has to be located as well in the undeniable failures of conventional narratives of progress and development. Paul Gifford notes that while Pentecostalism is a global phenomenon, its meanings are quite distinctive in Africa, the continent that has consistently been excluded from globalized circuits of wealth, technology, and education: "Africa's newest form of Christianity, while in many ways reinforcing traditional beliefs, also serves as one of Africa's best remaining ways of opting *into* the global order" (Gifford 2001, 78). Niger has not flourished under any of the many grand narratives provided in the past—the *mission civilisatrice* of the French colonial order certainly did not provide wealth or infrastructure, the uranium boom illustrated the country's vulnerability to the vagaries of the world market, military rule created havoc in the farm economy, and neoliberal structural adjustment has made the most ordinary of services extraordinary luxuries. Africans have turned inward, in many ways, to seek other answers to the enduring problem of poverty. Pentecostalism, for better or for worse, provides an answer of sorts.

The positive element of Pentecostalism, which is very appealing to those in deep economic distress, is the promise that the blessings of wealth and health are obtainable through a positive confession of faith. Personal prosperity, and by extension national prosperity, will follow from proper tithing combined with an openly articulated statement of needs (success in childbearing, promotion at work, a profitable transaction) through prayer. The outward success of Pentecostal preachers and churches as a result of both internal and external donations provides a kind of surface plausibility to this doctrine that has the effect of attracting ever more converts. The negative element in Pentecostalism is the necessary corollary to the first element, namely that any failure to obtain health and prosperity must be attributed to satanic forces. The negative pole is necessary because, as Gifford points out, "Faith preaching in so many cases cannot be said to have worked. Faith did not bring about all that was promised. Deliverance still allows the emphasis on success, as long as something more than faith is added" (Gifford 2001, 73). Deliverance, then, is more than simply healing through prayer—it is the active expulsion or reversal of forces that inhibit success. At the individual level this might imply expelling demons that entered in through improper participation in a pagan ritual; at the national level failures of development can be attributed to the demonic power of *bori* and Islam.

For this reason, Pentecostalism, paradoxically, is far more self-consciously engaged with the "traditional" than the conventional evangelical churches and SIM precisely because it aims to excise it. Where evangelical preachers may dress in traditional Hausa garb, their Pentecostal counterparts might sport a bright flowered Hawaiian shirt. Where evangelical women might wear traditional Hausa outfit, a Pentecostal woman might wear a Western-style blouse, slacks, and sunglasses. The access to the global signaled in these modes of dress is aggressively antitraditional and non-Islamic. Pentecostal pastors critical of the moderate style of the more mature evangelical churches argue that the evangelical community no longer knows how to distinguish Christianity from Islam and therefore has lost the vital spirit necessary to inspire conversions in others or generate prosperity. The Pentecostals also attribute any moral failing within the evangelical community to the loss of spirit that comes with an inability to distinguish "true" Christian belief from Islam.

If this way of thinking automatically implies a combative attitude toward Islam, it is also true that deliverance thinking implies a certain degree of self-loathing—there is nothing recuperative in this attitude toward the vernacular, the traditional, the *African*. Africa's failure to progress, within this logic, is the result of its own embrace of satanic practices. This is why Lamine Sanneh's work on translatability fails to capture the dynamism of contemporary Christianity in Africa—the newer Pentecostal movements see the past as a contaminant rather than an enhancement to the unfolding of Christian understanding. Progress will imply a rupture with conventional social relations, prior practices, and familiar vocabularies of belief. Pentecostal practices imply a deep attention to local ritual, local spirit beliefs, and local sites of spiritual potency, and that attention in a sense contributes to their ongoing salience. For in working assiduously to annihilate the past, Pentecostalism constantly revives it. So long as there are failures of prayer, there will be demons to eject.

It seems to me likely that Pentecostalism will before long find itself mired in many of the same practical dilemmas that SIM encountered. It is all very well to preach a gospel of prosperity, but until all the constraining demons are ejected it will undoubtedly seem to be a good idea to begin a school, a clinic, a program to improve farming. Vie Abondante is already engaged on a modest scale in just such interventions. Like SIM at its inception, it is relatively easy for newer missionary efforts to emphasize prayer and church-building, and it is relatively easy to demonize the practices of one's neighbors, one's family, and one's own past. Over time, however, as we have seen, SIM was drawn into physical interventions out of keeping with its initial self-conception. SIM's desire to generate a kind of vernacular Christian, however, may be less appealing to Pentecostal missions, given the prominence and near-sacred quality of English within such circles and given the demonization of traditional practices. Generating a global Christian, one whose glossolalia extends to fluency in English, may imply investment in schooling and facilitating circulation into the anglophone world. At the moment, Pentecostal movements are atomized, diffuse, and migratory, which makes it possible for them to evade the fierce and angry accounting that previous discourses of success, modernity, and development have been subject to. If in the short term the binary logic of demonization is likely to inflame tensions between Christians and Muslims in Niger, in the longer term ordinary Hausa-speakers are seeking *lafiya*—health, well-being, peace, and success. Any movement that, in the end, cannot produce this kind of well-being will at length be subject itself to the relentless logic of reform.

Glossary

addini	religion, monotheism, most commonly understood to mean Islam
ajami	the use of Arabic script to write texts in languages other than Arabic
aljanu	spirits, genies
Arna	non-Muslim populations of the Maradi region; a term used to describe a person who venerates spirits of the local landscape; Christians and Muslims in the region use the term to describe a pagan
arnanci	paganism, spirit worship
boka/bokaye	traditional healer(s), often understood to have occult powers
bori	spirit-possession cult typical on the Hausa speaking region; adepts are said to be mares ridden by the spirits
fadama	rich soils near river valleys and lakes that are flooded during the rainy season
Habe	Muslim rulers of the pre-jihad Hausa-speaking kingdoms
horo	discipline administered from without; taming
iska/iskoki	spirit(s) (from the Hausa word for wind)
iskanci	madness
jahilci	ignorance; the ignorance typical of the period of paganism prior to the coming of Mohammed; ignorance of monotheism; backwardness in general
jigawa	sandy dune soils
kafir/kafirai	pagan/pagans
madrasa	formal school for Islamic training
magani	remedy, any medicine, a cure, magical potion, any charm
majinya	a medical nurse; someone who nurses a family member
makaranta	a place for learning/reading; a school; an informal Koranic school (*makarantar allo*); a Christian church
malam	Islamic teacher or scholar, sometimes understood to have special powers to make healing and preventive medicines in the forms of drinks and charms
marabout	Muslim religious teacher
maye/mayu	evil sorcerer/sorcerers
ruhu mai tsarki	The Holy Spirit
salla/salat	ritual prayer of Muslims
sarauta	offices open to members of the Habe ruling aristocracy
Sarki	traditional ruler of Hausa-speaking kingdoms, chosen from among members of the sarauta class

tarbiyya	training, education, self-discipline, initiation into Sufi order
Ubangiji	Creator God, used by Christians to refer to God, epithet of Allah; father of all houses
wasa	dance, play, joking relations
'Yan Izala	Members of the Islamic reformist Movement for Suppressing Innovations and Restoring the Sunna
zummuntar mata	women's association; Christian women's fellowship groups, often implying membership in a singing group for married women

Notes

Introduction

1. In the current Bush administration, General William G. Boykin, a senior figure in the Pentagon, likened the war against Islamic militants to a battle against Satan while speaking to a prayer breakfast. He was not reprimanded (Jehl and Firestone 2003, A1). His way of thinking about the world has fearsome policy implications and, evidently, fund-raising potential.

2. Excellent historical studies would include Joseph-Roger de Benoist's 1987 study of the Catholic church in Soudan and Jean-François Zorn's 1993 study of the Mission de Paris. A very welcome departure from the pattern is Bernard Salvaing's comparative study of missionaries in the nineteenth century (1994). Political scientists do not seem to have the same blinders that historians of francophone Africa have; see, for example, Médard (1997).

3. Classic studies of missions in Africa focus on denominational missions of European origin. See Wright (1971), Beidelman (1982), Comaroff and Comaroff (1991 and 1997), and Ayandele (1966). More recent studies that have taken up the faith mission phenomenon globally include Carpenter and Shenk (1990) and Brouwer, Gifford, and Rose (1996).

4. There are, of course, exceptions, such as the long history of Firestone in Liberia.

5. Unless otherwise indicated, all citations from the Bible are from the King James Version. For alternate readings of this passage, see Walls 1996, 48. For the fundamentalist operationalization of this idea, see Patrick Johnstone and Jason Mandryk's "Operation World" Web site, available at http://www.gmi.org/ and annual "Operation World" publications (e.g., Johnstone 1993).

6. There is nothing "natural" about the absence or weakness of African states—current circumstances are, among other things, the result of systematic policies of the International Monetary Fund and the World Bank and the political dynamics of the post–Cold War period. Yet disaster in Africa is treated as if were natural or inevitable, and the replacement of the state with religious NGOs is heralded as heroic. See, for example, the enthusiasm of Kristof (2003, A15). Evangelical NGOs fill a void, but the larger question is why that void persists and how it was created.

7. Parallels with SIM in existing literature on missions in Africa would be studies of the East African stations of the Africa Inland Mission, with which SIM was in great sympathy, which is discussed in the work of Richard Waller (1999) and David Sandgren (1989). In West Africa, SIM felt most kinship with the Sudan United Mission (SUM) theologically, but after a brief romance in 1906–1907 the

two missions parted ways. It would be interesting to know more about why, given how much more politically engaged SUM eventually became in comparison with SIM (Corwin 1993; Turaki 1993, 69–72; on SUM in Nigeria, see Kastfelt 1994).

8. Today SIM resists the tag "fundamentalist"; however, interviews with older missionaries make it clear that the mission and major evangelical leaders such as Billy Graham were once comfortable with that self-designation (Burt Long interview, November 26, 1986).

9. SIM's doctrinal statement can be accessed on its Web site: www.sim.org. SIM is the largest and most significant of the missions operating in Niger; it began work in 1924 before the arrival of Catholic missionaries in 1931. Other Protestant missions followed, but none have had the long history and the broad scope that SIM has enjoyed. The African Christian Mission began work in the Niger River area near Niamey in 1929, the Baptist International Mission began work among the Tuareg of Agadez in 1966, and Southern Baptists began evangelization to Fulani in 1989. The Assemblies of God and Calvary Missions, which focus largely in Niamey, opened work in the mid-1980s. A smattering of other missions are also at work, including Youth with a Mission, Portes Ouverts, and Sahara Desert Mission, all of which focus on nomadic groups in northern Niger (Cunningham 1996, 6–7).

10. Marty and Appleby's influential if diffuse working definition of fundamentalism for their five-volume Fundamentalism Project is that it is a "habit of mind" in which "beleaguered believers" who feel their identity to be at risk in the contemporary era "fortify it by a selective retrieval of doctrines, beliefs, and practices from a sacred past" (Marty and Appleby 1993b, 3). Their approach, while opening the door to considerable scholarly discussion, is too loosely defined to be useful for thinking through the gender implications of fundamentalisms.

11. One of the most interesting of his discoveries is that in terms of class background, U.S. fundamentalists of the period were similar to the overall population of Protestants as a whole. Class distinctions are much more obvious between Protestant churches (compare Episcopalians with rural Southern Baptists, for example) than between fundamentalists and Protestants.

1. Anatomy of a Riot

1. For the sake of simplicity, I have named major neighborhoods of the city rather than the many administrative units into which Maradi is divided today. This map is adapted from Map 1.8 in Grégoire (1992) and from Carte no. 3 in Meunier (1997). I have also benefited from an unpublished schematic map produced by SIM.

2. I have indicated a few of the larger mosques and the *madrasas* that offer an all-day program that mirrors the broader education offered in public schools in terms of mathematics, language training, and exposure to the sciences. I have not attempted to show the countless small neighborhood mosques and Koranic schools (*makarantar allo*) that offer only instruction in reading the Koran. For an excellent study of Islamic schooling, see Meunier (1997).

3. The 80 percent figure appears in the CIA's *World Factbook* entry for Niger, which has been cited regularly elsewhere. See *The World Factbook*, available online at http://www.cia.gov/cia/publications/factbook (accessed June 15, 2005). The site offers no source for the figure, however.

4. Responses in northern Nigeria to the September 11 attack were equally mixed (see Danfulani and Fwatshak 2002, 251).

5. Niger ranks 176th of 177 countries listed in the 2004 human development index (United Nations Development Programme 2004).

6. I have decided not to offer the precise names of the individual parties to the conflicts in Maradi, although they are well known in Maradi and some of the names have been used in radio and print media. The names of minor players in what I describe are also pseudonyms. Where representatives of major associations in Niamey have chosen to be quoted and identified in the international press I do identify them by name; the reader should not assume that such protesters and spokespersons were themselves engaged in any subsequent violence. I quote them in order to suggest the nature of some of the local objections to FIMA.

7. It has recently been discovered that many children in the neighboring town of Tsibiri have been permanently deformed by overfluoridation of the state water supply (Mahamane 2001). Rumor has it that many children died in a previous state-supported anti-meningitis vaccination campaign when corrupt officials replaced the vaccine with a serum that turned out to be toxic. They sold the real vaccine on the black market to the highest bidder. The government's belated interest in promoting condom use in the context of an anti-AIDS campaign has been readily confused with the efforts of international agencies to promote family planning.

8. In Alphady's plan, new information technologies would link artisan and vendor and avoid opportunistic middlemen. Artisans would receive a fair price for their goods. Alphady's vision also included a school of fashion design in Niger.

9. A transnational Tuareg insurgency in the north wracked Niger and neighboring states for five years until a peace accord with the insurgents was signed in 1995. The ongoing violence caused serious disruption to Niger's modest tourist sector and was a severe disincentive to international investors.

10. Alphady's fashion initiative had given rise to tension in the past. The first FIMA was held in Agadez in 1998 and occasioned such friction that the organizers decided not to hold the event in 1999. The notion in 2000 was, one supposes, that Niamey is a more cosmopolitan setting than Agadez and that the financial stakes were high enough to make it worth trying again. After a brief hiatus in the wake of the riots, the festival was again held in Niger in 2003 with little disruption.

11. Subsequent to the events discussed here, single women accused of prostitution were systematically arrested in Niamey at the behest of Muslim leaders, who blame the poor rains on the sins of Muslims who were led into temptation by prostitutes (BBC 2002).

2. Love and Violence

1. SIM Quarterly Report, October–December 1943, Zinder Resumes 1935–1945, folder SR-2A, Box 188, SIM International Archive, Fort Mill, South Carolina (hereafter SIMIA).

2. SIM Quarterly Report, January–March 1944, Zinder Resumes 1935–1945, folder SR-2A, Box 188, SIMIA.

3. SIM Quarterly Report, January–March 1945, Zinder Resumes 1945–1968, folder SR-2, Box 188, SIMIA.

4. SIM Quarterly Reports, April–June 1949 and July–September 1949, Zinder Resumes 1945–1968, folder SR-2, Box 188, SIMIA.

5. For an excellent discussion of the "complex whole" of Pentecostal meetings of organizations such as Christ for All Nations in Africa, see Gifford (1987). Like me, Gifford is struck by the absence of attention to Jesus' ethical teachings in this strand of Christianity. The emphasis instead is upon healing and demonology.

6. Pastor Iro, guest sermon on Vie Abondante *Muryar Ceto* radio program, March 21, 1999. I am very grateful to Vie Abondante missionary Neal Childs, who lent me tapes of the sermons discussed here.

7. This is my translation into English of the Hausa text of II Timothy 2:22 that Pastor Iro used. The King James Version reads, "Flee also youthful lusts: but follow righteousness, faith, charity, peace, with them that call on the Lord out of a pure heart." The 1979 Hausa Bible consistently uses a single word, "*'kauna*," to translate several different Greek words associated with the concept "love." The English translations occasionally distinguish the Greek concepts: the King James Version of the passage from Luke quoted in the epigraph translates the word "*agape*" as "love," while it translates the word "*caritas*" in the letter to Timothy as "charity." But in the revised Hausa Bible, both words are translated with the word "*'kauna.*"

8. Pastor Daniel, *Muryar Ceto* radio program, March 28, 1999.

9. Pastor Huseini, *Muryar Ceto* radio program, April 11, 1999.

10. Pastor Isa, *Muryar Ceto* radio program, April 25, 1999.

11. Pastor Sahiru, *Muryar Ceto* radio program, May 9, 1999.

12. Pastor Sahiru, *Muryar Ceto* radio program, September 3 and 10, 2000.

3. From "Satan's Masterpiece" to "The Social Problem of Islam"

1. For a penetrating critique of American evangelicalism from within, see Mark A. Noll's cri de coeur, *The Scandal of the Evangelical Mind* (1994). He points out that evangelicalism need not imply either anti-intellectualism or fundamentalism. More than one non-American missionary with SIM remarked to me, only half in jest, that they experienced greater culture shock when dealing with the Americans than when they interacted with the Nigérien population they had come to serve.

2. Thus, despite some interesting commonalities, the tone and thrust of the

SIM endeavor differed in important ways from the worldview of the Noncon-formist missionaries Jean and John Comaroff studied (1991, 49–85).

3. Quoted in Isichei 1995, 209. For the works and philosophy of Hippolyte Berlier, which are so very different in spirit from those of SIM, see André Ber-thelot's useful biography of the bishop (1997).

4. The literature on evangelical women and their prominence despite the patriarchal strands within the movement is at this point quite rich. Noll provides a useful overview (2001), and central texts include Juster (1994), Robert (1997), Griffith (1997), and Brasher (1998).

5. By the late nineteenth century, women's work in missions was not so much unrecognized as it was unquantifiable. This has made it difficult to reconstruct their history (Kirkwood 1993, 28).

4. A Hausa Spiritual Vernacular

1. The notion of the middle figure was articulated by Nancy Hunt in 1999.

2. Philips (2000) has analyzed in detail the interweaving of mission and co-lonial interests that resulted in the emergence of Romanized Hausa print (boko) over ajami.

3. George Percy Bargery compiled A Hausa-English Dictionary and English-Hausa Vocabulary, which was regarded as indispensable among SIM missionaries in Niger in the 1940s and 1950s; it was first published in 1934 and was reprinted in 1951 and 1993. The Bargery dictionary supplanted the older Dictionary of the Hausa Language compiled by Charles Robinson (1899; reprint, Cambridge: Cam-bridge University Press, 1925), which, like the Bargery dictionary, was generated as a collaborative enterprise between missionaries and British colonial government authorities. Reverend Bargery served in the Nigerian Education Department and later was a lecturer in Hausa at the premier training institution for British colonial administrators, the School of Oriental Studies in London. The dictionary I have tended to prefer myself is R. C. Abraham's much richer Dictionary of the Hausa Language, which did not appear until 1958 and does not include an English-Hausa vocabulary, so it was of less use to missionaries in the field. Abraham assisted Bargery in compiling the 1934 dictionary along with a host of other helpers, in-cluding Malam Mamudu of Kano, whose contribution Bargery recognized in the preface (1934/1993, vii). The "helper" referred to by Ray de la Haye in the in-terview appears to be a different scholar, Malam Musa Nahann Danjuma.

4. Among the many demands on Miller was considerable secular translation work for the colonial government which he could ill afford to refuse (Philips 2000).

5. The Sudan United Mission was a faith mission in general sympathy with SIM that was founded in 1904 by Karl Kumm with the aim of creating mission stations where Islam and traditional religion came into contact. The motivations of the two missions were so similar that SIM and SUM briefly entertained a merger in 1926, but the venture collapsed (Isichei 1995, 89, 266).

6. For a similar process elsewhere, see James 1988, 227.

7. Compare Lamine Sanneh's theory of translatability, which argues that the

enrichment of Christianity through the vernacular principal renders it less static than Islam. Despite the dynamism of the model, it implies a prior authentic traditional spiritual practice and an identifiably distinct realm in Islam (1994).

5. African Agency and the Growth of the Church in the Maradi Region

1. Acting Lieutenant-Gouverneur Jore, "Rapport Politique Annuel 1924, Colonie du Niger," Affaires politiques: Niger, 2G24, (14miom/1705), Centre des Archives d'Outre-Mer (hereafter CAOM).

2. The period of relatively cordial relations between the French and British administrations from 1920 to 1935 stands in stark contrast with the tensions that emerged during World War II. Administrators regularly shared information about religious activities, medical problems, pilgrims to Mecca, and trade. Accused criminals were successfully extradited in both directions.

3. "Rapport Politique Annuel 1927," Affaires politiques: Niger, 2G27 (12), (14miom/1713), CAOM.

4. Drusille and David Osborne to "Dear Brother Trout," June 1928, Tsibiri Resumes 1930–1945, folder SR-2A, Box 188, SIMIA.

5. Drusille Osborne to Mr. Trout, March 20, 1928, Tsibiri Resumes 1930–1945, folder SR-2A, Box 188, SIMIA.

6. Murray Last has recently argued that the history of the Hausa-speaking region in the nineteenth and twentieth centuries can be told only by attending to the youth of the young men engaged in many of its most striking moments of change. He points out in particular the relative youth of the leaders of the jihad of Usman 'dan Fodio (2003).

7. Drusille and David Osborne to "Dear Brother Trout."

8. This region's first experience of the French was, sadly, the devastation caused by the Voulet-Chanoine expedition of 1899. For a full but rather journalistic account, see Simoën (1996).

9. "Rapport Politique 1930," Affaires politiques: Niger, 2G30 (11), (14miom/1729), CAOM.

10. Ibid.

11. "List of Professing Christians 1933," Tsibiri Church Records, Box 188, SIMIA.

12. Ibid.

13. "List of Professing Christians at Gidan Marafa, 1933," Tsibiri Church Records, Box 188, SIMIA.

14. "History to 1933," Tsibiri Church Records, folder SR-2, Box 188, SIMIA.

15. Ibid.

16. "A Trek Diary" Friday, June 21, 1946, letter from Rita Salls to her sisters. In author's possession.

6. Disciplining the Christian

1. The quote is a paraphrase of Ephesians 6:12 in prayer letter from D. V. and D. M. Osborne to "Dear Friends," July 31, 1937, Zinder Resumes, folder SR-

2A, Box 188, SIMIA. SIM missionaries sent "prayer letters" to large numbers of supporters with news from the field, requests for prayer support, and hints about financial and staffing needs for fund-raising. The letters were also used in the regional field offices (Zinder, Maradi, Tsibiri) to assist in writing colorful quarterly reports. They were forwarded from field offices to the central offices of SIM in Canada and later the United States, where they were copied and sent to lists of friends and donors through broader evangelical networks. Portions of prayer letters were often reprinted in *The Sudan Witness*.

2. Prayer letter from D. V. and D. M. Osborne to "Dear Christian Friend," November 1938, Tsibiri Church Records, folder SR-2A, Box 188, SIMIA.

3. Minutes of Tibiri Church Meeting, August 25, 1938, Tsibiri Church Records, folder SR-2, Box 188, SIMIA. Until 1945, Tsibiri Church meetings were open to the whole congregation and were held on weekday evenings on the SIM mission compound, just outside of Tsibiri town. After 1945, the Church meetings were replaced by Elders Council meetings, open only to members of the Church Elders Council. After the new church building was built in Tsibiri town in 1948, the Elders Council meetings were held in the church building rather than the SIM mission compound.

4. "List of Professing Christians 1933," Tsibiri Church Records, folder SR-2, Box 188, SIMIA.

5. Ibid.

6. "Les Chrétiens qui peuvent lire et écrire, 1945," Tsibiri Church Records, folder SR-2, Box 188, SIMIA.

7. Anonymous and undated prayer letter, "Encouraging word comes to us from Mr. and Mrs. D.M. Osborne of Tsibiri," n.d. [ca. 1934], Tsibiri Church Records, folder SR-2A, Box 188, SIMIA.

8. "List of Professing Christians 1933."

9. See, for example, "Minutes of Tsibiri Church Meetings," June 20, 1935, and August 5, 1935, Tsibiri Church Records, folder SR-2, Box 188, SIMIA.

10. "Encouraging word comes to us from Mr. and Mrs. D.M. Osborne of Tsibiri."

11. Prayer letter from David Osborne to "Dear Friends," January 1934, Tsibiri Church Records, folder SR-2A, Box 188, SIMIA. The other woman was Habsu.

12. Minutes of Tsibiri Church Meeting, December 23, 1935, Tsibiri Church Records, folder SR-2, Box 188, SIMIA.

13. The word *"tsibiri"* refers to an area of land surrounded by seasonal flood water—a kind of inland island. The town of Tsibiri is named for this phenomenon, as it was built next to the seasonal watercourse, the Goulbin Maradi. Often English-speakers spell the name of the town "Tibiri," omitting the "s." Conventional usage in French includes the "s."

14. Minutes of Tsibiri Church Meeting, June 4, 1933, Tsibiri Church Records, folder SR-2, Box 188, SIMIA.

15. "Tsibiri Church History," n.d., Tsibiri Church Records, folder SR-2, Box 188, SIMIA.

16. Prayer letter from D. V. and D. M. Osborne to "Dear Friends," July 31, 1937, Tsibiri Church Records, folder SR-2, Box 188, SIMIA.

17. Church Elders Council Meeting, Agenda, September 3, 1952, Tsibiri Church Records, folder SR-2, Box 188, SIMIA.

18. "List of Professing Christians 1933."

19. For the rich layers of symbolic meanings attached to numbers, cutting, and animal sacrifice that render the distinction between local animist practice and local Islamic practice slippery, see Nicolas (1975, 84–85, 232, 243).

20. Prayer letter from D. V. and D. M Osborne to "Dear Friend," May 1930, Tsibiri Church Records, folder SR-2A, Box 188, SIMIA.

21. Church Elders Council Meeting, Minutes, October 2, 1945, Tsibiri Church Records, folder SR-2, Box 188, SIMIA.

22. Church Elders Council Meeting, Minutes, February 5, 1946, folder SR-2, Box 188, Tsibiri Church Records, SIMIA.

23. Church Elders Council Meeting, Minutes, March 5, 1946, Tsibiri Church Records, folder SR-2, Box 188, SIMIA.

24. Church Elders Council Meeting, Minutes, June 4, 1946, Tsibiri Church Records, folder SR-2, Box 188, SIMIA.

25. Quarterly Report, October–December 1934, Tsibiri Resumes, 1930–1945, folder SR-2A, Box 188, SIMIA.

26. Marie Schroeder to "Dear Prayer Partner," June 1944, Tsibiri Resumes, folder SR-2A, Box 188, SIMIA.

27. Church Elders Council Meeting, Agenda, October 2, 1945, Tsibiri Church Records, folder SR-2, Box 188, SIMIA.

28. Ibid.

29. Church Elders Council Meeting, Minutes, April 8, 1948, and May 24, 1948; Church Elders Council Meeting, Agenda, September 16, 1948, all in Tsibiri Church Records, folder SR-2, Box 188, SIMIA.

30. Church Elders Council Meeting, Minutes, July 16, 1952, Tsibiri Church Records, folder SR-2, Box 188, SIMIA.

31. Church Elders Council Meeting, Agenda, July 23, 1952; "Horo," n.d. [ca. 1944], both in Tsibiri Church Records, folder SR-2, Box 188, SIMIA.

32. Quarterly Report, October–December 1942, Zinder Resumes, folder SR-2, Box 188, SIMIA.

33. Church Elders Council Meeting, Minutes, April 2, 1945, Tsibiri Church Records, folder SR-2, Box 188, SIMIA.

34. Church Elders Council Meeting, Minutes, June 5, 1945, Tsibiri Church Records, folder SR-2, Box 188, SIMIA.

35. Quarterly Report, April–June 1946, Tsibiri Resumes, folder SR-2A, Box 188, SIMIA; emphasis in original.

36. "1954 Niger Territory Regional Conference," Maradi Resumes, folder SR-1, Box 187, SIMIA.

37. Church Elders Council Meeting, Minutes, March 3, 1948, Tsibiri Church Records, folder SR-2, Box 188, SIMIA.

38. "Accursed for Christ's Sake," ca. 1957, Maradi Girls' School Resumes, folder SR-1, Box 187, SIMIA.

39. Elder's Council Meeting, Minutes, June 5, 1945, Tsibiri Church Records, folder SR-2, Box 188, SIMIA.

40. Fieldnotes, January 25, 2001

41. G. Bishop to R. J. Davis, June 29, 1956; R. J. Davis to G. Bishop, July 4, 1956, both in Zinder Miscellaneous, folder SR-2, Box 188, SIMIA.

42. Quarterly Report July–September 1948, Dogondoutchi Resumes, folder SR-1, Box 186, SIMIA.

43. See Quarterly Reports: April–June 1955, January–March 1956, and July–September 1957, Dogondoutchi Resumes, folder SR-1, Box 186, SIMIA.

44. Quarterly Report March 1958, Dogondoutchi Resumes, folder SR-1, Box 186, SIMIA.

45. Third Quarterly Report, 1963, Dogondoutchi Resumes, folder SR-1, Box 186, SIMIA.

7. "An Extremely Dangerous Suspect"

1. See also Inspecteur de 1ère classe des Colonies Bourgeois-Gavardin, "Mission d'Inspection au Niger," 1941, Fonds Ministériels, Affaires Politiques 634 (8), CAOM. Materials cited from the Centre des Archives d'Outre-Mer (CAOM) are of two kinds: paper documents that belonged to the different ministries in Paris or microfilmed documents that were all records of the AOF, the originals of which are in Dakar. Ministerial documents are designated Fonds Ministériels. The documents used in this work all come from a subset of the Fonds Ministériels that was generated by the Direction des Affaires Politiques, a section within the Ministère des Affaires Étrangers. These documents are divided up into boxes and dossiers, for which I have provided the numbers. I have then offered a descriptive name for the document, the author (where known), and the date (where known). Citations from the microfilmed records of the AOF include two kinds of locators. I have given the original designations of the documents as they were generated by the colonial administration in Dakar and I have also provided the microfilm number and reel number. All AOF documents consulted at COAM are to be found in the same microfilm set, designated 14miom.

2. Falvy, "Rapport Politique 1941," 2G41 (23) (14miom/189), CAOM.

3. Quarterly Report, October–December 1940, Tsibiri Resumes, Box 188, SIMIA.

4. Anonymous report, "Missions au Niger" 1941. 17G115 (14miom/2310), CAOM.

5. Quarterly Report, January–March 1942, Tsibiri Resumes, folder SR-2A, Box 188, SIMIA.

6. Guadalcanal was occupied by Japanese forces in July 1942 and recaptured by the Allies in February 1943 in a series of major battles. Missionaries were cut off from most sources of information about the war after 1940.

7. Extract of Annual Report, Côte d'Ivoire, 1940, Affaires politiques AOF, Missions: divers, 17G115 (14miom/2310), CAOM.

8. Gouverneur Falvy to Gouverneur Général de l'AOF, Dakar, 8 mai 1941, Confidential telegram 235, Affaires Politiques 17G115, CAOM.

9. See "Sabveutious à divers oeuvres missionaires" 1941–49, Fonds Ministériels, Affaires Politiques, 2196 (9) in CAOM on the regular subventions of the Vichy government to the Séminaire des Colonies, a Catholic seminary that trained Catholic priests for mission work overseas. The subventions ended with the close of the war, although the French government continued to help missionaries of all de-

nominations return home after being stranded during the war. For an extended and nuanced study of the relations between the Catholic church and Vichy, see Halls (1995).

10. Telegram from Vichy authorities to Gouverneur-Général in Dakar dated December 10, 1941, confirming safe conduct for a French Protestant pastor, Eugène Marchand, to "reinforce the numbers of French Protestant missions," 17G115 (14miom/2310), CAOM.

11. Letter from Sécrétaire Général Morel, Côte d'Ivoire, to Gouverneur-General of the AOF, Pierre Boisson, Dakar, dated March 22, 1942, on subject of Protestants and need for umbrella group, Affaires politiques AOF, Missions: divers, 17G115 (14miom/2310), CAOM.

12. Pastor J. Keller, Délégué général des Missions Protestantes en AOF in Dakar to Monsieur le Directeur de la Sureté Général, 29 décembre 1942, Affaires politiques AOF, Missions: divers, 17G115 (14miom/2310), CAOM.

13. In a "Bulletin hebdomadaire de renseignement" (weekly information bulletin) of November 13, 1939, marked "secret," Jean Rapenne, governor of Niger, reported on the loyalty of teachers and students to "la France menacée" and on the favorable response of the ministry of foreign affairs to SIM's request to expand its operations in Niger. Jean Rapenne, "Bulletin hebdomadaire de renseignement," 13 novembre 1939, Affaires politiques: divers, 11G31 (14miom/2208). See also Jean Rapenne, "Rapport Politique Annuel, 1939," Affaires politiques: Niger, 2G39 (4) (14miom/1803). Both in CAOM.

14. Jean Rapenne to Osborne 1543/ P/A, sujet "Construction d'une léproserie," le 13 juin 1940, Records of the Afrique Occidentale Française, 1H 73 versement 144, Archives du Sénégal, Dakar.

15. Jean Rapenne to Osborne 2354/S, sujet "Creation d'une léproserie Maradi," le 17 Septembre 1940, Records of the Afrique Occidentale Française, 1H73 versement 144, Archives du Sénégal.

16. Excerpt from the "Rapport Politique, Niger, 1941," Affaires politiques: divers, 11G21 (14miom/2204), CAOM.

17. Secret telegram from Governor Falvy to Genesuper, Dakar no. 101, transmission no. 53, 28 fev. 1941, Affaires politiques: divers, 11G32–36 (14 miom/2209), CAOM.

18. Excerpt from the "Rapport Politique, Niger, 1941."

19. David M. Osborne, Missionnaire in Tibiri (Maradi) to Monsieur le Gouverneur du Niger, Niamey, le 12 Décembre 1942, Affaires politiques AOF, Missions: divers, 17G115 (14miom/2310), CAOM.

20. African Christians I spoke with claimed that the "American" missionaries regarded Newton Kapp as a potential *German* spy. Kapp was an Armenian born in Georgia but schooled in American institutions in Egypt and the United States. He would have been very different from the Americans—he was fluent in several languages including Arabic and he rented a Hausa-style house in Maradi off the mission compound in 1940. During the war, he violated the anti-material bias of the mission by conducting trade to stay afloat. A true cosmopolitan, he had friends among the French, the Nigérien *evolués*, and the Lebanese traders (Ray de la Haye interview). Kapp's willingness to build ties with the Vichy administration probably contributed to tensions among the missionaries. The fact that Governor Toby seemed confident that correspondence was being carried across the border to Ni-

geria could also have given Osborne and others the impression that someone inside the mission was passing along information.

21. J. Keller, "Rapport de tournée," 12 janvier au 26 mai 1942, Affaires politiques AOF, Missions: divers, 17G115 (14miom/2310), CAOM.

22. Ibid.

23. Pasteur J. Keller to Monsieur le directeur de la Sureté Générale, Dakar 29 décembre 1942, Affaires politiques AOF, Missions: divers, 17G115 (14miom/2310), CAOM.

24. Roderick Kedward suggests that the long history of Protestant resistance in the face of religious persecution in some regions of France may have contributed to the Maquis outlaw culture of the resistance movement (1985, 232–251).

25. When the foreign ministry finally began to systematically collect materials on missions in French colonies in Africa, it had to turn to the Société des Missions Évangéliques de Paris, which itself had only partial data; Charles Folz, "Societés des Missions travaillant dous les Colonies françoises," 1946, Questions religieuses (missions), FM2192, CAOM.

26. Pasteur J. Keller, "Note sur la délégation général des missions Protestantes en AOF," 5 oct 1943, Affaires politiques AOF, Missions: divers, 17G115 (14miom/2310), CAOM.

27. Correspondence on Pasteur Keller's pro-Vichy leanings, Fonds Ministériels 2190 (1), CAOM.

28. "Enquête parmi les Missions Protestantes du Cameroun et de l'A.E.F. 19 juin 1943 au 1 avril 1944, par l'Aumonier Marcel J. Brun," Federation des missions Protestantes 1943, Fonds Ministériels 2190 (2), CAOM.

29. Ibid.

30. Pleven proposed Étienne Boegner as head of the Free French delegation in the United States in 1941, although de Gaulle eventually chose the socialist Tixier. It is possible that the fracas between Brun and Boegner contributed to Boegner's falling out with the Gaullists, who later accused him, according to Halls, of "poisoning the minds of the Americans against de Gaulle" (Halls 1995, 154).

31. "Situation Juridique Comparée des Missions, 1944," Fonds Ministériels 2190 (3); "Questions Religieuses: Missions," Fonds Ministériels 2192; "Enquête sur les Missions Religieuses au Niger," 1945, Fonds Ministériels 2190; G. Monod, "Influence des Missions Protestantes en Afrique noire," 1945, Fonds Ministériels 2190 (7); and Christian Merlo, "Fondement juridique d'une politique missionaire positive," 1955, Fonds Ministériels 3369 (4). All in CAOM.

32. "Enquête sur les Missions Religieuses 1945," Fonds Ministériels 2190, CAOM. SIM's Niger staff included five French citizens, three Canadians, one New Zealander, four English, and sixteen Americans. More than half of the personnel were from the United States.

33. Charles Foltz, of the Société des Missions Évangéliques de Paris, report to the Foreign Ministry, "Sociétés de Mission travaillant dans les Colonies françaises," 17 mai 1946, Questions religieuses (missions), Fonds Ministériels 2192, CAOM.

34. "Rapport Politique Annuel 1945," Affaires politiques: Niger, 2G45 17 (14miom/1863), CAOM.

35. "Rapport Statistique Annuel 1946," Fonds Ministériels 386, (77 bis/8), CAOM.

36. After the war and in the context of the growth of political activity as decolonization loomed on the horizon, Lieutenant-Colonel Cases, the head of the AOF police force, ordered the heads of the police in Niger, Togo, Bamako, Conakry, Porto-Novo, and Gao to produce secret studies of foreign missions in the AOF. Letter from Lieutenant-Colonel Cases, Commandant de détachement de gendarmerie de l'AOF, to the Gouverneur-Général de l'AOF Pierre Cournarie December 16, 1946, Afrique Occidentale Française, 17G141 (14miom/2318). The report on Niger was authored by Adjudant Fajole, the sergeant heading the police force in Niger, "Rapport sur l'importance, l'organisation, l'influence, et l'activité des missions religieuses installées au Niger," November 28, 1946, Afrique Occidentale Française, 17G141 (14miom/2318). Both in CAOM.

37. Confidential report: "Affaires Politiques, Niger," juillet 1946, Affaires politiques: divers, 11G21 (14miom/2204), CAOM; emphasis added.

38. "Renseignement: Origine: Maradi, 21/1/1947, Objet: activité des missions religieuses étrangères," Affaires politiques: divers, 11G21 (14miom/2204), CAOM.

39. Gouverneur du Niger Colombani, "Rapport Politique Annuel, 1948," Affaires politiques: Niger, 2G48 2 (14miom/1887), CAOM.

40. "Rapport politique 1949," Affaires politiques: Niger, 2G49 29 (14miom/1903), CAOM.

41. "Rapport politique annuel 1950," Affaires politiques: Niger, 2G50 30 (14miom/1917), CAOM.

42. "Rapport Politique annuel 1951," marked confidential by Gov. Casimir, Affaires politiques: Niger, 2G51 36 (14miom/1934), CAOM.

43. Letter from Directeur du Service Général d'Hygiène Mobile et de Prophylaxie to Monsieur le Directeur Général de la Sante Publique en A.O.F. no 1783, 4 mai 1953, Records of the Afrique Occidentale Française, 1 H 73 versement 144, Archives du Sénégal.

44. G. Monod, "Influence des Missions protestantes en Afrique noire," 1945, 19–20, Fonds Ministériels, Affaires politiques 2190 (7), CAOM.

45. Ibid., 59.

8. Impasses in Vernacular Education

1. "Rapport Politique 1949," Affaires politiques: Niger, 2G49 29 (14miom/1903), CAOM.

2. "Rapport Statistique Annuel 1946," 6, Fonds Ministériels Carton 386, Dossier 77 bis/8, CAOM.

3. "Rapport politique annuel 1950," Affaires politiques: Niger, 2G50 30 (14miom/1917), CAOM.

4. Rita Salls to Marie Murray, February 5, 1959, in author's possession.

5. Fieldnotes, February 22, 2001.

6. This is a rather familiar pattern of gendering mission education that is shaped at least in part through the predispositions of the colonial state; see Gaitskell (2002).

7. Minutes of Education Committee (Tsibiri school planning committee),

July 20, 1966, Dossiers: École Primaire Privée Tsibiri, Église Évangélique de la République du Niger Archives, Maradi (hereafter EERN Archives).

8. Ibid.; my translation from the Hausa. Words in quotes appear as in original.

9. Fieldnotes, February 22, 2001.

10. "Rapport d'activité de l'école primaire privée EERN 1992," from Claude Traoré to Monsieur le Président du Conseil d'administration, April 23, 1992, Dossiers: École Primaire Privée Tsibiri, EERN Archives.

11. "Minutes of Tsibiri Primary School committee meeting of September 27, 1973," Dossiers: École Primaire Privée Tsibiri, EERN Archives.

12. "Réunion du comité directeur," February 20, 1988, Dossiers: École Primaire Privée Tsibiri, EERN Archives.

13. "Minutes of Tsibiri Primary School Committee meeting," June 22, 1977, Dossiers: École Primaire Privée Tsibiri, EERN Archives. With the advent of independence the mission increasingly began to speak of African Christians as "nationals" of particular independent nations rather than as "natives."

14. The first hint of such an incident for which I found archival documentation appears in minutes for a meeting in 1976. A girl and two of her friends who helped her with her writing were disciplined for collaborating to send a letter to one of Pastor Kouloungou's daughters in Nigeria in which the girl alleged something "very bad." Sending a letter to the pastor's daughter was perhaps this girl's way of trying to address the issue without having to face telling an older man about a distressing problem. The girl was sent away from the school to live with a Christian family in the hope that she could be married off soon; her friends were disciplined as well. It seems rather odd to punish the children simply for sending a private letter. "Minutes of Tsibiri Primary School Committee meeting," February 28, 1976, EERN Archives.

15. "Proposition de règlement intérieure," February 10, 1978, Dossiers: École Primaire SIM, EERN Archives.

16. See, for example, "Minutes of Tsibiri School Committee Meeting," September 29, 1982, Dossiers: École Primaire Privée Tsibiri, EERN Archives.

17. "Rapport d'Activité de l'Année Scolaire 1988–1989," Dossiers: École Primaire Privée Tsibiri, EERN Archives.

18. "Convention entre SIM et l'EERN," authorizing transfer of École Primaire Privée de Tibiri to the EERN, le 19 fevrier 1990, Dossiers: EERN, EERN Archives.

19. "Rapport d'activité de l'école primaire privée EERN 1992."

20. Claude Traore to Monsieur le president de l'EERN in Zinder, May 14, 1992; Claude Traore to Monsieur le president du Conseil d'Administration, n.d., both in Dossiers: École Primaire Privée Tsibiri, EERN Archives.

21. Director of the École Primaire Privée EERN de Tibiri to Monsieur le President de l'EERN à Zinder, No. 28/E.P.T. Année Scolaire 1993–1994, Dossiers: École Primaire Privée Tsibiri, EERN Archives. According to the housemother, the teacher had repeatedly sent for the girl at night, but she refused him. One evening at sunset he asked her to bring him water and took advantage of the occasion to seize her violently and attempt to rape her. She managed to escape and wanted to leave the school permanently even though she had not yet sat for

428 / Notes to pages 290–294

the exam. In the wake of this allegation, other students claimed that this professor had been extorting money from them, threatening to beat them if they attempted to reclaim it. Director of the École Primaire Privée EERN de Tibiri to Monsieur le President de l'EERN à Zinder, No. 28/E.P.T. Année Scolaire 1993–94, EERN Archives.

9. Handmaid to the Gospel

1. Leprosy is caused by a bacillus commonly referred to as *M. leprae*, or Hansen's bacillus. While its effects can be horrifying, compared with other diseases such as smallpox and meningitis it is not easily transmitted—doctors and nurses treating Hansen's patients today simply take care to wash their hands regularly. Infection generally occurs through lengthy and close contact with an untreated person, which means that family members are at higher risk than non-family members. Not everyone who is exposed to the virus develops the illness, and once infected it can take four years before symptoms develop. The bacillus attacks skin and nerve cells, leaving discolored lesions with decreased sensitivity. In its more destructive lepromatous form, the disease spreads throughout the body causing widespread nerve and tissue damage to bones and organs (particularly the eyes, nose, testes, and larynx). Some patients with strong immunity heal spontaneously—they are "burnt out." But for those with weakened immunity, the condition may worsen. The disfiguring and debilitating loss of limbs, noses, and skin is an indirect consequence of the loss of nerves and skin cells rather than a direct result of the disease: patients lose sensitivity in areas infected by the bacillus and are easily wounded or damaged as a result. Wounds then result in infections and sores that destroy the appendages. Because there were no effective treatments for leprosy until the development of sulfone drugs in the 1950s, governments have often attempted to isolate lepers in "colonies" to prevent the spread of the disease rather than cure it. Mission leprosaria prior to the 1950s did attempt to treat the disease, but they had a great deal more success in treating its symptoms. For a fuller discussion see Silla (1998, 19–26).

2. The money AOF authorities budgeted for Niger was less than for any other colony of the AOF except Mauritania. Its facilities were less developed than those of other French colonies, and its medical staff was absurdly small. See, for example, Service de Santé, "Inspection General des Services Sanitaires et Médicaux, 1933," 1H4 versement 1, Records of the AOF, Archives du Sénégal. Extremely overworked medical officers decried the appalling state of the medical system, the colonial administration's lack of interest, and the inadequacy of the resources the administration made available; see le Médecin Lieutenant Colonel E. Le Cousse, "Rapports Médicaux mensuels, 1933," Affaires politiques: Niger, 2G33 (18) (14miom/1754), CAOM.

3. Service de la Lèpre, "Rapport Annuel de Santé, 1935," 2G35 (18), Records of the AOF, Archives du Sénégal.

4. Service de Santé, "Rapports, Hôpital de Niamey, 1945–50," 1H58 versement 163, Records of the AOF, Archives du Sénégal.

5. See, e.g., Ed Morrow's recollections of Bingham's thoughts on the limits

of prayer in a dialogue with Pentecostal missionaries in 1929; Edward Morrow, "Regarding Benin and Niger in Early Days" (transcription of interview, undated), SIMHIS 0007, SIMIA.

6. This does not mean that SIM missionaries today entirely divorce prayer and healing. As Pentecostalism has become mainstream, some missionaries have occasionally mentioned faith healing in their writings; see, for example, Brown (1993, 17).

7. Osborne's adoption of what must have been a familiar phrase is in some ways an unconscious acknowledgment that SIM was reiterating an earlier practice. See Comaroff and Comaroff (1997, 333).

8. "Rapport Médicale Annuel 1914 Territoire Militaire du Niger," 2G14 (17) (14 miom/1676), CAOM; "Rapport d'Ensemble Annuel—Niger 1920," 2G20 (14miom/1693), CAOM; Foerster, "Rapport Annuel 1943, Service de Santé, Niger," 2G43 (14) (14miom/1783), CAOM.

9. "Rapport Medicale Annuel 1914 Territoire Militaire du Niger," 2G14 (17) (14 miom/1676), CAOM; Service de Santé "La Lutte anti-amarile, 1933" 1H4 versement 1, Records of the AOF, Archives du Sénégal.

10. Kervingant, "Rapport Medicale Annuel, 1948," 2G48 26 (14miom/1891); Lorre, "Rapport sur l'épidémie de Méningite cérébro-spinale, 1950–51," 2G51 (16) (14miom/ 2732). Both in CAOM.

11. Lt. Col. Morvan, "Rapport Médical Annuel 1945," 2G45 (13) Records of the AOF, Archives du Sénégal; Lt. Gov. Jean Toby, "Rapport politique annuel 1950," 2G50 30 (14miom/1917). Both in CAOM.

12. Acting Commandant de Cercle Auge, "Rapport de Tournée dans le canton de Gober [sic] entre le 9 et le 27 mai 1936," 14.3.26, Archives nationales du Niger; Service de la Lèpre, "Rapport Annuel de Santé, 1935," 2G35 (18), Records of the AOF, Archives du Sénégal. The Service de la Lèpre was a government institution located in Bamako to serve all of the AOF. The Service at various times provided housing and experimental treatment for lepers, conducted research, and oversaw broader health campaigns related to leprosy. It also gathered data for reports on leprosy in all of the AOF. Its distance from Maradi meant that it had no utility for Hansen's sufferers in the region discussed in this book—patients would be far more likely to avail themselves of services across the border in British Nigeria than to travel all the way to Bamako.

13. Pinaud (1945); Cunin (1946).

14. Jean Rapenne to Osborne 2354/S, sujet "Creation d'une léproserie Maradi," le 17 Septembre, 1940, 1H73 versement 144; "Rapport de Sante, 1940," 2G40 (24). Both in Records of the AOF, Archives du Sénégal.

15. For an overview of missionary society attitudes toward the recruitment of women in the nineteenth century, see Williams (1993); on women's associations and their shifting relations with mission boards, see Tucker (1990); for a comprehensive treatment of American women in missions, see Robert (1997), especially 189–254; for a sympathetic study of American Protestant women in more conventionally denominational missions, see Beaver (1968/1998).

16. *The Sudan Witness* XIV, no. 1 (1938): n.p.

17. "Minutes of Leprosarium Board Meeting," Maradi Leprosarium, January 11, 1974, folder SR-1, Box 187, SIMIA.

18. "Rules of Leproserie de Maradi," November 1974, Maradi Leprosarium

Miscellaneous 1954–1978, Appendix C, pages 6K–7K, folder SR-1, Box 187, SIMIA.

19. Ibid., page 8K.

20. Ibid, page 6K.

21. This was one of the significant differences between the scientifically minded missions of the early nineteenth century and the evangelical revivalists. Where the earlier missionaries attempted to convince local populations that their spirit world was "superstitious" and that it, in effect, did not exist, later evangelicals envisioned exorcism as one of the benefits they would bring to the pagan (Ajayi 1969, 264).

22. *Bori* possession might not be madness, but *bori* ritual does seem to have a role in treating mental illness. It offers people who are suffering from acute confusion or emotional distress a way to interpret and inhabit a contradictory world. *Bori* gives them some measure of peace and hope and a community that can be a safe haven. Because of the gendering of religious practice (and perhaps of emotional distress), male Muslim reformists regularly reject *bori* as un-Islamic, and traditional Muslim women must struggle to reinterpret events in the world through the light of *bori* in ways that redeem spirit practices.

23. Masquelier's work suggests that Muslim reformists who reject *bori* do not have an alternative to offer those who are afflicted by spirits; Masquelier (2001, 78, 81). But see also O'Brien (2000, 214–270) on Muslim therapy to counter spirits in the context of northern Nigeria.

24. Older women may serve as *ungozoma*, generally translated as "midwife," but their role in childbirth is quite constrained, for they are not to enter the birthing chamber until after the baby has been born. Their task is to cut the umbilical cord. As a result, midwives in Niger have not been as useful as interfaces between "traditional" and "western" medicine as they were some other parts of Africa (see, for example, Davison 1989; Hunt 1999). *Ungozoma* often uphold local practices such as withholding the colostrum from the infant because it may be poisonous. Infants then miss out on the benefits of their mothers' antibodies and mothers suffer frequently from breast infections and abscesses.

25. *Bori* spirit cult practitioners believe that their activities can remove impediments to conception and protect the health of babies; spirit cult membership may also help women deal with the emotional crises of pregnancy (Masquelier 2001, 92–93, 80–81, 85). A woman may seek *bori* medicine to help her retain the love of her husband in a polygynous marriage that is perhaps rendered more complex by infertility, repeated pregnancies, and the rearing of small children. The community presents a haven for women rejected by their families for leaving an unhappy marriage.

26. There is a potentially tragic side to this coexistence. When the water supply in Tsibiri became contaminated with too much fluoride, parents did not seek medical treatment for their children, or even feel troubled by the growing pattern of illness, because the kind of paralysis they saw in the children was associated with a particular *bori* spirit.

27. Specialists such as bone-setters may have little relation to the occult. People in Maradi often claim that local treatments for skin ailments are far more effective than anything the pharmacy has to offer.

28. This explains somewhat Masquelier's misapprehension that there are very

few Protestant Christians in Dogondoutchi—no evangelical Christian would ever choose to be in the presence of a researcher who devoted her study to *bori*, for to do so would be to risk expulsion from the church.

29. The maternity ward substantially improved maternal health in the region as women began to seek help with unusual deliveries earlier in the process by 1988. The hospital had less success in transforming local *ungozoma* into *matrones*, or genuine midwives. Even after they had been trained, *ungozoma* still went into the home of a woman only after she had given birth and continued to cut the umbilical cord with dirty razor blades. Harry Enns, "An Evaluation of the Galmi Village Health Project" presented for the course Interventions in Public Health at Université Laval, Quebec, April 1988, SIMNIG 0019, SIMIA.

30. In 1969 and 1970, Dr. Jeanette Troup and nurse Charlotte Shaw succumbed to the Lassa virus; nurse Lily Pinneo, who survived the virus, provided the antibodies now used to fight the disease (SIM 1970a, 1970b).

31. Eric Silla points out that European doctors in the federation-wide mobile medicine agency organized to counter Hansen's Disease lost power to African staff in the late 1950s (Silla 1998, 111). Catholic missionaries eventually yielded to the preferences of African staff and came to emphasize treatment over conversion (146).

32. "Statuts Église Évangélique de la République du Niger EERN, 1964," Vertical File SIMRCH 0015, SIMIA.

33. "John Ockers, SIM Maridi, to Andrew Ng, Sécrétaire médicale, SIM Galmi," July 7, 1983, Dossiers: EERN, EERN Archives. Ockers copied this letter to both the EERN and SIM's central administration.

10. The Tree of Life

1. The sizes of the plots available to most Maradi farmers are well below the optimal size for the use of ox-drawn equipment (see Cooper 1997a, 57). Investing in such equipment may become rational if a farmer can hire animals and equipment out to other farmers to earn cash. Access to animal transport can also significantly improve a farmer's ability to reduce the costs of inputs and maximize the use of inputs (such as manure) that are available. Oxen are used to draw carts so that farmers can make the most of an expensive investment.

2. Seyni Kountché came into power through a coup d'etat in 1974 and governed the country under military rule until his death in 1989.

3. Under the leadership of French anthropologist Claude Raynaut, PDRM produced a number of detailed and substantial studies of the geomorphology of the region, rainfall patterns, use of natural resources, and sociological dimensions of adoption of technology using both macrolevel data and close studies of particular villages. The studies were impressive self-critical models of the kind of synergies that occur when scientific, social scientific, and development workers collaborate. The recent work of the Drylands Research group under geographer Michael Mortimore builds substantially from these studies, using them as baselines for their more positive assessments of agricultural intensification in the period since the project closed down in the late 1980s.

4. Emmanuel Isch, "Wholistic Development: An Overview of the Concept,"

Vertical File SIMNIM 0002, SIMIA; Don Stilwell, ed., "SIM Famine Relief Evaluation Report," August 1989, HV 630 S78 (spec.), 2, SIMIA.

5. Local populations suspect that western health care and aid organizations are really interested in reducing African population growth. This contributes to their skepticism and mistrust of the polio vaccine, which they believe has traces of human hormones that could act as a contraceptive.

6. In a 1999 assessment of MIDP project components to determine whether and how the mission should continue in its relationship with the secular funding agency of the Canadian government, C. Evans came to much the same conclusion as I have here (Evans 1999, 32). The mission nevertheless continues to promote "improved" stoves.

7. I am drawing from Isch, "Wholistic Development: An Overview of the Concept," Joel Matthews (1999), and Miller (1999). Special thanks to Joel Matthews for sharing his publication with me and drawing my attention to Miller's response, which most fully articulates my observation about the evident centrality of the eighth commandment. Matthews's view is rather more utopian than Miller's and Isch's; it posits the possibility of a transformed altruistic society with almost communal overtones.

11. Ça bouge

1. In this I find myself very much in sympathy with the arguments made by Wendy James in the rather different setting of Sudan (1988).

2. Adeline Masquelier has pointed out to me that ritual purity, or *tsarki*, is also important within *bori*, suggesting an even deeper shared Hausa substrate relating to cleanliness (personal communication with author).

3. I am grateful to Barbara Kapenga for many interesting and illuminating conversations about Hausa usage of Arabic loanwords in this context.

4. Fieldnotes, February 22, 2001.

5. Because I am a married woman with children, I take part in the women's group rather than the *kwaya* when I am in Maradi. My observations therefore reflect a certain bias in that direction.

6. For an interesting study of the creation of Christian songs in Tanzania, see King (2000). King was able to interview a hymnwriter, Motti Mbogo, about the creation of "youths' hymns" (which would be closer to the songs sung by the *kwaya*). The women's songs I discuss here tend to circulate a great deal, so it is difficult to determine which songs present a particular authorial interpretation of the Bible. King's point, though, is that Mbogo's hymns reflect a characteristically indigenous religiosity that emphasizes encouragement and inspiration rather than private introspection. It may be that there is a greater sense of an auteur among songs young men write for youth choirs.

7. Evangelical women in Maradi readily make a parallel between the fortuitous appearance of a ram to replace Isaac and the redemption of humans through the sacrifice of Jesus; in this song, they vividly imagine Abraham's willingness to sacrifice his son. Since women devote much of their energies to keeping children

alive, it perhaps is all the more striking to them that a parent would be willing to give up a child.

8. Washing, or *wanka*, is an important part of many major rituals aimed at healing or social transformation. A bride is washed in a decoction of various barks, for example, as part of the wedding rituals. Illnesses are sometimes cured when the patient washes in herbal medicines or in the ink washed from a board on which a suitable Koranic verse is written.

9. SIM, "Position actuelle sur la Polygamie," excerpt from *Manuel SIM*, ca. 1983.

10. The image is particularly striking in the context of Hausa architecture, for the high outer walls of most compounds mean that in order to see into someone else's house one has to find a high vantage point, such as the back of a camel, a hill, or an upturned mortar. Any similar attempt to peek into another home is at best very bad manners and at worst a crime. It is illegal to ride through the town of Maradi on the back of a camel, and many a misadventure in Hausa folktales begins with an arrogant prince on horseback looking over a compound wall at an innocent young woman.

Epilogue

1. Fieldnotes, February 14, 2001.
2. Letter to Immie Larsen from retired SIM missionary, n.d. (in author's possession).

Works Consulted

Archives

Archives du Sénégal, Dakar, Sénégal
    Fonds AOF

Archives nationales du Niger, Niamey, Niger
    Rapports de Tournée (Gobir)

Centre des Archives d'Outre-Mer, Aix-en-Provence, France (CAOM)
    Fonds Ministériels
    Afrique Occidentale Française

EERN Archives, Maradi, Niger
    Dossiers: École Primaire Privée

Maradi Integrated Development Project Records, Maradi, Niger

Private Papers of Rita Salls

SIM International Archive, Fort Mill, South Carolina (SIMIA)
    Dogondoutchie Resumes
    Maradi Girls School Resumes
    Maradi Leprosarium
    Maradi Resumes
    Tsibiri Church Records
    Tsibiri Resumes 1930–1945
    Zinder Miscellaneous
    Zinder Resumes

Interviews

Abdou, Barmo. Interview with author, November 8, 2000, Maradi, Niger.
Abdou, Madame. Interview with author, February 1, 2001, Kegel, Niger.
Buzu, Ali 'dan. Interview with author, February 9, 2001, February 19, 2001, and February 20, 2001, Maradi, Niger.

Chisholm, Liz. Interview with author, November 16, 1990, August 11, 1997, and August 12, 1997, Sebring, Florida.
Dama, Malam Labo. Interview with author, February 13, 2001, Jiratawa, Niger.
Dama, Yacoubou Labo. Unrecorded interview with author, February 26, 2001, Maradi, Niger.
Forster, Chuck. Interview with author, August 14, 1997, Sebring, Florida.
Hay, Ian and June. Interview with author, August 13, 1997, Sebring, Florida.
Haye, Ray de la. Interview with author, November 17, 1990, Sebring, Florida.
Ibrahim, Hajjiya Hawa. Interview with author, February 12, 2001, Kiriya, Niger.
Jacobson, Ruth. Interview with author, August 14, 1997, Sebring, Florida.
Jima, Malam Ibrahim 'dan. Unrecorded interview with author, February 16, 2001, Maradi, Niger.
Kashalu, Malam. Interview with author, January 30, 2001, Maradi, Niger.
Kooy, Genevieve. Interview with author, August 12, 1997, Sebring, Florida.
Lawali, Malam. Unrecorded interview with author, February 23, 2001, Maradi, Niger.
Lawali, Pastor Ayyuba. Unrecorded interview with author, February 14, 2001, Danja, Niger.
Long, Burt Elmer. Interview with Heather Conley, November 26, 1986. Collection 351, T1, Billy Graham Center Archives. Accessed online.
———. Interview with Heather Conley, December 3, 1986. Collection 351, T2, Billy Graham Center Archives. Accessed online.
Lullu'bi, Malam Yahaya. Interview with author, February 25, 2001, Maradi, Niger.
Mamayo, Pastor Adamu na. Interview with author, January 31, 2001, Danja Leprosorium, Danja, Niger.
Marafa, Jadi. Interview with author, February 5, 2001, Tsibiri, Niger.
Masoyi, A'i. Unrecorded interview with author, February 14, 2001, Danja, Niger.
Muni, A'i Mai. Interview with author, April 25, 1989, Maradi, Niger.
Nana, Pastor 'dan. Interview with author, October 24, 2000 and November 3, 2000, Soura, Niger.
Sabo, Malam. Interview with author, February 7, 2001, Maza Tsaye, Niger.
Saley, Malam. Unrecorded interview with author, February 15, 2001, Maradi, Niger.
Saley, Salamatou. Interview with author, February 6, 2001, Maradi, Niger.
Salls, Rita. Interview with author, November 16, 1990, Sebring, Florida.
———, and Ray de la Haye. Interview with author, August 12, 1997, Sebring, Florida.
Souley, Pastor Mahamane. Unrecorded interview with author, February 13, 2001, Jiratawa, Niger.
Watkins, Helen. Interview with author, August 14, 1997, Sebring, Florida.
Yacouba, Pastor Cherif. Interview with author, October 24, 2000, Maradi, Niger.
Zabriskie, Zeb. Interview with author, August 12, 1997, Sebring, Florida.

Primary Sources

Abdou, Laouali. 1999. "Le Monothéisme Trinitaire dans la relation Apologétique avec les Musulmans." Mémoire de Maîtrise en Théologie, Faculté de Théologie Évangélique de Bangui.

Abraham, R. C. 1958/1978. *Dictionary of the Hausa Language.* London: Hodder and Stoughton.

Anza, Souleymane. 2001. "Le phénomène islamiste prend de l'ampleur et inquiète au Niger." Panafrican News Agency. Available online at the Panafrican News Agency Web site, accessed October 8, 2001.

Arji, Saidou, and Noel Tadegnon. 2000. "Niger Bans Islamic Groups Opposed to Fashion Festival." Misanet.com/IPS, available online at the afrol.com Web site, accessed November 18, 2000.

Auge. 1936. "Rapport de Tournée, le commandant de cercle par interim Auge dans le canton de Gober [*sic*] entre le 9 et le 27 mai 1936." Rapports de Tournée (Gobir), 14.3.26, Archives nationales du Niger.

Bargery, G. P. 1934/1993. *A Hausa-English Dictionary and English-Hausa Vocabulary.* Zaria: Ahmadu Bello University Press.

BBC. 2002. "Niger Sinners Blamed for Drought." Available online at the BBC News Africa Web site, accessed July 22, 2002.

Beacham, Rev. C. Gordon. 1939. "Annual Field Report for Nigeria and French West Africa 1938." *The Sudan Witness* XV, no. 2: 1–3.

———. 1940. "Annual Field Report for Nigeria and French West Africa." *The Sudan Witness* XVI, no. 2: 1–3.

———. 1941a. "1941 Annual Field Report." *The Sudan Witness* XVII, no. 2: 1.

———. 1941b. "French West Africa." *The Sudan Witness* XVII, no. 3: 9.

Berdan, Elaine, R. N. 1953. "Islam Bowing!" *The Sudan Witness* XXIX, no. 3: 13–15.

Bingham, Rowland V. 1921/1952. *The Bible and the Body: Healing in the Scriptures.* Toronto: Evangelical Publishers.

———. 1938/1951. *The Burden of the Sudan.* New York: Sudan Interior Mission.

———. 1943. *Seven Sevens of Years and a Jubilee: The Story of the Sudan Interior Mission.* New York: Evangelical Publishers.

Bishop, G. 1957. "Wanted: Men Who Specialize in Preaching!" *The Sudan Witness* XXXIII, no. 2: 7.

Bourgeois-Gavardin. 1941. "Mission d'Inspection au Niger par Inspecteur de 1ère classe des Colonies Bourgeois-Gavardin." Fonds Ministériels, Affaires Politiques 634 (8), CAOM.

Brant, Howard E. 1988. "Niger—Land of Standing Millet Stalks: A Report on SIM's Ministry in Niger, West Africa." June 13, 1988. SIM Vertical Files SIMNIG 0001, SIMIA.

Brown, Wendy. 1993. "Niger: The Short and the Long of It." BV3625 N48, SIMIA.

Brun, Marcel J. 1944. "Enquête parmi les Missions Protestantes du Cameroun et de l'A.E.F. 19 juin 1943 au 1 avril 1944." Fonds Ministériels 2190 (2), CAOM.

Bulifant, Josephine C. ca. 1938. *From Pagan Child to Christian Mother: The Story of the Oro Girls' Bible School.* New York: Sudan Interior Mission.

Burt, Mark. 1994. "The Wodaabe Christians Living in the Dakoro-Maradi Axis." PGRFUW 0001, SIMIA.

CARE. 2000. "Rapport de l'Étude de Base." Projet Equité entre le Genres et Sécurité des Conditions de Vie des Ménages "Tatalin Arzikin Gida." PN51. Septembre.

Carpenter, Charles. 1959. "French West Africa: Not 1 Saved." *The Sudan Witness* XXXV, no. 1: 4.

Ceton, Dr. Jim. 1982. "There Are Times When You Can't Say 'No.'" *SIM Now* (May–June): 7.

Charlemagne, Catherine. 1996. "Le Projet de Développement de Maradi, au Niger: Un Espoir au Coeur de l'Afrique." Rapport de stage de deuxième année, été 1996, Institut National Polytechnique, École Nationale Supérieure Agronomique de Toulouse. Archived at Maradi Integrated Development Project Office.

Charles, Samuel. 1994. "Dandja: le refuge des lepreux" *Experiences* 93, no. 1: 6–12. SIM Vertical Files SIMNIG 0022 [clippings], SIMIA.

———, et Franck Keller. 1994. "Bâtir ici une église, c'est donner plus que son temps, sa sueur et ses larmes . . ." *Experiences* 93, no. 1: 23–30. SIM Vertical Files SIMNIG 0022 [clippings], SIMIA.

Chisholm, Elizabeth. 1954. "'Do They Really Want Help?'" *The Sudan Witness* XXX, no. 2: 4.

Corwin, Gary. 1993. "Events That Shaped SIM during 100 Years." SIM Vertical Files SIMHIS 0004, SIMIA.

Cox, Mrs. Harry L. 1938. "In Search of Lepers." *The Sudan Witness* XIV, no. 2: 20–21.

Cunin, M. Camille. 1946. "Rapport sur le recensement du village de Maradi Juillet-Sept 1946." Rapports de Tournée (Gobir), 14.3.98, Archives nationales du Niger.

Daniel, Pastor. 1999. Radio program. March 28. *Muyar Ceto* radio programs, Vie Abondante, Maradi, Niger.

Davis, Raymond J. 1944/1966. *Swords in the Desert.* Aylesbury: Sudan Interior Mission Books.

"Le Dispensaire, l'état et les missionaries." N.d. (Clipping from unidentified periodical.) SIM Vertical Files SIMNIG 0007, SIMIA.

Djadi, Illia. 1998. "Niger: Vives tensions politiques." SPP/01.05.98 (Service electronique).

———. 1999a. "Niger: menaces sur la cohabitation religieuse." SPP/29.07.99 (Service electronique) et *Bulletin SPP* 14, no. 19 (Aout 1999): 9–10.

———. 1999b. "Niger: Elaboration de nouveaux textes constitutionnels." SPP/15.06.99 (Service electronique) et *Bulletin SPP* 10, no. 17 (Juin 1999): 21–22.

Dorset, Verna S. 1963. "Glimpses of the Dogondoutchi Girl's Home." BV3625 N4D6, SIMIA.

Echert, Tim. 1993. "Fulani Team Strategy, July 1993." PGRFUW [no number], SIMIA.

Enns, Harry. 1988. "An Evaluation of the Galmi Village Health Project." presented for Interventions in Public Health course at Laval University, April 1988. SIM Vertical Files SIMNIG 0019, SIMIA.

Esperet. 1942. "Rapport de Tournée effectuée de 4 au 10 mai frontière ouest et limite Madaoua, Maradi par le commandant de cercle Esperet." Rapports de Tournée (Gobir), 14.3.66, Archives nationales du Niger.

Evans, C. 1999. "Comprehensive Evaluation of MIDP Program Components, 1999." CIDA/SIM Canada Agreement No. S 53491. Archived at Maradi Integrated Development Project Office.

Fajole, Adjudant. 1946. "Sur l'importance, l'organisation, l'influence, et l'activité des missions religieuses installées au Niger, le 28 novembre, 1946. Affaires politiques Afrique Occidentale Française 17G141 (14miom/2318), CAOM.

Foltz, Charles. 1946. "Sociétés de Mission travaillant dans les Colonies françaises." Report of the Société des Missions Évangéliques de Paris to the Foreign Ministry. Fonds Ministériels, Affaires Politiques, 2192, 10, CAOM.

Gosselin, M. 1934. "Tournées de recensement faites dans le sud du cantan de Maradi au cours des 1e et 2e trimestres 1934 par le Comandant de cercle de Maradi, M. Gosselin, le 30 juin 1934." Rapports de Tournée (Gobir), 14.3.21, Archives nationales du Niger.

Hall, John. 1923. "Atmosphere, Attitudes, Antagonisms." *The Sudan Witness* III, no. 3: 13–14.

Haye, Ray de la. 1943. "Hausa Bible Conference at Tsibiri." *The Sudan Witness* XIX, no. 2: 17–19.

———. 1946. "Encouragement in Gobir-land." *The Sudan Witness* XXII, no. 3: 20–21.

———. 1953. "A New Pilgrim's Progress." *The Sudan Witness* XXIX, no. 3: 27–28.

Hayes, Margaret. 1982. "'Middle Ages' Midwifery." *SIM Now* (May–June): 7.

Helser, Albert D. 1940. *The Glory of the Impossible.* Toronto: Evangelical Publishers.

The Holy Qur'an. 1946. Trans. Abdullah Yusuf Ali. Jeddah: Islamic Education Centre.

Huseini, Pastor. 1999. Radio program. April 11. *Muyar Ceto* radio programs, Vie Abondante, Maradi, Niger.

International Monetary Fund, African Department. 2002. "Niger: 2001 Article IV Consultation (January 17, 2002)." Washington: IMF Publication Services.

Iro, Pastor. 1999. Radio program. March 21. *Muyar Ceto* radio programs, Vie Abondante, Maradi, Niger.

Isa, Pastor. 1999. Radio program. April 4. *Muyar Ceto* radio programs, Vie Abondante, Maradi, Niger.

Isch, Emmanuel. 1989a. "Report on the Spiritual Impact of the Maradi Integrated Development Project (Niamey)." June. Archived at Maradi Integrated Development Project Office.

———. 1989b. "Rapport final de l'évaluation du projet EERN/SIM de Développement Intégré de Maradi." June. Dossiers: EERN, EERN Archives.

———. N.d. "Wholistic Development: An Overview of the Concept." SIM Vertical Files SIMNIM 0002, SIMIA.

Jackson, H. G. 1935. "Conversation with a Moslem." *The Sudan Witness* VII, no. 6: 18–19.

Jehl, Douglas, and David Firestone. 2003. "Rumsfeld Draws Republicans' Ire." *New York Times* (October 24): A1.

Kapp, N. A. 1934. "How Prejudices Are Broken Down." *The Sudan Witness* VII, no. 1: 20–21.

———. 1935. "Preaching in a Moslem Town." *The Sudan Witness* VIII, no. 2: 15–16.

———. 1939. "By One Spirit . . . Baptized into One Body." *The Sudan Witness* XV, no. 4: 9, 17.

———. 1940. "Station Flash, Tsibiri." *The Sudan Witness* XVI, no. 4: 19.

———. 1953. "Survey in French West Africa." *The Sudan Witness* (Jubilee Issue, 1893–1953) XXIX, no. 1: 19–20.

———. 1955. "Annual Report. Niger Territory, F.W.A., 1954." *The Sudan Witness* XXI, no. 2: 2–3.

Kapp, Rev. and Mrs. N. A. 1950a. "Business for the King." *The Sudan Witness* XXVI, no. 1: 13–15.

———. 1950b. "Missionary Mail: French West Africa." *The Sudan Witness Supplement* III, no. 2: 1.

Keller, J. 1942a. "Rapport de tournée, 12 janvier au 26 mai 1942." Affaires politiques Afrique Occidentale Française, 17G115 (14miom/2310), CAOM.

———. 1942b. Pastor J. Keller, à Monsieur le directeur de la Sureté Générale, Dakar 29 décembre, 1942. Affaires politiques Afrique Occidentale Française 17G115 (14miom/2310), CAOM.

———. 1943. "Note sur la délégation général des missions protestantes en AOF, oct. 1943." Affaires politiques Afrique Occidentale Française, 17G115 (14miom/2310), CAOM.

Kirk, H. A. 1950. "Annual Report, Nigeria and French West Africa." *The Sudan Witness* XXVI, no. 5: 7.

Kristof, Nicholas D. 2003. "God on Their Side." *New York Times* (September 27): A15.

Leroux, Henri. 1946. "Rapport de tournée de recensement effectuée par Monsieur Leroux Henri, stagiaire de l'administration coloniale dans le canton de Djirataoua du 3 au 11 et du 22 au 28 juillet 1946." Rapports de Tournée (Gobir), 14.3.97, Archives nationales du Niger.

Levin, Joseph. 1956. "Mud-Walled Cottage Her Home Amid Woe." *The Sudan Witness* XXXII, no. 3: 7.

Litafi Mai-Tsarki (The Holy Bible in Hausa). 1932. Lagos: The Bible Society of Nigeria.

Littafi Mai Tsarki duk da Afokirifa (The Bible in Hausa, with Deuterocanonical Books). 1979. Lagos: The Bible Society of Nigeria.

Lovering, Kerry. 1963. "Deep Roots." *Africa Now* 18: 8–9.

———. 1966. "Niger Republic's Newton Kapp, Man with the Big Back Yard." *The Sudan Witness* H3 (3): 2–4.

———. 1982. "Barefoot Doctors." *SIM Now* (May–June): 7.

———. 1985. "Hot New Items in the Desert." *SIM Now* (March–April): 2–4.

Lyons, Bill. 1979. "Some Thoughts on Our SIM Work in Niger." February 22. BV3625 N47, SIMIA.

Mahamane, Cissé Souleymane. 2001. "More Than 400 Children Handicapped by Error of the Niger Water Company." *Alternative* (January 4).

Massey, Joshua. 2004. "Should Christians Use Allah in Bible Translation?" Available online at http://www.sim.org/mag_104_19.asp, accessed January 9, 2004.

Matthews, J. 1999a. "Progress Report, Maradi Integrated Development Project #30-97230, Jan–March 1999." Archived at Maradi Integrated Development Project Office.

————. 1999b. "Annual Project Progress Report, April 1998–March 1999." Archived at Maradi Integrated Development Project Office.

Merlo, Christian. 1955. "Fondement juridique d'une politique missionaire positive" ("Legal Foundations for a Constructive Policy towards Missions"). Fonds Ministériels 3369 (4), CAOM.

Merryweather, F. 1925. "The Easy Way." *The Sudan Witness* IV, no. 6: 13–14.

Moncoucut. 1941. "Rapport de la tournée effectuée par l'élève administrateur Moncoucut dans l'est et le nord de la Subdivision de Maradi du 28 août au 12 septembre 1941." Rapports de Tournée (Gobir), 14.3.59, Archives nationales du Niger.

Monod, G. 1945. "Influence des Missions protestantes en Afrique noire" ("The Influence of Protestant Missions in Black Africa"). Fonds Ministériels 2190 (7), CAOM.

Morrow, Edward W. 1934. "From the Window." *The Sudan Witness* VII, no. 2: 3–4.

————. 1935. "Itinerating amongst Moslems." *The Sudan Witness* VII, no. 5: 22–24.

————. 1941. "Reaching the Moslem." *The Sudan Witness* XVII, no. 3: 8–9.

————. 1946. "Abba Musa of Zinder." *The Sudan Witness* XXIV, no. 4: 19–22, 24.

————. n.d. "Regarding Benin and Niger in Early Days." (Transcription of interview.) SIM Vertical Files SIMHIS 0007, SIMIA.

N.a. [probably Jean Toby]. 1945. "Enquête sur les Missions Religieuses au Niger" ("Survey of Religious Missions in Niger"). Fonds Ministériels 2190 (1), CAOM.

N.a. 1964. "Statuts Église Évangelique de la République du Niger EERN, 1964." SIM Vertical Files SIMRCH 0015, SIMIA.

Nobili, Pierre. 1928. "Rapport de Tournée, L'administrateur-Adjoint des Colonies Pierre Nobili a Monsieur l'Administrateur du cercle de Maradi, le 19 novembre 1928." Rapports de Tournée (Gobir), 14.3.3, Archives nationales du Niger.

Ockers, John. 1958. "Call of the Desert." *The Sudan Witness* XXXIV, no. 1: 3.

Ogilvie, Rev. H. L. 1942. "Preparation of Hausa Literature." *The Sudan Witness* XVIII, no. 4: 10–12.

Ohia, Paul. 2000. "Sharia Fever Grips Niger Republic Citizens." *Post Express*, July 3. Available online at www.postexpresswired.com, accessed July 2000.

O'Keefe, Mark. 2002. "Televangelist Falwell Paints Muhammad as a 'Terrorist.'"

Religion News Service, available online at New Jersey Online (www.nj.com), accessed October 4, 2002.

Oliver, Roland. 1952/1970. *The Missionary Factor in East Africa*. London: Longman.

Osborne, D. M. 1934. "Field Report for Niger and French West Africa for 1933." *The Sudan Witness* VI, no. 6: 5.

———. 1936. "The Gospel in the Niger Colony." *The Sudan Witness* IX, no. 4: 10–13.

———. 1937. "Mission Work in Niger Colony." *The Sudan Witness* XII, no. 5: 22–24.

———. 1939. "The Story of Tamu." *The Sudan Witness* XV, no. 3: 12–14.

———. 1944. "Prospecting." *The Sudan Witness* XX, no. 3: 1–6.

———. 1945. "Wandering Sheep Brought In." *The Sudan Witness* XXI, no. 1: 8–10.

———. 1946. "Outline of Mission Work in Niger Colony 1924–1945." *The Sudan Witness* XXIV, no. 4: 7–10.

———. 1950. "Missionary News: French West Africa." *The Sudan Witness Supplement* III, no. 3: 2.

Panafrican News Agency. 2000. "L'artisanat et la mode en lutte contre la pauvreté." Posted to the allAfrica.com Web site, accessed November 2, 2000.

Paternoster, Daniel. 1994. "Report of October 1993 Mission." February 20. SIMNIC0014, SIMIA.

Paumelle, Jean. 1945. "Compte-rendu de tournée de recensement effectuée par l'administrateur adjoint Paumelle Jean dans le Gober." Rapports de Tournée (Gobir), 14.3.80, Archives nationales du Niger.

Pinaud, Jean. 1945. "Rapport de la tournée de recensement effectuée du 6 au 14 avril 1945 dans le Gober par Jean Pinaud, du 6 au 20 avril." Rapports de Tournée (Gobir), 14.3.81, Archives nationales du Niger.

Petersen, Karen. 1938. "Small Beginnings." *The Sudan Witness* XIV, no. 2: 7–8.

Playfair, G. W. 1949. "Needed MEN Urgent." *The Sudan Witness Supplement* II, no. 5: 1–2.

"Prayer Guides." 1929–1985 PG-1; 1985–1995 PG-2, SIMIA.

Pujol. 1948. "Compte-rendu de tournée effectuée dans le canton du Gober [*sic*] secteur de Madeyena du 31 mai au 16 juin 1948 par l'élève administrateur Pujol." Rapports de Tournée (Gobir), 14.3.112, Archives nationales du Niger.

République du Niger, Ministère de l'Économie et des Finances. 1992. *Recensement Général de la Population 1988, Série 4: Caractéristiques socio-culturelles*. Niamey: Imprimière Albarka.

Rinaudo, Tony. 1988a. "Avoiding Hunger Trap." *SIM Now* (May–June): 4–5.

———. 1988b. "The Root of the Problem." *SIM Now* (May–June): 6.

———. 1994a. "Development among Nomads." Interview done by Bonnie Aebi, June 11, 1994. SIM Vertical Files PGRFUW 0003, SIMIA.

———. 1994b. "Rapport janvier 1994 à septembre 1994." Archived at Maradi Integrated Development Project Office.

———. 1995. "Report July–Sept. 1995." Archived at Maradi Integrated Development Project Office.

——. 1997a. "1997 Quarterly report, April–June." Archived at Maradi Integrated Development Project Office.

——. 1997b. "Rapport pour la periode d'avril–mai–juin 1997." Archived at Maradi Integrated Development Project Office.

——. 1997c. "Report July–Sept. 1997." Archived at Maradi Integrated Development Project Office.

——. 1998a. "Project Progress Report: Maradi Integrated Development Project #30-97230, July–Sept. 1998." Archived at Maradi Integrated Development Project Office.

——. 1998b. "Report Oct. 1998–Dec. 1998." Archived at Maradi Integrated Development Project Office.

——, and C. Evans. 1999. "Le Manuel Technique MIDP." Archived at Maradi Integrated Development Project Office.

Robinson, Charles Henry. 1899/1925. *Dictionary of the Hausa Language.* Cambridge: Cambridge University Press.

Sahiru, Pastor. 1999. Radio program. May 9. *Muyar Ceto* Radio Programs, Vie Abondante, Maradi, Niger.

——. 2000a. Radio program. February 1. *Muyar Ceto* Radio Programs, Vie Abondante, Maradi, Niger.

——. 2000b. Radio program. September 3. *Muyar Ceto* Radio Programs, Vie Abondante, Maradi, Niger.

——. 2000c. Radio program. September 10. *Muyar Ceto* Radio Programs, Vie Abondante, Maradi, Niger.

Salls, Rita. 1949. "Tsibiri, French West Africa." *The Sudan Witness Supplement* II, no. 3: 2.

Schön, James Frederick. 1876/1968. *Dictionary of the Hausa Language.* Farnborough Hants: Gregg Press Ltd.

SIM. 1932. *SIM Handbook.* Archived at SIMIA.

——. 1934. "Statistical Report for Nigeria and French West Africa." *The Sudan Witness* VI, no. 6.

——. 1938. "The Peaceful Invasion of the Northern Emirates of Nigeria." *Sudan Witness* XIV, no. 1.

——. 1939. "The Boys' Brigade." *The Sudan Witness* XV, no. 3: 15.

——. 1941. "Obituary: Mrs. D. M. Osborne." *The Sudan Witness* XVII, no. 1: 3–4.

——. 1948. "Moslems Need Christ!" *The Sudan Witness* I, no. 3: 1.

——. [ca. 1950] *Training the African Evangelist: The Story of West African Bible Training Schools of the Sudan Interior Mission.* Archived at SIMIA.

——. 1951a. "WANTED For French West Africa." *The Sudan Witness Supplement* (February: 1).

——. 1951b. ". . . But While the Men Slept . . ." *The Sudan Witness Supplement* (April: 1).

——. 1953. "The Last Letter of Walter Gowans (written in 1893)." *The Sudan Witness* (Jubilee Issue) XXIX: 29–31.

——. 1955. "Help Those Women." *The Sudan Witness* XXXI, no. 5: 1.

——. 1961. "More Women Than Men—Why?" *Africa Now* 9:2–4.

———. 1968. "Farmer-Evangelists Graduate in Niger." *Africa Now* 37 (March–April): 10.

———. 1970a. "Killer Virus Claims Third Missionary Victim." *Africa Now* (May–June): 11.

———. 1970b. " 'Killer Virus' Survivor Provides Antibody Bank." *Africa Now* (January–February): 13.

———. 1971. "Significant Events in Gospel Outreach in Africa." *Africa Now* (January–February): 2.

———. 1972. "Come . . . but live among my people!" *Africa Now* (January–February): 6.

———. 1973. "Blind Evangelist Draws Response from Niger Muslims." *Africa Now* (July–August): 12.

———. 1976. "Expanded Role for Niger Hospital." *Africa Now* (March–April): 10.

———. 1982. "Putting Down Roots." *SIM Now* (May–June): 60.

———. ca. 1983. "Position actuelle sur la Polygamie." *Manuel SIM.* Dossier: Correspendance EERN/SIM, EERN Archives.

———. 1988. "Guidelines for Muslim Ministry." May 28. SIM Vertical Files SIMMOU 0007, SIMIA.

Simms, A. L. 1949. "A Window on the Work." *The Sudan Witness* XXV, no. 6: 20–22.

Simms, Alberta. 1992 (December 4). "SIM Niger in the 1940s." SIM Vertical Files SIMNIG 0006, SIMIA.

St. Germain, E. 1935. "A Slave to Fear." *The Sudan Witness* VII, no. 5: 14–16.

Stilwell, Don, ed. 1989 (August). "SIM Famine Relief Evaluation Report." HV630 S38 (spec.), SIMIA.

Stirrett, A. P. 1932. "The Bible in Hausa." *The Sudan Witness* V, no. 1: 4–6.

———. 1935a. "Reminiscences." *The Sudan Witness* VIII, no. 1: 5–7.

———. 1935b. "Reminiscences." *The Sudan Witness* VIII, no. 2: 6–9.

———. 1935c. "Reminiscences." *The Sudan Witness* IX, no. 3: 22–24.

———. 1936. "Reminiscences." *The Sudan Witness* IX, no. 4: 20–22.

———. 1937. "A Message." *The Sudan Witness* XII, no. 5: 4–5.

———. 1945. "Translating the Hausa Bible." *The Sudan Witness* XXI, no. 4: 10–13, 20.

"Statistical History, 1970–1991." SIM Vertical Files SIMHIS [no number], SIMIA.

Tashibka. 1949. "An African Letter." *The Sudan Witness Supplement* II, no. 3: 1.

Troup, Roger. 1956. "The Women Do It!" *The Sudan Witness* XXXII, no. 3: 6.

Varenner. 1942. "Rapport de Tournée par le commis des Services civils Varenner sur la frontière de la Nigeria, 1942." Rapports de Tournée (Gobir), 14.3.67, Archives nationales du Niger.

Vatican Council II. 1964. *Lumen Gentium:* Dogmatic Constitution of the Church Promulgated by Holiness Pope Paul VI, November 21, 1964. Available online at http://www.vatican.va/archive/hist_councils/ii_vatican_council/index.htm.

Wall, Martha. 1952. "She Was Almost Broiled Alive!" *The Sudan Witness* XXVIII, no. 4: 5–10.

———. 1953a. "Help Those Women," *The Sudan Witness* XXIX, no. 2: 7–9.

———. 1953b. "The Light Must Not Fail." *The Sudan Witness* XXIX, no. 4: 5–6.

————. 1960. *Splinters Off an African Log.* Chicago: Moody Press.

Whale, Fred. 1937. "Vain Repetitions as the Heathen Do." *The Sudan Witness* XI, no. 4: 9–10.

Whale, Mrs. Fred. 1938. "On Visiting Terms (Zinder)." *The Sudan Witness* XIV, no. 3: 9–11.

Wright, Miss D. 1935. "A Call to Prayer." *The Sudan Witness* IX, no. 3: 9–10.

Zabriskie, Rev. C. K. 1947. "An Introduction to Dogon-Doutchi." *The Sudan Witness* XXIII, no. 1: 10–11.

Zwemer, Samuel Marinus. 1941. *The Cross above the Crescent: The Validity, Necessity and Urgency of Missions to Moslems.* Grand Rapids, Mich.: Zondervan Publishing.

Secondary Sources

Ajayi, J. F. Ade. 1969. *Christian Missions in Nigeria 1841–1891. The Making of a New Elite.* Evanston, Ill.: Northwestern University Press.

Akpo-Vaché, Catherine. 1996. *L'AOF et la seconde guerre mondiale.* Paris: Karthala.

Alidou, Ousseina. 2005. *Engaging Modernity: Muslim Women and the Politics of Agency in Postcolonial Niger.* Madison: University of Wisconsin Press.

Aliyu, Sani Abba. 2000. "Christian Missionaries and Hausa Literature in Nigeria, 1840–1890: A Critical Evaluation." *Kano Studies* (n.s.) 1: 93–118.

Ammerman, Nancy. 1991. "North American Protestant Fundamentalism." In *Fundamentalisms Observed,* ed. Martin E. Marty and R. Scott Appleby, 1–65. Chicago: University of Chicago Press.

Amselle, Jean-Loup. 1998. *Mestizo Logics: Anthropology of Identity in Africa and Elsewhere.* Trans. Claudia Royal. Stanford: Stanford University Press.

Anthony, D. 2000. " 'Islam does not belong to them': Ethnic and Religious Identities among Male Igbo Converts in Hausaland." *Africa* 70, no. 3: 422–441.

Austin, Alvyn J. 1990. "Blessed Adversity: Henry W. Frost and the China Inland Mission." In *Earthen Vessels: American Evangelicals and Foreign Missions, 1880–1980,* ed. Joel Carpenter and Wilbert R. Shenk, 47–70. Grand Rapids, Mich.: William B. Eerdmans Publishing Company.

Awaïss, Aboubakar. 2000. "Gestion des forêts et des arbres au niveau des terroirs dans la région de Maradi." Drylands Working Paper 31. Crewkerne: Drylands Research.

Ayandele, E. A. 1966. *The Missionary Impact on Modern Nigeria 1842–1914: A Political and Social Analysis.* London: Longmans.

Bado, Jean-Paul. 1996. *Médecine coloniale et grandes endémies en Afrique: 1900–1960: lèpre, trypanosomiase humaine et onchocercose.* Paris: Karthala.

Barnes, Andrew. 1995. " 'Evangelization where it is not wanted': Colonial Administrators and Missionaries in Northern Nigeria during the First Third of the Twentieth Century." *Religion in Africa* XXV, no. 4: 412–441.

Baier, Stephen. 1981. *An Economic History of Central Niger.* London: Oxford University Press.

Beaver, R. Pierce. 1968/1998. *All Loves Excelling: American Protestant Women in World Mission.* Grand Rapids, Mich.: William B. Eerdmans Publishing Co.

Beidelman, T. O. 1982. *Colonial Evangelism: A Socio-Historical Study of an East African Mission at the Grassroots.* Bloomington: Indiana University Press.

Benoist, Joseph-Roger de. 1987. *Église et pouvoir colonial au Sudan français: Administrateurs et missionaires dans la Boucle du Niger (1885–1945).* Paris: Karthala.

Bergstrom, Kari. 2005. "Gender, Livelihoods, Rights, Power and Development in Two Communities Near 'Dan Issa." Preliminary report for CARE and UNICEF, Niger based on field research in Niger, January to August 2004.

Berman, Bruce, and John Lonsdale. 1992. *Unhappy Valley: Conflict in Kenya and Africa.* Athens: Ohio University Press.

Berthelot, André. 1997. *Hippolyte Berlier, 1919–1992, Rédemptoriste: Premier Évêque du Niger en Terre d'Islam.* Paris: L'Harmattan, 1997.

Beynon, John. 1985. "Saint-Exupery's Pilote de Guerre: Testimony, Art and Ideology." In *Vichy France and the Resistance: Culture and Ideology,* ed. Roderick Kedward and Roger Austin, 91–105. London: Croom Helm.

Bowie, Fiona, Deborah Kirkwood, and Shirley Ardener. 1993. *Women and Missions: Past and Present.* Oxford: Berg.

Brasher, Brenda E. 1998. *Godly Women: Fundamentalism and Female Power.* New Brunswick, N.J.: Rutgers University Press.

Brouwer, Steve, Paul Gifford, and Susan D. Rose. 1996. *Exporting the American Gospel: Global Christian Fundamentalism.* New York: Routledge.

Brown, Karen McCarthy. 1994. "Fundamentalism and the Control of Women." In *Fundamentalism and Gender,* ed. John Stratton Hawley, 175–211. New York: Oxford University Press.

Carpenter, Joel. 1990. "Propagating the Faith Once Delivered: The Fundamentalist Missionary Enterprise, 1920–1945." In *Earthen Vessels: American Evangelicals and Foreign Missions, 1880–1980,* ed. Joel Carpenter and Wilbert R. Shenk, 92–132. Grand Rapids, Mich.: William B. Eerdmans Publishing Co.

―――, and Wilbert R. Shenk, eds. 1990. *Earthen Vessels: American Evangelicals and Foreign Missions, 1880–1980.* Grand Rapids, Mich.: William B. Eerdmans Publishing Co.

Central Intelligence Agency. 2005. *The World Factbook.* Available online at http://www.cia.gov/cia/publications/factbook.

Charlick, Robert. B. 1991. *Niger: Personal Rule and Survival in the Sahel.* Boulder, Colo.: Westview Press.

Cohen, William B. 1971. *Rulers of Empire: The French Colonial Service in Africa.* Stanford: Hoover Institution Press.

Comaroff, Jean, and John Comaroff. 1991. *Of Revelation and Revolution: Christianity, Colonialism and Consciousness in South Africa.* Vol. 1. Chicago: University of Chicago Press.

―――. 1997. *Of Revelation and Revolution: The Dialectics of Modernity on a South African Frontier.* Vol. 2. Chicago: University of Chicago Press.

Cooper, Barbara. 1997a. *Marriage in Maradi: Gender and Culture in a Hausa Society in Niger, 1900–1989.* Portsmouth, N.H.: Heinemann.

―――. 1997b. "Gender, Movement, and History: Social and Spatial Transformations in 20th Century Maradi, Niger." *Environment and Planning D: Society and Space* 15, no. 2: 195–221.

———. 1999. "The Strength in the Song: Muslim Personhood, Audible Capital and Hausa Women's Performance of the Hajj." *Social Text* 17, no. 3: 87–109.

Cox, Ruth. 2000. "The Lord's Work: Perspectives of Early Leaders of the Evangelical Church of West Africa in Nigeria Regarding the Spread of Christianity." Ph.D. diss., Intercultural Studies, Trinity International University.

Cunningham, Peter. 1996. "The Historical Development of the Christian Church in Niger." Unpublished paper.

Danfulani, Umar H. D., and Sati U. Fwatshak. 2002. "Briefing: The September 2001 Events in Jos, Nigeria." *African Affairs* 101: 243–255.

Davison, Jean, with the Women of Mutira. 1989. *Voices from Mutira: Lives of Rural Gikuyu Women*. Boulder, Colo.: Lynne Rienner Publishers.

Dipple, Bruce. 1994. "A Missiological Evaluation of the Sudan Interior Mission in French West Africa, 1924–62." Ph.D. diss., Trinity Evangelical Divinity School, Deerfield, Ill.

Draper, Jonathan. 2000. "The Bishop and the Bricoleur: Bishop John William Colenso's *Commentary on Romans* and Magema kaMagwanza Fuze's *The Black People and Whence They Came*." In *The Bible in Africa: Transactions, Trajectories and Trends*, ed. Gerald O. West and Musa W. Dube, 415–454. Boston: Brill Academic Publishers, Inc.

Erny, Pierre. 1982. *Écoles d'église en Afrique noire: poids du passé et perspectives d'avenir*. Fribourg: Nouvelle Revue de science missionnaire.

Esposito, John. 1998. *Islam: The Straight Path*. New York: Oxford University Press.

Fairhead, James, and Melissa Leach. 1996. "Rethinking the Forest-Savanna Mosaic: Colonial Science and its Relics in West Africa." In *The Lie of the Land: Challenging Received Wisdom on the African Environment*, ed. Melissa Leach and Robin Mearns, 105–121. Oxford: The International African Institute,

Findlay, James F. 1969. *Dwight L. Moody, American Evangelist, 1837–1899*. Chicago: University of Chicago Press.

Fuglestad, Finn. 1983. *A History of Niger 1850–1960*. Cambridge: Cambridge University Press.

———, and R. Higgott. 1975. "The 1974 Coup d'Etat in Niger: Towards an Explanation." *Journal of Modern African Studies* XIII, no. 3: 383–398.

Fuller, Harold. 1967. *Run While the Sun Is Hot*. New York: Sudan Interior Mission.

Gaitskell, Deborah 1982. "'Wailing for Purity': Prayer Unions, African Women and Adolescent Daughters, 1912–1940." In *Industrialisation and Social Change in South Africa*, ed. Shula Marks and Richard Rathbone, 338–357. London: Longman.

———. 2002. "Ploughs and Needles: State and Mission Approaches to African Girls' Education in South Africa." In *Christian Missionaries and the State in the Third World*, ed. Holger Bernt Hansen and Michael Twaddle, 98–120. Athens: Ohio University Press.

Gaiya, Musa. 1993. "A History of the Hausa Bible: 1980 Edition." *The Africa Journal of Evangelical Theology* 12, no. 1: 54–65.

Garba, John Mamman. 1989. *The Time Has Come: Reminiscences and Reflections of a Nigerian Pioneer Diplomat*. Kaduna: Spectrum Books Limited.

Gifford, Paul. 1987. "'Africa Shall Be Saved': An Appraisal of Reinhard Bonnke's Pan-African Crusade." *Journal of Religion in Africa* XVII, no. 1: 63–92.

———. 1998. *African Christianity: Its Public Role*. Bloomington: Indiana University Press.

———. 2001. "The Complex Provenance of Some Elements of African Pentecostal Theology." In *Between Babel and Pentecost: Transnational Pentecostalism in Africa and Latin America*, ed. André Corten and Ruth Marshall-Fratani, 62–79. Bloomington: Indiana University Press.

Göle, Nilüfer. 2002. "Islam in Public: New Visibilities and New Imaginaries." *Public Culture* 14, no. 1: 173–190.

Gray, Richard. 1990. *Black Christians and White Missionaries*. New Haven, Conn.: Yale University Press.

Grégoire, Emmanuel. 1992. *The Alhazai of Maradi: Traditional Hausa Merchants in a Changing Sahelian City*. Translated by Benjamin Hardy. Boulder, Colo.: Lynne Rienner Publishers.

Griffith, R. Marie. 1997. *God's Daughters: Evangelical Women and the Power of Submission*. Berkeley: University of California Press.

Halls, W. D. 1995. *Politics, Society and Christianity in Vichy France*. Oxford: Berg Publishers.

Hamidou, Seyni. 2000. "Politiques Nationales et investissement dans les petites exploitations agricoles à Maradi." Drylands Research Working Paper 33. Crewkerne: Drylands Research.

Hartmann-Mahmud, Lori Lynn. 2000. "Beyond Dichotomies and Assumptions of Development Discourse: The Case of Women and Gender Relations in Niger." Ph.D. diss., Graduate School of International Studies, University of Denver.

Hastings, Adrian. 1979. *African Christianity*. London: Geoffrey Chapman.

———. 1993. "Were Women a Special Case?" In *Women and Missions: Past and Present*, ed. Fiona Bowie, Deborah Kirkwood, and Shirley Ardener, 109–125. Oxford: Berg.

———. 1994. *The Church in Africa, 1450–1950*. Oxford: Clarendon Press.

Harrison, Christopher. 1988. *France and Islam in West Africa, 1860–1960*. Cambridge: Cambridge University Press.

Hintjens, Helen. 1999. "Explaining the 1994 Genocide in Rwanda." *Journal of Modern African Studies* 37, no. 2: 241–286.

Hodgson, Dorothy. 2005. *A Church of Women: Gendered Encounters between Maasai and Missionaries*. Bloomington: Indiana University Press.

Hoffman, Valerie J. 1995. "Muslim Fundamentalists: Psychosocial Profiles." In *Fundamentalisms Comprehended*, ed. Marin E. Marty and R. Scott Appleby, 199–230. Chicago: University of Chicago Press.

Hunt, Nancy Rose. 1997. "'Le Bébé en brousse': European Women, African Birth Spacing, and Colonial Intervention in Breast Feeding in the Belgian Congo." In *Tensions of Empire: Colonial Cultures in a Bourgeois World*, ed. Frederick Cooper and Ann Laura Stoler, 287–321. Berkeley: California University Press.

————. 1999. *A Colonial Lexicon of Birth Ritual, Medicalization, and Mobility in the Congo*. Durham, N.C.: Duke University Press.

Isichei, Elizabeth. 1995. *A History of Christianity in Africa*. Lawrenceville, N.J.: Africa World Press.

James, Wendy. 1988. *The Listening Ebony: Moral Knowledge, Religion, and Power among the Uduk of Sudan*. Oxford: Clarendon Press.

Johnstone, Patrick. 1993. *Operation World: The Day-to-Day Guide to Praying for the World*. Grand Rapids, Mich.: Zondervan Publishing House.

Juergensmeyer, Mark. 1995. "Antifundamentalism." In *Fundamentalisms Comprehended*, ed. Martin E. Marty and R. Scott Appleby, 353–366. Chicago: University of Chicago Press.

Juster, Susan. 1994. *Disorderly Women: Sexual Politics and Evangelicalism in Revolutionary New England*. Ithaca: Cornell University Press.

Kane, Ousmane. 1997. "Un pluralism en quête de démocratie. Mobilisations musulmanes et régime militaire à Kano (Nord Nigeria)." In *Religion et transition démocratique en Afrique*, ed. François Constantin and Christian Coulon, 51–79. Paris: Karthala.

Kastfelt, Niels. 1994. *Religion and Politics in Nigeria: A Study of Middle Belt Christianity*. London: British Academic Press.

Kedward, Roderick. 1985. "The Maquis and the Culture of the Outlaw (With Particular Reference to the Cevennes)." In *Vichy France and the Resistance: Culture and Ideology*, ed. R. Kedward and R. Austin, 232–225. London: Croom Helm.

Kessler-Harris, Alice. 1982. *Out to Work: A History of Wage-Earning Women in the United States*. New York: Oxford University Press.

Kirkwood, Deborah. 1993. "Protestant Missionary Women: Wives and Spinsters." In *Women and Missions: Past and Present*, ed. Fiona Bowie, Deborah Kirkwood, and Shirley Ardener. Providence, R. I.: Berg Publishers.

Koley, Glenda Dick. 1984. "Mission Primary School Dilemma: Day or Boarding School for the Nationals of the Republic of Niger." M.A. thesis, Columbia Bible College.

Kure, Reverend Mai Kudi. 1990. *Shaida Bishara ga Musulmi Hausawa da Fulani Musamman da Yadda za a Goyi Musulmi Wanda ya Tuba*. Jos, Nigeria: Covenant Press Limited.

King, Fergus J. 2001. "*Nyimbo za Vijana*: Biblical Interpretation in Contemporary Hymns from Tanzania." In *The Bible in Africa: Transactions, Trajectories, and Trends*, ed. Gerald O. West and Musa W. Duba, 360–373. Boston: Brill Academic Publishers, Inc.

Krapohl, Robert H., and Charles H. Lippy. 1999. *The Evangelicals: A Historical, Thematic, and Biographical Guide*. Westport, Conn.: Greenwood Press.

Last, Murray. 2003. "Towards a Political History of Youth in Muslim Northern Nigeria 1900–2000." Paper presented at the 46th Annual African Studies Association Meetings, Boston, November 2.

Lindley, Susan Hill. 1996. *"You Have Stept Out of Your Place": A History of Women and Religion in America*. Louisville: Westminster John Knox Press.

Lovejoy, Paul, and Jan Hogendorn. 1993. *Slow Death for Slavery: The Course of*

Abolition in Northern Nigeria, 1897–1936. Cambridge: Cambridge University Press.

Luxereau, Anne, and Bernard Roussel. 1997. *Changements écologiques et sociaux au Niger: des interactions étroites*. Paris: L'Harmattan.

Lyons, Marynez. 1992. *The Colonial Disease: A Social History of Sleeping Sickness in Northern Zaire, 1900–1940*. New York: Cambridge University Press.

Mack, Beverly, and Jean Boyd. 2000. *One Woman's Jihad: Nana Asma'u, Scholar and Scribe*. Bloomington: Indiana University Press.

Mahamane, Ali. 2001. "Usages des Terres et Évolutions Végétales dans le Département de Maradi." Drylands Working Paper 27. Crewkerne: Drylands Research.

Manning, Patrick. 1988. *Francophone Sub-Saharan Africa, 1880–1985*. Cambridge: Cambridge University Press.

Martin, Sandy. 1989. *Black Baptists and African Missions: The Origins of a Movement, 1880–1915*. Macon, Ga.: Mercer.

Marty, Martin E., and R. Scott Appleby, eds. 1991. *Fundamentalisms Observed*. Chicago: University of Chicago Press.

———. 1993a. *Fundamentalisms and the State*. Chicago: University of Chicago Press.

———. 1993b. *Fundamentalisms and Society*. Chicago: University of Chicago Press.

———. 1994. *Accounting for Fundamentalisms*. Chicago: University of Chicago Press.

———. 1995. *Fundamentalisms Comprehended*. Chicago: University of Chicago Press.

Masquelier, Adeline. 2001. *Prayer Has Spoiled Everything: Possession Power, and Identity in an Islamic Town of Niger*. Durham, N.C.: Duke University Press.

Massey, Joshua. 2004. "Should Christians Use Allah in Bible Translation?" *Evangelical Missions Quarterly* (July): 137–138.

Matthews, Joel. 1999. "Biblical Holism and Secular Thought in Christian Development." *Evangelical Missions Quarterly* (July): 290–298.

Médard, Jean-François. 1997. "Les Églises protestantes au Cameroun, entre tradition autoritaire et ethnicité." In *Religion et transition démocratique en Afrique*, ed. François Constantin and Christian Coulon, 189–220. Paris: Karthala.

Meunier, Olivier. 1997. *Dynamique de l'enseignement islamique au Niger*. Paris: L'Harmattan.

Miller, Darrow. 1999. "Biblical Holism: Critiquing a Critique." *Evangelical Missions Quarterly*, (July): 299–302.

Mojola, Aloo Osotsi. 2001. "The Swahili Bible in East Africa, 1844–1996." In *The Bible in Africa: Translations, Trajectories and Trends*, ed. Gerald O. West and Musa W. Dube, 511–523. Boston: Brill Academic Publishers, Inc.

Mortimore, Michael. 2000. "Profile of Rainfall Change and Variability in the Kano-Maradi Region, 1960–2000." Drylands Research Working Paper 25. Crewkerne: Drylands Research.

———, Mary Tiffin, Yamba Boubacar, and John Nelson. 2001. "Synthesis of Long-Term Change in Maradi Department, 1960–2000." Drylands Research Working Paper 39e. Crewkerne: Drylands Research.

Moussa, Bouzou. 2000. "Gestion des ressources naturelles et évolution des systèmes agraires dans la région de Maradi." Drylands Research Working Paper 28. Crewkerne: Drylands Research.

Nicolas, Guy. 1975. *Dynamique sociale et appréhension du monde au sein d'une société hausa.* Paris: Musée National d'Histoire Naturelle.

Noll, Mark A. 1994. *The Scandal of the Evangelical Mind.* Grand Rapids, Mich.: William B. Eerdmans Publishing Co.

———. 2001. *American Evangelical Christianity: An Introduction.* Oxford: Blackwell.

O'Brien, Susan. 2000. "Power and Paradox in Hausa Bori: Discourses of Gender, Healing and Islamic Tradition in Northern Nigeria." Ph.D. diss., University of Wisconsin-Madison.

Peel, J. D. Y. 2000. *Religious Encounter and the Making of the Yoruba.* Bloomington: Indiana University Press.

Peters, F. E. 1994. *The Hajj: The Muslim Pilgrimage to Mecca and the Holy Places.* Princeton, N.J.: Princeton University Press.

Peterson, Derek. 1999. "Translating the Word: Dialogism and Debate in Two Gikuyu Dictionaries." *Journal of Religious History* 23, no. 1: 31–50.

———, and Jean Allman. 1999. "Introduction: New Directions in the History of Missions in Africa." *Journal of Religious History* 23, no. 1: 1–7.

Philips, John Edward. 2000. *Spurious Arabic: Hausa and Colonial Nigeria.* Madison: African Studies Center, University of Wisconsin.

Rain, David. 1999. *Eaters of the Dry Season: Circular Labor Migration in the West African Sahel.* Boulder, Colo.: Westview Press.

Riesebrodt, Martin. 1993. *Pious Passion: The Emergence of Modern Fundamentalism in the United States and Iran.* Trans. Don Reneau. Berkeley: University of California Press.

Robert, Dana L. 1990. "'The Crisis of Missions': Premillennial Mission Theory and the Origins of Independent Evangelical Missions." In *Earthen Vessels: American Evangelicals and Foreign Missions, 1880–1980,* ed. Joel Carpenter and Wilbert R. Shenk, 29–46. Grand Rapids, Mich.: William B. Eerdmans Publishing Company.

———. 1997. *American Women in Mission: A Social History of Their Thought and Practice.* Macon, Ga.: Mercer University Press.

Robinson, Pearl. 1983. "Traditional Clientage and Political Change in a Hausa Community." In *Transformation and Resiliency in Africa,* ed. Pearl Robinson and Elliott Skinner, 105–128. Washington, D.C.: Howard University Press.

Salvaing, Bernard. 1994. *Les Missionnaires à la rencontre de l'Afrique au XIXe siècle.* Paris: L'Harmattan.

Sandgren, David. 1989. *Christianity and the Kikuyu.* New York: Peter Lang.

Sanneh, Lamin. 1994. "Translatability in Islam and in Christianity in Africa: A Thematic Approach." In *Religion in Africa: Experience and Expression,* ed. Thomas Blakely, Walter E. A. van Beek, and Dennis L. Thomson, 23–45. London: James Currey.

———. 1996. *Piety and Power: Muslims and Christians in West Africa.* Maryknoll: Orbis Books.

Saritoprak, Zeki. 2003. "The Legend of al-Dajjal (Antichrist): The Personification of Evil in the Islamic Tradition." *The Muslim World* 93 (April): 291–307.

Shankar, Shobana. 2003. "Children of the Mission in Kano Emirate: Conflicts of Conversion in Colonial Northern Nigeria, c. 1899–1953." Ph.D. diss., University of California, Los Angeles.

Silla, Eric. 1998. *People Are Not the Same: Leprosy and Identity in Twentieth-Century Mali*. Portsmouth, N.H.: Heinemann.

Simoën, Jean-Claude. 1996. *Les Fils de Rois: Le crépuscule sanglant de l'aventure africaine*. Paris: Éditions Jean-Claude Lattès.

Stanley, Brian. 2003. "Conversion to Christianity: The Colonization of the Mind?" *International Review of Mission* XCII, no. 366: 315–331.

Stoller, Paul. 1989. *Fusion of the Worlds*. Chicago: Chicago University Press.

Sugirtharajah, R. S. 2001. *The Bible and the Third World: Precolonial, Colonial and Postcolonial Encounters*. Cambridge: Cambridge University Press.

Thompson, Virginia, and Richard Adloff. 1957. *French West Africa*. Stanford: Stanford University Press.

Thornton, John. 1998. *The Kongolese Saint Anthony: Dona Beatriz Kimpa Vita and the Antonian Movement, 1684–1706*. Cambridge: Cambridge University Press.

———. 1992. *Africa and Africans in the Making of the Atlantic World, 1400–1680*. Cambridge: Cambridge University Press.

Tucker, Ruth. 1990. "Women in Missions: Reaching Sisters in 'Heathen Darkness.'" In *Earthen Vessels: American Evangelicals and Foreign Missions, 1880–1980*, ed. Joel Carpenter and Wilbert R. Shenk, 251–280. Grand Rapids, Mich.: William B. Eerdmans Publishing Company.

Turaki, Yusufu. 1993. *An Introduction to the History of SIM/ECWA in Nigeria, 1893–1993*. Jos, Nigeria: Challenge Press.

United Nations Development Programme. 2004. *Human Development Report: Cultural Liberty in Today's Diverse World*. New York: Human Development Report Office, UNDP.

Vaughan, Megan. 1991. *Curing Their Ills: Colonial Power and African Illness*. Cambridge: Polity Press.

Waller, Richard. 1999. "They Do the Dictating and We Must Submit: The Africa Inland Mission in Maasailand." In *East African Expressions of Christianity*, ed. Thomas Spear and Isaria Kimambo, 83–126. Athens: Ohio University Press.

Walls, Andrew. 1990. "The American Dimension in the History of the Missionary Movement." In *Earthen Vessels: American Evangelicals and Foreign Missions, 1880–1980*, ed. Joel Carpenter and Wilbert R. Shenk, 1–25. Grand Rapids, Mich.: William B. Eerdmans Publishing Company.

———. 1996. *The Missionary Movement in Christian History: Studies in the Transmission of Faith*. Maryknoll: Orbis.

———. 2002. "Africa as the Theatre of Christian Engagement with Islam in the Nineteenth Century." In *Christianity and the African Imagination: Essays in Honour of Adrian Hastings*, ed. David Maxwell and Ingrid Lawrie, 41–62. Boston: Brill.

West, Gerald O., and Musa W. Dube, eds. 2001. *The Bible in Africa: Transactions, Trajectories and Trends*. Boston: Brill Academic Publishers, Inc.

Williams, Peter. 1993. "'The Missing Link': The Recruitment of Women Missionaries in Some English Evangelical Missionary Societies in the Nineteenth

Century." In *Women and Missions: Past and Present*, ed. Fiona Bowie, Deborah Kirkwood, and Shirley Ardener, 43–69. Oxford: Berg.

Worger, William. 2001. "Parsing God: Conversations about the Meaning of Words and Metaphors in Nineteenth-Century Southern Africa." *Journal of African History* 42, no. 3: 417–447.

Wright, Marcia. 1971. *German Missions in Tanganyika, 1891–1941: Lutherans and Moravians in the Southern Highlands.* Oxford: Clarendon Press.

———. 1993. *Strategies of Slaves and Women: Life Stories from East/Central Africa.* New York: Lilian Barber.

Yamba, Boubacar. 2000. "Évolution des régimes de propriété et d'utilisation des ressources naturelles dans la région de Maradi." Drylands Research Working Paper 29. Crewkerne: Drylands Research.

———. 2001. "Les Politiques publiques de gestion des ressources ligneuses au Niger." In *Le Niger: État et Démocratie*, ed. Idrissa Kimba, 127–172. Paris: L'Harmattan.

Yates, Timothy. 1994. *Christian Mission in the Twentieth Century.* Cambridge: Cambridge University Press.

Zorn, Jean-François. 1993. *Le Grand Siècle d'une mission Protestante: La Mission de Paris de 1822 à 1914.* Paris: Karthala.

Index

Barbara M. Cooper is Associate Professor of History at Rutgers University. She is author of *Marriage in Maradi: Gender and Culture in a Hausa Society in Niger, 1900–1989*.